Ethics and Business

*An Integrated Approach for Business
and Personal Success*

INTERNATIONAL ADAPTATION

Ethics and Business

*An Integrated Approach for Business
and Personal Success*

INTERNATIONAL ADAPTATION

Paul C. Godfrey
William and Roceil Low Professor of Business Strategy
Marriott School of Business
Brigham Young University

Laura E. Jacobus
Professor, Santa Clara University

WILEY

Ethics and Business
An Integrated Approach for Business and Personal Success

INTERNATIONAL ADAPTATION

Cover image: © Shutterstock

Contributing Subject Matter Expert: Dr. Abhishek Singh, Assistant Professor, Indian Institute of Management Rohtak

Founded in 1807, John Wiley & Sons, Inc. has been a valued source of knowledge and understanding for more than 200 years, helping people around the world meet their needs and fulfill their aspirations. Our company is built on a foundation of principles that include responsibility to the communities we serve and where we live and work. In 2008, we launched a Corporate Citizenship Initiative, a global effort to address the environmental, social, economic, and ethical challenges we face in our business. Among the issues we are addressing are carbon impact, paper specifications and procurement, ethical conduct within our business and among our vendors, and community and charitable support. For more information, please visit our website: www.wiley.com/go/citizenship.

ISBN: 978-1-119-88921-2

ISBN: 978-1-119-88922-9 (ePub)

ISBN: 978-1-119-88923-6 (ePdf)

Printed and bound by CPI Group (UK) Ltd, Croydon, CR0 4YY

C9781119889212_091122

Preface

Ethics and Business: An Integrated Approach for Business and Personal Success equips students with business ethics concepts and pragmatic knowledge they need to identify and solve ethical dilemmas, understand their own and others' ethical behavior, promote ethical behavior in their organization, and begin the process of living a life rich in meaning and happiness.

This International Adaptation provides a systematic and logical framework for understanding ethical challenges and thinking about how to respond. The chapters build on each other. Part 1 (Chapters 2–7) lays a foundation for a holistic view of individual ethics (Chapters 2–3) and provides important knowledge and language about organizational realities and how they deal with issues of ethics and compliance (Chapters 4–7). Part 2 (Chapters 8–12) offers students the opportunity to apply what they've learned around five common ethical challenges in business: the use and abuse of power, conflict of interest, bribery, honesty/integrity, and corporate social responsibility. Part 3 (Chapters 13–14) takes up some larger issues of ethics: the ethical challenges that come with technological innovation and the role of ethics in a market-based or planned economy. The book features:

- **An Engaging and Applied Approach:** the text employs a "Harvard Business Review" writing style and tone that provide solid foundations in an organized and accessible manner. Frameworks, tools, and activities provide structure, help guide ethical decision making, and provide students a variety of opportunities to practice ethical decision making.

- **Varied Contemporary Examples to Address Different Work Experiences:** A mix of examples includes cases centered on the kinds of problems that most students, not just executives, will encounter now and in their future careers.

- **Latest Research on Ethics:** The book draws on current current academic research and company examples, and in many cases advice from case protagonists or professionals who have faced ethical challenges.

- **Career/Decision Focused Content and Examples:** Each chapter helps students understand issues and better prepare for their future careers and personal life related to ethical decision making. Every chapter contains exercises that allow students to think about how they see these issues playing out in their career.

- **Variety of Contemporary and High-Interest Cases:**
  - "Mini-Cases" provide students with a condensed opportunity to think about a very specific issue or general principle. These cases invite students to take a stand. Each issue provides enough merit on both sides that students will come up with, and argue for, different solutions.
  - "Opening Cases" offer students more context and detail than mini-cases. Opening cases are based on dilemmas facing actors, executives, managers, or employees and provide 60–80 minutes of discussion.
  - "Application Exercises" are located at the end of each chapter and contain exercises that require points of discussion. These exercises are organized into three categories: individual, organizational, and societal.

- **Author Lecture Videos:** Each learning objective in the chapters (approximately four per chapter) include a brief Author Lecture Concept video to support the learning objective content and bring the material to life for students. Some of these videos will provide additional stories and examples to support the concepts and some will feature the author answering questions related to the concepts. These videos will help students frame many ethical issues they will face during their careers and can be used to help kick-off discussions or as student assignments. Each video includes several supporting assessment type questions.

- **Expert Interview Videos:** About half of the longer company cases include unique original videos featuring key stakeholders (CEOs, VPs, etc.) from the companies who provide students with additional context about the company.

Course Resources

Custom-produced videos provide an engaging learning tool for students. Some of the videos will open up the chapters, some are applied and scenario based, and others will provide solutions/discussions surrounding the mini-cases.

Videos: We will have one brief (2-minute) video for each learning objective (LO) for each chapter (done by the authors) that will bring additional context to the learning objective. Some of these LO videos will provide additional examples and stories to support the concepts, and others will have the authors answering questions related to the concepts. Then we will have a number of expert videos with the cases (see below case list) where a senior manager from the company discussed in the case will provide additional context about the company.

Main cases are all written specifically for the text by Paul Godfrey. Many are accompanied by expert interview videos with company employees such as vice presidents, chief sustainability officers, and others.

Why Did We Bring Another Book to the Market?

"As we've written the book, we've consciously reflected on the thousands of real students we've taught and the great questions they've raised about leading an ethical life. Our combined fifty-plus years of working in, teaching about, or researching business and ethical behavior have taught us a valuable lesson: When people live their values and do what they are passionate about, they experience fewer ethical crises (they have no problem staying out of jail), and they have an overarching life plan to thrive that helps them integrate their personal and professional lives."

—PAUL C. GODFREY

"I teach a lot in Silicon Valley (at Santa Clara University) in the Leavey School of Business (undergraduate/MBA/OMBA programs). I need not only help students to understand theory/spot issues but also sync those with the roles they either are seeking or already have in the Valley. The work they do/will do is incredibly time-consuming in terms of hours in a week, and there are often exhaustion and/or depression issues as a result. They need to have the tools to spot issues and react incredibly quickly. In other words, sometimes there just isn't a lot of time to think. Students need to have developed their gut instincts to help them. Resources in business ethics courses they take must reflect the reality of where we are living."

—LAURA JACOBUS

Meet the Authors

PAUL C. GODFREY is the William and Roceil Low Professor of Business Strategy at the BYU Marriott School of Business. He has been honored with both the school's Outstanding Researcher and Outstanding Teacher awards. An active researcher, his work has appeared in a number of premiere scientific publications, including *Nature Biotechnology*, the *Academy of Management Review*, and the *Strategic Management Journal*. Paul's previous textbook, *Strategic Management: Concepts and Cases* (4th edition) provides students with a well-written, tools-driven approach to these important areas of business.

In 2019, Paul, John Bugalla, Kristina Narvaez, and Manny Lauria co-authored *Strategic Risk Management: New tools for competitive advantage in an uncertain age*. Paul has been an active consultant for businesses and not-for-profit organizations. His not-for-profit experience includes the Human Interface Technology Lab at the University of Washington, DINÉ (Developing Innovations in Navajo Education), Inc. and Newman's Own Foundation.

Paul received his MBA and PhD degrees from the University of Washington and a Bachelor of Science from the University of Utah.

PAUL C. GODFREY
William and Roceil Low Professor
of Business Strategy
Marriott School of Business
Brigham Young University

LAURA JACOBUS is a seasoned attorney and business leader. She has held strategic legal and business leadership roles in Silicon Valley global high tech companies including Cisco Systems and Juniper Networks. Her interest in business ethics began while working in Silicon Valley during the dot-com bubble. Laura now teaches in several different business and law programs, including those at Santa Clara University Leavey School of Business, SCU Law School, Widener Delaware Law School, Baker College and Drexel University School of Law (MLS program). She teaches primarily in the areas of ethics and compliance, risk management, international business and business communications. Laura has co-authored Essential Lawyering Skills: A Companion Guide for Neil W. Hamilton's ROADMAP (2021, American Bar Association). She received a Juris Doctor from SCU School of Law and a Bachelor of Arts in English from SCU. She is an attorney licensed to practice in California.

LAURA JACOBUS
Professor, Santa Clara University

Brief Contents

Contents

14   Ethics and a Market Economy   199

Cases

CHAPTER 1

Introduction: Why Study Business Ethics?

LEARNING OUTCOMES

At the end of this chapter, you should be able to do the following:

1. Define ethics and the domain of business ethics.

2. Discuss how the constraints on managers influence ethical decision making in business.

3. Use the business and ethics trade-offs framework to differentiate between four types of ethical temptations business professionals face.

4. Explain the two approaches to business ethics and use the DRAFT model to understand the key differences between the two.

5. Use the tools and frameworks in this chapter to analyze actual ethical situations and issues.

Opening Case | WeWork Doesn't Work: Ethical and Business Challenges Stop a Unicorn in Its Tracks

Bloomberg/Getty Images

Adam Neumann and Miguel McKelvey founded WeWork in 2010, when the pair recognized a scalable business opportunity in what they had done with their own office space. The two had subleased a workspace in New York City and remodeled it into a comfortable, inviting place for two millennial, digital-savvy workers to be more creative and productive. The company's value proposition centered on signing long-term leases for prime office space in the world's largest markets and creating a shared and collaborative work environment that was "hip and inviting" for a generation of knowledge workers, many of whom previously worked from home or in coffee shops.[1] Clients, at first individuals and then entire companies, would sublease space from WeWork on a short-term basis. The positive "vibe" in these new offices would boost collaboration and creativity, fueling entrepreneurial ideas and gains in worker productivity.[2]

WeWork built on the premise that work was the central axis around which people's lives rotated in the twenty-first century, and the company hoped that the new style of working would alter and raise the consciousness of people beyond work and contribute to the solution of global problems such as climate change, hunger, and poverty. Neumann proved an adept promotor of his vision and found investors willing to back his new venture. The largest investor, Japan's SoftBank, would pour more than $10.5 billion into the company over the 2010s.[3] By 2018, WeWork had expanded to 500 cities across the globe and was the largest lease holder of office space in London, New York City, and Washington, DC.[4] The company had revenues of $1.8 billion, a cash hoard of over $6.6 billion, and a valuation of $47 billion.[5] The time seemed right for an IPO, and the company targeted a fall 2019 date to go public.

Revenues and valuations had climbed over the decade, but so did losses. The company lost $1.6 billion in 2018, and by July of 2019 it racked up another $690 million net loss over six months on earnings of $1.5 billion.[6] When the company filed its

S-1 prospectus, investors wondered whether the company's fundamental business model, based on long-term costs and short-term revenue, would ever turn a profit. Investors and critics of the company also found reports of several questionable ethical practices, and the company's definition of success seemed out of touch for a company in the commercial real estate business.

The S-1 filing, the company's initial SEC-required registration document prior to an IPO, detailed several questionable transactions that raised concerns about conflicts of interest and the company's ability to manage them. In a 2014 funding round, Neumann had created a voting rights structure (his shares held ten times the voting rights of any other shares) that left him with 100% control of the company. He also had been an owner or investor in several of the properties WeWork leased and had even licensed the trademarked name of "We" to the company for $6 million. Neumann had sold, but not reported to investors, shares worth hundreds of millions of dollars, often at valuations not available to others inside the company, and he had borrowed over $740 million against the value of his remaining shares.[7]

Neumann was not alone in apparent self-dealing. Reports later surfaced that several members of the executive team, including the vice presidents of real estate and construction, had funneled money to relatives or entities in which they were owners. Former Twitter CEO Dick Costolo summed up what many in the market felt: "The degree of self-dealing in the S-1 is so egregious, and it comes at a time when you've got regulators and politicians and folks across the country looking out at Silicon Valley and wondering if there's the appropriate level of self-awareness."[8]

In addition to raising global consciousness, alleviating climate change, ending hunger, and solving poverty, Neumann had publicly stated his goal to be the world's first trillionaire, and he claimed the need for a high market capitalization this way: "I need to have the biggest valuation I can, because when countries are shooting at each other, I want them to come to me."[9] WeWork glorified its culture of work hard, play hard, and sometimes-unreasonable expectations. The company produced T-shirts and other swag with slogans such as "Hustle Harder" and "Thank God It's Monday." Free-flowing alcohol was a staple at formal company meetings.[10]

The combination of a questionable business model, sketchy ethical transactions, and an outlandish vision of success sank WeWork's IPO. The company's valuation went from $47 billion to just over $7 billion in a matter of weeks. SoftBank, with its investment deeply underwater, took control of the company and removed Neumann from an operating role. Neumann would play a reduced role in the company, now named We, going forward, but the deal with SoftBank left him a billionaire and with a $185 million consulting contract.[11]

Adam Neumann and WeWork exemplify the concerns people have about ethics in business. The WeWork story provides a short but sobering answer to the question: "Why study business ethics?" Greater attention to ethics might have helped WeWork avoid catastrophic losses, business failures, and the destruction of value both for shareholders ($40 billion in lost market value) and other stakeholders (4,200 employees lost their jobs when the IPO fizzled, and lessors and other suppliers found their payments in jeopardy). We don't know whether or not Adam Neumann took an ethics class when he studied business at Baruch College, but the presence of ethical challenges and problems at WeWork belies a serious consideration of the ethical dimension of business activity and decision making.

Introduction

Our goal in writing this book is to provide you with an integrated view of ethics and business that answers these two foundational questions: How do I avoid ethical and compliance quagmires such as conflict of interest (often translated as "How do I stay out of jail?"), and How do I create a life full of meaning and positive purpose (or "How do I lead a good life?")? After all, no one wants to (or intends to) go to jail, and all of us hope to live a happy, meaningful, and productive life. Ethical thinking and frameworks also can help you answer other important questions. Figure 1.1 lists these questions, describes the central frameworks and tools we'll introduce in the book to help you find answers, and gives you a road map of where you'll encounter each area of integration. We'll begin integrating ethics and business by defining the areas where ethics and business come into contact.

Ethics and Business Ethics

Ethics

Many definitions of ethics exist, from a basic dictionary definition of ethics as "a set of moral principles," or "principles of conduct governing an individual or group."[12] Aristotle, a

Integrating Ethics Helps You Answer These Questions	Using These Frameworks/Tools	Covered in These Chapters
How can I avoid creating moral harms?	The Ethical Tradeoffs Framework The DRAFT Model	Chapters 8–14 Chapters 1, 2, 4, 5
How can I create moral goods and live a meaningful life?	The PERMA Model Sustainability	Chapters 3, 4, 12
How can I balance personal values and professional obligations?	The PERMA Model Ethical Leadership	Chapter 3 Chapter 6
How can I apply ethical concepts in practical situations?	Situation Specific Guidelines	Chapters 8–12
How can I make better business decisions by considering the ethical component?	The Eight Questions Stakeholder Salience Model	Chapter 3, 6 Chapter 4, 6
How can I account for religious, philosophical, or scientific models of ethics?		Chapter 3, 7
How can I design ethics-based compliance systems?	Elements of Compliance	Chapter 5
How can I navigate ethics in a global setting?	The CAGE Framework	Chapter 7

FIGURE 1.1   The advantages of integrating ethics and business.

philosopher of Ancient Greece, used the Greek word hexis to describe individual moral virtue as a "stable disposition . . . [or] way of being."[13] Hexis provides the foundation of a person's *character*." The nineteenth-century British aristocrat Lord Moulton described ethics as that which lies between unbridled human freedom of choice and the strict confines of law. This third domain of human action requires "obedience to the unenforceable," or conformance with norms and principles where no punishment arises from nonconformance.[14]

Business Ethics

Business ethics involves the "ethical dimensions of productive organizations and commercial activities."[15] This definition covers both traditional business (commercial) activity and the work of many nonprofit or civil society (productive or service) organizations. Individual business professionals and organizations both deal with ethics in each of the three senses defined earlier.

You may ask: "Why study business ethics?" Having a serious and thoughtful consideration of the role of ethics in business life helps you answer several critical questions that will influence your professional success and personal fulfillment. We've already pointed out the two overarching and most critical questions in the opening case: How do I avoid ethical and compliance quagmires such as conflict of interest (often translated as "How do I stay out of jail?"), and How do I create a life full of meaning and positive purpose (or "How do I lead a good life?")? The first question, avoiding ethical harm, has concerned scholars, executives, and policy makers throughout much of the twentieth century.[16] The second question concerns more than just living a life free from moral harm and involves creating moral goodness. This question has been central to philosophers since the dawn of civilization.[17]

Many companies and individuals have clearly stated principles of conduct that define right and wrong behavior, often contained in a mission statement, list of values, or a code of ethics. Our Ethics in the Real World 1.1 feature provides an example of a famous mission and values statement: the Johnson and Johnson Credo. The language in many of these documents creates an aspirational goal of a type of character to be obtained by the company and its employees. Finally, much of business activity, from how we deal with coworkers to customers, depends on people being obedient to unenforceable norms of civility, kindness, and respect.

Ethics in the Real World 1.1 | The Johnson & Johnson Credo

Robert Wood Johnson served as CEO of Johnson & Johnson from 1932 to 1963. In 1943, he articulated the core values of his company in a document he termed the Credo:

> We believe our first responsibility is to the doctors, nurses and patients, to mothers and fathers and all others who use our products and services. In meeting their needs everything we do must be of high quality. We must constantly strive to reduce our costs in order to maintain reasonable prices. Customers' orders must be serviced promptly and accurately. Our suppliers and distributors must have an opportunity to make a fair profit.
>
> We are responsible to our employees, the men and women who work with us throughout the world. Everyone must be considered as an individual. We must respect their dignity and recognize their merit. They must have a sense of security in their jobs. Compensation must be fair and adequate, and working conditions clean, orderly and safe. We must be mindful of ways to help our employees fulfill their family responsibilities. Employees must feel free to make suggestions and complaints. There must be equal opportunity for employment, development and advancement for those qualified.

> We must provide competent management, and their actions must be just and ethical.
>
> We are responsible to the communities in which we live and work and to the world community as well. We must be good citizens—support good works and charities and bear our fair share of taxes. We must encourage civic improvements and better health and education.
>
> We must maintain in good order the property we are privileged to use, protecting the environment and natural resources.
>
> Our final responsibility is to our stockholders. Business must make a sound profit. We must experiment with new ideas. Research must be carried on, innovative programs developed and mistakes paid for. New equipment must be purchased, new facilities provided and new products launched. Reserves must be created to provide for adverse times. When we operate according to these principles, the stockholders should realize a fair return.

As you read the Credo, think of the different definitions of ethics. Where do you see a "set of moral principles" that govern behavior? What type of corporate character does J & J aspire to? What "unenforceable" norms does the company commit to obey? What relationships do you see between J&J's values and their business strategy?

The Dimensions of Ethical Choice

This textbook will expose you to several categories of ethical challenges and issues that business professionals, specifically managers, and their organizations face, such as conflicts of interest, bribery, promise keeping, and the use and abuse of power. These broad categories of challenges play out in daily business life in countless concrete decisions and situations; however, each of those situations will have two common elements. Each involves a moral component, and each requires a professional to choose a course of action.

The Moral Aspect of Ethical Decision Making

The **moral component** means that ethical challenges center on fundamental questions of good and bad, right and wrong. Good/right and bad/wrong, when considered as a part of morality, may consider both instrumental and ultimate ends. **Instrumental ends** are things that are good because they lead to something else. **Ultimate ends**, also called **intrinsic** ends, are things that are good or desirable in and of themselves. A college education has both an instrumental and intrinsic moral nature. A degree provides instrumental value as it facilitates higher wages, which allow people to purchase goods and services that bring contentment or pleasure.[18] A college education is intrinsically good as knowledge provides its own happiness and satisfactions, over and above economic or other benefits.

The moral component of an ethical challenge may be an input or output to an ethical decision. Consider workforce reductions. These moves, often called downsizing, rightsizing, or reductions in force, often create ill will among employees and other stakeholders as they are seen as a company focusing on "business" at the expense of "ethics." Workforce reductions appear to pit a company's obligations to shareholders and financial returns against employee loyalty and well-being. Managers who see the impact on employees as having a moral, as well as business, dimension can work to design restructuring programs that are transparent and fair and satisfy both business and ethical needs. French tire giant Michelin has a formal policy to ensure fairness:

> **"Restructures [the company's term for Reductions in Force] are inevitable in certain circumstances in order to maintain the company's global competitiveness. These restructures must, as far as possible, take place at times when the company's health allows mobilization of adequate resources to attenuate the social consequences. Whenever possible, staff at the entities concerned and their representatives are invited to work together to seek and suggest solutions for restoring competitiveness and reducing overcapacity, which may open up an alternative to closing an activity or site. When restructuring is unavoidable, it must be announced as soon as possible and carried out according to the procedures negotiated with the staff representatives. The ensuing changes on a personal level must be supported for as long as is necessary to ensure that the reclassified employees find a satisfactory solution in terms of standard of living, stability, family life and self-esteem."[19]**

Fair and transparent processes produce positive *instrumental* outcomes when people are more satisfied with the company and their jobs. Fairness and transparency are also *intrinsic* moral goods, valued in and of themselves. Many business decisions involve moral outcomes. Marc Tarpenning and Martin Eberhard founded Tesla Motors in 2003 with the goal of producing a high-end performance sports car that would not contribute to global warming. After a divorce from his first wife, Eberhard recalls: "I was thinking I should do what every guy does and buy a sports car. . . . I couldn't bring myself to buy a car that got 18 miles to the gallon at a time when wars in the Middle East seemed to somehow involve oil and the arguments for global warming were becoming undeniable."[20] Similarly, Heliogen, a start-up backed by Bill Gates and AOL's Steve Case, devised a way to use machine learning to focus hundreds of solar panels to generate 1,000 degree Celsius temperatures. Heliogen hopes to deploy its innovation in cement, petrochemical, and steel production plants. If their technology works, solar energy would replace fossil fuels in these massive facilities and could reduce global carbon emissions by up to 20%.[21] An ecologically sustainable world represents an ultimate moral end, good in and of itself. Ethics in the Real World 1.2 describes another organization acting to create ultimate moral ends.

Ethics in the Real World 1.2 | Celeste Mergens Empowers Girls in the Developing World

In 2008, Celeste Mergens (see picture) found herself working in an orphanage just outside Nairobi, Kenya. One night she asked what the young women at the orphanage did for feminine hygiene. The answer was, "Nothing. They wait in their rooms."[22] Girls would sit alone on whatever cardboard they could find, missing meals, school, and opportunities for social interaction during their periods. Mergens worked to find a solution to the taboo subject of female menstruation. She began by providing disposable pads to the girls, but found that these pads overwhelmed the capacity of communities to process the waste. Over the next several years, Mergens devised a new product, the DfG (Days for Girls) POD (for Portable Object of Dignity), a patented, cloth-based, reusable set of absorbent pads that allow girls full mobility and activity during their period. The cloth-based

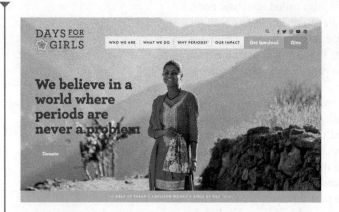

product dramatically reduces landfill waste and is cheaper to use. Each POD lasts up to three years. The product empowers girls by putting them out in the community, removes a substantial

barrier to education, and fosters gender equality. As of 2019, Days for Girls had provided hygiene kits to over 800,000 girls and women.

> "[Days for Girls] addresses something that frees and strengthens girls and women on a very foundational level," [friend Camille] Olson said. "By doing this, you really start changing the world and you can make a change happen instantaneously. From the moment they get one of those pads and learn how to take care of it, it's a new life for that girl, for that woman. It changes right there."[23]

Education and gender equality represent important instrumental, or intermediate ends. Education allows people to realize their full potential for happiness, and equality is an important element of human freedom. Happiness and freedom are intrinsic moral ends.

Moral Agency and Choice

The second characteristic that defines the ethical dimension is choice, the ability to freely decide among different options. When an actor has a real choice of alternative courses of action, that person has moral, and often legal, responsibility for the choices he or she makes.[24] Note that having choice does not mean that ethical decisions or challenges will be easy and convenient, nor will the course of action readily be clear. A part of what makes up many ethical choices is the difficulty and sacrifice actors must make to conform to ethical norms, standards, and values.

Sometimes actors don't have free choice. In this case. they make decisions under duress, the condition in which an actor faces two alternatives, but one course of action is perceived as so unreasonable as to not be a feasible choice. Contract law recognizes that sometimes people make decisions under conditions of coercion or duress, and the legal corpus has identified five conditions under which an actor is considered under duress:

1. The actor must be threatened with significant harm.

2. The actor must have no reasonable opportunity to escape from the coercive situation.

3. The threat must be itself illegal or immoral.

4. The threat of harm must be imminent in time or have a high probability of being carried out.

5. The actor must not have placed themself into this situation voluntarily, or where they could expect the situation to result in threat or coercion.

In organizational situations, duress is often a function of the power differential between a person requesting/demanding a certain action and the one being asked. Our experience is that those with power and a desire to abuse it can far too easily request unethical behavior of subordinates with either explicit or implicit threats, such as being demoted, fired, or transferred to a less attractive assignment. The fifth criterion becomes particularly important in many situations, as those without power sometimes voluntarily put themselves in situations where threats become more severe. For example, recent graduates in their first jobs will often incur personal debt, like buying a new car. This debt makes the threat of demotion or job loss more severe but fails to constitute duress as the graduate voluntarily incurred the debt and left themself open to coercion. In this case, our new hire still has free choice; however, one of the choices is reasonable, but very unattractive. Our Ethics in the Real World 1.3 feature describes a situation in which many women found themselves under duress.

dpa picture alliance/Alamy Stock Photo

Activist Tarana Burke first used the phrase "Me Too" in 2006 to bring attention to the problem of sexual abuse among women of color. The phrase would lie dormant for another decade until October of 2017, when actress Ashley Judd accused Oscar-winning media mogul Harvey Weinstein of soliciting sexual favors from her during a visit to his hotel room.[25] "Women have been talking about Harvey amongst ourselves for a long time,

and it's simply beyond time to have the conversation publicly," Judd said of her decision to disclose the harassment.[26] It soon came out that Weinstein had offered legal settlements to eight other women whom he sexually harassed, molested, or threatened. The threat was often cloaked in a promise: In exchange for sexual favors (or the lack thereof), Weinstein would use his power to advance (or destroy) the careers of young actresses. In 2020, Weinstein would be convicted of rape for some of his coercive actions.

Judd's revelation led to disclosures by other women that felled and sometimes jailed many powerful men, including NBC *Today* anchor Matt Lauer, CBS CEO Leslie Moonves, and comedian Bill Cosby. Other powerful men would also be accused, such as popular scientist Neil deGrasse Tyson, musician R. Kelly, and actor Cuba Gooding, Jr. #MeToo crossed the gender line in 2019 when US Representative, from California, Katie Hill resigned amidst the disclosure of an inappropriate sexual relationship with a male subordinate.

Common to each of these stories is the account by accusers of being coerced into sexual activity or harassed about it under the explicit or implicit threat of serious and sustained career damage. These threats placed the victims under extreme duress and resulted in emotional pain and decisions and actions all victims later regretted.

Business Agency and Fiduciary Responsibilities

Employees, executives, and managers in organizations have been hired to make choices. They act as agents of the organization that hired them. An agent is a person "who is authorized to act for or in place of another."[27] Some business leaders, the senior executives of the firm and the board of directors, are fiduciaries. A **fiduciary** is an agent who has custody over things of value to the principle, and a responsibility to act in the best interest of the principal that he or she represents. The executives of a firm have a fiduciary responsibility to pursue the best interests of the organization that hired them. A **fiduciary duty** has two components. The first is the **duty of loyalty**, which requires a fiduciary to act in good faith and in a manner that they reasonably believe is in the best interest of the organization. The second is the **duty of care**, which requires a fiduciary to avoid untoward risk or potential harm to the interests of the principal. For executives of exempt organizations, typically religious, charitable, scientific, public safety, literary, or educational organizations, a third fiduciary duty exists. They much make sure the organization conforms to the purposes that allow the organization it tax-exempt status from the IRS. Employees do not have the same formal fiduciary duties as executives and officers; however, when a person accepts a job and its compensation, they agree to work for the benefit of their employer and avoid taking risks that would jeopardize the business.

Ethical Challenges in Business

Ethical challenges fall into two broad categories, temptations, where the choice is between something right and something wrong, and dilemmas that pit right versus right or wrong versus wrong.

How to Develop Ethical Managers

The teaching pedagogy of business ethics plays a very vital role in developing ethical managers. In the first step, schools identify key ethical competencies for business students; they then can integrate with the outcome of various courses. Then, experiential learning teaching pedagogy can be used to transfer appropriate ethical knowledge to future business leaders by using appropriate context. Ethical decision making suggests that individual ethical decision is driven by awareness, decision, intent, and courage. Thus, along with business ethics course, management education should include some courses from philosophy and culture which will help increase the awareness of students to ethical practices. Moreover, we should remember that ethics is a multidisciplinary subject. Therefore, management education curriculum should cover various relevant practical ethical dilemmas and instructors should be able to discuss these issues with appropriate ethical models. We hope these efforts will help develop ethical orientation in future managers.

Ethical Temptations

For business executives, the root of most temptations is a conflict between their roles as agents of the busines owners and their personal ethical values. The matrix shown in Figure 1.2 captures the basic elements of an ethical temptation, where a business professional must decide between a course of action that's good for the business or that's ethically proper.

Note that the actor faces four potential decisions:

- Quadrant I—The situation where the action is good for the business but morally improper. This becomes a difficult decision, and represents a real temptation, as forgoing the ethically correct decision will bring clear rewards to the business.

- Quadrant II—The situation where the action is both good for the business and ethically correct. This is an easy decision, there is no temptation, and the decision is a clear yes.

- Quadrant III—The situation where the action is both bad for the business and ethically improper. Again, this is an easy decision with no temptation. No is the simple answer.

- Quadrant IV—The situation where the action is bad for the business but ethically correct. Like its diagonal counterpart, these choices represent tough decisions and real temptations as doing the "right thing" will lead to "wrong consequences" for the business.

When professionals face the temptations in quadrants I and IV, they resolve these temptations by employing **moral courage**, the willingness and ability to make the correct ethical choice in the face of negative consequences. Wise professionals will often employ **moral creativity** to

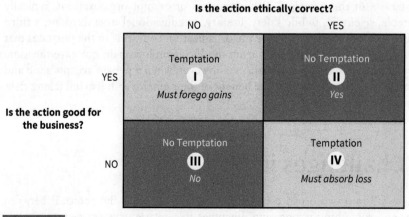

FIGURE 1.2   The business ethics tradeoff framework.

find a solution that resolves the temptation by finding a way to move the decision into either quadrant II or III. Take the issue of a reduction in force, or layoff, that we described earlier. Business conditions may worsen and require prompt action by managers to cut costs by reducing head count, and the temptation appears to pit two important stakeholder groups, investors and employees, against each other: profitability against fairness, transparency, and equity in honoring the informal or social contract between the firm and its employees.[28] Moral creativity enters the decision when managers focus on the potential increases in long-term costs, such as reduced productivity or innovation, that often accompany poorly handled layoffs.[29] Layoffs may still take place, but by attending to the process and context of the action, managers can remove the temptation to act unethically by showing that the predicted trade-off was false: There was a way to accomplish the business goal through more ethically correct means.

Ethical Dilemmas

The second set of ethical challenges are dilemmas, where the decision is between competing moral goods. In these cases, managers and employees must trade off competing ethical values such as respect for privacy with openness and transparency, or they may have two responsibilities and must choose which one to honor.[30] Dilemmas may arise from traditional fiduciary/employee duties and focus on problems of discretionary corporate activities. For example, Connecticut-based Newman's Own Foundation operates with a set annual budget and supports a number of organizations in predefined philanthropic categories. When Hurricane Sandy hit the New York area in 2012, executives felt the need to divert funds to support relief efforts in their local community. They had to sacrifice one good act in order to do another one.

Dilemmas may also arise from conflicts between our duties at work and obligations as life partners, parents, or as compassionate human beings. Managers and coworkers struggle with this balancing act all the time. How should we respond to a single parent on our work team who misses some deadlines due to the lack of childcare options? What is the appropriate level of tolerance for employees with a history of substance abuse? How can managers and leaders balance the need for safety and security and yet still offer compassion to the chronically unsheltered?[31] Dilemmas require that professionals disappoint one party or leave one responsibility undone in favor of the other, or they force people into compromises that leave neither party satisfied or both responsibilities partially unfilled.

How to Solve Ethical Dilemmas   Ethical dilemmas can be associated either with an individual or an organization. In case of an individual, moral reasoning could be an effective method to solve ethical dilemmas. In addition, various theories such as rational choice theory and ethical models such as PREMA may be useful to solve such dilemmas. In the case of organizational ethical dilemmas, stakeholder analysis that highlights short-term and long-term impacts of such ethical decisions on various stakeholders is of significance in resolving such issues.

Why are Ethics Important in Business?

The main objective of any business is to create value for the society. While ethics in any business increases its sustainability, ethical dilemmas test various situations for any organization. If the organization makes morally correct decisions in such situations, then it is able to increase its employer brand and customer trust. A good employer brand attracts exemplary employees who help grow the organization, while customer trust helps to make the company profitable by repeat consumption of a product. Further, research on ethics confirm that ethical decisions are beneficial for all stakeholders. Therefore, ethical decisions in any organization are likely to make it sustainable because ethical environment brings transparency, develops trust, and puts pressure on employees to have moral courage and moral creativity to find out solutions for ethical dilemmas at workplace.

The Need for an Integrated Approach

The WeWork case that opened the chapter introduced the two foundational concerns for business ethics: how to avoid moral harm, and how to create moral good. In common language, these become questions such as How do I stay out of jail? and How do I create a great, happy, and meaningful life?

Two Perspectives on Ethics in Business

These two questions represent two broad approaches to the ethical challenges and issues in business, which we label the *pragmatic* and the *philosophical* approaches to ethics. Table 1.1 displays important features and underlying assumptions that differentiate the pragmatic from the philosophical view. We use the mnemonic DRAFT to capture the key differences between the two views.

Employing an Integrated Approach

The vignettes of Harvey Weinstein and Celeste Mergens in this chapter provide evidence that both views have merit: Human beings can be greedy, power-hungry, and downright awful. They also be filled with concern for others, creative in finding solutions to vexing problems, and exhibit genuine love and charity toward each other. Humanity falls on some sort of moral distribution, with very small numbers of people who are purely immoral or moral. Most people fall in the middle of the distribution, capable of both good and evil, and swayed to engage in either one by formal laws and ethical principles, and informal norms and customs that prove unenforceable. Aristotle saw the development of a moral character as the outcome of a lifetime of moral actions or habits. For most people, the type of moral character they develop is the result of following base desires for acquisition, comfort, and power, or heeding the better angels of their nature by practicing kindness, altruism, and a concern for virtue.

This book title includes the words *An Integrated Approach* because our view is that a robust and helpful introduction to ethics requires deep and serious consideration of the two fundamental ethical questions: How do I stay out of jail? and How do I build a good life? We don't see integration as some sort of mash-up of the two views. There is no middle position between the pragmatic and philosophical view, and we'll take seriously each position. As you read this book, you'll come to understand the overarching frameworks, models, rules, and tools of ethical compliance that will allow you to navigate within the world of work. You'll also be exposed

TABLE 1.1 Approaches to Business Ethics.

	Pragmatic	Philosophical
Drivers of behavior	Greed and Power—Personal Gain	Benevolence and Love—Personal and Other's Gain
Relationship between actors and decisions	Ethical actors are constrained business agents acting in the face of incentives that limit moral choices.	Ethical actors are principals and have real moral choice even in the face of constraints and incentives.
Approach to ethical issues	Transactional—What should I do?	Theoretical—Why should I do it?
Fundamental governance mechanisms	Rules and sanctions and external controls to counter incentives for unethical behavior	Principles, intrinsic rewards, and self controls to facilitate the expression of positive ethical behaviors
Target	Compliance and avoiding harm	Happiness, fulfillment, and doing good

to the frameworks, models, principles, and tools that help you integrate the other elements we laid out in Figure 1.1. Each of these areas are important for you to consider as you plan to stay out of jail and build a good life—one filled with meaning and happiness.

The first section, of the book, which comprises chapters 2 through 7, provides you with some important fundamental knowledge about human nature and how smart people have thought about ethics throughout history (Chapter 2). Chapter 3 takes up the issue of how to create a morally good life and the role of integrating business and ethics in that process. Chapter 4 describes key features of organizations and gives you a set of tools to evaluate the different stakeholder groups that interact with a business or organization. Chapter 5 lays out the important role of compliance and related processes in organizations, and Chapter 6 discusses the critical role of organizational culture and individual ethical leadership in creating flourishing organizations. Chapter 7 provides you with some foundational frameworks for dealing with ethical issues in a global setting. In Chapters 8 through 12, the second section, we turn our attention to specific ethical challenges and issues common in twenty-first century business and nonprofit organizations: power, including bullying, cancelling, and coercion (Chapter 8), conflict of interest (Chapter 9), bribery (Chapter 10), promise keeping (Chapter 11), corporate social responsibility/sustainability (Chapter 12), The focus in these chapters is to provide you with practice facing ethical challenges and making decisions. With practice, you'll make better decisions when you arrive in the world of work. Section three zooms out and offers two essays that consider larger issues. Chapter 13 takes up the relationship between ethics and technology, and Chapter 14 invites you to think about both the role of ethics in a well-functioning market economy and the moral goodness of a market economy for society at large.

Key Terms

choice	fiduciary duty	moral courage
duty of care	hexis	moral creativity
duty of loyalty	instrumental ends	third domain
ethics	intrinsic	ultimate ends
fiduciary	moral component	

Chapter Summary

In this chapter, we've outlined the following key concepts:

- Ethics in business provides answers to two foundational questions: How can individuals and organizations avoid causing moral harm? How can individuals and organizations create morally good actions and outcomes? These questions are often expressed as follows: How can I stay out of jail? How can I lead a happy, meaningful life?

- Ethics is a system of moral principles and values that guide action. For Aristotle, the goal of ethics was to create an individual, or an organization, of great moral character. Ethics also entails conformance, or obedience, to unenforceable social norms or customs.

- Business ethics is the application of moral character, customs, norms, principles, and values to commercial and productive organizations. This includes business organizations as well as those in the not-for-profit sector.

- Ethical challenges take two forms: temptations that force individuals to choose between right and wrong, and dilemmas that require a choice between right and right. Working through both types of challenges requires moral courage and moral creativity.

- There are two broad and different approaches to business ethics. The pragmatic view sees individuals as motivated by the darker sides of self-interest and driven by a desire for acquisition (which easily becomes greed) and power. The goal of pragmatic ethics is to keep these destructive desires in check through rules, regulations, punishments, and other sanctions. The philosophical view holds that individuals can be motivated by positive moral virtues, such as altruism, benevolence, and charity. The goal of ethics is to encourage individuals and organizations to exercise and implement these moral motivations and actions into their lives. This book will integrate those two views by exploring how these two perspectives inform business activity and decision making.

Chapter Review Questions

1. Define business ethics. How do the three conceptions of ethics outlined in the chapter fit together? How does each notion of ethics help us understand the prevalence of the ethical dimension in business?

2. Should business ethics include a concern for personal well-being, or should it just focus on curbing the tendency of firms and managers to engage in harmful actions?

3. How does an ethical temptation differ from a dilemma? Provide an example from your own life about when you faced a moral temptation, and another when you faced a moral dilemma. How did you resolve them?

4. How can managers reconcile situations where a course of action is morally correct but will create negative consequences for their business? Would this be a more difficult decision than forgoing some gain to the business in order to avoid moral harm? Why or why not?

5. What things can individuals and organizations do to develop moral courage?

6. In your opinion and experience, which view of human tendencies, the pragmatic or the philosophical, better describes individuals and organizations?

7. Identify business activities that are unethical. Justify why they are unethical.

8. Discuss the challenges of business executives to choose the ethical path.

9. What motivates an organization to choose an unethical path?

Application Exercises

- *Personal Ethical Development.* Begin keeping an ethics journal. For this chapter, record your thoughts and feelings about the need for ethics to help you "stay out of jail" and "lead a happy life." As you reflect on your own history, record instances when you have been motivated by an unhealthy desire for acquisition (you have been greedy), or when you have used power inappropriately. Also think about and record times when you have acted according to the "better angels" of your nature.

- *Career Goals and Planning.* Throughout this book, we'll give you the opportunity to think about creating a career that fulfills the goal of ethics to lead a happy, meaningful, and productive life that blends and builds upon the following: (1) the type of life you are interested in leading, (2) your deepest and most important values, (3) the work you are interested in doing, (4) what you are good at, (5) your preferences for things like work versus free time, and (6) your personality. To begin this work, write down your initial responses to these questions. Think about your answers for a couple of days, and then revisit your answers and begin to add more depth. You'll do this throughout the course, and for now it's good to begin thinking seriously and rigorously about these issues.

- *Ethics in the Business World.* Identify two companies that have faced ethical challenges and find articles or other information about the specific challenges these companies have faced. How did these companies respond to these situations? What common actions do you see in both instances? In what areas did their responses differ? What were the results of each company's actions? Which company do you think did a better job?

- *Talking with and Learning from Others.* Choose a business professional you admire and aspire to be like. Engage that person in a brief interview. What types of ethical temptations and dilemmas has this person faced in their career? What did they do? How did they develop moral courage? When did they exercise moral creativity to resolve these issues? What practices can you adopt in your own life and career to help you be a more ethical person?

Mini-Cases

Case 1: How much cheating is wrong? In November of 2017, the Houston Astros won baseball's World Series. The championship was the first for the franchise, and after the devastation of Hurricane Harvey, the team lifted the spirits of many beleaguered Houstonians. Much of that joy turned to shock and anger in late 2019, when former Astros pitcher Mike Fiers claimed that the Astros 2017 championship came about because the team engaged in a sophisticated scheme of "sign stealing." Hitting a baseball is said to be the most difficult athletic maneuver. A batter is trying to use a 2.6-inch-wide bat to hit a ball flying in at up to 100 miles per hour, and sometimes "curving," "sinking," or "jumping" during its flight. The speed, spin, and trajectory of the ball are strategic decisions on the part of the pitcher, and the decision on which pitch to throw is communicated between the pitcher and the catcher (who needs to know which pitch is coming in order to successfully catch it). If the batter knows which pitch is coming, he is better able to hit the ball.

All teams engage in sign stealing, and the attempt to figure out which pitch is coming is considered a part of the game. Pitchers and catchers create elaborate sign systems, and often change signs in order to avoid sign stealing by opposing players and coaches. What is not part of the game, however, is using advanced technology to steal signs. The Astros had an employee in center field (directly behind the pitcher and in full view of the catcher and the sign-giving catcher). This employee would view video of the catcher's signs, and then note the ensuing pitch. After a couple of innings, the employee would match signs with pitches, and when the catcher signaled for a "breaking ball"—one that would curve, sink, or jump, the employee would send a signal to the Astros bench, and a player would bang on a garbage can. The batter would then know to expect a "breaking ball" and react accordingly.

In January of 2020, Major League Baseball, the sport's governing body, announced that it had confirmed that the Astros had cheated and suspended two of the team's leaders, who were later fired from the Astros. No players were sanctioned; in exchange for exposing the scheme, they were given immunity. Major League Baseball chose to punish those who organized and perpetuated the scheme, but not those who participated in it or were the direct beneficiaries of it.

Discussion Questions

1. Is cheating in sports wrong? How can some cheating be an accepted part of the game, and other cheating be unacceptable? Where should the line be drawn? How does modern technology change the game of sign stealing?

2. How can Major League Baseball control cheating? What rules and punishments might be effective?

3. What role does cheating play in living a happy and meaningful life? Does winning a championship through cheating diminish its value? Why or why not?

Case 2: Privacy in the digital age. The right to privacy is foundational for Americans, legally encoded into the Fourth Amendment to the Constitution of the United States. The 1948 United Nations Declaration of Human Rights includes language that acknowledges the right to privacy for people all over the globe. With the dawn of the Internet age, however, privacy has become a hotly contested issue. The revenue model of many technology companies, such as Google and Facebook, relies on gathering data on the private actions of individuals, on the Web and off, and providing/selling that data to advertisers to better target potential customers.

Discussion Questions

1. What should remain private and beyond the reach of technology? What role does privacy play in leading a happy and meaningful life?

2. What have we gained in exchange for our privacy? Are individuals and societies better off now? In what ways?

3. Can companies be trusted to self-police and self-regulate the data they collect and sell? What conflicts of interest are there, and how do these threaten self-regulation?

4. How much should companies disclose about what data they collect and how it is used?

5. Recently, California adopted a law that allows users to opt out of data sharing. The European Union has a similar data privacy law. What are the advantages and disadvantages of such laws?

6. What types of government regulation can protect our privacy? Does government have the capability to create effective regulations in the rapidly advancing technology world? What would be lost, in terms of innovation, safety, or convenience, if government regulates social media and technology companies?

Case 3: Satyam – The greed of one person. Satyam computers were founded as an information technology services company by Mr. Ramalinga Raju and his brother-in-law in 1987. The company was converted into a public limited company in 1991 and it was listed in the New York Stock Exchange in 2001. Satyam had nearly 40,000 employees working in India and abroad, with almost 600 global clients. From 2005 to 2008, the company grew steadily, both organically and inorganically. In 2008, the company decided to purchase 51% shares of the Maytas infrastructure development, construction, and project management company. The strategic goals of both companies were not aligned. In addition, Mr. Raju did not inform the investors about the bidding process. This led to trust issues between Satyam board members and investors from across the world. Thus, the shareholders of the company requested the Government of India to review this deal. The inquiry revealed that the financial statements showed inflated profits. Moreover, the board members, senior managers, and auditors of the company were not aware of the manipulated financial statements. Mr. Raju acknowledged all these allegations and informed that the Maytas company was owned by his son. This incident by the top management has changed the image of this organization from a symbol of trust to one of scams and frauds. The company is no longer operational in the software industry.

Discussion Questions

1. What was the reason for Mr. Raju's unethical behavior?

2. Analyze the impact of Mr. Raju's behavior by doing a stakeholder analysis.

3. What kind of ethical infrastructure should companies like Satyam develop to eliminate such incidents?

References

1. Eliot Brown, "How Adam Neumann's Over-the-Top Style Built WeWork. 'This Is Not the Way Everybody Behaves.',", *Wall Street Journal*, September 18, 2019, https://www.wsj.com/articles/this-is-not-the-way-everybody-behaves-how-adam-neumanns-over-the-top-style-built-wework-11568823827.

2. Lizzie Widdicombe, "The Rise and Fall of WeWork," *The New Yorker*, November 6, 2019, https://www.newyorker.com/culture/culture-desk/the-rise-and-fall-of-wework.

3. Ibid.

4. Judy Woodruff, John Yang, and Peter Eavis, "WeWork's spectacular rise and fall provide cautionary tale for startups," *PBS Newshour*,

November 26, 2019. Transcript available at https://www.pbs.org/newshour/show/weworks-spectacular-rise-and-fall-provide-cautionary-tale-for-startups.

5. Ruth Reader, "WeWork reported nearly $2 billion in losses in 2018," *Fast Company*, March 26, 2019, https://www.fastcompany.com/90325201/wework-reported-nearly-2-billion-in-losses-in-2018.

6. Ibid.

7. Ibid.

8. Ibid.

9. Taylor Telford, "Adam Neumann's chaotic energy built WeWork. Now it might cost him his job as CEO.," *Washington Post*, September 23, 2019,

https://www.washingtonpost.com/business/2019/09/23/adam-neumanns-chaotic-energy-built-wework-now-it-might-cost-him-his-job-ceo/.

10 Ibid.

11 Widdicombe, "The Rise and Fall of WeWork."

12 Definition taken from *Merriam Webster's Dictionary*, cf. ethic, https://www.merriam-webster.com/dictionary/ethic.

13 Pierre Rodrigo, The Dynamic of Hexis in Aristotle's Philosophy, *Journal of the British Society for Phenomenology* (2011), 42 (1): 6–17

14 Right Honorable Lord (John Fletcher) Moulton, "Law and Manners," *The Atlantic Monthly*, July 1924, http://www2.econ.iastate.edu/classes/econ362/hallam/NewspaperArticles/LawandManners.pdf.

15 Jeffrey Moriarty, "Business Ethics," *The Stanford Encyclopedia of Philosophy*, ed. Edward N. Zalta (Fall 2017), https://plato.stanford.edu/entries/ethics-business/.

16 For an early consideration of these issues, see Adolf Berle and Gardner Means, *The Modern Corporation and Private Property* (New Brunswick, NJ: Transaction Publishers, 1932).

17 See Norman Melchert, *The Great Conversation* (Oxford: Oxford University Press, 2010), for a discussion of this tradition in Western philosophy. Chinese and other philosophers have also considered these issues. For an extensive history, see Wing-tsit Chan, *A Source Book in Chinese Philosophy* (Princeton, NJ: Princeton University Press, 1969).

18 See, for example, "The Rising Cost of Not Going to College," Pew Research Center, February 11, 2014, https://www.pewresearch.org/social-trends/2014/02/11/the-rising-cost-of-not-going-to-college/.

19 Sandra J. Sucher and Sharlene Gupta, "Layoffs That Don't Break Your Company," *Harvard Business Review* (May–June 2018), https://hbr.org/2018/05/layoffs-that-dont-break-your-company.

20 Drake Baer, "The Making Of Tesla: Invention, Betrayal, And The Birth Of The Roadster," *Business Insider*, November 11, 2014, https://www.businessinsider.com/tesla-the-origin-story-2014-10.

21 Minda Zetlin, "This Bill Gates-Backed Solar Startup Just Had a Breakthrough That Could Cut the World's Carbon Emissions by 20 Percent," *Inc. Magazine*, November 21, 2019, https://www.inc.com/minda-zetlin/heliogen-bill-gates-backed-startup-solar-

breakthrough-manufacturing-cement-steel-petrochemicals.html.

22 Information on Days For Girls can be found at their website, daysforgirls.org.

23 Aubrey Eyre, "Honored among leading women of the world, Days for Girls founder stays true to the mission of the Lord," *Deseret News*, March 29, 2018, https://www.deseret.com/2018/3/29/20642632/honored-among-leading-women-of-the-world-days-for-girls-founder-stays-true-to-the-mission-of-the-lor#celeste-mergens-a-church-member-and-founder-of-days-for-girls-meets-with-a-member-of-parliament-in-kenya-to-discuss-the-importance-of-girls-and-women-having-access-to-menstrual-care.

24 Claire Oakes Finkelstein (1995), "Duress: A Philosophical Account of the Defense in Law," *Arizona Law Review* 37 (1995): 251–283.

25 "#MeToo: A timeline of events," *Chicago Tribune*, February 4, 2021, https://www.chicagotribune.com/lifestyles/ct-me-too-timeline-20171208-htmlstory.html.

26 Lindsey Bahr, "Harvey Weinstein to take leave of absence after bombshell New York Times sex harassment report," *Chicago Tribune*, October 5, 2017, https://www.chicagotribune.com/entertainment/movies/ct-harvey-weinstein-new-york-times-sexual-harassment-report-20171005-story.html.

27 *Black's Law Dictionary*, 7th ed., cf. agent. Bryan Garner, ed. (Minneapolis, MN: West Group, 1999).

28 Joe Mahoney (2012), "Towards a Stakeholder Theory of Strategic Management," in *Towards a new theory of the firm: Humanizing the firm and the management profession*, J. E. Ricart Costa and J. M. Rosanas Marti. ed. (Bilbao, Spain: Fundación BBVA, 2012): 153–182. See also Denise Rousseau, *Psychological Contracts in Organizations* (Thousand Oaks, CA: Sage Publications, 1995).

29 Sucher and Gupta, "Layoffs That Don't Break Your Company."

30 Joseph Badaracco, *Defining Moments: When managers must choose between right and right* (Boston, MA: Harvard Business School Press, 1997).

31 For an example of this struggle, see Jane E. Dutton and Janet M. Dukerich, "Keeping an Eye on the Mirror: Image and Identity in Organizational Adaptation," *Academy of Management Journal* 34, no. 3 (September 1991): 517–554.

CHAPTER 2

Theories of Morality and Business Ethics

LEARNING OUTCOMES

At the end of this chapter, you should be able to do the following:

1. Define unethical behavior and explain the challenge of hedonism.

2. Differentiate between a theory of moral actions versus moral outcomes.

3. Explain how the world's major religions view moral actions and outcomes.

4. Identify the strengths and weaknesses of the most well-known ethical theories in moral philosophy.

5. Critique the scientific theories of how people develop the capacity for moral reasoning.

6. Use the frameworks you learned in this chapter to evaluate moral choices that individuals and managers face.

Opening Case | SC Johnson Sacrifice Opts for Consumer Safety over Market Share

ZUMA Press, Inc./Alamy Stock Photo

In 1933, Ralph Wiley was working on a compound of hydrogen and chlorine and created a super-water-resistant new compound, polyvinylidene chloride (PVDC). Since it was the Great Depression, he named the new product eonite, after a fictional material in the then-popular comic strip *Little Orphan Annie*.[1] The compound was so water resistant that he couldn't wash it out of his test beakers.[2] Wiley's bosses at Dow Chemical used the compound to treat everything from combat boots to fighter planes, and in 1949 Dow sprayed the chemical into thin green sheets that could be used to wrap food products and introduced Saran Wrap. It would go on to become one of America's leading consumer goods.

The product's water resistance meant it also clung tightly to whatever bowl or plate it covered. It created an impenetrable barrier to odor and it proved able to withstand the rigors of the microwave oven.[3]

SC Johnson, the Racine, Wisconsin, consumer products company, bought the brand from Dow in 1998. At the time, Saran Wrap was the category leader with 18% market share.[4] As the millennium turned, however, scientific research began to show that PVDC created environmental and human harms. When incinerated, for example, PVDC emitted several dioxin compounds, which are potential carcinogens.[5]

CEO Fisk Johnson and the leadership team faced the tough decision of whether or not to abandon PVDC. To make this decision, the company initiated an internal review process called Greenlist. The Greenlist process considered each product category, from cleaning solvents to food products, at the company for biodegradability, human toxicity, and other factors. Figure 2.1 shows how SC Johnson scored products using the Greenlist. An ingredient scored zero (0) if no substitute existed. PVDC scored a zero.[6] This created a decision point for the company. Johnson explained the consequences of that categorization: "Under Greenlist criteria, PVDC rated 0, so we pledged to eliminate it from our external packaging altogether. When it comes to the safety of our ingredients, we prefer to err on the side of caution."[7]

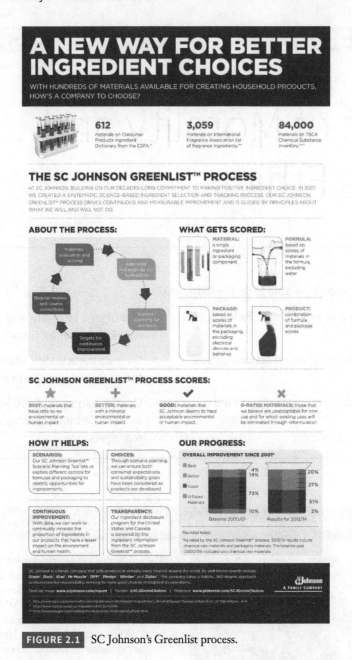

FIGURE 2.1 SC Johnson's Greenlist process.

The company committed to a replacement product by 2004, but finding a new ingredient proved difficult. Several alternative ingredients existed, but to get the same protection from odor and moisture would require multiple layers of film, and customers would likely not appreciate putting a "garbage bag" over their food.[8] Such a move would also require expensive new machinery that would make the product a money loser for the company. Eventually, Johnson settled on low-density polyethylene (LDPE), a film that is noticeably less effective than PVDC.[9] With its new formulation, Saran Wrap would be an inferior product, and the company could no longer support many its key claims, such as superior cling. SC Johnson reduced marketing support for the new formulation and watched as its share fell by a third to 11% in 2015.[10]

As he made the decision to change a popular product, Fisk Johnson looked back to the early history of the family company.

In 1975, the company had decided to move away from chlorofluorocarbons (CFCs), which had been implicated in damaging the Earth's ozone layer. That was twenty years before the federal government banned them for any use. Johnson had seen that move as successful, and so the Saran Wrap Decision was easier to make. He also relied on a fundamental business principle that had been with the company from the beginning. He explained: "For us, anything that risks the trust customers have in us is unacceptable. Once we learned about the possible toxic chemicals PVDC emitted from landfills, we never really considered retaining the original formulation. Doing the right thing for customers is always the right thing for us."[11] The decision has helped the business over the years, as Johnson noted: "As in the past when we eliminated ingredients, we gained a surer sense of who we are as a company and what we want SC Johnson to represent."[12]

Introduction

Most people would think of Fisk Johnson as an ethical leader. In the language of Chapter 1, Fisk and his company faced a moral temptation: They could do what was good for the business and keep Saran Wrap, or they could do what they believed was morally correct and replace the product. Their decision showed moral courage, and Fisk and the other employees at SC Johnson needed a strong idea of what was morally correct in this situation. Having a strong moral code of conduct helps all of us withstand moral temptations and resolve moral dilemmas. This chapter provides you with several different paradigms of what is morally correct conduct. We discuss how theologians, philosophers, and scientists have answered the two critical questions of **positive and normative ethics**: What constitutes morally correct action, and what are the moral outcomes that people and groups should work toward? This chapter gives you language and a set of frameworks to think more clearly about the elements of your own moral code. With this foundation, you'll be able to make better decisions about ethical issues you face. Before discussing what is right, we begin by considering the opposite of ethics: morally incorrect action and evil.

Human Nature and the Problem of Evil

The need for ethics arises because people have the capacity to engage in **unethical actions**; that is, they violate local ethical norms and customs or globally held notions of what is morally correct. Unethical actions arise from human nature and our penchant for **hedonism**, the pursuit of pleasure and the avoidance of pain. The English philosopher Jeremy Bentham outlined the power of our hedonistic desires: "Nature has placed mankind under the governance of two sovereign masters, *pain* and *pleasure*. It is for them alone to point out what we ought to do, as well as to determine what we shall do."[13] Seeking pleasure is not in itself wrong—in fact, it becomes one of the major perspectives on what is morally correct—but hedonism can easily degenerate into people pursuing their own physical, sensory, and sensual needs and desires at the expense of the desires and needs of others and the larger community. Evil is the extreme end of morally bad or wrong behavior. Ethics in the Real World 2.1 gives you a sense of the origins of the moral evils human beings are capable of.

Ethics in the Real World 2.1 | Thomas Hobbes on Human Nature

IanDagnall Computing/Alamy Stock Photo

Thomas Hobbes (1588–1679) lived in England during a period of social unrest and political division that culminated in the English Civil Wars of 1642–51. He outlined the problem of unethical and evil behavior in his classic book *Leviathan*: "Whatsoever therefore is consequent to a time of Warre [war], where every man is Enemy to every man; the same is consequent to the time, wherein men live without other security, than what their own strength, and their own invention shall furnish them withall. In such condition, there is no place for Industry; because the fruit thereof is uncertain; and consequently no Culture of the Earth; no Navigation, nor use of the commodities that may be imported by Sea; no commodious Building; no Instruments of moving, and removing such things as require much force; no Knowledge of the face of the Earth; no account of Time; no Arts; no Letters; no Society; and which is worst of all, continuall feare [fear], and danger of violent death; And the life of man, solitary, poore, nasty, brutish, and short." [spelling original].[14]

Hobbes has a very dark view of human nature, and of life in general. Left to their own designs, and unregulated by either ethics or government, the inevitable reality of people all wanting the same things creates a world of evil. People would care only for themselves, and life would be "solitary, poore, nasty, brutish, and short." The solution, for Hobbes, lay in setting up an all-powerful government, the Leviathan, that would deter people's natural tendency to fight and make social life possible.

Moral Development Process

The organizational moral development process has five stages.

Stage one – The amoral organization

In first stage of moral development process for an organization's productivity and profitability are the two important values of the organization. In this stage, the organization does not give much priority to an employee's concern but expects obedience from them.

Stage two – The legalistic corporation

In this stage, the organization decides right or wrong on the basis of legality of an action rather than its morality.

Stage three – The responsive corporation

In this stage, the organization goes beyond the productivity and legality of action and focuses on the demand of society. In addition, it also develops ethical code which includes values, integrity, confidentiality, quality, and compliance.

Stage four – The emergent ethical organization

In this stage, the organization tries to develop social contract between the business and society and focuses on development of ethical climate in it. The organization solves ethical dilemmas by considering both consequences of ethical decision (i.e., profit and ethical perception of stakeholder about the situation).

Stage five – The ethical organization

An ethical organization develops core values based on organization-wide acceptance of a common set of ethical values. It takes day-to-day decisions based on core organizational values and develops ethical culture within it.

Moral Action and Moral Outcomes

Theologians, philosophers, and (recently) scientists, have developed systems of morals, thoughts, actions, and outcomes that they consider to be correct, just, and right. The most important aspect of a system of morals is a definition of moral actions that produce moral goods. All notions of moral goods share two common elements. First, they are intrinsically valuable; that is, in and of themselves. Intrinsic value can be contrasted with instrumental value, actions or goods that bring about other goods. Many people value money and see it as a good; however, money is not in itself a moral good because it is a means to other ends, not an end in itself.[15] What people buy with their money may be goods of all types, including intrinsic goods like housing, food, vacations, and fun, but they may also include additional intrinsic goods, such as donating to help the homeless or continuing education. Second, moral goods are intrinsic goods that reasonable people would all prefer in contrast with their opposite.[16] If people have experienced both (either in total or some degree), what they would prefer is the moral good. Some examples are respect versus contempt, knowledge versus ignorance, health versus sickness, and liberty versus enslavement.

Moral action produces moral goods for each individual and it leads to moral outcomes for others, or states of being that are intrinsically valuable to others or society at large. To be an ethical person, one must act with integrity, or correspondence between what he or she believes to be good and the actions they engage in. Integrity produces a moral outcome of trust and feelings of esteem between the actor and others. Another example is the dyad of respect versus contempt. What are the behavioral elements of respect? Honesty and truth-telling would clearly be on the list; so would keeping appropriate confidences, acting kindly and with benevolence, and accommodating the needs and desires of the other when possible. Respect also includes listening to truly understand what a person says and means, which is a valuable business as well as moral skill. When we treat others with respect, they feel honored and valued, two feelings which are intrinsic moral goods. They also tend to be more willing to trust us and engage in economic and social transactions with us.

Religious Teachings of Moral Actions and Outcomes

Many people today don't describe themselves as religious; indeed, the number of people in the United States who describe their religious affiliation as "atheist, agnostic, or "nothing in particular" stood at 26% [in 2018], up from 17% in 2009."[17] A thorough discussion of ethics should include religious perspectives for two reasons: First, the principles taught in the world's great religions laid the foundation for many of the laws and institutions in societies around the world today. Think of the Ten Commandments as the basis for ethical thought and legal codes in much of the Western world. Second, for every person who doesn't hold a faith tradition, roughly five others do (see Figure 2.2).

Ethics in the Real World 2.2 describes the link between freedom of religion and business prosperity. To get a sense for how these traditions are spread over the Earth, there are several web-based tools that provide a census of world religious membership.

The Abrahamic Faiths. For this religious tradition, moral action is conformance with God's commands. The hoped-for moral outcome state for individuals is God's approbation in this life, and salvation in the next. Moral societies live together in peace and harmony. Judaism, as the oldest of these traditions, provides a common foundation. Moses admonished his people, "…. and you shall love the Lord, your God, with all your heart and with all your soul, and with all your means."[18] The primary duty is obedience to God and his commandments as contained

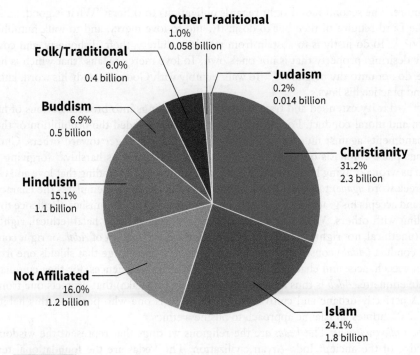

FIGURE 2.2 Global Religious Affiliation in 2015 (in billions).

Ethics in the Real World 2.2 | Religious Freedom Is Good for Business

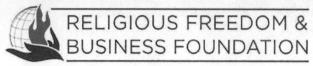

Religious freedom means accepting all religions and forms of worship in a society. Sometimes this freedom conflicts with other societal goals. Businesses are subject to employment discrimination laws. However, businesses may also hold to the religious protections of their owners. Many people think that the two must therefore be in conflict with each other but that is not true. Freedom of religion or belief is good for business according to research from the Religious Freedom and Business Foundation.

Freedom of religion is embodied in Article 18 of the UN Universal Declaration of Human Rights: *Everyone has the right to freedom of thought, conscience and religion; this right includes freedom to change his religion or belief, and freedom, either alone or in community with others and in public or private, to manifest his religion or belief in teaching, practice, worship and observance.*[21]

But why exactly is freedom of religion good for business? In general, religious freedom is a stabilizing force and businesses thrive where stability exists, increasing the opportunity to invest and conduct normal and predictable business operations, especially

in emerging markets. Specifically research shows that religious freedom:

- **F**osters respect—preserves the ability of all to worship (or not) as they please.
- **R**educes corruption—Studies link religious intolerance with higher levels of corruption.
- **E**ngenders peace—reduces religion-related conflict, oppression, and violence.
- **E**ncourages broader freedoms—Freedom of religion is linked to freedoms such as better health care to higher incomes for women.
- **D**evelops the economy—Faiths that must compete for adherents fosters more robust and civil competition between business firms.
- **O**vercomes over-regulation—Religious freedom is associated with more forms and types of entertainment, finance, and labor freedoms.
- **M**ultiplies trust—Companies that encourage religious freedom lower liability costs and improve employee morale.

Given that religious freedom contributes to better economic and business outcomes as shown here, businesses would benefit from taking religious freedom considerations into account in all aspects of their planning and operations. For more information on the relationship between religious freedom and business, visit https://religiousfreedomandbusiness.org/.

---

in scripture. The second moral right regards obligations to others: "What is good; and what does the Lord require of thee but to do justly, and to love mercy, and to walk humbly with thy God?"[19] To do justly is to abstain from murder, adultery, theft, dishonesty, and coveting (unduly desiring) property that is not one's own. To love mercy means "that which is hateful to thee, do not unto thy neighbor."[20] To walk humbly with God is to study his word, know his laws, and practice his laws.

Christianity extended and transformed these teachings into broader notions of human concern and moral conduct. For example, Jesus Christ expanded the prohibition of the Ten Commandments against murder to an admonition to avoid anger toward others. Christian teachings place emphasis on loving those who oppose or treat us harshly,[22] forgiving those who do us wrong,[23] living in love with friends and family,[24] and extending that love and charity (the Greek word *agape*) to all the human family.[25] By so doing, one emulates the character of Christ and accepts his grace. Like its Abrahamic cousins, Islam admonishes obedience to God. In dealing with others, Muslims must distinguish between what is halal (ethical, right) and haram (unethical, not right).[26] The goal of ethics is the development of *Adab*, or right conduct: "Right conduct (*Adab*) constitutes the sum of prudential knowledge that shields one from all error in speech, acts, and character. It signifies all the Arabic sciences, for they cumulatively promote etiquette. *Adab* is thus a habitus or disposition (malaka) that protects one from disgrace. A perfectly urbane and cultivated person (adib) is one who possesses this habitus."[27] Figure 2.3 outlines an Islamic approach to business ethics.

The Vedic traditions. The Vedas are the religious writings that represent the wisdom and knowledge of the ancient Indo-Aryan civilization. The Vedas are the foundational texts of Hinduism and Buddhism (22% of the world's population). The moral outcome in Hinduism is *moska*: freedom, liberation, or release. Moska encompasses both negative freedom, escaping suffering, and positive freedom, or the ability to create a life of one's own choosing.[28] People are

FIGURE 2.3   Ethical injunctions from the Islamic tradition.

moral agents constrained and defined by membership and standing in a particular society, and what is morally correct action depends on a number of social factors. Moral conduct is *dharma*, "that which strives for the benefit of creatures; dharma is so called because it is wedded to ahimsa (non-harmfulness)…Dharma is…friendliness, which [works for] the welfare of all."[29] A person living a life of dharma can be identified by his/her solicitude and kindness toward others. They know themselves and have an inner calmness, patience, and perfect balance of mind. Dharma requires active thought and effort, "at all times, one has several possible duties to perform, given one's location on numerous interlocking matrices of relationships. One must determine which duty is the most pressing at any one time and act accordingly."[30]

The moral outcome in **Buddhism**, similar to Hinduism, is freedom from suffering. People attain this moral good as they are able to see the world as it is, free from their own false impressions and biases. Morally correct conduct is captured in the Five Precepts, or injunctions against poor or evil conduct: to not kill, steal, engage in sexual misconduct, lie, or revel in drunkenness. Adherence to this code ensures rebirth that avoids a lower realm of more suffering. To find enlightenment, however, requires more than the mere avoidance of morally wrong behavior. One must actively see the Six Perfections: generosity (*dāna*), moral discipline (*śīla*), patient endurance (*kṣānti*), perseverance (*vīrya*), meditative stability (*dhyāna*), and wisdom (*prajñā*).[31]

Central to both the Abrahamic and Vedic traditions is the notion of right conduct toward others. As Figure 2.4 displays, this ethic of kindness, reciprocity, or the golden rule, is common to most faith traditions:

Philosophical Perspectives of Moral Action and Outcomes

In general, the moral outcome in any philosophical system is an optimal society, one in which people want to live and find happiness, opportunity, peace, and stability. Where these philosophies differ is in the nature and texture of what constitutes a good society and the moral behaviors and actions that build it. Table 2.1 provides both an overview and a summary of major ethical perspectives in Western and Eastern philosophy. In practice, these normative theories provide will provide the same moral guidance in most circumstance. The primary value of these theories in todays business world is that they serve as tools to help people reflect upon and justify their actions and practices in dialogue with one another.

TABLE 2.1   A Comparison of Major Ethical Philosophies.

	Deontology	Utilitarianism	Justice	Sentiment	Virtue	
What is good? The end result	Human rights, duties and obligations	The greatest good for the greatest number	Equal opportunities for all, protection of the least well off.	Sympathy towards others	Eudemonia (human flourishing)	A society of righteous moral agents
What is right? Behaviors	Treating others as ends, not means Universality	Calculating benefits and harms Objectivity	Designing systems for equity toward the least privileged	Acting according to sentiments of sympathy toward others	Ethics as habit—the doctrine of the mean	Ren (Benevolence) Xiào (Filial piety)—loyalty
Ethical focus	Moral intentions	Moral outcomes	Intentions and outcomes	Moral sentiments	Individual character	Social character
Exemplary philosophers	Immanuel Kant (1724–1804)	John Stuart Mill (1806–1873)	John Rawls (1921–2002)	Adam Smith (1723–1790)	Aristotle (384–322 BCE)	Confucius (551–479 BCE)
Strengths	Simple and clear rules for action	Understanding cost/benefit tradeoffs	Avoiding systematic bias and deprivation	Individual moral compass	Personal happiness and fulfillment	Focus on mutuality and social harmony
Difficulties	Rigidity in prescriptions	People can be treated as means to ends	Theories of justice may differ across cultures	Emotion vs. reason, cultural roles in sentiment	Little guidance on how to act, Individual, not collective virtue	Reconciling with market outcomes and inequalities
Business Applications	Promise keeping/ contracts	Profit maximizing decisions	Diversity, inclusion, plurality	Charitable giving, CSR, forgiveness	Honesty, trustworthiness, reputation	Organizational loyalty and commitment

Deontology. **Deontology** is a Greek word meaning duty, and the natural other side of the coin—rights. For deontologists, **intentions** matter, and provide the basis for judging whether an action is morally right or wrong. The world will be better, on balance, when people act according to their moral duties, even when that creates disadvantages for themselves or others. Immanuel Kant, the most famous deontologist, argued that humans should be guided by a **categorical imperative**, a moral rule that applies in all situations, without conditions.[32] The categorical imperative has two common formulations that most people are familiar with... The first is to act on a rule that, if adopted by everyone, would lead to a moral society. The second formulation is to treat others as "ends in themselves," never merely as means to someone else's ends. Because people have rights and independent value, they must be treated as a moral end. People should ask, "Would I want everyone to act as I am acting? Am I respecting the rights of others through my actions?" Deontological thinking manifests itself in business in how people obligate themselves to each other through contracts, whether formal or informal.

Utilitarianism. Utilitarianism holds that actions are morally right to the extent they promote happiness, benefit, or **utility**. Utilitarianism stands opposed to deontology in that the judgment of moral correctness depends on the **consequences** of actions and how much utility they generate. In the nineteenth century, John Stuart Mill proposed a more sophisticated notion than the individual pleasure and pain model of Jeremy Bentham: The moral society was the one that created the greatest good for the greatest number of people.[33] Utilitarianism comes with an inherent challenge: People can easily define what is good for them, but it takes more thought to define what is good for others. To overcome this challenge, Mill argued that when deciding what provides the most good, actors had to be **impartial**. They couldn't value their own pleasures above those of others. In practice, utilitarians adopt one of two practical stances. **Act utilitarians** calculate the net utility and benefits for every action. **Rule utilitarians**, in contrast, develop and live by a set of rules that will, in general, lead to the greatest good for the greatest number. Utilitarian moral logic underlies business decisions about the optimal way to allocate resources. For example, during the COVID-19 crisis of 2020, many Utilitarians argued against lockdowns as the total cost of the economic shutdown caused more pain (net dis-utility) than the expected cost from the number of deaths from the virus.

Justice. In the latter part of the twentieth century, John Rawls developed an ethical theory that focused on creating a just society. Moral action means that everyone has an equal opportunity to succeed, and social and political policies don't disadvantage the least well-off. Rawls's system begins with a question: If people knew that economic and social positions varied (e.g., there will be rich, average, and poor), but they didn't know which position they would occupy, what kind of economic, political, and social rules would they design for society? For Rawls, the answer was a society that would ensure a set of institutions and processes designed to create fair outcomes: "Fair terms of cooperation specify an idea of reciprocity, or mutuality; all who do their part as the recognized rules require are to benefit as specified by a public and agreed upon standard."[34] The best rules would be ones that ensure a fair process and equal access to important social goods, such as education and legal rights, that allow people of all socioeconomic conditions, ethnic backgrounds, or religious beliefs to live good lives. Such a fair system proves difficult to build as different cultures will define what is fair, just, and appropriate in different ways. The morality of justice is important in today's business climate because it underpins many business decisions about diversity, equality, and inclusion.

Moral Sense Theorists. A discussion of business ethics, in particular, should include the moral sentimentalists of the eighteenth-century Scottish Enlightenment because the most ardent advocate for a capitalist economy, Adam Smith (see Ethics in the Real World 2.3), was a dedicated moral sentimentalist. Smith believed that the morally good society was a prosperous one, but one also characterized by deep feelings of sympathy and compassion by its citizens toward each other. Morally right action would be driven by these sentiments of concern. People have not only base passions, which lead to selfishness, but also higher, noble sentiments that lead to morally right behavior. For Smith, the self-interest that drove economic activity would be naturally bounded by the control of people's more noble passions.[35] The morality of the sentimentalists helps leaders think about the business issues of philanthropy, community involvement, and sustainability.

Virtue Ethics. Some ethical systems see the goal of moral action as the development of individual moral virtue and character. As individuals develop these virtues, they begin to live a

---

Ethics in the Real World 2.3 | Adam Smith on the Noble Passions

ARCHIVIO GBB/Alamy Stock Photo

Adam Smith is known to most people for his writings on the power of free-market economies to increase prosperity. In *The Wealth of Nations*, Smith argues that it is the economic self-interest of actors for profit that guides a well-functioning economy. Most people are unaware that Smith was also a moral philosopher. As the following passage shows, Smith believed that people's economic self-interest would be constrained by their sympathies toward one another:

"When we are always so much more deeply affected by whatever concerns ourselves, than by whatever concerns other men; what is it which prompts the generous...to sacrifice their own interests to the greater interests of others?...It is reason, principle, conscience, the inhabitant of the breast, the man [or woman] within, the great judge and arbiter of our conduct.... It is from him [her] only that we learn the real littleness of ourselves, and of whatever relates to ourselves, and the natural misrepresentations of self-love can be corrected only by the eye of this impartial spectator. It is he who shows us the propriety of generosity and the deformity of injustice; the propriety of resigning the greatest interests of our own, for the yet greater interests of others, and the deformity of doing the smallest injury to another, in order to obtain the greatest benefit to ourselves. It is not the love of our neighbour, it is not the love of mankind, which upon many occasions prompts us to the practice of those divine virtues. It is a stronger love, a more powerful affection, which generally takes place upon such occasions; the love of what is honourable and noble, of the grandeur, and dignity, and superiority of our own characters."[36]

Vice of Deficiency	Virtuous Mean	Vice of Excess
Cowardice	Courage	Rashness
Insensibility	Temperance	Intemperance
Illiberality	Liberality	Prodigality
Pettiness	Munificence	Vulgarity
Humble-mindedness	High-mindedness	Vaingloriness
Want of Ambition	Right Ambition	Over-ambition
Spiritlessness	Good Temper	Irascibility
Surliness	Friendly Civility	Obsequiousness
Ironical Depreciation	Sincerity	Boastfulness
Boorishness	Wittiness	Buffoonery
Shamelessness	Modesty	Bashfulness
Callousness	Just Resentment	Spitefulness

FIGURE 2.5   Watch out! Every virtue can turn into a vice.

life characterized by the activity of **eudemonia**. They act in ways that allow them to flourish.[37] Aristotle (385–323 BCE), a philosopher of Ancient Greece, is the most well-known proponent of virtue ethics, morally right action is that driven by virtue, and "moral virtue comes about as a result of habit, whence also its name *ethike* is one that is formed by a slight variation from the word *ethos* (habit)...the virtues we get by first exercising them, as also happens in the case of the arts as well...we become just by doing just acts, temperate by doing temperate acts, brave by doing brave acts."[38] Aristotle listed twelve key moral virtues of focus. Each virtue was subject to the "doctrine of the mean." Each virtue had a proper or appropriate level, and the lack of virtue could be found in the deficiency or excess of any of the twelve virtues. For example, the proper amount of courage induces us to act in the face of fear; a deficit of courage leads to cowardice, but the excess of courage leads to rashness and foolhardiness.[39] The concern for virtue comes into play and leaders and their companies think about building a reputation as a company of character. Figure 2.5 illustrates these virtues, their deficits, and their excesses.

Confucian ethics. Like Aristotle in Ancient Greece, Confucius considered the core of ethics to be the development of virtue. Confucius focuses on the attainment of righteousness and virtue in the context of social and societal relationships. Proper relationships would exist in a reciprocal balance of two opposing yet interconnected forces, yin and yang. Dong Zhong-shu, a later writer in the Confucian tradition, describes the balance among five fundamental relationships:

> "The lord is yang 陽, the retainer is yin 陰; the father is yang, the son is yin; the husband is yang, the wife is yin. The way of yin cannot proceed anywhere on its own [nor can the way of yang].... Therefore, the retainer depends on his lord to gain merit; the son depends on his father; the wife on her husband [and vice versa], yin on yang, and the Earth on Heaven.... The Three [Fundamental Bonds] of the kingly way can be sought in Heaven."[40]

The pursuit of individual virtues constitutes moral action and virtuous action. Confucius saw many virtues as important, but five stood out in his teaching and have retained their importance over time:

- *Ren* (benevolence)—care and concern for the well-being of others
- *Yi* (righteousness)—doing that which is proper and right
- *Li* (propriety)—to engage and act, to do
- *Zhi* (wisdom)—intellectual and applied knowledge, discernment
- *Xin* (trustworthiness)—sincerity of purpose and honest interactions[41]

Confucius also emphasized *Xiào*, or filial piety. This can be narrowly interpreted as the obligations of children to parents but more broadly interpreted as loyalty.[42] The five virtues, along with deep loyalty, help people create moral outcomes—a set of mutual obligations for support, an orderly—often hierarchical, and well-integrated social order. The five key relationships typify a morally good society.[43] The Confucian ethic of loyalty and reciprocal relationships can help leaders choose organizational designs and promote cultural elements that foster loyalty and commitment to the organization.

Scientific Perspectives of Moral Action and Outcomes

Scientists and researchers, primarily psychologists, have created theories of moral action and outcomes. The research conversation between University of Chicago psychologist Lawrence Kohlberg and his critic, Harvard psychologist Carol Gilligan, focused on the ways in which human beings developed the capacity for moral reasoning and how that led to morally right behaviors.

Kohlberg and moral development. In the late 1950s, Kohlberg framed his dissertation work around the question of how people make moral judgments, and whether those judgments changed as they grew older.[44] Moral reasoning lay behind both how people thought about what was morally good and how those morally right actions would create such a world. Kohlberg studied a number of young men in Chicago, asking them to reason through a series of moral problems or dilemmas. (Mini-Case #2 is his most famous dilemma.) These young men were from nine to sixteen years old, and Kohlberg followed up with them over the next twenty years.[45] His work identified three distinct stages of moral development: preconventional, conventional, and postconventional reasoning. As expected, children around age nine and below used pre-conventional reasoning to solve problems. Most adolescents and adults engage in conventional moral reasoning, and fewer than one in six adults move on to the highest stage, post-conventional reasoning. Figure 2.6 describes the three broad levels and two substages for each level.

Carol Gilligan and the feminist response. Kohlberg found that, in general, men exhibited more advanced moral reasoning, typically reaching level four, whereas women tended to score consistent with level three. Carol Gilligan, a doctoral student at Harvard, noted that the original work had focused solely on men, and she believed that the differences arose not from men's

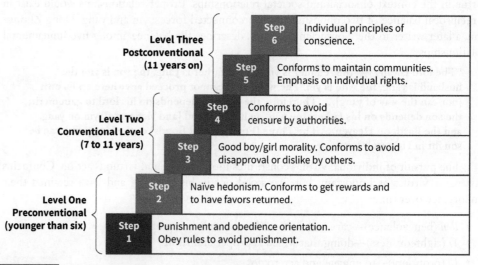

FIGURE 2.6   Kohlberg's theory of moral development.

superior reasoning but because women reasoned from a different position. As one ascended through Kohlberg's stages, he or she become less reliant on what others thought and were willing to stand alone in making moral choices. According to Gilligan, this did not represent moral advancement but rather the different ways men and women were raised: "Since masculinity is defined through separation while femininity is defined through attachment, male gender identity is threatened by intimacy while female gender identity is threatened by separation. Thus, males tend to have difficulty with relationships, while females tend to have problems with individuation."[46] Women weren't morally inferior to men; they made moral decisions according to a different standard, one of care and concern for others. Gilligan's work became a foundation for what would become known as the ethic of care, or a feminist approach to ethics. Other theories that are pillars to the feminist view of ethics are the liberal-equality approach and the radical feminist approach. Many believe that the ethic of care is not gender specific, and that males and females all incorporate elements of concern for others.

The moral outcome of a good society in this ethic mirrors the one of Rawls. It is one where all are treated equal and none are privileged through gender, race, or socioeconomic standing. It is a world of equal opportunity filled with people who care about and promote the achievement, belonging, and happiness of others.[47] The ethic of care focuses on relationships over rule following, which differs from deontology; however, both systems share many similarities, that all individuals have a set of basic, inalienable rights and that we have firm moral obligations to each other to protect and advance those rights. Gilligan's model also shares common elements with both Aristotle and Confucius in seeing virtue as paramount, and sees the highest manifestation of virtue in promoting a strong social order. This ethic would see a hierarchical division of society as problematic, unless it contained adequate safeguards against the exploitation of the weak by the strong. Actions that show concern and respect for others, such as benevolence, listening, and clear and heartfelt communications, become morally right actions as they create a world of caring concern.

Key Terms

act utilitarians	fair outcomes	morals
buddhism	hedonism	intentions
categorical imperative	hinduism	positive and normative ethics
christianity	impartial	rule utilitarians
consequences	islam	sympathy
deontology	judaism	unethical actions
eudemonia	moral actions	utility

Chapter Summary

This chapter discussed the major notions of moral goods and the moral behaviors that bring about those goods.

- Moral goods have two characteristics. They are intrinsically good, good in and of themselves and not as means to acquiring other things. Second, most people and cultures will agree that these are good and desirable things.

- A theory of what is morally right describes those actions and behaviors that will bring about the desired moral goods.

- Religious perspectives have different versions of what is morally good, but very similar versions of what is morally right. The Abrahamic faiths see the good as salvation, and the Vedic

traditions see the good as transcendence from human suffering. All religions believe in an ethic of reciprocity.

- There are five major philosophical perspectives: deontology (rights and obligations), utilitarianism (the greatest good for the greatest number), justice (fair treatment and opportunity), sentimentalism (the presence of moral passions), and virtue (the development of character).

- Psychologists have been concerned with moral development. Kohlberg outlined six stages of moral development. Carol Gilligan and the ethic of care argue that men and women make moral decisions on different criteria, and one is not better than another.

Chapter Review Questions

1. Define unethical behavior. What are the sources of unethical behavior?

2. What is the relationship between moral action and moral outcomes?

3. How have conceptions of correct moral action changed as you have grown up? Describe two experiences that have helped crystalize for you what is morally correct.

4. Compare and contrast the views of what is morally correct in the Abrahamic faith traditions and the Vedic ones.

5. What are the dangers of choosing among different visions of what is good and right? How can you avoid using different moral theories to come to different moral conclusions?

6. How can elements like organization design and compensation systems encourage ethical behavior? What role is appropriate for a leader to play in encouraging/demanding ethical behavior?

7. Identify and discuss five values of each religion. How will these ensure people to follow them?

8. Does any religion teach unethical practices? If no, then why do people engage in unethical practices?

Application Exercises

• *Personal Ethical Development.* If you began keeping an ethics journal as suggested in the first chapter, continue that writing work. Here are some prompts: What did you think about the different perspectives on the good and the right outlined in this chapter? Which ones resonate with you? Which one do you find most objectionable? If you accept a theory of what is good, what is your personal theory of what is right? Think of three to four things you can do to improve your capacity to act rightly.

• *Career Goals and Planning.* A happy, meaningful, and productive life blends and builds upon the following: (1) the type of life you are interested in leading, (2) your deepest and most important values, (3) the work you are interested in doing, (4) what you are good at, (5) your preferences for things like work versus free time, and (6) your personality. You have learned about some different, yet similar, ways of working through points 1, 2, and 6. For this exercise, work on connecting how your theory of what

is good and right influences points 3, 4, and 5. Create a plan to tighten the links between your values, the skills you need to develop, and how you plan to use your time.

• *Ethics in the Business World.* Identify two companies that have won awards for strong ethical behavior. What pathway have these companies followed? Has their view of what is good evolved over time? How have their actions changed to correspond to this evolution? What role does culture play? What role do individual leaders play in steering the ethical corporation?

• *Talking with and Learning from Others.* Make four or five groups in your MBA class and then assign one religion to each group. Ask each group to identify the important values of their assigned religion and process to develop these values. At the end of the course, each group can submit a report and give a presentation in class, followed by a question and answer session.

Mini-Cases

Case 1: A runaway trolley is heading down the tracks toward five workers who will all be killed if the trolley proceeds on its present course. Adam is on a footbridge over the tracks, between the approaching trolley and the five workers. Next to him on this footbridge is a stranger who happens to be very large. The only way to save the lives of the five workers is to flip a switch to release a trapdoor that will drop the stranger off the bridge and onto the tracks below, where his large body will stop this trolley. The stranger will die if Adam does this, but the five workers will be saved.

Discussion Questions

1. What should Adam do in this situation?[48]

2. What is a business situation in which leaders confront their own version of the "trolley problem"?

Case 2: Heinz and the druggist: A woman was near death from cancer. One drug might save her, a form of radium that a druggist in the same

town had recently discovered. The druggist was charging $2,000, ten times what the drug cost him to make. The sick woman's husband, Heinz, went to everyone he knew to borrow the money, but he could only get together about half of what it cost. He told the druggist that his wife was dying and asked him to sell it cheaper or let him pay later. But the druggist said "No." The husband got desperate and broke into the man's store to steal the drug for his wife.

Discussion Question

1. Should the husband have done that? Why do you think so?[49]

Case 3: Subhiksha, a retail outlet business, was started by Mr. R. Subramanian (an IIT and IIM alumnus) in 1997. It started with one retail outlet in Chennai. It sold FMCG, grocery, mobile products, fruits, and vegetables. Later, the outlet also started selling medicine at discounted rates. From 1997 to 2008, Subhiksha succeeded in establishing more than 1600 retail outlets and showed its presence in more than 90 cities. To grow very rapidly, Subhiksha required a large amount of money and thus took a huge business loan from banks to meet this requirement of the growth phase. The company unfortunately did not get the expected return on its investment and faced a cash crunch. The top management's focus then shifted to many money-saving activities and practices such as delay in payment of salaries, non-payment of employees' provident fund, and non-payment of rent and vendor payments. Further, retail stores also started selling expired food items and stored their FMCG goods in unhygienic places. Finally, Subhiksha also ensured that the official auditor (Deloitte) did not publish regular financial reports of the company from 2007 onwards. The management of the company did not pay much attention to these practices and kept on investing in opening new retail stores across the country. Subhiksha failed because it expanded fast with thin or zero margins, and there was a mismatch between cash outflow and inflow. On February 11, 2009, Subhiksha announced that it was closing down all its 1,600 outlets till May 2009. Today, many retailers are present and doing good business in India but Subhiksha stores have been closed.

Discussion Questions

1. Why did top management of Subhiksha not pay attention to unethical practices?
2. What is the main reason for the failure of Subhiksha?
3. How can management keep a track of unethical practices while growing?

References

1 Sarah Gibbens, "The sticky problem of plastic wrap," *National Geographic*, July 12, 2019, https://www.nationalgeographic.com/environment/article/story-of-plastic-sticky-problem-of-plastic-wrap.

2 "Plastic Wrap 101," U.S. Packaging & Wrapping, LLC, https://uspackagingandwrapping.com/plastic-wrap-101.html, accessed April 17, 2020.

3 Fisk Johnson, "SC Johnson's CEO on Doing the Right Thing, Even When It Hurts Business", *Harvard Business Review* (April 2015), https://hbr.org/2015/04/sc-johnsons-ceo-on-doing-the-right-thing-even-when-it-hurts-business?autocomplete=true.

4 Ibid.

5 "Polyvinylidene Chloride (PVDC)," GreenSpec, https://www.greenspec.co.uk/building-design/chlorinated-polyethylene-cpe-health-environment/, accessed April 17, 2020.

6 Michael Burke, "CEO explains why SC Johnson hobbled Saran Wrap," *Lake Geneva Regional News, The Journal Times*, April 25, 2015, https://journaltimes.com/business/local/ceo-explains-why-sc-johnson-hobbled-saran-wrap/article_55000b9a-88cb-5786-a36e-3835f1d820ce.html.

7 Johnson, "SC Johnson's CEO on Doing the Right Thing."

8 Johnson, "SC Johnson's CEO on Doing the Right Thing."

9 "Plastic Wrap 101."

10 Burke, "CEO explains why SC Johnson hobbled Saran Wrap."

11 Burke, "CEO explains why SC Johnson hobbled Saran Wrap."

12 Johnson, "SC Johnson's CEO on Doing the Right Thing."

13 Jeremy Bentham, "An Introduction to the Principles of Morals and Legislation," in *The English Philosophers from Bacon to Mill*, Edwin A. Burtt, ed. (New York: Modern Library, 1967), 791.

14 Thomas Hobbes, *Leviathan*, 1651, online edition through the Guttenberg Project, available at https://www.gutenberg.org/files/3207/3207-h/3207-h.htm#link2HCH0013 March 9, 2020.

15 Michael J. Zimmerman and Ben Bradley, "Intrinsic vs. Extrinsic Value," *The Stanford Encyclopedia of Philosophy*, Edward N. Zalta, ed. (Spring 2019), https://plato.stanford.edu/archives/spr2019/entries/value-intrinsic-extrinsic/.

16 See *Culture Matters*, ed. Samuel P. Huntington and Lawrence E Harrison (New York: Basic Books, 2000); and Thomas Donaldson and Thomas W. Dunfee, *Ties That Bind: A Social Contracts Approach to Business Ethics*, (Cambridge, MA: Harvard Business Press, 1999).

17 "In U.S., Decline of Christianity Continues at Rapid Pace," Pew Research Center, October 17, 2019, https://www.pewforum.org/2019/10/17/in-u-s-decline-of-christianity-continues-at-rapid-pace/e.

18 *Tanakh*, The Hebrew Bible, Devarim (Deuteronomy) 6:5., https://www.chabad.org/library/bible_cdo/aid/9970/jewish/Chapter-6.htm, accessed March 12, 2020.

19 Hilary Putnam, "Jewish Ethics?," in *The Blackwell Companion to Religious Ethics*, William Schweiker, ed. (Oxford: Blackwell Publishing, 2005), 162.

20 Ibid.

21 The UN Declaration of Human Rights can be accessed at https://www.un.org/en/about-us/universal-declaration-of-human-rights.

22 Matthew 5: 21–24 (New International Version).

23 Matthew 5: 43–45 (New International Version).

24 John 15: 12 (New International Version).

25 See 1 Corinthians 13, especially verses 4 and 13 (New International Version).

26 Samir Ahmad Abuznaid, "Business ethics in Islam: the glaring gap in practice," *International Journal of Islamic and Middle Eastern Finance and Management* 2, no. 4 (2009): 278–288.

27 Ufi Wafa Kandzada, quoted in in Ebrahim Moosa, Muslim Ethics? *The Blackwell Companion to Religious Ethics*, (Wm Shweiker, ed.) 2005 p. 238.

28 Arti Dhand, "The Dharma of Ethics, the Ethics of Dharma: Quizzing the Ideals of Hinduism," *Journal of Religious Ethics* 30, no. 3 (2002): 347–372.

29 All section notes here at to the Mahābāhrata, found in Dhand.

30 Dhand, p. 357.

31 Charles Goodman, "Ethics in Indian and Tibetan Buddhism," *The Stanford Encyclopedia of Philosophy*, Edward N. Zalta, ed. (Spring 2017), https://plato.stanford.edu/entries/ethics-indian-buddhism/.

32 The categorial imperative can be found in two places: Immanuel Kant, *Groundwork of the Metaphysics of Morals*, trans. H. J. Paton (New York: Harper Torchbooks, 1785/1948; and Immanuel Kant, *Critique of Practical Reason*, Mary McGregor, ed. and trans. (Cambridge: Cambridge University Press, 1788/1997).

33 John Stuart Mill, *Utilitarianism* (Buffalo: Prometheus Books, 1863/1987).

34 John Rawls, *Justice as Fairness: A Restatement*, Erin Kelly, ed. (Cambridge, MA: Belknap Press, 2001).

[35] For a discussion of the role of self-interest, see Adam Smith, *An Inquiry into the Nature and Causes of the Wealth of Nations*, 1776/1976, Book IV, Chapter II, 456.

[36] Adam Smith, *The Theory of Moral Sentiments*, 1759/1982, Book III, Section 3.5, 137.

[37] Rosalind Hursthouse and Glen Pettigrove, "Virtue Ethics," *The Stanford Encyclopedia of Philosophy*, Edward N. Zalta, ed. (Winter 2018), https://plato.stanford.edu/entries/ethics-virtue/.

[38] Aristotle, "Nicomachean Ethics," Book II, Ch. I, in *The Basic Works of Aristotle*, Richard McKeon, ed. (New York: Random House, 1941).

[39] The bulk of the Nicomachean Ethics takes up the discussion of the virtues.

[40] Quote found in Sangang Wuchang, "Three Fundamental Bonds and Five Constant Virtues," *Berkshire Encyclopedia of China*, Edwin A. Burtt, ed., (Great Barrington, MA: Berkshire Publishing Group, 2009), 2253.

[41] Wuchang, "Three Fundamental Bonds," 2254.

[42] Kit-Chun Joanna Lam, "Confucian Business Ethics and the Economy," *Journal of Business Ethics* 43 (2003): 153–162.

[43] Tu Wei-ming, *Centrality and Commonality: An Essay on Confucian Religiousness* (Albany: State University of New York Press, 1989), p. 48.

[44] Marie Doorey, "Lawrence Kohlberg, American Psychologist," *Encyclopedia Britannica*, 2020, https://www.britannica.com/biography/Lawrence-Kohlberg, accessed April 17, 2020.

[45] His work is summarized in Lawrence Kohlberg, *The Psychology of Moral Development: The Nature and Validity of Moral Stages* (San Francisco: Harper & Row, 1984).

[46] Carol Gilligan, *In a Different Voice: Psychological Theory and Women's Development* (Cambridge, MA: Harvard University Press, 2016), 8.

[47] Norlock, Kathryn, "Feminist Ethics," *The Stanford Encyclopedia of Philosophy*, Edward N. Zalta, ed. (Summer 2019), https://plato.stanford.edu/entries/feminism-ethics/.

[48] Valerio Capraro et al., "People making deontological judgments in the Trapdoor dilemma are perceived to be more prosocial in economic games than they actually are," *PloS One*, no. 10 (2018), https://doi.org/10.1371/journal.pone.0205066.

[49] This is a classic case in psychology. This version is taken from "The story of Heinz," http://labs.psychology.illinois.edu/~lyubansk/Kohlberg.htm, accessed April 16, 2020.

CHAPTER 3

Living a Great Life: PERMA, Mission Statements, and Ethical Decision Making

LEARNING OUTCOMES

At the end of this chapter, you should be able to do the following:

1. Define hedonia, eudemonia, and PERMA, and identify the types of happiness described in each concept.

2. Describe the three categories of values leaders must consider when they "manage by values."

3. Create your own personal mission statement and identify your key values.

4. Evaluate the ethical component of business decisions using the 8-Question Framework.

5. Apply the tools and concepts you've learned in this chapter to real-life business situations.

Opening Case | Martin Burt, Compassionate Social Engineer

NicoFurt/Wikimedia Commons/Public domain

Martin (pronounced Mar-teen) Burt was born in Asunción, Paraguay, in 1957. His father Daniel Burt, a lawyer who never practiced law but found a career in business, and his mother Deidamia Artaza, daughter of a Liberal Party businessman, belonged to the opposition party to dictator General Alfredo Stroessner. Martin was the third of three brothers, and a fourth brother, Richard, was born in 1966 with several disabilities. Martin grew up in a loving home, and much more, as he described:

It quickly became apparent to my brothers and sisters that we were among the very privileged in Paraguay, a poor country, and so we always heard from my parents and my grandparents that we had to take advantage of the opportunities we had but to also give back. So, giving back became a very honorable thing to do, at least in the ethos of my family. That is, I suppose, what influenced me. I have this ethos and so do my brothers and my cousins. There's a sense of work in the social sector, not as charity, but as extending opportunities. We deeply believe in equal opportunities for everybody. Mind you, equality of *opportunities*, not necessarily of results.[1]

After earning both his bachelor's and master's degrees in the United States, Martin returned to his native country and founded Fundación Paraguaya (FP) with a group of local businessmen in 1985. FP was one of the first nongovernmental organizations (NGOs) and microfinance providers in Paraguay. FP used solidarity groups; the organization lent money to groups of poor entrepreneurs who guaranteed, as a group, to pay back the money. FP began to see success in its efforts.

Martin left FP in 1991 to serve as the only nonpartisan official in a new national government. During his tenure as the deputy minister of commerce, he worked to introduce a number of free market reforms in the country. He served as mayor of the capital city of Asuncion from 1996 to 2001. Martin returned to FP, and by 2003 the organization had become the country's largest NGO with offices in 18 regions and 200 employees. In 2002, FP had taken over an in-residence agricultural high school located near the Chaco region in rural Paraguay. Martin and the staff transformed the school into an entrepreneurship laboratory for students. Students studied in the morning and then worked at everything from raising chickens to making yogurt the rest of the day. They also learned to market and sell their products in the local area and in Asuncion. By 2007, the school was fully self-funding, generating $300,000 a year.

Martin began exporting the model around the globe through his Teach a Man to Fish foundation. Based in London, the group is a global network of 3,000 members in 150 countries promoting the principle of "education that pays for itself." He has also developed the Poverty Stoplight, a poverty measurement tool and coaching framework that allows families to diagnose their level of poverty along multiple dimensions. With an accurate assessment, they can then develop their own plans to move out of poverty.[2] Martin earned a PhD from Tulane University in

2016. Martin describes his philosophy about the poor and his work with them:

> It's not a matter of throwing money at the poor or throwing charitable gifts at the poor but learning how to feel as one with them—that we are on this planet together and their fate is our fate. My vision is to develop social innovations to alleviate injustice in the world, that's what I want to do, and as I said, not from a position of guilt, because I don't feel guilty that the poor are poor—I don't feel responsible. . . . I refuse to accept that poverty cannot be addressed, or that running water cannot be extended to people, or that the quality of education cannot be improved.
>
> My experience is that poor people have great wealth and resources inside of them. I really believe that the poor have the wealth inside of them. This is the only explanation that I can find for all of the people that I have seen lift themselves out of poverty. Where was that money before? Where was that strength before? It was inside of them. So my work is really easy; that's because I know that the power is in them. "Hey I'm just going to go and stroke the lamp!" From my perspective, I see that it's just a matter of doing it.[3]

Introduction

Most people would consider Martin Burt a happy person who is living an ethical life. Chapter 2 introduced several differing conceptions of the morally good life for individuals and society. Each of the religious and philosophical traditions covered in that chapter has a positive view of ethics and moral goods; ethics should be about far more than compliance and staying out of jail. An ethical life should be a happy and fulfilling life. Aristotle captured the essences of a happy life in his notion of eudemonia, or flourishing. You'll learn about eudemonia and other important concepts for leading a happy life as you read this chapter. The discussion of working toward eudemonia forces individuals to consider how their personal and professional lives interface. The models you'll read about in this chapter view people as unified beings, and they need to have a sense of purpose and meaning and an ethical system that includes both work and leisure activities. This chapter also discusses the role of a mission statement in developing an ethical life of meaning and purpose. With a strong sense of personal/professional ethics and mission, leaders can utilize an ethics tool we refer to as the 8-Question Framework to guide decision making. This model helps leaders avoid a common trap: that business decisions can be separated from ethics; the 8 questions ensure that both business (pragmatic) and ethical concerns factor into each decision; it helps decision makers view business decision making from a unified perspective.

Hedonia, Eudemonia, Flourishing, and a PERMA Life

Everyone wants to be happy, and happiness is considered a part of an ethical life. Happiness can be defined in one of two ways: The first definition considers happiness as a high level of positive and a correspondingly low level of negative affect (feelings). The other considers the happy life as one lived in a deeply satisfying way.[4] The first definition creates, and builds upon, a hedonistic view of happiness, similar to the one described by Jeremy Bentham in Chapter 2. The second definition encompasses a eudaimonistic view of life, borrowing the concept from Aristotle in Chapter 2.[5]

Hedonism

Hedonism is the idea that happiness is positive affect, feeling good, or pleasure. Happiness is like an index, where people can add up their pleasurable feelings and subtract their negative ones. The net result is the level of happiness. Because of the close connection between philosophers' views of pleasure and pain and economists' views of utility, hedonism is often translated into economic terms. People will be happy if they have income, housing, and other material goods. Within organizations, hedonism presumes that being a boss is better than being a worker because bosses have the pleasures of formal authority, power, and status. The logic of hedonism suggests that if a little money is good, more is better. The popular media creates messages and impressions that fame, fortune, power, and happiness flow from material wealth. Ethics in the Real World 3.1 provides you with a way to measure your hedonic happiness.

A body of academic research that spans psychology and economics provides a surprising counterintuitive result: Having more material possessions does not make people happier.[6] The reason has to do with the way our bodies and minds are wired and is called the "**hedonic treadmill**,"[7] or **hedonic adaptation**.[8] These terms mean that our bodies and minds quickly adjust to the level of physical or psychic pleasure we have, and it takes an ever-increasing amount to provide the same level of happiness. The results of this research show that a focus on hedonia, or hedonistic pleasure, may bring short-term happiness and satisfaction, but this focus rarely leads people to long-term satisfaction and joy in their lives. The other models we discuss in this chapter are better equipped to provide long-term happiness.

Ethics in the Real World 3.1 | Measuring Levels of Happiness

Cantril Self-Anchoring Scale

Thriving
Present life = 7 or higher
Future life = 8 or higher

10
9
8
7
6

Struggling
Present life = 4–7
Future life = 4–8

5
4

Suffering
Present life = 4 or below
Future life = 4 or below

3
2
1
0

Happiness is often measured in terms of emotional (hedonic) well-being (How is a person feeling today?) and overall life satisfaction (How is a person feeling about the overall trajectory of their lives?). A common way to measure overall life satisfaction is the Cantril Self-Anchoring Scale:[9]

Please imagine a ladder with steps numbered from zero at the bottom to ten at the top. The top of the ladder represents the best possible life for you and the bottom of the ladder represents the worst possible life for you.

- *On which step of the ladder would you say you personally feel you stand at this time? (ladder-present)*
- *On which step do you think you will stand about five years from now? (ladder-future)*

Here are the scores for the scale:

1. Thriving (strong and consistent well-being): A score of 7 or above on the ladder-present item and 8 or above on the ladder-future score.

2. Struggling (moderate or episodic well-being): A score between 4 and 7 on the ladder-present item and 4 and 8 on the ladder-future item.[10]

3. Suffering (lack of well-being): A score of 4 or below on both the ladder-present and ladder-future item.

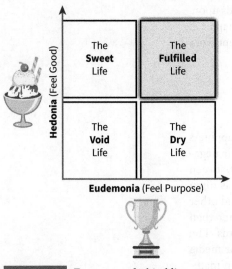

FIGURE 3.1 Four types of ethical lives.

Eudemonia and PERMA

Eudemonia is a Greek word that means "having a good guardian spirit," or leading a life that people would consider desirable. Eudemonia differs from emotional well-being because it may include times of sadness, grief, or disappointment as each of these emotional states is an important element of living a rich and full life.[11] After all, grief at the death of a friend is a manifestation of love and admiration for that person. Eudemonia has become relevant again in modern psychology through the work of Martin Seligman. See **Figure 3.1** for a comparison between hedonia and eudemonia. Western moral philosophies such as utilitarianism build on hedonia; our focus will be on the impact of building a life philosophy on eudemonia.

Seligman's work grew out of the search for the outcomes of a positive psychology, one focused on thriving and flourishing, not merely on eliminating neuroses and other negative mental conditions. For Seligman, the absence of illness does not equal health, particularly if flourishing requires active effort and investment on the part of individuals. Positive psychology defines the healthy life as one of well-being, but a well-being that goes beyond self-assessed life satisfaction. Life satisfaction may be an element of well-being, but well-being captures a rich and full life, which depends on more than just being satisfied with one's life.[12] Five elements create well-being, and Seligman titles these PERMA. **Figure 3.2** presents the main elements of the PERMA Model.

The first element, P, stands for *positive emotion*. Positive emotion goes beyond simple pleasurable emotions or sensations and captures deep feelings of lasting satisfaction. As Figure 3.2 notes, positive emotions endure through time as we find contentment and pride about the past (which utility theory discounts as "sunk"); joy, ecstasy, calmness, and a zest for life in the present; and faith, hope, optimism, and trust in the future.[13]

Engagement, or the E, can best be described by Mihaly Csikzentmihalyi's concept of flow: when people become so engrossed in an activity that they become completely absorbed in what they are doing and lose themselves.[14] Flow is not easily achieved and follows a specific recipe. To get into flow, people must operate at the edge of their current abilities; tasks that are too difficult frustrate and those that are too easy bore people. Flow is work, but rewarding work.

The R in the model stands for *relationships*. We need others, both for physical and psychological well-being.[15] People who are in committed, long-term relationships such as marriage report high levels of happiness, life satisfaction, and well-being.[16] Positive relationships build on the ethical virtues of respect for others, concern for their well-being, and a willingness to give of ourselves.

M stands for *meaning*. This construct gets at our deep need to live a transcendent life, one that is part of something bigger than the day-to-day elements of feeding, clothing, and

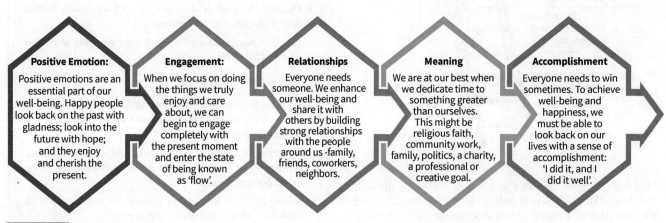

Positive Emotion:
Positive emotions are an essential part of our well-being. Happy people look back on the past with gladness; look into the future with hope; and they enjoy and cherish the present.

Engagement:
When we focus on doing the things we truly enjoy and care about, we can begin to engage completely with the present moment and enter the state of being known as 'flow'.

Relationships
Everyone needs someone. We enhance our well-being and share it with others by building strong relationships with the people around us -family, friends, coworkers, neighbors.

Meaning
We are at our best when we dedicate time to something greater than ourselves. This might be religious faith, community work, family, politics, a charity, a professional or creative goal.

Accomplishment
Everyone needs to win sometimes. To achieve well-being and happiness, we must be able to look back on our lives with a sense of accomplishment: 'I did it, and I did it well'.

FIGURE 3.2 The PERMA Model.

sheltering ourselves. True happiness and well-being come when people can answer two fundamental questions: Why am I here? What purpose does my life serve?[17] Meaning bestows a deep and persistent sense of happiness that creates long-term flourishing, even during times of sadness, grief, and loss (see Ethics in the Real World 3.2).

Ethics in the Real World 3.2 | Finding Meaning Amidst Suffering: The Work of Victor Frankl

United Archives GmbH/Alamy Stock Photo

Victor Frankl was an Austrian psychologist who spent most of World War II in a concentration camp because he was Jewish.

He survived and penned a book about his experiences, *Man's Search for Meaning*. Frankl believed that with a meaning to their lives, people could overcome tragedy and suffering, as the following story suggests:

> **Once, an elderly general practitioner consulted me because of his severe depression. He could not overcome the loss of his wife who had died two years before and whom he had loved above all else. . . . I refrained from telling him anything but instead confronted him with the question, 'What would have happened, Doctor, if you had died first, and your wife would have had to survive you?' 'Oh,' he said, 'for her this would have been terrible; how she would have suffered!' Whereupon I replied, 'You see, Doctor, such a suffering has been spared her, and it was you who have spared her this suffering—to be sure, at the price that now you have to survive and mourn her.' He said no word but shook my hand and calmly left my office. In some way, suffering ceases to be suffering at the moment it finds a meaning, such as the meaning of a sacrifice.[18]**

The final element of the PERMA model is *achievement*, or A. The type of achievement that allows people to flourish comes from reaching challenging goals, mastering new skills or difficult subjects, winning real contests, or witnessing fundamental progress along life's path. Achievement allows people to measure the growth of their skills and prowess in new or existing areas of activity; indeed, without achievement, development, growth, and progress do not occur. People should be optimistic about future achievement, joyful when it comes, and should look back with satisfaction about what they have accomplished (see Ethics in the Real World 3.3).

Ethics in the Real World 3.3 | Meaning: Where is it found?

Where Meaning is Found

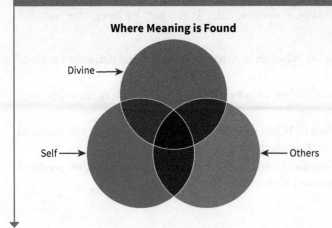

Divine
Self
Others

Seeking to help individuals and families find meaning in their lives, a company called Ampelis has studied and researched meaning as represented in philosophy, psychology, history, theology, and even neuroscience. Their exhaustive journey motivated them to analyze the lives and writings of individuals who have lived or written about meaning. Individuals like the Dalai Lama, Lao Tzu, Confucius, Jesus Christ, Mother Theresa, Albert Schweitzer, Friedrich Nietzsche, Victor Frankl, Martin Seligman, and Mihaly Csikszentmihalyi (to mention just a few) were included. As a result of their studies and readings a framework emerged that has provided guidance on where meaning is grounded in individuals, families, and organizations.[19]

Ampelis' proprietary model describes three essential activities that help people find meaning in their lives. A focus on meaning helps people decide where to focus their energy, money, and time.

1. **Development of Self:** Essential to a meaningful life is a focus of discovering and developing those unique gifts and talents we each possess. Whether "development of self" is expressed by focusing on education, a profession, an athletic pursuit, or any myriad of self-development endeavors, life is more purposeful when meaning is realized through growth, progress, and a sense of becoming.

2. **Relationship with Others:** Research abounds about how healthy and thriving relationships are core to a meaningful life. Meaning found in healthy relationships is linked to lower rates of anxiety and depression, higher self-esteem, greater empathy, and more trusting and cooperative relationships. Science confirms that strong, healthy relationships help to strengthen the immune system, help bodies recover from disease, and even lengthen life.

3. **Connection to Divine:** Finding the Divine in God, religion, nature, art, or in the multiple forms of mindfulness (e.g., meditation, yoga, or gardening), being part of something bigger than self is a salient feature of individuals who have lived, or are living, meaningful lives. Research indicates that knowing or believing that one is part of something bigger than themselves, enhances purpose, builds confidence, and brings a richness to life.

The PERMA model represents key tasks and important elements in a life that leads to eudemonia, or flourishing. Many of these elements produce hedonic pleasure as well (such as accomplishing a long-term goal), but the elements of the PERMA model combine to help us reach our full human potential. Each of the PERMA elements suggests that a satisfying life is one guided by strong principles and core values. Organizations and their leaders who conduct business guided by a set of principles face some unique challenges; however, they also enjoy certain advantages.

Sources of Unethical Behavior

Unethicality is the outcome of explicit/conscious or implicit/automatic subjective expected utility, or SEU (SEU is the product of individual expectations and the reward value of the outcome) maximizing behavior rather than an affect based, adaptive behavior. Moreover, SEU may involve gains from affiliation with other entities, or cost related to social exclusion. In other words, unethical behavior may not serve any immediate self-interest but may also be practiced in the interest of others with the aim of maintaining social cohesion or avoiding social exclusion. Unethical behaviors are determined by their utility and are reinforced by reward and punishment.

Types of Unethical Behavior

Individuals' unethical behavior can be divided into broad categories: (1) pro-self unethical behavior and (1) pro-other unethical behavior. Further, pro-self and pro-other behavior can be divided in to two categories: explicit and implicit. Sometimes, individuals indulge in unethical behavior because of others consciously or unconsciously. In this way, we categorize unethical behavior into four categories:

1. *Explicit pro-self unethical behavior.* When an individual takes unethical decisions for his or her own benefit.

2. *Implicit pro-self unethical behavior.* When an individual gives more credit to his or her work unconsciously.

3. *Explicit pro-other unethical behavior.* When an individual consciously engages in unethical behavior due to strong organization identification.

4. *Implicit unethical pro-other behavior.* When individual unconsciously exhibits unethical behavior due to in group biases or cultural relativism.

Rational Choice Theory

Rational choice theory (RCT) is useful in explaining a wide range of human behavior that are consequential in nature. RCT prediction about human behavior depends on six postulates:

1. First postulate – Any social phenomenon is the effect of individual decisions, actions, and attitudes (individualism).
2. Second postulate – Some human action can be understood (understanding).
3. Third postulate – Human actions have reasons (rationality).
4. Fourth postulate – These reasons derive from consideration by the actor of the consequence of his or her actions as he or she sees them (consequentialism, instrumentalism).
5. Fifth states – Actors are concerned mainly with the consequences to themselves of their own actions (egoism).
6. Sixth postulate – Actors are able to distinguish the costs and benefits of alternative lines of action and they choose the line of action with the most favorable balance (maximization optimization).

Further, RCT has three major limitations in identifying the rationality of human behavior: (1) social phenomena involving non-commonplace belief, (2) phenomena involving non-consequentialist prescriptive beliefs, and (3) social phenomena motivated by the individual's self-interest.

Leading by Values: A Tool for Organizational Leaders

The move to "managing by values"[20] became popular in the mid-1990s when business researchers Jim Collins and Jerry Porras published their bestselling book *Built to Last*.[21] They highlighted the importance of a set of core values as a key differentiator in companies that performed well over long periods of time; they were "built to last." Values are popular: A recent survey indicated that 57% of companies list the ethical Virtue of integrity as a core company value.[22]

Managing by values carries significant risk. The major risk is the risk of hypocrisy: A company may be seen as espousing a set of values it doesn't practice. For example, a generation ago, many hotels claimed to be environmentally sensitive in how they laundered towels, but investigators found the move was done purely to cut costs. The term greenwashing was born and referred to attempts by companies to either portray pure business practices as environmentally conscientious, or as an attempt to espouse values they never practiced.[23] When companies fail to "walk the talk," they discredit values and create cynicism and negative feelings among employees, customers, or other stakeholders.

Leading by values may bring rewards for companies, but it takes hard work to move beyond values as a mere slogan, as author Patrick Lencioni notes:

> **The debasement of values is a shame, not only because the resulting cynicism poisons the cultural well but also because it wastes a great opportunity. Values can set a company apart from the competition by clarifying its identity and serving as a rallying point for employees. But coming up with strong values—and sticking to them—requires real guts. Indeed, an organization considering a values initiative must first come to terms with the fact that, when properly practiced, values inflict pain. They make some employees feel like outcasts. They limit an organization's strategic and operational freedom and constrain the behavior of its people. They leave executives open to heavy criticism for even minor violations. And they demand constant vigilance.[24]**

Leading by values becomes easier when leaders understand the different categories of values and how those values relate to their business practices. There are three fundamental categories of values:

- *Basic beliefs*—These beliefs form the normative world view of the business, or the theory of how the business operates. Basic beliefs include the role of profit and what creates it, the role of people, and a firm's basic orientation. Some firms believe, for example, that making great products leads to profits, while others see the extra expenses to make a product great as a waste of profits. The people who work at the firm may be seen as assets or interchangeable cogs.

- *Business values*—These beliefs encompass the most important intangible values that a business prioritizes and focuses on. Common business values include things like relationships within the firm (e.g., everyone is "family"), individual behaviors that lead to success (e.g., hard work, perseverance), or orientations toward risk (e.g., innovativeness, prudence, risk-taking, caution).

- *Ethical values*—These principles often look like the virtues that Aristotle or Confucius taught. Ethical values include a commitment to honesty and integrity, respect for customers and employees, the promotion of diversity, equality, and inclusion, and other values around community membership or corporate citizenship.

These three categories of values are woven into the business in one of four ways, and understanding each level of values entrenchment is key to managing, or leading, by values.[25]

1. *Core values*. These are the central and enduring norms and priorities in a business. They form the core of the firm's identity. They aren't aspirations; they are the way people already act and behave. For ethics to be a competitive advantage, ethical virtues have to be core.

2. *Aspirational values*. Elements you want to incorporate in the future. After the Black Lives Matter protests in 2020, many companies began to adopt diversity and inclusion as values, but they realized their organizations did not yet measure up. Many created aspirational values around improving diversity, equality, and inclusion.

3. *Permission-to-play values*. The basic standards of conduct. Ethical values like honesty, integrity, and transparency fall in this category. The challenge with these values is that they are rarely well-defined, subject to interpretation, and often taken for granted rather than emphasized. For most companies, ethical values fall into the category of taken for granted and not emphasized.

4. *Accidental values*. Values that arise out of repeated behaviors by some group in the organization. Accidental values, such as the party culture at WeWork (see Chapter 1) often conflict with aspirational or core values such as inclusion, teamwork, and dedication to work tasks.

Leaders who successfully manage by values ensure that intangible and difficult-to-define values get translated into concrete policies, cultural artifacts, and incentive and promotion systems. These concrete manifestations reinforce core and permission-to-play values and can help an organization live its aspirational values. The most powerful way to define one's purpose is the creation of a mission statement, the topic of the next section of this chapter.

Mission Statements

Every business should have a mission statement. Each person reading this book is the CEO of a very important organization: ME, Inc. ME, Inc. will sell its products and services to employers, through a job, or directly to customers, through business ownership. ME, Inc. will make important contracts, such as marriage or mortgage, will acquire assets, and create liabilities. A mission statement covers the biggest issues of the organization or individual, their deepest aspirations, and their highest goals.[26]

The Elements of a Mission Statement

A mission statement is about identity, purpose, core values, and superordinate goals, broad objectives around which stakeholders can coalesce.[27] Good missions answer three fundamental questions: What does the organization do? What do members want? What values and principles guide decision making?[28] Figure 3.3 displays the three questions:

Business Definition. Defining the business answers three crucial questions: Who are the key stakeholders, the people or groups served, such as customers, suppliers, owners, and/or donors? Which needs of those stakeholders does the business aim to meet? How will those needs be met (which products or services will the business offer)? A clear mission helps an individual or organization focus their efforts on things that truly add value. Ethics in the Real World 3.4 shows how Federal Express captures these elements in a mission statement.

Superordinate Goals. A mission lays out the goals and objectives the organization hopes to accomplish and ways to measure success. How will stakeholders' lives be different? How will the organization measure success? At FedEx, goals include providing the *highest-quality* services (for customers), *superior* returns (for investors), and *mutually rewarding* relationships (employees).

Ethics in the Real World 3.4 | The Mission and Vision at FedEx

Take a look at how the FedEx corporation crafts their mission and vision statements. Think about what is says about the company and its leadership.

FedEx Corporation will produce superior financial returns for its shareowners by providing high value-added logistics, transportation and related business services through focused operating companies. Customer requirements will be met in the highest quality manner appropriate to each market segment served. FedEx will strive to develop mutually rewarding relationships with its team members, partners and suppliers. Safety will be the first consideration in all operations. Corporate activities will be conducted to the highest ethical and professional standards.

FedEx's long term goals include:

- Increase EPS 10%-15% per year
- Grow profitable revenue
- Achieve 10%+ operating margin
- Improve cash flows
- Increase ROIC
- Increase returns to shareowners[29]

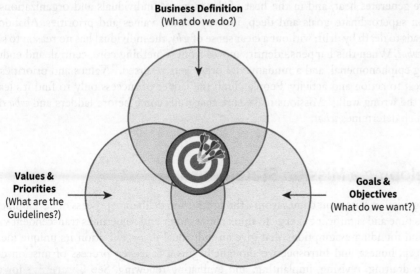

FIGURE 3.3   The elements of a mission statement.

Shared Values. Values delineate our priorities and tell stakeholders what the organization feels is important. While values can have moral components such as honesty, integrity, or respect, they may also be quite pragmatic; for example, whether the group plans for the long- or short-term is an expression of values and priorities.[30] Values play a decisive role in a mission statement as they should inform choices among competing alternatives, and perhaps most importantly, indicate when to say no.

The Purpose of a Mission Statement

A well-developed mission *communicates* to all stakeholders what the organization does, where it's going, and a fundamental sense of identity, or how the organization answers the question of "who we are." Missions *motivate* long-term commitments by various stakeholder groups, and they offer a way to *evaluate* potential courses of action.

Communication and Motivation. Missions that effectively communicate will also motivate stakeholders; the more clearly the mission communicates purpose, goals, and values, the deeper and more solid the motivation among relevant stakeholders. A good mission statement is concise and insightful. Potential stakeholders can quickly and clearly see what the organization stands for, and whether engagement with the organization will add value to them. They'll get a realistic sense of *what* the organization does, *why*, and *how* that purpose gets fulfilled, and *whether* that purpose meets their own needs. Clear objectives provide an honest look at core purposes and motivations. Finally, a strong mission statement gives potential participants (for example, a potential employer or romantic partner) an accurate sense of the organization's/person's identity or constitution and a set of principles they hope to live by. The commitment level of various stakeholders will correlate with the number of mission elements they agree with.

Evaluation. Bain and Company is a strategy consulting firm driven by hard data and results. Their most recent study of effective management practices indicated that mission statements rank as a popular management tool in the services they provide their clients. Eighty percent of clients *consistently* ranked the tool as highly valuable for over 25 years in Bain's annual report.[31] Why does a tool so pilloried by humorists continue to be so well liked and used by executives? Missions help us decide what to do and what not to do. The three core mission elements of a good mission statement raise insightful questions when deciding whether or not to pursue opportunities. How will this decision fit with what we do and our current activities? A good mission cuts to the chase and helps calibrate whether opportunities are consistent with organizational goals and values.

Employers, partners, or other stakeholders continually pressure organizations to increase the scale and scope of activities, or to behave in ways that violate their ethical values. This pressure generates heat, and in the heat of the moment, individuals and organizations lose focus on superordinate goals and deep, identity-central values and priorities. Abandoning these leads to death by drift; without a clear sense of *why*, the individual has no reason to say no to any *what*. When this happens, identity moves from something core, central, and enduring to being epiphenomenal, and a fundamental order gets reversed.[32] Values and priorities take a backseat to action and activity. People climb the ladder of success only to find it's leaning against the wrong wall.[33] Missions make sure that walls come before ladders and *who* drives *why*, which determines *what*.

Developing a Mission Statement

A strong mission statement comes from a thoughtful and deliberate process of development. It requires time and significant energy to think about larger and sometimes transcendent values, goals, and founding assumptions that give an individual or organization its unique identity. That deep, honest, and introspective thought begins a four-step process of mission development: drafting, revising, implanting, and evaluating/renewing. See Figure 3.4 for three examples of different mission statements.

	**The Alzheimer's Association's Mission** The Alzheimer's Association leads the way to end Alzheimer's and all other dementia—by accelerating global research, driving risk reduction and early detection, and maximizing quality care and support.
Linked 	**LinkedIn's Mission** The mission of LinkedIn is simple: connect the world's professionals to make them more productive and successful.
The **ⓦalⓣ Ðisney** Company	**Walt Disney's Mission** The mission of The Walt Disney Company is to entertain, inform and inspire people around the globe through the power of unparalleled storytelling, reflecting the iconic brands, creative minds and innovative technologies that make ours the world's premier entertainment company.

FIGURE 3.4 Compare the mission statements from these three organizations.

Drafting. To draft a mission statement, begin by focusing on each of the three elements. A mission should be both descriptive and aspirational, and the responses to each question need to reflect both realities. People should ask these questions:

- What am I good at today?
- What activities are core to my purpose, and how do I create value?
- What "business" do I want to be in as I grow older? In five years? In ten years? At retirement?
- What do I most want to accomplish in my life?
- How will I measure success?
- What's most important to me?
- What moral virtues matter most?
- Which pragmatic values do I hold dear?

People or organizational teams begin by brainstorming answers to these questions. The real insight comes when they go into the field and find out how key stakeholders answer these questions. External stakeholders such as parents, partners, or employers will have complementary, and competing, views in terms of the three questions. Internal stakeholders often know what's *intended*; those outside only see what's *produced*. The differences can be enlightening. Good work at this stage incorporates all the different perspectives gathered through the research process and leads to an initial draft. Initial drafts tend to be cumbersome and difficult. It helps to summarize answers into, respectively, a page, paragraph, sentence, phrase, and finally a single word. The single word unearths what's truly critical and nonnegotiable to answer each question.

Revising. Think of the draft as a rock dropped into a still pond that immediately creates ripples that spread out across the water. Something similar happens when individuals and organizations begin to think about their core identity and purposes. Allow ample time and opportunity for thoughtful feedback and critique to emerge from the author as well as other key stakeholders. Time matters because people need to ingest and digest the mission before they suggest substantive changes. Revising the draft usually proves far easier than the initial crafting. Look for common themes in thoughts and reactions to the draft; some will be substantive and lead to thoughtful changes, but others focus on wordsmithing. Drafting and revising may take several months or up to a year. The hard work is done, right? Wrong! Now comes the toughest phases: implanting the mission.

Implanting. If the mission process ends with the final revision and a sigh of relief, then you have not created a living and impactful mission. You've created something to layer over, or imprint, on the organization or your own life. Good missions encourage you to implant, not just imprint, the mission in everything you do. To implant implies to break the surface and to go deep. Unless those good feelings translate into real changes in behaviors, the mission exercise has little long-term value. The completed mission invites individuals or organizations to *rethink*, *rework*, and *retool* actions, habits, and rules for living. Elements that conflict with the mission are like weeds; they have to go or else they will choke off the development of the new mission-centered life. Begin with the low-hanging fruit of easy inconsistencies that you have little vested interest in maintaining. You have to prove you're serious, and the mission really represents both reality and worthy aspirations. Implanting and tending the new mission is hard work, but a well-husbanded mission statement becomes like a healthy plant, a living element that provides cover, meaning, and a sense of beauty to the process of living.

Evaluating and Renewing. Things change, and both people and companies mature over time. What might have been your mission at 25 might not be your mission at 40. The final step in the process is to periodically evaluate your mission to make sure that as your sense of meaning and purpose evolve, your mission will as well. Many people use significant mile posts in their lives, such as a birthday, or starting a new job, to evaluate and renew their mission statement to account for deep changes in their lives.

Decision-Making and Ethics: Eight Questions That Combine Business and Ethics

The 8-Question Framework provides a systematic method for making business (and personal) decisions that explicitly recognizes and includes the ethical dimension of each decision. The model builds on the "basic framework of ethical challenges" presented in Chapter 1. Figure 3.5 reproduces the matrix. The matrix helps managers focus on both aspects of good decision making: business success and ethical correctness.

The 8-Question Framework provides you with a systematic way to place decisions in each quadrant. The model can also help you think about alternative ways to approach the decision so that it will fit into either quadrant II or III—decisions where there is no conflict between what is profitable and ethical. The 8 Questions facilitate the use of moral imagination, or the ability to create new possibilities that meet moral objectives. The model also buttresses moral courage as it provides a clear rationale for why certain actions fail to meet moral (and often business) criteria for success. Table 3.1 illustrates the questions and overarching framework.

The 8 Questions give leaders four major areas of focus:

- *Fit with what matters most.* Good decisions are consistent with the economic and ethical "architecture" of the business. The strategic perspective helps maintain a focus on the long-term implications of the decision on the bottom line and the core ethical values that create a company's identity. If your original decision doesn't produce a "yes" to each of these questions, begin to think about "what would need to change for us to 'get to yes'" for each question.

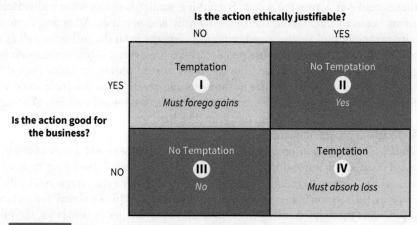

FIGURE 3.5 A basic framework for ethical temptations in business.

TABLE 3.1   The 8-Question Framework for Business Decision Making.

	Is This Decision Right for the Business?	Is This Decision Ethically Correct?
The Strategic Perspective	**Strategic fit** How does this decision improve our sustainable competitive advantage?	**Values fit** How is this decision consistent with who we are and who we want to be?
The Market Perspective	**Value added** Who wins through this decision? Who loses?	**Stakeholder impact** How does this decision treat stakeholders as subjects with intrinsic value?
The Financial Perspective	**Assumptions** What assumptions must be true for this decision to be profitable?	**Costs** Have we considered the (social) cost of the potential action?
The Risk Perspective	**Risks** What risks need to be factored into this decision?	**Options** What alternative courses of action do or might exist?

- *Real value for the business and its key stakeholders.* The first question forces you to spell out exactly why the company's core customers will approve of the decision with their wallets. The second question makes sure that business value is consistent with the human dignity and worth of each affected stakeholder.

- *The full costs of a decision.* Decision champions always create spreadsheets that show a positive return on investment. The first question unearths the assumptions that lead to a positive net present value. Leaders can then ask these questions: "Do these assumptions ring true?" "What happens if we consider a range of alternatives rather than a point estimate?" The second question asks, from a moral and values perspective, what line items have been omitted from the spreadsheet, or if those included have been appropriately priced. Have we, for example, factored in the costs to communities or the natural environment?

- *Risks and options.* Advocates of a decision tend to present best-case scenarios for impact of a decision on both business and ethical grounds. These last questions invite you to think about the risks—those uncomfortable things that can and often do go wrong—and factor them in to the decision calculus. The final question looks at the ethical downside and invites decision makers to consider other options that don't jeopardize value consistency.

Managing a project, unit, division, or organization according to the 8 Questions is not always easy. There are a number of decisions that won't get made, and the company will leave money on the table. Jack Welch, Chairman and CEO of General Electric from 1981 to 2001, articulated the most difficult challenge of managing by this framework in the company's annual report in the year 2000.

> **The toughest call of all: the manager who doesn't share the values but delivers the numbers. This type is the toughest to part with because organizations always want to deliver and to let someone go who gets the job done is yet another unnatural act. But we have to remove these [people] because they have the power, by themselves, to destroy the open, informal, trust-based culture we need to win today and tomorrow.**
>
> **We made our leap forward when we began removing [these] managers and making it clear to the entire company why they were asked to leave—not for the usual "personal reasons" or "to pursue other opportunities," but for not sharing our values. Until an organization develops the courage to do this, people will never have full confidence that these soft values are truly real.**[34]

Key Terms

eudemonia	Happiness	hedonic treadmill
greenwashing	hedonic adaptation	

Chapter Summary

This chapter discussed the reality that living an ethical life means living a good, purpose-driven life.

- Happiness can be defined in terms of hedonia or eudemonia. Happiness in the former consists of enjoying positive affect, pleasurable emotions, and avoiding negative affect and emotional or physical pain. The latter defines happiness as a rich and meaningful life, which will include a mix of positive and negative affect.

- The elements that lead to a rich and meaningful life are captured in the PERMA model: Positive emotion, Engagement, Relationships, Meaning, and Achievement.

- Many companies try to lead by values. This is hard work. Leaders must understand the three categories of values (basic beliefs, business values, moral values) and the four ways they are woven into the organization (core, aspirational, permission-to-play, accidental). Managing by values is hard work. Mission statements provide an orienting framework or compass for people to live a rich and meaningful life. Missions combine the real and the aspirational; they express who we are today and who we hope to become. A mission has three elements: a business definition (what we do), goals and objectives (what we want), and values and priorities (what guidelines direct our behavior). Missions help others understand who we are and whether they want to interact with us. Missions also help people evaluate different courses of action.

- Creating a mission statement involves three stages. Drafting entails the deep thinking, and feedback from key stakeholders, about each element of the proposed mission. Revising allows time for new thinking and clarification about each element. Implanting moves the mission from an abstract document to a lived reality.

- All business decisions have an ethical component. The 8 Questions presented in this chapter help people decide whether a proposed action makes good business sense and whether or not it is ethically correct. When the answer is yes in both areas, engage in the action. When the answer is a unified no, forego the action. Actions that are good for the business but bad ethically require moral courage to not engage in, and actions that are bad for the business but ethically correct invite moral imagination in creating a sustainable path forward.

Chapter Review Questions

1. Define hedonism and eudemonia. Why aren't these just different descriptions of the same goals in life?

2. What is necessary for an activity to lead to flow? Have you ever felt deep engagement or flow? If yes, describe two experiences where you've experienced this deep emotion. If no, why don't you think you've been able to get to flow?

3. What's the difference between imprinting and implanting a mission statement? Why does this difference matter?

4. What's the risk of ethical values being relegated to "permission-to-play" status?

5. How can the 8-Question Framework help leaders avoid making poor decisions?

6. How will you decide the important values for a leader?

7. How can PERMA model be operationalized in organizations?

8. What are the components of ethical infrastructure in any organization?

Application Exercises

- *Personal Ethical Development.* If you began keeping an ethics journal as suggested in the first chapter, continue that writing work. Here are some prompts: On which of the PERMA elements do you rate highest? Lowest? How can you leverage your strengths in each area? What can you do to overcome your weaknesses? Make some specific plans to improve your ability to live a rich and meaningful life throughout the rest of the course.

- *Career Goals and Planning.* A happy, meaningful, and productive life blends and builds upon the following: (1) the type of life you are interested in leading, (2) your deepest and most important values, (3) the work you are interested in doing, (4) what you are good at, (5) your preferences for things like work versus free time, and (6) your personality. If you have a mission statement, evaluate it through the lens of these six areas. If you don't have a mission statement, spend the next several weeks writing a first draft. What gaps do you see between where you are today and where you want to be in the near future (when you graduate or after your first year on the job)? What actions can you take to close those gaps?

- *Ethics in the Business World.* Identify an organization that you believe has strong missions and does meaningful work. This may be either a for-profit or not-for-profit organization. What roles does mission play for them? How do they implant their mission into organizational life? What key events in their history helped them refine their mission and purpose? What role do individual leaders play in making the mission real?

- *Talking with and Learning from Others.* Choose a business professional you believe has good business and ethical judgment. Engage that person in a brief interview. What questions do they ask themselves to judge whether an opportunity is good business and good ethics? How did they learn judgement? How long did it take? What advice would they offer you in developing your business and ethical judgment?

Mini-Cases

Case 1: Review the Rose Martinez case that accompanies Chapter 2. Assume that you were a member of the board of directors at the time the Belarussian plant was proposed. Work through the 8 Questions for the decision about building the plant. How might this have changed the outcome of your decision? Assume you are Rose Martinez at the end of the case. Work through the 8 Questions for this decision.

Discussion Questions

1. How do these questions influence the decision to speak up?

2. How would they help you see how to make the case for change?

Case 2: Does Google have a racially biased corporate culture? Google is a multinational technology company that works on artificial intelligence, search engine, and online advertising. Google is considered one of the most valuable brands in the world. It has grown rapidly in the market by developing products that are aligned with customers' needs. Some very popular Google products are YouTube, Google Map, and Gmail. Google is also known for its innovative and employee-friendly HR practices in all its global offices. However, it was recently reported in the media that a group of employees made a complaint against Google about racial biases in the organization. In the complaint, a group member highlighted that at Google, Black people comprise only 4.4% of employees and about 3% of leadership and its technology workforce. In addition, Black employees were being harassed at its California campus by being asked to produce identification proof and other questions related to security. Google responded that it did not stop any Black people from applying or joining Google but that they are unable to qualify for the selection process, which is same for everyone. The company also insisted that its HR practices are the best in the world, which is why it receives millions of applications every year. From these, candidates are shortlisted, selected, and rejected on the basis of well-defined criteria and without bias.

Discussion Questions

1. There are allegations that Google does not have sufficient representation from all groups. If this is statement is true, then is this practice unethical? Explain your answer.

2. Who is unethical in this case—Google or its black employees? Why?

References

1 Martin Burt, interview by the case writer, July 2011.
2 For more information, see povertystoplight.org.
3 Martin Burt Interview.
4 Edward L. Deci and Richard M. Ryan, "Hedonia, Eudamonia, and Well-being: An introduction," *Journal of Happiness Studies* 9 (February 2008): 1–11.
5 For Aristotle's view of eudemonia, see J. H. Randall, *Aristotle* (New York: Columbia University Press, 1960).
6 Sonja Lyubomirsky, *The Myth of Happiness* (New York: Penguin Books, 2013), provides a summary of much of this research.
7 Martin E. P. Seligman, *Authentic Happiness* (New York: Altria Paperbacks, 2002).
8 Lyubomirsky, *The Myth of Happiness*.
9 Hadley Cantril, *The Pattern of Human Concerns* (New Brunswick, NJ: Rutgers University Press, 1965).
10 Scoring scale taken from that used by the Gallup Organization: https://news.gallup.com/poll/122453/understanding-gallup-uses-cantril-scale.aspx, accessed April 28, 2020.
11 Lyubormirsky, *The Myth of* Happiness, 4.
12 Martin E. P. Seligman, *Flourishing* (New York: Free Press, 2011), 15.
13 Seligman, *Authentic Happiness*, 62.
14 Mihaly Csikszentmihalyi, *Flow: The Psychology of Optimal Experience* (New York: Harper Perennial, 2008).
15 For an insightful, early discussion of the role of relationships and organization in life, see Chester Barnard, *The Functions of the Executive* (Cambridge: Harvard University Press, 1938).
16 Seligman, *Authentic Happiness*, 187.
17 Victor Frankl, *Man's Search for Meaning* (New York: Washington Square Press, 1985).
18 Frankl, *Man's Search for* Meaning, 117.
19 Personal conversation with Ampelis Founders, July 2021.
20 Anat Garti and Simon Dolan, "'Managing by Values' (MBV): Innovative tools for successful micro behavioural conduct," *European Business Review* (November 25, 2019), https://www.europeanbusinessreview.com/managing-by-values-mbv-innovative-tools-for-successful-micro-behavioural-conduct/.

21 Jim Collins and Jerry Porras, *Built to Last* (New York: Harper Business, 1994).

22 "The Value of Integrity," Integrity Solutions, October 28, 2020, https://www.integritysolutions.com/insights/blog/business-integrity-in-practice#:~:text=A%20whopping%2057%25%20of%20Fortune,mean%20in%20a%20practical%20sense.

23 Karen Becker-Olsen and Sean Potucek, "Greenwashing," *Encyclopedia of Corporate Social Responsibility*, Samuel O. Idowu et al., ed. (Berlin: Springer, 2013).

24 Patrick M. Lencioni, "Make Your Values Mean Something," *Harvard Business Review* (July 2002): 113–117.

25 Lencioni, "Make Your Values Mean Something."

26 Patrick Lencioni, *The Advantage: Why Organizational Health Trumps Everything Else in Business* (San Francisco: Jossey-Bass, 2012).

27 David W. Johnson and Roy J. Lewicki, "The initiation of superordinate goals," *Journal of Applied Behavioral Science* 5, no. 1 (March 1, 1969): 9–24.

28 The original framework of the three questions came from my mentor Charles W. L. Hill and from Gareth Jones, "*Strategic Leadership: Managing the Strategy-Making Process*," in Strategic Management: An Integrated Approach (Mason, OH: *Cengage Learning*, 1995). See also Paul C. Godfrey, Chapter 8, "Mission and Vision: Leading the Fight with Values." *More Than Money* (Palo Alto: Stanford University Press, 2014).

29 Fed Ex, "Mission & goals," Company Overview, http://investors.fedex.com/company-overview/mission-and-goals/default.aspx, accessed April 29, 2020.

30 Peter F. Drucker, "Managing Oneself," *Harvard Business Review* 83, no. 1 (January 2005): 100–109.

31 See "Mission and Vision Statements," Bain and Company, April 2, 2018, https://www.bain.com/insights/management-tools-mission-and-vision-statements/.

32 Stuart Albert and David A. Whetten, "Organizational Identity," in *Research in Organizational Behavior*, Larry L. Cummings and Barry M. Staw, ed. (Greenwich, CT: JAI Press, 1985), 263–95.

33 Stephen R. Covey, *The Seven Habits of Highly Effective People* (New York: Simon and Schuster, 1991).

34 Jack Welch, Chairman's Letter, GE Annual Report, 2000, p. 5. Available at https://www.annualreports.com/HostedData/AnnualReportArchive/g/NYSE_GE_2000.pdf.

CHAPTER 4

Corporate Organization and the Role of Stakeholders

LEARNING OUTCOMES

At the end of this chapter, you should be able to do the following:

1. Explain the difference between the shareholder primacy model and the stakeholder perspective.

2. Classify an organization's stakeholders according to their characteristics and importance.

3. Compare the advantages/disadvantages of emerging business forms and models, such as Benefit Corporations and triple LLCs.

4. Use the principles you learned in the chapter to evaluate how managers account for and manage stakeholder interests.

Opening Case | Yvon Chouinard, Mountain Climber, Patagonia Founder, and Billionaire

Yvon Chouinard may be the world's most unlikely billionaire (*Forbes* estimated his 2020 net worth at $1.2 billion).[1] With the heart of a young mountain climber, Chouinard would later author a book that carried the title of *Reluctant Businessman*.[2] He noted that on his early adventure with friends, "We took special pride in the fact that climbing rocks and icefalls had no economic value in society."[3] Chouinard was born in Lewiston, Maine, and his family moved to Burbank, California, when he was about eight. Yvon joined the local falconry club at age 14, where he first learned to rappel to reach the falcons' aeries.[4] In 1957, he purchased a used forge and began to make his own pitons, which he sold for $1.50 each. The new company, Chouinard Equipment, became the largest seller of climbing hardware, but the company abandoned the piton business when leadership realized that pitons were creating irreparable damage to the rocks; the company developed an aluminum chock (a specialized piece of equipment used to secure climbing ropes) that was both more effective and less destructive.

Chouinard supplemented the hardware business by selling climbing clothing and in 1973 he incorporated under the name of Patagonia (see Figure 4.1). Clothing became a major source of business, and Chouinard worked with various suppliers to develop new materials, labeled Synchilla® and Capilene®, with greater functionality and performance to replace the age-old staples of cotton and wool, although the company continued to produce cotton clothing. Patagonia produced goods in a range of colors beyond traditional tan and forest green, and the clothing found

markets beyond climbing enthusiasts. During a product review, the company realized that the cotton it purchased came from farms that used toxic and harmful pesticides to increase production.

FIGURE 4.1 Yvon Chouinard in the early days.[5]

Robert Landau/Alamy Stock Photo

The company committed in 1994 to 100% use of organic cotton within two years. The company worked with a number of certified farmers, ginners, and spinners to make the transition.

Yvon had always been committed to protecting pristine natural environments, and in the early 1970s his company became involved with efforts to preserve and revive California's Ventura River. Patagonia began sponsoring small, grassroots organizations working to preserve or restore the environment. This evolved into a commitment in 1986 to donate 10% of corporate profits to support these causes. That promise morphed into a pledge to spend 1% of sales—regardless of profitability—to saving the environment. Chouinard founded the 1% For The Planet organization in 2002 to encourage other willing companies to support the cause. The company worked to save other environments, and by the late 1990s began to focus on its own environmental impact in its production and sales facilities. Patagonia was a pioneer in calculating its own footprint and took active steps to show internal stewardship and responsibility toward the environment.

The new millennium brought more changes to Patagonia. On Black Friday 2011, Patagonia famously printed a full-page ad in the *New York Times* encouraging customers to not buy its products, but rather to repair and reuse their existing clothing (see Figure 4.2). The company began offering free repairs for its apparel, because, as new CEO Rose Marcario noted in 2015, "the single best thing we can do for the planet is to keep our stuff in use longer."[6] The move was typical of Chouinard's philosophy. Susie Buell of competitor North Face explained, "I'm sure he's made what some people might consider not smart business decisions in order to have his ethics drive his business. He didn't create a culture of things you want. He tried to create a culture of things that would serve you."[7]

Patagonia became California's first benefit corporation—adopting a legal framework that enables, and commits, the company to it's environmental mission. The company is also a certified B-Corp, another signal to investors and stakeholders of Patagonia's commitment to preserving the natural world. Chouinard has invested some of his own wealth into Tin Shed Ventures, named after the location where he worked with his original forge. Tin Shed underwrites and provides guidance to start-ups hoping to thrive with a triple-bottom-line (economic, environmental, and social success) orientation.

By 2017, Patagonia had reached $1 billion in annual revenue.[8]

FIGURE 4.2 Patagonia's Black Friday advertisement was revolutionary.

Introduction

In prior chapters, we've focused on ethical thinking at the individual level, why people behave in unethical ways, what it means for us to act ethically, how individuals can craft the ultimate end of ethics—a meaningful and happy life—and how individual managers can make ethical business decisions. In this chapter and the two that follow, we shift our focus to the organizational foundations and ethical issues they create. It's vital for you to understand how being in an organization affects and shapes ethical choices, because the average American (including part-time workers) spends almost 35 hours per week at work.[9] The average for business leaders is much higher—CEOs spend a whopping 62.5 hours per week at work.[10] This chapter will cover two topics, the competing models of shareholder versus stakeholder capitalism, and the new forms of organization available to business leaders as they balance the demands of shareholders and other stakeholders.

Shareholders Versus Stakeholders: For Whom Do Managers Manage?

The firm that you learned about in your economics classes is an abstraction. Those firms are run by owners who seek to maximize the profits of each firm. Since they are the sole owners, these economic actors are also maximizing their own personal utility, as measured in dollars. While such firms may have existed in the time of Adam Smith, who noted that it's not from the benevolence, but the self-interest of the baker, brewer, and butcher that we obtain products,[11] the world in which we live and work is much different.

The modern corporation, run by professional managers for distant owners, is a relatively new phenomenon. In eighteenth- and early nineteenth-century America, corporations were the exception rather than the norm. Most economic activity was carried out by single individuals or families, where the same person owned and ran the business, or partnerships formed with a few individuals. If you wanted to form a corporation, you had to go to the state legislature and obtain a charter that granted you the right to form a corporation; however, that corporation had a very limited scope and purpose, such as road, canal, or turnpike construction.[12] The corporation accomplished a goal desired by the state (a key stakeholder) but was run to make a profit for its owners (shareholders).

As the nineteenth century drew to a close, states loosened restrictions on corporate purposes, and today you can form a corporation for whatever lawful purpose you decide, and that purpose does not have to be specified in advance. One advantage of the corporate form of ownership is that you can sell ownership shares (stock) to others and their liability for any losses the corporation incurs is limited to the value of their investment. Investors contribute money, but they hire professional managers to run the corporation and try to maximize the returns on their investment. In the eighteenth century, the owner and operator of the business was most often the same person; by the twentieth century, ownership of corporate assets had been separated from control of those assets.[13] In the 1930s, two law school professors, Adolf Berle and Merrick Dodd, debated the purposes of the corporation. Professor Berle articulated the commonly held position that the corporation should be run primarily for the benefit of the shareholders, while Professor Dodd wrote that the corporation should be run for the benefit of the entire community.[14] Berle's summary is best known today as the **shareholder primacy** model and Dodd's as the **stakeholder model**. The *shareholder model* states that managers' primary duty is to maximize shareholder returns, while the *stakeholder model* asks the manager to balance the shareholders' financial interests against the interests of other stakeholders even if it reduces shareholder returns. Table 4.1 displays the key features of each model. As you can see, the stakeholder model has two orientations that use terms you should be familiar with by now: the instrumental and intrinsic stakeholder models.

The Shareholder Model

Nobel Prize–winning economist Milton Friedman was a strong advocate for free market capitalism and the leading proponent of what we refer to as the shareholder primacy model. He stated:

> In a free-enterprise, private-property system, a corporate executive is an employee of the owners of the business. He has direct responsibility to his employers. That responsibility is to conduct the business in accordance with their desires, which generally will be to make as much money as possible while conforming to their basic rules of the society, both those embodied in law and those embodied in ethical custom.[15]

Friedman reasoned that an executive is essentially a tool of the corporation, hired to make sound business decisions and promote the profitability of the business. He declared that if an executive engaged in spending on anything that did not directly benefit shareholders, he or she "would be spending someone else's money for a general social interest. Insofar as his

TABLE 4.1 The Shareholder and Stakeholder Models.

	Shareholder Model	Instrumental Stakeholder Model	Intrinsic Stakeholder Model
Moral Premise: Shareholder Property Rights	Shareholders provide the capital for the firm and have a property claim on the residual earnings of the firm. It is unjust to dispose of that property without the consent of the owners.	Enhancing stakeholder welfare increases the value of shareholders' residual claims.	Shareholder property rights only meaningfully exist within an overarching framework of community institutions and basic human rights and concern for human dignity.
Moral Premise: Stakeholder Welfare	Corporations contribute most to stakeholder welfare through the production of economic goods (e.g., products, services, jobs, and tax revenues).	Corporate contributions can have a direct and measurable impact on both stakeholder welfare and a corporation's "strategic balance sheet" (e.g., increased trust, loyalty, and goodwill).	As a citizen of a larger community, a firm has an obligation to contribute to stakeholder welfare in a broad-based way (e.g., policies, strategies, technologies, and philanthropy).
Strengths	• Creates a clear stopping rule for managerial discretion, investments, and moral obligations. • Holds managers strictly accountable to shareholders for outcomes. • Mitigates agency problems related to mixed motives and messages.	• Presents a broad vision of a firm's roles and opportunities within society while retaining focus on shareholder wealth. • Fosters broader (more constituencies) and deeper (longer-term) commitments by firms to stakeholders.	• Models the firm as a citizen deeply embedded in a global society of communities and institutions. • Offers a broad agenda for meaningful contributions to stakeholder and social welfare.
Weaknesses	• Firms are independent/autonomous within the larger society with no obligations beyond shareholder wealth. • Limited view of business contributions to stakeholder welfare; many opportunities for social contributions may be unrealized.	• Many pressing stakeholder issues and problems may not fit a firm's "strategic objectives." • What is "strategic" is difficult to measure; thus, it is open to abuse of agency relationships and provides a fuzzy stopping rule for investment.	• No clear or simple stopping rule (in theory or practice) to limit managerial decision making, investments, and moral obligations in stakeholder issues. • Expansive view of business contributions to stakeholder welfare. Companies may fail as they try to meet all stakeholder demands.

actions in accord with his 'social responsibility' reduce returns to stockholders, he is spending their money. Insofar as his actions raise the price to customers, he is spending the customers' money. Insofar as his actions lower the wages of some employees, he is spending their money."[16] Friedman strongly believed that "there is one and only one social responsibility of business—to use its resources and engage in activities designed to increase its profits so long as it stays within the rules of the game, which is to say, engages in open and free competition without deception or fraud."[17]

Friedman's argument is consistent with the deontological focus on rights and duties. His focus on property rights and contracts is also consistent with utilitarianism and virtue ethics. Shareholders purchased shares that gave them the right to the profits of the firm, and executives have a responsibility to uphold those rights. Friedman would take issue with the way Yvon Chouinard runs Patagonia, not because Chouinard owns the company and has the right to do with his profits as he pleases but because philanthropists like Chouinard would create pressure on all business leaders to do the same. However, for publicly traded companies, or those with multiple investors, shareholder primacy dictates that when the interests of shareholders and stakeholders collide, shareholders win.

Legal scholars Frank Easterbrook and Daniel Fishel reached the same conclusion from a utilitarian perspective. They pointed to the environmental devastation in the former Soviet Union as evidence that market failures caused by the lack of a focus on profits actually harm stakeholders and societies much more than firms that must answer to markets and shareholders and their performance.[18] They argued that when managers shifted their focus from market competitiveness to social causes or political concerns, strong market incentives would fail and economic value would be destroyed. Vulnerable stakeholders would also suffer. Other researchers employ both positions. For example, researchers pointed out that when General Motors negotiated with its labor unions, the company looked after employee interests in ways that damaged GM's competitiveness for decades. This violated the responsibility of managers to manage for shareholder interests, and it put the company in a position that eventually jeopardized the jobs of thousands of employees.[19]

The Stakeholder Model

Stakeholder theory presents an alternative vision to the shareholder primacy model. It argues that managers should manage the corporation for the benefit of all its stakeholders, not just shareholders. *Stakeholders* are defined as entities "who [are] involved in or affected by a course of action."[20] A **business stakeholder** is someone, something, or some group that either has influence or is influenced by the corporation and its activities.[21] Many people assume that stakeholder theory is synonymous with corporate social responsibility (CSR), but many experts note that every company manages stakeholders, whether or not they engage in CSR practices. If you ask managers what they do all day, you'll find that much of what they do is manage stakeholders: customers, employees, suppliers, investors, regulators, or even members of the local community.[22]

Figure 4.3 displays the many stakeholders of a business firm. There are 12 different groups noted in the figure; each of the these could be subdivided into many specialty groups. While all stakeholders can affect, and are affected by, a business, the ways in which those effects appear allow us to create two broad groups of stakeholders: direct and indirect.

Direct stakeholders include those who transact with the firm on a regular basis, including creditors, customers, employees, investors, managers, suppliers, and some regulators. Each of these stakeholders has a clear and easy-to-define stake in the firm, and each has contact and interacts with members of the firm, its products, or processes.

Indirect stakeholders are not regular transaction partners of the firm, nor do they have regular and obvious interactions with the firm. Some of these stakeholders have their own voice, while some stakeholders rely on others to speak for them. Indirect stakeholders include activist groups, animal species, future generations, non-regulatory government actors, journalists, and the natural environment. It's much easier to manage direct stakeholders than indirect ones. Executives can clearly forecast the impact of changes in work rules on employees, but it's more difficult to think through and measure the impact of allowing employees to work a day for the local United Way.

Given that managers spend most of their day managing stakeholder demands, the real question is whether organizational leaders manage stakeholders well or poorly. Stakeholder theorists and researchers have created two broad models of effective stakeholder management:

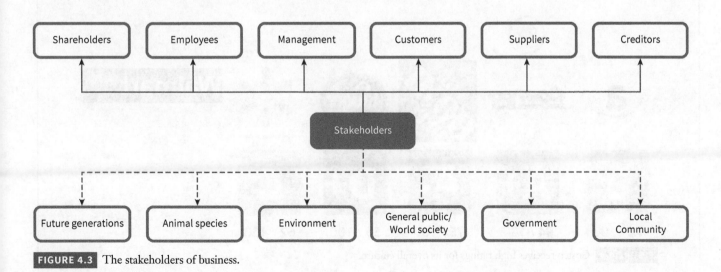

FIGURE 4.3 The stakeholders of business.

the instrumental and the intrinsic model.[23] Table 4.1 displayed the differences between the two, and we'll describe them in greater detail below.

The instrumental stakeholder model. When managers consider and act on the needs and desires of different stakeholders, this enhances the likelihood of broad regard for the moral interests at stake. Stakeholders see their needs satisfied, and the firm is more likely to benefit through higher revenues, lower expenses, or some combination of the two. Doing right by stakeholders can lead to doing well for the corporation. Some examples of such win-win relationships are the following:

- A focus on customer needs provides marketing managers and product development teams with more information into customer preferences and emerging needs.

- Fair and generous treatment of employees can lead to greater loyalty (lower absenteeism and turnover) and increased productivity.

- Transparent and accurate reporting to investors and the financial community can lead to lower interest rates or better loan terms in general.

- Attention to the suppliers' concerns and needs can improve efficiency along the supply chain and can encourage suppliers to share knowledge with operations managers that streamlines processes, reduces inventory needs, or leads to new products.

Ethics in the Real World 4.1 describes the instrumental stakeholder approach at bulk retailer Costco.

Ethics in the Real World 4.1 | Costco Wins by Treating Employees Right

Costco, the Kirkland, Washington, bulk retailer, invented the concept of the larger warehouse shopping club in the late 1980s. Costco is known for treating its employees well. The company pays above industry-average wages and provides employees with exceptional benefits. The job-hunting website Indeed describes Costco this way:

> So how did a warehouse chain beat out the top tech companies when it comes to benefits and salary packages? To start, the company pays well above the typical salary that other retail companies pay, even for entry-level workers.
>
> "They have a graduated wage program that's based purely on total hours worked. Show up, do your job, and your pay goes up on its own," says one employee.
>
> When it comes to insurance and other benefits, another employee describes the company as "second

to none." In general, employee reviews praise Costco's family-based philosophy, great treatment of its employees, and concern for their well-being.

> One employee sums it up well: "Costco believes that employees are the most important assets in the company."[24]

In fact, Costco is rated more highly by its employees than well-known stars such as Apple or Starbucks (see Figure 4.4 for how Costco rates compared to some of its retail competitors). Seventy-six percent of Costco Warehouse managers began as hourly employees (reducing hiring costs and preserving company knowledge and culture), and turnover is about 6% for employees who stay a year or more. How does the company compare to its closest rival, Walmart-owned Sam's Club? Weekly sales at Costco locations are 72% higher than at Sam's Club.[25]

FIGURE 4.4   Costco receives high ratings for its overall culture.

The intrinsic stakeholder model. The earliest proponent of the intrinsic stakeholder model was Harvard Law Professor Merrick Dodd. He stated: "If the unity of the corporate body is real, then there is reality and not simply legal fiction in the proposition that the managers of the unit are fiduciaries for it and not merely for its individual members, that they are . . . trustees for an institution rather than attorneys for the stockholders."[26] The language Dodd uses is the language of duties (including but not limited to being a fiduciary or trustee) the corporate leaders have toward a much larger set of stakeholders than just shareholders. The flip side of these duties and obligations is that stakeholders have rights. They have a set of fundamental rights, merely because they are other living beings or the natural environment that sustains us. Some of these rights include the following:

- Safe products for customers, ones free from known hazards or defects; clear information about the product, its uses, its potential hazards, and disposal

- Safe working environments and adequate wages for workers; work cultures that allow for individual differences to flourish and time and energy for people to meet multiple life objectives

- Transparent information about the state of the business for investors; information about what is working well, and what is not working well in the firm; clear communication of strategies, their potential upsides and downsides

- Mutually beneficial exchanges with suppliers, exchanges that do not exploit asymmetric positions by either side; fair and forthright information sharing

Ethics in the Real World 4.2 shows how Patagonia, the company we opened the chapter with, views its responsibilities toward an important indirect stakeholder, the planet.

Ethics in the Real World 4.2 | Intrinsic Stakeholder Management at Patagonia

You may not be surprised to know that Chouinard stated, "At Patagonia, we work hard to make high-quality, responsibly sourced clothing that lasts for years and can be repaired—and we guarantee it for life. . . . We go to great lengths to provide our customers with opportunities to fix their gear themselves, find it a new home, or recycle it if necessary. We ask our customers to use tools we provide to decrease the environmental impact of their stuff over time by buying only what they need, repairing what they have, finding ways to reuse items, and recycling when it's truly time. As we see greater impacts from climate change every year, we as individuals must reverse our current course of overconsumption. Let's behave like owners, not consumers, and repair rather than inflict something new on the planet if we don't truly need it. It's a radical thought, but change can start with just a needle and thread."[27] (See Figure 4.5.)

Notice the language that Chouinard uses. Patagonia is an owner of the planet, as we all are, and that ownership (or really stewardship) creates a set of moral obligations to act toward the natural environment.

patagonia

Shop   Activism   Sports   Stories

Ironclad Guarantee

We guarantee everything we make. If you are not satisfied with one of our products at the time you receive it, or if one of our products does not perform to your satisfaction, return it to the store you bought it from or to Patagonia for a repair, replacement or refund. Damage due to wear and tear will be repaired at a reasonable charge.

Where do I return my item(s)?

Need a different size or color? Contact our Customer Service team (1-800-638-6464) for a replacement. We'll waive the shipping fee on your new order and provide you with a free shipping label to return your original order.

If you'd like to ship it back, we offer a $5 flat rate return shipping label that includes tracking and insurance. This cost will be deducted from your refund or credit. You can also skip the shipping cost and return your item(s) at any official Patagonia retail store.

More Details

FIGURE 4.5 Patagonia's Ironclad Guarantee.

Stakeholder Characteristics and Importance

Figure 4.3 displayed twelve different stakeholder groups, and each of these groups may include hundreds (suppliers), thousands (employees or shareholders), or millions (customers) of individuals. Each of these stakeholders has a set of demands and needs that he or she wants to see the corporation meet. For example, customers prefer lower prices, but employees prefer higher wages. When stakeholder desires or needs collide, how can managers effectively decide which ones to focus on? Management scholars Ron Mitchell, Brad Agle, and Donna Wood have provided practical advice to managers about which stakeholders they should pay attention to at which time. They argue that stakeholders could be sorted along three high–low dimensions:

- The power a stakeholder has to press his, her, or its claims against the organization;
- the legitimacy, or perceived appropriateness, of those claims; and
- the urgency and need for immediate attention to those claims.

Their model is known as the "stakeholder salience model" and results in seven categories of stakeholders, using the helpful mnemonic that each category begins with the letter *D*. Figure 4.6 displays their model and we briefly describe each category below.

- **Dormant Stakeholders:** These stakeholders have power to influence the firm, but internal or external decision makers do not see these claims as appropriate, and there is no urgent need to respond to these claims. An example would be if Chevron (the customer) demanded that a pipeline provider, such as Williams Companies, reduce maintenance on the pipeline in order to lower transmission fees. Chevron's size gives it power, but the claim lacks legitimacy (it violates both industry standards and state laws), and the claim has no urgent need for action.

- **Discretionary Stakeholders:** Individuals or groups in this category make very appropriate and legitimate claims on a company, but they lack power to force the company to act, nor is there urgency to their demands. An example would be the Navajo Nation demanding that Chevron reduce drilling and production around designated wilderness areas on federal lands. These claims have merit, but the Navajo's have no power or leverage other than moral persuasion to encourage Chevron, and the claim lacks immediacy in its appeal.

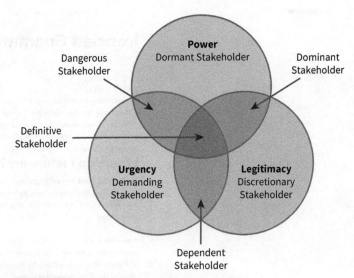

Source: Mitchell, R, Agle B, and Wood, D, (1997) Toward a theory of stakeholder identification and salience: Defining the principles of who and what really counts, Academy of Management Review, 22 (4): 853–886

FIGURE 4.6 The Stakeholder Salience Model.

- **Dominant Stakeholders:** Stakeholders with both legitimacy and power create this group. Imagine if the President of the Navajo Nation were to convince the *New York Times* to write an expose detailing Chevron's wilderness drilling policy. The claim would be legitimate, the *New York Times* would have the power to create reputational problems for Chevron, and company executives would feel a need to respond to the *Times'* demands to change drilling patterns.

- **Demanding Stakeholders**: These stakeholders have a very urgent claim, but the claim may not be legitimate, and the group has no power or leverage over the corporation. Continuing with the Chevron case an example of a demanding stakeholder might be the Southern Utah Wilderness Alliance (SUWA), a private activist group, protesting a new well on land on which Chevron had a legitimate lease to drill. The group sees stopping further drilling as critical to preserving wildlife and wildlands, but SUWA has little power to influence Chevron's actions.

- **Dependent Stakeholders:** These groups have an urgent and legitimate claim, but no power to leverage the corporation to respond to their claim. In our example, the animal species and natural landscapes that SUWA hopes to protect would be dependent stakeholders. Their "claim" for survival would be legitimate and urgent, but they would have no power in and of themselves to effect change. They are dependent on other stakeholders— those with power—to advance their claims.

- **Dangerous Stakeholders:** Imagine that a group of zealous SUWA advocates, frustrated by Chevron's lack of response to their claims, sabotaged the new wells. Their claim was urgent, and they used a form of power (coercive) to gain leverage; however, their claim, and their action, lacked legitimacy. This group would constitute dangerous stakeholders, groups willing to pursue their agendas through coercion or violence, to press their demands.

- **Definitive Stakeholders:** This group sits at the intersection of all three circles. Their claims are legitimate and urgent, and these stakeholders have power to force the corporation to deal with their demands. In our hypothetical drilling case, the U.S. Fish and Wildlife Service, the Department of Energy, or even an activist investor would all be definitive stakeholders. The government entities have legal authority to ensure their claims are heard and respected, while investors could use their rights of governance to make sure their agenda received attention and action.

In this section, you've read about a long-running debate concerning the purposes of business and who the main beneficiaries of corporate activity should be. One way that business and government leaders have resolved this issue is to create new, legitimate forms of corporate organization that allow executives to focus on more than a single, financial bottom line. In the next section, we review several of these emerging business forms.

Alternative Organizational Forms to Improve Stakeholder Management

In the seventeenth and eighteenth centuries, corporations could only be formed for a specific purpose. Once that purpose had been achieved, the corporation dissolved, and its assets were distributed to the owners. The nineteenth and twentieth centuries witnessed the rise of the corporate form in a more general sense; corporations could form for any purpose the owners desired, and the corporation had perpetual life. The purpose of the corporation was to enrich its owners, and a string of legal cases established shareholder primacy as the dominant model. These corporations are most commonly referred to by their shorthand designation in the U.S. Internal Revenue Code, C Corps. In the not-for-profit world, the dominant form of organization is also commonly referred to by its tax code designation: a "501(c)(3)."

In the twenty-first century, activists and legislators have provided people like Yvon Chouinard—committed to running a business that serves multiple stakeholders and focuses

TABLE 4.2   Comparing Different Types of Social Enterprise.

	C-Corp	Exempt Organizations	For-Profit Social Enterprises		
			L3C	Benefit Corporation	Philanthropic Enterprise
Legal Status	Subparagraph (C), Internal Revenue Code § 108(d)(7) of 1986	Internal Revenue Code § 501(c)(3) of 1986	L3C (10 States)[29]	Benefit Corporation (37 States)[30]	Internal Revenue Code § 4943(g), as amended Feb. 2018
Stakeholder/Social Mission	Voluntary	Exclusive in charter	Prioritized in charter	Articulated in charter	Exclusive in charter
Profit Mission	Primarily wealth maximization	No distribution	Limited by charter	Stakeholder constrained	Wealth maximization
Governance	Simple, single mission	Simple, single mission	Simple, prioritized	Complex, contested	Simple, single mission
Revenue Model	Unrelated	Embedded or related	Embedded or related	Related or unrelated	Unrelated
Funding Sources	Sales Equity capital Debt capital	Sales Grants Assets	Sales Equity capital Debt capital	Sales Equity capital Debt capital	Sales Debt capital Corporate profits
Wealth Transfer	Discretionary	Defined by charter	Defined by charter	Discretionary	Defined by charter
Financial Scalability	Easy	Moderate	Difficult	Difficult	Moderate
Examples	IBM www.IBM.com	Red Cross www.redcross.org	Civic Staffing, L3C www.civicstaffing.com	Better World Books www.betterworldbooks.com	Newman's Own www.newmansown.com

on solving social problems or creating a more sustainable world—with alternative ways to organize their businesses. These businesses are often referred to as social enterprises. These organizations, which Harvard Business School professor Julie Battilana terms "hybrid" organizations, seek to employ market-based solutions to create social and stakeholder benefit.[28] We discuss three alternative forms to conclude this chapter. Table 4.2 lays out these forms and highlights their key features in comparison to the traditional corporate or not-for-profit form.

Low-Profit Limited Liability Company (L3C)

Ten states in the United States, three Native American tribes, and Puerto Rico recognize the low-profit limited liability company as a legitimate business form. The form provides owners with the limited liability advantages of the corporate form but limits the amount of profit the business creates and reports to that needed to fund its stakeholder or social mission and provide some surplus funds to preserve the company's survival. Because the limitations on profit generation make scaling difficult, many L3Cs remain small, local organizations.

Benefit Corporations

Yvon Chouinard had a clear goal to provide some type of benefit to the broader world community while propelling Patagonia to be a market leader. In 2012, Patagonia applied for and became the first California corporation to be registered as a "benefit corporation."[31] What does the B stand for? Keeping Patagonia in mind, it comes as no surprise that the B stands for "benefit." Thirty-seven U.S. states recognize the benefit corporation as a legal business form; however, a company in any of the 50 states can apply for B Corp certification through B Lab.

THE B CORP
DECLARATION OF
INTERDEPENDENCE

We envision a global economy that uses business as a force for good.

This economy is comprised of a new type of corporation - the B Corporation -
Which is purpose-driven and creates benefit for all stakeholders, not just shareholders.

As B Corporations and leaders of this emerging economy, we believe:

- That we must be the change we seek in the world.
- That all business ought to be conducted as if people and place mattered.
- That, through their products, practices, and profits, businesses should aspire to do no harm and benefit all.
- To do so requires that we act with the understanding that we are each dependent upon another and thus responsible for each other and future generations.

FIGURE 4.7 The mission of a B Corp.

Jay Coen Gilbert and two of his friends, Bart Houlahan and Andrew Kassoy, created B Lab in 2006. B Lab formalizes what Chouinard did informally—by providing a certification to companies that actually provide social good, while meeting their business goals:[32] To qualify as a B Corp, a firm must have an explicit social or environmental mission and a legally binding fiduciary responsibility to take into account the interests of workers, the community, and the environment as well as its shareholders (see **Figure 4.7**). The directors of these corporations must consider the impact on all company stakeholders of doing business.

In addition to this lengthy list of requirements, "A B Corp must pay an annual fee based on revenues, biannually complete a B Impact Report (a lengthy questionnaire that measures social and environmental impact against a third-party standard), meet B Lab's comprehensive social and environmental performance standards and make that B Impact Report public, in order to receive the certification from B Lab." If the corporation passes the certification, it receives access to certain services, a community of likeminded corporations, use of a very recognizable logo, and so forth.[33] As of 2020, there were 3,393 Certified B Corporations representing 150 industries and 71 countries.[34]

Philanthropic Enterprises

In the early 1980s, actor Paul Newman and his friend, A. E. Hotchner, made a batch of Paul's secret recipe salad dressing and gave it away to friends. When the friends came back and asked for more, Newman decided that he might make a business of it.[35] Newman's acting career had left him a wealthy man and so he decided that his new company, Newman's Own, would give 100% of its profits to charity. Newman said, "I'm not running for sainthood. I just happen to think that in life we need to be a little like the farmer, who puts back into the soil what he takes out."[36] From the mid-1980s until his death in 2008, Newman owned both the company and his foundation. Upon his death in 2008, he bequeathed the corporation to the foundation so that the giving tradition could continue.

This bequest ran afoul of the provisions in the tax law that prohibited a foundation from owning 100% of a corporation. If the foundation retained ownership of the corporation after a grace period (eventually extended to 10 years), the foundation would be crippled by paying an excess holdings tax. The leaders of the foundation soon realized that the only way to preserve their unique business model of 100% to charity required a change in the tax law. The company began working on legislation in the early 2010s, and a few months before it faced a huge tax liability, Congress passed a provision changing the tax code and allowing philanthropic enterprises.

The philanthropic enterprise draws from two classical American traditions: the power of business corporations and an innate love for benevolent philanthropic activity. The philanthropic enterprise marries these two traditions to enhance the common good. A private foundation is the sole stockholder in the corporation and has a claim on all profits. The law requires that 100% of profits, save a reasonable reserve held for legitimate business purposes, be distributed to the foundation, which then funnels those funds to charitable causes. Since 1982, Newman's Own has given away over $550 million, and since the change to the tax law, other 100% of profits- to-charity enterprises are beginning to emerge.

Key Terms

business stakeholder
direct stakeholders
indirect stakeholders

legitimacy
power
shareholder primacy

social enterprise
stakeholder model
urgency

Chapter Summary

In this chapter, we addressed different types of objectives of corporations:

- We addressed the competing shareholder primacy and stakeholder models of Milton Friedman and Ed Freeman, respectively. While Freidman focused on the inherent duty of a business to bring wealth to the shareholder, Freeman and his colleagues hold that the purpose of corporation is to be aware of and take care of stakeholders of corporations. Stakeholders are those entities that either can impact a corporation or be impacted by the corporation.

- Stakeholders can be direct or indirect. Direct stakeholders include customers, employees, investors, regulators, and suppliers. Indirect stakeholders include local, regional, and global communities, future inhabitants of our planet, animals, and the natural environment. There are two approaches to stakeholder management. Companies can focus on instrumentally managing

stakeholders and satisfying their needs in ways that improve the profitability of the company. This is doing well by doing good. Companies can also manage stakeholders intrinsically because they see these stakeholders as having a set of fundamental rights and privileges.

- Stakeholders can be classified according to their salience, or how much attention managers should pay to each stakeholder group or claim. We discussed the seven categories of stakeholder salience based on the three overarching dimensions of stakeholder power, legitimacy, and urgency.

- We concluded by reviewing several new forms of business organization that facilitate stakeholder management. These include L3Cs, benefit corporations, and philanthropic enterprises. Each form allows entrepreneurs, managers, or owners to focus on both profitability and satisfying stakeholder needs.

Chapter Review Questions

1. Explain the shareholder primacy perspective. Why did it originate, and what is the moral premise for prioritizing financial investors in a corporation?

2. What is the moral basis of the stakeholder model? Does it have a single moral justification? Why or why not?

3. Do you think it is appropriate for a corporation to make strategic decisions while considering positive and negative impact to the world? How can investors be sure that a company truly wants to make money for them?

4. Name ten stakeholders of Patagonia. Why is each of these a stakeholder?

5. Using the stakeholder salience model, classify each of the stakeholders you identified in question 4. Which ones are dormant? Which are dangerous, and which are definitive? What does this mean for how Patagonia runs its business?

6. If you were to start a business focused on stakeholders, would you choose one of the new organizational forms? Which one? Why?

7. Do all employees have to always comply?

8. Identify and discuss the situations in any organization where compliance is not required.

9. Is non-compliance unethical?

10. How are shareholders different from stakeholders?

Application Exercises

- *Personal Ethical Development.* If you began keeping an ethics journal as suggested in the first chapter, continue that writing work. Here are some prompts: How important is it that a company you work for make money for its shareholders? Should that be the prime objective? Which stakeholders should corporations pay the most attention to? Create a list of questions you can ask during a job interview to assess a company's commitment to the shareholder or stakeholder model.

- *Career Goals and Planning.* A happy, meaningful, and productive life blends and builds upon the following: (1) the type of life you are interested in leading, (2) your deepest and most important principles, (3) the work you are interested in doing, (4) what you are good at, (5) your preferences for things like work versus free time, and (6) your personality. Create a stakeholder map for your own life. What "stake" does each stakeholder have in you and your career? How would attention to their interests affect your career path?

- *Ethics in the Business World.* Identify an organization that you believe treats its various stakeholders well. This may be either a for-profit or not-for-profit organization. What evidence from the company backs up your belief? What stakeholder-friendly activities does it engage in? How it measure success with its stakeholders?

- *Talking with and Learning from Others.* Choose a business professional you believe has good business and ethical judgment. Engage that person in a brief interview. How does he or she balance the conflicting need of making a profit and focusing on efficiency with the various demands and needs of stakeholders? Which stakeholders does the professional spend the most time working with? What advice would he or she give you about how to balance making money with meeting stakeholder needs?

Mini-Cases

Case 1: Distributing corporate profits. You are a director of a large, publicly held company. Although publicly held, the CEO and chair of the board is the founder and majority stakeholder. The company has been very successful selling consumer electronics and has built up a large cash reserve. The CEO has proposed to the board a plan to use that cash reserve in two ways. First, the company would expand the market for its products. One key element of that strategy is to lower the price of the final product to consumers; the plan would, in essence, give a large part of the cash reserve to customers through lower prices. Customers have always been willing to pay the premium prices the company charges. The second element of that strategy would be to increase the wages and benefits paid to workers, already well above industry averages. The CEO believes that workers should be paid more to build better lives for themselves and their families.

A group of minority shareholders, with significant holdings, has contacted you to register their opposition to the plan. They argue that the company should use the cash reserve to increase dividends paid out to shareholders, who have patiently invested capital over many years. Shareholder returns have been above average for the industry. Their analysis also suggests that implementing the CEO's plan may lead to a decline in the company's share price. You are a well-respected member of the board and your argument is likely to sway several directors, one way or the other.

Discussion Questions

1. Whose proposal would you support, the CEO's or the minority shareholders'? Why?

2. Is the purpose of a corporation to maximize returns to shareholders, or do other stakeholders have a claim on corporate earnings?

3. What are the benefits and risks to each proposal?

Case 2: Surviving during the coronavirus pandemic. Paleo is a restaurant located just outside the urban core of St. Louis. The chef and owner, McKenzie Goodwin, has always been committed to serving her customers fresh, locally grown, and certified organic ingredients made into wonderful appetizers, sides, and main dishes. The company employs a staff of 13 servers, assistants, and dishwashers. The year 2019 was a very good one for the restaurant and it enhanced its reputation with its prime customer group: upscale young millennials who work in the urban core. Sales were strong and McKenzie enjoyed record profits. The 2019 profits gave her a solid down payment on a beautiful new home with a state-of-the-art kitchen, and her forecasts for 2020 and beyond allowed her to take out a large mortgage.

In March of 2020, McKenzie's business cratered, along with most other restaurants during the COVID-19 lockdown. Her menu did not translate well to curbside pickup, but she and her staff worked to create a takeout/curbside pickup menu that allowed the business to limp along. She applied for a Paycheck Protection Program loan in April of 2020, which allowed her to keep her staff employed. Business picked up over the summer as the city of St. Louis allowed restaurants to use the parking strip as additional outdoor seating.

As summer turned to fall, McKenzie realized that her situation was not good. She would soon lose her outdoor seating, and the takeout menu would reduce her need for staff, as well as curb her purchases from local suppliers, many of them small farmers also limping through the pandemic. If she cut deep enough into her staff and purchasing, she could continue to meet her own income goals. She wondered how deeply she should cut her staff.

Discussion Questions

1. Who are McKenzie's major stakeholder groups? Which ones are discretionary stakeholders? Which ones demanding? Which ones definitive?

2. What would you advise McKenzie to do? How should she make trade-offs between her own needs and desires and those of her key stakeholder groups?

3. What risks and opportunities do different courses of action offer McKenzie?

Case 3: Tata Motors Limited is India's largest automobile company, which is committed to serve society by focusing on four thrust areas—employability, education, health, and environment. In March 2003, Mr. Ratan Tata revealed the company's plans to make the world's cheapest car—the Nano. The manufacturing unit was located at Singur in West Bengal, where there was a conflict in the values of different interest groups—farmers, government, and the company. The ethical challenge faced by Tata Motors in Singur was the purpose of business at the cost of society and the environment, since the land acquired for this purpose was a multi-crop farmland. Moreover, while 15,000 depended on the land for agriculture, Tata managed to create only 1,000 jobs, many of which were offered outside of the village. Tata Motors maintained silence over the farmers' protest and continued working on various corporate social responsibilities such as employment generating trainings for locals. There was also a lot of delay in starting the manufacturing plant of Ratan Tata's dream car, which added to the negative impact. Also environmental activists protested that the project would degrade the fertile land. On the other hand, if the company shifted to another location after investing time and money in building a manufacturing plant in Singur, it would be huge cost for the company. The relocation cost estimated by the company was about ₹2,000 crore. Tata Group has over the years built an outstanding image in India and it has always been considered as a socially responsible group. However, Tata Motors was not able to protect the interests of Singur, leaving behind a lasting negative impression. The company finally decided to change the location of the manufacturing unit due to all these issues.

Discussion Questions

1. Discuss the ethical role and responsibilities of each stakeholder (Tata Motors, government, farmers, and society) in this case.

2. What other alternatives did Tata Motors have to resolve this issue?

References

1. "#1750, Yvon Chouinard," *Forbes'* World Billionaires List 2021, accessed May 2, 2021, https://www.forbes.com/profile/yvon-chouinard/?sh=6091a1ae4fb5.

2. The bulk of information in this introduction was obtained through the Patagonia company history, available at https://www.patagonia.com/company-history/. For ease of reading, we have minimized the number of references.

3. Daniela Sirtori-Cortina, "From Climber To Billionaire: How Yvon Chouinard Built Patagonia Into A Powerhouse His Own Way," *Forbes,* March 20, 2017 https://www.forbes.com/sites/danielasirtori/2017/03/20/from-climber-to-billionaire-how-yvon-chouinard-built-patagonia-into-a-powerhouse-his-own-way/?sh=5af48832275c.

4. Ibid.

5. Photo from Yvon Chouinard, *Let My People Go Surfing: The Education of a Reluctant Businessman* (New York, Penguin Publishing Group, Kindle Edition, 2005), 35.

6. Patagonia (@Patagonia), "'The single best thing we can do for the planet is to keep our stuff in use longer,' our CEO Rose Marcario on @qz," Twitter, November 25, 2015, 10:47 a.m., https://www.patagonia.com/stories/repair-is-a-radical-act/story-17637.html.

7. Sirtori-Cortina, "From Climber to Billionaire."

8. "Patagonia stock price, funding rounds, valuation and financials," Craft, https://craft.co/patagonia/metrics.

9. Alison Doyle, "What is the Average Hours Per Week Worked in the US?," The Balance Careers, last modified January 21, 2021, https://www.thebalancecareers.com/what-is-the-average-hours-per-week-worked-in-the-us-2060631.

10. Sarah Berger, "Here's what CEOs actually do all day," *CNBC Make It,* last modified June 21, 2018, https://www.cnbc.com/2018/06/20/harvard-study-what-ceos-do-all-day.html.

11. Adam Smith, *An Inquiry into the Nature and Causes of the Wealth of Nations,* 1776/1976, Book IV, Chapter II, p. 456, para. 9.

12. Herbert Hovenkamp, *Enterprise and American Law, 1836–1937* (Cambridge, MA: Harvard University Press, 1991).

13. Adolf Augustus Berle and Gardiner Coit Means, *The Modern Corporation and Private Property* (New Brunswick, NJ: Transaction Publishers, 1932). See Book 1, Chapter 2.1, property in transition for an excellent exposition.

14. A. A. Berle, "Corporate Powers as Powers in Trust," *Harvard Law Review* 44, no. 7 (May 1, 1931): 1049–1074, doi:10.2307/1331341; and E. Merrick Dodd, "For Whom Are Corporate Managers Trustees?," *Harvard Law Review* 45, no. 7 (May 1, 1932): 1145–1163, doi:10.2307/1331697.

15. Milton Friedman, "The Social Responsibility of Business Is to Increase Its Profits," New York Times Magazine, September 13, 1970.

16. Ibid.

17. Ibid.

18. H. F. Easterbrook and D. R. Fischel, *The Economic Structure of Corporate Law* (Cambridge, MA: Harvard University Press, 1991), 38–39.

19 Paul C. Godfrey and Nile W. Hatch, "Researching Corporate Social Responsibility: An Agenda for the 21st Century," *Journal of Business Ethics* 70, no. 1 (2006): 87–98. See page 94.

20 Definition taken from *Merriam Webster's Dictionary*, SV stakeholders, https://www.merriam-webster.com/dictionary/stakeholder.

21 The early work that defined the field of *stakeholder theory was done by Ed Freeman. See R. Edward Freeman, Strategic Management: A Stakeholder Approach* (Marshfield, MA: Pitman, 1984).

22 R. Edward Freeman, Jeffrey S. Harrison, and Andrew C. Wicks, *Managing for Stakeholders: Survival, Reputation, and Success* (New Haven: Yale University Press, 2007).

23 Thomas Donaldson and Lee E. Preston, "The Stakeholder Theory of the Corporation: Concepts, Evidence, and Implications," *Academy of Management Review* 20, no. 1 (January 1995): 65–91.

24 Gina Acosta, "Why Costco is America's favorite workplace," *Retail Leader*, March 1, 2018, https://retailleader.com/why-costco-americas-favorite-workplace.

25 Brian Woolf, "What Makes Costco So successful?," BrianWoolf.com, April 7, 2015, http://www.brianwoolf.com/index?id=49&action=bw_article_read.

26 *Harvard Law Review*, Vol. 45, No. 7 (May 1932): 1160.

27 See note 6 above.

28 Julie Battilana et al., "In Search of the Hybrid Ideal," *Stanford Social Innovation Review*, Summer 2012.

29 Data from Hana Muslic, "A Jargon-Free Guide to Low-Profit Limited Liability Companies (L3C)," Nonprofit Hub, June 1, 2017, https://nonprofithub.org/starting-a-nonprofit/jargon-free-guide-l3c/#:~:text=Can%20I%20start%20an%20L3C,following%20places%2C%20yes%20you%20can!.

30 Data from "State by State Status of Legislation," Benefit Corporation, accessed May 2, 2021, https://benefitcorp.net/policymakers/state-by-state-status.

31 Patagonia, https://www.patagonia.com/home/.

32 Ellen Rosen, Working to Benefit Society, Not Just Companies, *New York Times*, Oct. 17, 2019, available at https://www.nytimes.com/2019/10/17/business/certified-b-corps.html. Patagonia, https://www.patagonia.com/home/.

33 See Benefit Corporation at benefitcorp.net for a complete description of the process, https://benefitcorp.net/.

34 Ibid.

35 For information on the Newman's Own Foundation, its history and activities, see https://newmansownfoundation.org/.

36 Paul Newman quotation available at https://www.goodreads.com/quotes/101598-we-are-such-spendthrifts-with-our-lives-the-trick-of.

CHAPTER 5

Ethics and Compliance in the Corporation

LEARNING OUTCOMES

At the end of this chapter, you should be able to do the following:

1. Describe the evolution of corporate compliance.

2. Discuss the objectives for the Federal Sentencing Guidelines for Organizations and the role these guidelines play in corporate compliance programs.

3. Identify the important elements of a corporate ethics and compliance department and discuss the key responsibilities of those working in this area.

4. Define the elements of a corporate code of conduct.

5. Describe the role of a chief ethics and compliance officer in a typical organization.

6. Apply the knowledge gained in this chapter to real situations managers face when trying to fulfill their compliance obligations.

Opening Case | Compliance Challenges at Pacific Gas and Electric

In 1852, Peter, James, and Michael Donahue received permission from the city of San Francisco to erect the first gasworks in the western United States. A gasworks was a company that manufactured and distributed gas to light homes in a city. In early 1854, the streets of the city were lit up at night, and within a year the new company—the San Francisco Gas Company—was providing gas for almost 200 streetlamps and over 500 homes.[1] An 1896 merger with the Edison Light and Power Company made the new San Francisco Gas and Electric Company one of the first integrated utility companies, and by 1905 further merger and acquisition activity resulted in the company known today as Pacific Gas and Electric (PG&E).[2] Today, the company provides electricity to over 5 million California customers and 4.4 million natural gas users over a service area that stretches from the Oregon border to the north to Bakersfield, California, to the south, and from the Pacific Ocean to the Sierra Nevada mountains to the east.[3] That's over 70,000 square miles, and the company has almost 107,000 miles of electric distribution lines.

Those miles of electrical lines represent a significant problem for PG&E, the state of California, and its residents because of the potential for faulty electrical wires to cause forest and range fires. In the 1990s, PG&E was found criminally negligent in three significant California fires: the Trainer fire (1994), a fire in San Francisco's Mission District (1996), and the Pendola fire in 1998 that burned over 12,000 acres in the Tahoe National

AP Images/Ben Margot

Forest. The company's problems with wildfires continued into the new millennium, and by 2019 PG&E had filed for bankruptcy protection because the company faced liabilities of over $30 billion for fires between 2015 and 2018.[4] PG&E also faced potential liability for over 1,500 other fires,[5] including the 2017 Tubbs fire (37,000 acres)[6] and the massive Kincaid fire (78,000 acres).[7] PG&E filed for bankruptcy, and experts estimated its total liability at $54 billion, although the company later agreed to pay only $25.5 billion to various insurance companies, government agencies, and victims' compensation funds. The company finally exited bankruptcy in 2020.[8]

As a public utility, PG&E reports to both federal and state regulators. The Federal Energy Regulatory Commission (FERC) has jurisdiction over any interstate transmission of electricity or natural gas, and PG&E's electric and natural gas grids both connect across state lines. FERC also regulates merger activity among utilities and sets accounting and reporting standards for compliance. The California Energy Commission (CEC) regulates all aspects of energy production and distribution in the state and sets compliance goals and standards around energy efficiency and migration to renewable energy sources. The California Public Utilities Commission oversees PG&E's pricing and access issues for consumers and sets numerous safety standards that PG&E must comply with. The utility also deals with county- and city-level officials in areas such as zoning and land use planning. As the company continues to operate, it must comply with court orders regarding financial payments and aspects of its operations.

Introduction

One of the most important elements for you in leading an ethical business life will be to understand the rationale for, nature of, and key tools in an effective compliance program. We warn you at the beginning that much of this chapter will cover what seem like irrelevant details; however, these details will help you understand how to navigate in a business world with increasing regulatory and compliance requirements. This is important stuff!

There are few companies today that have no concerns about regulation and compliance. Even the smallest businesses pay taxes and must comply with local regulations. As companies grow, they tend to formalize a compliance program. For small and medium-sized companies, compliance may be led by a single individual, and much of the work of compliance is outsourced to accountants, insurance brokers, law firms, payroll companies, and others. Large companies find it economical to bring many of these functions in-house, and they often have a compliance officer and a formal compliance program, or "a formal internal system of policies, procedures, controls, and actions to detect and prevent violations of laws, regulations, rules, standards, and policies."[9]

In this chapter, you'll learn about what a compliance program is, who oversees these programs from a corporate perspective, and some important government agencies that have an interest in compliance. As you read in the opening vignette, PG&E had several problems with compliance that created liabilities related to fires. An effective compliance program has two elements: a formal program and a culture that supports those efforts. In this chapter, you'll learn about the former; in the next chapter, we'll discuss the role of culture in sustaining compliance programs and ethical behavior in general. We begin this chapter with an overview of compliance.

The Evolution of Compliance

Martin and Daniel Biegelman noted that "Compliance has always been around, in some form or another, since the beginnings of organized commerce."[10] Compliance means "adherence to, or conformance with, rules, laws, standards, and policies. It also implies a sense of accountability and an obligation to uphold pertinent codes of conduct."[11] We noted in Chapter 1 that one element of ethics is obedience to the unenforceable, and compliance is both different from and similar to ethics. Compliance and ethics differ in their enforceability. Ethical violations don't bring about fines, imprisonment, or other penalties; failure to comply with formal compliance requirements leads to penalties. Compliance and ethics are very similar in that both are most effective when people practice voluntary adherence to unwritten expectations and norms of behavior. Most of us can think of instances when we have had to "comply" with policies or regulations, from not chewing gum in elementary school to learning our state's driving laws so that we could obtain a driver's license.

The Twentieth Century

How did we get from simple rules to formal corporate compliance programs? Some believe that a series of events, over multiple decades, led to the commonplace corporate compliance programs that exist today. The first large-scale regulation of business began in the late nineteenth century with the Sherman Antitrust Act, a law used to break up large monopolies; that law forms the foundation of today's regulation of mergers and acquisitions.[12] A generation later, the U.S. government passed the Securities Acts of 1933 and 1934. This legislation created the Securities and Exchange Commission and laid the foundation for today's financial reporting requirements. These acts also established an important precedent that underpins many compliance regimes: Making companies transparently report their activities would be a powerful check on behavior.

The 1960s and 1970s witnessed a number of instances of corporate misbehavior and saw a rise in environmental concerns. Two major regulatory and compliance efforts began during this time. Public outrage over bribery scandals and misdeeds by U.S. companies competing overseas led to the enactment of the Foreign Corrupt Practices Act of 1977.[13] You'll learn more about the FCPA in Chapter 7 on global ethics. A growing environmental consciousness led to the passage of the Clean Water and Clean Air Acts, and the beginning of the Environmental Protection Agency. Ethics in the Real World 5.1 gives you an overview of how social activism and concern for the natural environment changed the law.

Ethics in the Real World 5.1 | A Burning River Leads to Change[14]

Jasper Chamber/Alamy Stock Photo

FIGURE 5.1 People have protested pollution and asked the government to protect the environment for many years.

Toward the end of the 1960s, people in the United States began to realize that an unregulated manufacturing-based economy was destroying the nation's waterways. Several critical events happened:

1968: The U.S. Bureau of Sport Fisheries found the poison DDT in 584 of 590 samples, with some of the DDT levels up to nine times the FDA limit for safety.

1969: Over 41 million fish in America's lakes and streams were killed due to pollution. Twenty-six million fish died in Florida's Lake Thonotosassa due to chemical discharges from four food-processing plants.

1969: In January, a massive oil spill in Santa Barbara, California, sent over 3 million gallons of crude oil into the Pacific Ocean, leading to a 35-mile-long oil slick in the Pacific Ocean.

1969: In June, a huge oil slick formed on the Cuyahoga River near Cleveland, Ohio. A chemical discharge of "highly volatile petroleum derivatives" caught fire. The likely cause was a spark from a passing train.

1970: The U.S. government reported that up to 30% of the nation's drinking water had chemical pollutants that exceeded public health standards.

Many Americans knew that air and water pollution were becoming huge problems, and the scene of a major river literally burning led people to act.[15] Senator Gaylord Nelson (D-Wisconsin) and Representative Pete McCloskey (R-California) recruited a young activist, Denis Hayes, to organize a set of campus teach-ins to raise awareness. Hayes adopted the name *Earth Day* for the teach-ins. The national media caught wind of the event, and on April 22, 1970, 20 million Americans took to the streets and other public places to protest (see Figure 5.1). This represented 10% of the U.S. population. Within three years, Congress had strengthened protections for clean air and clean water.

Table 5.1 shows you the major regulatory agencies of the United States government. Note that the creation of these agencies tended to come in waves during the twentieth century. The Food and Drug Administration and the Federal Trade Commission appeared after the "trust-busting" era and the Sherman Antitrust Act. The vast majority of regulatory agencies

TABLE 5.1   Major U.S. Government Regulatory Agencies that Impact Business.[16]

Agency	Mission	Year Founded	Primary Stakeholder Group
Bureau of Alcohol, Tobacco, Firearms and Explosives	Protect against violent criminals, weapons trafficking, and terrorism	1972	Communities
Commodity Futures Trading Commission	Protect commodity markets from fraud, manipulation, and abuse	1975	Investors
Consumer Financial Protection Bureau	Supervise and regulate the consumer finance industry	2011	Customers
Consumer Product Safety Commission	Protect against risk of injury or death from consumer product use	1972	Customers
Drug Enforcement Administration	Protect against drug cartels, mobs, and drug trafficking	1973	Communities
Environmental Protection Agency	Protect human health and the natural environment	1970	Communities, natural environment
Equal Employment Opportunity Commission	Protect against discrimination in employment based on race, color, sex, national origin, age, or disability	1965	Employees
Federal Aviation Administration	Provide a safe and efficient aerospace system	1958	Communities, customers, suppliers
Federal Deposit Insurance Corporation	Maintain stability in the nation's financial system	1933	Customers, suppliers, investors
Federal Energy Regulatory Commission	Regulate interstate transmission of natural gas, oil, and electricity (including hydroelectric power)	1977	Customers, communities, suppliers
Federal Trade Commission	Prevent anticompetitive, deceptive, or unfair business practices	1914	Customers, competitors
Food and Drug Administration	Protect public health, including the food supply and human and veterinary drugs, medical devices, cosmetics, and more	1906	Customers
Securities and Exchange Commission	Protect investors, maintains fair and orderly markets, facilitates capital formation	1934	Investors

were born in the decades of the 1960s and 1970s, and the youngest agency, the Consumer Financial Protection Bureau, arose from the financial crisis of 2007–2008.

The Twenty First Century

Another wave of corporate scandal occurred in the early 2000s. You may have heard of Enron, one of the worst offenders. Enron was an energy-trading and utilities company based in Houston, Texas, that perpetrated one of the biggest accounting frauds in history. The company's executives employed accounting principles that falsely inflated the company's revenues and, for a time, made it the seventh-largest corporation in the United States. Enron's leaders employed a complex accounting procedure called a *special purpose entity* (SPE) to move high-risk assets and large amounts of debt off Enron's balance sheet.[17] This inflated the company's stock price. Enron's shares traded at a high of over $90 before the fraud was discovered, and then plummeted to around $0.25 after the scandal hit the news. Enron's auditor, the accounting firm Arthur Andersen, should not have certified these SPEs, but it faced its own conflict of interest. If Andersen exposed these questionable accounting tricks, it would lose millions of dollars of consulting contracts. When energy markets plunged and the Internet bubble burst in late 2001, the true state of Enron's financial situation came to light and the company

Stephen Chernin/Stringer/Getty Images

FIGURE 5.2   Enron's CEO became a symbol of what goes wrong when a company has unethical leaders.

collapsed in a matter of weeks. Enron filed for bankruptcy on December 2, 2001, and Arthur Andersen melted down in the early months of 2002.

Enron shareholders lost over $63 *billion* in total value, more than 20,000 Enron employees joined the ranks of the unemployed, and another 90,000 employees and partners of Enron's auditor Arthur Andersen saw their firm fail. Chief financial officer and architect of many of Enron's accounting tricks, Andrew Fastow, spent six years in prison and Enron CEO Jeff Skilling received a 24 year prison sentence for his leadership of the company (see Figure 5.2).

The collapse of Enron and Arthur Andersen and instances of equally fraudulent behavior by executives at other companies led to the passage of the Sarbanes-Oxley Act (otherwise known as SOX) into law in 2002. "The Act mandated a number of reforms to enhance corporate responsibility, enhance financial disclosures, and combat corporate and accounting fraud, etc."[18] SOX works to strengthen internal accounting and information controls within the organization. One of SOX's most significant features is that CEOs must personally sign to verify that the accounting numbers provided by the organization are correct to the best of their knowledge. A CEO's reputation—and sometimes legal culpability—is now on the line.

The financial collapse and Great Recession of 2007–2009 began when mortgage defaults began to climb. These defaults unearthed a complicated web of arcane and sophisticated financial products, each described by cryptic abbreviations, from CDSs (credit default swaps) to MBSs (mortgage-backed securities). In 2008, leading investment firms Bear Stearns and Lehman Brothers both failed, and many other banks and financial institutions teetered on the brink of disaster. For a few days in 2008, it appeared that the U.S. and global financial systems would fail.

The compliance/regulatory response to the crisis was the Dodd–Frank Act, passed in 2010. The Act created a new agency, the Financial Stability Oversight Council, that could be called upon to help liquidate and restructure troubled financial institutions. The Act established the Consumer Financial Protection Bureau to prevent predatory mortgage lending and to make it easier for consumers to understand the obligations they incurred when they took out a mortgage. Dodd–Frank established the Volcker Rule (named after former chairman of the Federal Reserve Board Paul Volcker), which restricted how commercial banks can invest in speculative or proprietary trading activities.[19]

The Federal Sentencing Guidelines for Organizations

In 2004, the U.S. Department of Justice made an amendment to an important document that was first released in 1991, and by doing so changed the landscape of corporate ethics and compliance. This document, the Federal Sentencing Guidelines for Organizations (FSGO),

is a set of rules that defines "the appropriate punishment for an organization that is convicted of a crime, which may range from probation to community service to the payment of hefty fines."[20]

The Rationale for the FSGO

The FSGO built on a simple premise, one consistent with what you learned about organizations in Chapter 4 and one we'll return to in ensuing chapters: Organizations create a context that either encourages or discourages ethical conduct. As such, an employer can, and in some cases should, be held responsible for the acts of employees. "The theory is that each organization shares a degree of culpability where an employee acts in an unlawful manner, even if the organization neither knew nor approved of their actions."[21]

Earlier iterations of the FSGO had focused entirely on compliance. However, the 2004 amendment broadened the guidelines to include ethics as well as compliance. For the first time, corporate culture became a specific point of reference. Perhaps the greatest practical impact for corporations was the inclusion of an actual definition for an effective compliance and ethics program. This set of amendments also "placed greater responsibility on boards of directors and executives for their oversight and management."[22] In a press release regarding the 2004 amendment to the FSGO, the United States Sentencing Commission stated the following:

> [D]irectors and executives now must take an active leadership role for the content and operation of compliance and ethics programs. Companies that seek reduced criminal fines now must demonstrate that they have identified areas of risk where criminal violations may occur, trained high-level officials as well as employees in relevant legal standards and obligations, and given their compliance officers sufficient authority and resources to carry out their responsibilities. Under the revised guidelines, if companies hope to mitigate criminal fines and penalties, they must also promote an organizational culture that encourages a commitment to compliance with the law and ethical conduct by exercising due diligence in meeting the criteria.[23]

Why would executives and their counterparts even care about following the FSGO guidance? The recommendations in these guidelines are not mandatory as related to compliance programs. However, if a company convicted of a federal crime can actually prove that, in spite of its violation of law, it actually did have in place an effective compliance and ethics program, then it may receive a reduced sentence.[24]

The FSGO Framework for Compliance

The original (1991) FSGO outlined what is commonly referred to as "the seven hallmarks of an effective compliance program." These hallmarks have become the guideposts every business and other public and private organization, from small to gigantic, can use to judge the effectiveness of its compliance efforts:

1. **Prevention and Detection Procedures**: Establish standards and procedures to prevent and detect criminal conduct.

2. **High-level Oversight:** Assign specific individuals within high-level personnel an overall responsibility to oversee compliance and provide adequate resources and authority to carry out such responsibility.

3. **Due Care:** Use reasonable efforts not to include within high authority personnel any individual who engaged in illegal activities or other improper conduct.

4. **Training and Communication:** Make effective compliance and ethics training a requirement for all of the organization's employees and agents, including the upper levels, and establish that this communication and training obligation is ongoing, requiring periodic updates.

5. **Monitoring:** Take reasonable steps to achieve compliance; specifically, use auditing and monitoring systems designed to detect criminal conduct and use internal reporting systems to report or seek guidance regarding potential or actual criminal conduct, allowing for anonymity and confidentially mechanisms.

6. **Consistent Enforcement:** Enforce and encourage compliance through, respectively, disciplinary measures and appropriate incentives to perform in accordance with the program.

7. **Response and Prevention:** Take reasonable steps to respond to and prevent further similar criminal conduct.[25]

The 2004 amendments added 10 items that clarify and detail compliance efforts and who in the organization has responsibility for effective compliance. The 10 additions are as follows:

1. **Tone at The Top:** Emphasize the importance within the guidelines of an organizational culture that encourages a commitment to compliance with the law.

2. **Conduct and Internal Control:** Provide better description of compliance standards and procedures; that is, the standards of conduct and internal control systems that are reasonably capable of reducing the likelihood of violations of the law.

3. **Leadership Accountability:** Specify the responsibilities of an organization's governing authority and organizational leadership for compliance.

4. **Resources and Authority:** Emphasize the importance of adequate resources and authority for individuals with the responsibility for implementing a compliance and ethics program.

5. **History of Violations:** Replace "propensity to engage in violations of the law" with a more objective requirement of determining if there is a "history of engaging in violations of the law."

6. **Conduct Training:** Include both training and dissemination of training materials within the definition of an effective compliance and ethics program.

7. **Evaluate Programs:** Add periodic evaluation of the effectiveness of a compliance and ethics program to the requirement for monitoring and auditing systems.

8. **Risk Assessment:** Provide for ongoing risk assessment as part of an effective compliance and ethics program.

9. **Encourage Employees:** Establish a system for employees not only to report actual violations, but also to seek guidance about potential violations, in order to encourage prevention of violations.

10. **Whistleblower System:** Require a mechanism for anonymous reporting.[26]

Governmental agencies continue to issue additional guidance, most notably from the Department of Justice in 2017 and 2020. Why would the government provide more guidance? As compliance becomes a bigger part of business life, and as the stakes for noncompliance continue to rise, the community of corporate ethics and compliance professionals seeks more guidance and clarity about what, exactly, the U.S. government would want to see to make a determination that a compliance program is actually "effective" and, therefore, worthy of "credit" in the event the company has a punishable event or series of events.

Effective Compliance Programs: Processes and Responsibilities

From reading the preceding U.S. government guidance, it seems rational that the role of a company's ethics and compliance department would be to implement these various compliance program elements. If you assumed this is the case, you would be correct! compliance departments may be a single individual in a smaller company or an enormous group in a global company. Regardless of number of employees, any compliance department has a herculean task. The work of the group consists of four major processes, and we'll describe and discuss each below.

A. Encourage Employees: Establish a system for employees not only to report actual violations, but also to seek guidance about potential violations, in order to encourage prevention of violations; and implement a whistleblower system: Require a mechanism for anonymous reporting.

Most companies have some type of mechanism for employees to report potential violations of company policy or even of laws or regulations. Typically, this takes the form of a hotline or helpline. Figure 5.3 shows an advertisement for a compliance hotline. A hotline may consist of several methods for employees to notify the compliance department and/or other management that they are concerned about some wrongdoing in the company, from a manager employing discrimination to an employee stealing company products to instances of bribery. "In organizations that have a formal reporting structure, telephone hotlines were the most common method to report a tip (39.5%). However, all forms of online reporting (such as email—34.1%—and Web-based or online form—23.5%) combine to make the Internet a more popular reporting method."[27]

The compliance department oversees a process (an external call center that handles international calls, if needed), collecting (sometimes anonymous) complaints and tips from employees from those call centers, live or email reports to managers and executives, or even a Web-based collection device. Then, the tips or concerns are sorted into categories (perhaps "fraud," "discrimination," "insider trading," etc.). Issues are then investigated, and management may need to take appropriate action if there are violations of policies or laws. As Ethics in the Real World 5.2 shows, employees choose different methods to report ethical misconduct.

Why would employees need to be *encouraged* to report potential misconduct? Most employees fear retaliation if they report some issue within the company, especially if they report wrongdoing of their manager. Retaliatory actions could include termination, lack of promotion (when the reporting employee would otherwise have received a promotion), unwarranted negative performance reviews, hours or shifts modified to be unfavorable, and so forth. Data from the Ethics & Compliance Initiative indicate that a significant portion of people who report compliance issues suffer retaliation of some type. The number depends on the type of misconduct observed, and the proportion varies between almost one-third and one-half.[29]

FIGURE 5.3 If you call an ethics hotline, you are protected throughout the process.

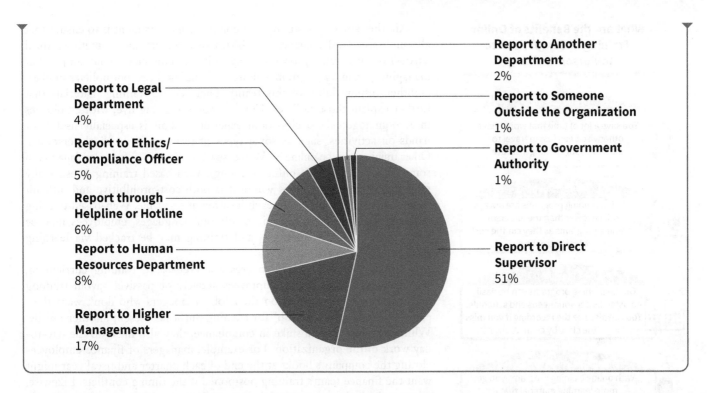

Report to Legal Department 4%

Report to Ethics/ Compliance Officer 5%

Report through Helpline or Hotline 6%

Report to Human Resources Department 8%

Report to Higher Management 17%

Report to Another Department 2%

Report to Someone Outside the Organization 1%

Report to Government Authority 1%

Report to Direct Supervisor 51%

How would a company then help them to report issues? Having a *culture* that supports this is key, and we will talk even more about this in Chapter 6. See **Figure 5.4** for an example of how a company might guide their employees in reporting ethics violations and reassure employees that they will not face retaliation. Also, having a policy that prevents retaliation is important. If such a policy exists, employees need to understand the policy. Typically, these policies state that the company will not tolerate retaliation for reporting. That means that if an employee reports harassment from his or her manager, the company will not permit anyone (likely this would be the manager) invoking negative, or retaliatory, consequences against the reporting employee. Knowing that the company is behind them, employees will be more likely to take the (sometimes frightening) step to report a concern.

B. **Conduct Training: Include both training and dissemination of training materials within the definition of an effective compliance and ethics program.**

FIGURE 5.4 Employees are encouraged to use Citibank's hotline if necessary.

What are the Benefits of Online Training in Comparison to In-Person Training?

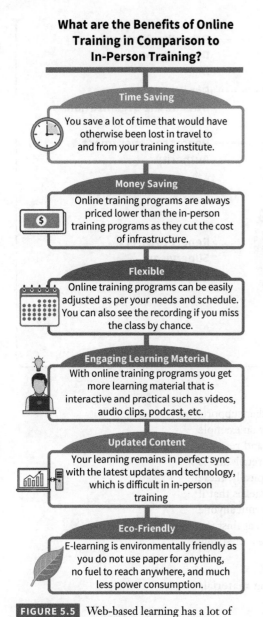

Time Saving

You save a lot of time that would have otherwise been lost in travel to and from your training institute.

Money Saving

Online training programs are always priced lower than the in-person training programs as they cut the cost of infrastructure.

Flexible

Online training programs can be easily adjusted as per your needs and schedule. You can also see the recording if you miss the class by chance.

Engaging Learning Material

With online training programs you get more learning material that is interactive and practical such as videos, audio clips, podcast, etc.

Updated Content

Your learning remains in perfect sync with the latest updates and technology, which is difficult in in-person training

Eco-Friendly

E-learning is environmentally friendly as you do not use paper for anything, no fuel to reach anywhere, and much less power consumption.

FIGURE 5.5 Web-based learning has a lot of benefits over the traditional model.

Another key responsibility of a compliance department is to ensure that all employees (and management, board of directors, and sometimes third parties) receive training on company policies. This may sound simple, but managing a training program is quite challenging. First, put policies in place (another responsibility of this team). Then, create training materials that further explain those policies. Conduct some training live, with employees in a room together—a classroom experience. This is especially useful for hands-on activities, such as some types of training for medical personnel. Other training may be online, or Web based (see **Figure 5.5** for an explanation of some of the benefits of online training). Web-based training is especially effective in large companies where it is both cost-prohibitive and difficult to include every employee in each location at one time. Web-based training may also be translated easily into different languages, employees may be given quizzes on the materials, and training may be tracked via learning management systems.

While it sounds simple to create a Web-based training curriculum, the challenges come when employees actively or passively avoid training because they want to focus on their jobs. Managers who don't want their employees taken "off the job" for training purposes present another hurdle. While managers have a stake in compliance, they also must do the day-to-day work of the organization. For example, managers of finance employees closing the company's books at the end of each quarter and fiscal year might want the finance team's training postponed if the timing conflicts. Likewise, salespeople might request that their teams be trained after meeting quarterly or annual sales goals. Managers and employees will always have a solid reason to avoid training, and the presence of strong cultural or financial incentives can help motivate them. Some companies, for example, require ethics and compliance training to be completed before performance reviews—and raises—can be administered.

New employees are a third group that needs training before they begin work. Wise ethics and compliance groups work closely with human resources during the employee onboarding process to ensure that required training happens when it will be the most valuable—before employees run into issues. At any point in time, if a company is training employees on multiple compliance and ethics topics, employees likely will be at different stages of training. That makes meeting necessary training goals difficult. Scheduling doesn't even consider changes in policies or regulations, or even company branding, that would necessitate updating training.

C. **Conduct and Internal Control: Provide better descriptions of compliance standards and procedures; that is, the standards of conduct and internal control systems that are reasonably capable of reducing the likelihood of violations of the law.**

This guidance point relates to the concept of monitoring that the compliance program must facilitate. Monitoring refers to capturing and reporting how well the company is doing in terms of ethics and compliance. Once companies have established policies and trained employees on those policies, the next step is trying to gather information about whether those policies, along with training and communication, are working. Monitoring can take various forms, from true surveillance of employees (like video cameras) to a hotline (noted earlier) that indicates where things aren't working well. Training is an episodic event, but monitoring and reporting tasks must be done constantly. Compliance professionals, particularly ones at smaller organizations, can easily become overwhelmed by the dual demands of training and monitoring.

D. **Consistent Enforcement: Enforce and encourage compliance through, respectively, disciplinary measures and appropriate incentives to perform in accordance with the program.**

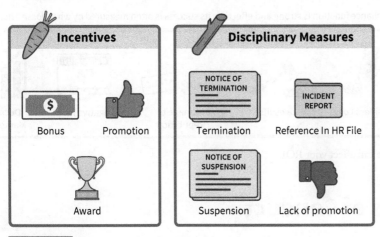

FIGURE 5.6   What motivates you to act?

Enforcement often relies on a combination of carrots and sticks as motivation (see **Figure 5.6**). Compliance programs should have clear procedures to discipline employees who violate policies; good programs also provide incentives to employees generally to act in accordance with company expectations. There are several day-to-day situations that raise issues that make enforcement challenging. For example, what would you do about a salesperson who submits an expense report to request reimbursement from the company that contains non-reimbursable expenses? While the employee would be terminated or suspended if he or she knowingly included fraudulent expenses on that report, what happens when employees make careless mistakes? What about items that might be appropriate in some situations (such as an expensive meal to close a big sale), but not others (treating a new and uncertain prospect to the same meal)?

While disciplinary measures may be easier to think of, offering incentives for compliance can be problematic. The first question is about appropriate incentives: What should you offer beyond the employment, benefits, pay, and so forth that employees already receive? The second question is about the appropriateness of incentives in general: If we reward people for doing what's right, what does that say about our theory of human nature? What happens if we stop incentivizing ethical behavior? These are all real considerations and challenges for compliance professionals, so it may seem reasonable that companies provide vast resources for these compliance departments. In fact, "[i]n a 2016 survey of risk management employers, two-thirds (68%) [felt] that their compliance department [was] 'insufficiently resourced for the demands made on it,' representing an increase from 55% in 2015."[30]

Even though boards of directors and executives may truly care about ethics and compliance, sometimes they may not provide the resources to compliance professionals that would help them to be very effective. Ethics and compliance are not "revenue-producing" functions in any company (except for law firms), and so a common budget strategy is to create a compliance department that meets the bare minimum standard. This logic fails to see the real role of the ethics and compliance function: It helps protect the company in the event of a worst-case scenario. In other words, money may be invested up front to help the company *if it gets into trouble.* Investing in compliance results in a long-term return on the investment. When viewed in this light, ethics and compliance have a very high return on investment (ROI) (see **Figure 5.7**). Most employees will sense fairly quickly whether their companies are the ones who choose to invest because ethics and compliance and business integrity are *priorities* (or whether they are companies that invest in ethics and compliance grudgingly and only when they feel in some type of danger). Likewise, there is great risk to and from organizations that invest heavily in ethics and compliance programs for the sake of appearances and to deflect or redirect attention as they mask unethical or illegal activities. Enron had an elaborate putative apparatus for its ethics and compliance program, including heartfelt endorsements for the program from its disgraced former chief executive, Kenneth Lay, in an ethics training video.

When a company's compliance function is strong and effective, its success is often measured by what *doesn't happen*...

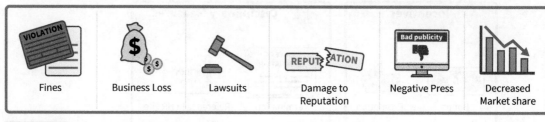

Fines   Business Loss   Lawsuits   Damage to Reputation   Negative Press   Decreased Market share

FIGURE 5.7   Compliance can affect your ROI.

Codes of Conduct

The key compliance policy of any public company is embodied in what is referred to as a "code of conduct." These "codes" come with a variety of names. Some examples are code of conduct, code of business ethics, standards of business conduct, code of ethical conduct, and so forth. Recent data indicate that more than 94% of organizations use a code of conduct to embed their compliance policies and procedures in a way that is accessible to all employees.[31] A code of conduct is similar to a mission statement in that both deal with core values; however, a code of conduct is about tangible behaviors and actions, while a mission statement focuses on aspirations. A code of conduct represents the expectations an entity has for its employees (and officers and others who are covered by the code). A code of conduct can best be thought of as an umbrella document. It references a multitude of stand-alone policies that the company has in place (such as bribery, discrimination, insider trading, use of company equipment, patent ownership, etc.). See Figure 5.8 for a framework that the Unilever Corporation uses to shape its code of conduct.

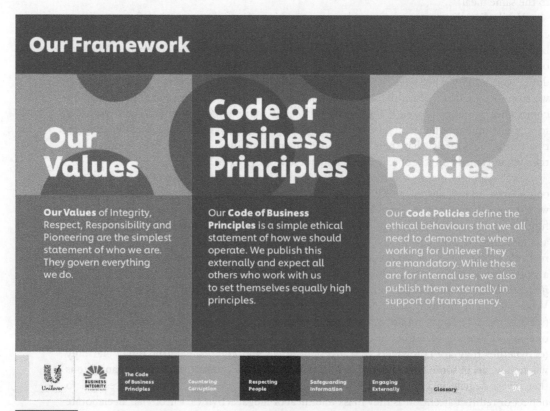

FIGURE 5.8   How does your company's framework compare to Unilever's?

Why Do Companies Need a Compliance Code?

"Section 406 of Sarbanes-Oxley Act (SOX) required public companies to disclose whether senior financial officers have adopted a code of ethics. Yes, it is actually the law for a public company (trading on an exchange) to have a code."

"Under SOX, code of ethics, means written standards that are reasonably designed to deter wrong doing and promote honest ethical conduct; avoidance of conflicts of interest; compliance with applicable laws, rules, and regulations; full, fair, accurate, timely, and comprehensible disclosure to the SEC; prompt internal reporting of any violations of the code; and accountability for adherence to the code."

The code really is more than just a summary document. "A well-written code of conduct clarifies an organization's mission, values, and principles, linking them with standards of professional conduct. The code articulates the values the organization wishes to foster, in leaders and employees and, in doing so, defines desired behavior." Ethics and Compliance Initiative (ECI/ethics.org) is a highly respected nonprofit organization in the ethics/compliance space.

FIGURE 5.9   Companies need a formal compliance code.

Codes typically state these polices in summary fashion. While a company's entire bribery policy may consist of 15 pages, the code section summarizing that policy might be only four or five paragraphs. Some codes are placed online (on a company intranet) for all employees to access. There may be an intranet link from the section of the code summarizing a policy to the actual policy. For printed codes of conduct, the code section on bribery, for instance, may simply include a statement of referral, such as "Please refer to the bribery policy for details."

You might wonder why a company would create a code of conduct when it already has policies on its books. Figure 5.9 lists a couple of reasons why this would not be sufficient.

Codes of conduct used to be dry and boring legal documents. The last several years have seen a real attempt by corporations to make these documents more engaging. Why? If a code is engaging and written in such a way that employees of all levels of education, backgrounds, and departments (not just the legal department!) can understand the policy, more employees will both want to read the code and understand it. Then they will be better able to comply with it. Codes now have slick graphics, bright colors, fonts that are inviting (no more only Times New Roman), shorter sentences and paragraphs, FAQs, Q&A sections, and so forth. They also typically have an inviting introduction by the CEO or other executive of the company. Those introductions, and the code itself, now tend to also reference the values of a company, which we'll take up in Chapter 6.

Ethics in the Real World 5.3 provides several examples of companies' codes of conduct. Our Ethics in the Real World feature 5.3 provides more modern takes on codes of conduct.

Ethics in the Real World 5.3 | Codes of Conduct

Every company should have a code of conduct outlining how employees are supposed to interact and behave while at work. By setting rules and expectations, employees know how to act at work and can be more successful in their roles. Employers need to consider many things to write a well-rounded code of conduct. The following samples, from different corporations, provide examples of what you may face in your organization or job.

An excerpt from the CVS Health Code of Conduct follows.[32]

When faced with business decisions that may affect the reputation of CVS Health, we use the framework below.

1. Should I be troubled by this? Is this consistent with CVS Health values?
2. Who will be affected by my decisions? How will they be affected?
3. What's my responsibility to act? What will happen if I don't act?
4. What are the ethical considerations?
5. Who needs to be involved in making this decision?
6. Am I being true to myself and to the values of CVS Health? How would my actions appear to customers or the public?

An excerpt from Lockheed Martin's Code of Conduct follows.[33]

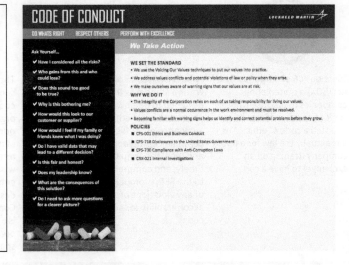

A page from hershey's code (with a familiar color and kisses):

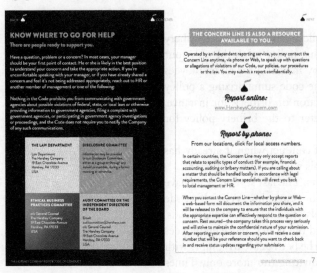

An except from Starbucks modern take on compliance:

Dear Fellow Partner:

Starbucks is the premier roaster and retailer of specialty coffee in the world and has become a truly global brand. From the beginning, we have recognized that you, our partners, are critical to our continued success. Starbucks reputation for the finest coffee in the world, legendary customer service and the highest integrity is the direct result of our collective efforts. We are all caretakers of Starbucks reputation. How we conduct our business and how we treat others—our fellow partners, customers, communities, suppliers and shareholders—will continue to determine how the world views Starbucks.

"Starbucks reputation for the finest coffee in the world, legendary customer service and the highest integrity is the direct result of our collective efforts."

Each of us is personally responsible for supporting our core values, which require compliance with the law as well as ethical conduct. We have issued the *Standards of Business Conduct* to restate our longstanding commitment to uphold that responsibility and to provide guidance to our partners.

As we move forward, the *Standards* will help ensure that our values continue to be reflected in each Starbucks store and business activity. A commitment to integrity, acting honestly and ethically, and complying with the letter and intent of the law are critical to our continued success.

Thank you for your partnership.

Warm regards,

Howard Schultz
chairman, president and
chief executive officer

The Structure of Ethics and Compliance Department

The structure of an effective ethics and compliance department has both a formal and informal element. We'll briefly describe each in the following sections.

Formal Structure

Today, many ethics and compliance departments are led by someone called a chief compliance officer (CCO) or chief ethics and compliance officer (CECO). Traditionally, however, the general counsel (GC) or chief legal officer (CLO), the top lawyer and head of the legal department inside a company, also managed compliance; however, given the complexity and professionalism required to run a compliance program, "the compliance obligations once given to the general counsel are exercised, instead, by the chief compliance officer."[34] While compliance and ethics are generally managed by the CECO or equivalent role, in many organizations this person still reports to the CLO. This is not ideal. Why not? Part of the role of the CECO is to ensure that the company complies with multiple regulations. In doing that job, a CECO needs to work with many people across a company (a tax employee in the finance department, a discrimination expert in the human resources department, an attorney in the legal department who manages anticorruption issues, etc.). In that work, the CECO may end up at odds with the CLO, whose job it is to protect the company and sometimes defend the company from accusations of noncompliance. For example, the CECO may encourage a company to "get out in front" of ethical issues and compliance challenges, while the CLO may urge the company to "stay behind" these issues to avoid admitting liability or culpability.

Likewise, working for any other C-suite executive (the CFO, CMO, etc.) may put the CECO in conflict if or when he or she discovers potential violations in a department managed by these executives. Therefore, there are various options and some emergent best practices in existence for placement and independence of a CECO:

a. [A] functional reporting line directly to the audit committee of the board of directors rather than to the chief executive officer or other management-level official;

b. An official job description that expressly recognizes the authority of the [CECO] to act independently of direction from senior executive officials;

c. Explicit guarantees of being invited to high-level meetings where matters pertinent to compliance are discussed;

d. Guarantees of adequate resources, enforced, for example, by assurances that the compliance department will have its own budget line rather than sharing one with the general counsel or internal audit;

e. Protections of tenure in office—for example, a requirement that the CECO can only be fired by the audit committee or full board of directors.[35]

To sum up, running an ethics and compliance function requires dedicating full-time personnel and resources to support them, even for small and medium-sized enterprises. Given the demands of different regulatory agencies and the general framework for compliance we've outlined here, the CECO (or other title for the head of the ethics/compliance department), and his or her team, will interact with people throughout the organization. The CECO and team must work to ensure compliance with a vast array of regulations, in addition to activities that include monitoring, training, and communicating with all levels of employees.

Informal Structure

Even in a company in which there is a department called ethics and compliance, the best response to the question "Who is responsible for compliance in a corporation?" is *everyone*. While the lawyers and professionals who run an ethics and compliance department carry the general responsibility for making sure that policies are well documented, training is rolled out to employees and third parties, monitoring of compliance processes happens, investigations occur, and there is a cycle of continuous improvement in terms of compliance, the reality is that it truly does take the combined efforts of every employee to make a compliant and ethical corporation. This reality links compliance and ethics—it takes everyone following formal rules and informal norms of conduct that create an ethical and compliant organization. Figure 5.10 shows how the formal and informal organization differ in an organization.

Let's look at a typical public company with 15,000 employees. Assume it has an ethics and compliance team, and it also has a lot of employees in different cross-functional roles whose direct responsibilities include something related to ethics and compliance—ensuring the supply chain is free from human trafficking and slave labor, handling tax matters for the company, training employees on the company's expectations on discriminatory or harassing behaviors, managing safety and health issues, and so on. Obviously, all these people have ethics and compliance in their sights every day. However, they sit within different departments. The tax matters likely are managed in the finance department; employment equity are managed out of the human resources department, and so forth. When each of these people engages in his or her work in ethical ways and complies with formal rules, the job of the ethics and compliance department is easier, and the department can be more effective.

Consider this: If even *one* employee does something illegal like bribing a foreign official, the consequences can include everything from bad press to a drop in stock price, loss of customers, investigations, jail time, and penalties. Likewise, if an employee goes onto social media and says untrue and slanderous things about the CEO or the company, the company's reputation may take a beating, resulting in employee morale dropping, investigations, fabulous new employees not wanting to apply to the company, and competitors picking up the slack. Those are the ethical land mines waiting to be triggered.

Beyond those policy and regulatory issues, employees who don't believe in the values of a company can just bring down the entire ship. If the same company's principles include integrity and respect, and management fails to enforce the policies that reflect these principles consistently, e.g., in expense reporting and equitable treatment of employees, then this could

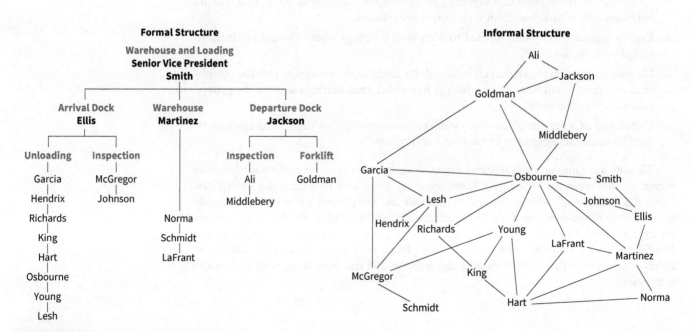

FIGURE 5.10 The formal and informal elements of a typical organization.

affect the morale and effectiveness of employees. As we discuss in the next chapter, it takes only one fish to turn a school of fish in a different direction, and it takes just one employee to do the same in a company. This is one reason companies invest so much time and money to ensure that employees understand policies and will take the time to speak up when they see a potential issue that conflicts with the regulatory requirements or ethical values. Part of the challenge in regulating behavior is that each individual employee has his or her *own* set of values. Yet, the company is asking that employees accept and live by the corporation's values. We will discuss corporate values more in the next chapter.

The Characteristics of Responsible Employees

Corruption in an organization, an employee's behavior in competition, and a leader's unethical behavior towards his/her subordinates has escalated the attention towards employees' moral responsibilities in the organization itself. Each employee in the organization is committed to human relationships, his/her duties, norms of behavior, personal ambitions, and decisions that bring him/her happiness. The employee has responsibilities in three areas—private life, organizational life, and societal life. In private life, an employee is deeply connected with family members, friends, and society; and these relationships are sources of happiness in his/her life. Sometimes, deep connections with family members, friends, and society become responsible for putting and individual in a dilemma or difficult situation. In such cases, the individual's integrity and character play a vital role in determining his/her behavior. Morality principles suggest that in such difficult situations, an individual should tell the truth, keep promises, and avoid harming others. Further, when employees work in an organization, it becomes important to work in the interest of shareholders. However, moral principles suggest that a manager should also think about society while making a business decision because it impacts people's happiness.

Chapter Summary

In this chapter, we addressed corporate ethics and compliance matters.

- Ethics and compliance are similar, yet distinct. They both are grounded in norms and ideas about what constitutes appropriate conduct. Ethical issues require obedience to the unenforceable, and compliance requires obedience to the enforceable.

- The general issue of compliance with rules and norms is an integral part of business. Most regulatory agencies, and many original rules, arose from ethical scandals in the business world. This has been true in the nineteenth, twentieth, and now twenty-first centuries.

- A compliance program has many well-defined components and responsibilities. Many of these components have sticks attached for noncompliance, and some businesses may choose to create carrots to encourage compliance. Of note, the FSGO process and rules mean that companies may receive credit criminal sentencing for having an effective compliance program.

- Compliance professionals work within converging global regulatory frameworks from public and private sources, including

U.S. law. The major duties of these professionals include responsibility for compliance policies, training, monitoring, and reporting compliance activities. Ethics and compliance departments are typically part of the legal department of a company or are independent in order to enable the head of the ethics and compliance department to maintain the ability to avoid conflicts with key department leaders and work directly with the board of directors.

- One key element of an organization's programs and controls to prevent, detect, and respond to incidents of fraud and misconduct is its code of conduct. While codes of conduct often have appeared in legalistic terms, organizations have been working to use more accessible language that takes account of the day-to-day issues and questions that employees and other covered persons encounter in their work. Such codes also emphasize development of conscientious decision making, e.g., through example cases, rather than a strict rule-based approach. Codes are umbrella policies, in that they contain summaries of other policies. Codes also refer to the principles of a company and expectations for behavior by employees.

Chapter Review Questions

1. Why would a corporation want to implement an ethics and compliance department?

2. What are five areas of guidance from the Federal Sentencing Guidelines that help companies decide on which activities to focus in their compliance programs?

3. Describe how a code of ethics and conduct may be thought of as an umbrella document.

4. Why would the head of an ethics and compliance department potentially have issues reporting to the CLO of a company?

5. Is non-compliance unethical in society and organizations? Discuss.

6. How will an organization ensure ethical compliance?

Application Exercises

- *Personal Ethical Development.* If you began keeping an ethics journal as suggested in the first chapter, continue that writing work. Here are some prompts: What is your personal attitude toward regulation and rule following? How happy would you be working in an environment that was highly regulated? What role do you believe leaders should play in enforcing compliance with rules? Create a list of questions you can ask during a job interview to assess a company's commitment to regulatory compliance.

- *Career Goals and Planning.* A happy, meaningful, and productive life blends and builds upon the following: (1) the type of life you are interested in leading, (2) your deepest and most important values, (3) the work you are interested in doing, (4) what you are good at, (5) your preferences for things like work versus free time, and (6) your personality. Create a set of commitments about your approach toward compliance with rules, regulations, and details. How will compliance issues impact your career path?

- *Ethics in the Business world.* Identify an organization that you believe complies with regulatory frameworks and guidelines. This may be either a for-profit or a not-for-profit organization. What evidence from the company backs up your belief? What internal processes do they have that drive compliance and ethical behavior? How do they measure compliance and report results to key stakeholders?

- *Talking with and Learning from Others.* Choose a business professional you believe has a good perspective toward regulatory compliance. Engage that person in a brief interview. How do they balance the conflicting need of making a profit and getting work done while complying with all rules and regulations? Where have they experienced challenges to compliance and how did they respond? What advice would they give you about working in an environment that requires compliance with multiple regulations and rules?

Mini-Cases

Case 1: Mark Johnson graduated with a finance degree from Drexel University and took a job with a local Philadelphia distributor of paints, coatings, and construction adhesives—ACME Paint and Coatings. His first job entailed doing financial analysis for a geographic expansion into the state of West Virginia. His attention to detail and willingness to go beyond analysis and help the management team with opening the new facility raised his profile within the company. The CFO, Elizabeth Narvaez, felt Mark would be perfect for a new role she and the general counsel were going to create: director of ethics and compliance. Mark accepted the job and dived in with his usual high energy. He soon found himself overwhelmed. Paints, coatings, and adhesives were all heavily regulated by both federal and state agencies, and as Mark delved into his role, he found many informal practices that violated existing regulations.

After poking around the various work groups, Mark saw two glaring problems. First, most employees were unaware of the different rules governing delivery, storage, and use of the materials their company sold. The company had no repository of Material Safety Data Sheets, for example. This meant that company sales reps often gave contractors false advice about how to safely use some of the most toxic products the firm sold. Second, the warehouse staff had no protocol to follow in disposing of old, unsold, or damaged inventory. His greatest fear was confirmed when he witnessed a "late night dump run" of old paint and expired adhesives. The materials were taken to the local landfill instead of a hazardous materials recycling facility. Mark approached the warehouse manager, a man in his mid-sixties named Chuck, about this apparent violation. Chuck responded simply, "Do you know how much it costs to take that stuff to the HazMat facility? Those fees would come directly out of my bonus. None of these materials are really 'hazardous' anyway. No harm, no foul."

Knowing that he needed help, Mark reached out to your firm, Compliance Advisors. Your firm helps new compliance officers like Mark create a road map for compliance. You had always found that the Federal Sentencing Guidelines for Organizations provided a great framework for setting up a compliance program. You accepted the contract to help Mark's firm and listened to his early finding about the state of compliance at ACME Paint and Coatings. He asked you which problem he should solve first: misleading sales information or the midnight dump runs? What steps should he take to solve either of these problems?

As you listened intently, you realized that Mark needed help with these short-term issues, but also that the company needed longer-term help in terms of training, reporting, and the other elements of the FSGO framework. You wanted to develop a plan that would help Mark solve both his immediate and longer-term compliance challenges. What elements should you include in your proposal to Mark? What are the real problems ACME should focus on?

Case 2: Zomato's 10 minutes delivery promise. Zomato is an online food delivery platform established in 2010. Zomato helps restaurants to understand the changing consumer behavior of customers and provides high-quality ingredients and kitchen products to restaurants. Zomato also fulfills the multiple needs of customers by providing an opportunity to search for restaurants, read and write reviews about them, and order food online, book a table, and make payments while dining out. From 2010 to 2022, the online food delivery market was very competitive. Therefore, Zomato decided to transform its brand by launching a new market campaign. The idea of 10 minutes delivery was taken from the Blinkit online grocery delivery

company. Zomato backed this plan and promised its customers delivery of online food orders within 10 minutes, without examining the impact on employees, customers, and society. This delivery model has raised many concerns in India including road safety and mental health of delivery personnel, highly possible violations of traffic rules, increased customer expectations and their uncivilized behavior towards delivery persons. But no one was concerned about its impact, and everyone involved was excited about its advantages such as customer expectations of delivery of fresh food. Finally, Zomato decided to purchase Blinkit without giving prior information to its investors. Zomato announced in the media one month before that they are going to purchase Blinkit, which led to investors filing a complaint against the company.

Discussion Questions

1. Should Zomato stop the 10 minutes delivery rebranding activity? Discuss.

2. Were investors right in filing a case against Zomato? Discuss.

3. Is there any unethical issue in this case?

References

1 Charles M. Coleman, *P.G. and E. of California: The Centennial Story of Pacific Gas and Electric Company, 1852–1952* (New York: McGraw-Hill, 1952).

2 Taken from timeline provided by PG&E Corporation, available at https://www.pgecorp.com/150_non_flash/index.html.

3 Material taken from PG&E website: https://www.pge.com/en_US/about-pge/company-information/profile/profile.page.

4 Jim Efstathiou and Romy Varghese, "A PG&E Bankruptcy May Be What California Needs for a Utility Fix," *Bloomberg*, January 14, 2019, https://www.bloomberg.com/news/articles/2019-01-14/pg-e-bailout-hopes-crushed-as-california-shows-little-interest.

5 Morgan McFall-Johnson, "Over 1,500 California fires in the past 6 years—including the deadliest ever—were caused by one company: PG&E. Here's what it could have done but didn't," *Business Insider*, November 3, 2019, https://www.businessinsider.com/pge-caused-california-wildfires-safety-measures-2019-10.

6 Priya Krishnakumar, Joe Fox, and Chris Keller, "Here's where more than 7,500 buildings were destroyed and damaged in California's wine country fires," *Los Angeles Times*, October 25, 2017, https://www.latimes.com/projects/la-me-northern-california-fires-structures/.

7 For information on the Kincaid Fire, see Cal Fire at https://www.fire.ca.gov/incidents/2019/10/23/kincade-fire/.

8 Alexandra Scaggs, "PG&E Is Emerging From Bankruptcy After Its Financing Plan Was Approved," June 22, 2020, Barron's, https://www.barrons.com/articles/pge-bankruptcy-financing-plan-wildfires-california-electric-utility-51592852472.

9 Martin T. Biegelman with Daniel R. Biegelman, *Building a World-Class Compliance Program: Best Practices and Strategies for Success* (Hoboken, NJ: John Wiley & Sons, 2008), 49.

10 Ibid., 49.

11 Nitish Singh, PhD, and Thomas J. Bussen, *Compliance Management: A How-to Guide for Executives, Layers, and Other Compliance Professionals* (Santa Barbara, CA: Praeger, 2015), 5.

12 "History of Corporate Compliance Regulations," LawShelf, https://lawshelf.com/shortvideoscontentview/history-of-corporate-compliance-regulations/.

13 Ibid.

14 Much of the data here is taken from "Troubled Waters," *NOW on PBS*, December 20, 2002, https://www.pbs.org/now/science/cleanwater.html and https://www.pbs.org/video/troubled-waters-a-turtles-tale-9mjvmg/. Information on the Santa Barbara Oil Spill comes from Christine Mai-Duc, "The 1969 Santa Barbara oil spill that changed oil and gas exploration forever," *Los Angeles Times*, May 20, 2015, https://www.latimes.com/local/lanow/la-me-ln-santa-barbara-oil-spill-1969-20150520-htmlstory.html.

15 See "The History of Earth Day," Earthday.org, https://www.earthday.org/history/.

16 Table created by authors from various web sources and histories. The addition of impacted stakeholder groups is our own.

17 C. William Thomas, "The Rise and Fall of Enron," *Journal of Accountancy* 193, no. 4 (April 2002): 41–48, https://www.journalofaccountancy.com/issues/2002/apr/theriseandfallofenron.html. See also Steven L. Schwarcz, "Enron and the Use and Abuse of Special Purpose Entities in Corporate Structures," *University of Cincinnati Law Review* 70 (June 6, 2002): 1309–1318.

18 Singh and Bussen, *Compliance Management*, 13.

19 Adam Hayes and Thomas Brock, "What Is the Dodd-Frank Wall Street Reform and Consumer Protection Act?," Investopedia, last modified, January 24, 2021, https://www.investopedia.com/terms/d/dodd-frank-financial-regulatory-reform-bill.asp.

20 *Corporate Counsel Business Journal*, June 1, 2005, https://ccbjournal.com/.

21 Ibid.

22 Ibid.

23 United States Sentencing Commission, "Sentencing Commission Toughens Requirements for Corporate Compliance and Ethics Programs," April 13, 2004, https://www.ussc.gov/about/news/press-releases/april-13-2004.

24 Ibid.

25 "Federal Sentencing Guidelines—An Interpretation," *Corporate Counsel Business Journal*, June 1, 2005, https://ccbjournal.com/articles/federal-sentencing-guidelines-interpretation.

26 Ibid.

27 "The Ultimate List of Compliance Program Statistics," Compliance Next, Navex Global, https://www.navexglobal.com/compliancenext/understanding-the-basics/the-ultimate-list-of-compliance-program-statistics/.

28 *Workplace Misconduct and Reporting: A Global Look*, 2019 Global Business Ethics Survey, Ethics & Compliance Initiative, 6, https://www.ethics.org/wp-content/uploads/Global-Business-Ethics-Survey-2019-Third-Report.pdf.

29 Ibid., 7.

30 *Corporate Governance Recruitment Market Report 2016—Compliance*, Barclay Simpson, 2016, accessed January 12, 2017, https://www.barclaysimpson.com/compliance-market-report-2016.

31 Nicole Stryker, "The Compliance Journey: Boosting the Value of Compliance in a Changing Regulatory Climate," KPMG, ed. Karen Staines, KPMG LLP, July 13, 2017 (as reported by Navex Global, https://assets.kpmg/content/dam/kpmg/pa/pdf/compliance-journey-survey-2017.pdf.

32 *Code of Conduct*, CVS Health, March 2021, https://cvshealth.com/sites/default/files/cvs-health-code-of-conduct.pdf.

33 "Code of Conduct," Lockheed Martin, https://www.lockheedmartin.com/en-us/who-we-are/ethics/code-of-ethics.html.

34 Geoffrey P. Miller, *The Law of Governance, Risk Management, and Compliance* (Riverwoods, IL: Wolters Kluwer, 2017) [VitalSource Bookshelf], 148.

35 Ibid., 147.

CHAPTER 6

Culture Matters

LEARNING OUTCOMES

At the end of this chapter, you should be able to do the following:

1. Identify the six ways that people can use culture to rationalize unethical behavior.

2. Describe how the 7S organizational elements create and sustain an organization's ethical culture.

3. Differentiate between symbolic and substantive elements of culture and their effects on ethical performance.

4. List ways in which corporate leadership can positively influence culture.

5. Apply the framework for ethical leadership to situations faced by organizational leaders.

Opening Case | Cultural Challenges and Ethics at PG&E

On November 8, 2018, a live wire broke away from a 100-foot-tall electrical tower in the foothills near Paradise, California. The resulting power failure affected a single Pacific Gas and Electric (PG&E) customer; however, within 15 minutes it was clear the downed line had started what would become known as California's worst wildfire to date, the Camp Fire (see Figure 6.1).[1] Within

FIGURE 6.1 Camp Fire overtaking a suburban neighborhood (from Rebecca Smith, "PG&E's Long Record of Run-Ins With Regulators: A 'Cat and Mouse Game,'" *Wall Street Journal*, September 5, 2019).

AP Photo/Michael Sah

days the fire had burned over 150,000 acres (234 square miles) of land, destroyed almost 19,000 structures, devoured the town of Paradise, California, and killed 85 people.[2] While PG&E claimed that high winds an unusually warm temperatures caused the fire, investigators determined that the company's own failures in maintaining equipment were major causes of the fire.

Internal PG&E memos noted that the tower that failed (Tower 27/222) should have been replaced 25 years ago, and the tower was one of many the company had failed to maintain.[3] That PG&E's lack of concern for maintenance and safety would spark a wildfire came as no surprise to the company's critics, who added the Camp Fire tragedy to a growing list of violations by PG&E:

- After a 2010 natural gas pipeline explosion in San Bruno, California, investigators determined that PG&E had an unhealthy and casual relationship with its main regulator, the California Public Utilities Commission (CPUC). CPUC teams coached PG&E on how to sidestep or avoid many regulatory requirements.[4]

- PG&E failed to identify threats and manage pipeline risks proactively. Before the San Bruno explosion, PG&E diverted $100 million for safety and operational repairs to other uses.[5] The lack of repairs on electrical Tower 27/222 resulted from continuing diversion of maintenance funds, specifically authorized by the CPUC, to other business purposes.

- An independent audit found "numerous critical deficiencies" in training, supervision, reporting, and an overall "impression that quality was not a high priority" in the company. Pipelines that were good enough was what people hoped for.[6]

- Workers who marked the ground (to protect against damaging buried lines and pipes) for new construction work falsified reports about their progress. The reports made them appear "caught up" with the workload, but in fact they were behind.[7]
- PG&E's ethical violations had even made Hollywood: Legal clerk Erin Brockovich's whistleblowing activities became the subject of a 2000 movie bearing her name that garnered a best female lead Academy Award for star Julia Roberts.[8] The film documented Brockovich's efforts to hold PG&E accountable for polluting drinking water in Kettleman City, California.

The root cause of PG&E's problems traces back to its organizational systems and its corporate culture. For example, the company's compensation system offered bonuses to managers who reported fewer pipeline leaks. The compensation system created a conflict of interest between public safety and individual reward. When the bonus system changed in 2015, PG&E identified 10 times the number of "high-priority" leaks as before.[9]

What mattered most at PG&E was quarterly financial performance. "There was very much a focus on the bottom line over everything: What are the earnings we can report this quarter?" said Mike Florio, a utilities commissioner from 2011 through 2016. "And things really got squeezed on the maintenance side."[10]

A number of PG&E's human resources policies encouraged employees to avoid maintenance and safety issues. When some PG&E managers noted problems with the ground-marking reports, for example, they found themselves transferred to other divisions and demoted. Managers who encouraged false reporting were promoted. Former CPUC commissioner Catherine Sandoval explained that PG&E had both "a trust issue and a conduct issue," and its violation of regulations represented a clear pattern. She judged PG&E as "definitely the worst" among all the utilities she had responsibility for.[11]

PG&E brought in new leadership after the company filed for bankruptcy in 2019. New Chief Executive Officer Bill Johnson recognized the challenges ahead. He noted that PG&E was a very old company with an entrenched culture and that "things accrete over time." He promised to change the culture, and noted that under his administration, PG&E would feature "transparency and openness and telling the truth as fast as we can."[12]

Introduction

We introduced Pacific Gas and Electric (PG&E) in Chapter 5. As a public utility, PG&E is heavily regulated, and looking at companies like this can help you understand the many challenges companies face when they must comply with many regulatory demands. PG&E created an office of ethics and compliance in 2015 and made a formal commitment to becoming "best-in-class."[13] As our opening case notes, having officers and organizational units is not enough when the culture of the corporation encourages people to avoid complying with regulations and engage in ethically questionable behavior. In this chapter, you'll learn about the role of culture in creating an environment that encourages and supports ethical behavior. You'll also learn about what it means to be an ethical leader. Let's begin by defining culture and explaining the different elements in the business that contribute to it.

Corporate Culture and Ethics

What comes to mind when you hear the phrase "corporate culture"? Innovation, inclusion of new ideas from all employees, management that acts with integrity, the manifestation of the vision of the founders? "Corporate culture is a set of certain ideas, attitudes, and values that are generally accepted in the enterprise. . . . These are not only elements visible externally, such as symbols, signs, logos, a company's uniformity, but especially certain patterns of behavior in certain situations."[14] Culture arises from the shared experiences of people who work together and solve problems. The term *culture* captures common assumptions and beliefs about how the world works, how people frame and solve problems, and how they act. An important aspect of culture is its "taken-for-granted" nature.[15] People who live in a culture don't usually question whether their way of living is right; it just is. Every organization has a culture, from businesses to families.

The Role of Culture in Ethics

Culture plays a pivotal role in guiding people toward ethical or unethical behavior at work. Consider two extreme examples. Some company cultures see the world working through authenticity, collaboration, and transparency; when individuals and organizations behave this way, everyone wins. Other companies believe that the world is about façade, competition, and secrecy; only those organizations and actors who are cutthroat and aggressive will win in the marketplace. These deep assumptions drive how people act and do their jobs.

Most people who join an organization will come to adopt the worldview and culture of the organization. Figure 6.2 presents the Ethical Behavioral Continuum, and we'll discuss its implications for creating an ethical organization. In any distribution of people, there is one "tail" that believes that honesty, integrity, and caring for others is the way to success. They'll behave in ethical ways in any organization. There is also an opposite "tail" that believes the opposite: Success is about grabbing everything a person can, and there are no rules that prohibit what behaviors are inappropriate. This tail will act unethically as much as possible. There is a large group in the middle of the distribution—the vast majority of people—who will adopt the organization's cultural assumptions about ethics as correct and will act accordingly. If the assumption is that ethical behavior wins the day, people will act ethically; however, if the culture stresses cutting ethical corners at every opportunity—such as at PG&E—then most people will cut ethical corners.

Culture, as a set of shared assumptions about how the world works and how people ought to behave, creates an environment that allows people to believe that actions they might feel are unethical are justified or appropriate. Scholars Vikas Anand, Blake Ashforth, and Mahendra Joshi identified three ways in which shared beliefs and assumptions can justify (and encourage) unethical behavior by members of a business:[16]

- **Denial of Responsibility:** The first way cultures justify unethical behavior is through a reference to industry practices, or the rules of the game. "What you are doing is how everyone in this industry does business. It's just how this industry works." Denial of responsibility often references corporate authority, or the rules of the particular organization. "I didn't want to do it, but my manager made me. My hands were tied."

- **Denial of Injury:** This argument accepts that actions may have been less than ethical or purely unethical; however, everyone involved in the situation was a willing participant, and so everyone knew the potential outcomes. "This customer knew what she was getting into in this kind of transaction." Similarly, people deny injury when no apparent harms occurred to the other party. "Sure, it wasn't right, but no one was disadvantaged. No harm, no foul."

- **Appeal to Higher Loyalties:** This justification admits ethical error, and even harm, but claims that such harms were committed in pursuit of a higher cause. "We had to act that way, or our company would go out of business." "Business is war." "I had to lie. It was that or my family would be out on the street."

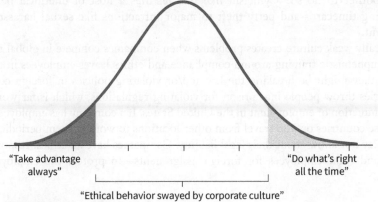

"Take advantage always"

"Do what's right all the time"

"Ethical behavior swayed by corporate culture"

FIGURE 6.2 The Ethical Behavior Continuum.

Culture also plays a role in training and socialization into a firm that creates another set of putative justifications for unethical behavior. New members of an organization can accept corrupt and unethical behaviors as normal through the following:

- **Incrementalism:** This process represents a clear effort by those in authority to downplay the harm or evil that might have occurred. The goal of incremental language and enculturation is to turn questions of ethical "black and white" into shades of gray. Incrementalism muddies the lines between unethical, mildly unethical, and grossly unethical behavior.

- **Euphemistic Language:** A euphemism is a mild or indirect word used in place of a harsher word. Euphemisms are fine in many situations, but they can often create ethical ambiguity. For example, companies don't lay people off; they "rightsize." People aren't fired for breaking rules; they simply "leave the organization." Similarly, "selective amnesia" makes lying or failing to tell the whole truth seem accidental and morally acceptable. Euphemistic language shades the truth, making something painful appear painless, or something ethically questionable seem all right.

- **Social Cocoon:** Many technical professions, such as accounting, engineering, and law, have their own unique language, skills, tools, and ways of doing work. It's easy for people in these careers to become isolated from others and insulated by their professional culture such that they fail to see many ethical challenges. Other views and opinions become hidden from view, and unethical behavior seems to be acceptable because everyone we come in contact with behaves in the same way.

The Consequences of an Unethical Culture

No companies, except perhaps those owned by the mafia, have cultures that openly encourage unethical behavior. The six ways that culture justifies and encourages unethical behavior that you just read about aren't part of the new employee orientation. These cultural forces help employees see how things are "really done" in the organization. You can easily see that when these elements are present, ethical behavior and compliance will be a problem throughout the organization. PG&E managers who skirted regulations and failed to invest in safety and maintenance could easily justify their behavior by denying responsibility (my hands are tied) or by an appeal to higher loyalties (If I report problems, I'll be demoted/fired and those I love will suffer).

The conflict between stated values and "the way things really work here" drives cynicism and saps productivity. When employees think that stated core values and cultural missives are just words on a page rather than meaningful guides, they will likely resent management's behavior, and they will be less likely to fully invest in work that will help the organization thrive. Employees may be embarrassed to work for a company that allows executives and others to act badly. Many employees may feel that their own bad acts are excused. If management doesn't have to live by a code of conduct and values, why should employees bother to do so? Cynicism like this justifies a host of unethical behaviors, from falsifying timecards and petty theft to major infractions like sexual harassment or embezzlement.

An ethically weak culture creates problems when companies compete in global markets. Cryptic or euphemistic training around compliance and ethics leaves employees in the dark about when they might be breaking the law and/or violating policies in foreign countries. Some countries throw people into prison for violating regulations, which is far worse than the mere termination of employment in the United States. If a company has employees either living in these countries or who travel from other locations to work in them periodically, the employees may not know about their legal liability. Companies have an ethical responsibility to prepare and train employees for foreign assignments—to protect the employees and the company.

Using Culture to Enhance Ethics

Given the power of culture to shape ethical behavior, a natural question arises: How can we use culture as the foundation of an ethical organization? We take up this topic in the next section. Before we can respond to the question, however, we provide a model to help you understand where culture—a set of unspoken assumptions, world views, and norms—is found inside an organization. Once you know where to look for culture, you'll see how it can be used to foster ethical, rather than unethical, behavior.

The 7S Model and Organizational Culture

The 7S model, originally developed by McKinsey and Company consultant Tom Peters, serves as an excellent framework to see how culture operates in a business, and how managers can leverage culture to enhance a commitment to ethics. The origin of the 7S model traces back to 1977 when McKinsey Managing Director Ron Daniel summoned a newly minted Stanford PhD, Tom Peters, to his New York office and tasked him to find the "Next Big Thing" for McKinsey to sell to its clients.[17] Daniel asked Peters to think about "organizational effectiveness" and "implementation," as the lack of these two elements often frustrated the strategy process. Peters traveled the globe in search of answers and began working with Bob Waterman, another McKinsey consultant, on the project. They interviewed the leading minds in academia and business to find what worked. After two years of hard work, Peters and Waterman identified key organizational elements that drove success, effectiveness, and for our purposes, ethical behavior.[18] The alliteration of these elements into the 7S' made the model ready to pitch to clients. Figure 6.3 displays the seven elements of the model: *Strategy, Structure, Systems, Staffing, Skills, Style,* and *Shared Values.*[19]

You learned in the last chapter that the federal sentencing guidelines for organizations were amended in 2004 to include, in part, a commitment to culture. Emphasizing a commitment to ethical action is one way that values establish and maintain an ethical culture. Ethics in the Real World 6.1 gives you examples of the explicit shared values at several companies.

In Figure 6.3, you see different colors for different elements of the 7S model. This is not by accident. Strategy, Structure, and Systems, the three elements in green, are usually referred to as the hard triangle. Hard doesn't mean difficult; it means tangible, or things people can

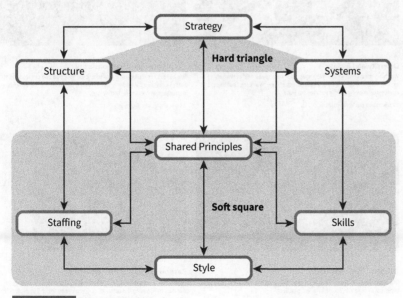

FIGURE 6.3 The 7S model.

see and feel. Managers can (relatively) quickly change each of these elements; indeed, nothing is easier than to draw a new organization chart on a napkin at lunch. Similarly, many new leaders shift strategy hoping to be more effective, and changes to elements like information systems create easy-to-see changes for employees and other stakeholders. Strategy, structure, and systems tend to reflect shallow, easily articulable, or tangible elements of the organization and its culture.

The remaining four elements of the 7S model constitute the soft square and are the major drivers of culture. Staffing and skills are outlined in orange because they represent primarily *intrapersonal* parts of culture, while shared principles and style, outlined in blue, identify the *interpersonal* elements of culture. Soft does not mean easy to change or weak; soft means intangible and difficult to see. While some shared principles have been written down, as you saw in Ethics in the Real World 6.1, most shared principles—the ones that drive day-to-day behavior, are usually not written down and passed in stories or other activities. Managers work long and hard to change the soft square, which led Tom Peters to offer this guidance to executives: "Hard is soft, soft is hard."[20]

Ethics in the Real World 6.1 | Company Commitments to Shared Values

You may wonder how companies take a very "soft" element like shared values and communicate them in ways that resonate with all stakeholders and that they can understand. We've chosen several great examples for you to consider. Each of these companies competes in the "tech" space, but notice that their core values have common themes (such as diversity and social value). Note how each company interprets these values differently. If you founded a company, what would your core values be?"

Microsoft[22]

Our mission in action

Innovation
We believe technology can and should be a force for good and that meaningful innovation can and will contribute to a brighter world in big and small ways.

Check out the latest research >   Explore innovation stories >

Diversity and inclusion
We thrive on diverse voices. We engage our employees' and customers' experiences, strengths, and different points of view to inform, challenge, and stretch our thinking. This is how we innovate.

Learn about our commitment >

Corporate Social Responsibility
We believe technology is a powerful force for good and are working to foster a sustainable future where everyone has access to the benefits and opportunities created by technology.

Learn about our approach >

AI
We believe that, when designed with people at the center, AI can extend your capabilities, free you up for more creative and strategic endeavors, and help you or your organization achieve more.

Learn more about AI >

Trustworthy Computing
Check out how we deliver secure, private, and reliable computing experiences based on sound business practices.

Learn about the Trust Center >

Responding to COVID-19 together
As the world responds to the outbreak of COVID-19, we're working to do our part by ensuring the safety of our employees, striving to protect the health and well-being of the communities in which we operate, and providing technology, tips, and resources to our customers.

Read more about our response >

Oracle[23]

Oracle core values

The following core values are the foundation of our company and are essential to Oracle's business.

Integrity

We are honest and make responsible decisions. We speak up for what is right.

Mutual respect

We treat each other with respect and dignity. We value the unique contributions that each individual brings.

Teamwork

We work together to make things the best they can be. We collaborate, share ideas, and give constructive feedback.

Communication

We share knowledge effectively with one another. We respect the need for confidentiality regarding certain information.

Innovation

We welcome new ideas and dare to try new things. Problems are solved where creativity and technical expertise meet.

Customer satisfaction

Our customers are our top priority. We make every effort to understand their needs.

Quality

We strive for excellence. We hold ourselves to the highest possible standards and always try to improve.

Fairness

We treat everyone we work with fairly. We do everything we can to make sure our decisions are free from bias.

Compliance

We comply with all laws, regulations, and policies that govern Oracle's business and our own actions.

Ethics

We uphold the highest standards of moral behavior and we act ethically at all times.

Facebook[24]

Former McKinsey consultant Lou Gerstner validated this guidance as he described the turnaround he led as CEO of IBM in the 1990s: "If I could have chosen not to tackle the IBM culture head-on, I probably wouldn't have. My bias coming in was toward strategy, analysis, and measurement. In comparison, changing the attitude and behaviors of hundreds of thousands of people is very, very hard. [Yet] I came to see in my time at IBM that culture isn't just one aspect of the game—it is the game."[21] Culture plays a role in every aspect of business success, and ethical behavior is no exception. With the 7S framework in hand, you now have a framework and language to talk meaningfully and sensibly about how executives can create a culture that values ethics.

Using the 7S Model to Create an Ethical Culture

The 7S model provides employees, entrepreneurs, or leaders with a road map of specific areas they can address and some specific actions they can take to create or strengthen an ethical culture. An organization's commitment to ethics begins with its mission, purpose, and contribution to creating a better society. With an ethical foundation for all it does, the 7S model offers leaders a tool to embed a call to ethical action in every aspect of the business. We'll begin by describing how each of the 7S elements can signal and strengthen a commitment to compliance and ethics. We'll then turn to two larger, "umbrella" elements of culture—symbols and substance—and illustrate how leaders can leverage these elements to encourage ethics.

- **Strategy:** Strategy is about competitive advantage, and leaders need to determine what role ethical behavior plays in creating and sustaining strategic advantage. Strategy may be the most important S because it's the foundation for everything the firm does or should be doing. Some organizations, such as PG&E and Enron (from Chapter 5), decided that ethics was a cost and constraint that would limit strategic advantage. Most organizations, such as Microsoft or Toyota, see a commitment to ethics as a fundamental citizenship obligation of the firm that has little impact on competitive advantage. Other organizations, such as Patagonia (Chapter 4) see a commitment to ethical practices as a key differentiator in their markets.

- **Structure:** As we noted, structure is about who does what, who has authority, and who reports to whom. Structure is found in the organization chart; the boxes answer the "Who does what?" question, the placement of those boxes above or below others answers the "Who's in charge?" question, and the connecting lines (horizontal and vertical) answer the "Who reports to whom?" question. As you learned in Chapter 5, the organizational location of the ethics and compliance function will, in larger measure, determine the effectiveness of that group. If ethics and compliance reports to the general counsel or another functional member of the C-suite, this function will face conflicts with the goals and objectives of each of those functions. When the chief ethics and compliance officer (CECO) reports directly to the CEO or the board, he or she will enjoy a greater degree of independence and have greater influence.

- **Systems:** These are the processes that coordinate and control activity across the business. Companies can install systems to make sure that employees have the opportunity to pass information about ethical violations to senior managers. These systems allow the organization to react to ethical issues and violations, and include hotlines, mandatory reporting structures, or formal compliance review processes throughout the company. Organizations with a commitment to ethics also install proactive systems in the areas of compensation and initiatives around corporate social responsibility. The CECO will work with human resource leaders to ensure that compensation systems encourage, not stifle, ethical behavior. You can think of the PG&E case where managers received bonuses for not reporting problems. What people get paid for will determine what they will do. Similarly, commitments to positive social initiatives (discussed in Chapter 12) signal to employees a commitment to ethics; the best initiatives provide employees with a way to engage in these good causes.

- **Staffing:** This S is about how organizations hire, train, retain, and promote human capital. The impact of staffing on ethics is easy to see, and it is substantial. The first area is professionalism in hiring through protocols that include a commitment to ethics and values as a screen for entry into the organization. Chapter 5 addressed the second area, the issues of onboarding training, and ongoing training, as a key element for creating an ethical organization. Remember, training articulates culture as it teaches new and existing employees how an organization perceives the world, the business, and appropriate behaviors. Performance reviews that explicitly incorporate compliance with organizational guidelines for ethical behavior as a condition for promotion or raises help the organization reinforce its commitment to ethics.

- **Skills:** Skills outline the critical KSAs (knowledge, skills, and abilities) that lead to organizational success. Training helps instill those KSAs into the organization, but activities that require employees and managers to practice and refine those skills can reinforce a commitment to ethics. Corporations that become leaders in ethics and compliance will often, for example, send teams to conferences to teach others what they do, and learn from others to enhance their own practices. Similarly, knowledge sharing between business units or with other leaders in ethics and compliance improves the core KSAs of the entire business.

- **Shared Values:** These are the shared outlooks, assumptions, and norms that guide the organization. Ethics in the Real World 6.1 displayed the formal values of a number of leading corporations. We like to think of shared values, and culture in general, as an iceberg. Formal values statements are like the part that everyone sees above the water, which is only about one-eighth of the total iceberg. The majority of shared values, the seven-eighths, is invisible to most people. This part of the cultural iceberg comes from the implied values found in the 5 S's that we've just discussed. When the leaders of PG&E, for example, created the position for the CECO in 2015, they made a visible commitment to act in accord with leading practices in ethics and compliance. That formal commitment ran afoul of the values implied by strategy, structure, reward systems, training programs, and commitment to skills. The bottom line is that when the formal shared values build upon, reflect, and reinforce the implied principles of the organization, there is a real commitment to ethics.

Building an Ethical Culture: Symbolic and Substantive Actions

As organizational leaders begin to change the culture, they'll employ both symbolic tools, like stories and legends, and substantive tools like policies and procedures (see Figure 6.4). It's important that you understand the role that each plays in creating and maintaining a strong and ethical culture.

Symbolic Actions

We invoked the metaphor of an iceberg to describe an organization's culture. The symbols and artifacts of culture represent the visible, but smaller, part of an organization's living culture, the part that an outsider can easily see. Symbols and artifacts (physical manifestations of

StunningArt/Shutterstock.com

FIGURE 6.4 Symbols and substance often differ.

symbols) like the mission statement, values statement, formal commitments to social involvement such as philanthropy or ecological sustainability, company-wide or divisional awards given to employees, and other visible elements communicate the core outlooks, priorities, and values that guide the organization. Reports, from financial reporting such as 10-Ks for public companies, social responsibility, or sustainability reports, plus the reporting requirements of particular regulatory agencies also embody visible elements of the organization's culture.

When leaders work to create a more ethical culture and climate, these symbols matter and wise leaders pay significant attention to detail. A good mission or vision statement will have both an actual (where we are today) and an aspirational (where we hope to be tomorrow) component. They articulate what people in the organization see as the result of their delivering on the mission. The attention to detail in regulatory filings and amount of emphasis given to voluntary reports such as sustainability reporting signal an increased commitment to ethics and compliance. Formal rewards, such as awards, recognition, or bonuses, for employees displaying exemplary behavior act as an important symbol that emphasizes ethical behavior.

Substantive Actions

Substantive actions have, as the term suggests, substance. These are the daily activities and interactions that people have around ethics and compliance. Few of these substantive actions are formal; most are found in the informal interactions among people in the organization. Substantive actions include the informal stories and legends that are told every day about what happens to people who are either ethical or unethical. Substantive actions represent the way ethics and compliance "really are" inside the organization.

Obedience to rules and norms by people at all levels is the largest substantive element of culture. If the culture emphasizes safety, an issue of compliance but also ethics, then how safely people actually do their work speaks volumes about the culture and commitment to not only safety, but other ethical concerns as well. When shop floor employees fail to wear safety equipment or report safety incidents, they reinforce a culture that doesn't "walk the talk" of company principles. Accounting and finance staff who cut corners while closing the books or processing payments, or sales and marketing people who submit inflated expense accounts all create a culture that devalues honesty and integrity.

You might have noticed that our discussion of the 7S model in this section omitted one S: Style, the way people interact with each other in the organization. In terms of ethics, style is critical because it sets the tone at the top of the organization and represents a company's commitment to ethical leadership.

Tone at the Top and Ethical Leadership

In Chapter 5, we discussed the reality that all employees in a company have responsibility to make the company an ethical entity that is compliant with laws. You also read how the federal sentencing guidelines were amended to include an expectation that companies have leadership that actively promotes compliance. So, while all employees have a responsibility to act ethically, with integrity and in accordance with the policies and values of a company, leadership has a special responsibility. Managers, particularly those in the C-suite, have a responsibility to set the "tone at the top" of the organization (or work group) and to exhibit ethical and moral leadership.

Tone at the Top

The phrase *tone at the top* means that

> **the behavior exhibited by the topmost executives sets the standard for the rest of an organization and thus will influence the credibility and success of an organization's**

compliance program. Executives, starting with the CEO, must demonstrate and reinforce the importance of ethical and compliant behavior. While there are many other factors contributing to an effective compliance program, none can be truly effective if the CEO is unethical.[25]

Figure 6.5 describes elements that create the "tone at the top."

What does *tone* refer to? Put simply, tone refers to the responsibility of top managers, who are the visible leaders in the company, to act as role models for all the employees below them. When management feels that their position exempts them from following the policies of a company, everyone who works for that person will soon believe the same thing. The logic of "If it's good enough for the CEO, it's good enough for me" will become the excuse that others use to skirt rules, to fudge numbers, or to abuse their power and position. "Issues with management tone can be pervasive because others in the company soon learn that the company doesn't care about ethics."[26]

What can a company do about a bad tone at the top? You might be surprised to learn that "[b]y far the most common remedy is getting rid of the bad apples."[27] We might all believe that members of the board could simply approach management about bad behavior and suggest that they act as real leaders for the rest of the company, or that additional training or counseling might solve the problem. This might work if this is the first report of unethical or poor behavior; however, in many instances the offending executive has engaged in similar behaviors in other roles. The board has a fiduciary duty to guard shareholder interests and monitor the behavior of the people in the C-suite (see Figure 6.6).

When the board removes an offending executive, or when higher-level managers remove lower-level ones for ethical lapses, the company benefits in two ways. Substantively, the offending manager is removed and that means that poor behavior should cease, particularly when the new occupant of the position is brought in, at least in part, because he or she has

HOW DO COMPANIES BUILD WORKPLACE CULTURE?

An organization's mission and principles should be at the forefront of its communications strategy

Include mission and principles in onboarding	68%
Include mission and principles in company communications	67%
Include cultural elements in learning and development	54%
Build culture into work processes	50%
Hire for cultural fit	49%
Include culture as part of the employee review process	39%

FIGURE 6.5   How do companies build a workplace culturetone?

C-Level Executive
A top corporate executive whose job title begins with the letter "C", which stands for "Chief".

CEO
Chief Executive Officer

CHRO
Chief Human Resources Officer

CMO
Chief Marketing Officer

CFO
Chief Financial Officer

COO
Chief Operating Officer

CIO
Chief Information Officer

CTO
Chief Technology Officer

CIO
Chief Investment Officer

FIGURE 6.6 There are different types of positions at the top who all need to be aware of their tone.

a reputation for strong ethics. Common sense dictates that a manager who presided over a major ethical breach or compliance failure should not be the person to lead the repair.[28] Symbolically, the harsh penalty of dismissal sends a powerful signal to others in the organization: "This drastic step can have the advantage of signaling to employees and outside stakeholders that the [organization] is very serious about creating a new culture of ethics and sound control in the company."[29]

Attention to the tone at the top of an organization or work group is the first element of ethical leadership, but it is only the first element. Let's look at other elements of being an ethical leader.

Ethical Leadership

It's easy to think of "tone at the top" as referring only to the CEO and other leaders in the C-suite. As we noted in Chapter 5, however, everyone has a responsibility for compliance. That means that everyone in a leadership role—either formal or informal—contributes to the "tone at the top" of his or her own team, work group, or division. Ethical leaders do six specific things, which we highlight:

- **Live** by a code of ethics; they are **authentic**. Leaders can't model and they can't lead if they aren't authentic. Some ethical leaders draw from a religious tradition, others from the study of philosophy, and a third group simply catalogs great moral choices in their own experience. The most effective leaders have a strong and deliberately derived set of moral principles that guide them; they have a well-functioning moral compass.[30]

- **Define** ethical behavior for others. Leaders live their moral principles, and they don't impose those values on others. What they do, however, is clearly define what ethical behavior means in their sphere of authority. They don't use phrases like "Just do the right thing." They define what the right thing is, such as honesty and total truth telling. They also don't "look the other way" when they see questionable behavior. They call out what's appropriate and what's not, in very clear terms that are easy to understand.

- **Teach** ethical action to those who work for and with them. Leaders don't rely on corporate training to instill ethical behavior. The best leaders use every possible interaction, from formal memos to informal conversations, to help their teams understand what's right and wrong. That constant reinforcement proves far more effective than the annual training session or performance review.[31]

- **Expect** ethical behavior from others. The best ethical leaders use both formal and informal methods to communicate their expectations. Formal methods include training, performance reviews, and settings such as staff meetings or retreats. Informal methods include "ethical management by walking around," which includes the opportunity to observe people in action and reinforce expectations. Along with expectations (backed up by clear definitions and training) leaders communicate to their associates a clear confidence that they can live up to those expectations.

- **Measure** ethical performance. Any behavior that we measure will improve. We all want targets to shoot for; no one wants to be the one who falls below the performance standard. As with the other elements of ethical leadership, some measures will be formal and others informal. Formal measures include mandatory training, attendance at conferences or events, or formal ethics and compliance reviews. The most effective informal methods are conversations and debriefs of both ethically challenging situations and ethically easy situations. When team members have the opportunity to report on what they did, how they decided, and why they chose to act as they did, the leader helps people calibrate their own actions and make plans for future improvement.

- **Reward** ethical behaviors. We noted in Chapter 5 that compensating people for ethical behavior is a double-edged sword. Rewards can encourage behavior, but if the reward ceases, what happens to the behavior? Smart leaders use more frequent and informal rewards to encourage ethical behaviors. These rewards range from highlighting exemplary actions in staff meetings to simple but heartfelt expressions of thanks and admiration. These small rewards often mean more than larger ones.

To put the point simply and sharply: Everyone in any leadership role in an organization contributes to an ethical culture when he or she becomes an ethical leader! Everyone leads in everything they do, all the time, even when they see themselves as individual contributor. See Ethics in the Real World 6.2 for an example of exemplary ethical leadership.

Ethics in the Real World 6.2 | Ethical Leadership: the example of Warren Buffett

Daniel Zuchnik/WireImage/Getty Images

Warren Edward Buffett (b. 1930) is known worldwide as the Oracle of Omaha for his investing prowess and business wisdom. He was born and raised in Omaha and he graduated from the University of Nebraska at age 19. He went on to earn a Masters' Degree from the Columbia Business School. He began working as an investor for legendary value investor Benjamin Graham in 1954 and put together enough capital to found Buffett Partnership Ltd. in 1956. By 1962, Buffet had over $1 million in personal assets. He bought his firm, Berkshire Hathaway, in 1965 and continued to invest in companies for the long haul. His net worth reached $1 billion in 1990, and by 2021 his net worth was estimated to be over $100 billion.[32]

Not only is Buffet a wealthy and wise investor, but he's also seen as one of Wall Street's most ethical leaders, and his embrace of a company can help restore its reputation. In 1991, Wall Street firm Salomon Brothers almost went bankrupt due to cheating while trading U.S. government bonds. Buffet had invested $700 million in Salomon Brothers, and during the bond crisis he increased his personal investment in the firm by becoming board chair.[33] While some critics dubbed him "Jimmy Stewart" (who played moral and kindhearted George Bailey in the movie, *It's a Wonderful Life*) for his firm moral stance, many investors and regulators trusted Buffets reputation for integrity in cleaning up the firm, and his nine months as chair saved the company and returned it to financial health.[34]

Buffet is often known for his wise words, and here are some of his best quotes about ethics:[35]

- If you're not sure if something is right or wrong, consider whether you'd want it reported in the morning paper.

- Lose money for the firm, and I will be understanding. Lose a shred of reputation for the firm, and I will be ruthless.

- You're looking for three things, generally, in a person: intelligence, energy, and integrity. And if they don't have the last one, don't even bother with the first two.

Key Terms

appeal to higher loyalties	euphemistic language	soft square
authentic	hard triangle	symbols
corporate culture	incrementalism	tone at the top
denial of injury	shared values	
denial of responsibility	social cocoon	

Chapter Summary

In this chapter, we addressed various topics related to corporate culture and ethical leadership:

- We defined culture as a set of taken-for-granted assumptions that tell members of an organization what is appropriate. Culture includes assumptions about how the world works, how problems should be approached and solved, and how people should interact with each other. Culture influences ethical behavior because the majority of people in the organization will use the culture as their compass to determine what's right and wrong.

- Culture contributes to unethical behavior through two major mechanisms. Cultural assumptions provide members with rationalizations for engaging in behavior they might believe is unethical. These rationalizations work on principles of denial, or an appeal to higher loyalties. Cultures also socialize people into accepting unethical behavior as normal. For example, the language leaders use can make unethical behaviors seem normal.

- The 7S model can help you understand where culture "comes from and lives" in an organization. The 7S model contains two large groupings, the hard triangle, and the soft square. The 7S model is a helpful tool for helping create and maintain an ethical culture in an organization. Leaders should pay attention to both symbolic and substantive aspects of each S as they work to strengthen their culture.

- Tone at the top refers to how well the upper echelons of the organization set the example for the organization. Top managers of the organization need to model ethical behavior for members of the firm because people throughout the organization will take behavioral clues from their top leaders. When leaders behave badly, employees tend to do the same. Even if they don't violate ethical standards, employees will become highly cynical.

- Finally, managers and supervisors at all levels of the organization have the opportunity to become ethical leaders. Ethical leadership at all levels is critical for a truly ethical culture to arise and flourish. Leaders at all levels must employ six specific behaviors to point the way for others. These behaviors, in regard to ethical behavior, are the following: Live it, define it, teach it, expect it, measure it, and reward it.

Chapter Review Questions

1. What are the elements of corporate culture? Why is a culture taken for granted by members of the organization?

2. How can a culture contribute to unethical behavior by employees or managers? Which of the justifications and socializations do you believe is most effective? Which ones have you seen the most often in your experiences in organizations of all types?

3. How can managers use the "hard triangle" elements of the 7S model to strengthen their culture? The "soft square"? Which of these do you think will be more effective? Why?

4. What is tone at the top? Where have you seen good (and bad) examples of top leadership's "tone at the top"?

5. Which of the six behaviors of ethical leaders do you believe is the most important? Which of these behaviors would be the most difficult for you to do? What steps can you take to work on that behavior?

6. What is the difference between corporate culture and national culture?

7. What should be the process to align corporate culture with national culture?

8. How can ethical culture be developed in an organization?

Application Exercises

- *Personal Ethical Development.* If you began keeping an ethics journal as suggested in the first chapter, continue that writing work. Here are some prompts: Which organizations (schools, jobs, sports teams, or clubs) have you been a part of that had strong ethical cultures? Which of the 7S elements helped contribute to that culture? Where have you seen good and bad examples of ethical leadership? Create a list of questions you can ask during a job interview to assess a company's ethical culture.

- *Career Goals and Planning.* A happy, meaningful, and productive life blends and builds upon the following: (1) the type of life you are interested in leading, (2) your deepest and most important values, (3) the work you are interested in doing, (4) what you are good at, (5) your preferences for things like work versus free time, and (6) your personality. Create a set of commitments about the importance of an ethical culture at places you want to work. Would you be happiest in a strongly ethical culture, or would you prefer a culture where "anything goes"?

- *Ethics in the Business World.* Identify an organization that you believe has a strong ethical culture. This may be either for-profit or not-for-profit organizations. What evidence from the company backs up your belief? What are the key elements of their culture? How do leaders nourish and sustain that culture?

• *Talking with and Learning from Others.* Choose a business professional you believe is an ethical leader. This may be a top manager, or someone deep inside an organization. Engage that person in a brief interview. How did they develop their own moral code? How do they define and model ethical behavior for others? How do they expect and reward ethical behavior among those who report to them? What advice would they give you about becoming an ethical leader?

Mini-Cases

Case 1: Jared Berger and the "Canary in the Coal Mine." In his first year as the CEO of Diamond Tire and Rubber, a $10 billion Cleveland, Ohio-based maker of tires, hoses, and belts for construction machinery and vehicles, Jared Berger had seen many things he wanted to change. The organization had outdated information systems, its human resources and training capabilities could hardly be considered a strength, and the company's centralized decision-making processes stretched new product time horizons too far into the future. What troubled Berger most, however, was his impression that Diamond's culture did not support ethical behavior. His interviews with members of the company revealed several issues: The company's outside sales force often misled customers about products, features, and the terms of the warranty for Diamond's products; shop floor employees skirted OSHA requirements in their attempts to extract every ounce of productivity from machines and people; managers often resorted to tyrannical bullying tactics to get things done; and employees seemed to "borrow" company assets and supplies for their own use.

About six months ago, Berger had decided to focus on safety as a priority in the company. This would solve the immediate compliance problems, and associated liability, of safety violations. Berger also felt that safety was a "canary in the coal mine" for solving other ethical issues. Safety would be the first element in his work to strengthen Diamond's commitment to ethics and compliance across the board.

He found employees and supervisors largely supportive of his efforts, and the company's committee on safety adopted a stringent "zero tolerance" policy toward safety violations. That meant that any safety violation, from gross negligence by a forklift driver to a clerical employee with a paper cut, had to be reported by the individual within 24 hours. If a report of a safety incident came from someone other than the person directly involved, that person would be subject to discipline. The first unreported incident led to a negative performance review report, the second to a 10% reduction in a month's salary, and the third to termination.

Jared found his commitment to "zero tolerance" tested one Wednesday morning. Robert Stokes, the company's executive vice president of sales and marketing, was a popular member of the C-suite and had proven to be a critical ally in his work to remake Diamond into a better company. Jared's executive assistant had noted in her morning report that Stokes had cut his arm on a loose screw on one of the employee cubicles during their early morning walk-through. The incident happened on Monday morning. Stokes had put a bandage on the cut. After this debrief, Jared checked the safety logs. Bob had not reported the incident, and Jared knew why.

This was Bob's third offense. Jared spent some time talking to others, and no one had seen Bob cut his arm except his assistant. Losing Bob would mean that a talented leader and key ally in the executive suite for strategic change would be gone. Bob and Jared had a very positive working relationship, and they genuinely liked and respected each other. No one other than Jared's assistant had witnessed the event, and she would likely do whatever Jared felt was best for the company.

Jared struggled with what to do about Bob. What would happen to his change efforts at Diamond without a key player on the team? What was his real commitment to safety? Was it really a "canary in a coal mine" for an ethical culture, or could he make an exception for Bob?

Case 2: Incentives. Thomas International Publishing Company (India) Pvt. Ltd. is an American multinational company (MNC). They are into publishing business directories for industrial buyers across the country. John Damsy had been working for this company for more than a decade. He was stationed in New Delhi at the headquarters of the organization. His job profile included handling three departments—Finance, Administration, and Human Resources. The first few years of his career at the organization went well. However, the problem started in his professional life after seven years. The organization was very rigid in giving increments to the staff members and hence most employees resorted to making personal problems an issue and started asking for extra money in the form of fringe benefits. The Managing Director of the company supported most of the employees, feeling that they were really in trouble. However, Damsy decided to back his personal values at his workplace and did not tell lie to the Managing Director. Therefore, he received lesser salary and incentives than his juniors, which demotivated him and forced him to leave his job.

Discussion Questions

1. What other alternative did Damsy have in this situation?

2. Should Damsy's junior lie to get more financial benefits at work? Discuss.

3. How will the fringe benefits impact Thomas International Publishing Company (India) Pvt. Ltd. in the long run?

Case 3: Thomas Sedway is working as a sales manager at a German multinational company (MNC) and headed a state in the southern part of India. The company sells luxury kitchen appliances that are imported as completely built units (CBUs) and have a niche set of customers. As a sales manager, Thomas has to manage the channel, primarily by taking care of the channel partners such as the distributors, dealers, retailers, and sometimes customers. As a state head, he has all the autonomy and power to make decisions locally. The decision-making process in the company is majorly decentralized. It is up to the state heads to ensure that sales and operations are smooth and hassle-free to its customers and, in turn, to the organization.

There was an incident where he was at the crossroads of an ethical dilemma. A customer had bought a refrigerator worth over $3,100, in addition to the overall purchase of $13,000. The customer happened to purchase from a key dealer, who was an exclusive dealer of the company and a significant contributor to the sales figures in Thomas's territory. Due to the pandemic, the construction works were delayed and came to a standstill during lockdown. After four months of delay, the construction was completed, and the refrigerator's installation was ready to put into operation. When the carton box was opened, it was found that the glass door of the side-by-side refrigerator was shattered due to physical damage at the site. The customer informed the dealer, who in turn called Thomas, demanding replacement of the item. As per the company's policy, any damage to a product should be informed to a company representative within seven working days from the date of purchase. As it was over four months, Thomas was faced with an ethical dilemma—whether to act against company policy and provide a replacement to the dealer or deny replacement of the item stating the company's policy. He had to choose between "doing the morally right thing and end up with a bad outcome" and "doing the morally wrong thing and end up with a good outcome". Looking at the bigger picture, the dealer, an exclusive partner of the company,

would not want to lose his reputation by denying a replacement to the customer. Thomas had to decide which side to choose, either the dealer or the company that trusts him. On one hand, Thomas has managed to get some personal credibility from his hard work over the years. The organization has blind trust in his decisions, but not at the cost of crossing the line and taking advantage of it. On the other hand and looking at the long term, he could not afford to lose this particular dealer. He chose to manipulate the data and changed the purchase date, and gave the product's replacement to the customer.

Discussion Question

1. Use a appropriate approach to solve the ethical dilemma of Thomas.

References

1. Ivan Penn, Peter Eavis, and James Glanz, "How PG&E Ignored Fire Risks in Favor of Profits," *New York Times*, March 18, 2019, https://www.nytimes.com/interactive/2019/03/18/business/pge-california-wildfires.html.
2. "CAL FIRE Investigators Determine Cause of the Camp Fire," CAL FIRE News Release, May 15, 2019, https://www.fire.ca.gov/media/5121/campfire_cause.pdf.
3. Penn, Eavis, and Glanz.
4. Rebecca Bowe, Lisa Pickoff-White, "Five years after deadly San Bruno Explosion: Are we safer." KQED, 08 September 2015. Available at https://www.kqed.org/news/10667274/five-years-after-deadly-san-bruno-explosion-are-we-safer.
5. Eric Nadler, PG&E diverted safety money for profit, bonuses. *SFGate*, 12 Jan 2012, Available at https://www.sfgate.com/bayarea/article/PG-E-diverted-safety-money-for-profit-bonuses-2500175.php.
6. Jaxson Van Derbeken, PG&E shorted gas-system safety, audit finds, Consumer Federation of California, 05 June, 2013. Available at https://consumercal.org/pge-shorted-gas-system-safety-audit-finds/.
7. Rebecca Smith, "PG&E's Long Record of Run-Ins With Regulators: A 'Cat and Mouse Game,'" *Wall Street Journal*, September 5, 2019, https://www.wsj.com/articles/a-cat-and-mouse-game-pg-es-long-record-of-run-ins-with-regulators-and-courts-11567707731.
8. *Erin Brockovich* Awards, IMDB, https://www.imdb.com/title/tt0195685/awards.
9. Kelly, "An Unethical Culture That Bred Death."
10. Penn, Eavis, and Glanz.
11. Smith, Record of Run-Ins With Regulators: A 'Cat and Mouse Game'."
12. Ibid.
13. "PG&E Appoints Julie M. Kane to New Position as Senior Vice President and Chief Ethics and Compliance Officer; Company Takes Next Step Toward Goal of Establishing a Best-in-Class Corporate Ethics Program," News Release, PG&E, March 24, 2015, https://www.pge.com/en/about/newsroom/newsdetails/index.page?title=20150324_pge_appoints_julie_m_kane_to_new_position_as_senior_vice_president_and_chief_ethics_and_compliance_officer_company_takes_next_step_toward_goal_of_establishing_a_best-in-class_corporate_ethics_program.
14. Petra Urbanovičová, Justina Mikulášková, Milos Čambál, and Milan Edl, "How Millennials Affect Corporate Culture," *Research Papers*, Faculty of Materials Science and Technology, Slovak University of Technology, 27 (2019): 76–83, Quotation appears on page 79. Available at https://www.researchgate.net/publication/338211994_How_Millennials_Affect_Corporate_Culture/link/5e07591392851c8364a00bfd/download.
15. Clayton M. Christensen, "What Is an Organization's Culture?" Harvard Business School Note, August 2, 2006, HBS #9-399-104, p. 1.
16. Vikas Anand, Blake E. Ashforth, and Mahendra Joshi, "Business as usual: The acceptance and perpetuation of corruption in organizations," *Academy of Management Perspectives* 18, no. 2 (May 1, 2004), https://doi.org/10.5465/ame.2004.13837437.
17. The material in these two paragraphs comes from Tom Peters, "A Brief History of the 7-S ('McKinsey 7-S') Model," *Tom Peters! Blog*, January 9, 2011, https://tompeters.com/2011/03/a-brief-history-of-the-7-s-mckinsey-7-s-model/.
18. Robert H. Waterman, Jr., Thomas J. Peters, and Julien R. Phillips, "Structure Is Not Organization," *Business Horizons* 23, no. 3 (June 1980): 14.
19. For a complete description of the 7 elements, see Weber, "A Leader's Guide to Understanding Complex Organizations: An Expanded 7S Perspective" (University of Virginia Darden School Foundation, 1998).
20. Tom Peters, "A Brief History of the 7-S ('McKinsey 7-S') Model."
21. Ibid.
22. "What we value," Microsoft, About, https://www.microsoft.com/en-us/about/values.
23. See Oracle Core Values, available at https://www.oracle.com/corporate/citizenship/values-ethics.html.
24. "Facebook's 5 Core Values," Facebook, September 8, 2015, https://www.facebook.com/media/set/?set=a.1655178611435493.1073741828.1633466236940064&type=3.
25. Susan Diehl and Monica Batsford, "Auto Industry Compliance: Will the Tone at the Top Go Tone Deaf in the Wake of Deregulation?," *Wayne State University Journal of Business Law* 2, no. 1 (2019).
26. Dana R. Hermanson, Daniel M. Ivancevich, and Susan H. Ivancevich, *Tone at the Top*. DigitalCommons@ Kennesaw State University, (2008): 40.
27. Ibid.
28. Susan Diehl and Monica Batsford.
29. Ibid., 43.
30. Stephen R. Covey, Developing True North, 08 December 2006. Available at https://crimson2810.blogspot.com/2006/12/developing-true-north-by-stephen-covey.html.

[31] John P. Kotter, *Leading Change* (Boston: Harvard Business School Press, 2012). Chapter 6 provides a detailed set of actions managers can take to effectively communicate with those they lead.

[32] Yun Li, Warren Buffett's net worth surpasses $100 billion for the first time as Berkshire shares hit record, CNBC, 11 March 2021, Available at https://www.cnbc.com/2021/03/11/warren-buffetts-net-worth-surpasses-100-billion-for-the-first-time-as-berkshire-shares-hit-record.html#:~:text=His%20fortune%20was%20estimated%20at,in%20a%20statement%20in%20July.

[33] Dealbook, Warren Buffett and the Salomon Saga, New York Times, 24 September 2008. Available at https://dealbook.nytimes.com/2008/09/24/warren-buffett-and-the-salomon-saga/.

[34] Linda Grant, Taming the Bond Buccaneers at Salomon Brothers: How Warren Buffet and friends swept up after the Salomon scandal, possible *[sic]* saving the firm from federal regulators furious after a decade of skullduggery on Wall Street, Los Angeles Times, 16 February 1992. Available at https://www.latimes.com/archives/la-xpm-1992-02-16-tm-4654-story.html.

[35] Marcel Schwantes, Warren Buffett Agrees That Having This 1 Leadership Trait Will Help You Find True Success, *Inc. Magazine*, no date. Available at https://www.inc.com/marcel-schwantes/warren-buffett-agrees-that-only-1-leadership-trait-among-many-will-find-true-success.html.

CHAPTER 7

Ethics in a Global Society and Economy

LEARNING OUTCOMES

After reading this chapter, you should be able to do the following:

1. Explain why ethical principles differ across countries and regions.

2. Identify cultural, administrative, governmental, and economic sources of global ethical differences.

3. Describe common ethical challenges global businesses face in different parts of their value chains.

4. Differentiate between effective and ineffective behaviors of ethical leaders in a global setting.

5. Apply the concepts you've learned in this chapter to real-world ethical challenges.

Opening Case | Global Engagement at Nike

Nike has always been a global company. The company began in 1962 when founder Phil Knight convinced executives of the Onitsuka shoe company to allow him to sell its Tiger brand in the Western United States.[1] The company proudly notes on its website that it produces its finished goods in 486 factories in 39 countries, paying almost 1.1 million people to produce its products.[2] It sells its products in 170 countries, using either traditional retailers or its own stores. The company is committed to giving back to its communities in a unique way: encouraging sports among youth and adults, particularly young women.

During 2019, the company was active across the world. In China, its Boundless Girls program worked with 10 schools in Beijing and Shanghai to reimagine sports for girls through a unique curriculum, expert speakers, and targeted products. Nike's Made to Play fund brought 17 young women from South Africa to London for advanced leadership training. In Tokyo, Nike's support of Jump-Jam helped provide trained staff to encourage play for 2,450 young women. Since 2004, the company has donated $200 million through its Girl Effect program (see Figure 7.1) to help young women around the world more successfully navigate adolescence and make good choices about health, education, and career.[3]

In its 2019 report, Nike President and CEO John Donahue noted that he had only been on the job for two months and he was surprised at the impact Nike had on the countries in which it operates. Like many companies, Nike has generated such impact

© girleffect.org with Nike

GIRLS ARE THE MOST POWERFUL FORCE FOR CHANGE ON THE PLANET. WELCOME TO THE GIRL EFFECT.

EXPLORE. DISCOVER. TAKE WHAT YOU NEED...

FIGURE 7.1 The Nike Foundation is making global change possible at girleffect.org.

in multifaceted ways and not always positively. He noted that Nike had set goals to convert to 100 percent renewable energy in its facilities by 2025, improve pay equity between women and men around the world, increase the diversity of its workforce, and continue its philanthropic efforts to promote sports and physical activity. Leading an organization to become a more ethical global citizen would certainly capture more of Donahue's attention as the years went by.

In spite of its efforts to improve the societies in which it operates, Nike has come under severe criticism for some of its global practices. In 2020, a Nike supplier facility in China faced accusations that it employed Uyghur Muslims in conditions of "highly disturbing coercive labor practices."[4] In the United States, when Olympian Alysia Montano became pregnant, Nike threatened to drop her sponsorship contract. After a public outcry, the company announced a new maternity policy for female athletes.[5] The company's location choices in Bermuda, Delaware, the Netherlands, Taiwan, Hong Kong, and Singapore are all considered at a high risk for corporate tax avoidance. Finally, Nike received Ethical Consumer Research Organization's (ERCA)—a global activist organization—worst rating for its use of cotton; the company used some organic cotton but has not committed to sourcing cotton that avoids pesticide and herbicide pollution.[6]

The company follows a tried-and-true formula as it locates/establishes its plants abroad; it chooses countries based on the swoosh index: "When choosing factory sites, Nike looks for cheap labor. However, it also picks countries with stable—usually authoritarian—leadership, decent infrastructure, a pro-business government, and a liberal trade regime."[7] Nike pulls out of countries as wages rise and it moves to the next tier of low-wage countries. Those countries are better off to the extent that they have diversified their manufacturing base, but if they have relied solely on Nike, the gains are fleeting.

The challenges Nike faces are not unique to the apparel business; any company that operates in multiple countries faces a host of business challenges, and some of these involve serious ethical issues. We presume that a part of your business education includes a course on international business, and we won't try to duplicate that education here. What we will do, however, is use some common frameworks for thinking about international business to highlight the ethical and moral challenges companies and their leaders face. When most people think of ethical challenges in global business, they often think of bribery and corruption as the main challenges. The ethical issues of bribery and corruption are important enough that we've dedicated an entire chapter (10) to them in the applications section of our book. In this chapter, we'll focus on the drivers of differences in ethical principles and practices around the world, we'll discuss ethical challenges every company faces along its value chain, and we'll outline the skills leaders need to operate in an ethical manner across the globe. We'll begin by considering the roots of ethical differences between cultures and countries.

Differences in Global Ethical Norms

All humans share a common biology and capacity for reason, everyone hopes to be individually happy, and all desire to live in a moral or good society. Our common humanity means that most people believe in a similar set of virtues; indeed, you saw that Aristotle (a leading philosopher in the Western tradition) and Confucius (an equally important philosopher in the Eastern tradition) wrote about many of the same aspects of moral formation and practices. Most of us agree that things like a commitment to truth, justice, human dignity and moral obligations are important elements of an ethical life.

Thick and Thin Ethical Principles

Those common virtues may stem from our common humanity; however, when we get down to defining what those concepts actually mean, we find dramatic differences across the globe. Moral philosopher Michael Walzer refers to this as the difference between thick and thin moral systems.[8] Thin systems include abstract concepts such as justice, freedom, happiness, and obligation. Thick systems are what justice, freedom, happiness, and obligation mean to a group of people trying to implement those virtues. For example, whether justice means a distribution based on equality (giving the same to everyone) or equity (giving more to some based on need or merit) differs across cultures. The ordering of ethical virtues within a society also differs. Western cultures, such as the United States, place a high priority on human freedom and autonomy, while cultures that draw on the Confucian tradition place a higher priority on our obligations to families. Figure 7.2 gets at the differences between cultures in things as simple as body language and movements, but these often have moral connotations. In Europe, for example, hugging and kissing are common greetings, but in other countries those types of greetings among strangers could be construed as unethical sexual advances.

As philosopher John Rawls noted, we live in a globally pluralistic world, one with competing, and sometimes even mutually exclusive, conceptions of what is morally right, and people often use contracts as a way to live and work together when they have different values.[9] Business ethics scholars Tom Donaldson and Tom Dunfee use the idea of ethics as a social

Eye contact
- In most Western cultures, eye contact shows that you are being attentive and sincere.
- Constant eye contact in Japan can make others feel awkward.

Physical Contact
- Physical touch varies in different cultures. Some countries where it can be considered rude to touch others include: Japan, New Zealand, Portugal, and Scandinavia.
- It's generally okay to touch in: Turkey, France, Italy, Greece, and Spain.

Arm Gestures
- In Italy and Spain, making grand gestures with the arms and hands while speaking is completely normal.
- Don't cross your arms in Finland though, where it is considered extremely offensive and arrogant.

Proximity
- In China, it's common for people to stand very close to each other.
- Americans are accustomed to a lot of physical space.
- Latin American cultures are very tactile and affectionate, so they stand closer to one another.

Head Movement
- Be careful in Iran, Syria, and Egypt, where a single nod of the head means "no."
- In India, a side-to-side head tilt is an affirmative gesture.

Lips
- Kisses are a normal way to say "hello" or "goodbye" to a loved one in Belgium and Switzerland.
- In some Asian cultures, these gestures are considered more intimate and private.
- In Filipino culture, the lips are used to point toward something!

Posture
- Bad posture is a sign of disrespect in Japan and Taiwan.
- In the US, slouching can indicate tiredness or vulnerability.

FIGURE 7.2 Even simple things differ around the world.

contract to help us understand how ethical norms and virtues are common and differ around the world. People share ethical **hypernorms**, which are a set of general moral principles that people across cultures all accept as legitimate and binding.[10] Hypernorms "[reach] to the root of what is ethical for humanity, precepts [that . . .] should be discernible in a convergence of religious, political, and philosophical thought" across countries and cultures.[11] **Figure 7.3** displays a set of hypernorms, the Universal Declaration on Human Rights, developed and adopted by the members of the United Nations in 1948.

The general nature of hypernorms creates **moral free space**, or the room to create localized, specific norms of behavior that fit both the economic context of a society and its religious, political, ethnic, and cultural heritage. Hypernorms represent a macro-social contract; localized norms at the level of countries and states can be thought of as meso-social contracts. Norms that apply to particular communities, such as an ethnic enclave or specialized industry, would represent micro-social contracts between these groups of people.[12]

Moral Relativism and Moral Imperialism

The fact that ethical norms differ from country to country creates two problems for business leaders engaging in economic transactions around the world. The first problem is **moral relativism**. Rawls, Walzer, and Donaldson and Dunfee would all agree that we live in a pluralistic world, one where there is substantial variation among thick, localized moral norms, but there exists a common set of hypernorms, or thin universal values. Moral relativism accepts the existence of thick, localized norms, but denies the existence of thin hypernorms. Moral relativism has two variations. **Cultural relativism** holds that no culture's ethical norms are better (more correct, more universal) than those of any other culture.[14] **Extreme relativism** argues that each individual builds his or her moral code from his or her own perspective, and no one's perspective is inherently better than another's.[15]

THE UNIVERSAL DECLARATION OF
HUMAN RIGHTS

Adopted by the General Assembly of the United Nations in 1948, the Universal Declaration states fundamental rights and freedoms to which all human beings are entitled.

You have the responsibility to respect the rights of others.

We are all born free and equal.
Everyone is entitled to these rights no matter your race, religion, sex, language, or nationality.
Everyone has the right to life, freedom, and safety.

No one can take away any of your rights.

No one has the right to hold you in slavery.

No one has the right to torture you.

You have a right to be recognized everywhere as a person before the law.

We are all equal before the law and are entitled to equal protection of the law.

You have the right to seek legal help if your rights are violated.

No one has the right to wrongly imprison you or force you to leave your country.

You have a right to a fair, public trial.

Everyone is innocent until proven guilty.

You have the right to privacy. No one can interfere with your reputation, family, home, or correspondence.

You have the right to travel.

You have the right to seek asylum in another country if you are persecuted in your own.

Everyone has the right to a nationality.

All consenting adults have the right to marry and to raise a family.

You have the right to own property.

Everyone has the right to belong to a religion.

You have the right to think and voice your opinions freely.

Everyone has the right to gather as a peaceful assembly.

You have the right to participate in the governance of your country, either directly or by helping to choose representatives in free and genuine elections.

You have the right to social security and are entitled to economic, social, and cultural help from your government.

Every adult has the right to a job, a fair wage, and membership in a trade union.

You have the right to leisure and rest from work.

Everyone has the right to an adequate standard of living for themselves and their family.

Everyone has the right to an education.

Everyone has the right to freely participate in the culture and scientific advancement of their community, and their intellectual property as artist or scientist should be protected.

We are all entitled to a social order in which we may enjoy these rights.

Everyone's rights and freedoms should be protected unless they obstruct the rights and freedoms of others. FREEDOM

No State, group, or person can use this Declaration to deny the rights and freedoms of others.

This is a simplified version of the UDHR. For the complete text, visit www.un.org

Source: Adapted from The Universal Declaration of Human Rights, Facing History, https://www.facinghistory.org/holocaust-and-human-behavior/chapter-11/universal-declaration-human-rights.

FIGURE 7.3 The Universal Declaration of Human Rights.[13]

A business leader who accepts cultural relativism would live by the maxim "When in Rome, do as the Romans do." These leaders would see global ethics policies and rules as counterproductive, as likely to be wrong as right, and almost sure to offend some element of a local culture. A leader who adopts extreme relativism lives by the maxim, "When in doubt, do what I think is best in this situation." The problem with this view is that what seems best is often (1) the most *convenient* or easiest solution that avoids conflict or (2) what is *personally* the best (read "most profitable") for the individual making the decision. Extreme relativism is a cover for blatant unethical behavior under the guise that it fits the situation.

A mirror image of ethical relativism is the problematic practice of moral imperialism, or the belief that the moral system of one's culture of origin is superior to all other moral systems. Moral imperialism builds on the idea of moral universalism, that there is a single set of ethical principles and virtues that are binding for all people.[16] There are hypernorms that are legitimate, and those happen to be the same as the local norms of the home country. Other ethical norms are considered illegitimate and inferior. Moral imperialists do more than just believe that their moral system is superior; they seek to impose their moral code on other cultures, either through coercive means or withering criticism of elements of other moral codes.[17] Moral imperialists deny the legitimacy of a pluralistic moral world and, in so doing, act on a distorted sense of social justice and moral right. Moral imperialism builds from, and in turn reinforces, stereotyped notions of other cultures and their commitments and practices. Moral imperialism is a close cousin to racism, sexism, or any other type of "ism" that puts one group over another.

The business leader who practices moral imperialism works on the premise of "my way or the highway." This mindset leads to strict rules of behavior and conduct that are developed in the home country and exported into the host country. The fundamental objective, in relation to host country partners, is a form of moral colonialism, and the moral imperialist becomes aloof in relation to local business partners and will not seek feedback on ethical, or usually even cultural, norms and practices. Imperialists are frustrated that others adopt different principles and practices and they often express contempt toward those with whom they work.

Understanding Global Ethics: The CAGE Framework

In the previous section, we described the differences between thin, global hypernorms and the thick localized norms that guide people in their day-to-day moral decision making. In this section, we focus on the root causes of why those thick, localized norms differ from country to country. To do so, we use the CAGE Model developed by Harvard Business School professor Pankaj Ghemawat.[18] CAGE is an acronym for four major areas of cultural differences: cultural, administrative (usually governmental and political), geographic, and economic bases of difference across countries.

Cultural Influences

Anyone who has traveled very far from home, even as little as a couple hundred miles, knows that culture is a very local thing. Culture, in a global context, is "the collective programming of the mind that distinguishes the members of one group or category of people from others."[19] Culture arises as people adopt a set of rules that allow them to live and work together in peace and builds on a foundation of traditional values and practices, religious doctrines and teachings, and the set of unique historical conditions that give groups a *Weltanschauung*, or world view. In the latter part of the twentieth century, IBM employee and professor of organizational behavior Geert Hofstede found that employees felt differently about IBM, but that employees from the same countries had remarkably similar views.

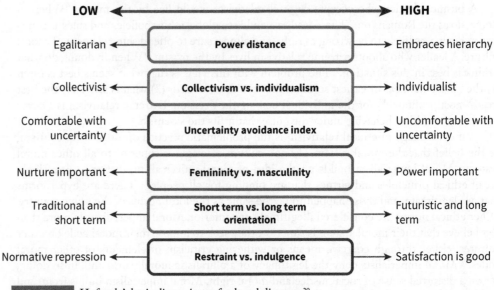

FIGURE 7.4 Hofstede's basic dimensions of cultural distance.[20]

He identified six dimensions that defined the cultural differences between countries. Figure 7.4 displays these six dimensions.

Each of these dimensions has implications for ethical decision making. Cultures that differ on power distance, for example, will likely have vastly varying views about the ethical obligations of those in power, such as what constitutes an abuse of power. They will also differ on the ethical responsibilities of people in responding to those in power; the moral worth of "speaking truth to power" will differ across cultures. We'll leave it to you to think about the moral implications of the other dimensions.

Administrative Differences

The administrative aspect of the CAGE model covers items such as the type of government, legal frameworks, institutional strength, and the degree of formality versus informality in economic activities. Governments may be democratic, authoritarian, or a mix of the two types. Legal systems may build on common law or statutory foundations.[21] Institutions such as education, healthcare, social services, and a civil society sector may be well developed and sophisticated or rudimentary. Most developed countries have very formal economies (legally registered businesses, a well-developed and transparent financial system, and an advanced regulatory apparatus), while much of the emerging and developing world relies on the informal economy ("off-the-books" businesses, cash or barter transactions, and/or sporadic regulatory interventions).[22] Figure 7.5 details one outcome of administrative difference—the perceived level of corruption—in countries around the world.

Corruption represents the most obvious ethical implication of administrative structure; however, it is not the only one. States with highly elaborated legal and regulatory systems have, to a large extent, replaced ethical norms with laws and statutes. Obedience to the enforceable replaces obedience to the unenforceable. In countries that lack many formal institutions in areas such as education, healthcare, or financial services, thick, localized norms will play a larger role in determining what is right and wrong.

Geographic Influences

The range of economic activity in a country depends in no small measure on the types of natural resources available to people. For example, countries with large tracts of arable

CORRUPTION PERCEPTIONS INDEX 2020

The perceived levels of public sector corruption in 180 countries/territories around the world.

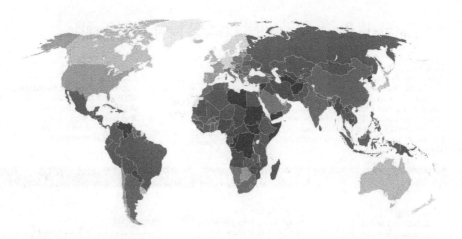

SCORE	COUNTRY/TERRITORY	RANK
88	Denmark	1
88	New Zealand	1
85	Finland	3
85	Singapore	3
85	Sweden	3
85	Switzerland	3
84	Norway	7
82	Netherlands	8
80	Germany	9
80	Luxembourg	9
77	Australia	11
77	Canada	11
77	Hong Kong	11
77	United Kingdom	11
76	Austria	15
76	Belgium	15
75	Estonia	17
75	Iceland	17
74	Japan	19
72	Ireland	20
71	United Arab Emirates	21
71	Uruguay	21
69	France	23
68	Bhutan	24
67	Chile	25
67	United States of America	25
66	Seychelles	27
65	Taiwan	28
64	Barbados	29
63	Bahamas	30
63	Qatar	30
62	Spain	32
61	Korea, South	33
61	Portugal	33
60	Botswana	35
60	Brunei Darussalam	35
60	Israel	35
60	Lithuania	35
60	Slovenia	35
59	Saint Vincent and the Grenadines	40
58	Cabo Verde	41
57	Costa Rica	42
57	Cyprus	42
57	Latvia	42
56	Georgia	45
56	Poland	45
56	Saint Lucia	45
55	Dominica	48
54	Czechia	49
54	Oman	49
54	Rwanda	49
53	Grenada	52
53	Italy	52
53	Malta	52
53	Mauritius	52
53	Saudi Arabia	52
51	Malaysia	57
51	Namibia	57
50	Greece	59
49	Armenia	60
49	Jordan	60
49	Slovakia	60
47	Belarus	63
47	Croatia	63
47	Cuba	63
47	Sao Tome and Principe	63
45	Montenegro	67
45	Senegal	67
44	Bulgaria	69
44	Hungary	69
44	Jamaica	69
44	Romania	69
44	South Africa	69
44	Tunisia	69
43	Ghana	75
43	Maldives	75
43	Vanuatu	75
42	Argentina	78
42	Bahrain	78
42	China	78
42	Kuwait	78
42	Solomon Islands	78
41	Benin	83
41	Guyana	83
41	Lesotho	83
40	Burkina Faso	86
40	India	86
40	Morocco	86
40	Timor-Leste	86
40	Trinidad and Tobago	86
40	Turkey	86
39	Colombia	92
39	Ecuador	92
38	Brazil	94
38	Ethiopia	94
38	Kazakhstan	94
38	Peru	94
38	Serbia	94
38	Sri Lanka	94
38	Suriname	94
38	Tanzania	94
37	Gambia	102
37	Indonesia	102
36	Albania	104
36	Algeria	104
36	Cote d'Ivoire	104
36	El Salvador	104
36	Kosovo	104
36	Thailand	104
36	Vietnam	104
35	Bosnia and Herzegovina	111
35	Mongolia	111
35	North Macedonia	111
35	Panama	111
34	Moldova	115
34	Philippines	115
33	Egypt	117
33	Eswatini	117
33	Nepal	117
33	Sierra Leone	117
33	Ukraine	117
33	Zambia	117
32	Niger	123
31	Bolivia	124
31	Kenya	124
31	Kyrgyzstan	124
31	Mexico	124
31	Pakistan	124
30	Azerbaijan	129
30	Gabon	129
30	Malawi	129
30	Mali	129
30	Russia	129
29	Laos	134
29	Mauritania	134
29	Togo	134
28	Dominican Republic	137
28	Guinea	137
28	Liberia	137
28	Myanmar	137
28	Paraguay	137
27	Angola	142
27	Djibouti	142
27	Papua New Guinea	142
27	Uganda	142
26	Bangladesh	146
26	Central African Republic	146
26	Uzbekistan	146
25	Cameroon	149
25	Guatemala	149
25	Iran	149
25	Lebanon	149
25	Madagascar	149
25	Mozambique	149
25	Nigeria	149
25	Tajikistan	149
24	Honduras	157
24	Zimbabwe	157
22	Nicaragua	159
21	Cambodia	160
21	Chad	160
21	Comoros	160
21	Eritrea	160
21	Iraq	160
19	Afghanistan	165
19	Burundi	165
19	Congo	165
19	Guinea Bissau	165
19	Turkmenistan	165
18	Democratic Republic of the Congo	170
18	Haiti	170
18	Korea, North	170
17	Libya	173
16	Equatorial Guinea	174
16	Sudan	174
15	Venezuela	176
15	Yemen	176
14	Syria	178
12	Somalia	179
12	South Sudan	179

SCORE

Highly Corrupt — Very Clean

0-9   10-19   20-29   30-39   40-49   50-59   60-69   70-79   80-89   90-100   No data

#cpi2020
www.transparency.org/cpi

This work from Transparency International (2020) is licensed under CC BY-ND 4.0

FIGURE 7.5 The Global Corruption Perceptions Index 2020.[23]

land might have robust agricultural sectors, where ethical norms build from traditional elements of an agrarian economy and are more likely to be "conservative" in the sense that preserving time-honored traditions is more important than social change. Given that many indigenous groups lack representation in political affairs, the United Nations developed a declaration of rights for these groups. **Figure 7.6** shows a timeline of the development of this declaration.

A major impact of geography on ethics has to do with the ease of transportation across regions or a country in general. When transportation is difficult and people interact mainly with like others, thick norms tend to be more rigid and traditional. Outsiders can easily violate ethical norms, often without knowing it. When people can travel easily and interact with others, or as more people move to cities, the social group becomes more heterogeneous in its ethnic and religious makeup. That heterogeneity and exposure to differences naturally broaden ethical frameworks. Diversity tends to "thin out" the thick values of each enclave.[24] Outsiders more easily adapt to and live within these broader notions of right and wrong.

Timeline of UN Declaration on the Rights of Indigenous Peoples

AUGUST 18, 1971
José Ricardo Martínez Cobo is appointed as Special Rapporteur of the Study of the Problem of Discrimination against Indigenous Populations. The Cobo Report is presented to the Sub-Commission on the Prevention of Discrimination and the Protection of Minorities (Sub-Commission) during its 1981–1983 sessions.

JULY 1993
WGIP agrees on a final text for the draft Declaration and submits it to the Sub-Commission.

AUGUST 26, 1994
Sub-Commission Resolution 45/1994 approves the draft text without a vote and passes it on to the Commission on Human Rights (Commission).

NOVEMBER 20–DECEMBER 1, 1995
A joint Indigenous People' Caucus Statement calls for the immediate adoption of the Declaration as submitted by the Sub-Commission without change, amendment, or deletion. Only three governments indicate willingness to accept the text without changes.

BEGINNINGS | **DRAFTING & DEBATING PHASE**

MAY 7, 1982
Sub-Commission establishes an annual Working Group on Indigenous Populations (WGIP) to take up work related to the Cobo Report.

AUGUST 27, 1985
WGIP formalizes production of a Draft Declaration on the Rights of Indigenous Peoples to fulfill the second aspect of its mandate "to give attention to the evolution of international standards concerning Indigenous rights."

MARCH 3, 1995
Commission Resolution 32/1995 establishes a Working Group of the Commission on Human Rights to elaborate a draft declaration (Working Group). The text is to be considered for adoption by the General Assembly within the International Decade of the World's Indigenous People (1995–2004).

NOVEMBER 1997
Article 5 (Every Indigenous individual has the right to a nationality) and Article 43 (All rights are equally guaranteed to male and female Indigenous individuals) are provisionally adopted by the Working Group.

NOVEMBER 20–DECEMBER 1, 2000
The Inuit Circumpolar Conference and Saami Council deliver and lobby a joint statement indicating a willingness to consider changes in the Sub-Commission text if such amendments strengthen or clarify the text and conform to international legal standards. Guatemala and Mexico adopt a no-change position. With "no-change" groups in both government and Indigenous Peoples' camps, any progress in the negotiations is effectively blocked.

NOVEMBER 29–DECEMBER 3, 2004
Norway proposes that Guatemala and Mexico take over Norway's responsibilities to facilitate consensus on proposed text amendments, forcing the two delegations to seek consensus.

NOVEMBER 28, 2006–SEPTEMBER 13, 2007
At the General Assembly's 61st session Namibia, acting on behalf of the African Group, tabled a proposal to postpone consideration of the Declaration to allow time for 'further consultations' essentially blocking its adoption. The main issue of self-determination was at the core of this move. Indigenous Peoples, led by their Global Steering Committee, and supportive governments, led by Guatemala, Mexico, and Peru, collaborated throughout the year, continuously lobbying to overcome some governments' efforts to derail the Declaration.

APPROVAL PERIOD | **IMPLEMENTATION**

SEPTEMBER 13–24, 2004
Representatives of New Zealand, on behalf of Denmark, Finland, Iceland, New Zealand, Norway, Sweden, and Switzerland submit a comprehensive package of proposed changes to the Sub-Commission text. The majority of proposed changes are included in the text adopted by the General Assembly in September 2007.

DECEMBER 5–16, 2005 AND JANUARY 30–FEBRUARY 3, 2006
The Working Group ends its 11th and final session with 16 preambular paragraphs and 21 articles ready for adoption. Fundamental issues such as self-determination, lands and resources, the nature of collective rights, third party rights, and the rights of all other citizens still lack consensus.

SEPTEMBER 13, 2007
The Declaration is finally adopted by the General Assembly with a majority of 143 states in favor, 4 votes against (Australia, Canada, New Zealand, and the United States), and 11 abstentions.

Source: Taken from "Celebrating 13 Years of the UN Declaration on the Rights of Indigenous Peoples," Retrieved from: https://www.culturalsurvival.org/news/celebrating-13-years-un-declaration-rights-indigenous-peoples.

FIGURE 7.6 The UN declaration on indigenous peoples.[25]

Economic Factors

The type, nature, and configuration of the economic system influence the ethical frameworks different societies use. The broadest distinction would be between market- and non-market-based economies, but each major classification can be subdivided. Non-market economies range from the household economy, where a small group produces for its own needs, to large planned, state-owned property systems.[26] Market economies also come in several varieties, from pure laissez faire entrepreneurial economies through markets dominated by large firms,

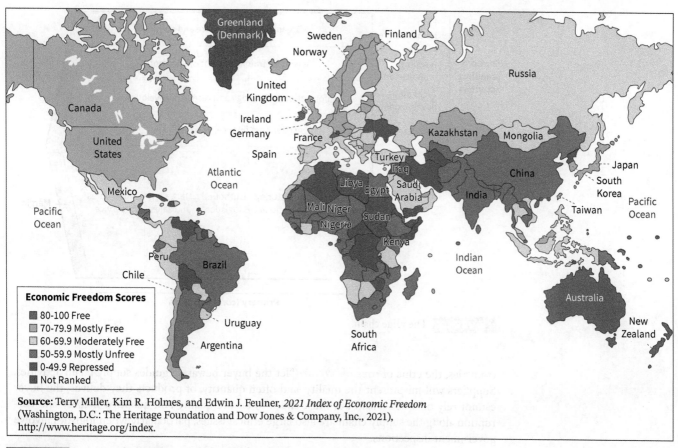

Source: Terry Miller, Kim R. Holmes, and Edwin J. Feulner, *2021 Index of Economic Freedom* (Washington, D.C.: The Heritage Foundation and Dow Jones & Company, Inc., 2021), http://www.heritage.org/index.

FIGURE 7.7   How countries differ in economic freedom.[28]

to state-directed, oligopolistic markets.[27] **Figure 7.7** breaks the world down in terms of market versus non-market economic systems.

Some impacts of an economic system on the moral frameworks of a society are easy to see. Market-based, capitalist economies see hard work, risk-taking, and individual initiative as virtues; however, many in such economies also see virtue in consumption of material goods, the accumulation of wealth, and the promotion of self-interest.[29] Non-market systems might allow people to elevate loyalty, self-sacrifice, and devotion to the larger social group as a virtue. These economies can create an ethic where obedience and subservience to the interests of the ruling group—family or state—become the sole measure of moral virtue. Market economies run the moral risk of overemphasizing individual satisfaction, and non-market economies run the risk of under-emphasizing individual achievement.[30]

Ethical Challenges Along the Value Chain

The last section helped you understand the drivers of ethical differences between countries. We focused on inputs and causes. In this section, we'll focus on the results, or outcomes, of differing ethical systems and frameworks. We'll employ a tool from the field of strategy, the value chain, to frame this discussion. The value chain, developed by strategy guru Michael Porter in the 1980s, offers a way to categorize the functional activities of a business. **Figure 7.8** presents the value chain,[31] and we'll consider the challenges for each segment.

Logistics (inbound, outbound). These categories capture the supply chain of the firm, how it gets supplies in and products out to market. Several ethical issues appear here. First, standards and representations of product quality are an ethical challenge. In many

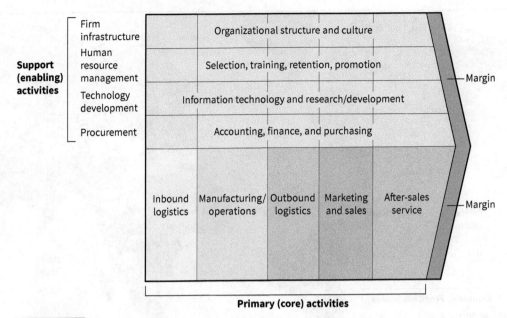

FIGURE 7.8 The value chain.

countries, the ethic of *caveat emptor* ("let the buyer beware") guides supply chain activities. Suppliers will mispresent the quality, and often quantity, of products they deliver; the buyer cannot rely on what is said but must check to ensure quality and quantity. Bribery and corruption along the supply chain are also large ethical issues, particularly when logistics involve government inspections.

Manufacturing/operations. This is the element of the value chain where transformation occurs, or where services are actually delivered. Manufacturing and operations raise two ethical concerns: environmental sustainability and worker safety. Care for the natural environment is as much an ethical obligation as a legal requirement. Many countries have laws against pollution or environmental exploitation, but enforcement is weak or nonexistent. Local ethical practices often do not sanction pollution or other environmental abuse in the name of fostering employment. Worker safety issues are very similar. Communities may prefer more jobs over safer jobs. If safety equipment reduces employment, and workers must take care for their own safety, then workers typically won't report safety violations.

Marketing. This includes not only traditional marketing of advertising and branding but also sales. The major ethical issue here is the risk of deceptive claims about products or services and dishonesty in the sales process. Many countries have no formal rules to ensure truth in advertising of the listing of product ingredients. Advertising representatives or salespeople in some markets will often misrepresent product features, functionality, and benefits as they reach for a sale. Delivery dates may have no correspondence to reality, and prices charged often depend on perceptions of the gullibility or wealth of the buyer. As with issues along the supply chain, *caveat emptor* is the operative ethical norm. Ethics in the Real World 7.1 highlights the problem of pricing products in different international markets.

Ethics in the Real World 7.1 | Canada Cracks Down on "Drip Pricing"

In its effort to protect its citizens against false price advertising, the Canadian Competition Bureau goes after companies that engage in the questionable practice of "drip pricing." Drip pricing occurs when a company advertises a product or service for a certain price, but then adds fees and surcharges—each charge "drips on" to the

advertised price—so that customers never pay the advertised price.[32] There are several industries where "drip pricing" is common:

- Delivery or "convenience fees" on tickets to entertainment and sports events

- Cleaning charges or local taxes on hotel rooms
- Insurance and fuel surcharges on rental cars
- Title insurance and other mortgage-related fees
- ATM withdrawal and other banking fees
- Baggage charges for airlines

In the United States, it is common practice in many industries to list a base price and then add on taxes and other fees. In Canada, the practice is not only unethical, but also illegal. Canadian regulators have gone after, and fined, every major rental car company in Canada for the practice, and in 2019, the Competition Bureau fined U.S. company Ticketmaster $4.5 million for drip pricing on its tickets to Canadian events.[33]

After-sales Service and Warranty. This important element of the value chain captures what happens after the sale and the customer has problems. The ethical challenge here is around promise making and promise keeping. Warranty terms may be overly restrictive or extremely vague; the former case dismisses most claims as out of warranty, while the latter claim gives sellers opportunities to limit what they seemed to have promised to do. Sellers may guarantee product performance, but a culture that values saving face may keep customers from invoking product guarantees and actually returning products. Other cultures that encourage shaming may encourage customers to raise every complaint and result in higher levels of after-sales support and warranty issues.

Firm Infrastructure and Culture. This element spans each of the functional areas of the firm and covers issues of formal organizational and management structure and the informal element of culture. The key ethical challenges in this area are racism, sexism, discrimination, and harassment. Organizational structures, such as span of control and reporting requirements, may make discrimination and harassment (especially sexual harassment) both easy and give them the appearance, or the reality, of organizational approval. Managers can often use formal authority to justify excluding minority groups from participating in decision making. Informal cultures often perpetuate the day-to-day harassment and oppression of women, ethnic minorities, or people with disabilities.

Human Resources (HR). This is the function of hiring, training, retaining, and compensating the firm's human capital. The biggest issue in HR is often not discrimination or harassment, but worker exploitation around working hours and wages. In pursuit of employment, many people around the world work for whatever wages they can get, and far too many employers feel no obligation to pay workers living, or even subsistence, wages. Figure 7.9 shows wage levels around the world that will help lift adults and their children out of poverty. Note that several countries have no minimum wage and well over one-half of the world's population live in countries with wages that will not lift people out of poverty. You should also remember that in many countries with adequate minimum wage laws, enforcement of those laws is spotty at best.

Information Technology (IT) and Research and Development. We combine these two functions because they both build on the firm's technology base. There are a number of ethical issues here, but three stand out. The first is cyber security around individual data and privacy and how employers use that data. Unethical employers can easily misuse the personal data of their employees and customers. The second is the use of IT systems for questionable surveillance of employee activities. The third is the theft of intellectual property and the lack of attention to patents, copyrights, and trademarks in the research and development process.

Accounting and Finance. These two functions help external investors and internal managers understand the business performance and value of a firm. We'll highlight two ethical challenges in this area. The first is "cooking the books," or engaging in accounting fraud and misrepresentation. Although the International Accounting Standards Board (IASB) has global accounting standards, ethical norms in many countries support the practice of "broadly interpreting" these standards to put their business in its best possible light, or better. The second challenge is operating "off the books." Informal activity may be done to evade taxes, or to engage in illicit transactions such as selling illegal products or selling legal products to prohibited customers, such as a country under international sanctions.

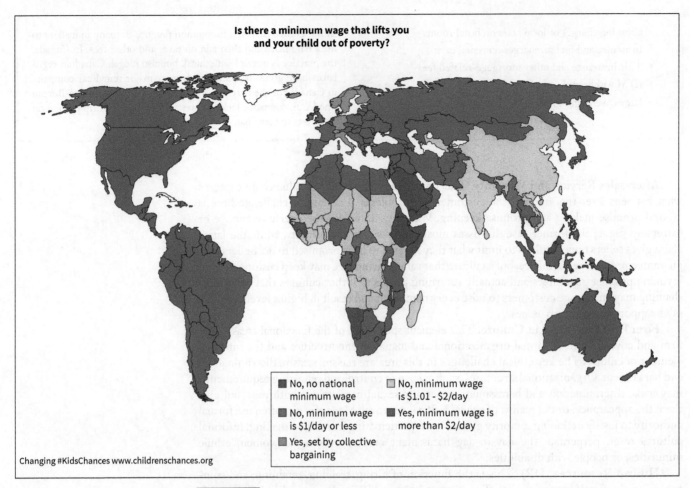

Is there a minimum wage that lifts you and your child out of poverty?

- ■ No, no national minimum wage
- ■ No, minimum wage is $1/day or less
- ■ Yes, set by collective bargaining
- ▨ No, minimum wage is $1.01 - $2/day
- ■ Yes, minimum wage is more than $2/day

Changing #KidsChances www.childrenschances.org

FIGURE 7.9 Minimum wage levels around the globe.[34]

Ethical Leadership in a Global Setting

This chapter has provided you with a framework to think about how ethical commitments and practices differ across cultures, thick localized norms, and thin hypernorms. You should have a better grasp of where those ethical differences come from, the elements of the CAGE model, and how they affect business practices, e.g., via the lens of the value chain. We conclude this chapter by providing you with seven things you can do to prepare to live an ethical life while working abroad:

1. *Be deeply grounded in the ethical principles of your home country.* Your commitment to ethics must be more than just "It's what I've always done." Understand how your own culture, administrative architecture, geography, and economic system ground your ethical principles. You must know why you consider certain practices to be ethical and what defines a good life for you. Knowing why provides a solid foundation from which to view other perspectives.

2. *Articulate which ethical principles are most important to you, and how you rank them.* Be clear about your "universal truths" and inviolate ethical principles and which ones grow out of the culture in which you grew up. Having a clear sense of what is right and wrong for you helps you overcome the challenge of moral relativism and the moral temptation to bend your own moral lines based on what is common practice in different areas of the world.

3. *Understand the principles, policies, and rules of your own organization.* Good companies will have well-articulated principles and guidelines that govern how business is done in other countries. If your company has an informal policy of "Just do the right thing," be careful. Seek clarification from managers and others who have worked in the country. Is the right thing conformance to home or host country ethical norms? Realize that even the best policies are not ironclad and there will be situations that (1) aren't covered or (2) may justify an exception. Know whom you can talk to when these situations arise.

4. Adopt the following principle as a guide to action: *In essentials, unity, in doubtful matters liberty, in all things, charity.* The source of this saying is unknown,[35] but this attitude helps you remain true to your own principles and the thin hypernorms you share with others. When localized, thick norms differ from yours, the principle is liberty or tolerance. In every situation, we should show kindness and respect to others. This moral maxim helps you avoid the challenge of moral imperialism.

5. *Learn to listen to understand before you speak to be understood.* In matters of differing views of morality, we are often too quick to listen to differing views while we are preparing a defense of our own. This practice is an invitation to misunderstand others. There are two important remedies. First, make sure that you understand the words and phrases the other person is using to explain their moral commitments. Words have different meanings across contexts. Second, seek to learn about the configuration of the elements of the CAGE model that contributed to the ethical system of the person with whom you are talking. You will know more, and you may help those you are interacting with to learn about the history and source of their own commitments.

6. *Trust, but verify.* This phrase became popular when Ronald Reagan was president of the United States.[36] The practice guided his dealings with what was then the Soviet Union. "Trust" suggests acting with goodwill toward those with whom we are interacting. "But verify" is a reminder to make sure that we learn about local ethical customs from multiple sources. It is not uncommon for the person across the table to persuade you to believe that he or she is acting in an ethical manner. Ask others that you trust, don't just take someone's word for it.

7. *Travel abroad whenever you can.* Mark Twain once said that "Travel is fatal to prejudice, bigotry, and narrow-mindedness, and many of our people need it sorely on these accounts. Broad, wholesome, charitable views of men [*sic*] and things cannot be acquired by vegetating in one little corner of the earth all one's lifetime."[37] We know that travel is expensive, in both money and time. We are well aware that travel, particularly foreign travel, raises many legitimate concerns, but also many unfounded fears. Foreign travel will help you in your quest to live an ethical life in two ways: First, by experiencing different ethical systems around the world, you'll become clearer about both what you hold dear and why you hold it that way. Second, travel enables you to experience many elements of PERMA: deep satisfaction at seeing new and different things, engagement as you stretch your skills and knowledge, the opportunity to create new and lasting relationships, a greater sense of your personal purpose and contribution in life, and the ability to overcome the fears and self-doubt that keep many of us from traveling.

Key Terms

administrative	culture	moral free space
CAGE Model	economic	moral relativism
caveat emptor	extreme relativism	moral imperialism
cultural	geographic	thick systems
cultural relativism	hypernorms	thin systems

Chapter Summary

- This chapter discussed ethics in a global environment. Ethical norms differ between countries because of the "thick" elements of a nation's ethnic diversity, unique history, and traditions about what is ethically right and good. While there are many localized ethical norms, there are a series of "hypernorms" that all cultures seem to accept.

- Differences in ethical principles can be traced back to, and sustained by, four different factors: cultural supports, administrative (political) structures and practices, geographic realities, and economic systems. It's helpful to think of culture in the six dimensions proposed by Geert Hofstede: power distance, collectivism versus individualism, uncertainty acceptance versus avoidance, femininity versus masculinity, short-term versus long-term orientation, and indulgence versus restraint.

- Michael Porter's concept of the value chain provides a helpful way to think about broad ethical challenges firms and leaders face in a global environment. There are eight elements of the value chain, and each carries a unique set of ethical issues and challenges. These challenges run from anticorruption issues to worker safety. Leaders within each operational area of a global firm should be attentive to the challenges they will face.

- Navigating the challenges of global ethics requires you to do more than merely learn the foundations of different ethical value systems. To succeed in a global environment, you must also learn and clarify your own principles and your company's policies, learn to listen to learn from those in other cultures, and rely on multiple sources of information when making decisions about what is correct in different global environments.

- As Mark Twain pointed out, travel is deadly to prejudice. The opportunity to work in a global setting can help you become a more well-rounded and open-minded ethical leader.

Chapter Review Questions

1. What is the difference between a hypernorm and a localized one? Provide examples of each. Do you believe that the world is moving toward or away from a set of recognized hypernorms in business?

2. Why do global ethics give rise to the acceptance of moral relativism? What's the danger in moral relativism? What about moral imperialism?

3. Of the ethical challenges categorized in the CAGE framework, which one do you believe is most problematic for business? How does your choice depend on which industries or markets a firm competes in?

4. Choose one element of the value chain. Identify two examples of ethical challenges for that element. What types of policies could a corporation establish to minimize these ethical issues?

5. How can you practice the principle of trust, but verify? What are good and objective sources to learn about the ethical systems and teachings in other countries?

6. Do you believe ethical practices vary from one country to another? Explain.

7. Is global travel an essential element of a PERMA life? Why or why not?

8. Identify and discuss global unethical practices and their sources. Suggest some ways to overcome them.

Application Exercises

- *Personal Ethical Development*. If you began keeping an ethics journal as suggested in the first chapter, continue that writing work. Here are some prompts: How important is it to you that you experience life in a country other than the one you grew up in? Where have you seen differences in how people from different cultures think about ethical issues? What are the areas where you are most likely to engage in moral imperialism? How can you hold to your ethical principles without becoming an imperialist?

- *Career Goals and Planning*. A happy, meaningful, and productive life blends and builds upon the following: (1) the type of life you are interested in leading, (2) your deepest and most important ethical commitments (3) the work you are interested in doing, (4) what you are good at, (5) your preferences for things like work versus free time, and (6) your personality. How important is it to you to work abroad? Develop a plan for finding opportunities to work in a foreign setting. What personal and professional skills will best prepare you for this experience?

- *Ethics in the Business World*. Identify a company that has faced ethical challenges in its global operations. What were the root causes of these ethical challenges? How did the organization and its leaders respond to the problems when they came to light? Did they do well? What would you have done differently? What changes has the organization made to avoid problems in the future?

- *Talking with and Learning from Others*. Choose a business professional you respect and admire who has lived and worked abroad. Engage that person in a brief interview. What motivated him or her to live abroad? What risks did he or she face? How was the experience beneficial for him or her? What advice would he or she give you as you begin your career?

Mini-Cases

Case 1: Is global pay equity a virtue or a vice? Charlie Buttars received an MBA from Creighton University in 2016, with a double emphasis in human resources and international business. She took a job at Maximus Apparel, a multi-line manufacturer and wholesaler of athletic and leisure clothing. She spent her first three years in the company's Omaha, Nebraska, headquarters as a human resources (HR) generalist. Because of her solid work and background in international business, Charlie was named director of HR for Maximus's new production facility in Vietnam. The factory would produce Maximus's first branded clothing line for the retail market, an athleisure line targeted toward Millennial and Gen Z women.

Maximus had bought the factory from its former owner, a global shoe producer, and had spent several million dollars retooling the plant and retraining the 200-plus production employees on the new equipment and procedures. Charlie arrived in hot and humid Ho Chi Minh City in early July of 2019. After a few short weeks, she developed and began to implement the HR plan for the operation. The plant and its former owners had garnered substantial negative publicity in the United States over a poor safety record, accusations of child labor, and extremely low wages. Since the new factory would produce Maximus-branded products targeting a socially conscious demographic, Charlie recommended raising wages to the U.S. equivalent, offering health insurance to employees, and building an on-site daycare center.

By mid-September, Charlie began to have second thoughts about the new policies. Vietnam had no integrated health system like that in the United States; *if* people accessed medical care, they paid out of pocket. More troubling, however, was the change in people applying for open positions at the factory. In the last month, she had interviewed an increasing stream of doctors and nurses for entry-level jobs operating a sewing machine. Each applicant had told her that the Maximus job paid between two to three times what they earned in their "professional" jobs at the local hospital. These people were clearly better off working for Maximus, but Charlie wondered if her new company policy seemed poised to gut the local market of its well-trained healthcare workers. Was paying U.S.-level wages in Vietnam the right thing to do? Was it ethical?

Case 2: Challenges in the supply chain. Omar Diaz had worked for Moynihan Fruits for 11 years. Moynihan, headquartered in Fresno, California, had a reputation as a vendor of high-quality fruit and Diaz had enjoyed working for a company with a great reputation and a strong commitment to ethics and developing its people. Diaz's family had immigrated to the United States when he was a child. His parents had saved enough for a house in Merced. After graduating from high school, Omar had gone to work for Moynihan as a field supervisor. After four years, the regional manager nominated Omar for the company's tuition scholarship and education program. With the company's full support, Omar attended UC Merced and received degrees in business management and agricultural economics.

About a year ago, Moynihan had begun selling fruit through Costco. The contract was very high volume at very low margins. Moynihan had begun importing blueberries, blackberries, and raspberries from Mexico to meet demand. Last month, Omar had been promoted; he was now the director of raspberry production for the company. His first task was to visit the Tamarillo farm in Baja, Mexico. Tamarillo had become Moynihan's largest supplier of raspberries, producing an average of 35 percent of Moynihan's total. In the winter, that percentage could grow to 55 percent.

As Diaz drove up to the facility, he knew things weren't right. The roadside was full of ragtag tent sites and he could smell the stench of open latrines. There were a number of women by the roadside cooking on open fires; Omar recognized the distinctive dress of the women and knew that the encampment was filled with Guatemalan refugees who had fled violence in their home country. As he walked the fields with the Tamarillo manager, he noticed many families, both adults and children, picking raspberries. Upon examining the books, he found that most workers were paid survival wages; he realized that it took the effort of most of the family to earn enough to scrape together any kind of savings and hope for a better life.

He brought up the issue at lunch with his Tamarillo counterpart, who spoke of the opportunities that the farm provided these refugees. If they didn't work at Tamarillo, they had no income and would wander the Baja countryside looking for food. Diaz knew that this was likely true, and that working in the fields was safer than running drugs or turning to sex trafficking. He knew that the situation at Tamarillo violated a number of U.S. laws and Moynihan policies. As he lay in bed that night, he wondered what he should do. Should he ditch the contract with Tamarillo? Who else could provide that quantity of berries? Should Moynihan help Tamarillo improve its operations? What were his, and his company's, ethical obligations to the refugees?

Case 3: There are several instances occurring in everyone's life that requires an employee to take unplanned leave to support their personal commitments. An employee of a company, Anne Henderson, had taken special leaves to care for her elderly mother who had fallen ill. Since then, Anne, a junior staff member, has recently returned to work full-time for financial reasons. However, she's been having problems with her mother's home care arrangements, which has caused her to skip many team meetings (which are normally held at the start of each day) and to leave work early. She is an expert in what she does, but due to the long intermittent leaves, she is being pushed by added pressure due to overflow of work. Being her Manager, Henry Colbert is aware that she has been an extraordinary employee with a habit of working day and night to meet timelines. But this time she is going through a genuine problem which might need her to take more leaves to support her ill mother. In addition, some male colleagues are passing comments that "women's place is in the home" and "women look better in aprons", which is demotivating for an associate who always accepted challenges and delivered work well on time. Her teammates are also forcing Colbert to take action against her.

Discussion Questions

1. How does an organization deal ethically with this situation?
2. What should Colbert do in this situation?
3. Why are Anne's teammates behaving in this way?

References

[1] Phil Knight, *Shoe Dog* (New York: Scribner, 2016), pp 26-31.

[2] See Nike Manufacturing Map, accessed March 23, 2021, http://manufacturingmap.nikeinc.com/.

[3] Information in this paragraph is from "FY19 Nike, Inc. Impact Report," https://purpose-cms-preprod01.s3.amazonaws.com/wp-content/uploads/2020/02/11230637/FY19-Nike-Inc.-Impact-Report.pdf.

[4] Anna Fifield, "Nike to review supply chains in China after reports Uighurs forced to make shoes," *Washington Post*, March 11, 2020, https://www.washingtonpost.com/world/asia_pacific/nike-to-review-supply-chains-in-china-after-reports-uighurs-forced-to-make-shoes/2020/03/11/6137df9e-6380-11ea-912d-d98032ec8e25_story.html.

[5] Alysia Montano, "Nike Told Me to Dream Crazy, Until I Wanted a Baby," *New York Times*, May 12, 2019, https://www.nytimes.com/2019/05/12/opinion/nike-maternity-leave.html.

[6] For more information, see Ethicalconsumer.com. Information on Nike is available at https://www.ethicalconsumer.org/company-profile/nike-inc.

[7] Dan Harris, "Nike Likes Manufacturing Outside China and You Should Too," Harris-Bricken, August 7, 2019, https://harrisbricken.com/chinalawblog/nike-likes-manufacturing-outside-china-and-you-should-too/.

[8] Michael Walzer, *Thick and Thin* (Notre Dame, IN: Notre Dame Press, 2006), see chapter 1 for an overview, and chapter 4 for the international implications of this argument.

[9] John Rawls and Erin Kelly, *Justice as Fairness: A Restatement* (Cambridge, MA: Harvard University Press, 2001), 3–8.

[10] Thomas Donaldson and Thomas Dunfee, "Toward a Unified Conception of Business Ethics: Integrative Social Contracts Theory," *Academy of Management Review*, 19, no. 2 (1994): 252–284.

[11] Thomas Donaldson and Thomas Dunfee, *Ties that Bind* (Boston, MA: Harvard Business School Press, 1999), 44.

[12] Ibid.

[13] The Universal Declaration of Human Rights, Facing History, https://www.facinghistory.org/holocaust-and-human-behavior/chapter-11/universal-declaration-human-rights.

[14] Donaldson and Dunfee, *Ties that Bind*, 23.

[15] See ibid. *Ties that Bind*, 23, and also Emrys Westacott, "Moral Relativism," *Internet Encyclopedia of Philosophy*, accessed June 3, 2021, https://iep.utm.edu/moral-re/#:~:text=Moral%20relativism%20is%20the%20view,uniquely%20privileged%20over%20all%20others.

[16] Donaldson and Dunfee, *Ties that Bind*, 23.

[17] R. Jenkins, "Moral Imperialism," in D. K. Chatterjee, ed., *Encyclopedia of Global Justice* (Dordrecht, Netherlands: Springer, 2011), https://doi.org/10.1007/978-1-4020-9160-5_754, and https://link.springer.com/referenceworkentry/10.1007%2F978-1-4020-9160-5_754#:~:text=Broadly%2C%20moral%20imperialism%20is%20the,force%20or%20through%20cultural%20criticism.

[18] Pankaj Ghemawat, *Redefining Global Strategy: Crossing Borders in a World Where Differences Still Matter* (Boston, MA: Harvard Business School Press, 2007).

[19] Geert Hofstede, *Culture's Consequences* (Thousand Oaks, CA: Sage Publications, 2001), 9.

[20] Taken from Hofstede's Cultural Dimensions Theory, Corporate Finance Institute, https://corporatefinanceinstitute.com/resources/knowledge/other/hofstedes-cultural-dimensions-theory/.

[21] For insight on the differences, see Giacomo Ponzetto and Patricio Fernandez, "Case Law versus Statute Law: An Evolutionary Comparison," *Journal of Legal Studies* 37, no. 2 (2008): 379–430.

[22] See, for example, Paul C. Godfrey, *Management, Society, and the Informal Economy* (New York: Routledge, 2015).

[23] Material available at and downloaded from https://www.transparency.org/en/cpi/2019/media-kit.

[24] A similar argument about the effect of diversity on economic heterogeneity comes from Quamrul Ashraf and Oded Galor, "Cultural Diversity, Geographical Isolation, and the Origin of the Wealth of Nations," National Bureau of Economics working paper series, 2011, https://www.nber.org/papers/w17640.

[25] Taken from "Celebrating 13 Years of the UN Declaration on the Rights of Indigenous Peoples," https://www.culturalsurvival.org/news/celebrating-13-years-un-declaration-rights-indigenous-peoples.

[26] William Booth, *Households: On the Moral Architecture of the Economy* (Ithaca, NY: Cornell University Press, 1993).

[27] William Baumol, Robert Litan, and Carl Schramm, *Good Capitalism, Bad Capitalism*, (New Haven, CT: Yale University Press).

[28] "2021 Index of Economic Freedom," The Heritage Foundation, accessed March 22, 2021, https://www.heritage.org/index/heatmap.

[29] Max Weber, *The Protestant Ethic and the "Spirit" of Capitalism and Other Writings* (New York: Penguin Books, 2002).

[30] John Paul II, *Centesimus Annus*, Washington, D.C., United States Catholic Conference, 1991.

[31] Michael Porter, *Competitive Advantage* (New York: Free Press, 1985), 46–47.

[32] "Changing the status quo for car rental pricing practices: ensuring that the prices you see are the prices you pay," Competition Bureau of Canada, Government of Canada, March 4, 2020, https://www.competitionbureau.gc.ca/eic/site/cb-bc.nsf/eng/04520.html#sec04out.

[33] "Ticketmaster to pay $4.5 million to settle misleading pricing case," Competition Bureau of Canada, Government of Canada, news release, June 27, 2019, https://worldpolicyforum.tumblr.com/post/70335434461/minimum-wage.

[34] "Is there a minimum wage that lifts you and your child of poverty?," World Policy Forum, accessed March 25, 2021, https://worldpolicyforum.tumblr.com/post/70335434461/minimum-wage.

[35] For a discussion of the origin of this statement, see "A common quotation from 'Augustine'?," https://faculty.georgetown.edu/jod/augustine/quote.html#:~:text=But%20the%20common%20saying%2C%20expressed,%3B%20in%20all%20things%2C%20charity.

[36] Barton Swaim, "'Trust, but verify': An untrustworthy political phrase," *Washington Post*, March 11, 2016, https://www.washingtonpost.com/opinions/trust-but-verify-an-untrustworthy-political-phrase/2016/03/11/da32fb08-db3b-11e5-891a-4ed04f4213e8_story.html.

[37] Mark Twain, quote from *The Innocents Abroad*, Goodreads, https://www.goodreads.com/quotes/1716-travel-is-fatal-to-prejudice-bigotry-and-narrow-mindedness-and-many#:~:text=%E2%80%9CTravel%20is%20fatal%20to%20prejudice%2C%20bigotry%2C%20and%20narrow%2D,the%20earth%20all%20one's%20lifetime.%E2%80%9D

CHAPTER 8

Power and Its Uses

LEARNING OUTCOMES

At the end of this chapter, you should be able to do the following:

1. Define the different bases of power and detail the effects of bullying.

2. Define sexual harassment and identify the three types of conduct that could support allegations of sexual harassment.

3. Describe potential formal and informal interventions to help prevent abuses of power.

4. Evaluate yourself in terms of the seven characteristics of people who acquire and successfully use power, and assess the strategies and plans you have developed to help you to use power effectively in your career and life.

5. Apply what you have learned about power in this chapter to situations where power is being used properly or improperly.

Opening Case | Steve Easterbrook: Misconduct at the Golden Arches

Tannen Maury/EPA-EFE/Shutterstock.com

Steve Easterbrook joined McDonald's in 1993 as a financial reporting manager in London, after a stint as an auditor for Price Waterhouse.[1] He quickly moved up in a variety of finance and operations roles, eventually running the UK Operation by 2006, and all of the company's 1,800 locations in Northern Europe in 2007. He left the Golden Arches in 2011 to become CEO of PizzaExpress, and he later moved to Wagamama (a British restaurant chain serving Asian food based on Japanese cuisine). He returned to McDonald's in 2013 as Executive Vice President and Chief Brand Officer and became CEO in 2015.

Easterbrook quickly developed a reputation for innovation and change as he worked to turn McDonald's fortunes around. He noted early in his tenure that "We were and we are a great

operational company, but perhaps you start naturally to run out of ideas and need fresh perspectives. Whether that's in communications or marketing or strategy, you need people to come in with a fresh perspective."[2] Easterbrook focused on increasing the number of locations owned and operated by franchisees, running company stores, improving food and beverage menu options (think upscale burgers and chicken sandwiches),[3] and, most important, serving breakfast all day.[4] The moves paid off for the company and by 2019, the company's stock price had doubled.

Easterbrook was fired by the board in November of 2019 for engaging in a consensual sexual relationship with a company employee. This violation "demonstrated poor judgment" according to the board's statement at the time. Easterbrook agreed, noting, "This was a mistake," he wrote. "Given the values of the company, I agree with the board that it is time for me to move on."[5] Despite the board's action, some employees believed that a culture that tolerated sexual harassment and other employee abuses persisted. Said one employee, "It's clear McDonald's culture is rotten from top to bottom. McDonald's needs to sit down with worker-survivors and put them at the center of any solution." The employee noted that McDonalds had refused to even talk with employees who filed claims of sexual harassment.[6]

The board softened Easterbrook's departure with a $42 million severance package. In August of 2020, eight months after the firing, the board discovered information that Easterbrook had had four separate sexual relationships with employees (instead of just the one that was originally reported). In one of those cases, Easterbrook awarded the employee hundreds of thousands of dollars in a "special retention grant" of stock that executives could offer high-performing employees without board approval.[7] The board filed suit to recoup Easterbrook's severance package, accusing him of lying to the board during its earlier investigation, concealing evidence, and fraud. Evidence of the three additional affairs came in response to a whistleblower complaint. The initial investigators had searched Easterbrook's company iPhone—where he had deleted many text messages—but had not looked into his email account.

The lawsuit cast Easterbrook in a terrible light as a serial abuser of his managerial power. McDonald's board also looked bad, however, for not pursuing a thorough investigation when the initial reports of misconduct came to light. The board appeared to do what many other companies do: Force a leader to resign, send them off with a comfortable severance package, and move on. The 2020 lawsuit signaled a change in how McDonald's viewed executive malfeasance, and it may set a standard for other companies as well.

The case of Steve Easterbrook introduces, and highlights, the ethical challenges around power. When used well, power helps drive organizational change and performance; however, when it is abused, power creates pain for people and organizations. Power and authority are central features in organizational life. Without the authority and power to direct work, many of the benefits of organized action prove difficult to attain; without power, very little would get done.[8]

This chapter has two goals. First, it will provide you with an understanding of power and its negative, unethical manifestations. Particular emphasis will be given to two abuses of power that are, unfortunately, far too common in business situations: bullying and sexual harassment. This understanding, and the chapter exercises, will allow you to develop strategies for avoiding unethical power plays or dealing with bullying and abuse. Second, the chapter also outlines ways in which you can use your power to accomplish much good in the organizations where you work.

Power and Bullying

The *Oxford English Dictionary* defines power in three insightful ways. At a basic level, power is the "ability to act or affect something," or the ability to do work and get things done. In social and organizational settings, power is the "capacity to direct or influence the behavior of others, personal or social influence." This definition captures the informal and social aspects of power. Finally, power is "control or authority over others."[9] Authority is the formal and accepted recognition that one person, the one holding authority, has the right to direct the activities of others. Ethics in the Real World 8.1 provides more information about the nature of authority and its limits.

Ethics in the Real World 8.1 | Authority and the Zone of Indifference

Twentieth century management thinker Chester Barnard wrote in 1938 that "The phrase 'zone of indifference' may be explained as follows: If all the orders for actions reasonably practicable be arranged in order of their acceptability to the person affected, it may be conceived that there are a number which are clearly unacceptable, that is, which certainly will not be obeyed; there is another group that is more or less on the neutral line, that is, either barely acceptable or barely unacceptable; and a third group unquestioningly acceptable. This last group lies within the 'zone of indifference' (see Figure 8.1). The person affected will accept orders lying within this zone and is relatively indifferent as to what the order is so far as the question of authority is concerned. Such an order lies within the range that in a general way was anticipated at the time of undertaking the connection with the organization.... The zone of indifference will be wider or narrower depending on the degree to which inducements exceed the burdens and sacrifices which determine the individual's adhesion to the organization."[10]

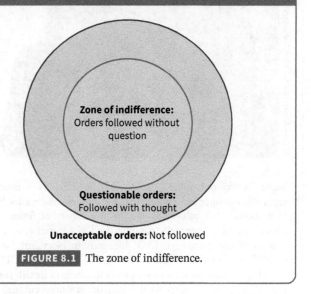

Zone of indifference: Orders followed without question

Questionable orders: Followed with thought

Unacceptable orders: Not followed

FIGURE 8.1 The zone of indifference.

Bases of Power

Social psychologist Adam Galinsky provides another window on power. Power is defined as who holds the resources in relationships. "When I have all the resources I need," he says,

"I'm not dependent on others; therefore, they don't have power over me. But if I have resources other people want, then I have power over them,"[11] Scholars have identified six ways in which resources may be controlled and serve as sources of power, as shown in Figure 8.2:[12]

When power is deployed in ways that objectify or demean others, those uses are unethical. We'll focus on and define two major unethical (and often illegal) uses of power—bullying in the next section and sexual harassment in the following one.

Bullying

The Workplace Bullying Institute defines bullying as "sub-lethal (non-homicidal) and non-physical violence."[13] That violence most often takes the form of psychological abuse and manifests itself as emotional or verbal abuse. Bullies have an unhealthy need for control, which they meet by creating oppressive and harsh conditions for those they work with. Bullying

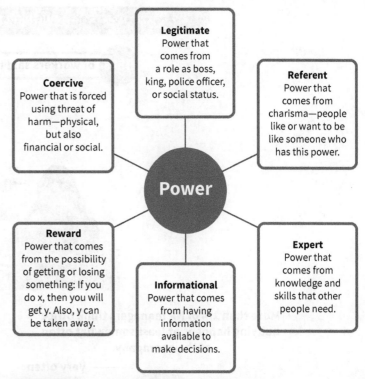

FIGURE 8.2 The bases of power in an organization.

- is driven by perpetrators' need to control the targeted individual(s);
- is initiated by people who choose their targets, timing, location, and methods;
- can include acts of commission (doing things to others) or omission (withholding resources from others);
- may escalate to involve others who side with the bully, either voluntarily or through coercion; and
- is akin to domestic violence at work, where the abuser is on the payroll.

Victims and bystanders often use disguising language to describe bullying, such as "incivility," "disrespect," "he or she is just a difficult person," or "we have a personality conflict."[14] This trivializes the behavior and is a strategy used to blame the victim through comments like "You just need to toughen up. Don't be so sensitive." When bullying does not get called out, bullies are empowered to continue their abusive behavior. Figure 8.3 shows the prevalence of workplace bullying and how average employees respond to the situation.

Harassment

The U.S. Equal Employment Opportunity Commission (EEOC) offers an excellent and comprehensive definition and description of harassment:

> Harassment is unwelcome conduct that is based on race, color, religion, sex (including pregnancy), national origin, age (40 or older), disability or genetic information. Harassment becomes unlawful when (1) enduring the offensive conduct becomes a condition of continued employment, or (2) the conduct is severe or pervasive enough to create a work environment that a reasonable person would consider intimidating, hostile, or abusive. Antidiscrimination laws also prohibit harassment against individuals in retaliation for filing a discrimination charge, testifying, or participating in any way in an investigation, proceeding, or lawsuit under these laws; or opposing employment practices that they reasonably believe discriminate against individuals, in violation of these laws.
>
> Petty slights, annoyances, and isolated incidents (unless extremely serious) will not rise to the level of illegality. To be unlawful, the conduct must create a

WORKPLACE BULLYING

35% **of workers said they have had an office bully.**

More than 1/4 of HR managers think office bullying happens at least somewhat often at their company:

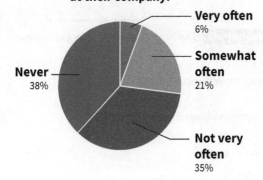

Very often 6%

Somewhat often 21%

Never 38%

Not very often 35%

How workers responded to office bullies:*

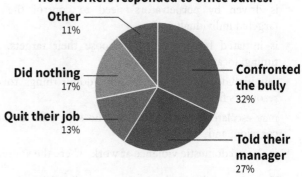

Other 11%

Did nothing 17%

Quit their job 13%

Confronted the bully 32%

Told their manager 27%

*Respondents who said they have had an office bully

Source: OfficeTeam survey of 317 workers and 307 human resources managers in the United States.

FIGURE 8.3   Bullying is more prevalent than many employees and HR managers would like to see.

work environment that would be intimidating, hostile, or offensive to reasonable people.

Offensive conduct may include, but is not limited to, offensive jokes, slurs, epithets, or name calling, physical assaults or threats, intimidation, ridicule or mockery, insults or put-downs, offensive objects or pictures, and interference with work performance.[15]

Sexual Harassment

Sexual harassment is a particular type of harassment. The EEOC defines sexual harassment as follows:

Title VII [of the Civil Rights Act of 1964] does not proscribe all conduct of a sexual nature in the workplace. Thus it is crucial to clearly define sexual harassment: only *unwelcome sexual conduct that is a term or condition of employment* constitutes a violation. The EEOC's Guidelines define two types of sexual harassment: "quid pro quo" and "hostile environment." The Guidelines provide that "unwelcome" sexual conduct constitutes sexual harassment when "submission to such conduct is made either explicitly or implicitly a term or condition of an individual's employment."[16]

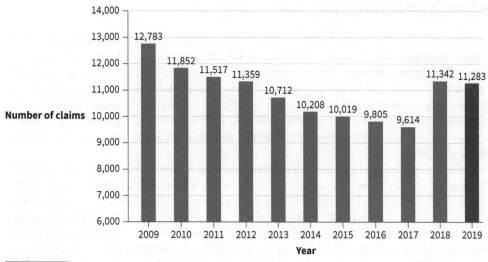

FIGURE 8.4   Claims of sexual harassment have risen recently.

Quid pro quo is a Latin term that means "this for that." Quid pro quo sexual harassment occurs when sexual favors of some sort are made an implicit (implied) or explicit (formally stated) condition of compensation, advancement, or employment. Quid pro quo sexual harassment is most common when people hold different power positions, either formal or informal. A hostile work environment is created when conduct or language of a sexual nature in the workplace is so strong and prevalent that it creates an intimidating or oppressive situation for those subject to the harassment. Inappropriate touching, groping, bumping, or rubbing up against someone to make sexual contact creates a hostile work environment. So do jokes of a sexual nature, sexually provocative or pornographic art, pictures, or posters. Unceasing requests for dates or other out-of-work contact also create a hostile environment.[17] Hostile work environments limit people's ability to participate in work activities.

The EEOC and the U.S. courts have clarified what constitutes unwelcome conduct:

> **Because sexual attraction may often play a role in the day-to-day social exchange between employees, "the distinction between invited, uninvited-but-welcome, offensive-but-tolerated, and flatly rejected" sexual advances may well be difficult to discern.... But this distinction is essential because sexual conduct becomes unlawful only when it is unwelcome. The Eleventh Circuit provided a general definition of "unwelcome conduct": The challenged conduct must be unwelcome "in the sense that the employee did not solicit or incite it, and in the sense that the employee regarded the conduct as undesirable or offensive."[18]**

Sexual harassment is more common than most people realize. We saw a reduction in claims of sexual harassment beginning in 2010, as shown in Figure 8.4. Unfortunately, incidents began to rise again as of 2018. The numbers for 2020 are expected to be an aberration in the data as a majority of offices in the United States closed for at least a period of time due to COVID-19.

Preventing and Controlling Abuses of Power: Informal and Formal Methods

In this section, we'll focus on preventing abuses of power, and in the next section we'll talk about how to use power to make a positive difference in your life, the lives of those you work with, and the world in general. Organizations can employ a number of formal and informal tools to help prevent bullying from occurring or persisting in an organization.

Informal Mechanisms

A priority element, as in most other issues of ethical behavior in business, is to create and nurture an organizational culture of inclusion, kindness, respect, and tolerance.[19] As we've discussed in earlier chapters, the accepted norms of behavior, supported by organizational leaders, both define and model the values of inclusiveness and civility that prevent abuses of power. Myths, stories, and legends about rewards for culturally consistent behavior—and sanctions for its opposite—communicate core values throughout the organization's informal networks.[20] The company mission statement and explicitly declared values can also prevent abuses of power.

Missions, stories, and values work together to create a solid platform to prevent, detect, and respond to bullying and harassment in all its forms. The most important element, however, is to hire, retain, and reward people in the organization who speak up to report abuses of power. In other words, people with moral courage. Bullying and harassment, especially sexual harassment, flourish in the shadows of organizational life and depend on networks of tacit approval and secrecy. When employees, managers, or executives prove willing to give voice and call out behavior they know is wrong, they shine a light on these behaviors that can change very old cultural norms that abet and perpetuate abuses of power of all kinds. See Figure 8.5 for some informal methods companies can utilize to create a more positive environment.

FIVE STEPS TO END
WORKPLACE HARASSMENT

COMMIT TO BATTLING BIAS
Promote activities and discussions that focus on behaviors the organization wants to encourage.

ENCOURAGE BYSTANDER INTERVENTION
Its's important that bystanders step forward when they witness harassment.

HOLD PEOPLE ACCOUNTABLE
Harassment will only stop when people are held accountable, regardless of who they are or where they work.

CREATE A SPEAK-UP CULTURE
Employers should create a culture in which everyone in the organization feels comfortable speaking up when there is a problem.

ASSESS AND ADDRESS
Investigate all claims, regardless of how much responsibility or "star power" the alleged harasser has in the organization.

SHRM
BETTER WORKPLACES
BETTER WORLD

Source: Society for Human Resource Management (SHRM).

FIGURE 8.5 Five steps to end workplace harassment.

Formal Mechanisms

In addition to mission statements, formal mechanisms include policies, procedures for reporting, and training. Leaders begin by crafting proactive and unambiguous *policies* that condemn bullying, harassment, or other abuses of power.[21] Policies must follow EEOC and other legal guidelines. Policies for reporting abuses of power are the next step. These policies should outline how complaints will be investigated and what protections will be afforded both accusers and alleged perpetrators. Potential outcomes and sanctions should be unambiguous.[22] *Training* follows and helps implement policies. Leaders should design training with clear goals that go beyond providing a defense against legal liability. Best-practice programs work to create and sustain an organizational culture and operating environment that are open, safe, and welcoming for all organizational members. Best-practice training defines and provides everyday examples of bullying or harassment and uses "real-world" cases that connect with the organization's business activities and industry challenges to help people see the nuances that define the boundaries of acceptable conduct.[23] Training should also include steps for bystanders and observers to take. See Ethics in the Real World 8.2 for an example of a well crafted anti-harassment policy.

Ethics in the Real World 8.2 | Major League Baseball Creates an Anti-Harassment Policy

In February of 2021, Major League Baseball responded to repeated claims of harassment and other inappropriate conduct by releasing a code of conduct. Here are important excerpts from that policy:

Major League Baseball Code of Conduct: Harassment and Discrimination

All people working in and around Major League Baseball must be treated equally—with dignity and respect—regardless of race, color, creed, national origin or citizenship status, ancestry, religion, gender, sexual orientation, actual or perceived gender identity, physical or mental disability, age, or any other characteristic protected by applicable federal, state, or local laws ("Protected Characteristics").

MLB's Principles

- Major League Baseball and its Clubs strive to create environments in which all individuals, including MLB and Club personnel, employees of MLB's business partners, and members of the press, are accepted and respected. Moreover, when an individual believes this standard is not upheld, they are comfortable speaking up without fear of recrimination, retaliation, or ostracism. The environments include any venue in which MLB and/or Club personnel are engaged on behalf of the League or Club, including in a Club's front office, in the Clubhouse, on the playing field, and any location in which people working in and around the game of Baseball interact. All MLB and Club personnel will be held accountable for inappropriate conduct, regardless of their seniority, rank, or stature. . .

Major League Baseball and Club Employees' Commitments

- *Treating all co-workers, partners, and individuals associated with the game of Baseball with dignity and respect.*

- *Understanding that inappropriate comments or conduct based on an individual's Protected Characteristic(s) have no place within MLB regardless of whether such words or actions are in the workplace, on social media, in electronic communications, or in casual conversation.*
- *Not engaging in conduct contrary to these principles, such as (i) making demeaning comments, slurs, insults, or jokes regarding an individual's or groups' Protected Characteristic(s); (ii) bullying; (iii) distribution or display of pornography; and (iv) physical, verbal, or visual sexual harassment, or any other harassment, towards any individual associated with the game of Baseball.*

Reporting Behavior Contrary to MLB's Principles

For MLB to achieve an inclusive culture, we must all take responsibility for addressing behavior that is inconsistent with these principles. There is no requirement to confront an alleged wrongdoer; however, victims of inappropriate conduct may attempt to resolve issues or disagreements on their own if they choose. If attempts to do so are unsuccessful or if an individual does not feel safe or comfortable addressing an incident directly, it is imperative that either MLB or the Club is made aware of inappropriate conduct. There are several options to do so. First, an MLB or Club employee can speak to a supervisor, or an individual in their respective Human Resources or Legal Departments. Alternatively, individuals, including those not employed by MLB or a Club, can make a complaint by calling MLB's *Speak Up* hotline at 1-844-993-0562. The hotline system is operated by an outside third party.

Finally, fighting the abuse of power requires *reporting* systems that specify who must report and the types of actions that are "reportable." For example, all supervisors or managers must promptly report any disclosed or witnessed incidents of sexual harassment or bullying. Strong reporting systems establish and maintain clear and easy-to-understand ways for people to report potential cases of bullying, harassment, sexual harassment, or other abuses of power. Hotlines, anonymous online submission forms, and dedicated personnel in HR or other departments all provide opportunities for employees to report bullying and understand how they can help victims and prevent perpetrators. Audits or other mechanisms to strengthen compliance with policies and procedures help assess the degree to which cultural values and norms of respect are embedded within the organization. Our Ethics in the Real World feature shows you the anti-harassment policy of one organization trying to improve: Major League Baseball.

Acquiring and Using Power Appropriately

So far in this chapter, you've learned about how power can be abused in unethical ways. Power creates ethical challenges because the ability to control or influence others can lead to treating others as objects, tools for us to gain what we want without concern for their well-being. Bullying and harassment, particularly sexual harassment, destroy the victim's sense of personal power and safety, and these acts degrade and demean others. As we saw with Steve Easterbrook, abuse of power also can lead to broader negative ethical outcomes, such as dishonest or criminal behavior that generates a pool of victims much larger than the individuals directly affected.

Power is a necessary part of organizational life. Without power, many of the gains of cooperation and coordination that come through organized activity would not be possible.[24] You've probably heard the phrase "power corrupts." The actual phrase comes from a nineteenth-century British gentleman, Lord Acton: "Power *tends* to corrupt, and absolute power corrupts absolutely."[25] Power does not inevitably corrupt people. Power is not, in and of itself, unethical. In the rest of this section, we'll outline how you can obtain power and how you can use it for ethical ends.

Acquiring Power

Stanford business professor Jeffrey Pfeffer has spent his career researching, teaching, and consulting organizational leaders about power.[26] Pfeffer outlines seven essential traits that people need if they hope to acquire and use power. None of these seven traits are morally bad; the moral problem with power comes when those who have it choose to abuse it for their own ends. The seven traits are outlined in Table 8.1.

Using Power Wisely

As you read through the list of those traits, we hope you see in the examples a number of people who have used power in very positive ways, such as ending the practice of slavery, helping patients who need brain surgery, or becoming a professional athlete. Power tends to corrupt, as Lord Acton said, but that's only a tendency, not an inevitable outcome. How can you use power wisely? The response is simple and builds on the concepts you've learned already: the PERMA model from Chapter 3. Here's how the elements of the PERMA model can help you use power in ways that contribute to a good life.

- **P—Positive Emotion**—The abuse of power often accompanies the pursuit of hedonistic pleasures, such as money, position, or the feeling of security that accompanies dominating others. These emotions are fleeting, and all are subject to hedonic adjustment. Commit to using power in ways that bring about more lasting emotional states such as beauty, joy, and satisfaction.

TABLE 8.1   Seven Traits Associated with Power.

Trait	Description	Example
Ambition	People accrue power over time want to have it. They desire it. That desire helps them make decisions about actions that help them build a base to acquire power.	Apple founders Steve Jobs and Steve Wozniak exemplify the role of ambition. The two founded the company, but Jobs's desire for power led him to the C-suite. Wozniak's ambition was to be a great programmer, and he never moved beyond his love for the technology of computing, working on technology-related projects throughout his career.[27]
Energy	It takes work and energy to obtain and use power. People who want power work long hours, and they often work weekends. They make investments in knowledge and relationships that create and solidify a base of power.	Margaret Thatcher, Prime Minister of the United Kingdom in the 1980s and 1990s, worked long hours and studied hard so that she would have expert power in any meeting she attended. Thatcher used expert power to overcome existing gender bias in politics at the time.[28]
Focus	Power comes to those who develop expertise, skill, or relationships in a particular area. Focus means the ability to concentrate, to intently attend to details and data for long periods of time, and apply mental energy toward mastering a craft.	Legendary NFL running back Walter Payton was famous for his off-season workouts that allowed a mere 200-pound running back to become a Hall of Fame performer. Payton said, "You get to a point where you have to keep pushing yourself. You stop, throw up, and push yourself again. There's no one else around to feel sorry for you."[29]
Self-Knowledge	Power comes to those who continually learn and grow. Paradoxically, many powerful people don't see themselves as experts in all things, and they are willing to continually learn from their experiences. Learning is an active process and reflects a strong "growth mindset."[30] They realize that the more they learn, the more control and influence they have over situations and the more willing people are to follow them.	Billionaire philanthropist Bill Gates has a yearly ritual of self-reflection. At the end of each year, Gates takes stock by asking two questions: "What was I excited about?" and "What could I have done better?" Reflection helps him make plans for the next year and continue to improve.[31]
Confidence	Powerful people project assuredness, steadiness, and courage in every situation, especially in new ones where they may lack deep knowledge.	Dr. Frances Conley was the first female full professor of neurosurgery. Yes, she was a brain surgeon. With her colleagues she would exhibit uncertainty, but with patients she always projected confidence about the treatment options. She knew that her confidence was a source of power that increased the confidence, trust, and calmness of her patients.[32]
Empathy	Empathy is the ability to understand and relate to another person.[33] We often think of the most powerful people as only interested in themselves or their own needs; however, people who can understand, relate to, and work with others are those who accrue power.	Abraham Lincoln was smart and clever, but he was also kind and generous. The stories of his concern and empathy for those he met are too numerous to mention, and that generosity created a strong bond of loyalty between Lincoln and those who knew him.[34]
Ability to tolerate conflict	Powerful people are willing and able to put up with disagreement. They may not initiate conflict, but they don't back down when it comes, and they are willing to use verbal and argumentative force to defend and advance what they believe is the right course of action.	During the Cuban missile crisis, John F. Kennedy encouraged conflicting opinions and debate among his subordinates as they contemplated a course of action. That conflict refined and improved both the decision and the president.[35]

- **E—Engagement**—Engagement comes when we operate at the boundary of our competence, but the unethical user of power prefers to remain solidly in a "comfort zone." Abusers and harassers rarely move beyond people they know—these abuses of power just repeat well-used scripts and patterns of behavior. Power—as influence—can allow you to stretch your competence and experience flow, which requires you to cast away those well-worn scripts and learn new behaviors.

- **R—Relationships**—The unethical use of power turns relationships from equal interactions of sharing and mutual benefit to ones of hoarding and gains for the powerful. Abusers of power always treat others as objects and see all interactions as transactions. A focus on building and maintaining healthy relationships requires us to accept others as subjects, with feelings, goals, and needs just as valid as our own. Strong relationships are an antidote to the abuse of power.

- **M—Meaning—**Those who abuse power often see themselves as the center of their universe. They have no overarching or transcendent goal or belief system to guide their lives; they have no larger purpose in their life that helps channel power into positive uses. Power serves the self. As we gain a deep sense of life mission and purpose, those things naturally limit our desire to abuse power. Power furthers a larger purpose than our simple self-interest. Some of the most ethical uses of power come as we employ our control and influence to serve larger causes that work to reduce poverty, illiteracy, inequality, injustice, or sickness and disease.

- **A—Achievement—**Achievement is a double-edged sword because it depends on what we want to achieve. Goal accomplishment provides a strong incentive to engage in unethical power plays, bullying, harassing, or seeking sexual favors in inappropriate ways. The goal is power and domination, there is little emphasis on growth, relationships have no meaning, and the self is the center of the universe. Goals that center on and facilitate the other elements of the PERMA model invite positive, ethical uses of power. When achievement is measured in terms of the other elements of the PERMA model, you have placed some strong guardrails around your use of power.

Key Terms

Authority	moral courage	Quid pro quo
hostile work environment	power	unwelcome

Chapter Summary

- Power is the ability to control or influence the behavior of others or organizational processes. There are six bases of power: legitimate or formal, control of rewards, threats of sanction or coercive power, control of vital information or access to it, expertise and knowledge, and charisma and charm (referent power). Power is an essential feature of organizational life.

- Bullying may include physical batter, but most often it is systematic and persistent nonphysical violence aimed at another individual. The most common forms of bullying are emotional abuse (such as shaming) and verbal abuse. Bullying often stems from insecurities in the bully and may include acts of commission (such as direct verbal abuse) or acts of omission (withholding resources or praise).

- Harassment is any unwelcome conduct that targets a person because of some category to which they belong, such as race, gender, or age. When that unwelcome conduct is of a sexual nature, it becomes sexual harassment. Sexual harassment can either be a quid pro quo (a supposed exchange of favors) or it can create a hostile work environment for victims.

- Traditional organizational levers such as written policies, training programs, and reporting mechanisms help prevent bullying and harassment in organizations. When training programs focus on business/industry-specific issues, they are more likely to succeed, and reporting mechanisms should use up-to-date technology. A set of strong cultural values of dignity, inclusion, and respect help prevent bullying or harassment, but the best defense is morally courageous individuals who speak up and refuse to tolerate these behaviors.

- Power is not morally bad, in and of itself. There are seven key characteristics that will help people acquire power: ambition, energy, focus, self-knowledge, confidence, empathy, and a tolerance for conflict. Using power in ethical ways is facilitated when individuals have a strong sense of the PERMA values guiding their lives.

Chapter Review Questions

1. Define power. How does harassment differ from bullying?

2. What are the bases of power? Which of these bases are easiest for managers or leaders to abuse? How can organizations curb the potential of managers to use their power in inappropriate ways?

3. What conditions must be present for conversation or behavior at work to constitute sexual harassment?

4. Why won't the presence of formal policies and procedures prevent abuses of power such as bullying or sexual harassment? What else must be in place?

5. What is your personal approach to power? How much power do you want in your career? Rate yourself on each of the seven necessary elements for acquiring and using power.

6. Discuss, with examples of some organizational practices, when the use of power is ethical and when it is not.

7. How will a leader ensure that his use of power is ethically correct?

Application Exercises

- *Personal Ethical Development.* If you began keeping an ethics journal as suggested in the first chapter, continue that writing work. Here are some prompts: Where and when have you seen power used well and poorly? When have you been bullied or harassed? How did you react? What feelings or values conflicts make it (or made it) difficult to respond? What is the right response?

- *Career Goals and Planning.* A happy, meaningful, and productive life blends and builds upon the following: (1) the type of life you are interested in leading, (2) your deepest and most important values, (3) the work you are interested in doing, (4) what you are good at, (5) your preferences for things like work versus free time, and (6) your personality. What types of organizational structures and controls, and checks on power, bullying, and harassment would you like to see in place where you work? How can you evaluate a company's real abilities to protect people from abuse, bullying, or sexual harassment?

- *Ethics in the Business World.* Identify a company that faced the problem of sexual harassment in the workplace. How did managers and organizational leaders respond? Did they do well or poorly? What were the outcomes? How has that organization adjusted its policies, culture, or style to prevent such incidents in the future?

- *Talking with and Learning from Others.* Choose a business professional you respect. Engage that person in a brief interview. Where have they seen bullying or harassment in their careers?

How have they responded? What do they wish they had done differently? What advice would they give you as you begin your career?

- *Be an Ethics Professional for a Day!* The following activities are all typically part of the role of compliance department professionals:

  a. Choose a company that you are familiar with and draft an email to all employees reminding them of the importance of complying with laws on bullying and sexual harassment. Be sure to tie compliance with these policies and laws to the values of the company. You will also want to remind employees of the penalties for violations, both for the company and for individual employees.

  b. Prepare a brief set of slides for a live training session. The audience is the product development team of a start-up software company, and the problem you are targeting is a report of the situations described in the mini-case. You have thirty minutes to provide them with guidelines that will help prevent future occurrences of these types of behaviors. You will want them to understand the relevant laws and ethical considerations in this area. You also want to help them navigate everyday work situations and common scenarios where harassment may occur. Your training should include some case situations or role-plays to help them understand what behaviors constitute harassment.

Mini-Cases

Case 1: Was it harassment or just a power play? Estelle took a job at a San Francisco investment bank just after she graduated with a finance degree from the University of Arizona in the early 1990s. She worked for the research arm of the bank. There were junior and senior analysts and there was usually a large age gap between the two groups. She was single, as was one of the senior analysts at the bank. Richard was not liked by many in the division for his abrasive and arrogant attitude, but he was a very good analyst and knew how to get great data on the future plans of the companies he followed. He let others in the department know he was better than any of them, or all of them combined.

One afternoon Richard, twenty years older than her, asked Estelle if she'd like to go on a date. The request was both surprising and shocking and caught Estelle off guard. Richard was not Estelle's boss, but he wielded significant power in the group. Estelle had no interest in dating Richard, but she was concerned about the career effects of saying no to a star in the firm. She declined his offer. That was the end of the matter.

A few months later, Estelle mentioned her concerns about the potential career impacts with a few colleagues. She had seen no repercussions, and Richard had seemed earnest in his desire to get to know Estelle better. She was surprised when, a couple days later, her boss Susan came into her office and asked if she could talk. Susan was a powerful boss, a type-A personality. She liked Estelle and many times said she would do everything she could to help her move up in the firm. Susan asked Estelle if she would be willing to file a sexual harassment claim against Richard. That would be an easy way for Susan—and perhaps the whole office—to get rid of Richard.

Estelle put Susan off, and after work that night she sat in her Mission District apartment and pondered what to do. Estelle loved her work and the investment banking culture, and she really loved living in San Francisco. She had a lot of respect for Susan and saw her as both a role model and mentor. Up until this moment, that is. As she thought about Richard, he was certainly full of himself, but had done nothing more than ask Estelle for a date. While she had been upset at his request, her only dealings with Richard had been professional in every respect. Estelle could think of several other office romances at the time, some of them between coworkers and some between senior and junior analysts.

Richard's request had broken no laws or company regulations. Richard's request for a date had upset her, but Susan's request was just awful. She felt a moment of déjà vu; she worried if saying no to Richard those months ago would harm her prospects, and now she wondered what saying no to Susan would mean for her future. She felt good about telling Susan no, but wondered how to frame her response.

Case 2: A company manufactures and produces a wide range of industrial motion control and industrial power transmission solutions. With exact engineered components and systems that provide the essential control of safety equipment speed, torque, positioning, and other functions, the products can be used in nearly any machine, process, or application involving motion. From precision motors embedded in medical robots to heavy-duty brakes used in rugged mining applications, the company has been solving complex customer challenges worldwide for decades. Stephen Hamilton works in this big multinational corporation as an operations manager. He faced an ethical dilemma wherein he had to decide what affected the career prospects and economic wellbeing of the employees. The decision involved incorporating artificial intelligence (AI) and machine learning (ML) based automation system into business processes, which meant laying off certain positions and losing specialization for others who were retained. In the annual meeting held, it was decided to implement AI and ML-based automation systems in all the manufacturing units to gain competitive advantages over competitors. The decision to change had both pros and cons.

The pros involved increased efficiency, competitiveness, and smooth flow of business processes; automation typically performs all the manufacturing processes that have less variability than human workers. And this results in greater control of the process and the consistency of the quality of the product. Some of the units are very small. By streamlining processes and equipment with AI and ML-based automation, the amount of scraps would be reduced. The small space can be utilized entirely; moreover, automation uses less energy.

The company also decided to add a few robots in the manufacturing process designed on a compact basis to fit in a confined space. In addition to mounting machines on the floor, these robots can be mounted on the factory wall, rail tracks, ceilings, and shelves. As the robots can perform tasks in confined spaces, apart from monetary savings, this will also save valuable floor spaces. Implementation of AI and ML-based automation system in the manufacturing system will help achieve the following:

1. The manufacturing unit will be 24/7 production with JIT manufacturing-friendly.
2. More uptime with historic efficiency figures above 90 percent.
3. Secondary operations capability—washing, deburring, gauging, etc.
4. Real-time factory communication with machines and automated cell.
5. Quick changeover for multiple parts, programs, and tooling.
6. Flexible multi-operation capability (i.e., Op 10, Op 20, etc.).

Implementation of AI and ML-based automation system has several cons as well. The most critical drawbacks that create an ethical dilemma are resistance from employees, fear, and apprehension due to change in working methods, and damage to employees' loyalty, and commitment. Work displacement is also a big factor in resistance to implementation of AI and ML-based automation systems. A third-party inspection done by the HR department concluded that by adding one robot in the manufacturing unit, it reduced employment by 3.3 workers. In turn, the company would save on its balance sheet. However, Hamilton had the ethical dilemma that workers will lose their jobs for the corporate decision in which he was involved.

Discussion Questions

1. How should Hamilton make a decision in this situation?
2. What is the type of ethical dilemma in this case?
3. How should an organization make a decision in this situation?

References

[1] *Encyclopedia Britannica Online*, s.v. "Steve Easterbrook," by John P. Rafferty, accessed May 10, 2021, https://www.britannica.com/biography/Steve-Easterbrook.

[2] Will Racke, "McDonald's CEO embracing change at fast food giant," *Chicago Business Journal*, November 22, 2016, https://www.bizjournals.com/chicago/news/2016/11/22/mcdonalds-ceo-embraceing-change-at-fast-food-giant.html.

[3] Paul R. La Monica, "McDonald's CEO promises better food," *CNN Business*, May 4, 2015, https://money.cnn.com/2015/05/04/investing/mcdonalds-turnaround-plan-steve-easterbrook/index.html.

[4] Tove Danovich, "Why McDonald's All-Day Breakfast Was Years in the Making," Eater.com, September 25, 2015, https://www.eater.com/2015/9/25/9393077/mcdonalds-all-day-breakfast-franchise-how-it-works.

[5] David Yaffe-Bellany, "McDonald's Fires C.E.O. Steve Easterbrook After Relationship With Employee," *New York Times*, November 3, 2019, https://www.nytimes.com/2019/11/03/business/mcdonalds-ceo-fired-steve-easterbrook.html.

[6] Yaffe-Bellany, "McDonald's Fires C.E.O. Steve Easterbrook After Relationship With Employee."

[7] Information in this paragraph is taken from David Enrich and Rachel Abrams, "McDonald's Sues Former C.E.O., Accusing Him of Lying and Fraud," *New York Times*, August 10, 2020, https://www.nytimes.com/2020/08/10/business/mcdonalds-ceo-steve-easterbrook.html.

[8] Chester Barnard, *The Functions of the Executive* (Cambridge, MA: Harvard University Press, 1938). See also Richard L Daft, *Organization Theory and Design* (Mason, OH: South-Western Publishing 2020), Chapter 12.

[9] Definition taken from *Oxford English Dictionary*, cf power, available at https://www.oed.com/search?searchType=dictionary&q=power&_searchBtn=Search (by subscription), accessed May 23, 2020.

[10] Chester Barnard, *The Functions of the Executive*, 168–169.

[11] Kristen Weir, "Power Play," *Monitor on Psychology* 48, no. 4 (2017): 40, https://www.apa.org/monitor/2017/04/power-play.

[12] The classic description of these sources of power comes from John R. P. French and Bertram Raven, "The Bases of Social Power," in *Studies in Social Power*, Darwin P. Cartwright, ed. (Ann Arbor: Institute for Social Research, University of Michigan, 1959), 150–167. A review of any college library's website will identify a stream of research that continues to build in these half-century-old insights. For example, see Antonio Pierro, Arie W. Kruglanski, and Bertram Raven, "Motivational underpinnings of social influence in work settings: Bases of social power and the need for cognitive closure," *European Journal of Social Psychology* 42 no. 1 (2012): 41–52.

[13] Definition and supporting material found at https://workplacebullying.org/, accessed May 21, 2020.

[14] Workplace bullying, see note 8, Chester Barnard, *The Functions of the Executive*.

[15] The material in the extract is taken from "Harassment," U.S. Equal Employment Opportunity Commission, accessed May 21, 2020, https://www.eeoc.gov/harassment.

[16] "Protections Against Discrimination and Other Prohibited Practices," Equal Employment Opportunity Commission, Federal Trade Commission, accessed May 27, 2021, https://www.ftc.gov/site-information/no-fear-act/protections-against-discrimination.

[17] "What are the different types of sexual harassment?" SHRM, September 11, 2019, https://www.shrm.org/resourcesandtools/tools-and-samples/hr-qa/pages/typesofsexualharassment.aspx.

[18] Material from "Policy Guidance on Current Issues of Sexual Harassment," U.S. Equal Employment Opportunity Commission, March 19, 1990, https://www.eeoc.gov/laws/guidance/policy-guidance-current-issues-sexual-harassment.

[19] Lisa Nagele-Piazza, "Workplace Bullying and Harassment: What's the Difference?" SHRM, March 28, 2018, https://www.shrm.org/resourcesandtools/legal-and-compliance/state-and-local-updates/pages/workplace-bullying.aspx.

[20] For a discussion, see Edgar H. Schein, *Organizational Culture and Leadership* (San Francisco: Josey-Bass, 2010).

[21] Nagele-Piazza, "Workplace Bullying and Harassment."

[22] Geoffrey P. Miller, *The Law of Governance, Risk Management and Compliance* (New York: Wolters Kluwer Law and Business, 2014).

[23] Brendan L. Smith, "What it really takes to stop sexual harassment," *Monitor on Psychology* 49, no. 2 (February 2018): 36, https://www.apa.org/monitor/2018/02/sexual-harassment.

[24] Jeffrey Pfeffer, *Power: Why Some People Have It and Others Don't* (New York: Harper Collins, 2010).

[25] John Emerich Edward Dalberg, "Letter to Bishop Creighton" (1887), Online Library of Liberty, accessed Jul 6, 2021, https://oll.libertyfund.org/quotes/214.

[26] Pfeffer's complete bio and list of works is available on his website, https://jeffreypfeffer.com/.

[27] Mary Bellis, "Biography of Steve Wozniak, Apple Computer Co-Founder," ThoughtCo.com, last updated October 28, 2019, https://www.thoughtco.com/steve-wozniak-biography-1991136.

[28] Charles Moore, *Margaret Thatcher: The Authorized Biography*, vol. 1 (New York: Alfred A. Knopf, 2013).

[29] Joseph Staph, "Walter Payton's off-season training," Stack.com, last updated November 1, 2006, https://www.stack.com/a/walter-paytons-off-season-training.

[30] Carol Dweck, *Mindset* (New York: Ballantine Books, 2008).

[31] Zameena Mejia, "Bill Gates asked himself these questions at the close of 2018," *CNBC Make It*, Power Players, last updated December 31, 2018, https://www.cnbc.com/2018/12/31/bill-gates-asked-himself-these-questions-at-the-close-of-2018.html.

[32] Story told in Pfeffer, *Power: Why Some People Have It and Others Don't*, 50.

[33] Stephen R. Covey, *The 7 Habits of Highly Effective People* (New York: Simon and Shuster, 2004).

[34] Doris Kearns Goodwin, *Team of Rivals: The Political Genius of Abraham Lincoln* (New York: Simon and Shuster, 2005).

[35] David Garvin and Michael Roberto, "What you Don't Know About Making Decisions," *Harvard Business Review*, 79, no. 8 (2001): 108–16; see also Kathleen Eisenhardt, Jean Kahwajy, and L. J. Bourgeois III, "How Management Teams Can Have A Good Fight," *Harvard Business Review* 75, no. 4 (1997): 77–85.

CHAPTER 9

Conflicts of Interest

LEARNING OUTCOMES

At the end of this chapter, you should be able to do the following:

1. Define and describe a "conflict of interest."

2. Identify several common examples of workplace conflicts of interest.

3. Describe ways that individuals and organizations can avoid or mitigate conflicts of interest at work.

4. Illustrate how personal values can help avoid the adverse effects of conflicts of interest.

5. Use the tools and information in this chapter to consider how to resolve real-world conflicts of interest.

Opening Case | JEDI: Competitive Bidding or Conflict of Interest?

The United States Department of Defense (DOD) is the nation's largest organization, with a budget of almost $750 billion dollars, more than 4,800 locations in 160 countries, and 2.9 million civilian employees and uniformed service members.[1] In 2017, the agency's CEO, Secretary of Defense James Mattis, issued an order for the department to upgrade and update its information technology (IT) infrastructure. Individual branches of the military had their own IT departments and protocols, but Mattis wanted to centralize all DOD data under one platform and he wanted to move most of the data to cloud management and storage. Early in 2018, the DOD announced project JEDI—Joint Enterprise Defense Infrastructure—and put a $10 billion, 10-year, winner-take-all contract out to bid.

The bidding process attracted all the major players in the cloud computing and storage market: Amazon, Google, IBM, Microsoft, and Oracle. The project had tight specifications and requirements that each company had to meet. Google dropped out of the bidding early when the company decided that JEDI raised potential conflicts with its recently announced principles around artificial intelligence and its use in developing weapons and/or surveillance systems.[2] Oracle and IBM were later eliminated when the DOD determined that these two competitors could not meet its stringent security requirements. Microsoft's Azure system was awarded the contract in October of 2019, beating out the presumed front runner, Amazon's giant cloud service AWS (Amazon Web Services). The company's shares rose about

4% upon the announcement.[3] The jubilation among Microsoft's team at winning the contract would be short-lived, however.

A group of Microsoft employees, naming themselves Microsoft Workers 4 Good, immediately protested. The group issued a tweet that said, "We are disheartened that Microsoft accepted the JEDI contract. As Microsoft workers, we are now complicit in 'increasing the lethality' of the U.S. Department of Defense."[4] Amazon also cried foul. They claimed that President Trump, who saw Amazon owner Jeff Bezos as an enemy, had improperly intervened to award the contract to Microsoft. Oracle had already filed its own lawsuit shortly after it was eliminated from the competition. Oracle claimed that AWS had received a preferential review due to a clear conflict of interest: DOD employees working on the JEDI project had cozy relationships with AWS.[5]

The potential conflicts surrounded two JEDI project leaders, Deap Ubhi and Anthony DeMartino. Ubhi worked for AWS until 2016, spent a year at the DOD's Defense Digital Service, and left the DOD in late 2017 to become the AWS general manager. Oracle's suit claimed that "While engaged in the JEDI Cloud procurement, Ubhi held discussions with AWS regarding AWS buying one of Ubhi's businesses, and had employment discussions with AWS."[6] Oracle further alleged that Ubhi's electronic messages on the Slack platform disparaged AWS competitors, calling those who supported anyone but AWS "dum-dums."

DeMartino's position on the JEDI team was alleged to have violated DOD conflict of interest policy, as he began work on JEDI with a known conflict of interest (prior consulting revenue from AWS) without approval from the DOD's Standard of Conduct Office. Although DeMartino later left the project, Oracle claimed that his participation had already created a bid process and specification set that privileged AWS.[7]

As of early 2021, the JEDI contract with Microsoft had not been finalized. Oracle's suit continued to move through the courts, and the Amazon charge that former President Trump had improperly intervened for Microsoft awaited a ruling from a federal judge. To date, the DOD has already spent over $5 million in contract-related issues, not including attorney's fees. Many experts wondered if the government would have to redo the entire process, from design and specification to the final award.[8]

The JEDI contract and its problems introduce you to one of the most common and ongoing ethical challenges facing business professionals: situations where professional duties and responsibilities conflict with personal goals, or situations where organizations face competing and conflicting goals or policies. These are conflicts of interest. Google resolved its conflict of interest by backing out of the JEDI bidding process. Deap Ubhi and Anthony DeMartino played ongoing roles in the process; whether their conduct created actual conflicts of interest that swayed the bidding process is yet to be determined. Their actions created a strong *perception* of a conflict of interest, which can often be as harmful to a reputation as an actual conflict. In this chapter, we'll introduce you to the concept of conflict of interest and provide you with some tools to navigate these challenges in your own career. We'll also provide you with a set of cases and exercises to help you practice identifying and resolving conflicts of interest.

Conflicts of Interest

Conflicts of interest are some of the most pervasive ethical challenges you will face. There are, as always, different definitions. A legal definition sets a strong framework:

> [A conflict of interest is] a situation in which a person has a duty to more than one person or organization but cannot do justice to the actual or potentially adverse interests of both parties. This includes when an individual's personal interests or concerns are inconsistent with the best for a customer [or employer], or when a public official's personal interests are contrary to his/her loyalty to public business.[9]

What are we really talking about here? Conflicts arise when there is a difference between what loyalty to an employer and loyalty to one's own interests may dictate (see Figure 9.1). Conflicts of interest represent a class of moral temptations when loyalty to the business (the firm, its customers, or other stakeholders) conflicts with immediate or long-term gains available to an individual. For example, people who work in sales and business development face these conflicts when they decide whether to pitch and sell products that best meet customer needs or to sell those on which they earn the highest commissions.[10] Moral courage and self-control are virtues that help to keep one's self-serving impulses in check and manage these conflicts ethically and productively. It takes moral courage for people to identify conflicts of interest, reflect on potential courses of action, and then respond to the conflict of interest.

Conflicts of interest become ethical dilemmas when loyalty to the organization is opposed by loyalty to other beliefs or systems. Google had a conflict between bidding on the JEDI contract and its principles and so it dropped out of the bidding. The group Microsoft Workers 4 Good faced a conflict of interest between executing a hard-won contract and upholding values they stood for, and ones they believed the company should stand for as well.

FIGURE 9.1   Conflicts of interest arise when there are differences between personal and organizational interests.

These employees exhibited moral courage. They also engaged their moral imagination as they chose to give voice to their values in a way that would encourage productive dialogue about appropriate uses of technology and Microsoft's business practices.[11]

How Conflicts of Interest Arise

In this section and the rest of the chapter, we'll pay attention to the first type of conflicts of interest, those where your business responsibilities lead you into situations where you must choose between what's best for the business or what appears to be best for you. Figure 9.2 presents a model of these conflicts of interest.

There are, unfortunately, almost a limitless number of conflicts of interest; however, real conflicts will have each of the three elements in Figure 9.2. Making sure that a situation has all three elements will help you avoid playing "whack-a-mole" and viewing each situation as a new and unique challenge. Employment agreements help sensitize you to sources of potential conflicts. Figure 9.3 displays some common language used in these agreements to help you identify conflicts of interest. In the next sections, we'll consider some of the ways in which conflicts of interest arise based on the three elements of Figure 9.2.

Transactions in Which an Employee Represents the Company and Could Benefit Personally

Relationships with vendors are a very common source of conflicts of interest. Every company has some type of process for buying items. Conflicts arise from simple things like spending more for supplies to buy brands that are your personal preference to more complex situations like steering business to a vendor you have worked for or may want to work for. This was Deap Ubhi and Anthony DeMartino's issue. It may also include giving certain vendors overly favorable contract terms or paying them more quickly than others. When you think about how many vendors a company has, you can see the potential for conflicts of interest.

Transactions in which employee represents company, or makes recommendations or decisions about transactions	**+**	Personal Considerations (profit, gain, etc.) from outside activities related to job activities	**+**	Situations that could lead to divided loyalties OR represent even the appearance of a conflict	**=**	**REAL CONFLICT**

FIGURE 9.2 A framework for thinking about conflicts of interest.

It is the policy of _____ Company that every employee should be free from the influence of personal considerations when representing the company in transactions with others, when making recommendations relating to such transactions, or when making decisions about such transactions. Company employees should not obtain any personal profit or gain from any outside activity related in any way to their responsibilities at Company. They should also avoid any situation which could lead to divided loyalties or present the appearance of a conflict of interest.

(Taken from a sample policy available at www.acca.com/protected/policy/employment/conflictofinterest.pdf.)

FIGURE 9.3 Sample employment policy language around conflicts of interest.

Hiring decisions are also rife with potential conflicts of interest. The most common challenge is **nepotism**, or giving a job to a family member whether or not that person is qualified. An ethical hallmark of a meritocracy is that jobs should go to the most qualified, not the most related. Hiring extends beyond nepotism to include friends of all sorts. We noted above that marketing and selling create opportunities for conflicts of interest. People who receive **bonus compensation** or are paid on **commission** have incentives to arrange their activities in ways that benefit them, but not necessarily the firm they work for. For example, pushing a sale into the next quarter may help with my commission structure, but it may not be good for the company's overall performance. Accountants and financial managers also face conflicts of interest around when and how to report income and expenses on internal and external financial statements.

As employees become proficient in their fields, they may be asked to speak at an event. Sometimes these speaking engagements come with perks. Those perks can include anything from free travel to and from a conference or free lodging and meals to an actual payment for speaking. How might perks like these be potential conflicts of interests? If the speaker fee or the trip could be something that influences the speaker to perhaps do business with a vendor or customer on a preferential basis in the future, this would be a conflict of interest. Finally, companies need to be able to rely on their employees not to divulge company **confidential information**. There are circumstances in any aspect of a business where employees have an incentive to release confidential information such as strategic plans, financial data, or contractual terms. When an employee is tempted to disclose confidential information for personal gain, a potential conflict of interest arises.

Situations Leading to Divided Loyalties or Presenting the Appearance of a Conflict

The most common conflict here is about the **use of equipment**. Many companies have policies about how employees may or may not use company equipment, such as computers, printers, company-provided mobile phones, tablets, and so forth. Preserving company confidential data on these devices is one of the reasons these policies exist. Another reason is that when the devices are owned by the company, employees should not be using them for activities unrelated to work. It may be more efficient to use the company laptop and software, or cheaper to use the 3D printer, but you may be putting your interest over the legitimate interest of your employer. The legitimate interests of your employer, including neglecting work projects or wear and tear on equipment that decreases its useful life.

Employees' personal **social media** accounts may create conflicts of interest. Office gossip may disclose confidential or unflattering information, or employee anger over company policies may lead to very different posts than those of the Microsoft Workers 4 Good. Employees may be serving their own interests at the moment but also doing something to harm the reputation of the company.

One of the aspects of conflicts that compliance departments generally make sure to train employees about is to *beware of the second job*. Employers don't want their employees working another job (or multiple jobs!) that might somehow interfere with the job they are paying their employee to do. We live in a gig economy where "alternative work arrangements are growing faster than traditional full-time jobs, and are only projected to keep growing."[12] In fact, an estimated "30–40% of today's workforce are self-employed either part- or full-time, and the numbers are only expected to grow."[13] What does a job conflict look like if workers are part of that gig economy and work multiple consulting, part-time, and/or temporary gigs? The onus, unfortunately, is on the employee to be aware of potential conflicts about time use, equipment use, confidential information, and divided loyalties.

Work is such a significant portion of our lives and we all establish **relationships** at work. These can be enjoyable and contribute to our PERMA life, but they may also create conflicts in the workplace, especially when we have close relationships with teammates or those we supervise. In these situations, it's easy to serve our own interests instead of looking out for the company's. The same goes for romantic relationships. What if you were dating your boss? Would he or she treat the other team members fairly? This is one of the reasons that many companies either have a prohibition on dating among coworkers or at least require that relationships be reported to management.

Finally, many employees come up with an idea about starting a business that is in some way related to their employers' existing business. They may actually, outside of their work role, establish a start-up company. While at first, these "side hustles" such as a consulting firm or a product sales website, may not appear to be related to the company (and the only conflict may be the time and energy focused on the start-up, which detracts from the main job of the employees), sometimes it is apparent that the new company does rely on plans, concepts, and/or processes, among other things, of the employees' main company.

Special Conflicts of Executives, Officers, and Directors

Members of boards of directors and executive officers have a legal duty to the company due to their position as fiduciaries. In addition to the conflicts of interest above that potentially impact all employees, there are some conflicts that typically arise only for executive officers and board members of a company. Their fiduciary duty means they must pay special attention to looking out for the interests of the company and not their own.

The Corporate Opportunity Doctrine comes from *Guth v. Loft, Inc.*, a 1939 court case.[14] In that case, the court held that

> if there is presented to a corporate officer or director a business opportunity which the corporation is financially able to undertake, is, from its nature, in the line of the corporation's business and is of practical advantage to it, is one in which the corporation has an interest or a reasonable expectancy, and, by embracing the opportunity, the self-interest of the officer or director will be brought into conflict with that of the corporation, the law will not permit him to seize the opportunity for himself.[15]

The corporate opportunity doctrine means that executives or officers of a company cannot take advantage of an opportunity that creates "a conflict between the fiduciary's duties to the corporation and the self-interest of the [officer]."[16] What types of opportunities might actually come to an officer or director of a company that the company itself might like to take advantage of? Sales of assets such as buildings or intellectual property, consulting arrangements, certain speaking opportunities, or authorship of books would be activities that could violate the corporate opportunity doctrine. Officers can manage conflicts of interest ethically and legally by bringing the matter to others on the executive team and having them make the decision about the opportunity. This avoids the perception and reality of self-dealing. Companies should also have formal policies and procedures that help executives identify, report, and review opportunities for self-dealing.

Mitigating Conflicts of Interest

As you might think, the mechanisms that organizational leaders use to avoid and mitigate conflicts of interest come from the same basic toolkit that you learned about in Chapter 5 on compliance. We won't provide an exhaustive review, but we will highlight some features about conflicts of interest that leaders ought to think about, and we'll provide examples of how companies have used these tools to help employees avoid and navigate conflicts of interest.

The first tool is a basic conflict of interest policy that is easily accessible, clear and simple for all employees to understand, and available in every language spoken in the organization. As we noted above, policies are usually described in employment agreements and contracts; however, these policies should also appear in employee handbooks and other materials that departments and work groups reference for operating procedures. Every employee, contractor, or director should receive a copy of the policy, and should certify in writing their receipt of the policy, their understanding of it, and their intent to comply with it. Good policies will also require employees to disclose any potential conflicts of interest as they arise.

Many organizations supplement individual policies with a **code of conduct**. A code of conduct is basically an umbrella policy for a company because it tends to cover all of the major policies of a company. It provides an ethical baseline for expected behavior of all of its employees, officers, board members, and so forth. Publicly traded companies generally have codes of conduct, as this is a legal requirement put into place as part of the Sarbanes-Oxley Act. Ethics in the Real World 9.1 displays retailer Target's code of conduct.

In recent years, as codes of conduct have gone Web-based for employees who have constant access to computers or other mobile devices, it is not uncommon for codes of conduct to include a brief overview of a policy with a hyperlink to the full policy for the topic.

Ethics in the Real World 9.1 | Target's Code of Conduct

Brian Cornell, CEO of Target Corporation, states "Target's commitment to ethical standards is reflected in the way we conduct business and through our actions. As team members, at any level, we must always consider the impact on our guests, team members, stakeholders, community and the Target brand when making business decisions. By holding ourselves and each other accountable to these standards, we deliver on our brand promises while deepening the trust of our guests, team members, stakeholders and communities."

Figure 9.4 shows the Conflicts of Interest section from Target's *Business Conduct Guide* (with reference to Target's full Conflict of Interest policy).

avoid conflicts of interest.

We have interests and relationships outside of work, but we act in Target's best interest and avoid even the appearance of a conflict of interest.

our commitment

We never allow our personal interests to impact the business decisions we make as Target team members. When our outside activities conflict or even appear to conflict with our responsibilities as a Target team member, we avoid and disclose any activity that could be considered a conflict of interest.

how it's done

The best way to avoid a conflict of interest is to know and avoid the types of situations where conflicts typically arise between personal and business interests and relationships. Seek guidance immediately if you see, hear or suspect a potential conflict. Always prioritize Target's business interests when making decisions.

in your daily work

Be alert to the activities of family members. Conflict of interest situations extend beyond your own activities – they also apply to the activities of your family members. Always disclose any personal or family relationships or activities that have the potential to influence decisions you make on the job. If you're not sure if a particular situation creates a conflict, always ask for guidance by contacting ethics@target.com.

Know when to say "No." Offers of gifts, entertainment or accommodations that do not further a legitimate business purpose or don't comply with our policies can also create a conflict of interest and cause others to question your objectivity. Know what's allowed – and what isn't – and turn down anything that is, or could be perceived as a violation of our policy.

Consider your influence. Never misuse the authority of your position for personal benefit. Your role should never be used to acquire anything of value or pressure a business partner for personal gain.

Disclose potential conflicts. Despite your efforts, conflicts of interest can still arise, even if you're careful to avoid them. Promptly disclose any actual, potential or perceived conflict to your leader, Human Resources partner or the Ethics team so it can be addressed and resolved. Depending on the job you hold, you may be required to complete an annual Conflicts of Interest Disclosure Statement.

Be aware. It's not possible to list every situation that could pose a conflict, but here are some that often arise:

- A business partner offering to pay for a meal, gift or entertainment that does not further a legitimate business purpose or exceeds our policy guidelines
- Investing in a company that competes with, does business with or seeks to do business with Target
- Transacting business on behalf of Target with a company in which you or a family member has a substantial financial interest
- Using your position or authority at Target, or company property, resources or information, for personal gain instead of putting Target first
- A family member performing services for a current or prospective business partner or for an entity that competes with Target
- Becoming a member of an outside board of directors or advisory board

consider this

Not sure if there's a conflict of interest? Ask yourself:

- Could it affect my objectivity?
- Could it influence the decisions I make on behalf of Target?
- Could an outside observer view it as a possible conflict?

If the answer to any question is "yes," or "I'm not sure," seek guidance.

what if

Q: A business partner that works with Target asked if I would be willing to do a little work for them "on the side." Is this OK?

A: It depends. If the work is unrelated to Target's business, it may be OK. If the work competes with our business, or interferes with your ability to do your job or could influence your judgment, you should not accept it. It is also a conflict if you are responsible for managing or making decisions about that business relationship on behalf of Target. The best course of action is to contact ethics@target.com and ask for guidance before proceeding.

policy spot

Conflicts of Interest Policy

Conflicts of Interest Business Amenities Table

Travel and Expense Policy

Code of Ethics | maintaining trust | avoid conflicts of interest

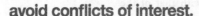

FIGURE 9.4 Target's Conflict of Interest Policy.

Policies and codes of conduct provide the first line of defense against conflicts of interest. **Training** and **education** provide an important second line of defense. Effective training will provide employees with a framework, such as in Figure 9.2, to help them think about conflicts of interest; however, it also invites employees to think through actual situations they are likely to face in their jobs and to learn where they can seek guidance. The best training occurs annually and requires employees to both exhibit competence and certify compliance. Best-in-class

CONFIDENTIAL CONFLICT OF INTEREST CERTIFICATION

_____
Identification of Matter (Case Number, Name, etc.)

I, _____ hereby certify that to the best of my knowledge, neither I nor my spouse, dependent child, general partner, or any organization for which I am serving as an officer, director, trustee, general partner or employee, or any person or organization with whom I am negotiating or have an arrangement concerning prospective employment has a financial interest in this matter.

I further certify to the best of my knowledge that this matter will not affect the financial interests of any member of my household. Also, to the best of my knowledge, no member of my household; no relative with whom I have a close relationship; no one with whom my spouse, parent or dependent child has or seeks employment; and no organization with which I am seeking a business relationship nor which I now serve actively or have served within the last year are parties or represent a party to the matter.

I also acknowledge my responsibility to disclose the acquisition of any financial or personal interest as described above that would be affected by the matter, and to disclose any interest I, or anyone noted above, has in any person or organization that does become involved in, or is affected at a later date by, the conduct of this matter.

_____   _____
Signature   Date

_____
Position

FIGURE 9.5 A sample conflict of interest certification form from the US Department of Justice. Available at https://www.justice.gov/jmd/deo-confidential-conflict-interest-certification.

training also has a **post-training disclosure** component. At the culmination of any training that includes conflicts as a topic, while the concepts are fresh for employees, it is ideal to ask employees (1) to certify that they understand and agree to comply with the conflicts of interest policy of the company and (2) to disclose if they have any concerns about potential or actual conflicts of interest. Figure 9.5 shows you a confidential conflict of interest certification from the US Department of Justice (DOJ).

The final tool in the kit for avoiding/mitigating conflicts of interest is a **disclosure process** that allows employees to disclose potential conflicts as they arise. Some companies make this disclosure part of an ethics or compliance "hotline" process. Employees can simply dial the company hotline and leave their concern with the hotline operator; someone—likely from the legal or compliance department—would reply to the employee. Other times, companies want employees to contact a specific person. The colleague to contact might be someone who handles conflicts on a regional basis (for the Middle East region of a global multinational enterprise, for example). If the company is rather small, perhaps this contact would be the chief legal officer or chief compliance officer.

As companies grow however, and because there are so many potential types of conflicts of interest, they may establish some type of process to manage conflicts. For many, this includes some type of Web-based disclosure portal, to which employees may submit potential conflicts of interest and provide details prompted by a survey mechanism. An administrator can collect these disclosures and refer them to appropriate decision makers or investigators. This method enables the compliance department to track metrics (how many disclosures are submitted on certain topics, from specific areas; time to respond to employee, etc.). Given that officers and directors have unique constraints on conflicts of interest, many companies have, separate from the basic disclosure process, a process for disclosure of corporate opportunities. This process may include officers presenting the opportunity to a certain executive, a team of executives, or some combination of board members and executives. Ethics in the Real World 9.2 contains the corporate opportunities code of conduct at Gulfport Energy.

The following code of conduct comes from Gulfport
Energy:[17]

Corporate Opportunities.
Employees and directors
owe a duty to the Company
to advance the Company's
legitimate business interests when the opportunity to do so
arises. Generally, employees and directors are prohibited from
taking for themselves (or directing to a third party) a corporate

opportunity that is discovered through the use of corporate
property, information or position, unless the Company has first
been offered the opportunity and turned it down. Additionally,
employees and directors are prohibited from using corporate
property, information or position for improper personal gain or
competing with the Company.

If an employee or director has any question about corporate
opportunities or whether any use of Company property or services is improper, such person should consult with the General
Counsel or other designated compliance officer in advance.

Resolving Conflicts of Interest as Individuals

Because conflicts of interest are pervasive in business, the question is not *if* you will encounter
a conflict—small or large—but *when*, and the next issue is *how* you will react. Policies, training,
and disclosure processes are all valuable resources for you; they tend to be good at helping you
identify conflicts. Sometimes they'll provide guidelines or principles you can use to resolve
conflicts, but you'll always have a decision to make. Our colleagues Brad Agle, Aaron Miller,
and Bill O'Rourke provide a list of five questions you can ask to help you resolve conflicts of
interest, and we add another two to their list:[18]

1. *What do company policies and guidelines say?* If there is a clear policy, you have an easy
   answer. If not, you can ask yourself about the "spirit" and "intent" of other policy
   statements. What would they recommend as a course of action?

2. *How will others interpret your actions and motivations?* How might your actions impact your
   reputation? Remember that you want to avoid real conflicts, *and* those that might appear
   as conflicts to others. Would you be pleased if someone told your mother about how you
   chose to act?

3. *Who else has a right to know and should be involved in the decision?* Your managers, officers in
   human resources, and significant others in your personal life may all be affected by your
   choice. Let them know about the conflict and share with them how you intend to move
   forward. Their reaction and advice will often help you make the right decision.

4. *Is there a way out?* As with any ethical temptation, if we can turn a conflict from a
   "win-lose" into a "win-win," we have an easy decision. Moral imagination and advice
   from trusted mentors can often help us see potential "win-win" opportunities. Mentors
   are also quite good at helping us see self-deception, and sometimes the conflict really is a
   "win-lose" situation.

5. *Can the other party in the conflict help us resolve the situation?* Sometimes the person across
   the table can alter the situation in a way that makes a conflict evaporate. It's always worth
   asking for their help.

6. *Whom can I rely on for good advice?* There may be people who don't have a right to know
   but who can give us very good advice. Friends and mentors can help us avoid the sense
   that we are all alone resolving the conflict. Their advice can bring comfort as well as practical wisdom.

7. *How does my desire to live a life filled with PERMA inform my choice?* Sometimes a conflict of
   interest trades off a short-term gain for long-term moral pain. When we frame conflicts
   of interest in terms of our long-term aspirations and values, we find resolution to many
   conflicts. Figure 9.6 presents a set of questions that the PERMA model suggests for
   dealing with conflicts of interest.

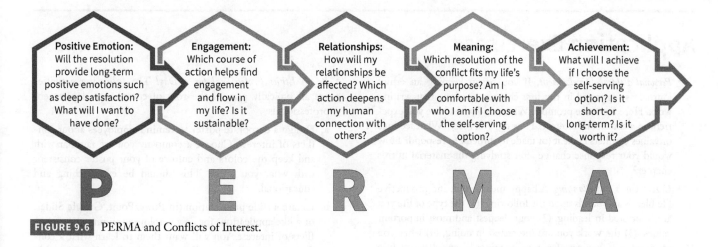

FIGURE 9.6 PERMA and Conflicts of Interest.

Key Terms

bonus compensation
code of conduct
commission
confidential information
corporate opportunity doctrine
disclosure process
education
ethical dilemmas

fiduciaries
loyalty
moral courage
moral imagination
moral temptations
nepotism
policy
post-training disclosure

relationships
second job
social media
start-up
training
use of equipment
vendors

Chapter Summary

- Conflicts of interest in the workplace take the form of any and all activities that interferes with an employee's obligations or loyalties to their employer. A conflict occurs when the employer's and employees' interests diverge and only one interest can be satisfied. Conflicts of interest are pervasive. They arise from three sources: first, transactions in which the employee represents the company or makes recommendations or decisions about transactions; second, situations in which the potential exists for personal profit or gain from outside activities related to job activities; and third, situations that could lead to divided loyalties or present even the appearance of a conflict.

- Because of their fiduciary duties, officers, directors, and executives also may face decisions involving *corporate opportunities*, situations

where something may be good for the firm and good for the officer, but it creates a real or perceived conflict of interest. The compliance and risk mitigation tools you've learned about in other chapters can all be employed to help employees and officers avoid conflicts of interest. These include policies, codes of conduct, codes of ethics, training, and disclosure policies and protocols.

- Individuals also need a values-based set of tools to help them avoid and resolve conflicts of interest, including company policies and communication strategies. When individuals have a strong foundation for a PERMA life, they will find themselves better equipped to resolve many conflicts of interest.

Chapter Review Questions

1. Explain what a conflict of interest is.

2. What could be the consequences of conflict of interest?

3. What are the three basic categories into which workplace conflicts of interest fall?

4. What tools do companies use to help individuals avoid or mitigate conflicts of interest?

5. Why would a CEO having a romantic relationship, even if it is consensual, with another employee always create a conflict of interest?

6. How can your values help you to recognize and avoid conflicts of interest?

Application Exercises

- *Personal Ethical Development.* If you began keeping an ethics journal as suggested in the first chapter, continue that writing work. Here are some prompts: Where and when have you experienced a conflict of interest? How did you react? What feelings or values conflicts make it (or made it) difficult to respond? How would your response change after studying the material in this chapter?

- *Career Goals and Planning.* A happy, meaningful, and productive life blends and builds upon the following: (1) the type of life you are interested in leading, (2) your deepest and most important values, (3) the work you are interested in doing, (4) what you are good at, (5) your preferences for things like work versus free time, and (6) your personality. What types of organizational policies and controls would you like to see around conflicts of interest where you work? What are the major conflicts of interest in the firms and industries where you'd like to work?

- *Ethics in the Business World.* Identify an individual or company that faced a conflict of interest. How did the individuals and organizational leaders respond? Did they respond well or poorly? What were the outcomes? How has that organization adjusted its policies, culture, or style to prevent such incidents in the future?

- *Talking with and Learning from Others.* Choose a business professional you respect. Engage that person in a brief interview. Where have they experienced conflicts of interest in their careers? How have they responded? What do they wish they had done differently? What advice would they give you as you begin your career?

- *Be an Ethics Professional for a Day!* The following activities are all typically part of the role of compliance department professionals:

  a. Design a corporate poster to remind employees about conflicts of interest. Choose a company you are familiar with and keep the colors and culture of your poster consistent with what you know. This should be eye-catching and educational.

  b. Create a slide presentation (in PowerPoint, Google Slides, or a like application) for new employee training about conflicts of interest. You will want them to learn what a conflict of interest is generally, some examples of conflicts that they should be aware of, and what they should do in the event that they believe they may have a conflict situation. You only will have fifteen minutes to present this information, so keep your presentation to five slides maximum plus a cover page.

  c. Draft an email for your company CEO to send to all employees, following an unfortunate situation that has just come to light. One of the company's top executives, the chief marketing officer (CMO), has just been terminated because it was discovered that he had created a list of company employees to hire for his new start-up, and that he had reached out to a few at the top of that list. The CEO will review your email, possibly revise it, and then email it herself to all employees. Consider what you want employees to know, both about the CMO situation and the company's expectations about conflicts of interest.

Mini-Cases

Case 1: Playing favorites among employees. Ben Alvarez's first "real" job out of college has been with IntelliShip, an Internet-based global trading and logistics firm. Ben started out as a product manager, with responsibility for making sure the company had shipping containers in the right locations, the right volume, and at the right time to efficiently move products around the globe. After about six months, Ben was promoted to his current role as the project manager over the company's Pacific Rim container business. He manages a team of four other employees, Tina, Rinda, Jorge, and Ace. During the first meeting, as the team members got to know each other, Ben learned that Ace is a scuba diver, and scuba diving is Ben's passion! This shared hobby is a fantastic perk for both Ace and Ben at work—they love being able to compare diving notes. Tina, Rinda, and Jorge often roll their eyes when they hear Ace and Ben discussing their latest fish photos or diving depth. They also call Ace "Ben's favorite" employee. Each time that a new and exciting project comes up, Ben often approaches Ace first, even when he's not the most qualified for the job. At the last annual review and bonus distribution, Ben found it hard not to rate Ace highly, even though his performance on some projects was just OK. When dividing up the bonus pool, Ben knew

that Ace was hoping to use his bonus for an amazing dive trip to the Maldives.

Discussion Questions

1. Does Ben have a conflict of interest here? What type is it? What should Ben do?

2. What would you do if you were in this situation?

Case 2: A questionable recommendation. Ben knows that his cousin, Andi, really needs a job because she was laid off from her last position. She pleaded with Ben to turn in her resume to the finance department at IntelliShip. Ben isn't actually sure why Andi was laid off from her other job, but he doesn't think she will be called in for an interview anyway since she doesn't have a lot of finance experience. He also owes her a favor from their days in school together. Andi had tutored Ben through his final business writing class so he could graduate. Ben carries her resume to one of his friends in finance. "Anyone you refer to us, Ben, would have to be a fabulous addition to our team," his friend says. And that is exactly when Ben feels that pit in his stomach. Andi does, in fact, get an interview with IntelliShip.

Discussion Questions

1. Should Ben have turned over the resume?

2. When he started to feel that he might have made a mistake, should he have talked with his friend in finance and explained the situation and retracted Andi's resume?

3. How could he have avoided this situation?

4. How can he make sure this doesn't happen again?

Case 3: Two sister companies of a powerful conglomerate merged into one. To keep the confidentiality of the organizations, let us call them HCCL and HVL. HCCL is a sinking ship, with its revenues coming down from $850 million to a mere $150 million in 2–4 years. On the other hand, HVL is a product company in the storage devices and server business. With the advent of cloud technologies, there were few buyers. So, HVL tried taking a chance on analytics by acquiring a company in this field. Eventually, they started selling their boxes with analytics software as a solution. To save HCCL, the top management and the holdings company merged HCCL and HVL into HJP. Until then, HCCL was like a competitor to HVL to sell HVL solutions. HCCL and HVL maintain the same ERP software for their financials, HR SCM, projects, and payroll domains. So, they have internal teams to manage, support, develop, etc. On the other hand, the HCCL ERP team was not as experienced as HVL. The ERP manager of HCCL, Vinod Chandra, was known for his poor leadership qualities. There were rumors that many of his team members escalated matters to the HR department due to his bad-mouthing them. Unfortunately, the HCCL top management

(CxO) has a strong connection with HJL. In this merger process, it is observed that the majority of layoffs were in HVL than in HCCL. Vinod was then made the manager of Daren Cross. Every now and then, Vinod would warn Daren that he would not have a career at HVL. Though Daren was shocked, he did not act on it as he thought he would get support from his former boss, who is now a site lead, and Vinod reports to him. But eventually, things worsened, and Daren was let go. Vinod did not like Daren talking to his counterparts in the US and other countries, as he thought it was a threat to himself. Though many in the team knew this was a game plan of Vinod, there was no concrete proof. Daren's former boss also did not have much say in the matter. The undocumented reason was that the HCCL ERP Manager was with the organization for more than 30 years and is more aged. So, he was assigned as to be Daren's manager. This was shocking to Daren, as he thought everyone who performs well would be elevated, which made this quite unethical. Even if Daren talks about it now, there were significantly fewer chances that HR would believe or support him due to various reasons. Daren even talked to his former boss and informed him about this case, but he did not receive any support. So he decided to focus on getting a new job while he had three months to go out. Eventually, in three months' time, he managed to get a better job.

Discussion Questions

1. Analyze Daren's decision in this situation.

2. Discuss the ethical role and responsibilities of Vinod in this situation.

References

1 See U.S. Department of Defense, About, https://www.defense.gov/our-story/.

2 Liam Tung, "Google: Here's why we're pulling out of Pentagon's $10bn JEDI cloud race," ZDNet, October 9, 2018, https://www.zdnet.com/article/google-heres-why-were-pulling-out-of-pentagons-10bn-jedi-cloud-race/.

3 "Microsoft Wins $10 Billion JEDI Contract, Pentagon Says," *Industry Week, Bloomberg*, October 28, 2019, https://www.industryweek.com/technology-and-iiot/article/22028481/microsoft-wins-10-billion-jedi-contract-pentagon-says.

4 Ibid.

5 David Harris, "Oracle Slams AWS 'Conflicts Of Interest' In JEDI Cloud Lawsuit," CRN, December 11, 2018, https://www.crn.com/news/cloud/oracle-slams-aws-conflicts-of-interest-in-jedi-cloud-lawsuit?itc=refresh.

6 Ibid.

7 Ibid.

8 Aaron Gregg, "With a $10 billion cloud-computing deal snarled in court, the Pentagon may move forward without it," *Washington Post*, February 10, 2021, https://www.washingtonpost.com/business/2021/02/10/jedi-contract-pentagon-biden/.

9 See "Conflict of Interest," Law.com, https://dictionary.law.com/Default.aspx?selected=292.

10 For an excellent example, see "Patrick Kuhse, Former International Fugitive and Convicted Felon, Addresses HBS Students," The Harbus, December 1, 2003, https://harbus.org/2003/patrick-kuhse-former-international-2423/.

11 Mary Gentile, *Giving Voice to Values* (New Haven, CT: Yale University Press, 2010).

12 Lawrence F. Katz and Alan B. Krueger, "The Rise and Nature of Alternative Work Arrangements in the United States, 1995–2015," last updated June 18, 2017, https://scholar.harvard.edu/files/lkatz/files/katz_krueger_cws_resubmit_clean.pdf.

13 Diane Mulcahy, "Will the Gig Economy Make the Office Obsolete?," *Harvard Business Review*, March 17, 2017, https://hbr.org/2017/03/will-the-gig-economy-make-the-office-obsolete.

14 Guth, [5 A.2d 503 (Del.1939)].

15 Guth, 510–511.

16 William Klein, John Ramseyer, and Stephen Bainbridge, *Business Associations, Cases and Materials on Agency, Partnerships, LLCs, and Corporations* (St. Paul, MN: Foundation Press, 2018), 319.

17 Gulfport Energy Corporation: Code of Business Conduct and Ethics, Amended and Restated, accessed May 11, 2021, https://www.sec.gov/Archives/edgar/data/874499/000119312506031437/dex14.htm.

18 Brad Agle, Aaron Miller, Bill O'Rourke, 2016. *The Business Ethics Field Guide* (Provo, UT: https://meritleadership.com/, 2016).

CHAPTER 10

Bribery and Corruption

LEARNING OUTCOMES

At the end of this chapter, you should be able to do the following:

1. Define and explain the differences between bribery, graft, and corruption.

2. Differentiate between a gift, a tip, and a bribe and identify the conditions when a gift or tip can become a bribe.

3. Describe the legal frameworks around bribery in the United States and other countries.

4. Explain how you can use your personal values to avoid and mitigate situations of bribery, graft, and corruption.

5. Apply the tools and information in this chapter to real-world issues of bribery, graft, and corruption.

Opening Case | College Admissions for a Hefty Price

William "Rick" Singer had always been competitive, with an incredibly strong desire to win. In 2002, Singer sold his first college-counseling business and took up coaching a youth basketball team in Omaha, Nebraska, to fill his time. His hard-driving style, including cursing his own players, the opposing team's parents, and officials, turned a mediocre team into a junior juggernaut. Singer once brought in a "ringer"—a talented player from another team—to help his team compete in a tournament. His win-at-all-costs mentality and his willingness to bend every rule in order to win led to his role, almost two decades later, as the architect of a college admissions bribery scandal that ensnared some of the United States' most prestigious universities, including Stanford, UCLA, the University of Southern California, and Yale.[1]

Fast forward to 2012. Rick Singer had started a new college admissions company, the Edge College & Career Network, with a clear vision of exploiting the admissions system to help wealthy parents get their children into elite colleges. Singer's scheme relied on two realities: First, elite colleges used different admissions criteria for certain groups of students, including athletes. Colleges had a "back door" for special admissions, which Singer hoped to open for the right price. Second, the wealthy were ultracompetitive and willing to blur ethical and legal lines to "win" the college application game for their children.

Singer used several methods to help students gain admission. In some cases, he would pay test administrators to help students improve their ACT or SAT performance. Some administrators looked the other way as a "ringer" took the test for a student, while others would correct answer sheets before submitting them for grading.[2] *Desperate Housewives* star Felicity Huffman paid Singer

Varsity Blues Exposes Bribery at Elite U.S. Schools

$15,000 to have her daughter's SAT score altered. In other cases, Singer worked with parents to create a false resume for their children that portrayed the children as athletes. *Full House* star Lori Loughlin and her husband, designer Mossimo Giannulli, paid Singer $500,000 to create the illusion that their two daughters were competitive crew athletes. Neither girl had ever participated in the sport.

Sometimes parents paid Singer's firm directly, as in the case of Felicity Huffman. There seemed nothing untoward about writing a $15,000 check for test prep and admissions guidance. In other cases, such as that of Lori Laughlin, the family made large donations to the Key Foundation, owned and operated by Singer, who would then funnel the money to university admissions gatekeepers for their help in shepherding a questionable packet through the admissions process. Parents could claim a charitable deduction for their donation, which meant they committed tax fraud as well as bribery.

Singer also used a variety of bribes to influence coaches and administrators. At Stanford, Singer initially approached seven different coaches about participating in his scheme. He eventually enrolled sailing coach John Vandemoer, who agreed to "recruit" two of Singer's students in exchange for donations to the sailing program. Vandemoer explained that he was under intense pressure to fund his program: "If I could take the development [money] and get recruits at the same time that I thought were going to help my team, I thought that was a no-brainer."[3] In other cases, Singer paid coaches directly, such as Yale women's soccer coach Rudolph Meredith. Meredith received almost $900,000 in direct bribe payments for designating Singer's clients as soccer players. In another case, Singer paid University of Texas men's tennis coach Michael Center $100,000 to designate a potential student as a tennis recruit.[4]

By 2018, federal authorities became aware of Singer's crimes, and he agreed to help the government gather evidence against his clients in exchange for leniency. In March of 2019, the government went public with criminal indictments for bribery and fraud against parents, coaches, and admissions administrators. Operation Varsity Blues, the government's code name for the investigation, eventually charged twenty-two parents and thirty-three others with bribery-related crimes. In sentencing Loughlin to jail, U.S. District Judge Nathaniel Gorton said that Ms. Loughlin had led a "fairy-tale life, yet you stand before me a convicted felon, and for what? For the inexplicable desire to grasp even more."[5]

The Varsity Blues case introduces you to the issue of bribery. When most people think of bribery, they think of people secretly paying off government officials in some developing country; advanced countries are supposed to have moved beyond bribery. Bribery is a pervasive and global problem that affects the private, public, and not-for-profit sectors. Our discussion of bribery comes after you've learned about power and its abuse and conflicts of interest because bribery and related corrupt behaviors represent an abuse of power and a conflict of interest. In this chapter, you'll learn about what bribery is and what it is not. We'll spend time discussing how a bribe differs from two ethical but neighboring practices: tips and gifts. You'll learn about the legal frameworks and rules that different countries employ to stop bribery. Finally, as with each of our other applied chapters, we'll provide you tools to help you avoid bribery and other forms of corruption.

Bribery, Graft, and Corruption

Black's Law Dictionary expands on the common notion of bribery as secretly given envelopes of cash by specifying the broad range of potential bribes and who can be bribed: "The receiving or offering any undue reward by or to any person whomsoever . . . in order to influence [their] behavior, and to incline [them] to act contrary to [their] duty and the known rules of honesty and integrity."[6] **Bribery** is related to several other unethical and illegal actions: corruption, fraud, and graft. *Black's Law Dictionary* defines corruption in stark terms: "a vicious and fraudulent intention to evade the prohibitions of the law. The act of an official or fiduciary person who unlawfully and wrongfully uses [their] station or character to procure some benefit for [themselves] or for another person, contrary to duty and the rights of others."[7] **Fraud** is the first close cousin of bribery: "Fraud consists of some deceitful practice or willful device, resorted to with intent to deprive another of [their] right, or in some manner to do [them] an injury. As distinguished from negligence, it is always positive, intentional."[8] Fraud usually refers to activities outside a government context. **Graft** is closely related and typically involves activities related to government. It is limited to public officials and is a "colloquial term referring to the unlawful acquisition of public money through questionable and improper transactions with public officials."[9]

An example helps clarify this quadrangle of dishonesty. Let's say that your business hopes to win a large contract from a city where you operate, and you make a secret payment to the project administrator to win the contract. *What* you and the administrator *are* is corrupt, *how* you engage in corruption is *through* bribery, and the *result* was graft. If you fail to report the payment (and who would want to report an illegal payment?), then you *act* fraudulently as well. As Figure 10.1 shows, corruption is the umbrella practice; bribery, fraud, and graft are actual corrupt behaviors.

Corrupt economic actions and actors have a significant impact on organizations and society at large. As Kofi Annan, then Secretary-General of the United Nations, stated in the foreword to the UN Convention on **Corruption**, "Corruption is an insidious plague that has a wide range of corrosive effects on societies. It undermines democracy and the rule of law, leads to violations of human rights, distorts markets, erodes the quality of life and allows organized crime, terrorism and other threats to

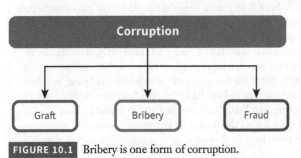

FIGURE 10.1   Bribery is one form of corruption.

human security to flourish."[10] Thankfully, good people everywhere recognize the risk of bribery and corruption. Business leaders craft company policies and public officials enact many laws and regulations to prevent both bribery and corruption. Most of our focus in this chapter will be on bribery, but you should look for and make connections among bribery, fraud, and graft as examples of corruption.

Social Norms, Bribes, and Gift Giving

Humans are gregarious; we live in groups. One strong bond that holds those groups together is the principle of **reciprocity**, returning like for like in social behaviors.[11] Reciprocity has many positive elements. Many of our day-to-day transactions are lubricated and facilitated by the expectation that when we extend help, kindness, tolerance, or understanding to others, they'll reciprocate by doing the same. The ethic of reciprocity is an example of obedience to the unenforceable. Recent evidence indicates that kindness, for example, not only facilitates social life, but being kind to others makes people happier as well.[12] Reciprocity has a dark side, however. When reciprocity becomes a transactional requirement rather than a hoped-for expectation, it becomes a source of moral harm and unethical conduct. This type of reciprocity is known as a *quid pro quo*. **Quid pro quo** is a Latin term that means "this for that." You learned about quid pro quo in the context of sexual harassment, where the request for sexual favors is given with the promise of either a reward (promotion, raise, bonus), or a penalty (demotion, career stagnation, etc.). Bribery, from the perspective of both the bribed and the briber, is a quid pro quo transaction.

Tips, Gifts, and Bribes

Table 10.1 shows three common types of reciprocity and social exchanges in our society, tips, gifts, and bribes.

These descriptions seem pretty straightforward; however, the lines that separate the three can become blurry in certain contexts. For someone who wants to live an ethical life, the natural question is: When does a tip or gift become a bribe? Here are some general principles. A tip becomes a bribe when the purpose changes from a *"Thank you"* to a *"Will you?"* Notice that reciprocity becomes expected rather than hoped for. In business practice, this happens in two ways: First, a tip may be outsized for the commensurate service rendered, and second, the

TABLE 10.1   Tips and gifts differ from bribery.

	A Tip	A Gift	A Bribe
Purpose	Remuneration for work performed	Expression of personal affection	Seeking to serve the briber's interest
Context	Custom-sanctioned situations of service (e.g., travel, restaurants)	Situations that involve personal feelings	Economic transactions or consequences
Goal	No goal, an expression of thanks	Deepen personal connection	Sway the recipient to certain behavior
Size	Proportional to service rendered	Size appropriate to occasion	Proportional to the level of expected outcome
Transparency	Yes—always public	Yes or No—public or private	No—secrecy and essential element
Result	Affect employee discretion, morale, and performance	Satisfaction and pleasure of both	Creates an expectation between briber and bribee
Reciprocity	No—given for a single event	No—given with no expectation	Yes—given as quid pro quo
Conflict of Interest	No—culturally accepted practice	No—given freely	Yes—goal is to create a conflict of interest for bribee

large tip is given in the context of a set of ongoing interactions and transactions. Both conditions must be present. The large amount creates the expectation, and the ongoing nature of the interaction provides the opportunity for the expectation to be met. A gift becomes a bribe when the objective changes from *"I care about you,"* to *"Will you take care of me?"* Again, note the forced reciprocity. This happens most often when the scale of a gift seems inappropriate for the current state of the relationship (e.g., You bought me a Tesla just because it's Friday?), or the gift is given in an unusually secretive manner. The outsized gift is usually accompanied by subtle hints or communications about what is expected.

Social and Business Conditions Ripe for Bribery

Now that you are familiar with bribery and the ways in which gifts and tips factor into business interactions, we can discuss the conditions and contexts that encourage the giving and taking of bribes. To make them easy to remember, we'll name them:

7 Deadly Signs of Bribery

1. A *sole decision maker* who has large amounts of authority. This invites corruption because a single individual has the power to make something happen or not.

2. Decision makers who have a *high degree of autonomy*. This means there are few checks on behavior, little oversight, and the potential for even less transparency.

3. Situations where *perks are a regular* and normal part of the job. Sales professionals, for example, work in situations where travel, food, entertainment, gifts, or honoraria are given to potential or existing customers.[13] These things are not bribes *per se*; however, the overall costs and level of perks can be a signal that any of these things are more than just "normal business" benefits.

4. Donations or other *signs of goodwill are involved* in closing a deal. Sometimes a decision maker will have a private pet cause, or the organization will have a charitable arm, and donations to those causes create goodwill during a transaction process.

5. Business dealings where parties have *different cultural norms*. Practices such as Guanxi (strong systems of networks) in China, or other cultural traditions that blur the boundaries between professional and personal relationships, can set the stage for bribery, particularly among outsiders to that culture.[14] In some countries, refusing a gift is seen as rude, and refusing to give gifts is an insult to the host. The Mid-Autumn Festival in China is typically a time to gift others with mooncakes, which are fairly expensive tiny cakes, as shown in **Figure 10.2**.[15]

6. The level of formality of the transaction. Bribery always entails people being in their formal roles, but many times the bribes are paid or requested in informal settings. Bribery is most often an *informal mechanism (secretive, off the books)* for influencing how people perform their formal roles.

FIGURE 10.2 A Chinese mooncake.

Bloomberg/Getty Images

7. *Ambiguous language* or cloaked requests. The most talented bribers always use language and phrases with a ready defense of "I was joking" or "You misunderstood what I said." Requests for bribes may not come as direct requests for money; they may be couched in statements about how much the recipient would enjoy a certain something.

In addition to the 7 deadly signs of bribery, we see that bribery happens more often in certain industries, business contexts and locations. See Ethics in the Real World 10.1 for an explanation of where bribery and corruption are most common.

Ethics in the Real World 10.1 | Where Is Bribery and Corruption Most Common?

Every business professional might face the ethical temptations of bribery and corruption, but people who work in some industries are more likely to experience these challenges than others (see Figure 10.3). If you work in any of these industries, you may find challenges of bribery and corruption to be more common:[16]

Extractive industries include businesses such as mining, timber, oil and gas. These businesses depend on access to fixed physical assets, mainly land. Owners of resources, or issuers of permits, understand the great value of the resources they hold and can, and sometimes do, extract "extra" payments or favors in exchange for permission. Bribes might also be requested of and paid by producers who fail to follow environmental, labor, or other regulations.

Construction. Most construction projects are awarded based on competitive bids, and those awarding contracts can use their power to extract bribes or other favors that will tip the balance in a "competitive bidding process" toward a contractor who makes illicit payments. Bribery may be especially common in public projects, as moderately paid government employees use their power in the contracting process to supplement their own income.

Transportation and Storage. This sector includes over the road trucking and railroads, but also includes the movement of goods over the ocean or through the air. Bribes arise as shippers are willing to pay to ensure that shipments of questionable or illegal goods can get through the customs office without scrutiny. Customs officials extract bribes before they release goods out of their custody.

Investing and Finance. In these industries, including banking and investment activities, bribes are often paid to skirt regulatory scrutiny, such as several large money transfers that you will read about in the Goldman Sachs and 1MDB case. Bribes can also be extracted because of asymmetric information; those hold valuable information can require additional payments from those who want that information.

The Multinational Industries where Bribery is Most Common
Percentage of total bribes by multinational industry

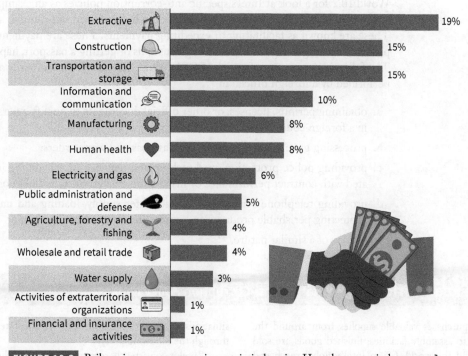

Industry	Percentage
Extractive	19%
Construction	15%
Transportation and storage	15%
Information and communication	10%
Manufacturing	8%
Human health	8%
Electricity and gas	6%
Public administration and defense	5%
Agriculture, forestry and fishing	4%
Wholesale and retail trade	4%
Water supply	3%
Activities of extraterritorial organizations	1%
Financial and insurance activities	1%

FIGURE 10.3 Bribery is more common in certain industries. How does your industry rate?

Legal Frameworks for Bribery and Gift Giving

We noted above that good people everywhere oppose bribery, and most countries have enacted strong laws to discourage the offering and taking of bribes. In this section, we'll provide some rather technical guidance on U.S. law and that of other countries.

The United States—The Foreign Corrupt Practices Act

The United States put into place the Foreign Corrupt Practices Act (FCPA) in 1977. This Act makes it unlawful for

- *any U.S. company or any officer, director, employee, agent, or stockholder*—The FCPA applies to anyone basically related in some way to a U.S. company.
- *acting on behalf of such company*—Whatever this person does that may land them in trouble must be while they act on behalf of the company.
- *to corruptly offer, pay, or authorize the payment*—Even the *offer!* of a payment with an intent for a personal gain is problematic.
- *directly or indirectly through any other person or firm of anything of value*—Remember, that's anything!
- *to a foreign official*—"Any officer or employee of a foreign government and . . . those acting on the foreign government's behalf."[17]
- *in order to obtain or retain business*[18]—The reason the bribe is being offered is economic gain.

The FCPA is a U.S. law that applies to U.S. companies, but it extends to the company's transactions anywhere in the world. If a U.S.-based company is doing business with the Sultan of Bhutan, the FCPA can be violated depending on the conversations that take place *in Bhutan*. It is this "long arm of the law" that terrifies many corporate executives. See Ethics in the Real World 10.2 for a look at Intel's specific anti-corruption policies as an example.

There is a certain class of payments that can be made without running afoul of the FCPA. These are known as facilitating or expediting payments. These are payments made to make a process, such as getting products through customs or getting a passport, happen more quickly. The following are exempt from the FCPA: "those actions which ordinarily and commonly are performed by a foreign official in

a. obtaining permits, licenses, or other official documents to qualify a person to do business in a foreign country;

b. processing governmental papers, such as visas and work orders;

c. providing police protection, mail pick-up and delivery, or scheduling inspections associated with contract performance or inspections related to transit of goods across country;

d. providing telephone service, power and water supply, loading and unloading cargo, or protecting perishable products or commodities from deterioration; or

e. actions of a similar nature."[19]

Ethics in the Real World 10.2 | What an Anti-Corruption Policy Looks Like

Intel corporation purchases valuable supplies from around the world, ships them to assembly facilities; finished goods are sold to customers around the world. Given Intel's global reach and the breadth of industries it spans, company employees will face situations where someone will ask for a bribe. Intel offers guidance through the following policy:

"Intel is consistently recognized as one of the world's leading corporate citizens and most ethical companies. We are committed

Intel's Anti-Corruption Policy

- Intel strictly prohibits all forms of bribery

- We must never offer, promise or accept bribes or kickbacks and must not participate in or facilitate corrupt activities of any kind

- Intel expects all suppliers to comply with Intel's Anti-Corruption Policy and Code of Conduct

- Intel further expects its Suppliers, their employees to prohibit bribery and corruption in any form and to communicate these expectations to their third parties as well.

Supplier Ethical Expectations (00018883) (Rev. 5)
6

(intel)

FIGURE 10.4   How does your company's anti-corruption policy compare to Intel's.

to maintaining our reputation as a well-respected, trusted, and admired company.

Intel's anti-corruption policies strictly prohibits all forms of bribery (see Figure 10.4). Our policy is to comply with all anti-corruption laws, and to accurately record all transactions. We don't offer or accept bribes or kickbacks. We don't participate in, or facilitate corrupt activity of any kind. Many countries' laws define facilitation payments to government officials as bribes.

For this reason, Intel doesn't make facilitation payments to government officials.

Our prohibition against offering, promising, or paying bribes also applies to third parties who provide services, or act on Intel's behalf, such as: suppliers, agents, contractors, consultants, and distributors. We don't engage with third parties that we believe may attempt to offer a bribe in connection with company business."[20]

Bribery Laws in Other Countries

Just as the United States has the FCPA, other countries and regional entities have their own bribery and corruption laws. Here are a few:

- *The United Nations.* Adopted in 2003, the United Nations Convention Against Corruption (UNCAC) has now been ratified by more than 160 countries (including the United States).[21] "The Convention covers five main areas: preventive measures, criminalization and law enforcement, international cooperation, asset recovery, and technical assistance and information exchange. The Convention covers many different forms of corruption, such as bribery, trading in influence, abuse of functions, and various acts of corruption in the private sector."[22]

- The OECD's Anti-Bribery Convention (see Figure 10.5) has three dozen countries that have signed on. These include the United States, all member states of the European Union, Australia, Brazil, Canada, Chile, Japan, Korea, Mexico, New Zealand, and Turkey.[23] "It is a criminal offence under its law for any person intentionally to offer, promise or give any undue pecuniary or other advantage, whether directly or through intermediaries, to a foreign public official, for that official or for a third party, in order that the official act or refrain from acting in relation to the performance of official duties, in order to obtain or retain business or other improper advantage in the conduct of international business."[24]

- The Inter-American Convention Against Corruption (IACAC), adopted by members of the Organization of American States, which now has more than thirty signatories.[25] This convention uses similar language to other organizations noted above.

- *The United Kingdom.* One of the most frequently referenced of these laws is the UK Bribery Act of 2010 (UKBA). The UKBA is similar in many ways to the FCPA, but it actually is even broader in its application. It not only covers bribes to foreign officials

Source: Obi, Ndifon Neji & Sovereign Felix Nyong, Rethinking Civil Society Participation in the Implementation of the UN Convention Against Corruption in Nigeria, Journal of Economics and Sustainable Development, Vol.9, No.16, 2018. Licensed under CC BY 3.0.

FIGURE 10.5   The OECD Anti-Bribery Convention has made a difference for more than twenty years.

but also between private companies. Facilitation payments are prohibited under this Act, and the penalties of the Act include "onerous sanctions such as imprisonment, large fines, potential confiscation of property, and disqualification of directors."[26]

- *China* has both the **Anti-Unfair Competition Law** of the PRC and **Criminal Law** of the PRC, which each address different types of bribery. What is a standout component of the Criminal Law? *The death penalty is a possible consequence of breaking the law.* Figure 10.6 displays a sample of infractions and the penalty they would receive in China.[27]

- **Singapore's Prevention of Corruption Act** is another law that makes bribery illegal both in the private sector and in attempting to influence foreign officials.[28] This law is aimed at catching both the giver and the receiver of the bribe. Under this legislation, the punishment for bribery is a fine of up to $100,000 and/or a jail term of up to 5 years. Because government officials are held to a high standard, the punishment for bribery involving a member of parliament is a fine of up to $100,000 and/or a jail sentence of up to 7 years.

- Brazil introduced its **Clean Company Act** in 2014. This Act holds companies responsible for the corrupt acts of their employees.[29] The timing of the Act is likely not coincidental as it went into effect prior to the 2016 Rio Olympics, which, like all large events, could give rise to significant opportunities for corruption.

Infraction	Penalty
Where the total bribes exceed RMB 3,000,000, or the total bribes range between RMB 1,500,000 and RMB 3,000,000 if it also has an aggravating factor	10 years' to life imprisonment or the death penalty, and monetary penalties or confiscation of property
A bribe involving an extremely large monetary amount and serious damage to the interests of the state and the people	Life imprisonment or the death penalty and confiscation of property

FIGURE 10.6   Some penalties for bribery under Chinese law.

Tools for Individuals

People who practice bribery and corruption do so for their own good and do not consider the interests of others, regardless of their putative claims, e.g., that everyone is doing it, it is a cost of doing business, and/or it increases efficiency. There are several ways that individuals and organizations can protect themselves against the temptation to engage in bribery or other forms of corruption.

First and foremost among these is a strong personal and organizational commitment to not engage in bribery. This commitment should be formally enshrined in policies and documents. Firms should have a clear and unambiguous *anti-corruption and bribery* policy. These policies should be very clear and detailed, because of the severe penalties and reputational harm that companies face when confronted with a potential bribery issue and/or investigation. Policies should cover both domestic and foreign definitions of bribery.

Clear policies should also exist for *gifts, hospitality, and other perks.* While these policies tend to have varied names, the idea is the same. If you are giving or receiving gifts or engaging in meals, events, or travel in conjunction with your job, you have a policy to consult for guidance and rules. Generally, companies will limit the amount of money spent on gifts, meals, travel, and so forth. For example, dinner might be limited to $50. A gift might be limited to a value of $15 or possibly just a company branded gift (like a pen or T-shirt with the company logo). **Figure 10.7** displays the gift policy at FedEx.

Many companies, in an effort to get out in front of any possible bribery issues, implement some type of tool or process that requires employees to enter information about gifts, travel, hospitality, donations, and the like prior to the actual purchase of the item, prior to the meal taking place, and so forth. This creates the opportunity for a preview of items to flag any that look suspect. Questions can be asked of the employees submitting the requests (e.g., *Why do you need to make this donation?*), parameters can be set (e.g., *You need to cap this dinner at $50/ attendee*), and so forth.

Reviewing employee expense reports is a key way to flag potential bribery issues. When employees submit receipts for expenses that they would like to have reimbursed by the company, reviewers will be able to see details of gifts purchased, donations made, dinners paid for, and similar expenses. Also, these expense reports flag when processes are not being followed.

Accepting Gifts, Meals & Entertainment from Third Parties

Accepting Gifts from Third Parties

- Gifts include (but are not limited to):
  - Tickets to sports, music or cultural events where FedEx employees and representatives of the Third Party providing the tickets do not attend the event together
  - Merchandise (for example, gift baskets, wine, clothing, mugs, pens, collectibles and hospitality bags)
  - Travel or lodging not associated with a business conference, meeting or event
  - Favorable terms or discounts on a product or service for the employee's benefit that are not otherwise available to all FedEx employees

- Subject to any local law restrictions, employees may accept nominal gifts with a combined market value of US$75 or less from the same Third Party per year.
- Acceptance of individual gifts greater than US$75, or multiple gifts in one year from the same Third Party totaling greater than US$75, must be approved by your company's General Counsel.
- Gifts of cash or cash equivalents (such as gift cards, gift certificates or "red packets" commonly offered in Asia) must never be accepted.

- Employees may not solicit gifts from Third Parties.
- Please refer to the Policy on Company-Provided Gifts and Awards for Employees for guidance regarding accepting gifts from FedEx.

Q: A supplier has sent me an expensive gift basket for the holidays. I have never received a gift from this supplier before. Can I accept it?

A: You can accept the gift basket if it is valued at US$75 or less. You should use your best judgment to estimate the value. If it is valued over US$75, you will need to receive approval from your company's General Counsel in order to accept it.

Q: A customer was really happy with the service I provided. To thank me, she sent me an Amazon gift card for US$50. Can I accept it?

A: A gift card that allows you to choose from a range of goods or services is considered a cash equivalent. Accepting gifts of cash or cash equivalents is strictly prohibited, regardless of the amount involved. You should politely return the gift card to the customer and explain that FedEx's policies do not allow you to accept it.

FIGURE 10.7 Gift and entertainment policy at FedEx.

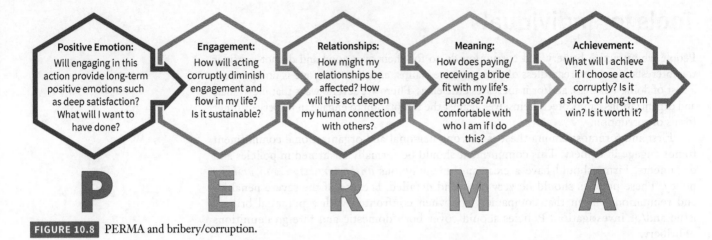

Positive Emotion: Will engaging in this action provide long-term positive emotions such as deep satisfaction? What will I want to have done?

Engagement: How will acting corruptly diminish engagement and flow in my life? Is it sustainable?

Relationships: How might my relationships be affected? How will this act deepen my human connection with others?

Meaning: How does paying/ receiving a bribe fit with my life's purpose? Am I comfortable with who I am if I do this?

Achievement: What will I achieve if I choose act corruptly? Is it a short- or long-term win? Is it worth it?

P E R M A

FIGURE 10.8 PERMA and bribery/corruption.

Beyond company policies, there are several things you can do to avoid situations of potential corruption:

- *Keep* your ears and eyes open when working with third parties and especially those who are in non-U.S. locations. Be careful to understand what is "business as usual," and consult all local laws and regulations. Ask questions when you don't know the answers.

- *Listen* to your gut. If you feel suspicious, there probably is reason to be suspicious. Even in unfamiliar surroundings, when you aren't necessarily familiar with international practices, if you feel that you need to stop, call off a meeting or conversation, and just give yourself time to think (or to call someone at your company), do that. Anyone you are working with who is not trying to put something over on you will appreciate your care and dedication to making sure you are doing the right thing.

- *Reach* out for help. We talked in the last chapter about the power of mentors in helping you identify and resolve conflicts of interest. The same applies here. It's easy to believe that we are isolated and alone in our decisions. In fact, that's a key element that those asking for bribes depend on, that we won't bring up the request with others. Even if you have a mentor, reach out to one of the people below—or at least start to gain some clarification in policies:

  - Legal Compliance Department
  - Your manager
  - An executive in the company
  - Human Resources

- *Educate* yourself about how corruption impacts the daily lives of so many people around the world before taking on any type of role in a company. Stay up to date on the news, study the real people impacted by corruption on the sites of nonprofit organizations,[30] and take time to reflect about how our actions can impact others. *In other words, slow down and be educated and aware!*

- Be sure to ask yourself the PERMA questions we raised in the last chapter. We reproduce them in **Figure 10.8**, in the context of bribery.

Key Terms

anti-bribery convention	bribery	criminal law
anti-corruption and bribery	clean company act	fraud
anti-unfair competition law	corruption	gifts, hospitality, and other perks

graft
inter-american convention against corruption
(IACAC)
offer!

quid pro quo
reciprocity
singapore's prevention of corruption act
UK bribery act

united nations convention against corruption
(UNCAC)

Chapter Summary

- Bribery is the act of offering something of value to someone for his or her personal benefit, with the intent that he or she violate his or her official roles and responsibilities and in exchange for a benefit to which the payor otherwise would not be entitled. Corruption is broader than bribery and can consist of other crimes in addition to bribery (e.g., organized crime, embezzlement, human trafficking). Corruption has a very negative impact on society.

- There are many ways that bribery can happen in the workplace. Working with clients, third parties, or potential customers that are owned partially by foreign governments; receiving or giving gifts; providing travel and/or hospitality to certain people; and giving donations are just a few of the ways that bribery may arise.

- In order to prevent employees from engaging in bribery, companies design, implement, and evaluate programs and controls to prevent, detect, and respond to incidents of bribery and other misconduct, including clear policies regarding bribery and gifts;

training and communications for complying with these policies; guidance via managers, ethics and compliance professionals, and helplines; and audits and continuous monitoring.

- The framework for identifying and resolving workplace bribery and corruption encompasses being wary when others belittle company and/or legal department strategies for avoiding bribery; keeping eyes and ears open when working with third parties in non-U.S. locations; paying close attention to company training and communications; and listening to your gut and always asking appropriate company employees in the event you have questions.

- Part of being aware of our values is staying educated about what those values mean. If we value freedom and want to live in a society that has limited corruption, it is important to stay educated about the various impacts of bribery and corruption around the world. Understanding how certain actions impact others personally will help us to live our own values.

Chapter Review Questions

1. What is bribery? How is it connected to the broader concept of corruption?

2. Which of the 7 Deadly Signs of potential bribery do you think is hardest to overcome? What are some common euphemisms used for corrupt practices?

3. What is a facilitating payment? Do these constitute bribery?

4. Why is a prereview and authorization for purchasing gifts a good idea?

5. Where can you turn if you have questions about a situation you feel might be corrupt?

6. Do all sectors and professions have the same rules for personal gifts? Discuss.

Application Exercises

- *Personal Ethical Development.* If you began keeping an ethics journal as suggested in the first chapter, continue that writing work. Here are some prompts: When have you felt uncomfortable about giving a gift or attending an event because you thought it might be a quid pro quo? How did you react? What feelings or values conflicts make it (or made it) difficult to respond? How would your response change after studying the material in this chapter?

- *Career Goals and Planning.* A happy, meaningful, and productive life blends and builds upon the following: (1) the type of life you are interested in leading, (2) your deepest and most important values, (3) the work you are interested in doing, (4) what

you are good at, (5) your preferences for things like work versus free time, and (6) your personality. What types of organizational policies and controls would you like to see around bribery and corruption where you work? What are the major activities where bribery might arise in the firms and industries where you'd like to work?

- *Ethics in the Business world.* Identify an individual or company that faced a situation where they were asked to pay a bribe. How did the individuals and organizational leaders respond? Did they do so well, or poorly? What were the outcomes? How has that organization adjusted its policies, culture, or style to prevent such incidents in the future?

- *Talking with and Learning from Others.* Choose a business professional you respect. Engage that person in a brief interview. Where have they experienced issues with corruption, bribery, or gift giving in their careers? How have they responded? What do they wish they had done differently? What advice would they give you as you begin your career?

- *Be an ethics professional for a day!* The following activities are all typically part of the role of compliance department professionals:

  a. Choose a company that you are familiar with and draft an email to all employees reminding them of the importance of complying with both the company's anticorruption policies and anticorruption laws. Be sure to tie the compliance with these policies and laws to the values of the company.

  b. Several sales department employees have submitted requests seeking approval to purchase gifts for their customers for an upcoming tailgate party and NFL game the company has invited its best customers to attend. What are the questions you would want to ask those sales employees about the intended gift recipients and the actual gifts?

  c. Draft an email for your company CEO to send to all employees, following an unfortunate situation that has just come to light. One of the company's top executives, the chief marketing officer (CMO), has just been terminated because it was discovered that she accepted large gifts from the graphic design firm that now is designing all of the company's marketing materials. The CEO will review your email, possibly revise it, and then email it himself to all employees. Consider what you want employees to know, both about the CMO situation and the company's expectations about accepting gifts and the appearance or reality of bribery.

Mini-Cases

Case 1: Gift giving and cross-cultural ethics. Megan Jordan had been enjoying her time in Shanghai. She had graduated last spring with her degree in operations management from Colorado College and had been thrilled to land a job with Ace Technologies, a supplier of circuits and motherboards to several companies in the automotive sector. Her excitement for her new job increased when she found out she had been assigned to monitor a team that was part of the company's Chinese contract manufacturer, QuiJin Industries. Over the past six months, Megan had mastered the intricacies of circuit and motherboard manufacturing and the most likely production bottlenecks and quality-failure points. She had also become friends with her counterpart at QuiJin, Ms. Wang.

Ms. Wang was in her late forties and had been a quality control specialist at QuiJin for over twenty years. She had started at QuiJin right after her graduation from a prestigious Chinese university. Ms. Wang had married early and had a daughter, Ying Yu, who had just graduated from college. One day, Ms. Wang told Megan that her daughter had gotten engaged to a wonderful engineering student she had met at school and the two planned to marry very soon. Megan congratulated Ms. Wang when she first heard the news and wished the new couple all the best.

This morning, some of the luster and excitement of her job faded when Megan found an invitation to Ying Yu's wedding on her desk. At first, Megan felt honored by the invitation and was pleased to attend. She then realized that attending the wedding created an ethical challenge. She knew that the local community norm required wedding guests to provide a cash gift to the new couple. Any amount under $200 would be considered a slight and insult.

Megan immediately realized that such a gift would violate Ace's Code of Conduct, which limited any gift giving to $50. Megan had no desire to offend Ms. Wang and wondered how the problem of the gift would affect their future working relationship. Megan also wanted to adhere to Ace's Code of Conduct, and she recalled that she had signed a form after the last ethics training which stated that she understood and would follow the policy. She had not anticipated this situation, however, and Megan wondered how she should respond to the invitation and the problem of the wedding gift.

Discussion Questions

1. What are the risks in this situation for Megan?
2. What would you advise Megan to do?

Case 2: Too good to be true. Jeff McDonald worked as a construction projects manager for St. Elmo's hospital. St. Elmo's was one of the oldest and most prestigious not-for-profit healthcare groups in Cleveland, Ohio. The hospital had been founded by Jesuit missionaries in the 1840s in a simple log cabin to provide relief for local women, with a clean place to give birth. St. Elmo's had grown over the centuries to become a sprawling 800-acre medical campus that provided care to residents of Cuyahoga County. True to its roots, St. Elmo's had just announced an $80 million addition to its Women's Center. The addition would provide state-of-the-art cancer care for women of all ethnicities and socioeconomic standards. McDonald was the project manager in charge of collecting and evaluating bids from a number of local and national general contractors.

McDonald had received dual degrees in construction management and business finance from Case Western University about a decade ago. One October evening, Jeff received a call from Max Cook, an old friend and confidant from his days in the Delta Epsilon fraternity at Case. Cook, who McDonald had lunch with about every year, told Jeff that he had an extra seat to the upcoming Cleveland Browns–Pittsburgh Steelers game and asked Jeff if he would attend. Jeff, a lifelong Browns fan, accepted the invitation almost before Cook had finished speaking. The day of the game, Max picked up Jeff and they took an Uber to the stadium.

Jeff soon found himself in one of the stadium's luxury boxes, one owned by Jacob's Brothers construction, an Akron, Ohio-based general contractor with a large healthcare business. Max explained that he had received the tickets from a work colleague who knew Peter Jacobs, a principal owner of Jacob's Brothers. Jeff soon found himself in conversation with Peter and about a dozen other Jacob's Brothers executives. He began to feel very uncomfortable.

Discussion Questions

1. What are the ethical risks in this situation?
2. What would you advise Jeff to do now?
3. What should Jeff do later?

Case 3: Liam Kent and Noah Centeno were working in the manufacturing unit of a reputed company. Liam was heading the mechanical department and Noah was responsible for instrumentation. Both had completed their B. Tech but Noah had passed out four years prior to Liam and thus had more experience. Since both men belonged to two different departments on the technical side, they would work, interact, argue, and compete with each other. Noah had very good relations with both the immediate Technical Head and his superior Unit Head. Noah was very good at his work; his behavior and team building efforts were examples for others to learn. His reputation in the organization was admirable, and overall, he was a very well-balanced professional. Liam used to follow him, learn from him, and address him as 'Sir'. As time passed on, some clashes occurred between the Unit Head and the Technical Head. The team members of the plant had different opinions and sided between the two of them. Although Noah was neutral in this situation, the Technical Head somehow felt he was inclined to side with the Unit Head. Things got worse for him when the Unit Head retired and the Technical Head was promoted to his position. He started troubling Noah by misusing his power at work. The others also started teasing him to please their superior. But the worst was yet to come. The Unit Head promoted Liam as Technical Head even when everyone knew Noah was a better choice and fit. This was a matter of concern for Noah but he could not do anything. Liam became his reporting manager and it was really tough for Noah to address him as 'Sir'. For Liam, it was the biggest ethical dilemma of his career as his boss (i.e., the Unit Head) was looking to ruin Noah's career. This led to Noah being very depressed and Liam to be in the middle of a dilemma (i.e., to support management and misbehave with Noah).

Discussion Questions

1. Why was the new Unit Head unable to control his emotions towards Noah?
2. What should the new technical head (Liam) have done in this situation?
3. How should Noah deal with this situation ethically?

References

1. Jennifer Levitz and Melissa Korn, "The making of a college-admissions con man," *Wall Street Journal*, July 17, 2020, https://www.wsj.com/articles/the-making-of-a-college-admissions-con-man-11594998156?mod=searchresults_pos15&page=1.

2. Melissa Korn, Jennifer Levitz, and Erin Ailworth, "Federal Prosecutors Charge Dozens in College Admissions Cheating Scheme," *Wall Street Journal*, March 12, 2019, https://www.wsj.com/articles/federal-prosecutors-charge-dozens-in-broad-college-admissions-fraud-scheme-11552403149?mod=searchresults_pos6&page=4.

3. Melissa Korn, "College-Admissions Mastermind Tried to Recruit Seven Stanford Coaches, School Says," *Wall Street Journal*, December 3, 2019, https://www.wsj.com/articles/college-admissions-mastermind-tried-to-recruit-seven-stanford-coaches-school-says-11575390744.

4. Jennifer Levitz and Jon Kamp, "Former Yale Soccer Coach Pleads Guilty in College-Admissions Scheme," *Wall Street Journal*, March 28, 2019, https://www.wsj.com/articles/former-yale-soccer-coach-appears-in-boston-court-in-college-admissions-scheme-11553791156?mod=searchresults_pos20&page=3.

5. Jennifer Levitz, "Lori Loughlin Sentenced to Two Months in College-Admissions Scandal," *Wall Street Journal*, August 21, 2020, https://www.wsj.com/articles/lori-louglin-and-husband-to-be-sentenced-in-college-admissions-scandal-11598011212?mod=searchresults_pos11&page=1.

6. *Black's Law Dictionary*, cf bribery, https://thelawdictionary.org/bribery/.

7. *Black's Law Dictionary*, cf corruption, https://thelawdictionary.org/corruption/.

8. *Black's Law Dictionary*, cf fraud, https://thelawdictionary.org/fraud/.

9. *The Legal Dictionary*, cf graft, https://legal-dictionary.thefreedictionary.com/Graft.

10. Kofi A. Annan, Secretary-General of the United Nations, United Nations Convention Against Corruption Foreword, 2004.

11. S. Bowles and H. Gintis, "The Evolution of Strong Reciprocity," Santa Fe Institute, Research in Economics Working paper 98-08-073E, 1998.

12. Oliver Scott Curry, Lee A. Rowland, Caspar J. Van Lissa, Sally Zlotowitz, John McAlaney, and Harvey Whitehouse, "Happy to help? A systematic review and meta-analysis of the effects of performing acts of kindness on the well-being of the actor," *Journal of Experimental Psychology* 76 (May 2018): 320–329.

13. Jeffrey MacDonald, "When does a gift become a bribe?," *The Christian Science Monitor*, January 25, 2006, https://www.csmonitor.com/2006/0125/p13s01-lire.html.

14. Alan Smart, "Gifts, Bribes, and Guanxi: A Reconsideration of Bourdieu's Social Capital," *Cultural Anthropology* 8, no. 3 (1993): 388–408.

15. Kim Bellware, "Here Are 5 Photos Of Mooncakes To Get You All Excited For the Mid-Autumn Festival," *HuffPost*, last modified September 20, 2014, https://HuffPost.com/entry/mid-autumn-festival-mooncake_n_5784738.

16. Andres Beattie, Why These Industries Are Prone to Corruption, Investopia, 08 February 2020. Available at https://www.investopedia.com/articles/investing/072115/why-these-industries-are-prone-corruption.asp.

17. *A Resource Guide to the U.S. Foreign Corrupt Practices Act* by the Criminal Division of the U.S. Department of Justice and the Enforcement Division of the U.S. Securities and Exchange Commission, Chapter 2.

18. https://justice.gov/criminal-fraud/foreign/corrupt/practices/act.

19. "Investor Bulletin: The Foreign Corrupt Practices Act – Prohibition of the Payment of Bribes to Foreign Officials," U.S. Securities and Exchange Commission, accessed June 2, 2021, https://sec.gov/investor alerts/fcpa.pdf.

20 Available at https://www.intel.com/content/www/us/en/support/articles/000022536/programs.html.

21 G. P. Miller, *The Law of Governance, Risk Management, and Compliance*, 2nd ed. (VitalSource Bookshelf), 574, https://bookshelf.vitalsource.com/#/books/9781454887133/.

22 United Nations Convention against Corruption, accessed June 2, 2021, https://www.unodc.org/unodc/en/corruption/uncac.html.

23 Miller, *The Law of Governance, Risk Management, and Compliance*, 574.

24 "OECD Convention on Combating Bribery of Foreign Public Officials in International Business Transactions," accessed June 2, 2021, https://www.oecd.org/corruption/oecdantibriberyconvention.htm.

25 Miller, *The Law of Governance, Risk Management, and Compliance*, 574.

26 Ibid.

27 "Bribery & Corruption Laws and Regulations 2021," Global Legal Insights, accessed June 2, 2021, https://www.globallegalinsights.com/practice-areas/bribery-and-corruption-laws-and-regulations.

28 Singapore Statutes Online.

29 "Brazilian Clean Company Act," Anti-Corruption Legislation, Risk & Compliance Portal, accessed June 2, 2021, https://www.ganintegrity.com/portal/anti-corruption-legislation/brazil/.

30 Transparency International (https://transparency.org) and Corruption Watch (https://corruptionwatch.org).

CHAPTER 11

Integrity and Mercy

LEARNING OUTCOMES

At the end of this chapter, you should be able to do the following:

1. Define *integrity* and *mercy* and describe the two manifestations of each.

2. Classify the different challenges people face in questions of integrity.

3. Explain the conditions where organizational forgiveness and mercy may be the most appropriate

ethical response. Evaluate the trade-offs in the decision to be just or merciful.

4. Apply the tools and concepts you've learned about integrity and mercy to situations you will face in the workplace.

Opening Case | The Cost of a Lack of Integrity

In 1852, Henry Wells and William Fargo met in New York City and formed a new company to provide banking and delivery services to the rapidly growing California Territory. As the decades passed, Wells Fargo earned a reputation for reliability and trustworthiness in transporting shipments of gold and cash over its stagecoach network. Today, few images in the financial services industry are more iconic than the stagecoach and galloping horses of Wells Fargo & Company (Wells).

Wells grew organically and through a series of acquisitions to become one of the nation's largest banks. What held the expanding empire together was a clear set of core values, contained in a thirty-seven-page vision and values book that outlined and reinforced an unyielding commitment to customers, ethics, and trust.[1] Wells Fargo's adherence to prudent banking principles helped it survive and thrive through the 2007–2009 meltdown that killed or crippled some of the nation's most well-known banks. By 2015, Wells was the nation's most valuable bank,[2] and mutual fund giant Morningstar named its chief executive, John Stumpf, CEO of the year, recognizing how he had "guided the bank through a difficult period in the industry and shunned activities that put profits ahead of customers."[3] Many experts considered Wells Fargo as the one bank that could withstand any crisis.[4]

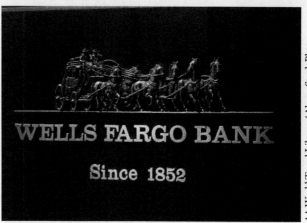

AA World Travel Library / Alamy Stock Photo

Wells could survive almost any external threat, but the bank was slowly rotting from the inside. On September 8, 2016, three federal and local agencies announced that Wells Fargo had agreed to pay a $185 million fine related to over two million fraudulent accounts the bank had created for its retail customers without their knowledge.[5] The *Wall Street Journal* noted the extent of this deception, as shown in **Figure 11.1**.

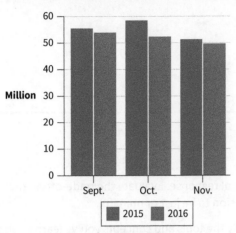

Customer interactions with bankers and tellers at Wells Fargo branches

$3.2 million
refunded to customers as of
December 2016

5,300
employees fired over
sales practices

1.5 million
deposit accounts may
have been unauthorized

565,000
credit cards may have
been unauthorized

Source: Wells Fargo Is Trying to Fix Its Rogue Account Scandal, One Grueling Case At a Time, By Emily Glazer, Christina Rexrode and AnnaMaria Andriotis, The Wall Street Journal, 27, Dec 2016.

FIGURE 11.1   The early cost of Wells Fargo's deception.

What drove such a massive deception? Aggressive incentives and an executive team that welcomed dishonesty when it padded revenue figures. In 2011, the bank rolled out an incentive program with aggressive quotas for new account openings. The program contained both carrots (bonuses) and sticks (demotion or termination).[6] The *Los Angeles Times* described one result:

> **Employees opened duplicate accounts, sometimes without customers' knowledge. . . . Workers also used a bank database to identify customers who had been preapproved for credit cards—then ordered the plastic without asking them, [Erik] Estrada [former Wells Fargo Personal Banker] said. "They'd just tell the customers: 'You're getting a credit card.'"[7]**

Risk advisors and operations leaders, who may have spotted problems, had no voice or authority to solve them. A strong personal relationship between community banking head Carrie Tolstedt and CEO John Stumpf meant that the senior team had no real idea of what was happening at the bank. Dishonesty and deception had become so rife at the bank that a succession of CEOs, three since Stumpf stepped aside in 2016, have been unable to right the ship. In 2018, the U.S. Federal Reserve essentially forbade the bank from growing until it rectified its internal controls and ethics.[8] Between 2016 and early 2020, the bank paid out almost $8.5 billion in fines and lawsuits.[9]

Introduction

This chapter deals with core questions of ethics: How do I have integrity in my business life? What does it mean to be honest? What does loyalty mean and how do I decide to whom to be loyal? When should organizations forgive misbehavior and show mercy, and when should justice and natural consequences carry the day? We emphasize these questions for two reasons: First, they are the most common ethical challenges most people face, and they underlie some challenges you've learned about earlier. For example, many conflicts of interest involve dishonesty or deception toward another person or organization. Second, as you think about leading a life rich in PERMA, the ability to resolve some of the knotty challenges around integrity and mercy is an important component in the PERMA elements of Relationships, a life of Meaning, and a sense of true and lasting Accomplishment.

Integrity and Mercy: Key Definitions

Before discussing the ethical challenges and issues that surround integrity and mercy, we begin with some definitions. The first major concept in this chapter is integrity, defined as "Soundness of moral principle; the character of uncorrupted virtue, esp. in relation to truth and fair dealing; uprightness, honesty, sincerity."[10] *Black's Law Dictionary* adds the following detail "[for] public officers, trustees, etc., this term means soundness of moral principle and character, as shown by one person dealing with others in the making and performance of contracts, and fidelity and honesty in the discharge of trusts."[11] In the language of the twenty-first century, a person of integrity is one who is both authentic (true to him- or herself) and transparent (honest and open in all his or her dealings).

People of integrity are **honest**; they don't mispresent facts or situations. A misrepresentation is an untrue statement, and can be offered fraudulently, with deliberate intent to deceive, negligently—without careful thought or confirmation of the truth of a statement—or innocently, a statement is given that the giver believes is true, but in fact is not.[12] People of integrity keep promises. A **promise** is "a declaration or assurance made to another person (usually with respect to the future), stating a commitment to give, do, or refrain from doing a specified thing or act, or guaranteeing that a specified thing will or will not happen."[13] It is important to note that a promise is not a contract, but only the first step in making a contract. A promise may be given by one person but must be accepted by another to become a contract. When both parties reach agreement about joint promises, a contract exists.[14]

The concept of **mercy** has a long history in language. The word traces back to the old Latin word *merces* or *merced*, meaning reward, which carried into the French language as pity, and on to the English language as mercy. Mercy has several meanings, two of which are particularly relevant for business ethics.[15] In the first sense, mercy is "an act or exercise of forbearance or good will." To **forbear** is to abstain from seeking justice against someone who has violated a contract or promise.[16] During the COVID-19 crisis, for example, many owners of real estate engaged in forbearance with those who rented or leased property from them (see Ethics in the Real World 11.1). They chose not to pursue contractual remedies on tenants who could not make payments.

Ethics in the Real World 11.1 | Mortgage Forbearance During COVID-19

In March 2020, the economies in many countries ground to a halt as businesses closed due to the COVID-19 pandemic. Millions of people in the United States lost their jobs and their ability to make the mortgage payments on their homes. The US government initiated mortgage forbearance programs through its major loan guarantee agency, Freddie Mac. Did that help people stay in their homes and were they able to repay their mortgages? The data in Figure 11.2 from November of 2020 provide some indication:

As the pandemic-related lockdowns continued through the summer, the rate of people in delinquency increased. As people began to return to work, a majority were able to become current on their mortgages or pay them off. Notice that the percentage of people 90 days or more delinquent is the second-largest group. Mortgage forbearance likely allowed many of these people to stay in their homes and weather the COVID storm until they could return to work.[17]

Month Since the Start of Forbearance	Delinquency Status				
	Current (%)	D30 (%)	D60 (%)	D90+ (%)	Paid Off (%)
Month before forbearance	92.8	6.0	0.9	0.2	0.0
Month forbearance begins	38.3	56.8	4.1	0.9	0.0
2nd month	17.7	31.6	46.0	4.0	0.6
3rd month	26.6	8.2	24.4	39.5	1.2
4th month	34.5	5.6	6.6	51.8	1.6
5th month	39.1	5.1	4.2	50.0	1.7
6th month	45.1	4.4	3.3	45.4	1.9
7th month	50.5	4.1	2.6	40.7	2.1

Note: The exhibit includes the performance through October 2020 for loans that entered forbearance from March through August 2020. All loans in the sample were active for at least one month in forbearance, which meant the earliest any borrower could have paid off a loan was in the second month the forbearance plan started.

FIGURE 11.2 Delinquency behavior of loans in forbearance during COVID-19.

In the second sense, mercy is a "disposition to forgive or show compassion" toward others. To be merciful is to abstain from punishing or administering justice to another person for their actions; it is also a component of being a kind and caring person. To forgive has a practical and emotional component. It is to pardon an offense, to not seek retribution, but it is also "to give up, cease to harbor resentment or wrath."[18] Forgiveness impacts both the offender through the withholding of punishment and the offended as they must let go of the hurt and anger caused by some triggering event.

Integrity: The Ethical Challenges

In this section, we'll provide you with a framework to think about the ethical challenges of integrity, based on its two major components.

Integrity as Honesty

Honesty appears rather straightforward, and you've probably heard phrases such as "honesty is the best policy (see Ethics in the Real World 11.2 for an example of how Americans view each other with regard to their honesty)." Honesty is also usually the easiest policy because

---

Ethics in the Real World 11.2 | Which Professions Do Americans See as Most Honest and Dishonest?

The Gallup organization regularly polls Americans to gauge their trust and confidence in different institutions and professions. The data for 2021 shown in Figure 11.3 revealed the following as professions seen as most and least honest:[19] Medical professionals, including both doctors and nurses, received the highest marks for honesty.

Group	Honesty Ranking				
	Very High	High	Average	Low	Very Low
Members of Congress	1%	7%	29%	39%	24%
Car Salespeople	1%	Y%	53%	29%	8%
Advertisers	1%	9%	45%	31%	12%
Business Executives	2%	15%	46%	26%	10%
Lawyers	3%	18%	48%	24%	6%
Journalists	6%	22%	31%	18%	22%
Bankers	5%	24%	48%	16%	5%
Nursing Home Operators	8%	28%	43%	15%	4%
Clergy	10%	29%	41%	11%	4%
Judges	9%	34%	40%	12%	4%
Police Officers	16%	36%	30%	11%	7%
Pharmacists	20%	51%	23%	4%	1%
Grade School Teachers	26%	49%	17%	5%	2%
Medical Doctors	27%	50%	19%	2%	1%
Nurses	41%	48%	10%	1%	N/A

FIGURE 11.3 Which professionals do you trust the most?

people only have to remember one thing—the truth—rather than two things, the truth and the lie. There are, however, three major complications when applying rules of honesty. First, what is true may be in doubt or subject to multiple interpretations. Second, what constitutes honesty, particularly in business situations, is often bounded and defined by social rules. Third, the pressure to be honest often runs into other moral imperatives, such as the desire to not offend others.

Honesty and multiple truths. How much money is in the U.S. economy at any one time, or what is the rate of unemployment? While the answers to these questions seem simple, there are *three* measures of the money supply, and *six* different measures of unemployment.[20] In accounting, restatements of earnings may occur through deliberate misrepresentation but may also be driven by errors of interpretation. The number of fraud-based restatements seems to be decreasing, while the number of error-based (including errors of judgement) restatements increases.[21] Sometimes the truth is not spoken because what is truth is debatable.

Honesty and social rules. Some social rules advocate for withholding true information from others, and two of these play significant roles in business. The first comes in negotiations. Each participant in a negotiation has a desired outcome and also what economists refer to as a "reservation price," or the outcome they'll be satisfied with. If asked, "What's the least you'll take for that item?" you are under no moral obligation to reveal your reservation price because keeping your reservation price to yourself is a well-accepted rule of negotiations.[22] The second situation is when your organizational role requires you to hold information confidential. Managers may have advance notice of events such as layoffs, losses, or mergers; however, they have an organizational duty to not reveal this information to others, even when asked.

Honesty and Kindness. There are a number of occasions where we might withhold the truth, or at least the whole truth, in an effort to be kind or preserve a relationship. Put yourself in the following situation: You just finish a long and exhausting bike ride with a group of friends. You had a flat tire, you're hungry and thirsty, and your bottom hurts from miles on the bike. The friend who invited you asks: "How did you enjoy the ride?" The truth may be that you hated the ride, but you may choose to say something different because of your friendship.

In all situations where honesty is the issue, it requires a mix of moral courage and creativity to find an ethical solution. In the case of the bike ride, moral courage would lead us to say, "Riding isn't my thing," or moral creativity might lead us say "I enjoyed the chance to get out and spend a day with people I care about."

Integrity as Promise-Keeping and Loyalty

Most people will respond, when asked, that promise-keeping is a moral virtue, and yet we often break our promises. Why? One answer is simply moral weakness or a strong passive-aggressive streak.[23] In this case, you might make a promise to do something rather than voice your true feelings that you have no intention of fulfilling your promise. More often, however, we break a promise because something of substance changed between the time of the promise and its fulfillment. The COVID-19 crisis caused a number of promises to be broken, everything from promised delivery dates from suppliers to promised completion dates for contractors. Keeping the promise became either impossible or imprudent in the new environment.

In some cases, the thing that changes after we make the promise is that we find out troubling information. This could be something we'd rather not know, or something we feel a need to disclose. The starkest example is when someone exacts our promise not to tell, and then confesses to the commission of a crime such as abuse. For most of us, we are under no obligation to keep such a promise because the act was a crime, or planned actions will lead to direct physical harm to others in the near future. There are five major relationships that require, or allow, us to keep promises of confidentiality as shown in Figure 11.4:[24]

Most promise-keeping is outside of these unique relationships, and when circumstances change, the question of whether or not to keep a promise becomes one of loyalty (see Figure 11.5 to learn how employee loyalty changed as a result of COVID-19). To be loyal is to be true and faithful to someone or something such as a group, an organization, an institution, or a government.[25] Loyalty is the basis of belonging to any group or team, and loyalty

• **Wife–husband or spousal roles.** This exemption is designed to uphold the sanctity of marriage.

 • **Clergy–communicant.** This exemption values the role of religion and repentance in society.

 • **Psychotherapist–patient.** This exemption encourages the proper use of confidentiality and full disclosure of information in the healing of psychological disorders and damage.

 • **Doctor–patient.** Similar to the one above, information disclosed between doctors and patients (with exceptions for some cases of abuse) facilitates physical healing by patients.

 • **Attorney–client.** This exemption allows for accused individuals to obtain and receive effective legal representation without fear of the truth being revealed.

FIGURE 11.4 The five relationships that allow confidential and protected communication.

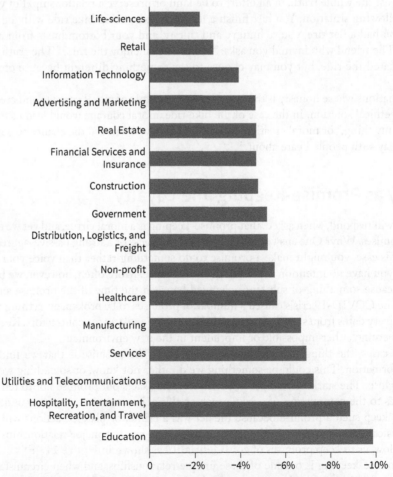

Source: Employee Loyalty Reaches Lowest Level in More Than a Year, According to Energage Research, Business Wire, 27 July 2021.

FIGURE 11.5 Employee engagement/loyalty changes due to the COVID-19 Pandemic.[26]

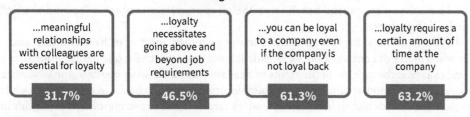

What is Company Loyalty?

Percentage who believe ...

...meaningful relationships with colleagues are essential for loyalty	...loyalty necessitates going above and beyond job requirements	...you can be loyal to a company even if the company is not loyal back	...loyalty requires a certain amount of time at the company
31.7%	46.5%	61.3%	63.2%

Source: Survey of 1,002 full-time employees.

FIGURE 11.6   How employees perceive loyalty in today's world.[27]

is paramount in our most cherished relationships (see Figure 11.6 for a view of how people view company loyalty).

While a virtue, loyalty creates its own set of ethical challenges. When answering ethical questions surrounding loyalty, it helps to classify loyalty into one of four types.[28]

- *Loyalty in concern.* When we prioritize one person's interests over another because we want the best for them. This type of loyalty leads to action, as questions of loyalty are often about whether we will do something that advances the interests of friends, coworkers, or organizations.

- *Loyalty in ritual.* This type of loyalty involves engaging in practices that show our allegiance to someone or something. Ethical challenges arise when we are asked to participate in rituals and practices such as stealing company property or attending off-work events that contribute to workplace discrimination (such as all male employees attending a strip club after work).

- *Loyalty in identification.* Identification is the essence of being a loyal fan of a sports team, product, celebrity, or politician. Our identification may lead us to engage in unethical behavior, such as looting or lying because that's what loyal fans do.[29]

- *Loyalty in belief.* We may loyally believe in others in ways that keep us from seeing what is wrong or unethical in their behavior. We may commit unethical acts because of our beliefs, but far more common is the case where we deny or excuse the unethical acts of others because of our beliefs about their character and integrity.

Mercy and Forgiveness: The Ethical Challenges

In Chapter Two, we introduced the moral philosophy of John Rawls, which emphasized the moral virtues of justice and fairness. Rawls described justice as "the first virtue of social institutions,"[30] and philosophers since Plato have believed that justice was one of the four cardinal virtues (the others being courage, temperance, and wisdom). Justice is, broadly speaking, the idea that people get a reward, or a punishment, equal to their action, or "to each his [or her] due."[31] Mercy, which is a virtue in many religions and moral philosophies, seems to run counter to the notion of justice; mercy is a manifestation of the moral sentiment of compassion and sympathy.

Mercy as Forbearance

Forbearance means not seeking a just punishment when the situation would clearly call for one. Forbearance exposes the fundamental dilemma and challenge: When is it right or good to exact a just punishment for an act and when is it good to offer compassion and sympathy? Think of a time when you missed points on an exam, but the instructor showed some mercy by offering partial credit, or a time when you made a mistake at work that should have drawn reprimand but did not. We all appreciate mercy and a "second chance" to make things right.

While we all hope for second chances in our own lives, most of us have also seen situations when mercy did not work out as intended. Sometimes mercy for one person prioritizes a second chance at the expense of the rights or needs of others. Showing mercy toward someone who has harassed another employee, for example, offers a second chance to the offender while demeaning the needs and rights of the offender's target. Other times, mercy may not result in a change of behavior. Extending mercy to a manager who bullies, or employees who exploit conflicts of interest for their own gain, may be helpful in the short run and avoid conflicts; however, that mercy may not invite or lead to real changes of behavior.

What criteria can you employ to make decisions about when mercy as forbearance might be appropriate? The following questions provide some helpful guidance for managers making determinations about extending mercy to offending stakeholders:

- *Do organizational policies or rules preclude mercy?* Organizations may have "zero tolerance" policies around things like employee theft, some addictive behaviors, or some forms of discrimination and harassment. Managers may question these policies, and they may appeal to HR staff or other executives for a change in policy; however, the first obligation is to uphold the policies of the firm.

- *Would mercy for one person violate the rights or jeopardize the safety of others?* Mercy for one person may mean injustice for another, and ethical actors need to weigh the benefits of mercy against the cost of injustice. Organizational actions, such as bullying, harassment, or other forms of discrimination violate the rights of targets to fair treatment, and often expose others to similar treatment in the future.

- *Would mercy be consistent with what experts know about behavioral change?*[32] Scientists and therapists have developed a series of interventions that help people with addiction problems, for example, to make real and lasting changes. Often these interventions require "tough love" or the administration of justice to help those addicted to make real and lasting change.[33] Mercy works best when it helps people get at the root causes of their problems. For example, managers who are bullies are very often insecure, and so forbearance that encourages and helps those individuals to process and resolve their own insecurity will be effective and helpful acts of mercy.

As with other questions of honesty and integrity, managers need both moral courage and creativity to consider when and how mercy might be the appropriate ethical response. Extending mercy requires courage when the decision may be seen as weak or run against the sentiment of others in the organization. Moral creativity comes into play in the specific design of how and under what conditions mercy will be extended.

Mercy as Forgiveness

Forgiveness is most often an individual, informal action. Forgiveness requires action by the forgiver, which enables a return to peace, both within the offender and the offended individual, and in the relationship between them. In spite of the many benefits of forgiveness, it proves a difficult thing for many of us to do. The most common difficulty is our desire for justice, which is not wrong. Justice and forgiveness can work together, however, leading to both change and peace. Here are three facets of forgiveness that often make it difficult:

- *Forgiveness is proactive.* Forgiveness doesn't naturally happen; time heals all wounds only when the "wound" is properly cleaned and set. Forgiveness comes from the one who has been harmed or offended, and ultimately *does not depend* on the behaviors or responses of the offending individual. If we say, "I'll forgive after they apologize," we deceive ourselves.

An apology may rationalize or encourage our forgiveness, but the grant of mercy comes from the offended person as a proactive behavior.

- *Forgiveness is an emotional as well as a cognitive act.* The definition of forgiveness as "ceasing to harbor resentment or wrath" toward an offender is insightful. Forgiveness has a cognitive component and leads us to think we have forgiven, but resentment and wrath are emotions, not cognitions. "Ceasing to harbor" is in part a conscious act, but what those who forgive actually do is emotionally let go of hate, anger, hurt, and resentment.

- *Forgiveness is about the past; reconciliation is about the future.* Forgiveness is letting go of the personal hurt and feelings of anger toward those who offended us in the past. We can forgive someone for what they did in the past, but we must reconcile with others to move forward into the future. Forgiveness enables reconciliation, but moving on from offenses requires its own active work.[34]

Key Terms

confidentiality	honest	mercy
forbear	loyalty	promise
forgive		

Chapter Summary

- This chapter dealt with two important topics in business ethics: integrity and mercy. Integrity concerns people doing what they say they will do and is most often exhibited in issues of honesty and promise-keeping. Mercy entails not seeking justice when the circumstances would clearly call for its application. Mercy manifests itself in the formal forbearance of sanctions, and the informal, personal process of forgiveness.

- Honesty is truth-telling, or the lack of misrepresentation. Business challenges around honesty involve the issues of multiple truths, social rules that may define what constitutes honest behavior, and the need to balance honesty and kindness.

- Promise-keeping is a virtue. People most often break promises when circumstances change. In most cases, changed circumstances become questions, and tests, of loyalty. Loyalty may be loyalty of concern, loyalty of ritual, loyalty of identification, or loyalty of belief.

- Mercy as forbearance is usually an organizational action where managers decide not to pursue sanctions against an individual for wrongdoing. Mercy may be prohibited by policy or rule, and mercy should only be extended when there is a high likelihood, based on evidence, that it will get at the core behavioral problems.

- Forgiveness, in contrast, is most often between individuals and involves the cognitive and emotional work of letting go of anger, hurt, and resentment. Forgiveness is a proactive response that, ultimately, does not depend on the actions of the offender, but only the offended.

Chapter Review Questions

1. Define honesty. Give an example of each type of misrepresentation.
2. How does a promise differ from a contract? Why is this important in issues of ethics?
3. What does loyalty mean? What are the different types of loyalty?
4. How should an organization develop employee loyalty?
5. Is loyalty and commitment both same? Explain.
6. What are the advantages and disadvantages of extending forgiveness and mercy? When would mercy be unhelpful?
7. What is your personal approach to integrity? Is integrity a matter of black and white, or does it depend on circumstances?
8. When should a leader forgive his subordinates?

Application Exercises

- *Personal Ethical Development.* If you began keeping an ethics journal as suggested in the first chapter, continue that writing work. Here are some prompts: When have you been most tempted to be dishonest or deceitful? To whom are you loyal and what are the boundaries of that loyalty? When would you violate a promise you made?

- *Career Goals and Planning.* A happy, meaningful, and productive life blends and builds upon the following: (1) the type of life you are interested in leading, (2) your deepest and most important values, (3) the work you are interested in doing, (4) what you are good at, (5) your preferences for things like work versus free time, and (6) your personality. How can you figure out how honest a company is before you join it? How do you define loyalty toward your employer, and how can you learn how the company defines employee loyalty? How important is mercy and forgiveness for you in a work environment?

- *Ethics in the Business World.* Identify a company that engaged in dishonest or deceitful behavior. What were the root causes that encouraged people to lie? How did the management team respond to the issue when it was discovered? Did they do so well, or poorly? What changes have leaders made to create a more honest and forthright culture?

- *Talking with and Learning from Others.* Choose a business professional you respect and whom you admire for their integrity or mercy. Engage that person in a brief interview. What challenges to integrity or mercy have they seen as common throughout their career? How have they changed their views on honesty, integrity, and forgiveness over time? What pitfalls and traps do they see now that they didn't see before? What advice would they give you as you begin your career?

- *Be a Compliance Professional for a Day!* The following activities are all typically part of the role of compliance department professionals:

  a. Choose a company that you are familiar with and draft an email to all employees reminding them of the importance of being honest and truthful. Be sure to tie the compliance with these policies to any relevant laws and to the core values of the company. You will also want to remind employees of the penalties of violations, both for the company and for individual employees.

  b. Prepare a brief set of slides for a live training session on dealing with organizational forgiveness. The audience is the senior management team of an established food-processing company, and the problem you are targeting is a report of the situations described in Mini-Case 2.

Mini-Cases

Case 1: A question of integrity. Jason Isaacson had worked for Duncan, Elliot, and Robinson, CPAs, as an accounting manager for just under eight years. He started at the firm right after earning his Master of Accountancy degree from the University of Georgia. DE&R, a San Antonio, Texas, firm employs over 100 CPAs and serves as auditors, tax advisors, and IT consultants for many of the city's largest, medium-sized, and most respected firms. Jason had worked his way up from audit associate to a management position in four years, timing that was on par with others in the firm and industry. Jason's work as a manager had been very solid on the technical side of the business. He knew how to manage a project and deliver high-quality audit results. He had some challenges as a team manager as many of the audit staff and junior associates felt that he was not a strong motivator and that his vague initial instructions left them with a lot of unnecessary rework. Jason was also not strong on the business side of public accounting; he was uncomfortable around the senior executive teams at his client companies, did not present well to this level of leadership, and had yet to sell any additional services to the accounts he worked on.

In the parlance of accounting, Jason was a good "minder"—supervisor of the work of others, but not a good "finder"—generator of new revenues for the firm. In fact, some other managers with the same time-in-role as Jason had already proven able to sell more services to existing clients and attract new clients as well. Since the ability to bring in new business was the key criterion for promotion to partner, Jason had definitely fallen off the partner track at DE&R.

Jason approached Karen Hyde, the managing partner of the firm, and requested a performance review coupled with a discussion about Jason's promotion to partner. Jason let it slip that he and his partner, Ruth, were planning on buying a condo together and he was excited to make a long-term commitment to his adopted city and the firm. He hoped the salary increase that would come with his promotion would allow them to move into an expensive condo.

Karen met with the other partners to discuss Jason's request, and the tone of the discussion confirmed what Karen already believed, that Jason would not be offered partner status within the firm.

Jason's request could not have come at a worse time. Three of the client engagements he managed were in the early stages of extensive financial and regulatory compliance audits. Because of his close knowledge of the clients and his strong relationships with their internal accounting team, Karen knew that replacing Jason at this stage would jeopardize critical client relationships—with losses in future auditing revenues and other consulting projects with these clients. The firm needed Jason to manage these projects—some of the compliance audits would require the better part of the next year to complete.

As Jason passed Karen in the office last Friday afternoon, he pressed hard for a performance review the next week. As Karen returned to her office she mulled over her options.

Case 2: Justice and mercy. Zach Hall had worked for Briggs Construction for almost twelve years when this incident happened. Our company is one of Chicagoland's larger commercial floor-covering contractors. We now have annual revenues just north of $200 million, and we capture about 15 percent of that as net income. We do all types of commercial construction, from office space to hospitals, clinics, and hospitality properties. For the last twenty years or so we've built out a very profitable niche doing clean-room installation and maintenance for the region's big pharmaceutical manufacturers.

Zach worked as an expeditor in that arm of our business. He had earned a bachelor's degree in construction management in 2005 from Purdue University, and we recruited him for his easygoing yet highly detailed personality. An expeditor is our term for a logistics specialist. Installing flooring and wallcoverings in the clean-room space is exacting. On any given day, you might have twenty types of materials that installers needed to install on these highly complex jobs. Zach's job was to make sure that the right quantity of the right stuff was in the right place at the right time. Small mistakes were very costly. For example, if the wrong size container of a specially formulated adhesive caused a job to pause, that $1,000 five-gallon container could cost our firm upward of $25,000. The flooring had to be laid in one continuous process to follow the manufacturer's recommendations and not void the warranty, so that container not being the right size would mean ripping out the entire sheet and starting over.

Zach learned the business well, and during the slowdown following the 2008–2009 financial meltdown, his attention to detail saved our company hundreds of thousands of dollars in installation and inventory costs. He had always been a valued employee, but about two years ago, his performance started to decline. He was often late to work and used all his paid time off over a couple of months. That wasn't the biggest problem, however. Remember that adhesive I told you about? On two jobs a couple months apart, he in fact sent the wrong size container to the job. The total cost of those two mistakes was about $60,000.

We all knew that Zach loved a good party. He had been president of his fraternity at Purdue and would come back to work on many Mondays full of stories about his exploits over the weekend. He had married about five years ago, and he and his wife had a three-year-old son and one-year-old daughter. As Zach's problems escalated, so did the office rumors about his heavy drinking. Rumor had it Zach had been a functional alcoholic who was becoming less functional.

Six months ago, things really blew up. Zach made another critical error. This time he sent the wrong flooring to a very large clean room job for one of our clients at a Missouri facility. This was his worst mistake yet. That error put the entire project back four days, costing us a cool $20,000 in direct costs, and we faced a $15,000 per-day "time is of the essence" penalty from the general contractor. That was job one. The flooring was supposed to go to another job in Wisconsin.

We lost another two days on that job, at a cost of $7,500. So, all told, we faced a loss of almost $90,000.

His coworkers were angry, and so was I. His administrative assistant told me that Zach had been extremely hungover that morning and had "bitten the hair of the dog" at work to calm his nerves. Company policy was clear: Drinking on the job was an offence that justified termination. I quickly scheduled a meeting with Zach for 1 p.m. that day. That gave me some time to consult our HR group about what my options were.

Case 3: James Hendricks and William Durst both joined at the same time at Careers360, an organization that provides counseling and preparation services to students. James was the Technical Lead of the team that creates exam preparation modules and William was the Module Lead responsible for the overall completion and decision analysis of various modules related to entrance exams. William and his team had worked very hard in completing a particular module that showed expected results and ranking in colleges across India, when a test is taken by any student. The module was to be completed before the exams season and thus there was a lot of pressure. James had already asked for clear specifications prior to development, as this would have helped the team plan better and create a better algorithm for marks calculation and data analysis. However, due to time constraint and lack of planning from William, James and his team could not get any clarity on how the module should be created. Despite all this, the team worked day and night trying to provide something meaningful to the customers. Finally, the date of the entrance exam was announced, which meant that they had to deliver on/before the deadline (which was before the exams) otherwise the contracts would become null and void. In order to cut the line and deliver faster, William asked team members to show bogus data to students whenever they attempted a test and give uncertain results. The team members knew this was completely wrong but they wanted to complete the project before the deadline.

To address this problem, James went to the Engineering Manager and asked him for a better solution as it was ethically and morally wrong to present incorrect data to students. This would also create a total lack of trust in the customers in future and hurt the company's reputation in every way. The problem was finally presented in the managerial meeting and the Chief Technical Officer resolved it by assigning more people to the team and removing William as the Module Lead. The company was then finally able to ship the product with correct data and it was a huge success.

Discussion Questions

1. Why did the Module Head, William, suggest manipulating the data?

2. Why did James not accept William's solution?

References

[1] Oliver Staley, "Wells Fargo just became the poster child for when external and internal values don't match," *Quartz Media*, September 8, 2016, https://qz.com/777241/wells-fargos-fake-accounts-scandal-makes-it-the-perfect-poster-child-for-when-external-and-internal-values-dont-match/.

[2] Ibid.

[3] The most valuable bank data is from Oliver Staley, "Wells Fargo Just Became the Poster Child for When External and Internal Values Don't Match, Quartz Media, September 8, 2016, https://qz.com/777241/wells-fargos-fake-accounts-scandal-makes-it-the-perfect-poster-child-for-when-external-and-internal-values-dont-match; and "Wells Fargo's John Stumpf Receives Morningstar's 2015

CEO of the Year Award," *PR Newswire*, January 26, 2016, https://www.prnewswire.com/news-releases/wells-fargos-john-stumpf-receives-morningstars-2015-ceo-of-the-year-award-300209920.html.

4 Alex Dumortier, Sean Williams, and Dan Caplinger, "3 Banks That Will Stand the Test of Time," October 12, 2015, The Motley Fool, https://www.fool.com/investing/general/2015/10/12/3-banks-that-will-stand-the-test-of-time.aspx.

5 The agencies were the Consumer Financial Protection Bureau, the Los Angeles City Attorney, and the Office of the Comptroller of the Currency. See Paul Blake, "Timeline of the Wells Fargo Accounts Scandal," *ABC News*, November 3, 2016, http://abcnews.go.com/Business/timeline-wells-fargo-accounts-scandal/story?id=42231128.

6 Former employees Alexander Polonsky and Brian Zaghi sued the bank, claiming they had been wrongly treated for failing to hit "impossible" new account goals. See Blake, "Timeline of the Wells Fargo Accounts Scandal."

7 E. Scott Reckard, "Wells Fargo's pressure-cooker sales culture comes at a cost," *Los Angeles Times*, December 21, 2013, http://www.latimes.com/business/la-fi-wells-fargo-sale-pressure-20131222-story.html.

8 "Responding to widespread consumer abuses and compliance breakdowns by Wells Fargo, Federal Reserve restricts Wells' growth until firm improves governance and controls. Concurrent with Fed action, Wells to replace three directors by April, one by year end," Federal Reserve, February 2, 2018, press release, https://www.federalreserve.gov/newsevents/pressreleases/enforcement20180202a.htm.

9 Author estimates, drawn from "Violation Tracker Parent Company Survey," accessed May 29, 2020, https://violationtracker.goodjobsfirst.org/parent/wells-fargo.

10 *Oxford English Dictionary*, sv "integrity", accessed June 2, 2020, https://www.oed.com/view/Entry/97366?redirectedFrom=integrity#eid.

11 *Black's Law Dictionary*, sv "integrity", *The Law Dictionary*, accessed June 2, 2020, https://thelawdictionary.org/integrity/.

12 *Black's Law Dictionary*, sv "misrepresentation", accessed June 3, 2021, https://thelawdictionary.org/article/3-types-misrepresentation-matter/.

13 *Oxford English Dictionary*, sv "promise", accessed June 2, 2020, https://www.oed.com/view/Entry/152432?rskey=5oqY8t&result=1.

14 Chilton J. Estes, "Contract: A promise or an agreement," *Washington University Law Review* 11, no. 4 (1926): 293–296.

15 Mercy, *The Online Etymology Dictionary*, accessed June 2, 2020, https://www.etymonline.com/word/mercy.

16 *Black's Law Dictionary*, sv "forbearance", *The Law Dictionary*, accessed June 2, 2020, https://thelawdictionary.org/forbearance/.

17 Research Note, Mortgage Forbearance and Performance during the Early Months of the COVID-19 Pandemic, Freddie Mac, 08 Feb 2021. Available at http://www.freddiemac.com/research/insight/20210208_mortgage_forbearance_rate_during_COVID-19.page?

18 Oxford English Dictionary, sv "Forgive".

19 Madison Troyer, America's most and least trusted professions, Stacker, 31 March 2021. Available at https://stacker.com/stories/561/americas-most-and-least-trusted-professions.

20 For the money supply, see Raphael Zeder, "Three measures of money supply," *Quickonomics*, last modified October 13, 2020, https://quickonomics.com/three-measures-money-supply/#:~:text=There%20are%20three%20measures%20of,public%2C%20and%20other%20checkable%20deposits. For unemployment, see "Measuring Unemployment," Lumen (Boundless Economics), accessed June 3, 2020, https://courses.lumenlearning.com/boundless-economics/chapter/measuring-unemployment/#:~:text=Six%20Measures%20of%20Unemployment,-The%20U.S.%20Bureau&text=Unemployment%20Rate%3A%20The%20U.S.%20Bureau,States%20from%201950%20to%202010.

21 Kyle Backman, "Trends in the reasons for restatement," Honors Thesis, Ohio State University, 2016, https://kb.osu.edu/handle/1811/76651.

22 See, for example, Roger Fisher and William Ury, *Getting to Yes* (New York: Penguin Books, 1991). They make clear that parties to a negotiation should know their reservation price (BATNA), but are under no obligation to reveal that to others.

23 Kendra Cherry, "What Is Passive-Aggressive Behavior?," *Very Well Mind*, September 18, 2019, https://www.verywellmind.com/what-is-passive-aggressive-behavior-2795481#:~:text=Passive%2Daggressive%20behaviors%20are%20those,expressing%20sullenness%2C%20or%20acting%20stubborn.

24 "Privileged Communication," JRank, accessed June 3, 2020, https://law.jrank.org/pages/9428/Privileged-Communication.html.

25 Adapted from the *Oxford English Dictionary*, sv "loyalty", accessed June 3, 2020, https://www-oed-com.erl.lib.byu.edu/view/Entry/110751?redirectedFrom=loyal#eid.

26 Employee Loyalty Reaches Lowest Level in More Than a Year, According to Energage Research, Business Wire, 27 July 2021.

27 Exploring the Nature and Motivations Behind Company Loyalty, Paychex Worx, 01 April 2019. Available at https://www.paychex.com/articles/human-resources/motivations-behind-company-loyalty.

28 Simon Keller, *The Limits of Loyalty* (Cambridge: Cambridge University Press, 2007). Most of this material is from Chapter 1.

29 Elizabeth Umphress and John Bingham, "When Employees Do Bad Things for Good Reasons: Examining Unethical Pro-Organizational Behaviors," *Organization Science* 22, no. 3 (2011): 621–640.

30 John Rawls, *A Theory of Justice* (Cambridge, MA: Belknap Press, 1971), 3.

31 David Miller, "Justice," *The Stanford Encyclopedia of Philosophy* (Fall 2017), Edward N. Zalta, ed., https://plato.stanford.edu/archives/fall2017/entries/justice/.

32 For youth, the tension between justice and mercy has been investigated. The same principles apply to adults. Curtis J. VanderWall, Alissa R. Mayer, Krista Cooper, and Laura Racovita-Szilagyi, "Balancing Justice and Mercy: Redemptive Ways of Dealing With Adolescent Substance Abuse," *Faculty Publications* 6 (2013), https://digitalcommons.andrews.edu/socialwork-pubs/6.

33 C. D. Clark, "Tough love: A brief cultural history of the addiction intervention," *History of Psychology* 15, no. 3 (2012): 233–246, https://doi.org/10.1037/a0025649.

34 Alfred Allan and Marietjie M. Allen, "The South African truth and reconciliation commission as a therapeutic tool," *Behavioral Sciences and the Law* 18, no. 4 (2000): 459–477.

CHAPTER 12

Corporate Social Responsibility and Social Entrepreneurship

LEARNING OUTCOMES

At the end of this chapter, you should be able to do the following:

1. Define what constitutes corporate social responsibility (CSR) and explain how it fits within a business's other responsibilities.

2. Identify how CSR creates value for different stakeholder groups.

3. Explain how social entrepreneurs affect corporations' social responsibility.

4. Describe how CSR fits within a meaningful and PERMA life.

5. Apply the concepts of CSR you learn in this chapter to situations you will face in the business world.

Opening Case | Ronald McDonald Is Good to Children

Fred Hill was drafted by the Philadelphia Eagles in 1965 as a tight end out of the University of Southern California. During the 1971 season, Hill's daughter Kim was diagnosed with leukemia.[1] For the next three years, Hill and his wife spent many nights sleeping in their car or in hospital lounges as they stayed with Kim during her treatments. They noticed that several other families did the same thing. Hill worked with his Eagles teammates and General Manager Jim Murray to do something about the situation. They teamed up with Dr. Audrey Evans, a local oncologist with a dream of building a permanent "temporary home" for the families of cancer patients.[2]

Murray and Hill also connected with Ed Rensi, the McDonald's regional manager in Philadelphia. Rensi used the chain's "Shamrock Shake" (a green mint shake) promotion to donate all funds to help purchase an old house near Evans's hospital. The house soon became the Ronald McDonald House. Within five years, there would be ten houses in the United States, and by 1984 that number had swelled to 365 houses in 45 countries.[3]

Ronald McDonald House Charities (RHMC) has three primary operating areas. The first is temporary housing for

families who travel to be with their children during medical care. Each house conforms to standards and guidelines set out by RMHC, but each house is independently owned and operated. Families who stay at a local Ronald McDonald House receive meals, a quality place to sleep, shower, and renew themselves, and playtime for accompanying children. Many facilities offer educational support for siblings of sick kids, art and music therapy, and gardens where families can plant and grow vegetables.[4] RMHC touts research that shows their houses provide services for the families of the sickest children who travel the farthest and stay the longest for medical care.[5]

The second core program is the Family Room program. These 260 rooms, located inside hospitals, provide families with the opportunity to rest, reset, clean up, and eat while they stay with their children during endless hours of testing and treatment. Parents can do laundry, catch up on email, or just enjoy a cup of coffee in a quiet setting. The charity's third core program area is the RMH mobile program. The charity brings medical and dental care to underserved communities around the world on semi-trailer trucks (see **Figure 12.1**).[6]

FIGURE 12.1   Ronald McDonald House's community mobile program provides communities with needed dental services.

The relationship between Ronald McDonald House Charities (RMHC) and McDonald's is close today, but that has not always been the case. The company ran the initial promotion and gave the charity permission to use the iconic Ronald McDonald image; however, the relationship between the charity and the company has not always reflected well on both of them. A 2013 report found that McDonald's Corporation accounted for less than 20% of RMHC's annual funding, and corporate contributions constituted 0.08% of their net income.[7] The corporation now contributes cash from its own operations, covers several administrative and fixed costs for RMHC, engages in a number of cause-related marketing promotions, and provides opportunities for customers to donate directly at the restaurants. In 2019, the chain helped raise $126 million, from all sources, for RHMC-related programs.[8]

RMHC is more than just a charity helping kids. It's a large organization in its own right. It operates on a budget of over $56 million a year and coordinates local chapters in all fifty U.S. States and sixty-four other countries around the world, each with their own budgets. The charity provides capacity-building grants to chapters as well as experts to help with every area of operations.[9] RMHC engages with over 500,000 volunteers each year, as well as McDonald's corporation and its almost 14,000 franchisees in the United States alone. All told, the organization provides over 2.5 million overnight stays for families each year. In spite of running a multinational organization, the charity remains remarkably focused on providing quality services for each family that stays. Rachel Jolivard, whose son Daniel underwent a bone marrow transplant, offered a comment typical of many residents: "Nothing else matters when I see the boys' smiles and excitement in being together. And the other families in the House have become a part of our own family, giving that much more support for Daniel as he battles back."[10]

Businesses face increasing pressure, and are under increasing scrutiny from stakeholder activists, to prove that their activities benefit more than merely their shareholders or direct stakeholders.[11] In an ethical society, businesses should create social and not merely economic value. Leaders in the private sector, both business and not-for-profit, have approached these demands in two ways. First, they engage in corporate social responsibility (CSR) activities in their own operations. Second, many have experimented with innovative solutions that target our most intractable social challenges. This chapter will provide you with a framework to think about CSR and social entrepreneurship. Many students today want to be involved in social innovation, and so we'll focus on the skills needed to engage in this type of work.

Corporate Social Responsibility (CSR)

Corporate Social Responsibility refers to activities that companies engage in that target social challenges and that lie *beyond* the direct economic interests of the firm.[12] The logic of the stakeholder model underpins the ethical foundations of CSR. You will read about how CSR has both instrumental and intrinsic stakeholder logic. CSR builds on the notion that businesses have a number of obligations they must meet as members of a society.

CSR and the Activities of a Firm

Figure 12.2 arranges these obligations in a pyramid that highlights their interdependence.[13] At the base is the firm's **economic responsibility**. Unless the firm produces profitable products and can pay its employees, suppliers, and investors, it cannot meet any other obligations. **Legal responsibility** obligates managers and others in the firm to obey laws and conform to all regulations in countries where they operate. The obligation of **ethical responsibility** binds managers to the unwritten standards, norms, and values that underlie social interactions. This is obedience to the unenforceable that we've written about in several places.

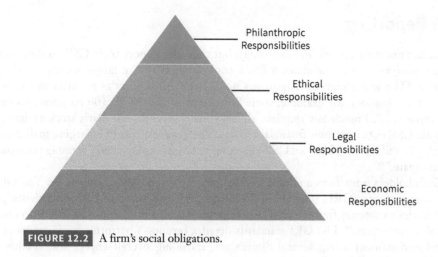

FIGURE 12.2 A firm's social obligations.

Philanthropic responsibility, the fourth obligation of business, implies an obligation to better the communities through giving back in ways that strengthen communities and the larger society. The first three obligations have clear and straightforward measures of success: economic revenues and profits, legal compliance, and obedience to the unenforceable. Managers and leaders have significant discretion in how, and how well, they fulfill their philanthropic obligations. **Philanthropy** means to promote the good or well-being of others through gift giving.[14] The most traditional form of philanthropy is donations of money. Nike founder Phil Knight, for example, has donated over $2 billion to the University of Oregon and Stanford University.[15] Firms also donate "in-kind" when they allow employees to spend work time in assisting individuals or not-for-profit organizations; many also donate products or services to local community organizations. After Hurricane Katrina hit New Orleans and the Gulf Coast, for example, Walmart donated 100 truckloads of relief supplies to affected residents (see **Figure 12.3**).[16] Following Hurricane Ida, which occurred exactly 16 years after Katrina, the city again saw relief samples pour in from many organizations.

CSR is more than philanthropy, however. It also includes producing safe and healthy products for customers, providing employees with adequate wages and a great place to work, fostering diversity and inclusion, acting transparently with shareholders and investors, and working to preserve and sustain the natural environment. CSR extends from a firm's direct stakeholders out to a number of indirect stakeholders.[17]

FIGURE 12.3 Walmart donates to communities in need after natural disasters.

CSR Reporting

Businesses not only engage in CSR today, but they also report their CSR to those stakeholders who want to know about a firm's commitments to the larger society in which it operates. "The world's largest companies now issue CSR reports as a matter of course. In the United Kingdom, for example, some 86 percent of the FSTE 100 corporations issued CSR reports. . . . French law requires all large firms listed on the Paris stock exchange to integrate CSR data into their financial reports. The governments of emerging markets such as Malaysia and South Africa see CSR as a competitive advantage and encourage companies to participate."[18]

Stakeholders want facts and data, not just anecdotes and feel-good stories. The Global Reporting Initiative (GRI), founded in Boston in 1997 by a group of business activists, gives stakeholders a common framework to assess how a business has performed in relation to the natural environment.[19] The GRI standards detail a business's performance in terms of the natural environment along several dimensions, including overall energy use, biodiversity protection, and levels of emissions and waste.

The first version of the GRI guidelines appeared in 2000, and the framework has expanded over time. It now covers many areas of a firm's performance, including economic impacts for shareholders, stakeholders, and communities. The social category of the GRI report holds firms accountable for their labor practices, compliance with human rights standards and goals, contributions to local communities, and the production of safe and responsible products. The GRI has developed a set of reporting guidelines firms use to produce an annual report, much like the Securities and Exchange Commission Form 10-K filing that public U.S. firms provide for their shareholders. Over 95 percent of the world's largest companies regularly create and publish sustainability reports based on the GRI guidelines.[20] As Figure 12.4 shows, the GRI framework is one of many that businesses can use to report their CSR activities.

While all CSR reports have some areas of commonality in terms of the categories that they address, these reports really "are attempting to serve one essential purpose: They portray the relationship between a corporation and society. They seek to improve communications between the corporate world and the broader society within which companies report."[21] They demonstrate to external stakeholders the actual value a company attempts to add to society.

CSR and Business Performance

The premise of CSR reporting in the GRI is that a firm's social performance is an intrinsic obligation it owes to stakeholders as a citizen of the communities where it operates. You learned about the intrinsic view of stakeholder obligations in Chapter 4. If we use this logic, then the question of whether firms do well (in terms of financial or strategic performance) by doing good (CSR) is irrelevant. CSR is an obligation firms have; they must work for the benefit of society and its many stakeholder groups.[22]

The instrumental view of stakeholder management argues that firms should do well by doing good.[23] The academic literature on this issue over the past half-century has provided a lively debate about the question of whether or not firms do well when they do good.[24] Do firms profit from their CSR activities?[25] What does the evidence say? In one comprehensive review of over 100 research studies, the evidence came out decidedly mixed.[26] In just over half the studies, CSR seemed to improve financial performance, but in just under half, CSR either had no effect or it seemed to decrease earnings. These scholars see financial performance increasing through the following mechanisms:

- *Customers* who trust a company's products for safety and reliability will be more likely to make repeat purchases. Customers also receive social and psychological benefits from their affiliations with companies with a reputation for doing good.[27]

The Top Five Sustainability Frameworks You Should Know

Standard	Focus	Why Report	Scoring	Who Reports	Reporting Period
CDP DISCLOSURE INSIGHT ACTION	Primarily GHG emissions, but has grown to address water and forestry issues as well	CDP holds the largest repository of corporate GHG emissions and energy use data in the world and is backed by nearly 800 institutional investors representing more than $90 trillion in assets. Its transparent scoring methodology helps respondents understand exactly what's expected of them. CDP was regarded as the world's most most credible sustainability rating in 2013	Companies receive two separate scores for Disclosure and Performance using a 100-point scale. CDP recognizes top scoring companies in the Carbon Disclosure Leadership Index [CDLI]	Public and private companies, cities, government agencies, NGOs, supply chains	• Climate Change program: Feb.1– May 29 • Supply Chain program: April 1–July 3 • Cities program: Jan.1–Mar. 31 • Water and Forestry programs: Feb.1 to June 30
Dow Jones Sustainability Indexes	Industry-specific criteria considered material to investors, Equal balance of economic, social and environmental indicators.	Membership in the DJSI is prestigious as it represents the top 10% of the 2,500 largest companies in the S&P Global Broad Market Index. The Corporate Sustainability Assessment [CSA] brings a sector-specific focus and need-to-know simplicity to disclosure for public companies. This index was regarded as the world's second most credible sustainability rating after CDP	Companies receive a total Sustainability Score is between 0-100 and are ranked against peers; includes a Media and Stakeholders Analysis; those scoring within the top 10% are included in index	The 2,500 largest public companies in the world	April 3–May 28
GRI	Corporate social responsibility with an equal weight on environmental, social and governance factors. Heavy on stakeholder engagement to determine materiality	GRI was announced as the official reporting standard of the Global Compact, making it the default reporting framework for the compact's more than 5,800 associated companies. It's among the oldest; most widely adopted and most widely respected reporting methodologies in the world. Its thorough focus on social and governance aspects of ESG is unparalleled	Focus is on transparency so on true scoring methodology; new G.4 framework requires entity reporting to choose "Core" or "Complete" reporting	Public and private companies, cities, government agencies, universities, hospitals, NGOs	Anytime, but typically integrated into a company's traditional annual report
GRESB	Environmental, social and governance performance in the global commercial real estate sector only. Includes asset- and entity-level disclosures	Private and public institutional investors look to GRESB's annual survey as the barometer of sustainability performance in the commercial real estate industry. Its niche target audience allows it to give deeper and more accurate insights into industry performance and reveal "investment grade" results	Responses scored out of a possible 140.5 points distributed across two categories of data. Heavy weighting placed on implementation and asset-level performance	Commercial real estate owners, asset managers and developers	April 1–June 30
VALUE REPORTING FOUNDATION SASB STANDARDS	US public companies only. Industry-specific issues deemed material to investors	SASB's standards enable comparison of peer performance and benchmarking within an industry, Studies by Goldman Sachs and Deutsche Bank have shown the stock of companies who disclose on sustainability outperforms that of companies who do not. SASB is backed by the likes of Bloomberg LP and the Rockefeller Foundation, giving it extra clout with capital markets	No scoring system. Instead, SASB is a standardized methodology for reporting sustainability performance through the Form 10-K	No one yet – they've just released their first sector reporting guidelines	Integrated into quarterly 10-K filings.

FIGURE 12.4 Sustainability Reporting Frameworks.

- *Employees* will be more productive, and more innovative, when they work for companies that engage in CSR. Companies that care about their communities will have an easier time attracting and retaining high-quality employees.[28]

- *Suppliers* are more willing to do business with companies that they trust. Engagement in CSR signals to suppliers that a company has strong values and can be trusted, which may lead to suppliers doing things like extending more credit to firms with active CSR initiatives.[29]

- *Investors* like to invest in companies with forward-thinking management teams. Engagement in CSR is a signal of a quality management team. Also, firms that report their CSR are most likely to engage in transparent and honest financial reporting.[30]

Table 12.1 summarizes these links between CSR and a firm's direct stakeholders. It also describes other ways in which CSR can improve business performance. CSR can focus on and create benefits for stakeholders in the firm's indirect stakeholders and strategy toward the natural environment. As businesses engage in CSR that has positive social outcomes, they also need to avoid involvement in hot-button social issues, many of which can lead to a decline in business value.

Recent research suggests that CSR activities help preserve a company's resource base when things go wrong. These researchers believe that the positive reputation for creating social value through CSR acts like an insurance policy that protects the underlying economic value of the firm when accidents or other negative events occur.[31] Several academic studies suggest that CSR may have an insurance-like effect that preserves shareholder value, particularly when CSR focuses on the strategic elements and environment of the firm, as noted in Table 12.1.[32]

CSR, when done thoughtfully, creates value for the societies in which firms operate. Sometimes, however, the traditional tools of CSR such as philanthropy, involvement in particular social issues, or direct stakeholder initiatives prove ill-suited to attack some of society's most vexing and intractable problems, such as the fight against global poverty. In these instances, companies or individuals often create innovative and entrepreneurial approaches to these problems that fall under the rubric of social entrepreneurship.

TABLE 12.1   CSR Initiates.

Focus of initiative	Affected stakeholder groups	Representative actions	Examples
Operational elements	Direct stakeholders		
	Customers	Products for disadvantaged R&D spending and innovation	Whole Foods' dedication to high-quality groceries
	Employees	No-layoff policy Generous benefits	Costco's above-industry wages, profit sharing, and benefits
	Investors	Reporting transparency Political accountability	Intel's extensive CSR reporting and commitment to transparency
Strategic elements	Indirect stakeholders		
	Communities	Charitable giving Innovative giving programs	Target's commitment to giving in its local communities
	Gender diversity	Promotion of women. Minorities Hiring disabled workers	IBM's history of hiring minorities and training the disabled
	Natural environment	Pollution prevention Recycling programs	Dow Chemical's efforts to reduce or eliminate toxins in production
Controversial social issues	Society at large	Abstain from Tobacco, alcohol, or nuclear power	Cerberus Capital sells its stake in Bushmaster rifle company after Newtown, Connecticut, shootings

Social Entrepreneurship and Innovation

You first met Martin Burt, the founder of the micro-credit organization Fundación Paraguaya, in Chapter 3. Martin is a social entrepreneur. **Social entrepreneurship** uses innovative organizational and business models to generate value for the larger societies in which people live and work.[33] Fundación Paraguaya enhances social value, as students at the San Francisco School have the skills to work themselves out of poverty, and they can use those skills to build stronger farming communities that improve the Paraguayan economy.

Social entrepreneurs may or may not use business models and market principles to solve social problems; some operate in the not-for-profit or civil society sectors. They are entrepreneurs in the sense that they look for and implement innovative approaches to solve problems. Social entrepreneurs come from many work disciplines, including government, religious organizations, large corporations, and small private businesses. Most social entrepreneurs depend on market principles and business logic to make their contribution. Finding philanthropic donors or government grantmakers willing to bet on untried models often proves to be a very difficult task, and running a business helps create a sustainable solution to social problems.

Types of Social Entrepreneurship

Social entrepreneurs generate social value in one of three ways: They attempt to build capacity, they sell products or services, or they drive institutional change.[34] **Capacity building** means transferring knowledge, skills, and abilities (KSAs) from one organization to another. Fundación Paraguaya builds capacity in its micro-credit operation by teaching Paraguayan entrepreneurs how to effectively run their own businesses. **Products and services** are typically custom designed for the social niche the entrepreneurs work in. For example, Hindustan Lever, the Indian subsidiary of Unilever, uses a business model that employs local women in rural communities to sell its low-cost and small-size products.[35] Ethics in the Real World 12.1 highlights another organization selling products and services that improve social welfare.

Ethics in the Real World 12.1 | Community Enterprise Solutions

Greg Van Kirk cut his professional teeth in the investment banking world.[36] After reading a biography of Muhammad Yunus, Van Kirk had a change of heart: "I had just turned 30 and knew I wanted to work in economic development, but I knew nothing about the field. I joined the Peace Corps to gain grassroots experience."[37] His assignment took him to Guatemala, where he saw individuals and communities living in poverty and despair. At the end of his Peace Corps stint, Van Kirk joined with George "Buckey" Glickley to form Community Enterprise Solutions, or CES. They later changed the name to Community Empowerment Solutions. They produced a concrete wood stove that replaced open-fire cooking. The stove would help individuals, families, and communities reduce the health risks of open-fire cooking, particularly the risks to children. CES wanted to engage local entrepreneurs, but the price of the stove meant that most people could not afford to purchase an inventory of stoves.

CES pioneered a new business model, micro-consignment, as an innovative solution (see Figure 12.5). CES lends the stove to the entrepreneur, who then repays CES for each unit sold, but only for each unit sold. Micro-consignment solved the cash flow problem for entrepreneurs and shifted the inventory risk to CES. The micro-consignment proved successful, and CES now offers its partners a number of different products on consignment. Van Kirk and CES have now exported the model to other Latin American countries.

FIGURE 12.5 The Micro Consignment Model at Community Empowerment Solutions.

Institutional change means that social entrepreneurs work to change the way communities frame problems and look for solutions. They use innovation to change institutions—from formal government policies and agencies to informal social values and norms. Institutional entrepreneurs usually work on large-scale social problems that have eluded easy solution by governments or others. Ohio-based Cardinal Health Foundation, for example, invests in several social entrepreneurial groups attacking the problem of prescription drug abuse. Cardinal does not build capacity, nor sell products; it hopes to create change within the health care sector as a whole.

Skills of Social Entrepreneurs

Social entrepreneurs need a specialized set of skills to work effectively. Table 12.2 matches leadership skills and the types of social entrepreneurship we just discussed.[38] Capacity building requires the skills of a **social bricoleur**, which comes from the French word *bricolage* and means building something new by combining existing things in new ways.

Social constructionists build new and innovative products or services. Mohammed Yunus, the Nobel Prize winner who founded the Grameen Bank, was a constructor. Yunus observed that Bangladeshi basket weavers, primarily women, paid exorbitant fees to intermediaries to finance their inventory, who then captured most of the value of the baskets. This left the women in a state of perpetual poverty. Yunus constructed a new type of loan, the micro-loan, targeted to groups of women entrepreneurs, and the group assumed responsibility for the loan and insured repayment. Women's incomes rose because of Grameen's micro-loans.[39] **Social engineers** design and work to create more effective large-scale social systems to solve problems. Advertising executive Phillip Joanus founded the Partnership for a Drug-Free America in the early 1980s (now Drugfree.org) to combat the problem of rampant drug abuse.[40] He employed the traditional tools of advertising to get people to view the problem of drug use in a new way. He changed the most fundamental social institution: the collective mindset and attitude about drug abuse. Joanus helped his advertising industry colleagues—and others in society—see drug abuse as a business problem, and not just a social problem.

TABLE 12.2　Types of Social Entrepreneurship.

Focus on SE Activities	Role of social entrepreneur/leader	Examples
Capacity Building	Social bricoleur: Combines existing resources in new ways to solve social problems	Highlander Research and Education Center (USA): adult education for community problem solving in Appalachia
		BRAC (Bangladesh): organizes and trains poor communities to create economic and social development
Products/Services	Social constructor: Develops new models products, or services	Grameen Bank (Bangladesh Worldwide): developed unique model for delivery/repayment of microcredit
		Unilever (India): Project Shakti uses rural women to sell hygiene products. Improves local health and incomes
Institutional Change	Social engineer: Creates momentum for change focuses on large institutional systems	Bono (Ireland): becomes a voice for worldwide poverty alleviation
		Nelson Mandela (South Africa): reconciliation commissions allow wounds from apartheid to heal

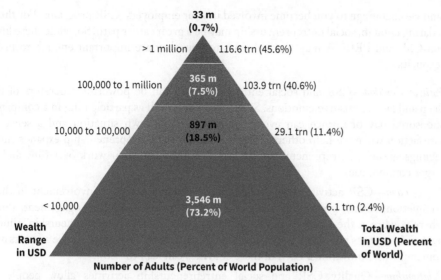

Source: James Davies, Rodrigo Lluberas and Anthony Shorrocks, Credit Suisse Global Wealth Databook 2016.

FIGURE 12.6 The global wealth pyramid.

Challenges for Social Entrepreneurs

Many colleges and universities have centers, institutes, and even majors devoted to advancing social entrepreneurship and entrepreneurship. If you want to become involved in social entrepreneurship, there are a number of ways to do so. In spite of all the momentum, however, serious challenges remain that may limit the potential of social entrepreneurship to create the large-scale social change its advocates hope for.

First, social entrepreneurs often work in unstable and harsh conditions, particularly those working at the **Base of the Economic Pyramid** (see **Figure 12.6**) to help the world's poor, or people living in extreme poverty.[41] Entrepreneurs work in environments with poor physical infrastructure and typically a poor set of legal and regulatory institutions. Corruption tends to be pervasive and makes progress difficult and halting. Many times, entrepreneurs must build their own infrastructure, physical or institutional, *before* they turn their attention to the problem they hope to solve. Second, social entrepreneurs face the difficulty of managing a **hybrid organization**, one that focuses equally on both social and economic goals. Entrepreneurs must make tough trade-offs between an exciting social mission and the realities of generating positive cash flow. Making these trade-offs sometimes requires sacrificing one in the name of the other.[42]

Finally, social entrepreneurs face a series of ethical and political challenges. Nelson Mandela won the Nobel Prize, and he transformed life in his native South Africa; however, he spent years in prison for what the South African Government of the day considered at the time to be seditious views. Social entrepreneurs also face the challenges of moral imperialism that we wrote about in Chapter 7. They often work tirelessly to bring their preferred solution to the poor, even if the poor do not want or need what they have to offer. Social entrepreneurs must be cautious about not overpromising and creating false hope. Social problems are not solved over the long term on promises of capacity building that never materialize, products or services that disappear shortly after they appear, or ineffective attempts to change institutions.

CSR and a PERMA Life

We conclude this chapter by returning to a common theme of this book: One goal of dealing with ethical issues in business is to lead a moral and happy life. CSR and social entrepreneurship represent excellent vehicles for people to increase the level of PERMA they have in their lives, and we encourage to you become involved in your employers' CSR programs. For those of you daring enough, social entrepreneurship may be a great career path. So, while these links between CSR and PERMA may seem obvious to you, they are important enough to make them explicit:

- *Positive Emotion*—CSR and social entrepreneurship can be powerful generators of the deep and lasting positive emotions. Simple CSR acts such as participating in a company-sponsored day of service can evoke gratitude for our own situation and a sense of satisfaction when we help others along the way. Social entrepreneurship expands these feelings as social entrepreneurs see the positive impact of their work over time and in larger communities.

- *Engagement*—CSR activities, particularly those that require your involvement in their completion, stretch your skills and put you in situations ripe for engagement, those where you are at the limit of your knowledge and skill. Social entrepreneurship, almost by definition, puts people on the frontier of their skill sets. They must devise answers and come up with innovations. Each of these activities can lead to "flow."

- *Relationships*—Quality CSR and social entrepreneurship activities allow people to cooperate and work with others in ways we are not used to. Through this engagement, we can find new areas of common skill or interest, and a set of similar human needs, that we share with others. When we work with others on projects with human and ethical meaning, we share positive emotions and flow with others.

- *Meaning*—CSR involves activity beyond just economic profit and success; it naturally places us in a realm of working on projects that transcend our own immediate needs. The same is true for social entrepreneurship. These activities force us to focus on challenges and issues that are too big for an individual to solve but are worth solving in their own right. Our life steps out of our own day-to-day problems through the projects of CSR or the life of a social entrepreneur.

- *Achievement*—CSR activities and social entrepreneurship allow us to achieve difficult goals and grow. There is a sense of having accomplished something when we paint a house or clean up a riverbank. That feeling and confidence are magnified when we help a child learn to read or master math skills. For social entrepreneurs such as Martin Burt who help others gain the skills that allow them to thrive on their own, there is a thrilling feeling of having achieved a very worthwhile goal.

Key Terms

base of the Economic Pyramid	institutional change	products and services
capacity building	instrumental view	social bricoleur
corporate social responsibility	intrinsic view	social constructionists
economic responsibility	legal responsibility	social engineers
ethical responsibility	philanthropic responsibility	social entrepreneurship
hybrid organization	philanthropy	

Chapter Summary

- This chapter dealt with an important topic for today's business leaders. Corporate Social Responsibility (CSR) is the engagement by a business in activities that are (1) not directly related to the profit-making work of the firm and (2) directed toward some societal issue or social good. All firms have economic, legal, and ethical responsibilities they must fulfill, but CSR is a discretionary or philanthropic responsibility.

- CSR is a sophisticated activity with its own reporting requirements and frameworks, such as the GRI.

- CSR may be either an intrinsic responsibility of a firm, or an instrumental activity that helps the firm earn greater profits. CSR helps firms "do well by doing good" as it deepens the relationships between the firm and its stakeholders.

- Many people today, including many college students and young professionals, hope to engage in social entrepreneurship, the use of innovative business models and approaches to solve social problems. Social entrepreneurs may work to build capacity in a given sector, they may introduce innovative products or services to help solve social problems, or they may attempt to change large-scale social institutions.

- Capacity building utilizes the skills of social bricolage, products and services call on the skills of social construction, and the skills needed to bring about large-scale change are those of the social engineer.

Chapter Review Questions

1. Define corporate social responsibility. Give an example of each of a firm's four responsibilities and obligations.
2. Should organization use CSR activity as marketing tool? Discuss.
3. In what ways can CSR and social involvement benefit both society and the business?
4. Is it ethical to make laws for CSR activities? Discuss.

5. What activities of social entrepreneurship help build the capacity of the social sector? What is the difference between capacity building and institutional change?
6. If you were to become a social entrepreneur, which skills would be the easiest for you to develop and deploy? Which ones would be hardest?
7. How does our involvement in social initiatives at work contribute to a PERMA life?

Application Exercises

- *Personal Ethical Development.* If you began keeping an ethics journal as suggested in the first chapter, continue that writing work. Here are some prompts: How important is it to you that your work life create social as well as economic good? What types of philanthropy would you like to become involved in? How might you begin/continue to make positive contributions to society while in school? In your first job?

- *Career Goals and Planning.* A happy, meaningful, and productive life blends and builds upon the following: (1) the type of life you are interested in leading, (2) your deepest and most important values, (3) the work you are interested in doing, (4) what you are good at, (5) your preferences for things like work versus free time, and (6) your personality. How can you figure out the level of dedication companies have to CSR or philanthropy? What types of CSR do you think are appropriate for the industries you want to work in? How important is it for you that your company is a leader in CSR?

- *Ethics in the Business World.* Identify a company that is considered a leader in CSR or philanthropy. What areas are they involved in? How did they decide on these areas, and what is their level of ongoing commitment? How does top management encourage people to become involved? What changes has the organization made to stay current in its CSR activities?

- *Talking with and Learning from Others.* Choose a business professional you respect and who you admire for their involvement

in social causes or philanthropy. Engage that person in a brief interview. When did they first become involved? What motivated them to become active in the areas they work in? What advice would they give you as you begin your career?

- Be an ethics professional for a day. Assume you are an intern in the ESG (Environment, Social, Governance) office of TeaCo, a $50 million import/export company that deals in varietal teas. TeaCo is considering publishing some type of CSR statement or goals on its website, and you have been asked to do a number of tasks to help management be prepared to make some decisions.

  a. Review CSR reports of several different companies, including those of food product companies. Prepare a slide deck presentation for TeaCo senior management that summarizes the different sections in these reports (sustainability, safety, CEO introduction, etc.). Your presentation should help the management team understand how others have become involved in CSR and how they report their involvement to their stakeholders.

  b. Prepare a brief set of slides for a live educational session that you will give to the ten regional managers at TeaCo. What are the key elements of a successful CSR program, and what do these managers need to do to ensure that TeaCo's CSR program gains traction? What are the most important formal and informal actions these managers need to take?

Mini-Cases

Case 1. Deciding among CSR options. Ben Jones works as a social media marketing specialist for DogMa, a regional chain of pet-care product

retailers in the Northeastern United States. The company produces its own line of high-quality dog food as well as selling all major national brands, and each store has a large dog-washing area. True to its name, DogMa provides both dog-walking services and a kenneling service for when customers leave town. DogMa is growing rapidly and believes that a CSR program would be good for the company and its employees.

Dogma's founder has two children with disabilities and wants to see the company support early childhood programs for children with disabilities. Others in the company feel that DogMa should focus on something related to dogs, either supporting rescue shelters or training programs for service animals. There is also a group that believes the company should support efforts to ban the use of dogs as landmine sniffers. Ben has been assigned to a CSR committee that will recommend a focus area to DogMa's executive team. The assignment for the first meeting is to come with a list of pros and cons for each of these three options, plus at least one other idea. Ben asks himself several questions as he prepares:

What are the benefits of being involved in each activity? What are the risks? What criteria should the committee use to evaluate each option?

Case 2: The Indian Railways is the lifeline of the nation and Karan Sharma is proud to work for it. Karan is a civil engineer and by virtue of his job is always connected with public safety. In his career, Karan made one decision that he believes was ethical, even if he did not follow the rules set by the Indian Railways. An incident occurred when he was posted at Masaipet village in Medak district adjacent to Hyderabad in Telangana. On July 24, 2014, at an unmanned level crossing near Masaipet village, the Nanded–Secunderabad passenger train rammed into a school bus in the morning hours. Twenty-eight schoolgoing children were killed on the spot in the accident, including the driver of the school bus. As per the law, the railway did not bear any responsibility for the accident at the unmanned level crossing

since the accident was due to the negligence of the driver. But Karan felt that the existing rules of the railway were not ethical. To ensure that such an incident did not occur again, a simple solution was to convert the unmanned level crossing to manned level crossing, or if there was less traffic, the unmanned level crossing could be closed directly with the permission of local authorities. Karan was in-charge of the adjacent section at Nanded during the period of the accident. The death of the young children disturbed him. He was also very worried in case the same incident occurred on the unmanned level crossing in his jurisdiction. Karan was already working on the closure/manning of the unmanned level crossing gate. By 2017, all unmanned level crossing gates from his section were to be eliminated. This involved a lot of paperwork and permissions, and the most difficult was getting permissions from local representatives.

There were two options in front of Karan. First was to go ahead with the existing plan and close the gates by 2017, but this does not guarantee that a similar accident does not happen again. Second was the immediate closure of the gates and completion of the formalities at a later date. Option one was by the book so it would have been easy, but it would take time. But Karan's personal values pushed him to do whatever he could to remove such a threat as fast as possible. Thus, he chose the second option, going against the rules, where he was questioned and faced major protest. He identified nine unmanned level crossing gates that closed overnight. There was a lot of resistance from the public and local villagers, but he convinced them by telling them that he did not want an accident like Masaipet to happen in their village. This convinced most people and they came to terms with the situation.

Discussion Questions

1. Why did Karan not follow the existing rules of the railway?

2. How did Karan convince local people?

References

[1] Jim Gehman, "Where Are They Now? TE Fred Hill," Philadelphia Eagles, December 21, 2018, https://www.philadelphiaeagles.com/news/where-are-they-now-te-fred-hill.

[2] "Our History: Learn how the 'House That Love Built' came to be," Ronald McDonald House Charities of the Capital Region, accessed June 4, 2021, https://rmhcofalbany.org/about-us/our-history/.

[3] Ibid.

[4] "Our Houses are filled with more than help, they're filled with hope.," Ronald McDonald House, accessed June 4, 2021, https://www.rmhc.org/our-core-programs/ronald-mcdonald-house-programs.

[5] Ibid.

[6] Ibid.

[7] Beth Hoffman, "Report Finds McDonald's Skimps On Charity Donations," *Forbes*, October 30, 2013, https://www.forbes.com/sites/bethhoffman/2013/10/30/report-finds-mcdonalds-skimps-on-charity-donations/?sh=1b7a56cc28b3.

[8] "McDonald's support helps benefit Chapters around the world, RMHC website," accessed June 4, 2021, https://www.rmhc.org/about-us/RMHC-and-McDonalds.

[9] "Ronald McDonald House Charities, Inc., Financial Statements," December 31, 2019, and 2018, https://www.rmhc.org/-/media/

Feature/RMHC-Production-Images/About-Us/Files/Media-Resources-and-Financials/2019-Audited-Financial-Statements.pdf.

[10] "The Jolivard Family: 'This is more than a place to sleep and eat…a place to be supported together.'," accessed June 4, 2021, https://www.rmhc.org/rmhc-family-stories/the-jolivard-family.

[11] Michael Porter and Mark Kramer, 2011, Creating Shared Value, Harvard Business Review, 89 (Feb), 62–77.

[12] Abagail McWilliams and Donald Siegel, "Corporate Social Responsibility: A Theory of the Firm Perspective," *The Academy of Management Review* 26, no. 1 (January 1, 2001): 117–127, doi:10.2307/259398. For an understanding of how CSR has been defined over the years, see Archie B. Carroll, "Corporate Social Responsibility: Evolution of a Definitional Construct," *Business & Society* 38, no. 3 (September 1, 1999): 268–295, doi:10.1177/000765039903800303.

[13] Archie B. Carroll, "The Pyramid of Corporate Social Responsibility: Toward the Moral Management of Organizational Stakeholders," *Business Horizons* 34, no. 4 (1991): 39–48.

[14] Definition adapted from the one given by the *Oxford English Dictionary*, accessed June 12, 2013, http://www.oed.com/view/Entry/142408?redirectedFrom=philanthropy#eid.

15 "Phil and Penny Knight's charitable contributions top $2 billion," *The Oregonian*, last modified January 9, 2019, https://www.oregonlive.com/business/2016/10/phil_and_penny_knights_charita.html.

16 Michael Barbaro and Justin Gillis, "Wal-Mart at Forefront of Hurricane Relief," *Washington Post*, September 6, 2005, http://www.washingtonpost.com/wp-dyn/content/article/2005/09/05/AR2005090501598.html.

17 J. E. Mattingly and Shawn Berman, "Measurement of corporate social action: Discovering taxonomy in the Kinder Lydenburg domini ratings data," *Business and Society* 45 (2006): 20–46.

18 "How to Read a Corporate Social Responsibility Report: A user's guide," Boston College Center for Corporate Citizenship, accessed June 4, 2021, https://iri.hks.harvard.edu/files/iri/files/how_to_read_a_corporate_social_responsibility_report.pdf.

19 Data in this section is taken from the GRI website, www.globalreporting.org, and the GRI guidelines handbook, available at https://www.globalreporting.org/about-gri/mission-history/ accessed September 16, 2013.

20 Taken from the GRI annual report, 2012. Available at https://www.globalreporting.org/about-gri/news-center/2020-12-01-sustainability-reporting-is-growing-with-gri-the-global-common-language/ accessed September 16, 2013.

21 "How to Read a Corporate Social Responsibility Report."

22 Donna Wood and Jeanie Logsdon, "Business Citizenship: From individuals to organizations," *Business Ethics Quarterly* 12, no. 1 (2002): 59–94. See also Jeanie Logsdon and Donna Wood, "Business Citizenship: From Domestic to Global Level of Analysis," *Business Ethics Quarterly* 12 no. 2 (April 2002): 155–187.

23 Paul C. Godfrey, "The Relationship between Corporate Philanthropy and Shareholder Wealth: A Risk Management Perspective," *The Academy of Management Review* 30, no. 4 (October 1, 2005): 777–798, doi:10.2307/20159168.

24 See Joshua Daniel Margolis and James P. Walsh, *People and Profits?: The Search for A Link Between A Company's Social and Financial Performance* (New York: Psychology Press, 2001). Also see Joshua D. Margolis and James P. Walsh, "Misery Loves Companies: Rethinking Social Initiatives by Business," *Administrative Science Quarterly* 48, no. 2 (June 1, 2003): 268–305, doi:10.2307/3556659. For a recent review of the key literature, see Qian Wang, Junsheng Dou, Shenghua Jia, A Meta-Analytic Review of Corporate Social Responsibility and Corporate Financial Performance: The Moderating Effect of Contextual Factors, business and Society, 2015, doi 10.1177/0007650315584317.

25 M. Friedman, "The Social Responsibility of Business Is to Increase Profit," *New York Times Magazine* (1970): 33.

26 Margolis and Walsh, *People and Profits?* See also Margolis and Walsh, "Misery Loves Companies."

27 Jeremy Galbreath and Paul Shum, "Do customer satisfaction and reputation mediate the CSR–FP link? Evidence from Australia," *Australian Journal of Management* (2012): https://doi.org/10.1177%2F0312896211432941.

28 Seth Carnahan, David Kryscynski, and Daniel Olson, "When does corporate social responsibility reduce employee turnover? Evidence from attorneys before and after 9/11," *Academy of Management Journal* 60, no. 5 (August 16, 2016): 1932–1962.

29 Min Zhang, Lijun Ma, Jun Su, and Wen Zhang, "Do Suppliers Applaud Corporate Social Performance,"? *Journal of Business Ethics* 121 (2014): 543–557.

30 Yi-Hung Lin, Hua-Wei Huang, Mark Riley, and Chih-Chen Lee, "Corporate Social Responsibility and Financial Reporting Quality: Evidence from Restatement," *Accounting and the Public Interest* 20, no. 1 (2020): 61–75.

31 Godfrey, "The Relationship between Corporate Philanthropy and Shareholder Wealth."

32 Michael D. Pfarrer, Timothy G. Pollock, and Violina P. Rindova, "A Tale of Two Assets: The Effects of Firm Reputation and Celebrity on Earnings Surprises and Investors' Reactions," *Academy of Management Journal* 53, no. 5 (October 1, 2010): 1131–1152, doi:10.5465/AMJ.2010.54533222.

33 The exact definition of social entrepreneurship has been hotly debated in the academic literature. For excellent reviews of the number of definitions, see Dacin, Dacin, and Matear, "Social Entrepreneurship." Cited above. See also Weerawardena and Gillian Sullivan Mort, "Investigating Social Entrepreneurship: A Multidimensional Model," cited above.

34 Sarah H. Alvord, L. David Brown, and Christine W. Letts, "Social Entrepreneurship and Societal Transformation: An Exploratory Study," *The Journal of Applied Behavioral Science* 40, no. 3 (September 1, 2004): 260–282, doi:10.1177/0021886304266847.

35 Basic information on project Shatki can be found at https://sellingwithpurpose.unilever.com/?p=43, accessed August 30, 2021. For a review, see V. Kasturi Rangan et al., "The Complex Business of Serving the Poor: Insights from Unilever's Project Shakti in India.," *Business Solutions for the Global Poor: Creating Social and Economic Value* (2007): 144–154.

36 Data and information for this feature are drawn from Paul C. Godfrey, "Community Enterprise Solutions: Replicating the MicroConsignment Model," GlobaLens (William Davidson Institute, University of Michigan), case # 1-429-331, April 1, 2013.

37 G. Van Kirk, "The Microconsignment Model: Bridging the 'last mile' of access to products and services for the rural poor," *Innovations/Tech4Society* (2010): 137.

38 Material in this section and the table are adapted from Alvord, Brown, and Letts, "Social Entrepreneurship and Societal Transformation," and Shaker A. Zahra et al., "A Typology of Social Entrepreneurs: Motives, Search Processes and Ethical Challenges," *Journal of Business Venturing* 24, no. 5 (September 2009): 519–532, doi:10.1016/j.jbusvent.2008.04.007.

39 See Alex Counts and Alex Counts, *Small Loans, Big Dreams : How Nobel Peace Prize Winner Muhammad Yunus and Microfinance Are Changing the World* (Hoboken, NJ: John Wiley & Sons, 2008). See also M. Yunus, "All Human Beings Are Entrepreneurs," in *Kauffman Thought Book 2009* (Kansas City: Kauffman Foundation, 2008), 127–130.

40 https://drugfree.org/article/our-history/works accessed April 2, 2014.

41 Ted London and Stuart Hart, *Next Generation Business Strategies for the Base of the Pyramid: New Approaches for Building Mutual Value* (Upper Saddle River, NJ: FT Press, 2011).

42 Paul Tracey and Owen Jarvis, "Toward a Theory of Social Venture Franchising," *Entrepreneurship Theory and Practice* 31, no. 5 (2007): 667–685, doi:10.1111/j.1540-6520.2007.00194.x.

CHAPTER 13

Ethics and Technology: Issues for the Twenty-first Century

LEARNING OUTCOMES

At the conclusion of this chapter, you should be able to do the following:

1. Articulate the moral benefits of technology on organizations and societies.

2. Discuss the morally negative consequences of technological innovations for society.

3. Explain the ways in which technology can help individuals lead more fulfilling lives.

4. Identify and distinguish the potential for technology to create and sustain ethical harms to individuals and small groups.

5. Develop and evaluate moral arguments for and against technological innovations in the real world.

Note to readers: This chapter is formatted as an essay, not as a traditional textbook chapter. The goal of the essay is to introduce you to several arguments about the ethical issues associated with advanced technology for individuals, organizations, and societies. As an essay, the goal is to stimulate your thinking rather than to present and explain key concepts. This essay invites you to agree with, or disagree with, its main arguments and to create a reasoned position for yourself regarding these important issues.

Introduction

The Industrial Revolution

The birth of the economy that we live in can be traced back to a Sunday in the spring of 1765, and the birthplace to the College Green in Glasgow, Scotland, a large park that served as a public laundry for most of the week. James Watt, an engineer and instrument maker, had spent months trying to improve on a half-century-old invention: a crude steam engine created by Thomas Newcombe. As he walked the Green, Watt had an insight that "flashed on [my] mind at once and filled [me] with rapture."[1] That insight would lead to the creation of the sophisticated steam engine that powered the Industrial Revolution. The Industrial Revolution radically restructured British, and eventually global, society.

The economic effects became apparent shortly after Watt's engine spread through British manufacturing. Between 1700–1780, Britain's gross domestic product (GDP) grew around 0.65 percent per year, but between 1780–1801 that rate doubled to 1.4 percent. It would rise to as high as 1.9 percent annually between 1801 and 1831, just about 300 percent greater than a century before. Innovation, as measured by patent activity, grew as well. In the 1760s, the government awarded 205 patents, more than double the 92 in the 1750s. Patents doubled again to 477 in the 1780s, and again by 1800, with 924.[2] Entrepreneurship, innovation, and business growth took off, and economic expansion fueled population growth. In 1701, the English population numbered just over five million. Six decades later, it would grow to six million. The country added another million by 1781 and another by 1796. That population increasingly lived in cities. In 1700, Leeds was a community of between 5,000 and 7,000 people. By 1750, its population tripled. It would triple again by 1800 to 53,000.[3] Economic and population growth were positive impacts.

Wages and standard of living tell a more complex story. Evidence suggests that wages increased between 1700 and 1750, but then declined significantly between about 1770 and 1800. Numbers are challenging, however, because the composition of the labor force changed, as did family earning patterns. This meant that, although wages went down, the standard of living often improved as more family members brought home an income. Wages rose for skilled laborers such as blacksmiths or the growth careers of boilermakers or iron puddlers. Earnings remained stagnant, or declined, for unskilled labor. The percentage of poor, known as vagrants, rose nine-fold, from 0.9 percent in 1759 to 8.2 percent by 1801. The Industrial Revolution produced winners and losers.[4]

Two longer-term trends in the economy should be noted. First, wage labor became the primary method of work. As people migrated to cities and the factories located nearby, wages became the sole source of people's livelihoods. For Karl Marx, wage labor was a form of slavery that he would feature in his attacks on capitalism.[5] Second, the shift to factory production altered the nature of the economic ecosystem. Textile work, for example, shifted from cottage (home) production to the factory, and skilled hand labor could now be commoditized through steam-powered machinery. For one critic, the change represented "nothing less than catastrophic, a violation of the sacred nature of the home."[6]

By the early nineteenth century, entrepreneurs and engineers figured out how to make the steam engine truly portable, and the consequence was the rise of rail transportation. By the end of the century, entrepreneurs had developed a portable engine powered by gasoline, which gave rise to the automobile industry. The development of the steam engine, and the Industrial Revolution it fostered, produced both positive and negative effects for British society. The Industrial Revolution had moral consequences, as does any significant economic or social change. *Any* technologically driven development produces winners and losers and good and bad outcomes.

The steam engine changed the world, and if you are thoughtful you can trace a line from Watt's steam engine to the U.S. space program of the 1960s, which led to many of the technological innovations that define today's economy. You'll also see that the moral consequences of the Industrial Revolution, such as economic growth, innovation, income inequality, and changes to the accepted ways of living, are challenges our economies face today. There is little doubt that technology can help us build a better world and facilitate individual happiness. It's also clear that technological innovation creates significant negative moral outcomes, from environmental degradation, species loss, pollution, and overcrowded cities to powerful weapons of mass destruction. We'll present a set of arguments about the positive and negative impacts of technology at the individual, organizational, and societal level. We hope you will think deeply about these arguments and come to your own conclusions. We really hope that you will gain the ability to use technology in morally positive ways to increase your own level of happiness and promote social benefit, or the common good.

Technology, Organizations, and Society: The Positives

Many of the technological innovations we live with today have changed, or are changing, our economy and society as much as, if not more than, James Watt's steam engine changed life in the eighteenth and nineteenth centuries. There are too many changes to create a complete catalog and so we'll focus on two broad categories: economic and social benefits. Most of the normative moral frameworks we discussed in Chapter 2 would find morally positive outcomes from technological innovation. We'll highlight a few here. A utilitarian moral perspective finds much to like in the economic sphere, while believers in Kantian rights, Rawlsian justice, or Aristotelian virtue can find praiseworthy elements of our current technology-based society.

Economic Benefits

The Watt steam engine dramatically increased the speed and efficiency of manufacturing. As machines replaced humans, economies of scale reduced costs and consequently the prices of finished goods. People in the middle class could now afford goods that had been the purview of the wealthy.[7] The scaling of products, and increasingly services, in the latter twentieth and early twenty-first century has been made possible by the continual application of Moore's law, which holds that the power of silicon chips doubles about every two years, meaning that costs fall in half.[8] Computers, smartphones, and a host of other devices become cheaper each year, when based on the cost of computing power or memory, and have become affordable to most people. Figure 13.1 provides a stark reminder of how quickly the Internet age has spread knowledge and information throughout society.

Farmers in remote villages in India can now access global markets for their products; websites like Etsy allow local craftspeople to sell their wares to national and global markets. Digitization has reshaped industries from airlines to zippers, and the emerging wave of the "Internet of things" promises to make our lives ever more convenient. New markets, new opportunities, and new industries all help create new jobs and raise income levels. Figure 13.2 displays income growth in England since the Middle Ages. Note that incomes began to creep up during the Industrial Revolution, and at the end of the World War II they began a steep rise. The end of World War II corresponds (roughly) with the commercialization of computing technology.

Social Benefits

The economic benefits noted above mean that technological innovation increases the level of economic utility in a society.

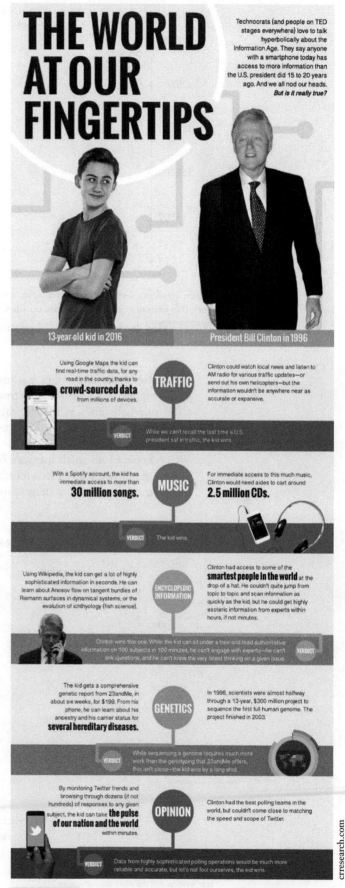

FIGURE 13.1 The spread of information throughout society.[9]

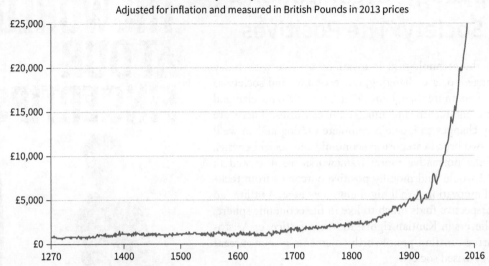

Source: Broadberry, Campbell, Klein, Overton, and van Leeuwen (2015)   OurWorldInData.org/economic-growth
Note: Data refers to England until 1700 and the UK from then onwards.

FIGURE 13.2   Income growth in UK over the centuries.[10]

Non-economic utility has increased in many areas, and we'll highlight one: health care. Figure 13.3 shows data from the World Bank: People today live on average two and one-half times as long as they did at the dawn of the Industrial Revolution. The rise in life expectancy has deep roots in technological development, including better nutrition brought about by technological improvements in agriculture. The rise of modern medicine, driven in no small measure by the access to better information, knowledge, and research equipment, has reduced mortality and certain morbidities through drug discovery and other equipment (such as better mosquito netting to fight malaria). Individuals have made better

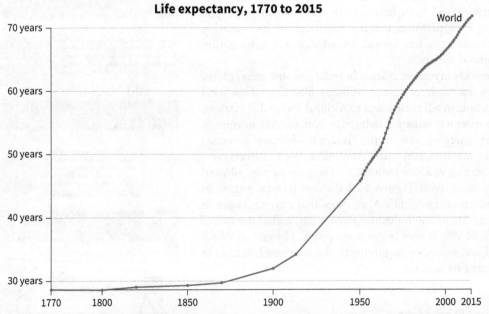

Source: Riley (2005), Clio Infra (2015), and UN Population Division (2019)   OurWorldInData.org/life-expectancy
Note: Shown is period life expectancy at birth, the average number of years a newborn would live if the pattern of mortality in the given year were to stay the same throughout its life.

FIGURE 13.3   Global life expectancy since 1770.[11]

lifestyle choices because they have better health education and knowledge. A longer life means more utility.

Improved access to education and knowledge predates the Industrial Revolution: We can go back to the invention of the Gutenberg printing press (1440) for the beginning of access to literacy and educational opportunities for the majority of people. Technological advances related to the Internet have changed the way people learn. A generation ago, the challenge was finding information: You had to search the "card catalog" at your local library to find what you wanted. Today, searching for information is easy; the challenge comes in making sense of it all and fitting it into integrated wholes. Students today can rely on YouTube for help, or they can access resources such as Khan Academy to improve their knowledge or Plural Sight to earn skill certifications. Education creates utility and Kantians would consider the acquisition of knowledge as both a right of people in a knowledge-rich society and a foundation of moral action. Virtue ethicists, either Aristotelean or Confucian, would also see knowledge as a virtue that characterizes a life of development and eudemonia. A Rawlsian framework of justice as fairness sees moral benefit in the continued diffusion of knowledge and democratization of education. Even the most disadvantaged have greater access and opportunity.

The justice perspective would approve of another by-product of technology: improved access to, and influence over, the political process. The famed Arab Spring uprisings of 2010–2011 provide a case study. Social media didn't foment the uprisings that changed government regimes and policies in countries from Egypt to Yemen. Protests began in individual countries and were led by courageous individuals agitating for change. Social media—Twitter, Facebook, and other sites—acted as accelerants that amplified the voices of protestors, coordinated the activities of disparate individuals and groups, and mobilized the forces for change.[12] It is morally good when technology helps people activate their rights of political participation; however, the use of technology for political ends points toward the negative moral consequences of technology, which we discuss next.

Technology, Organizations, and Society: The Negatives

Technology has made life better economically, socially, and politically for most people; however, the moral benefits of technology have been offset (at the very least) or outweighed (at the very most) by negative moral consequences. Again, all of the normative theories we discussed in Chapter 2 would see many moral harms through technological progress, and we'll focus on a few here. Few of these consequences are utilitarian. The moral costs of technology become apparent within the paradigms of Kantian Rights, Rawlsian Justice, and Virtue ethics. We'll focus on three ethical issues: the disappearance of reliable information, inequality and the digital divide, and the problem of technological substitution.

Unreliable Information

Technology companies, from Facebook to YouTube, make their money by selling your attention (metaphorically your eyeballs) to advertisers. The more time you spend on their sites, the more they get to monetize you. These sites have dedicated massive amounts of resources to figuring out how to keep your attention. They found that the more you see, read, or hear things you like, the more likely you are to stay on the site, and they've designed their algorithms to feed you more of what you want.

This may be harmless when you are seeing photos of dogs doing tricks or pictures of your Aunt Ruby; however, when you rely on these sites as your source for news and information (particularly political information), you end up with an incomplete picture of what's going on in the world. This is known as the "echo chamber," where all you see on social media is information that you agree with and "like"; much of it is not factual, but is either opinion or spin.[13] The echo chamber gives rise to unreliable information. Modern news providers

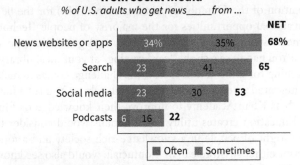

Americans more likely to get news on digital devices from news websites, apps and search engines than from social media

% of U.S. adults who get news_____ from ...

Source: Survey of U.S. adults conducted Aug. 31-Sept. 7, 2020.
PEW RESEARCH CENTER

FIGURE 13.4   Where Americans Get their news.[14]

have figured out this economic equation and they now skew their stories to reach an ideologically friendly audience. Figure 13.4 puts this problem in perspective because it shows where Americans turn for their news.

Unreliable, biased news and information demean the moral worth of human beings and violate Kant's categorial imperative—people as ends in themselves deserve the truth and real facts. Reliable facts and information contribute to the foundation of a virtuous and PERMA life; they also help us create a just society for all. Some of our colleagues have developed a guide (see Ethics in the Real World 13.1) for everyone to use in their search for reliable and veridical information.

Ethics in the Real World 13.1 | Seeking Information from Reliable Sources

BYU Strategy Group, Management Department

Our faculty have created a list of questions we can all use as we seek information from reliable sources.

1. What is the source of the information? Does the source have a track record of providing accurate information? Is the source trained to provide objective information (e.g., studies that follow the scientific method)? Is the source subject to journalistic standards or some type of review body in which sources are verified? Does the source have a bias, an agenda, or a desire to influence community beliefs and behaviors or to obtain attention or benefit financially?

2. How did the source obtain the information? Was it through primary research from firsthand observation? Even if firsthand, was it from a biased sample or an unreliable source? If it was secondhand, was it from reliable sources as defined above?

3. How did you find the information? If you are relying on information sent to you via social media or even friends or family, it is more likely to be inaccurate than if you had gone out and conducted an unbiased search for accurate information on the issue from credible sources as defined above.

4. Do multiple reliable sources corroborate the information? Look for multiple, credible, nonbiased sources that provide the same information.

5. Is the information sensational or difficult to believe and getting lots of attention? Research shows that false information is forwarded/shared six times faster through social media than factual information.[15]

6. Have you considered that all of us experience confirmation bias, which is the condition of believing something is true and then looking for information and "facts" that confirm our belief? Can you truly be objective and open to different points of view? Are you open to the idea that what you currently think to be true might not be true?

Inequality and the Digital Divide

Technology and its tools can provide many benefits to people if they have access to those tools. In the earliest days of the Internet, many people had early and easy access to computers and the Internet. These people, the "information-haves," tended to be economically and socially well off. The poor became the "information have-nots." Psychologist and Children's Television Workshop founder Lloyd Morrisett called it the "digital divide," or "a discrepancy in access to technology resources between socioeconomic groups."[16] The digital divide meant that the rich would get richer as they leveraged technology and the poor would get poorer, on either an absolute or relative basis. As the cost of technology dropped and Internet connectivity became relatively ubiquitous, people believed that the digital divide had closed. The COVID-19 pandemic that closed schools and sent children (and adults) home to learn and work via the Internet revealed that the digital divide is still there. A 2020 study by the Rand Corporation found that a mere "30 percent of teachers in high-poverty schools reported that all or nearly all of their students had access to the Internet at home, compared with 83 percent of teachers in low-poverty schools."[17] It's hard to create a just world for all when certain groups lack access to the tools that could help them improve their situation.

The digital divide has another morally negative outcome: It creates a knowledge inequality that moves in to the workplace. Technological innovation creates great job opportunities for those with the educational and skill background to navigate in this world. That means job opportunities, and better incomes, will continue to skew toward those with college degrees, particularly those in STEM fields and those with graduate education. That's good news for you because you're a student. It's not great news for those who fail to complete or even go to college. They will continue to see their job opportunities narrow, face greater odds of unemployment, and continue to see slow wage growth. The digital divide means that the data reported in Figure 13.5 should persist into the future.

The final negative moral outcome we'll discuss is the problem of technological solutionism. Technological solutionism is the belief that "all problems have tractable technical fixes"[18] and we can look to technology to solve the world's problems. There are two flaws to this argument, one empirical and the other moral. Empirically, there appear to be a number of problems that technology has not solved, and possibly cannot solve. Technology has not yet solved problems of poverty, even as it has democratized information and computing equipment. The causes of poverty extend beyond the technological sphere and have their origins in social, political, and ethical systems. Morally, when we look to technology to solve problems it is suited for, such as climate change, we have to remember that previous iterations of technology and decisions about how it should be used (from the steam engine to the automobile to air conditioning) brought about climate change. It's hard to claim the moral high ground for

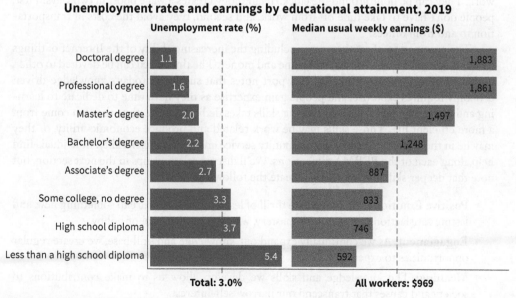

Unemployment rates and earnings by educational attainment, 2019

	Unemployment rate (%)	Median usual weekly earnings ($)
Doctoral degree	1.1	1,883
Professional degree	1.6	1,861
Master's degree	2.0	1,497
Bachelor's degree	2.2	1,248
Associate's degree	2.7	887
Some college, no degree	3.3	833
High school diploma	3.7	746
Less than a high school diploma	5.4	592

Total: 3.0% All workers: $969

Source: U.S. Bureau of Labor Statistics, Current Population Survey.

Note: Data are for persons age 25 and over. Earnings are for full-time wage and salary workers.

FIGURE 13.5 Employment outcomes by educational level.[19]

technology (in either utilitarian, justice, or virtue terms) if one of its key benefits is the ability to belatedly fix problems it has created.

In this section, we've argued that technology has created a number of moral challenges and problems for our society. In the next two sections, we'll change the level of analysis and look at ways in which technology impacts individuals.

Technology and Individuals: The Positives

We begin by noting that many of the positive impacts of technology on organizations and societies flow directly to individuals. Individuals and families are the beneficiaries of higher wages, increased life expectancy, better health, greater educational opportunities, and political participation. We'll take these for the most part as given, and we'll highlight two other positive moral outcomes of advanced technologies: increased personal efficiency and the time created for high-value activities, and the ways technology builds relationships.

Personal Efficiency and High-value Activities

One positive impact of technology is **personal efficiency**, we now spend far less time in lines dealing with the bureaucratic elements of twenty-first-century life. A generation ago, you had to stand in long lines to make changes to your class schedule or pay tuition. You also had to spend significant amounts of time standing in lines anytime you dealt with any level of government, from paying a parking ticket to registering your car, and in many cases registering to vote. Medical care for routine things, from physicals to pink eye to prescription refills, all required a visit to the doctor's office. And you had to do each of these things between 8 A.M. and 5 P.M., Monday through Friday. One positive impact of Internet technologies has been to automate many of these mundane, time-consuming tasks. Technology has created personal efficiency.

The ability to register for school or register your car online doesn't seem like a big moral victory, but the benefits to people on the low end of the wage spectrum have been profound. People no longer have to miss time off from paid work or use paid time off to accomplish these mundane tasks. In the best case, people perform these tasks during break time or lunchtime at work. They can be done around the clock. Technology creates a wage boost in two ways: First, people don't have to take time off from work, and second, they avoid the costs of transportation to and from offices.

The automation of routine tasks, including the increasing ability of the Internet of things to automate other routine tasks, saves time and money. The time saved can be devoted to other, higher-value activities. Author Cal Newport notes that success in today's knowledge-driven economy requires expertise, and people gain expertise as they have time to dedicate to learning and mastering new skills.[20] Mastering skills takes dedicated time, time that can come from a more efficient life. Those skills may be work related and produce economic utility, or they may lie in the realm of a hobby or community service and create social utility. Individuals find help along each of the PERMA dimensions. We'll discuss relationships in the next section, but note that deeper skill and knowledge create the following:

- **Positive Emotion:** The immediate thrill of learning and exposure to something new, and lasting satisfaction of acting with mastery, whether professional or hobby.
- **Engagement:** As we continually expand our knowledge and skill base, we create regular opportunities to experience flow.
- **Meaning:** The knowledge and skills we develop allow us to make contributions to society and causes that transcend our narrow self-interest.
- **Achievement:** We learn new things and work to gain mastery. That mastery may be formally measured through certifications or informally by acceptance into "expert" groups.

Fulfilling Relationships

Advanced technology allows us to build more fulfilling relationships by broadening the reach of our relationships and deepening the content and connections we have. Breadth comes through two mechanisms. Tools such as Facebook (personal) and LinkedIn (professional) allow us to extend the reach of our personal network at a very low cost. It's easy to build out a network that we never use, but if well-tended and pruned, a strong network builds our social capital. Social capital increases our economic utility as we gain access to the knowledge and resources of others. It also enhances our personal utility as we have more friends we can call on, interact with, and learn from.

Social media, other Internet resources, and the twentieth-century technology of airplanes allow us to broaden our networks geographically. New economy companies like Airbnb reduce the cost of lodging and can facilitate longer stays wherever we travel and provide us with more money and time to spend with those we love. Travel, particularly the foreign travel that we noted in Chapter 7, creates not only moral benefits for individuals by helping them understand where cultures and values differ, but also the common humanity that binds people together. Our cognitive knowledge of the world we live in expands, as does our emotional and spiritual connection with people we meet as we travel. Travel provides us with all the PERMA elements, and with dedicated effort, it can turbocharge the number of relationships we have around the globe.

Technology, from autos to cell phones to social media, helps us deepen relationships as well. There are advantages to being constantly available via cell phone technology. We are able to enjoy the good things that happen to friends and family in real time. We can rejoice with them at a new job offer or the birth of a child. Photos, blogs, and other tools allow us to see what others are doing and to share what we are doing as well. If we can avoid the jealousy and frustration that exemplify the Facebook syndrome (why isn't my life as wonderful and beautiful as my friends'?), we deepen and intensify relationships with those we love.

Technology not only helps us share the good times with others, but it also lets us provide help and support during challenges. A text message, or a meme, sent to a friend the morning of a big test, job interview, or major project presentation can lift their spirits and let them know of our hope for their success. Crises, from flat tires to strokes, can be reported more easily and quickly through talk or text, and earlier notification means that we can respond earlier, and often more effectively. Technology opens opportunities for individuals and groups to serve their communities beyond their personal circle. Websites such as www.volunteermatch.org and www.justserve.org provide geographically sorted lists that connect volunteers with local community needs. Community service of this type both broadens our relationship set and deepens the relationships we have with the organizations in the communities where we live and work.

Technology is, however, a double-edged sword. Used wisely and properly, technology complements and supplements many of our activities, enhances our personal development, and generates positive contributions to a PERMA life or eudemonia. Used unwisely and improperly, however, the tools of advanced technology can degrade and demean our humanity. We take up this topic in the last section.

Technology and Individuals:
The Negatives

Critics of modern technology have existed since the dawn of time. In the opening case of this chapter, one critic noted that the Industrial Revolution had "catastrophic" impacts on traditional family life. There are a number of moral critiques we could offer of technology, but we'll focus on two: the rise of anomie and the atomization of social life, and the addictive nature of Internet-based and smartphone technology.

Anomie and Atomization

In the late nineteenth century, French sociologist Emile Durkheim wrote about the emerging consequences of the Industrial Revolution. For Durkheim, industrialization resulted in the continued advance of science and human reason as the bases for governing society.[21] This was a moral positive for Durkheim. The Industrial Revolution and social advancement created a strong moral negative: the rise of anomie and the atomization of humanity.[22] Anomie is an outcome of social change that leads to disintegration, when the formal and informal bonds that hold social groups together collapse. The result is that individuals become atomized. They act as individuals, solely in their own perceived interest, and they have difficulty creating lasting bonds with others.

Walk around your campus any afternoon, and you'll find a crowded public square with most people's gazes solidly focused on a small handheld device. Instead of viewing the animated natural beauty of the day, they'll be focused on the latest inanimate picture someone posted on Instagram, checking out the scores of sporting events half a world away, or reading a post from some social or political pundit designed to enflame. What they aren't doing is dealing with each other; everyone exists as an atom. Advanced social media technology works to refute John Donne's centuries-old claim that "no [one] is an island, entire of itself."[23]

Technology works to make each of us our own island in two ways. First, the same apps that allow us to organize our lives and efficiently dispense with mundane tasks remove the opportunity to interact with others, from the worker at the DMV to the person ahead of us in line. We become an island by default. More insidious, however, is the subtle shift of technology that, by making everything more efficient, sets saving time—and being timely—as a central virtue. Technology encourages us to move from a world of Kairos (things like relationships) to one of Chronos (the management of time).[24] We become an island unto ourselves as we become enamored with, and driven by, the need for effective time management when that desire jeopardizes deep relationships.

Second, the "echo chamber" feature of social media newsfeeds creates divisions among us. Mark Zuckerberg's original vision for Facebook was a tool to bring people together; however, the advent of the newsfeed as a means for lengthening attention and engagement by users and selling more advertising has meant that Facebook has driven people apart. The goal of many in the echo chamber, either through deep personal belief or deliberate design, is to drive wedges between people, provide purity tests for those whose beliefs are "right," and vilify those who are wrong as enemies. The impact on individuals is devasting, and that devastation scales up through communities to societies at large. The echo chamber helps us become and remain an island of ourselves.

Addiction

The introduction of the smartphone in 2007 changed the world forever. It might be the early twenty-first century's first steam engine. As we noted above, the smartphone puts more information in the palm of your hand than world leaders had a generation ago. That's the positive. The negative aspect of smartphones is that they can be highly addictive. Yes, you can develop an addiction. It begins with all that information, plus games and photos, constantly at our fingertips. We now have an easy solution for one of our oldest problems: boredom. We find ourselves, innocently at first, going to our phones when we have nothing else to do, and that pleasurable relief from boredom gives us a psychological boost. That pleasurable feeling comes from a boost of dopamine, a neurotransmitter chemical in the brain, that we get from using our phone.[25] The pattern of addiction evolves from using the phone when we are bored to using our free time—any unstructured time—to "catch up" on the latest, be it the latest news, the latest picture, or the latest score. That dopamine release now becomes a pattern, and soon it becomes more difficult for us to leave the phone alone.

Smartphone and Internet use aren't physiological addictions such as heroin or cocaine addictions; they are psychological addictions more like gambling. The addictions are similar in the following ways:[26]

- **Loss of control**—You can't help yourself from accessing your smartphone.
- **Persistence**—You continue to use your phone even when you commit not to.
- **Hedonic treadmill**—You need to use your phone more, or more often to get the same feeling.
- **Negative consequences**—You miss appointments or damage relationships because you are on your phone.
- **Withdrawal**—When you can't use your phone, you are cranky and anxious.
- **Ease of relapse**—Even after you stop using your phone, you pick up right where you left off.

There is a robust test to judge the role of your smartphone in your life.[27] You can take the test online (ironic if you suffer from Internet addiction), and we reprint the test in Ethics in the Real World 13.2.

Technology, particularly social media, smartphones, and Internet technology, is neither intrinsically moral nor immoral. These are tools. The ultimate moral outcomes of the technological world we live in, and the constant emergence of new technology, depend on how, why,

---

Ethics in the Real World 13.2 | The Smartphone Compulsion Test

This test was developed by Dr. David Greenfield of The Center for Internet and Technology Addiction. This test is not presented as a medical or psychological diagnostic tool. It is for your education and information only. If you are concerned about the results of this test, you should seek out professional help. For each question, answer yes or no.

1. Do you find yourself spending more time on your cell or smartphone than you realize?

2. Do you find yourself mindlessly passing time on a regular basis by staring at your cell or smartphone?

3. Do you seem to lose track of time when on your cell or smartphone?

4. Do you find yourself spending more time texting, tweeting, or emailing as opposed to talking to people in person?

5. Has the amount of time you spend on your cell or smartphone been increasing?

6. Do you wish you could be a little less involved with your cell or smartphone?

7. Do you sleep with your cell or smartphone (turned on) under your pillow or next to your bed regularly?

8. Do you find yourself viewing and answering texts, tweets, and emails at all hours of the day and night—even when it means interrupting other things you are doing?

9. Do you text, email, tweet, or surf while driving or doing other similar activities that require your focused attention and concentration?

10. Do you feel your use of your cell or smartphone decreases your productivity at times?

11. Do you feel reluctant to be without your cell or smartphone, even for a short time?

12. Do you feel ill-at-ease or uncomfortable when you accidentally leave your smartphone in the car or at home, have no service, or have a broken phone?

13. When you eat meals, is your cell or smartphone always part of the table place setting?

14. When your cell or smartphone rings, beeps or buzzes, do you feel an intense urge to check for texts, tweets, emails, updates, and so forth?

15. Do you find yourself mindlessly checking your cell or smartphone many times a day, even when you know there is likely nothing new or important to see?

The results are indicative as follows:
Scoring:

1–2: Your behavior is normal, but that doesn't mean you should live on your smartphone.

3–4: Your behavior is leaning toward problematic or compulsive use.

5 or above: It is likely that you may have a problematic or compulsive smartphone use pattern.

8 or higher: If your score is over 8, you might consider seeing a psychologist, psychiatrist, or psychotherapist who specializes in behavioral addictions for a consultation.

and when we use that technology. Technology has the power to raise individuals and societies to new levels of productivity, happiness, and well-being. That's if it's used well. If used poorly, these same technologies can ruin our world, make people miserable, and break the ties that bind us together. The choice is ours.

Key Terms

addiction

anomie

digital divide

echo chamber

industrial revolution

life expectancy

personal efficiency

unreliable information

Chapter Summary

- Technological innovation and progress create many benefits for organizations and societies. The rise of innovation since the late eighteenth century has been accompanied by a dramatic increase in global standards of living. Technology has improved human longevity and improved the quality of life through scientific breakthroughs that have increased human health and helped disseminate information to people around the globe.

- Technology has either created or helps to create several negative outcomes for society. One impact is that newsfeeds and Internet sources of information are often unreliable and untrustworthy. The digital divide, different access to technology among socioeconomic groups, perpetuates income inequality. We also depend on new technologies to solve problems created by old technologies, and the cycle might never stop.

- At the individual level, technology has many positive influences that can help people lead ethical, PERMA lives. Technology can alleviate and make efficient many mundane tasks we all engage in. This frees up our time for more valuable pursuits. Technologies such as social media can help us create more and deeper relationships with others. Social media and other platforms have been used to help people become involved in their communities in meaningful and productive ways.

- Technology can harm individuals in many ways and make it harder for them to live PERMA lives. Technology can atomize and isolate people from each other. The more time we spend alone on our devices, the less time we have to spend with each other. Technology has elements that encourage people to become addicted to it.

Chapter Review Questions

1. Describe three ways in which technological progress enables economic progress for individuals, organizations, and societies. In your opinion, how strong is the link between technological innovation and economic development?

2. What is the "digital divide"? Why, after one-quarter of one century of effort, does the digital divide still exist? What role do business organizations have in helping to close the digital divide?

3. In what ways has technology helped you lead a more productive and meaningful life? If you were to rank order its benefits, what aspect of technology is the most beneficial for you?

4. What is atomization? Do you believe that technology increases anomie and atomization in our society? Why or why not?

5. How has technology created negative impacts in your life? What are your biggest challenges with the problems of atomization and addiction?

6. How does technology influence ethical decision making?

7. If a user spreads fake news about his competitor on social media platforms Facebook and Twitter, then is the user or the social media owner unethical?

Application Exercises

- *Personal Ethical Development*. If you began keeping an ethics journal as suggested in the first chapter, continue that writing work. Here are some prompts: How has technology benefited your life

so far? Where are you vulnerable to the problem of atomization? Where have you seen yourself engage in addiction-like behaviors with technology? What steps can you take to ensure that technology is a positive force in your life? What changes do you need to make?

- *Career Goals and Planning.* A happy, meaningful, and productive life blends and builds upon the following: (1) the type of life you are interested in leading, (2) your deepest and most important principles/commitments (3) the work you are interested in doing, (4) what you are good at, (5) your preferences for things like work versus free time, and (6) your personality. What types of company policies would you be comfortable with around technology use? What about policies about technology use during personal time? How comfortable are you with the need to always be available for work needs?

- *Ethics in the Business World.* Identify a company or organization that you believe uses technology well. What are the behaviors

they engage in? What role have things like organizational mission and top management leadership played in creating a positive technology environment? What elements of the organization sustain their ability to use technology in positive ways? What crises have they faced, or what challenges do you foresee in their future?

- *Talking with and Learning from Others.* Choose a business professional you respect and who you admire for his or her ability to use technology in positive ways. Engage that person in a brief interview. What are his or her "rules" for using technology? Where did those rules come from, and which are the most challenging for him or her to follow? What advice would he or she give you as you begin your career?

Mini-Cases

Case 1: The future with artificial intelligence. One emerging area of technological innovation is artificial intelligence (AI), defined as "machines that respond to stimulation consistent with traditional responses from humans, given the human capacity for contemplation, judgment, and intention."[28] The challenge of AI comes in that machines, robots, computers, and some other types of machines, can eventually learn to do some jobs better than people. A recent study by McKinsey & Company estimated that AI could impact roughly one-half of the jobs people currently do; about six in ten jobs have more than 30 percent of their activity set that AI would replace. The report sees up to 30 percent of jobs being replaced by AI by 2030, in the fastest rollout scenario.[29] AI may dramatically increase productivity while having devastating effects on people.

Figure 13.6 illustrates this point:

As you think about the moral impacts of AI, please think about the following questions:

1. What assumptions have to be true for AI to displace 30–50 percent of the workforce? Do you agree with these assumptions? Why or why not?

2. What are the moral and ethical trade-offs involved as AI becomes more central to economic activity?

3. How can AI be good for business firms but bad for society as a whole?

4. What should we do about AI in the workplace?

Case 2: Project Blackbird. Melanie Anderson worked as a project manager for FaceTek, a small Iowa software company that developed facial

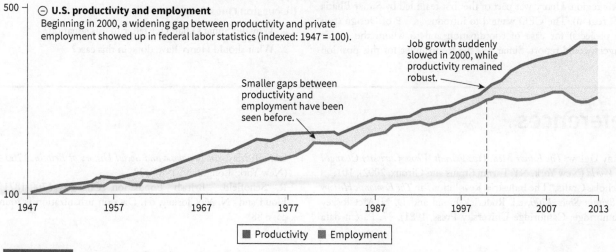

Decoupling Productivity and Employment
Digital technologies have boosted productivity in the United States without also spurring the expected job growth, argue Erik Brynjolfsson and Andrew McAfee. A result of this decoupling is that while gross domestic product (GDP) has risen, median income has not, and inequality has grown.

FIGURE 13.6 Mapping productivity and employment gains, 1947–2013.[30]

recognition software solutions for some of Silicon Valley's largest social media and technology companies. Melanie had graduated with her MBA, with a focus in project management, from the University of Iowa in 2018. In her role, Melanie managed a team of FaceTek engineers working on "facial recognition at a distance (FRD)"—the ability to quickly generate facial images that could be quickly and easily identified from distances of several hundred feet. Ticketmaster and several professional sports teams were interested in the technology for crowd control and security at large events. Melanie was always looking for opportunities for her team to push the limits of its development capabilities and expand the technology.

One afternoon she was looking on BidWorld, a site that gathered requests for proposals from government agencies. She noticed that the Defense Advanced Research Projects Agency (DARPA) was looking for a contractor to help it build an FRD platform for use aboard drones. The contract would stretch her team's development capacities as FRD technology had never been applied to a mobile platform. The contract would also generate significant revenue for FaceTek and would complement its work with other federal agencies. At the weekly staff meeting the next day, Melanie signaled her interest in the project. She was surprised at the response of Ben Schmidt, a talented computer engineer with an MBA from the University of Michigan. Schmidt told Melanie that he would not work on a project for "Satan."

When she questioned him, Ben explained that FRD technology was particularly vulnerable to "weaponization." Schmidt noted that one use of an FRD drone could be the assassination of political or military enemies "from a distance." Schmidt wanted no part of such a project. As she left the meeting, Melanie had several questions: Was Ben right? Was it morally wrong to develop technology that could be "weaponized" in unexpected ways? If FaceTek didn't take the contract, someone else would, and should the company give up a very profitable and learning-rich project if the technology would be developed anyway?

Case 3: Henry Smith is working as Manager Architect in a well-established real estate company in Gurgaon. The company has multiple commercial and residential ongoing projects across multiple locations in India. The organization has a big design department with a staff strength of 50 people. Structurally, the company has three senior managers—for NCR, Mumbai, and West India, and for the rest of India. All three senior managers report to the CEO. Each of the managers have their own design team to cater to projects specific to their region. Henry was part of the first team led by Simar Bhatia (NCR region). The CEO wanted to introduce a VP of Design (pan India projects) for ease of coordination and to whom the senior managers would report. Simar was the frontrunner for this position

and was working very hard to achieve this position. He had been with the company for nearly two decades and was steadily progressing through the ranks. Simar was a strong supporter of the company and a star performer; he was a role model for most of his team members. Henry knew something was wrong when Simar got back to his desk after his meeting with the CEO. After a couple of hours, he learned that the CEO had decided to hire an external person as VP and Simar would be reporting to this new external person within the next three months. Simar was very upset at this denial of position and told to Henry that he had been working 60–70 hour weeks all these years and the management was now making him answerable to an external person. Soon after, Henry started noticing Simar behaving differently. He started coming late and leaving work early, or would go to sites more often during the day. He would also prioritize live project issues at the site and disregard strict deadlines to some upcoming projects, which was usually not done. One day, Henry went into his office for some files and found Simar copying some of the software the company used for 3D models rendering and printing project drawings from the office printer. A couple of weeks later, at a dinner party, Henry overheard a conversation about Simar doing design consulting work for some competitive firm/external clients. This is when Henry realized that he had been making some of the team members work on designs related to personal projects, which were not for the organization, and were denoted as feasibility studies for upcoming projects. Simar also started asking the company's existing suppliers to give him samples or supply materials free of cost or below cost for his personal projects. It was clear that Simar's commitment to the company had degraded significantly, and this was impacting the team and organization as a whole. Henry could clearly see that Simar's character and personal integrity had faltered and that he was making his team unknowingly compromise their integrity and values as well. This was against the ethical code of conduct laid down by the organization as team members were not permitted to use company resources, intellectual property, or time for consultancy work for external clients. Simar was compromising on professional ethics due to a lack of achievement of his extrinsic motivation (promotion). One day, Henry gathered the courage to confront Simar. He told Henry that he was filling up the performance appraisal forms. He said that he would put the blame on Henry for misusing company resources and that he might even end up losing his job. Henry was shocked! He knew that Simar was much more senior and well respected in the company and that it would be his word against him.

Discussion Questions

1. Why did Simar's character falter in this situation?
2. What should Henry have done in this case?

References

[1] Jenny Uglow, *The Lunar Men: Five Friends Whose Curiosity Changed the World* (New York, NY: Farrar, Straus and Giroux, 2002), 101.

[2] Nicholas Crafts, "The Industrial Revolution," in *The Economic History of Britain Since 1700*, ed. Roderick Floud and D. N. McCloskey (Cambridge: Cambridge University Press, 1981), 47. Patent data

from T. May, *An Economic and Social History of Britain, 1760–1970* (New York: Longmans, 1987), 23.

[3] R. Schofield, "British Population Change, 1700-1871," in Floud and N. McCloskey, 64. Data on urbanization is found on page 88.

4 R. Brown, *Society and Economy in Modern Britain, 1700–1850* (New York: Routledge, 1991). Chapter 15, "Wages," discusses the challenges to measuring changes in real wages as well as the secular trend in British working life.

5 Karl Marx, *The Communist Manifesto*, in *Karl Marx: Selected writings*, ed. D. McLellan (London: Oxford University Press, 1848/1977).

6 Brown, 319.

7 Alexis de Tocqueville noticed the same phenomenon during his visit to the United States in the early 1800s. See Alexis de Tocqueville, *Democracy in America* (New York: A. Knopf, 1835/1994), see chapter 1, but also chapters 2 and 3.

8 Matt Peckham, "Could Nanowire Transistors Rescue Moore's Law from Obsolescence?," *Time*, May 1, 2013, https://techland.time.com/2013/05/01/could-nanowire-transistors-rescue-moores-law-from-obsolescence/.

9 "The World at Our Fingertips," C + R Research, accessed June 11, 2021, https://www.crresearch.com/cell-phone-information-age.

10 Max Roser, "Economic Growth," Our World in Data, https://ourworldindata.org/economic-growth.

11 Max Roser, Esteban Ortiz-Ospina, and Hannah Ritchie, "Life Expectancy," Our World in Data, last modified October 2019, https://ourworldindata.org/life-expectancy.

12 Gadi Wolfsfeld, Elad Segev, and Tamir Sheafer, "Social Media and the Arab Spring: Politics Comes First," *The International Journal of Press/Politics* 18, no. 2 (January 16, 2013): 115–137.

13 Zeynep Tufekci, "Facebook Said Its Algorithms Do Help Form Echo Chambers. And the Tech Press Missed It.," *Huffington Post*, last modified May 11, 2016, https://www.huffingtonpost.com/zeynep-tufekci/facebook-algorithm-echo-chambers_b_7259916.html.

14 Elisa Shearer, More than eight-in-ten Americans get their news from digital devices. Pew Research, 12 January 2021, available at https://www.pewresearch.org/fact-tank/2021/01/12/more-than-eight-in-ten-americans-get-news-from-digital-devices/.

15 See Soroush Vosoughi, Deb Roy, and Sinan Aral, "The spread of true and false news online," *Science* 359, no. 6380 (March 9, 2018): 1146–1151, American Association for the Advancement of Science, https://science.sciencemag.org/content/359/6380/1146.

16 Laura L. Burchett, "What is the Digital Divide?," University of Iowa Education Technology Center, last modified by Sarah N. Armstrong October 27, 2010, https://wiki.uiowa.edu/display/edtech/Definition+of+the+Digital+Divide.

17 Laura Stelitano et al., "The Digital Divide and COVID-19," Creative Commons Attribution 4.0 International Public License, 2020, https://www.rand.org/pubs/research_reports/RRA134-3.html.

18 Emanuel Moss and Jacob Metcalf, "The Ethical Dilemma at the Heart of Big Tech Companies," *Harvard Business Review*, November 14, 2019, https://hbr.org/2019/11/the-ethical-dilemma-at-the-heart-of-big-tech-companies.

19 "Employment Projections," U.S. Bureau of Labor Statistics, last modified April 21, 2021, https://www.bls.gov/emp/chart-unemployment-earnings-education.htm.

20 Cal Newport, *Deep Work* (New York: Grand Central Publishing, 2016), see particularly chapters 1 and 2.

21 Emile Durkheim, *The Elementary Forms of Religious Life* (New York: Free Press, 1912/1995).

22 Idem, *The Division of Labor in Society* (New York: Free Press, 1893/1984), see Book 3, Chapter 1.

23 John Donne (1572–1631), "Meditation XVII," in M. H. Abrams, general editor, *The Norton Anthology of English Literature* (New York: W. W. Norton & Company, 1979), 1108.

24 For a nice summary of this, see Naomi Matlow, "More Kairos, Less Chronos (Live More. Work Less.)," Unsettled, accessed June 11, 2021, https://beunsettled.co/blog/more-kairos-less-chronos-live-more-work-less/.

25 Rebecca Joy Stanborough, "How to Tell If You Could Be Addicted to Your Phone," Healthline, October 17, 2019, https://www.healthline.com/health/mental-health/cell-phone-addiction.

26 Ibid.

27 "Smartphone Compulsion Test," The Center for Internet and Technology Addiction, accessed June 11, 2021, https://virtual-addiction.com/smartphone-compulsion-test/.

28 Shula Shubhendu and J. Vigay, "Applicability of Artificial Intelligence in Different Fields of Life," *Computer Science*, 2013, quoted in Darrell M. West, "What is Artificial Intelligence?," Brookings Institution, October 4, 2018, https://www.brookings.edu/research/what-is-artificial-intelligence/.

29 James Manyika et al., "Jobs lost, jobs gained: What the future of work will mean for jobs, skills, and wages," McKinsey & Company, November 28, 2017, https://www.mckinsey.com/featured-insights/future-of-work/jobs-lost-jobs-gained-what-the-future-of-work-will-mean-for-jobs-skills-and-wages.

30 Calum McClelland, "The Impact of Artificial Intelligence - Widespread Job Losses," IOT for all, July 1, 2020, https://www.iotforall.com/impact-of-artificial-intelligence-job-losses.

CHAPTER 14

Ethics and a Market Economy

LEARNING OUTCOMES

At the end of this chapter, you should be able to do the following:

1. Explain how ethical behavior reduces transaction costs in an economy.

2. Distinguish among different types of trust and their impact on business performance.

3. Identify ethical actions business professionals can take to help build communities of business.

4. Describe the ways in which a market economy fosters personal development and growth.

5. Explain how market economies foster innovation through a process of "creative destruction."

6. Craft an argument for or against the problem of economic inequality in a market economy.

Note to readers: This chapter is formatted as an essay, not as a traditional textbook chapter. The goal of the essay is to introduce you to several arguments about the critical role of ethics in a market-based economy, and the ethical arguments for a market-based economy. As an essay, this chapter will be text heavy as the goal is to stimulate your thinking rather than to present and explain key concepts. This essay invites you to agree with, or disagree with, its main arguments and to create a reasoned position for yourself regarding these important issues.

Opening Case | The Evolution of Microsoft

Anthony Bolante/Alamy Stock Photo

Bill Gates dropped out of Harvard in 1975 to found Microsoft with his partner, Paul Allen. The two wrote the original software to run the Altair, one of the first personal computers, and founded their company by combining the words *microcomputer* and *software*. Microsoft hit it big in 1980 when IBM chose Microsoft's operating system to run its first personal computer.[1] The company went public in 1986 at $21 per share, making both Gates and Allen millionaires.[2]

Over the next 34 years, Gates would become the world's richest person, although by 2020 he would drop to number two on the list.[3] Gates started a charitable foundation, today known as the Bill and Melinda Gates Foundation, in 1994. The foundation seeks to improve lives by funding initiatives around education, lifting people out of poverty, and fighting infectious diseases.[4] In 2008, he stepped away from Microsoft to devote his attention to the foundation, and in 2020, 34 years to the day after founding Microsoft, he retired from the company's board of directors.

While his focus shifted to philanthropy, Gates remained an investor in several start-up companies.

One of these investments came shortly after he gave a 2010 TED Talk about the need for innovation to solve the world's energy problems.[5] Gates was approached by Bill Gross, a Caltech-educated scientist and entrepreneur, about investing in a new start-up, Heliogen, which hoped to develop clean energy solutions, primarily solar, to solve one of the world's most vexing energy challenges: creating enough heat to fuel industrial processes, such as cement production. Production of cement, steel, and petrochemicals and mineral extraction require temperatures greater than 1,000° Celsius, far beyond the capabilities of traditional solar power systems.

By 2017, Heliogen and its team of engineers were hard at work on the problem.[6] The temperatures necessary for industrial applications preclude using traditional solar panels or mirrors. They top out at about 600°. The team at Heliogen developed a tracking device that employs artificial intelligence and machine learning so that solar panels track the sun throughout the day. Advanced software and hardware move a two-acre plot of 400 panels to concentrate their reflective heat to a tower. That large array broke the 1,000° barrier in November 2019. While the technology continues to emerge, Gross noted the potential: "For the first time, we can now heat chemical reactions directly using solar power instead of fossil fuels. That opens up the huge trillion dollar-plus industrial market to the use of renewable energy."[7] Cement production, the first targeted application of the Heliogen technology, contributes 8 percent of global carbon emissions, so the ability to move away from fossil fuels in industrial applications could dramatically shift the world's response to changing climates and pollution problems.

Heliogen sees two major areas for applying its technologies: industrial production and the generation of green fuels such as hydrogen. HelioHeat, as the company refers to it, would provide a viable alternative to fossil fuels for several heavy industrial applications. HelioFuel would use the thermal process to split water into its components, oxygen and hydrogen, which would replace gasoline to fuel autos, industrial equipment, and aircraft. Hydrogen may also be able to heat homes.[8]

Heliogen's work is in an early stage and many problems remain. The technology might be useful in the sunny desert regions of the world, but it's not clear how the technology would work in major industrial zones, such as the Northeastern United States or Northern Europe, where sunny days are less common. Heliogen must also become price competitive against alternatives such as natural gas.[9] In spite of this, the company's technology represents a promising response to the challenges of global climate change.

Gates explained his interest in the project: "If we're going to get to zero carbon emissions overall, we have a lot of inventing to do. I'm pleased to have been an early backer of Bill Gross's novel solar concentration technology. Its capacity to achieve the high temperatures required for these [industrial] processes is a promising development in the quest to one day replace fossil fuel."[10]

Introduction

Bill Gates, one of the richest people in the world, helps us introduce one of the core challenges of ethics in a capitalist system. Gates made his money by creating a scalable and global product, and he had a reputation as a hard-nosed, competitive, and even ruthless boss. His innovation created tremendous wealth for him and his family. He has used that wealth to focus on creating a better, healthier society through the Gates Foundation, and, as the Heliogen case shows, he's using his wealth and business acumen to create market-based, innovative responses to the world's problems. This chapter is not written as a typical textbook chapter but is an essay about two topics: the role of ethics in supporting a market economy, and the ethics of market economies in helping build a good society. We'll discuss six important issues concerning ethics and market economies.

1. Ethics and transaction costs

2. Ethics and trust

3. Ethics and a strong business community

4. Market economies and personal development

5. Market economies and innovation

6. Market economies and inequality

You'll pick up some important frameworks in this chapter to help you think though these issues, but the major goal of this chapter is to invite you to think deeply about the importance of ethics in our society and the ways in which our economy creates ethical, and perhaps unethical, outcomes.

To many casual observers, the tenets of a capitalist economy of individual autonomy, materialism, and wealth maximization appear to be at odds with ethical goals such as a good society or a PERMA-based life (Positive Emotion, Engagement, Relationships, Meaning, and Accomplishments, a model developed by psychologist and educator Martin Seligman). People committed to living ethical lives, under this view, abandon goals like wealth maximization because the pursuit of wealth (supposedly) requires the abandonment of ethical principles and requires us to treat others as objects to our own material ends. Ethical habits such as honesty or kindness impede economic efficiency and hold us back from engaging in certain transactions; indeed, it is the self-interest, or "greed" of the baker, brewer, and butcher that drives economic activity.[11]

In what follows, we argue that this view is wrong. An economy filled with people committed to living by ethical principles such as honesty, promise keeping, fair dealing (avoiding conflicts of interest or bribery), and compassion/concern for the well-being of others is more efficient, productive, and wealth maximizing than one in which people are engaged in the ruthless pursuit of their own interest.[12]

Ethical Behavior Helps Reduce Transaction Costs

Most microeconomics textbooks focus their discussion of costs on the costs of production because a fundamental simplifying assumption of economic theory is that both buyers and sellers have all the information they need for any market which they operate, and that information can be obtained at no cost.[13] In the real world, that assumption proves quite false, and traders incur transaction costs every time they exchange goods and services.

Transaction costs. These costs can be thought of as the economic equivalent of friction in physical systems.[14] These frictional costs break down into three broad categories: search and information costs (how buyers and sellers find each other), bargaining costs (over prices, delivery options, etc.), and policing and enforcement costs (contracts and contingencies for failed performance).[15] Figure 14.1 displays these three categories of transaction costs.

Search and information costs. For consumers, this includes the time, energy, and money they spend in finding products or services and establishing the relevant characteristics of a product, such as durability, fit, and quality. The time you spend researching a pair of shoes on Zappos, a vacation destination on Expedia, or a particular stock or bond you're thinking of purchasing counts as a transaction cost. The money a firm spends on advertising and

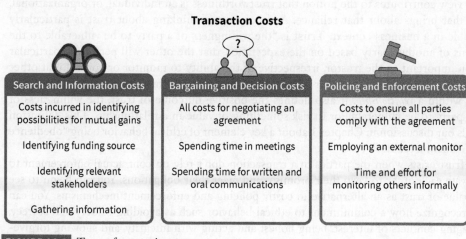

Transaction Costs

Search and Information Costs	Bargaining and Decision Costs	Policing and Enforcement Costs
Costs incurred in identifying possibilities for mutual gains	All costs for negotiating an agreement	Costs to ensure all parties comply with the agreement
Identifying funding source	Spending time in meetings	Employing an external monitor
Identifying relevant stakeholders	Spending time for written and oral communications	Time and effort for monitoring others informally
Gathering information		

FIGURE 14.1 Types of transaction costs.

marketing is designed to help customers get the relevant information they need about what's for sale, where, and when. They are transaction costs, as are the salaries and commissions that salespeople earn. Money spent on developing a brand or warranty costs is also included as such expenditures signal quality to a potential buyer.

Bargaining costs. Bargaining costs include money, time, and energy spent haggling over the price of a product or service. The purchases of big-ticket items such as houses and cars are prime examples where bargaining and negotiating are essential to the purchase process. Many people engage a real estate broker to help buy and sell a house or engage a broker to buy and sell financial securities. Their fees represent transaction costs. Amazon's Prime membership service provides free shipping on a number of products and free or reduced prices for products such as audio and video streaming. The cost of Prime for both Amazon and members is a bargaining-related transaction cost.

Policing and enforcement costs. Search and information costs help buyers and sellers know what they are buying and who they are dealing with; however, sometimes the product or service is flawed or doesn't meet expectations. Other products may be delayed in transit, or services may take longer to perform, and cost more, than the buyer and seller originally intended. Return policies represent a form of enforcement cost for many products. Quality control for incoming shipments is another type of policing cost. For complex products or services, buyers and sellers write contracts that specify how they will resolve disputes or other problems involving transactions. These contracts help protect each party against unforeseen contingencies such as bad weather that delays a shipment, and discourage opportunistic behaviors, where one party tries to take advantage of the other party.[16]

You can see how commitments to ethical behavior on the part of both buyers and sellers work to minimize, but not eliminate transaction costs. Basic search costs will remain, but commitments to honest and fair practices by sellers make it easier for buyers to understand which products will fit their needs and the quality of those products. When buyers don't have to worry about sellers exploiting conflicts of interest or information advantages this will help minimize bargaining and other costs. When sellers abstain from exploiting their power in business relationships and view other parties with justice and equity, policing and enforcement costs fall dramatically. The ethical concept many people still hold that "their word is their bond" makes some contracts unnecessary. When someone says, "My word is my bond," he or she claims to be a trustworthy business partner. Over repeated exchanges, the other party can verify the commitment to honoring promises.

Ethics and the Economic Value of Trust

A common definition of trust is "to have faith or confidence in someone or something."[17] This view contributes to the notion that trustworthiness is an individual, or organizational, trait that brings about that reliance. Another way of thinking about trust is particularly valuable in a business context. **Trust** is "the willingness of a party to be vulnerable to the actions of another party based on the expectation that the other will perform a particular action important to the trustor, irrespective of the ability to monitor or control that other party."[18] This definition moves trust beyond a trait of individuals or organizations and sets trust within a *relationship*. It also defines the positive outcome of trust, the willingness of each party to be vulnerable or to risk something of value in a relationship. This definition recalls our discussion in Chapter 1 about a key element of ethical behavior being "obedience to the unenforceable."[19]

Trust exists when the parties to a transaction don't rely on contractual enforcement to motivate each other to keep their promises and meet their obligations. You can begin to see the value of trust as an alternative to costly policing and enforcement mechanisms. You can also recognize how a commitment to ethical behavior such as avoiding bribery and secrecy, managing conflicts of interest, being honest and acting with integrity, and showing forgiveness and mercy can encourage other people to take risks in their relationships with us. Long-term commitments such as joint property ownership, marriage, and parenthood all become

	Weak Form Trust	Semi-Strong Form Trust	Strong Form Trust
Risk Level	Low	Moderate	High
Advantages	Reduces search & information costs	Reduces contracting and enforcement costs	Create new sources of joint value
Best for	Commodity transactions With many substitutes	Customized transactions with high levels of integration	Innovation, joint projects or ventures
Ethical requirement	Conform to standard norms and rules	Conform to partner specific norms and agreements	Partners abide by deep principles that generate trust
Typical manifestation	Spot market transactions	Contracts	Joint ventures, co-production work

FIGURE 14.2   Types of trust.

more attractive when our partners create in us the confidence that we can take risks and be vulnerable together.

Trust also pays off professionally. Buyers and sellers can develop one of three types of trust with each other (see **Figure 14.2**).[20] **Weak form trust** grows when neither party to the transaction is taking a big risk, such as putting one company's valuable brand behind a transaction. Each party is willing to put some assets at risk because, even if things don't go well, they don't have much to lose. These parties reduce the search and information costs they incur because each party will only put at risk assets that can be easily measured or are commodity-like in nature. Weak form trust reduces the transaction costs of search and information gathering. Weak form requires conformance to basic ethical norms of behavior by both parties.

Semi-strong form trust arises when parties put significant assets at risk but employ standard governance mechanisms to resolve disputes or handle unexpected contingencies. The most obvious of these are contracts or independent mediators or arbitrators whom the parties assign to help resolve disputes. These formal mechanisms won't resolve many situations, and so the trading parties rely on social mechanisms, such as shared norms and principles or threats of exclusion from membership in important groups, to provide more powerful incentives to avoid violating the trust of the other party.[21] Semi-strong trust creates competitive advantage by reducing the (often) substantial costs of contracting or enforcement through the court system, although both parties incur costs at the beginning to establish governance measures. Semi-strong form trust requires commitment to generalized ethical norms, but also commitments to observe specific and idiosyncratic ethical norms specific to their relationship. It's crucial that each party keep its promises.

Strong-form, or hard-core, **trust** is evident when the parties to an exchange put assets of significant value at risk because they believe, according to the definition above, that the other party will not exploit those vulnerabilities. Strong-form trust is also known as **principled trust** and is developed as trading partners engage with each other over time and observe the principled (ethical) behavior of their trading partner.[22] Strong-form trust not only reduces search, information, and policing/enforcement costs, but it also enables the parties to put at risk significant assets to create value.

When people and organizations operate in an environment of strong-form trust, they gain the following advantages:[23]

- Effective communication and collaboration across groups and teams inside the organization that save time and money and reduce work-related errors and improve quality

- Effective collaboration with external stakeholders such as customers, suppliers, and regulators that saves time, reduces bargaining and haggling between parties, and creates opportunities to find solutions that prove advantageous to the needs of all

- High levels of energy and engagement contributed by all stakeholders toward meeting joint goals
- Fewer disagreements and problems because of principles-based communication and ease and speed in resolving conflicts that do arise, based on a spirit of openness and fair dealing
- Greater creativity and improved innovation by all parties as people and groups are willing to share knowledge and ideas and invest the effort in experimentation and development that generate innovative processes, products, or services

When companies and their important stakeholders create and maintain strong-form trust, they move from being an economic ecosystem that creates value to being a diverse community that creates economic and social value. Strong form trust, based on firm commitments to ethical behavior, underlies the development of community and shared values that reduce friction in an economic system but also lead to a strong sense of community meaning and the deep relationships that characterize a PERMA life.

Ethics and Strong Business Communities

Ethical behavior improves efficiency as it reduces transaction costs for individuals and organizations and fosters the trust that can create innovation. The economic value of ethical behavior extends to communities as well, and the respect for individuals as subjects, a commitment to justice and fairness, and the principles of forgiveness and reconciliation all contribute to strong and vibrant trading communities. This makes economic exchanges more efficient, and it also brings non-economic benefits related to the PERMA model. Ethical behavior strengthens intrinsic relationships, the bonds between people that bring lasting satisfaction.

Respect and subjectivity. The idea of treating individuals as subjects, or ends in themselves, is a foundation of the deontological ethical theory of people like Immanuel Kant. The ethical issues we've discussed in previous chapters around conflict of interest, bribery, power, and many questions of honesty stem from a view of others as objects, not subjects worthy of respect in themselves. You can see that a commitment to ethics that includes a view of others as subjects eliminates many of these challenges. Two other benefits flow from this respect. First, when we treat others with respect and as subjects, we often discover unmet economic needs that we can develop products and services to satisfy. Treating people with respect can be a source of innovation. Second, when we show respect for others, we invite them to show respect for us. Put simply, when people respect each other, transactions go more smoothly and we develop and strengthen relationships.

Justice and Fairness. The commitment to justice and fair treatment is the main concern of John Rawls. It's easy to see how justice and fairness reduce transaction costs and build trust, especially strong-form trust. One problem with innovation is the problem of knowing how much value each party contributes to the project.[24] A commitment to ethics as fair treatment encourages people to bring their ideas and contribute to economic transactions with the confidence that the value they bring will help create value for all. Fairness, like respect, is a lubricant that encourages people to trade and contribute, and like respect, it produces non-economic benefits of personal satisfaction and friendship as well.

Forgiveness and Reconciliation. The death of George Floyd at the hands of a Minneapolis police officer in the summer of 2020 brought to the surface calls for racial equality and justice. These calls are overdue, and both business and government must work to redress these wrongs and strengthen the social fabric. A commitment to justice, however, will prove insufficient to create the lasting change American and other societies need. Forgiveness must work hand-in-hand with justice so that not only the economic and social impacts of wrongs can be redressed, but the emotional bitterness held by victims (and paradoxically perpetrators) also can resolve and dissipate. No one can force others to forgive or reconcile; these come only from the people and groups involved. Reconciliation is all about moving forward and will be critical as people learn to live together in trust.

Just as personal relationships require healthy doses of forgiveness and trust to move beyond problems, so social groups, and society at large, must forgive and reconcile to realize the promise of a society that respects all members.

The first three topics in this essay made the case that ethical behavior lays a solid foundation for an efficient economy, and we also noted that ethics can help an economy be effective as well. By effectiveness, we mean an economy that meets the deep needs of people, their desires for good products and services, and also deeper engagement, better relationships, and higher levels of achievement. To complete the argument, we return to the logic of the opening case of Heliogen and Bill Gates. Heliogen highlights the power of capitalism and market economies to spawn innovations that can help solve economic and social problems. Bill Gates reminds us of one outcome of a capitalist economy that troubles many—capitalism allows some to amass great wealth while others live in poverty. Before we turn to these features of a capitalist economy, we discuss another ethical outcome of a capitalist economy: Free markets facilitate personal freedom and growth.

Market Economies: The Ethics of Personal Development

One fundamental assumption of a market economy is that producers have free choice about which markets they'll compete in and what they'll produce, and they select the level of quality and quantity at which they'll produce.[25] The information they use to make such a choice is the level of sales and prices for different products in the marketplace. Those prices and quantities reflect the decisions of individual consumers and households, who also are exercising their free choice in decisions about the quality and quantity of goods they want to consume. Autonomous economic actors are the foundation of a market economy. Consumer sovereignty, and that of all economic actors, underpins all free market economies.

Autonomy comes from an ancient Greek word, αὐτονομία, or eleutheria, which means "liberty" or "freedom." To make autonomous choices is to choose freely, without being coerced or controlled by someone else.[26] Autonomy is a characteristic of individuals as ends, not merely as means, and is consistent with a deontological ethical system. Autonomy and freedom would also be considered a source of utility; indeed, most people would consider the ability to make free choices as producing both instrumental (freedom allows me to buy what I want) and intrinsic satisfaction (being free is valued in its own right). The ethical and political theory of libertarianism, not covered previously in this book, is built on the notion that the good society is one where people are left free to make most decisions about their lives and happiness.[27] Human freedom is intrinsically valuable. For libertarians, governments and other institutions should provide the minimum support needed to facilitate freedom and impinge upon freedom as little as possible.

Autonomy is intrinsically valuable, but it has instrumental utility that goes beyond merely choosing, for example, what products and services to purchase. Autonomy is the foundation for development, growth, and living a PERMA life. The assumption behind each of the PERMA elements is that an individual can choose for themselves the activities that yield the fruits of positive emotion, engagement, meaning, and achievement. Autonomy also allows people to develop, invest in, and sustain relationships of their choosing that meet their deep needs.

Autonomy also spawns another valuable ethical good: free and complete information. Autonomous journalists and marketers want to produce honest and forthright information, for they know that citizens and consumers with free choice will demand nothing less. In today's online world, which features access to information of all types, marketers quickly realize that false claims can be easily detected and exposed. Free and complete information is valuable in its own right as autonomous, subjective actors value truth for its own sake. The market forces that encourage the production of complete information also make economic and social exchanges more valuable as they reduce transaction costs, build trust, and encourage the treatment of others as subjects worthy of respect.

Market Economies, Innovation, and Ethical Benefits

One instrumental outcome of autonomous economic actors is creativity and innovation; people are free to bring to market new products and services through the process of entrepreneurship. As the chapter's opening case illustrates, the range of activity for creativity includes traditional products and services as well as applying business principles and technologies to respond to societal problems. In the early part of the twentieth century, the economist Joseph Schumpeter contrasted the process of entrepreneurship with the static view of economics that provides the foundation for microeconomics.[28] In a static world, price signals for existing products help producers make decisions about the quantity they'll produce and help consumers decide how much they'll purchase. When the economy reaches equilibrium, then the traditional model implies that the market will "clear" each year as the amount of a good produced will equal the amount consumed.

Markets clear, but there is no innovation, as everyone is focused on meeting existing needs and existing demand. Where does innovation come from? Schumpeter provides this explanation: "Innovations in the economic system do not as a rule take place in such a way that first new wants arise spontaneously in consumers and then the productive apparatus swings round through their pressure. . . . To produce means to combine materials and forces within our reach. . . . Development in our sense is then defined by the carrying out of new combinations."[29] The people who "carry out" those new combinations are entrepreneurs, individuals with a different set of skills from traditional producers. First, entrepreneurs don't see themselves as constrained by current reality, either in meeting the needs of consumers or in the processes and resources it will take to satisfy unmet needs. They "pursue opportunities without regard to the resources they currently control."[30] Entrepreneurs create new resources through two processes: invention or innovation. Invention is the creation of something brand new, a new product, process, or technology that was previously unknown. Innovation occurs when existing assets, processes, or products are used in different ways.

Second, entrepreneurs differ from Schumpeter's traditional producers in their views of risk. They are willing to incur the costs of developing new products and bringing them to market without knowing what the demand for that product might be, or the exact price point that consumers will be willing to pay. They are willing to operate under very uncertain conditions.[31] For example, Bill Gates and Paul Allen developed their first software business while they were still in high school.[32] They saw an opportunity to automate the State of Washington's traffic-flow management system and so they wrote a program that used a computer to do what employees had been doing by hand. They found a partner who developed the hardware that would support their software, and the Traf-O-Data machine was born. All of this happened before they knew whether a market for their machine existed. The two eventually made about $20,000 from this venture, but the knowledge they gained prepared them for the creation of their next company, Microsoft.

When entrepreneurs create new products that solve real problems for consumers, the result is economic development. The economy moves from the static model of market equilibrium of planned production and consumption to one of dynamic movement and change, where new products come on the market and either complement or substitute for existing products. Schumpeter referred to this process as "creative destruction." The driver of creative destruction is the potential for the entrepreneur to profit from his or her creativity and risk taking. When a new product appears on the market, it has no rivals and so the entrepreneur may enjoy a season of high prices, and equally high revenues. Whether entrepreneurs create through innovation or invention, they often can utilize legal mechanisms such as patents, trademarks, and other protections for intellectual property that allow them to profit from their creations by forestalling competition.

The benefits of a dynamic, entrepreneurial economy, and the social order that supports it, come in the form of a constantly evolving economy that satisfies new and unmet consumer needs.[33] These needs range from the fully private, such as the development of smartphones and the thousands of apps that support them, to the social, such as Heliogen and its work to earn potential profits by bringing new, clean, and green technologies to the markets of industrial production. The disadvantages of a dynamic, entrepreneurial market economy arise from the profit motive: Market economies create huge disparities in wealth, and they only work when all parties can compete on equal terms.

Market Economies, Inequalities, and Ethical Harms

The promise of a market economy, in moral terms, is to preserve individual autonomy and try to maximize total utility; indeed, an optimally functioning economy—a state known as **Pareto optimality**—is one where no person can be made better off (or have more utility) without someone else being worse off.[34] **Figure 14.3** provides a model of a Pareto optimal solution in Economics. Points M and N are corner solutions, where all consumption is of good X or Y, respectively. Point E is not optimal, because it's a mix of X and Y that is below the line of maximal bundles of X and Y. Point D is on the maximizing line, but does not intersect with the highest possible social indifference curve. Point Z, where the two curves are tangent, is the Pareto optimal point. At point Z, no one can be made better off without someone else being worse off.

Pareto optimality looks at utility at a very high level, and critics of free market systems note that maximizing societal utility is not the same as each individual maximizing his or her own utility. A free market economy that is functioning very well and producing large amounts of total wealth may both create and tolerate massive inequalities in the distribution of that wealth.[35] Paradoxically, providing more wealth to the rich (or the "rich get richer") may create more total utility than a more equal distribution.

The mini-cases at the end of this chapter will provide you with some data about the level of income disparity in the United States, presented in terms of the disparity between chief executive officer (CEO) pay and that of the average worker. You'll also see data on the global distribution of wealth. Our purpose here is to provide you with some ethical reasoning on both sides of this important social issue. While some may hold that these significant differences in income and wealth are "good" outcomes, most people would like to see wealth gaps reduced. The challenges, however, come in the details of how that should be done and what the consequences of closing the gap might be.

Income disparities have a moral basis. The ethical arguments that tolerate such large disparities in income focus on the negative outcomes of attempts to remove these disparities. This belief holds that to create caps or ceilings on income would lead us further from the good society that we all desire rather than closer to it. First, high levels of wealth that come from wise management of economic resources reflect the value those assets bring to our society. Chief executive officers earn outsized paychecks because they manage those resources in ways that create economic value for many people. A significant portion of CEO pay comes from stock grants and options, and so executives only win when other investors, including many retirement funds, do. For entrepreneurs, particularly those in the technology sector, the huge paydays they receive reflect the scaled value of their products to society at large. High levels of pay are fair because they reflect the amount of economic value added.

Second, the promise of those big paydays is the incentive and motivation for the hard work of executive management or entrepreneurship. Without the carrot of high pay and wealth, the best and brightest in society would not engage in the hard and taxing work of managing and leading enterprises, including making difficult decisions about how to help the business grow. Similarly, without the potential for great wealth through an initial public offering (IPO), fewer people would engage in the creative activities of entrepreneurship, thus depriving society as a whole of new, value-creating products and services.

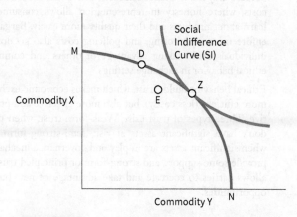

FIGURE 14.3 The economists view of Pareto optimality.

Income disparities have no moral basis. The argument against income inequality centers on the impact of inequality itself. Extreme income inequality inequality, in this line of reasoning, fails to treat people with the dignity and respect due to each person as a member of the human family.[36] This is a fundamentally deontological argument: We can't treat people as true subjects with their own desires, feelings, and needs and not provide some with enough income for them to meet even the most basic of those needs. Utilitarians would argue that extreme poverty reduces the overall utility that a society could produce and people like John Rawls would see these outcomes as unjust. Another aspect of unequal distributions of wealth objectifies people: the informal societal attitude that ties individual status to wealth. The rich are perceived as "winners" and the poor as "losers," and thus not deserving of help.[37] Treating others as ends in themselves would not require that all incomes be equal, just that the disparity shrink.

Others take the position that John Rawls advocates in the ethic of justice as fairness. For Rawls, income disparities aren't unjust *per se*, only when income inequality leaves those who are the worst off in an intolerable position. It's okay for some to enjoy outsized wealth as long as the poorest among us have adequate means to meet their needs. Income inequality has a ripple effect that further harms those at the bottom. Low income may *arise* from poor educational opportunities, the lack of access to healthcare that allows illness to breed, or systemic racial bias; however, low income also *leads* to limited healthcare choices, consigns the next generation to lower-quality education, and perpetuates systemic racism. Justice as fairness expands our view and argues that an unfair distribution of income—one that fails to provide for those at the bottom—is only one element in a basket of unjust outcomes.

Ethical people differ on how, or whether, to reduce the income gap. There is no right or wrong answer here as all arguments have some merit. You should be a part of these debates, but we believe that you should take part in them after having reasoned through the problem from multiple perspectives.

Key Terms

autonomy
pareto optimality
principled trust

semi-strong form trust
strong-form trust

trust
weak form trust

Chapter Summary

- Ethical behaviors make a capitalist economy more efficient because they lower transaction costs. These costs include search costs, where honesty in representation allows consumers to learn about products and their quality more easily. Bargaining, enforcement, monitoring, and policing costs also go down as individuals avoid taking advantage of others and commit to ethical behavior in exchange settings.

- Ethical behavior builds trust, which makes economic exchanges more efficient (less costly), but also more effective and productive. Three types of trust exist: Weak-form trust, when parties don't have significant assets at risk, semi-strong-form trust, when significant assets are in play and governance mechanisms provide some support, and strong-form or principled trust that allows parties to cocreate and take advantage of new business opportunities.

- The ethical principles of respect, justice, fairness, forgiveness, and reconciliation strengthen the ability of communities to engage in value-creating economic trades. When people behave in these ways, non-economic benefits also arise, namely, it becomes easier for all members of a community to lead PERMA lives.

- One argument for the ethical value of capitalism is that it builds upon and reinforces fundamental ethical values of human autonomy and freedom. The *free* in a free market economy refers to the freedom of choice that producers and consumers have in their economic lives. Freedom of choice is an instrumental and intrinsic value.

- Another argument for the ethical value of a capitalist system is the dynamic process of innovation. The allure of profit and wealth induces entrepreneurs to develop new products and services to meet consumer needs. These needs may be purely economic, or they may have a social focus. The application of entrepreneurship to social problems may yield new and effective responses to social problems.

- The opportunity for profit and wealth creation spawns income inequality, with some having great wealth and others living in poverty. Some tolerate income inequality as the price for a dynamic and innovative economic system. Others argue that income inequality fails the key moral test of treating others with respect and as subjects, and that it represents an unjust outcome.

Chapter Review Questions

1. Define transaction costs. How do costs of search differ from policing and enforcement costs?

2. What are the different types of trust? What is the relationship between different types of trust and economic efficiency? Competitive advantage for firms?

3. One benefit of capitalism is that it provides consumers with choice and the agency to make choices. Visit a local grocery store and look in the dental hygiene section. Does a society really need so many different types of toothpaste and toothbrushes? What arguments justify this level of product diversity in a society?

4. What is the process of creative destruction? How does it relate to the ethics of a capitalist system?

5. If capitalism and a market economy have so many problems, would society be better off adopting a more socialist political economy? Why or why not?

6. In what ways can the ethical behavior of organizations influence the market?

7. Is capitalism ethical? Discuss.

Application Exercises

- *Personal Ethical Development.* If you began keeping an ethics journal as suggested in the first chapter, continue that writing work. Here are some prompts: Where have you experienced "opportunistic" behavior in your school or work career? When have you been tempted to act opportunistically? What types of personal ethical principles/commitments will help you avoid taking advantage of the trust others place in you? How can you more comfortably trust others in business situations?

- *Career Goals and Planning.* A happy, meaningful, and productive life blends and builds upon the following: (1) the type of life you are interested in leading, (2) your deepest and most important principles/commitments (3) the work you are interested in doing, (4) what you are good at, (5) your preferences for things like work versus free time, and (6) your personality. What level of trust would you like to see in a company you work for? How can you identify what kind of trust exists in organizations you

interview with? What responsibilities do employees and managers have in creating a climate of trust?

- *Ethics in the Business World.* Identify a company or organization that engages in social innovation, either products, processes, or services. What roles do mission, vision, and ethical principles play in their innovative efforts? What challenges have they faced over time? How have they learned to sustain those innovations over time, or how have they effectively scaled their products, processes, or services to reach more people?

- *Talking with and Learning from Others.* Choose a business professional you respect, who you believe is trustworthy. Engage that person in a brief interview. What, for him or her, are the key elements of signaling trustworthiness in business relationships? What types of things has he or she sacrificed to maintain his or her reputation for trustworthiness? What advice would he or she give you as you begin your career?

Mini-Cases

Case 1: Executive compensation. Consider the following:

- In 2019, average CEO compensation for the S&P 500 firms was $13.1 million. That represents an 8% increase over 2018. The median investment return at these firms was 30%. Eight percent of CEO pay came in the form of straight salary, 19% in bonus and cash incentives, 51% in stock compensation, 12% in options, and 10% in deferred compensation (the portion of an employee's income that is paid out after the income is earned) or other perks.[38]

- In 2020, in the wake of the COVID-19 pandemic, 102 companies in the S&P 500 cut CEO pay. Of those companies, one-third cut CEO salaries completely.[39]

- In 1965, the ratio of CEO pay to that of the average worker was 20:1. That ratio peaked in 2000 at 368:1. As of the end of 2018, it stood at 278:1 From 1978–2018, CEO compensation, adjusted for inflation, grew 940%, while pay for the average worker, again adjusted for inflation, grew 12%.[40]

- U.S. CEO pay disparity is the highest in the world. For 2018, the ratio of CEO pay to that of the average worker was 127:1 in

China, 136:1 in Germany, 171:1 in the Netherlands, 201:1 in the United Kingdom, and 229:1 in India.[41]

- From December 1978 to December 2018, the S&P 500 increased roughly 600%, from 364 to 2,560.[42]

- Between 2015 and 2017, CEO tenure fell by one year to five years for consumer goods companies, and to 5½ years for industrial companies.[43]

- Is CEO pay too high? To combat the meteoric rise in CEO compensation, some have argued for policies, such as higher marginal tax rates on CEO income, making corporate tax rates dependent on the ratio of top executive pay to that of the average worker, or creating a "luxury" tax on companies where they would pay $1 in taxes per dollar that executive pay exceeded a certain amount.[44]

- Others argue for different reforms such as greater transparency by boards that link compensation to key strategic and risk-management milestones, greater attention by investors to who sits on a company's board, and especially the compensation committee, and a willingness of boards to signal that they won't engage in "arms race" competitions around executive compensation to retain talent.[45]

As you consider these facts, ask yourself, "Is this a morally good outcome for a society? Is it fair? Should we be concerned about fairness?

Case 2: The distribution of global wealth. As you consider the following data displayed in Figures 14.4 and 14.5, think about whether these outcomes of a capitalist system are fair and equitable. Create a strong argument that supports your position. What changes would you make to change the global distribution of wealth? What are the risks of making the changes you recommend?

The World's Ten Richest People in June of 2020:

Individual	Net Worth
Jeff Bezos	$156.9 B
Bill Gates	$111.3 B
Bernard Arnault & Family	$108.0 B
Mark Zuckerberg	$87.8 B
Warren Buffet	$77.8 B
Larry Ellison	$68.6 B
Amancio Ortega	$67.8 B
Steve Ballmer	$67.4 B
Larry Page	$65.4 B
Sergey Brin	$63.7 B

Source: The World's Real Time Billionaires, *Forbes*, available at https://www.forbes.com/real-time-billionaires/#2bece1143d78, accessed June 9, 2020.

The Distribution of Global Wealth: Percentage of Wealth by Population, 2018

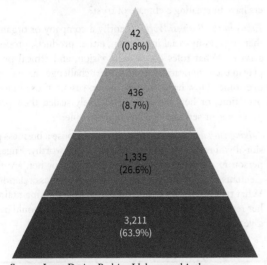

Source: James Davies, Rodrigo Lluberas, and Anthony Shorrocks, Credit Sulsse Global Wealth Databook, 2018.

FIGURE 14.4 Global population, in millions.

The Distribution of Global Wealth: Percentage of Wealth by Population, 2018

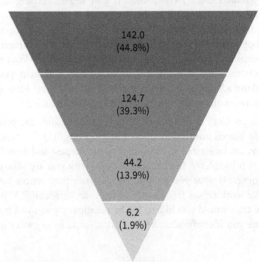

Source: James Davies, Rodrigo Lluberas, and Anthony Shorrocks, Credit Sulsse Global Wealth Databook, 2018.

FIGURE 14.5 Global wealth, in trillions USD. The net result: A small percentage of the world's population holds most of the world's wealth.

Case 3: Finley Miller was working as Deputy Manager in Adani Total Gas Ltd. (ATGL) and handled city gas distribution projects. As part of his job responsibility, he was project lead for Surat, Navsari, Tapi, and Dang geographical areas to develop steel, CNG, and PNG infrastructure projects. Most of the city gas distribution projects were capital intensive projects. A capital expenditure of ~70–80 crore was invested yearly for a specific geographical area

for the initial six to seven years as per the business development plan. ATGL made a significant investment in green fuel development and the company revised its project scheduling from moderate to intense expansion phase. Thus, all projects were to be completed with minimum lead time and required project permission. At the company, there was a Geographical Area (GA) Head concept, where all project, operational, finance, admin, and HSE functional leads reported to him/her. Being a project lead, Finley was assigned nine team members who worked in different departments of CNG, steel, and other verticals. In addition, third party inspectors from reputed firms were present for QA/QC as per the Petroleum and Natural Gas Regulatory Board (PNGRB) inspection requirement. Based on the site deployment, the inspectors needed to certify project activity and payment of running bills of contractors was then accordingly released to them. During the COVID-19 pandemic, projects were running slow and sourcing field manpower was challenging. During this time, Finley was puzzled to see an email from a steel project contractor complaining about the unnecessary monetary demand from a third party inspector for clearing project DPR for billing purposes. The situation became worse as most of the financial cycle for steel contractors was stuck due to the pandemic lockdown. It was essential to clear the running bill to maintain cash flow of the project and at the same time, there was no other third-party inspection available to make third-party verification for a contractor job at the site. As per the company policy, we needed to hold third-party inspections, which were to be undertaken by different people until the audit was completed. In case of any policy lapse or any sign of corruption or undue practice, a show-cause notice would be issued and the contract terminated. Because of this dilemma, Finley during an afternoon meeting discussed it with the GA Head. However, due to the large financial stake of ~50 crore due to delay in the project and target pressure, he was instructed to manage the site progress activity and was cautioned about his personal loss with reference to promotion and other financial implications. After the meeting, he received a call from the Human Resources team to take appropriate action for conducting an audit and to submit closure reports for necessary termination.

Discussion Questions

1. What should be the role and responsibilities of Finley in this situation?
2. Is it correct to put pressure on Finley?

References

[1] *Encyclopedia Britannica Online*, s.v. "Microsoft Corporation," by Gregg Pascal Zachary and Mark Hall, accessed June 9, 2020, https://www.britannica.com/topic/Microsoft-Corporation.

[2] Emmie Martin, "If you had invested $1,000 in Microsoft at its IPO, here's how much money you'd have now," *CNBC Make It*, November 19, 2018, https://www.cnbc.com/2018/11/19/how-much-a-1000-dollar-investment-in-microsoft-at-its-ipo-is-worth-now.html.

[3] "The World's Real-Time Billionaires," *Forbes*, https://www.forbes.com/real-time-billionaires/#2bece1143d78, accessed June 9, 2020.

[4] For more, see the Bill and Melinda Gates Foundation, https://www.gatesfoundation.org/, accessed June 22, 2020.

[5] Todd Bishop and Alan Boyle, "Company backed by Bill Gates claims solar breakthrough, looks to replace fossil fuels in industrial plants," *GeekWire*, November 19, 2019, https://www.geekwire.com/2019/company-backed-bill-gates-claims-breakthrough-concentrated-solar-energy-promising-replace-fossil-fuels-industrial-plants/.

[6] Howard Fine, "Solar Startup Heliogen Looks to Power Plants, Refineries," *Los Angeles Business Journal*, November 29, 2019, https://labusinessjournal.com/news/2019/nov/29/startup-heliogen-industrial-solar-power/.

[7] Ibid.

[8] See "How it Works," Heliogen, https://heliogen.com/, accessed June 9, 2020.

[9] Fine.

[10] Bishop and Boyle.

[11] See Adam Smith, *An Inquiry into the Nature and Causes of the Wealth of Nations* (New York: Modern Library, 2000), Book IV, Chapter II, 456, paragraph 9.

[12] The latter notion is the war of all against all, popularized by Thomas Hobbes in the *Leviathan*. See Thomas Hobbes, *Leviathan* (Cambridge: Cambridge University Press, 1651/1996).

[13] Walter Nicholson and Christopher Snyder, *Intermediate Microeconomics*, 10th ed. (Mason, OH: Thomson Business, 2007). See Chapters 9 and 10.

[14] This argument is made powerfully by Oliver Williamson, See Williamson, 2012, Transaction Costs: What are the questions, Berkeley Working Paper. Available at https://businessinnovation.berkeley.edu/wp-content/uploads/businessinnovation-archive/WilliamsonSeminar/williamson040512.pdf.

[15] "What are Transaction Costs?," Corporate Finance Institute, https://corporatefinanceinstitute.com/resources/knowledge/economics/transaction-costs/, accessed June 10, 2020.

[16] Williamson's book, *The Economic Institutions of Capitalism*, devotes many chapters to the causes and consequences of opportunism on the part of contracting parties.

[17] Definition taken from *Oxford English Dictionary*, sv "trust" available at https://www-oed-com.erl.lib.byu.edu/search?searchType=dictionary&q=trust&_searchBtn=Search, accessed June 10, 2020.

[18] Roger Mayer, James Davis, and David Schoorman (1995), "An Integrative Model of Organizational Trust," *Academy of Management Review*, 20, no. 3 (1995): 712.

[19] Right Honorable Lord (John Fletcher) Moulton, Law and Manners, *The Atlantic Monthly*, July 1924, http://www2.econ.iastate.edu/classes/econ362/hallam/NewspaperArticles/LawandManners.pdf.

[20] The three types of trust are described in Jay Barney and Mark Hansen, "Trustworthiness as a Source of Competitive Advantage," *Strategic Management Journal* 15 (1994): 175–190.

[21] William Schulze and Paul C. Godfrey, "Organization and Contract in the Informal Economy," in *Management, Society, and the Informal Economy*, Paul C. Godfrey, ed. (New York: Routledge, 2015), 60–76.

[22] Barney and Hansen, 179.

[23] See Stephen M. R. Covey, *The Speed of Trust* (New York: Free Press, 2006).

[24] Arman Alchain and Harold Demsetz, "Production, Information Costs, and Economic Organization," *American Economic Review* 62, no. 5 (1972): 777–795.

[25] Nicholson and Snyder. See Chapter 3.

[26] Oxford English Dictionary, sv autonomy, https://www-oed-com.erl.lib.byu.edu/view/Entry/13500?redirectedFrom=autonomy#eid, accessed June 22, 2020.

[27] For a description of libertarianism, see Robert Nozick and his book *Anarchy, State, and Utopia* (New York: Basic Books, 1974). See also

Michel J. Sandel, *Justice* (New York: Farrar, Straus, and Giroux, 2010).

[28] Joseph Schumpeter, *The Theory of Economic Development* (Cambridge, MA: Harvard University Press, 1934). See Chapters 1 and 2.

[29] Ibid., 65–66.

[30] Howard H. Stevenson and J. Carlos Jarillo, "A Paradigm of Entrepreneurship: Entrepreneurial Management," *Strategic Management Journal* 11, no. 5 (1990): 17–27, 23.

[31] Frank H. Knight, *Risk, Uncertainty and Profit* (New York: Houghton Mifflin, 1946).

[32] Zameena Mejia, "Microsoft exists because Paul Allen and Bill Gates launched this high school business first," *CNBC Make It*, October 16, 2018, https://www.cnbc.com/2018/10/16/microsoft-exists-because-paul-allen-and-bill-gates-launched-this-high-school-business.html.

[33] William J. Baumol, Robert E. Litan, and Carl J. Schramm, *Good Capitalism, Bad Capitalism, and the Economics of Growth and Prosperity* (New Haven, CT: Yale University Press, 2007).

[34] Nicholson and Snyder. See Chapter 13.

[35] Amartya Sen, *On Ethics and Economics* (Oxford: Basil Blackwell, 1987). See Chapter 1.

[36] See John Paul II, *Centesimus Annus* May 1, 1991, Rome. John Paul II frames the argument in terms of obligations we owe to each other as children of a divine creator, but the argument can be made on similar grounds without the religious foundation. See section III, especially 29.

[37] Michael B. Katz, *The Undeserving Poor: America's Confrontation with Poverty*, 2nd ed. (Oxford: Oxford University Press, 2013). See Chapter 1 for an overview and history of this argument.

[38] Chip Cutler and Theo Francis, "CEO Salaries decline, stock awards remain," *Wall Street Journal*, June 4, 2020, B1.

[39] Ibid., B6.

[40] Lawrence Mishel and Julia Wolfe, "CEO Compensation has grown 940% since 1978: Typical worker compensation has risen only 12% during that time," The Economic Policy Institute, August 14, 2019, https://www.epi.org/publication/ceo-compensation-2018/#:~:text=CEO%20compensation%20in%202018%20(stock%2Doptions%2Dgranted%20measure),the%20recovery%20began%20in%202009.

[41] Data from Statista, https://www.statista.com/statistics/424159/pay-gap-between-ceos-and-average-workers-in-world-by-country/, accessed June 8, 2020.

[42] Data from Macrotrends, https://www.macrotrends.net/2324/sp-500-historical-chart-data, accessed June 8, 2020.

[43] Lauren Silva Laughlin, "Many C.E.O. Tenures Are Getting Shorter," *New York Times*, October 23, 2018, https://www.nytimes.com/2018/10/23/business/dealbook/ceo-tenure-kimberly-clark.html.

[44] Mishel and Wolfe.

[45] Simon C.Y. Wong, "A Remedy for Soaring Executive Pay: Focus Less on It," *Harvard Business Review*, March 8, 2012, https://hbr.org/2012/03/a-remedy-for-soaring-executive.

Introduction—The Overwhelmed Ethics Student

Thursday, March 11 was a beautiful, bright, and sunny day in Claremont, California.[1] The afternoon block of classes was just ending when it occurred: that horrible, treacherous feeling that I loathed more than anything else. As I made my way out of the classroom door, I anxiously turned my cell phone on. I was yearning, longing to hear that sharp, pulsing sound that emanates from the phone whenever a message has been left. To my dismay, there was nothing but silence—an eerie, nerve-wracking, pit-in-the-bottom-of-your-stomach silence.

The Situation

I was a second-year MBA student at St. John's University of California, known as Cal-St. Johns, or just CSJU, with an emphasis in marketing. I had worked in marketing after receiving my undergraduate degree and fell in love with it. I knew that in order to build a solid, successful career out of this passion, I would need the educational foundation provided by an MBA degree.

Marketing was not a strength of the CSJU MBA. From the first day of orientation, Career Services made it clear to each of us thirty marketing students that, with a few exceptions, we would be on our own in finding post-MBA employment. I had turned down offers from strong marketing MBA programs because of the ethical character and life-long learning objectives of CSJU. I wanted to surround myself with bright, classy characters who sought to grow not only academically and professionally but ethically as well.

Most CSJU marketing students have fewer than one to two years of marketing experience, compared to the national MBA average of five-plus years. Our limited experience and limited name recognition from the school made it very difficult to compete with other students vying for the coveted corporate, post-MBA marketing opportunities. This limited our opportunities to smaller companies in Southern California and/or whatever companies came to CSJU to recruit.

BioPharma

BioPharma was a mid-sized San Diego-based corporation with an open position for a product brand manager. While the pay wasn't as high as some MBAs would expect, the opportunity would be perfect for me and serve as a springboard for better opportunities down the road. I began interviewing with them at the end of January and by mid-February I had completed a detailed phone interview, a one-on-one interview with the hiring manager, and an office visit where I had great interviews with four executives from the marketing department. A few days later, the company phoned asking for references. As the pressure of impending graduation grew, I felt comfort in what I thought was a pretty sure thing.

When there was no message on my phone, I faced the brutal reality: It was mid-March and I had no offers, no leads, no upcoming interviews, nothing. An ominous sense of failure and hopelessness

began setting in and weighing on my mind. As I made my way out of class that Thursday, I could feel a deep, pressing, piercingly painful feeling slowly creep into my gut as I made my way toward my car. After just a few minutes of driving, I pulled over in a random neighborhood and wept.

A part of me felt sorry for myself. Part of me questioned why I ever came to CSJU and was foolish enough to attend a school not known for the career path I hoped to pursue. But mostly, I blamed myself. I was the one ultimately responsible for securing post-MBA employment. I had carried the hope of a BioPharma dream for more than a month. This was my fault. I had no one else to blame. I decided right then and there that no matter what I had going on, nothing was more important to me than solidifying a job offer.

Moments after my emotional breakdown, a sense of optimism, determination, and resolve replaced my despair. I was inspired and focused like an eagle stalking its prey. I returned to school with a plan. I was going to get a job. No matter what the cost. I was going to make it happen. I thought to myself, "I have worked way too long and way too hard to give up now, and there is no way I am going to endure the same torture I did last summer."

Last Summer

Over the course of my first year at CSJU, I emailed over 200 companies, applied for over 100 marketing internships, and contacted almost every networking opportunity I could think of. After several anxious months of internship hunting, I ended up taking an offer from a small, local video game start-up. The pay was $3,000 a month. I didn't know how I'd survive on such a low income, but it truthfully was the only option I had. I accepted the position. After a month, I finally realized that this start-up never had any intention to pay me. I was devastated.

A few stressful weeks later, I accepted an unpaid internship with a local venture capital (VC) firm. While there was no compensation for the forty hours of work I put in every week, I felt the prestige and the experience of working with a VC firm might be enough to justify my effort. Essentially, I spent my entire summer banking on the slim hope that this venture capital internship would put me in a better position to get a job coming out of my second year in the MBA program. And I was now deeper in debt, having lived off my credit cards over the summer.

Resolve

It was often said that the first job you get following your MBA studies would be a key determining factor in your lifestyle and standard of living for the rest of your life. It would have a direct influence on the industry you would work in, the city you'd live in, and the income you would earn for the rest of your professional career.

That March afternoon I made ambitious goals. I would contact fifteen potential employers a day with a personalized cover letter.

I would apply to twelve openings online a day and would accept every interview opportunity availed to me.

I had been working since September four nights a week as a server at Red Lobster in an attempt to keep at bay the $12,000 in credit card debt I accumulated over the summer. To save money, I moved to a cheaper apartment in Chino, which added a twenty- to thirty-minute commute each way. Balancing time between work, full-time MBA studies, job search, and an hour of commuting was nearly impossible.

My typical Mondays, Wednesdays, and Fridays would begin at 7 a.m. I'd awake and finish up any last-minute assignments, leave for school at 8 a.m., and from 9 a.m. to 4 p.m., I was in class, studying, doing group work, and job hunting. By 4:30, I'd change in the restroom and leave for work at Red Lobster. I'd return home sometime between 11 p.m. and midnight and spend the remainder of the night preparing for the following day's studies. I'd get some sleep if I could.

Tuesdays and Thursdays were a little different. My first class began at 12:30, but the last class ended at 6:20. Tuesday and Thursday mornings and evenings were the only time during the week without explicit demands on my time. This is when I spent most of my time sending out resumes, preparing for interviews, and getting whatever rest I could to keep going.

Business Ethics 604

My tight schedule forced me to alter the normal second-year MBA core class schedule. In order to take a key marketing elective, I would have to take the required ethics course in the second term of my last semester. I'd be with a section of first-year MBA students. At the time I made this decision (in the fall), I was preparing for a flyback interview opportunity with Delta Airlines. I was confident that I would find employment either through this or some other opportunity that would present itself. Once I landed a job, I would quit Red Lobster and then devote 100 percent of my time to school, working out, and enjoying the last semester of my MBA program.

None of these things panned out, and I began the ethics course full of stress. I was in a class full of first-year MBA students, none of whom I knew. These students had assigned groups and shared multiple classes together; they also did not have the time commitment of a part-time job. This led to a glaring problem as my schedule would not be compatible with others in the class, a notion I was overly self-conscious about.

Perhaps the biggest mistake I made at this time was missing the first day of class. I thought Dr. Sanderson would go over the syllabus and outline the goals and requirements of the course, but he did much more. After the first day, student groups were already hard at work on the ethics practicum, a field project that had groups teaching financial literacy skills in local elementary schools. I was terrified of two things: having to introduce myself to a bunch of people I didn't know and the reality that my super-tight schedule would make being a good team member very difficult.

Realistically, it was time that I should have made available, as successfully completing school should have been my top priority, but subconsciously, the pressure and anxiety of finding a job and mining for job leads were too great. As a result, I succumbed to the thinking that the practicum was too much effort, too much time, for something that was too low on my priority list. Once I got a job, I could quit Red Lobster and regain my focus on academics. I had to complete the course to graduate, so dropping at this late date was not an option.

Job Fortunes Reverse

By early April, things on the job front were very promising. I had maintained contact with BioPharma and continually expressed a deep passion in working for them. I had very successful initial interviews with Toyota and Lockheed Martin, two excellent corporations that had indicated interest in continuing the interview process. On March 30, Software Now, a leader in the software as a service (SaaS) market, became the first corporate recruiter to visit campus and be willing to interview second-year marketing MBAs for a full-time position.

During my first interview with Software Now, I had the feeling this that was the dream job I had always hoped I would get following the completion of my MBA. I received an invitation to fly to their headquarters in Silicon Valley in three weeks. I was ecstatic. However, not knowing much about the SaaS industry, I knew that to have a successful interview experience, I had some serious homework to do.

A couple days before I flew out, BioPharma finally made me an offer, followed the next day by Lockheed Martin. BioPharma gave me an exploding, forty-eight-hour offer. I now had two firm job offers, and a flyback for my dream job. I'd been through hell finding a job, and I didn't want to settle for BioPharma or Lockheed Martin, both stable jobs but not what I was passionate about. I turned both of them down, flew to Silicon Valley to interview with Software Now, and by the first week of May had landed my dream job.

The Final Paper

Now I had to complete my course work and graduate. A few days later, Dr. Sanderson emailed me asking for my (late) reflective essay assignment, a major part of my grade. My goals of completing the coursework as best I could made me want to respond immediately. I viewed the reflective essay as an opportunity to synthesize the great takeaways and lessons learned from the class.

The problem was the essay required integration of the practicum experience with the course content. My initial reaction was to tell Dr. Sanderson that I did not participate and would have to make up the assignment in some other way. But my mind and my anxieties were focused on what I'd just been through and where I was now going. I made the horrible decision to write the essay as if I had participated on a practicum team. I would pass the class, prepare to move to Silicon Valley, and start the next phase of my life.

I explained that, for me, ethics had been a great course. I was passionate about the topic of financial literacy (living through my own financial crisis), and I wrote about the importance of teaching it to students and of practicing ethics as virtue and being involved in our local community. I contacted several people who had worked on the practicum, and I wove their insights into my essay. While I never explicitly lied and claimed that I played a specific role on my team's project, the overall tone of the essay, and the way I quoted other people, created a clear impression—to me and anyone else who might read it—that I had participated in the practicum.

Dr. Sanderson called me the day after turning in the essay to ask which team I had been on. When the teams filled out their peer evaluations, I was not listed as a member of any team. He asked me what was up, and I admitted that I had not been a part of a team. Rather than fail me, he gave me an assignment: Figure out and write about what would lead someone who came to CSJU because of its reputation for ethics to engage in unethical conduct.

As I wrote, I realized that the pressure of finding a job led me to rationalize not participating in the practicum. I would have to integrate with a new group, and the project would take precious time from my job search. I had been blind to the ultimate consequence, that I would have to falsify my participation in the practicum in order to pass the class. My intentions were good. I meant to do the project. I meant to do everything required for the course, but I fell into a trap caused by my optimistic thinking. I let extreme amounts of pressure influence my actions, and the result was a series of very questionable decisions.

Did the end of finding a job justify dishonesty? Was I justified in allowing the pressure of finding employment to supersede other priorities, including the practicum project? For me, landing the job with Software Now was as important, if not more important, than any other activity accomplished during my MBA. It would be easy to say that *this* end justified *this* means in *this* case. I'm not sure it's that black and white.

Reference

[1] Note: All locations, and many company names have been changed to protect the privacy of all involved.

Ethical Theories—Rose Martinez and TriHydraChlorafine

Rose Martinez, twenty-seven, grew up in a working-class home in Bakersfield, California.[1] Her parents were first-generation immigrants to the United States and had made substantial sacrifices to help Rose earn a degree in business at Chico State University. They, like Rose, had been thrilled when she accepted a job with MicroPower, Inc., a producer of lithium-ion and lithium-polymer batteries for smartphones. Rose had been impressed with the quality of people she met at MicroPower and the company's commitment to diversifying its workforce and gender-blind, merit-driven promotion policies. She had benefited from those policies. After her first assignment in Silicon Valley, Rose had spent the last eighteen months in a global supply chain leadership development program.

That program entailed four six-month assignments in different areas of MicroPower's supply chain. She spent the first rotation in Silicon Valley working on logistics for a new battery for Apple devices. The second rotation took her to South Africa and the third to a manufacturing facility in Wichita, Kansas. Her final rotation was as supply chain director at MicroPower's newest production facility in Vitovka, Yamuskistan, just outside the capital city of Pringhosk. She found Yamuskistan to be bursting with cultural and economic activity. Since the fall of the Iron Curtain a generation earlier, Yamuskistan, like many Eastern European countries, had tried to move toward a market economy. The old Soviet socialist system, overburdened with bureaucracy and sprinkled with corrupt officials, had been hard to displace, but progress had been made. Yamuskistanians had a strong work ethic, and annual income had continued to grow, reaching just over $4,000 per worker per year in 2019.

The Yamuskistanian government saw foreign investment as key to economic growth and established many policies that would entice manufacturing firms to locate in the country and generate significant numbers of high-wage jobs. MicroPower completed a new, $730 million lithium-polymer assembly facility in 2016. The plant employed 5,000 Yamuskistanian production workers and managers, and with a starting wage of $10 per hour, the workforce earned about five times the national average. These high wages attracted talented workers, and Rose learned that many of them saw a job at MicroPower as a way to build a better life for their children. Economists estimated that MicroPower's plant contributed three indirect jobs for each production job, bringing a total employment gain of 20,000 to the country.

The plant was good for the country and also for MicroPower. In spite of its landlocked location and rudimentary logistics, the plant punched above its weight in contribution margin. The facility serviced the company's EMEA (Europe, Middle East, and Africa) customers and distribution partners. Its 2019 revenue of $2.2 billion represented 25 percent of total company revenues, and its $627 million in EBITDA (earnings before interest, taxes, depreciation, and amortization) accounted for 30 percent of the MicroPower total. Rose marveled at that EBITDA number. Yamuskistan was by no means the least expensive country in which to locate; at least three others in the region offered lower labor costs, and the logistical infrastructure

in the country was satisfactory but still more expensive than locations closer to ocean ports.

Rose knew that her time in Yamuskistan would be limited and she had spent the last four months exploring the country and enjoying its rich culture. While most employees spoke some English, Rose had worked to learn the rudiments of Yamuskistanian. She often spent her lunch hour in the cafeteria in conversation with the women who worked on the production line. This gave her the chance to learn about life in Yamuskistan and practice her language skills. While she lunched with several women, she had become particularly close to Elena Solokova, a woman in her early fifties. Elena told Rose with great pride about her two children who were now at Pringhosk University and how grateful she was for her high-wage job that was providing her kids with the chance to build a much better life than she enjoyed.

One afternoon as Rose and Elena lunched, Rose practiced her pronunciation of Yamuskistann words for different body parts. When she spoke the word for feet, she saw Elena grimace and turn her gaze away. "Did I mispronounce it?" Rose asked.

"No," Elena replied, "but you obviously haven't seen many Yamuskistanian feet, particularly the women here. If you did, you would have said *zailony nohi*. It means green feet. We all refer to our feet as green feet because the greenish discoloration of our feet is the first sign of Kohoroshovsky syndrome."

"What's that?" Rose asked.

"It's a weakening of the body's immune system that increases the risk of deadly melanomas. KS, our shorthand for the syndrome, is linked to the use of TriHydraChlorafine, or THCF, one of the chemicals we use in the polymer production process. My nephew, who is a physician, has told me that THCF has been classified by many countries as a carcinogen.

"My colleagues and I have all talked about the risk of THCF, but the jobs we have here allow us to build a better life for ourselves and especially for our children."

That night after her work ended, Rose spent several hours looking into KS and THCF. The chemical had been linked to KS and cancer in some studies, but not in others. The science around the issue was not settled, but new research with better methods pointed toward THCF as a carcinogen. Cutting-edge thinkers called for replacing THCF with a close chemical cousin, TetraHydroChlorolol, or THCL. THCL was benign, but the chemical had two drawbacks for industrial use: It was expensive to produce and rare. Suppliers were limited to a small number of facilities in South Asia. Second, because it was benign and had fewer abrasive abilities, it involved a four-step rather than two-step process to be effective.

After two solid weeks of research and financial modeling, Rose began to form some conclusions:

- MicroPower was doing some things in Yamuskistan that U.S. law would likely prohibit if done there. The company *could* use THCF in the United States, but it would cost a lot more for compliance issues and would pose the risk of expensive lawsuits and activist pressure. It seemed to Rose that the company did not choose Yamuskistan because of logistics or market access, or even because of low labor costs; basically, MicroPower chose the country because of its weak legal system and lax enforcement of worker safety and pollution laws.

- Of course, MicroPower could switch to THCL and eliminate the health problem, but at a cost of twice that of THCF, costs would rise between 9 to 11 percent. Strong price competition among smartphone suppliers meant that price increases of that magnitude would be difficult to push through. The combination of rising costs and shrinking demand would reduce the plant's EBITDA to 23 percent. The plant would move from being a "star" to a "dog."
- The women who work at the plant know the risks of THCF, and they have chosen to work there. If costs increase, the company may cut jobs, wages, or both. The workers seemed comfortable with the trade-off of high wages for reduced safety. Rose couldn't help but compare women like Elena to her own mother, who had sacrificed to provide Rose with a much better life.

- She had fewer than six weeks left in this assignment. She would return to Southern California and, at MicroPower's expense, begin the UCLA Anderson Executive MBA program. This would be the next step in her professional advancement, and she knew she had a good shot at eventually ending up in a very senior leadership position. That would be a great prize for a young woman from a working-class childhood in California's Central Valley.

The next morning as Rose arrived in the office, she opened an email from Steve Ferguson, MicroPower's executive vice president of the global supply chain. He wanted to set up time in the next day or so for a video conference and exit interview. Steve wanted to know about Rose's experience in Yamuskistan and gauge her feelings toward her upcoming transfer. Steve also invited Rose to make any recommendations for change. Rose had several recommendations for improving the efficiency of production in the plant. That was the easy part. As Rose turned and looked out on a beautiful Yamuskistanian spring day, she wondered what, if anything, she should say about the use of THCF at the plant.

Reference

[1] Certain elements of this case including names, corporations, locations and chemical formulas have been changed to protect e privacy of all involved.

Living an Ethical Life—Peter Olson

Peter Olson was thirty-four years old and an assistant to the head of the Polymers and Synthetics (P & S) Division of United Chemical Corporation (UCC). Peter had been with UCC for twelve years. UCC was a large chemical company with annual sales of approximately $50.25 billion. The P & S Division, with over $6.75 billion in sales, was one of UCC's fastest-growing and technologically sophisticated divisions.

Peter Olsen graduated from Case Western Reserve University in finance and went to work for UCC immediately upon graduation. He began as a financial analyst for special projects, but he had moved from finance into a line-management role at P & S's largest production plant. Peter had performed well in all his assignments, and the company's senior management let him know on many occasions that his career trajectory should land him in the C-suite. In 2012, Peter graduated from the University of Michigan's executive MBA program. As a part of a leadership development program, Pete was asked to assume responsibility for the division's R&D and new product development group in 2015. He and his family moved to the division's headquarters office, located in White Plains, New York, just thirty-three miles from the corporate office in New York City. Early in 2018, he became assistant to the president of the division for strategic planning and corporate development. His salary was $325,000.

Peter Olson and his wife Toni had married just before he entered his MBA program at Michigan. Toni was a graduate of Wellesley and Dartmouth Law School and had lived on the East Coast most of her life. When they married, they had both pictured the happy life of a successful dual-career couple. Pete's work with UCC required a number of moves, and although Toni made them without complaint, Pete knew that she missed the East Coast. Toni had put her career on hold to move to the South and Midwest. Over time, Pete and Toni welcomed two children into the family: Kara was six, and Spencer was four. They both wanted children, and Toni was happy to stay home with the kids while they were young. She was actively planning on returning to her legal career when Spencer entered kindergarten next year and had found a firm in White Plains willing to work with her on a flex-time basis.

When they moved to the White Plains area, Pete and Toni were delighted to find an old saltbox colonial in the legendary community of Sleepy Hollow, with a population of about 10,000. Both Toni and Peter found it easy to make friends in the area, and Toni was particularly happy to find so many women her age with interests similar to hers. The local school system was excellent, and great options were available for after-school activities for the kids. Toni looked forward to working.

Peter found that his new job as assistant to the president placed heavy demands on his time. Frequent trips to divisional plants were required, as were visits to large customers and branch sales offices. Peter believed that he was away from home on an average of one and one-half weeks each month. Work in his White Plains office could be exhausting as well. His boss was a driver who expected a lot from his team, and Pete spent many evenings at the division office and many others working from home. However, he loved his work and he continued to perform well.

The Olsons had always been a close-knit family, and Peter had realized for months that his absence from home and his long working hours put heavy demands on Toni and the kids. After one particularly long trip to South America, Toni told Peter she was not sure "it's worth the rat race." Those feelings subsided, and Peter's enthusiasm for his work, his renewed dedication to the family when he was in town, and Toni's own sense of balance succeeded in avoiding any serious problems. On two or three occasions, Peter and Toni discussed how their lives would change once Toni went back to work, how they would create space for the family, and where they wanted their professional and personal lives to go. The demands of Peter's job continued, and they made little progress on implementing any plans.

On a pleasant spring evening in late April of 2019, Peter returned home about 9 o'clock to tell Toni that he had just been offered a position as the president of the recently spun-off carbon fiber unit, which would now become its own division. Annual sales would be in the neighborhood of $1.5 billion, and the demand for the unit's new lines of products, growing rapidly, should drive fast-paced growth. Pete talked delightedly about the challenges of sales, production, engineering, and organization that would be his responsibility and the opportunity for advancement that the job represented. From this new position, the next move up would be into the corporate executive suite. He was so excited that he talked without stopping for forty minutes, and only mentioned in passing that the job brought a substantial raise to $450,000 a year, plus bonus income.

It finally dawned on Peter that Toni had said nothing. Trying to find some way to wind down his oration, he concluded with a final announcement, "Of course, we'll have to move out to St. Louis. I've got to go out week after next, but you and the kids don't have to come until school finishes here."

Toni stared fixedly at her husband. Finally, she said, "Peter, dinner is cold. You'll have to warm something up." Peter rose and turned to go to the kitchen. As he got to the kitchen door, Toni said coldly, "Peter, who the hell wants to live in St. Louis?"

The Corporation and its Stakeholders—Ecolab and the 2030 Sustainability Goals

by Paul C. Godfrey and Emilio Tenuta

Emilio Tenuta, Ecolab's chief sustainability officer, turned away from his desk and looked out the window at the beautiful St. Paul summer skyline. It was July of 2020 and he had just posted the video announcing Ecolab's 2030 sustainability goals.[1] The goals represented the latest evolution in the company's century-long commitment to creating a better world through economically and ecologically sustainable products. Exhibit 1 displays the 2030 goals. These goals were not platitudes or aspirational statements; they created clear metrics for success that would drive business growth for the company and its customers while ensuring wise stewardship of precious natural and human resources. As he finished watching, Emilio felt a deep sense of satisfaction at the culmination of eighteen months of hard work. The 2030 goals represented state-of-the-art thinking in several areas: working with customers to show that sustainable approaches meet both business and social goals, walking the talk by focusing on internal operations as well as external markets, and focusing on measurable outcomes that would connect everyday actions to high-level goals.

As he gazed out at the Mississippi River from his office, he began to think about the next steps. It had been hard work to define the goals and gain consensus around the metrics and commitments the company had just made. It would be harder work to achieve those goals through the work of Ecolab's 44,000 employees spread over 170 countries. The goals pointed the way forward, but now his challenge was to figure out how to get all parts of a diversified global company to march in the same direction. Exhibit 2 provides details on Ecolab's business and recent performance.

ECOLAB: A CENTURY OF COMMITMENT TO PROFITABLE SUSTAINABILITY

Merritt J. (M. J.) Osborn founded the company that would become Ecolab in 1923. Osborn's early work as a traveling salesman put him on the road many nights a year. He noticed that the hotels where he stayed had to take rooms out of service for up to two weeks every time they cleaned the carpets. Osborn developed a carpet cleaner—Absorbit—that cleaned carpets in less time and used less water, meaning that rooms would be out of commission for a much shorter period. Although customers paid more for Absorbit than other cleaners, their total cost of cleaning—factoring in labor, water usage, and downtime—would be lower.[2]

Osborn named his company Economics Laboratory (EL). "Economics" to signify that products lowered overall customer costs of cleaning, and "Laboratory" because each product had been developed through laboratory research. In 1924, EL introduced Soilax, an easy-to-measure dishwashing detergent, and in 1928, the company's addition of Soilax dispensers and other dishwashing equipment made EL a leading provider of dishwashing solutions, not just soap. Over the next ninety-seven years, the company adhered to the same basic business model: Identify a customer pain point around cleaning or sanitation, develop a scientific solution that saved labor, maintenance, downtime, and equipment costs, and charge customers a premium based on a lower total cost of using the EL system. Osborn hired technical people as field representatives so that EL people would "know more about the cleaning processes of that industry

---

By 2030, we aim to:

Water
Help customers conserve **300 billion** gallons of water, equivalent to the drinking water needs of **1 billion people**

Climate
Help customers become carbon neutral by reducing greenhouse gas emissions by **4.5 million** metric tonnes, preventing **7.3 million** pollution-related illnesses

Food
Help customers provide high-quality and safe food to **1.8 billion** people for an entire year, preventing **11 million** foodborne illnesses

Health
Help clean **50 billion** hands and provide safe medical care for **116 million** people each year, reducing more than **1.7 million** infections

For more information about our 2030 impact Goals, visit ecolab.com/sustainability

EXHIBIT 1 Ecolab's 2030 Sustainability Goals

EXHIBIT 2   Ecolab's Financial Performance, by Business Segment

Net Sales (millions)	2019	2018	2017	2016	2015	2014
Global Institutional	$ 5,569.9	$ 5,220.2	$ 4,895.8	$ 4,617.1	$ 4,485.5	$ 4,261.9
Global Industrial	$ 5,235.5	$ 5,066.0	$ 4,785.8	$ 4,495.6	$ 4,210.9	$ 3,982.8
Global Energy	$ 3,334.0	$ 3,388.8	$ 3,205.8	$ 3,035.8	$ 3,470.8	$ 3,815.8
Other	$ 907.5	$ 855.7	$ 910.7	$ 806.5	$ 747.1	$ 705.2
Subtotal	$15,046.9	$14,530.7	$13,798.1	$12,955.0	$12,914.3	$12,765.7
Effects of Foreign Currency Translation	$ (140.6)	$ 137.5	$ 37.8	$ 197.8	$ 630.8	$ 1,514.8
Total Reported Net Sales	$14,906.3	$14,668.2	$13,835.9	$13,152.8	$13,545.1	$14,280.5
Operating Income (millions)						
Global Institutional	$ 854.7	$ 724.4	$ 722.0	$ 703.0	$ 626.4	$ 538.8
Global Industrial	$ 1,042.2	$ 1,007.3	$ 962.7	$ 966.7	$ 876.6	$ 772.6
Global Energy	$ 379.1	$ 338.5	$ 322.9	$ 337.1	$ 465.5	$ 534.8
Other	$ 167.3	$ 160.0	$ 140.7	$ 148.1	$ 127.5	$ 109.9
Corporate	$ (409.2)	$ (303.6)	$ (210.3)	$ (272.1)	$ (663.8)	$ (252.4)
Subtotal	$ 2,034.2	$ 1,926.6	$ 1,938.0	$ 1,882.8	$ 1,432.2	$ 1,703.7
Effects of Foreign Currency Translation	$ (20.4)	$ 20.4	$ 12.1	$ 32.2	$ 129.1	$ 251.3
Total Reported Operating Income	$ 2,013.8	$ 1,947.0	$ 1,950.1	$ 1,915.0	$ 1,561.3	$ 1,955.0
Corporate-Level Items						
Other (Income) Expense	$ (76.3)	$ (79.9)	$ (67.3)	$ -	$ -	$ -
Interest Expense, Net	$ 191.2	$ 222.3	$ 255.0	$ 264.6	$ 243.6	$ 256.6
Income Before Income Taxes	$ 1,898.9	$ 1,804.6	$ 1,762.4	$ 1,650.4	$ 1,317.7	$ 1,698.4
Provision For Income Taxes	$ 322.7	$ 364.3	$ 243.8	$ 403.3	$ 300.5	$ 476.2
Net Income Including Noncontrolling Interest	$ 1,576.2	$ 1,440.3	$ 1,518.6	$ 1,247.1	$ 1,017.2	$ 1,202.8
Net Income Attributable to Noncontrolling Interest	$ 17.3	$ 11.2	$ 14.0	$ 17.5	$ 15.1	$ 19.4
Net Income Attributable to Ecolab	$ 1,558.9	$ 1,429.1	$ 1,504.6	$ 1,229.6	$ 1,002.1	$ 1,202.8
Basic (in dollars per share)	$ 5.41	$ 4.95	$ 5.20	$ 4.20	$ 3.38	$ 4.01
Diluted (in dollars per share)	$ 5.33	$ 4.88	$ 5.12	$ 4.14	$ 3.32	$ 3.93

Source: Ecolab 10-K Filings, various years

than anyone else, including the customer."[3] Economics Laboratory sales and field service representatives offered customers high levels of support, including being on call 24/7.

As EL grew, the company moved beyond simple cleaning solutions. For example, throughout the first half of the twentieth century, milk had a useful shelf life of only three days, due to poor cleaning practices at dairies. In 1961, EL bought a dairy equipment supplier, Klenzade, and combined EL's cleaning and sanitation expertise with Klenzade's clean-in-place (CIP) system to improve cleaning milk production lines without having to dismantle the entire system. Former chief executive officer (CEO) Doug Baker would note a half-century later that EL, with its clean-in-place technology, probably made the single biggest contribution to extending milk shelf life. This technology soon spread to other food and beverage operations.[4]

In 1986, EL changed its name to "Ecolab" and began to shift its identity. The "eco" now stood for ecology and environment, while the "lab" continued the focus on science and technology.[5] The following year, the company sold its consumer dishwasher detergent business to focus solidly on serving its institutional (hospitality, restaurants) and industrial (food and beverage, manufacturing) businesses. Ecolab remained true to the original philosophy of M. J. Osborn through its emphasis on hiring and training technical experts who could help customers solve problems and provide high levels of service and support. In 2002, the company launched its EcoSure business, an assessment, evaluation, and training service that expanded the company's offerings from a focus on "end-of-use" cleanliness and sanitation to "beginning-of-use" product safety and "in-use" process integrity. In recognition for the company's impact, Ecolab won the 2006 Black Pearl Award for

The Four Pillars

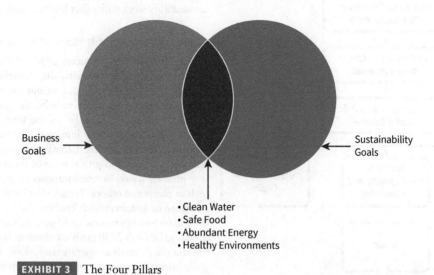

Business Goals

Sustainability Goals

- Clean Water
- Safe Food
- Abundant Energy
- Healthy Environments

EXHIBIT 3 The Four Pillars

Corporate Excellence in Food Safety and Quality, presented by the International Association for Food Protection (IAFP).[6]

In 2011, Ecolab purchased Nalco Water, an acquisition that nearly doubled the size of the company and brought sophisticated water-management expertise and technology. Nalco's advanced technology, such as its 3D TRASAR™ water-management system, complemented and expanded Ecolab's expertise in helping customers manage water. Prior to this acquisition, Ecolab's customers were already expanding their focus beyond efficiently delivering high-quality products and services to also operating sustainably. Ecolab realized that its unique solutions, technology, and newly acquired water-management expertise offered the company a new source of competitive advantage: Ecolab could help customers achieve both their profitability and sustainability goals. Christophe Beck, Ecolab CEO since July of 2020, explained that "the essence of sustainability is the fundamental proposition that you improve business performance and lower cost as you reduce the use of natural resources. It's a win-win-win proposition."[7] The customer, Ecolab, and the environment would all win through sustainable solutions.

Ecolab shifted its strategic position and messaging to focus on sustainability, and the company continued its historical trajectory of creating innovative systems to solve customers' toughest problems. Emilio Tenuta, who was Nalco's first director of sustainability, developed the notion of eROI to help Nalco service staff and their customers understand the business value of sustainability and brought that platform to Ecolab. eROI stands for exponential return on investment and allowed customers to see how Ecolab's services and technologies impacted their bottom lines. eRoi focused on five areas:

- **Safety:** Nalco products, services, and systems helped create cleaner, safer, and healthier operating environments for employees and customers, reducing losses from accidents and illnesses.
- **Water:** Nalco solutions conserved water and optimized water quality, preserving the environment and reducing costs.
- **Energy:** Nalco solutions saved energy by enabling more efficient operations or helped produce more energy by supporting the extraction of new oil and gas reserves.
- **Waste:** Efficiency, recycling, and reuse solutions helped keep waste out of landfills.

- **Assets:** Products and services improved asset efficiency and lengthened asset life.

As Ecolab integrated Nalco into the organization, several synergies became apparent. Tenuta, for example, moved from his role as director of sustainability at Nalco to vice president of sustainability at Ecolab. The emphasis on sustainability became more pronounced as Ecolab adopted what it termed its *four pillars*. The four pillars represented an integrated approach to sustainability throughout the corporation, and they highlighted key challenges that lay at the intersection of its business and sustainability goals. Exhibit 3 shows the four pillars.

The four pillars captured the four major impacts of Ecolab's business: Clean Water, Safe Food, Abundant Energy, and Healthy Environments. While the four pillars provided strategic and mission-centric guidance, they lacked specific impact goals. In 2015, Tenuta and his team used the four pillars to create the 2020 Sustainability Goals, which represented measurable targets for Ecolab to achieve:

- Help customers save 300 billion gallons of water annually by 2030.
- Prevent more than one million foodborne illnesses by 2020.
- Reduce internal use of CO_2 by 10 percent by 2020.
- Reduce the risk of health-care–associated illnesses (HAIs) for as many as 10,000 people.

The four pillars also supported the United Nations Sustainable Development Goals (SDGs). The four pillars linked to SDGs 6 (Clean Water) and 7 (Affordable and Clean Energy), and the customer-facing goals connected to SDGs 3 (Good Health and Well-Being), 12 (Responsible Consumption and Production), and 13 (Climate Action). Ecolab's internal talent and performance efforts already aligned with SDGs 8 (Decent Work and Economic Growth) and 9 (Industry, Innovation, and Infrastructure).

SUSTAINABILITY AT ECOLAB

Tenuta led a team of eight professionals in the corporate sustainability group. Exhibit 4 shows the structure of the group. The team works most closely with three corporate-level functions: marketing;

Sustainability at Ecolab, 2020

EXHIBIT 4 The Sustainability Group at Ecolab in 2020

research, development, and engineering (RD&E); and supply chain. However, they also engage regularly with their functional counterparts in each Ecolab business unit. The team reports formally through the marketing channel, and Emilio reports to Gail Peterson, chief marketing officer. Tenuta has an informal reporting relationship with Christophe Beck, CEO. In fact, rarely a week goes by without Tenuta bringing issues and opportunities to Beck for feedback and advice.

Tenuta also reports to the Sustainability Executive Advisory Team (SEAT). Christophe Beck chairs the SEAT, and the committee is composed of the presidents of Ecolab's industrial, institutional, and health-care businesses, as well as the heads of RD&E, marketing, communications, the chief legal officer (CLO), and the chief human resources officer (CHRO). The SEAT acts as the internal board of directors for Ecolab's sustainability programs; it exercises oversight

of all initiatives, provides input and advice for advancing initiatives, and approves policy changes throughout the organization to align sustainability work with other business goals.

Sustainability and Strategy at Ecolab

The 2030 goal-setting process provided the team with the opportunity to rethink how sustainability contributes to Ecolab's overall strategy. For most companies, a serious commitment to sustainability begins as an internal initiative, with the goal of improving performance within the "four walls" of the firm. Activities could include everything from recycling initiatives, fleet-management changes to decrease carbon emissions, manufacturing and operational changes to redesign products and processes to eliminate pollution and unnecessary product waste, or commitments to transition away from fossil fuels in plants and offices. Tenuta refers to these initiatives as the *first generation* of sustainability.[8] Ecolab's 2020 goal to reduce CO_2 emissions in its own operations by 10 percent represented first-generation thinking. Ecolab's 2030 goals continue to lay out clear objectives for the company's internal operations. Exhibit 5 displays these internal goals, which position the company as "a responsible and sustainable partner."

Second-generation activities build on these important foundations and include initiatives that move beyond the four walls of the firm to span the value chain and the impact the company has through its customers. Initiatives such as sustainable supply chains and "fair-trade" or "conflict-free" product-sourcing commitments typified second-generation thinking. The 2020 goals included second-generation thinking as Ecolab explicitly focused on how it helps customers save water, produce safe food, and reduce health-care–acquired infections. Second-generation goals tended to be incremental improvements over the first generation, with the firm simply expanding its horizon and leveraging its growing capabilities into its larger market.

Tenuta hoped that the 2030 goal-setting process could move Ecolab into the *third generation* of sustainability, where the focus shifted to societal impacts and sustainability would become a driver of strategic growth through collaboration with other companies, non-governmental organizations (NGOs), and governments. Third-generation goals would be ambitious and bold, and they would more closely link a company's work with other efforts in the governmental and civil society sphere to address large-scale societal challenges. The idea of ambitious and bold goals sounded appealing but ran several risks. For example, bold goals were by definition harder to achieve than moderate ones. If Ecolab failed to achieve its

---

Our 2030 operational goals will focus on:

Water	Carbon	Diversity and Inclusion	Safety
Achieving net positive water use in our operations	Tackling carbon emissions by meeting the UN Business Ambition for 1.5C and achieving 60% renewable energy by 2030	Supporting a diverse, inclusive workforce, committing to the UN Sustainability Development Goal 5 (Gender Equality for Woman and Girls) and advancing pay equity and gender and diverse representation	Training and educating 100% of our associates to work safely 100% of the time

EXHIBIT 5 Ecolab's 2030 Operational Targets for Sustainability

targets, critics and stakeholders could lodge claims of greenwashing or hypocrisy that could damage the brand and demoralize employees.

Foremost for Tenuta, however, was the reality that sustainability was such a broad notion that a company could become stretched too thin by trying to be all things to all people. To avoid this loss of focus, Emilio used four questions as guardrails to tighten the scope of the new goals:

1. **What's relevant and good for Ecolab's success?** In 2019, Ecolab's sales were around $13 billion, and the company had ambitious growth goals. The 2030 goals needed to reduce water and energy use, but they also needed to suggest and inspire new lines of business, new products, and expanded service offerings that would generate more revenue from existing customers and expand the company's customer base. Sustainability needed to become a driver of strategic evolution and revenue growth, building on the company's core assets and capabilities.

2. **How do we work with our customers to improve their business performance?** Sustainability represents a strategic opportunity for Ecolab's customers as well. Customers bought from Ecolab, and paid more for its products, because the company's solutions improved their business results, either by reducing costs or increasing revenues. They also were setting ambitious sustainability goals themselves. The 2030 sustainability goals had to deliver on all counts.

3. **How does our work impact the planet?** Thinking about global impact on our planet would be the essence of a bold and ambitious goal. The water business provided a great example. Ecolab's technology could help individual companies reduce, recycle, and reuse water in their own operations, which also reduced their costs. Water requires lots of energy to heat, cool, move or treat, and so water conservation led to energy conservation as well. Given that water is one of the scarcest resources on the planet, if Ecolab could find new ways to scale its water business, the impact on arid countries and regions of the world could be dramatic.[9]

4. **What are the implications of our work for people and society?** Ecolab's ambitions had to extend beyond the impact of business on the natural environment. The goals needed to include the human factor. Some 2020 goals had a human focus, such as preventing food-borne illnesses, but ambitious and bold meant helping more people and being more explicit about ways in which people's lives would improve through Ecolab actions. Water scarcity meant, for example, that almost three billion people faced water shortages in drinkable water at some point during an average year. Ecolab's water goals would need to be communicated in ways that connected to human impact.

DEVELOPMENT OF THE 2030 GOALS

Tenuta and his team began work on the 2030 sustainability goals in early 2019. Ecolab's internal cadence focused on having a new set of goals ready when the 2020 goals would naturally sunset, and the team hoped to have the goals ready to launch in June of 2020. They set out a four-phase process to lay the foundation for the 2030 goals. Phase I entailed a deep-dive review of relevant sustainability standards laid out by oversight and advisory bodies. The team reviewed the Global Reporting Initiative (GRI) topics to ensure that the company was addressing all key areas, consulted the Sustainability Accounting Standards Board (SASB) Chemical Standards for insights into measurement and reporting requirements, and mapped Ecolab's alignment with relevant United Nations Sustainable Development standards.

This review yielded forty-eight areas where the company needed to examine its practices and take action.

Phase II led the team outside to see how peer companies approached sustainability; companies included Exxon, Chevron, BASF, and Dow Chemical. Insights from this phase helped Ecolab gauge its position among a set of other global organizations and uncover ideas for new initiatives and potential opportunities. Phase III turned the team's focus to Ecolab's internal performance around the 2020 goals. The team worked to measure performance but also learned from business unit leaders and field personnel what worked well and what had proven difficult. Phase IV brought together all the data, and the team worked to cull areas for action most relevant for Ecolab. The team selected fourteen topic areas with high strategic relevance.

The Sale of Nalco Champion

When Ecolab bought Nalco in 2011, it picked up a business focused on the "upstream" segment of the oil and gas market. Ecolab later acquired another company serving this segment and formed Nalco Champion. This business provided solutions to support drilling, completion, and energy production, with a focus on water treatment. In February of 2019, Ecolab announced it would be spinning out Nalco Champion.[10] The business would merge with Apergy Energy and become Champion X. The transaction closed in June of 2020.[11] The spinout freed Ecolab of a highly cyclical business unit (see Exhibit 2 for details) and allowed the company to focus on its core institutional, industrial, and health-care/life sciences businesses.

In terms of the 2030 sustainability goals, the spinout effectively removed the "abundant energy" pillar as a core area of work. Tenuta realized that it would be easy, but deceptive, to abandon thinking about energy in the 2030 goals. First, Ecolab retained its downstream business, which serves refineries and petrochemical plants. Second, Ecolab and its customers used massive amounts of energy in their own operations and were a part of the "demand-side" of energy production. It was clear that Ecolab needed to address energy and climate issues in the 2030 goals. The team replaced Abundant Energy with Climate as a bolder and more expansive "fourth pillar" for the company.

Finalizing the 2030 Goals

As the team finalized the goals, they realized that the fourteen final areas of consideration all targeted impacts for the planet and society through a focus on the new four pillars. The remaining issue was to filter the options through the two other framing questions: Which efforts would be most relevant for Ecolab and which would help its customers best improve their business and sustainability performance? Bold goals also needed to yield clear and measurable outcomes. This work proceeded in a straightforward way because the four pillars reflected where Ecolab's businesses had the most impact through their work with customers.

For several years, Ecolab had measured gallons of water conserved through reuse and recycling. The 2030 goal of conserving 300 billion gallons of water annually represented a 50 percent increase from the company's 2019 performance of 206 billion gallons conserved.[12] With individual drinking needs estimated at just over 3 liters of water/day, 300 billion gallons would provide the equivalent of drinking water for 1 billion people. The 2030 goal would require the company to help more customers become more efficient, which would grow Ecolab's business while helping customers meet their goals. It would also challenge the company to find new ways to profitably deploy its resources and capabilities in water management.

Safe food would be free from bacteria or other microbial pests; it also would be higher quality overall. Rolling up their customer numbers (food producers), their customers' customers (food service and food retail), and adding a growth factor, Tenuta and the team set the target of helping to provide safe food for 1.8 billion people. Using the best available public health data and medical research, the team determined that those numbers translated into 11 million fewer foodborne illnesses each year. These goals represented a 46 percent increase from Ecolab's 2019 performance.[13]

In 2019, Ecolab provided soap and hand sanitizers for 40 billion hand washes. The goal for 2030 would be to increase that by 25 percent over the next decade. Clean hands are essential for public health, especially in health-care settings, where reaching this goal would prevent 1.7 million related infections. Ecolab's business in cleaning medical equipment and hospital rooms would result in 116 million people receiving safer hospital care.

Climate represented a new pillar. The 2020 goals had focused on internal CO_2 use, as well as helping oil and gas customers produce more energy, use less water, and reduce their own emissions. Climate represented the team's most ambitious and bold goal: to help Ecolab's customers become carbon neutral. Its products and services had helped customers conserve 28 trillion BTUs in 2019, which translated to 1.5 million tonnes of greenhouse gas emissions. The 2030 goal would *triple* that contribution to 4.5 million tonnes. Ecolab also would focus on achieving 60 percent total renewable energy in its own operations. Using the best available data, the team estimated that such savings also would translate into better health, preventing over seven million pollution-related illnesses.

Tenuta, his team, the members of the SEAT, and the safety, health, and environment (SHE) committee of the board had worked together to craft an ambitious vision for the company that would make it a global best-practice leader in sustainability and would help grow revenues by 60 percent.

THE IMPLEMENTATION CHALLENGE

The creation and rollout of the goals had been heady times, some of the most enjoyable in Tenuta's career. As he turned back from his Mississippi River view and toward his desk, he realized that the real work began now. To achieve these goals, every business unit would have to stretch, and he needed to help 44,000 people move from current performance toward driving these ambitious and bold goals, both in the market and in their own operations. He mentally created four buckets of work that would harmonize the organization around the 2030 goals:

Products and Services: How should Ecolab translate the goals into innovation efforts and metrics? How could the RD&E pipeline expand to introduce new products that could reach these stretch goals? How could his group help business units win new customers?

Value Capture: How should the company merchandize the concepts and metrics of eROI throughout the business units? What new measures would the company need for measuring carbon neutrality progress and many of the illness-prevention goals? What leading indicators might he employ to measure progress?

Operations: How should the team work with the supply chain group to make sure that Ecolab's suppliers helped it reach its own operational goals? How would functions like fleet management respond to the need to accelerate their move away from fossil fuels?

Diversity, Equality, and Inclusion: The company, like many others in the United States, had taken many positive steps to increase diversity; however, the company needed a stronger roadmap for sustained progress in areas such as hiring and compensation. What role should his team play, and what should fall to corporate and business unit HR?

There were other, larger questions as well. How much should the team focus on working on the "vital few," the 20 percent of initiatives that would produce 80 percent of the gains, versus the "important many" that also mattered in reaching the new goals? How could his team, the SEAT, the SHE committee of the board, and the entire C-suite, create a "line of sight" that would link the everyday actions of Ecolab's 44,000 employees with the sustainability goals? With so much work to do, and an aggressive time line, which of the four buckets should he focus on first? These seemed to be the most important questions to answer and would be the focus of the work ahead as Tenuta and the team mapped out their plans to achieve the ambitious goals they had set. Those goals would inspire them and help the company achieve its purpose: to make the world cleaner, safer, and healthier, protecting people and vital resources.

References

[1] *Our 2030 Impact* Goals, Ecolab, July 15, 2020, https://www.youtube.com/watch?v=fAiEC7aVXjI.

[2] "Ecolab, Celebrating 75 years of history," Ecolab internal company document, 1998, 5–6.

[3] "Ecolab, Celebrating 75 years of history," 10.

[4] Doug Baker, interview by Paul Godfrey, October 30, 2017.

[5] "Ecolab, Celebrating 75 years of history," 46.

[6] Ecolab Fact Book.

[7] Christophe Beck, interview by Paul Godfrey, October 12, 2017.

[8] The three generations model is summarized from internal Ecolab documents and presentations.

[9] "Water Scarcity Overview," World Wildlife Federation data on water scarcity, accessed September 9, 2021, https://www.worldwildlife.org/threats/water-scarcity#:~:text=Only%203%25%20of%20the%20world's,one%20month%20of%20the%20year.

[10] Dee DePass, "Ecolab to spin off its $2.4 billion Upstream oil chemicals business," *Minneapolis Star Tribune*, February, 5, 2019, https://www.startribune.com/ecolab-to-spin-off-its-2-4-billion-upstream-oil-chemicals-business/505333352/#:~:text=Ecolab%2C%20with%20%2413.8%20billion%20in,in%202013%20for%20%242.3%20billion.

[11] "Apergy and ChampionX complete merger to create the new ChampionX," *World Oil*, June 5, 2020, https://www.worldoil.com/news/2020/6/5/apergy-and-championx-complete-merger-to-create-the-new-championx.

[12] "2019 Sustainability Report," Ecolab, available for download at https://www.ecolab.com/corporate-responsibility/sustainability-reporting-resources.

[13] "2019 Sustainability Report."

Ethics and Compliance in Corporations—Valeant Pharmaceuticals

Robert Ingram glanced away from his computer screen after checking the stock price of Valeant Pharmaceuticals. As board chairman, Ingram was pleased to see that the stock price had climbed after the announcement of the hiring of new CEO Joseph Papa. Papa replaced Michael Pearson, who had led Valeant through a period of phenomenal growth and a phenomenal collapse. Valeant had, at one point, lost almost 90 percent of its market value as its stock fell from $262 per share to a little more than $26. (Exhibit 1

displays Valeant's stock price during the Michael Pearson era.) The recent release of the company's long-delayed 2015 financial statements restated its 2014 revenue downward by $57.5 million; its net income dropped by $26.8 million. The release of the financial statements eased creditor concerns that Valeant would violate key debt covenants, and Ingram hoped that Valeant could leave its troubled past behind. As he thought about the future direction of the company, Ingram wondered how the board had missed so many signals that

EXHIBIT 1   Valeant (VRX) Share Price

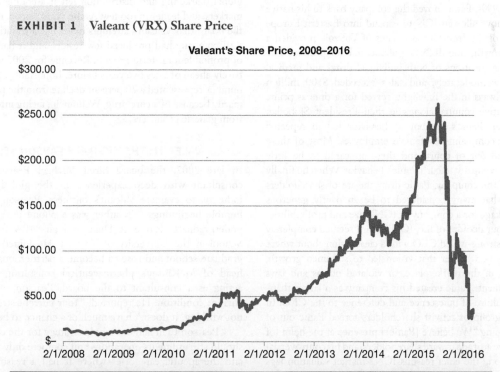

Valeant's Share Price, 2008–2016

Valeant Stock Highlights			
Date	Closing Price	Date	Closing Price
31-Mar-16	$ 26.30	31-Dec-13	$ 117.40
31-Dec-15	$ 101.65	29-Jun-12	$ 44.79
30-Sep-15	$ 178.38	30-Dec-11	$ 46.69
31-Jul-15	$ 257.53	30-Jun-11	$ 51.96
31-Mar-15	$ 198.62	31-Dec-10	$ 28.29
31-Dec-14	$ 143.11	31-Dec-09	$ 13.96
30-Jun-14	$ 126.12	31-Dec-08	$ 9.45

Source: NASDAQ Data, http://charting.nasdaq.com/ext/charts.dll?2-1-14-0-0-5120-03NA000000VRX-&SF:715-BG=FFFFFF-BT=0-WD=635-HT=395-XTBL-April 23, 2016.

Valeant's business model was unsustainable, and many of its business practices were ethically problematic. What changes should be made to Valeant's governance structure and business strategy to help the company compete both profitably and ethically?

VALEANT PHARMACEUTICALS

ICN Pharmaceuticals, the company that would become Valeant, enjoyed a storybook birth. ICN started in 1960, its first office the Los Angeles garage of founder Milan Panic.[1] Panic was a former member of the Yugoslavian Olympic cycling team who defected to the United States during the team's 1956 tour. Panic had just $200 to begin his new life, but from that humble start he was able to attend the University of Southern California and found ICN. The company initially grew by acquiring a niche product to treat dermatological conditions, while it worked on its first home-grown drug. Ribavirin (marketed as Virazole), was an antiviral that treated adults suffering from hepatitis-C and children with respiratory syncytial virus (RSV). Panic later marketed Ribavirin as a cure for the deadly virus that causes AIDS, a claim that drew formal charges of misleading information from the Securities and Exchange Commission in 1991.[2]

In the early 1990s, Panic moved the company back to his native Yugoslavia. The move allowed ICN to expand into Eastern Europe following the fall of the Iron Curtain. Sales of Virazole provided a foundation for growth, and ICN supplemented its product line through selective acquisitions of both individual drugs and medical devices. ICN grew moderately, and sales exceeded $500 million by 1996.[3] Panic, always in the limelight, served for a time as prime minister of his native country alongside then–President Slobodan Milosevic; however, Panic's flamboyant behavior led to repeated sexual harassment complaints by female employees. Most of these claims were settled out of court, and there appeared to be little appetite inside the company to curb Panic's behavior. When he finally was forced out of the company, Panic drew the ire of shareholders concerned with what many considered to be an overly generous compensation package for a company of ICN's size and profitability.

For its first four decades of life, ICN's board seemed completely happy to follow a strong-willed CEO with a clear vision about where to lead the company, whether that vision led to sustained growth, untruthful actions in the marketplace, or violated norms and laws of employee treatment. Panic created his company as a larger-than-life CEO, and a culture of quiescence and deference to the CEO. In 2002, however, a group of activist shareholders forced Panic out of the company, claiming "We believe [Panic's] presence at the helm [of ICN], his dismissive attitude toward shareholders, and his controversial reputation are among the chief reasons ICN's market valuation lags those of its peers and fails to adequately reflect [ICN's] fundamentals."[4] The board hired Robert W. O'Leary to take the helm; O'Leary brought a strong history in health care and medical devices, but also experience in business spin-offs and corporate reorganizations.[5] The board appointed three new directors, and the new leadership team began a comprehensive review of the company's product and business strategies with an eye toward improving shareholder returns.

When ICN changed its name to Valeant Pharmaceuticals in 2003, the company issued a statement: "Our new name represents our focus on value and supports our vision to be a leading, fully integrated specialty pharmaceutical company with a robust research and development capability and a worldwide capacity to commercialize products."[6] Valeant intended to pursue a strategy of developing its own drug pipeline of neurological drugs. The company also produced its own branded generic drugs to supplement its existing product line of skin care medications. The new strategy attempted to make Valeant look and act like other major pharmaceutical companies that all relied on internal research and development to create a strong pipeline of ethical (prescription) drugs. Once again, the board and company seemed willing to follow a CEO with a clear vision; strangely, the board failed to ask about the viability and long-term sustainability of this strategy before tasking O'Leary to implement it.

Valeant's first problem was size. With $823 million in 2003 revenue and $87 million in R&D spending, Valeant had little hope of developing the depth or breadth of a new drug pipeline that could compete with major pharmaceutical houses.[7] By comparison, Merck's 2003 sales exceeded $22 billion and its R&D expenditures were more than $3 billion.[8] Valeant pursued a "Big Pharma" strategy, but its lack of size and scale made it difficult (at best) to create an internal pipeline of innovative new drugs. The second problem was Valeant's lack of product and regional focus. With a small R&D budget to begin with, the company placed its investments in increased product breadth and geographic reach. By 2007, the company sold 2,200 different versions of its 370 core products around the globe, using 85 different third-party suppliers.[9]

The company's lack of adequate staff, resources, and skills in global marketing and distribution left it a competitor in too many markets, and leader in too few. As the years passed, it became clear to the board that Valeant's attempts to act like a traditional pharmaceutical company had produced few results, and it had little likelihood of profitable long-term growth. Revenue for 2007 was $842 million, barely ahead of sales five years before. Importantly, the 2007 revenue number represented a 20 percent decline from the previous year, primarily because of a core drug, Wellbutrin, facing intense competition from generic producers.

VALEANT: THE MICHAEL PEARSON STRATEGY

In late 2007, the board hired Michael Pearson, a McKinsey consultant with deep experience in the global pharmaceutical industry, to evaluate Valeant's business. Pearson had risen from humble beginnings (his father was a phone installer) to earn his undergraduate degree at Duke and an MBA from the Darden School at the University of Virginia. He joined McKinsey after graduate school and rose to become a partner, board member, and head of McKinsey's pharmaceutical consulting practice. While acting as a consultant to the board, Pearson surveyed Valeant's current condition. He reported: "Your current strategy is not only not working, it doesn't have much of a chance to be successful."[10]

Pearson then laid out a bold strategy for the company: Valeant should streamline its operations and compete only in global regions and therapeutic categories where it had a reasonable chance of success. The product portfolio needed to shift away from highly competitive categories such as cardiovascular and infectious disease drugs in which Valeant competed head to head with Big Pharma. The company would always be outgunned in these categories, both in terms of R&D and marketing and sales budgets. The company should instead focus on niche categories such as dermatology (skin care). Dermatology offered adequate demand and a stable base of customers who often needed lengthy, ongoing treatments to treat chronic conditions. The dermatology market also featured a broad range of specialty, niche ailments that required unique treatments, and a payer base of primarily private individuals rather than government agencies.

Pearson also suggested cutting R&D and focusing on mergers and acquisitions (M&A) to drive growth. Valeant could acquire smaller companies or individual products that produced enough revenue to create growth but were too small to interest Big Pharma buyers. Pearson, and the Valeant board, believed that there were enough of these undervalued, orphan products to drive substantial future growth. The board liked Pearson's bold vision, and they appreciated his direct management style. "[His] leadership style wasn't a cult of personality or a force of will—though he's extremely willful—but one where the decision making was going to be based on facts, which was a breath of fresh air," said one director. "He felt like a much better fit for what we needed to do."[11] In short, Pearson displayed the clarity and boldness of vision that typified the founder, Milan Panic; however, Pearson did not appear as iconic or eccentric as Panic. Pearson joined Valeant as CEO in February 2008. During that month Valeant's stock price averaged $13.88, ranging from $13.24 to a high of $14.17.

IMPLEMENTING THE NEW STRATEGY

As Pearson and the board began to execute the strategy, they enjoyed three advantages. First, the company had a well-established pipeline that would generate current revenue. Second, the company's balance sheet provided ample room for leverage. In 2008, cash or equivalents represented 60 percent of total assets; importantly, the company had no long-term debt (Exhibit 2 provides selected financial data for Valeant from 2008 to 2015.). Third, it appeared that there were, in fact, a number of just the right types of drugs, and companies, that Pearson identified as attractive targets. The company was poised to create value by implementing what, to all accounts, was a sound strategy for growing a small, specialty pharmaceutical company.

In 2008 and 2009, Valeant acquired four companies selling dermatology or aesthetics (beauty) compounds around the world. The moves added more than $300 million in long-term debt, but the immediate effect of the new strategy had yet to be realized in significant stock price appreciation. As 2010 began, Valeant pressed ahead with its strategy, spending more than $400 million for Aton Pharmaceuticals (ophthalmology care) and a private label Brazilian producer of generic drugs. Pearson's boldest move to date came on June 21, when he announced that California-based Valeant would sell itself to Canada's largest publicly owned pharmaceutical maker, Biovail, for $3.3 billion.[12]

Biovail brought its own checkered business history to the new combination. The company's original patent was a timed-release drug delivery technology that allowed many drugs to be taken once a day rather than multiple times. Biovail's founder, Eugene Melnyk, built a high-flying company, but some accused Melnyk of using questionable accounting methods to inflate the company's performance. In 2003, a Biovail truck was involved in a fatal accident; Melnyk claimed that between $10 and $20 million worth of Wellbutrin XL was destroyed in the crash, an amount significant enough to have an impact on earnings.[13] The next year the company admitted that only $5 million of Wellbutrin had been lost, and the ensuing accounting scandal consumed Biovail over the next few years. The company settled by paying a $10 million fine to the SEC in 2008.[14]

Although Biovail bought Valeant, the deal represented a form of a reverse merger that would later be known as an inversion. Biovail bought Valeant, which made Valeant a Canadian company. The new firm, in which Valeant held a 49.5 percent ownership stake, would keep the Valeant name, CEO, and business strategy. The deal benefited shareholders of both companies in the short term as Biovail's shareholders enjoyed a 15 percent premium on their shares and Valeant shareholders received a cash dividend of almost $17 per share.[15] The big winner, however, was Valeant. Valeant's US tax credits were about to expire, and the company lowered its effective tax rate from 35 percent (as a California company) to 10–15 percent as a company headquartered in Ontario. Pearson said, "We had to do this sooner rather than later from a standpoint of gaining this tax rate."[16]

With the Biovail deal, Valeant's long-term debt jumped more than tenfold, to just under $3.5 billion. Valeant's shares rose 12 percent, moving from $16.67 to $18.87. They would rise to $28.29 by year's end, and the Biovail purchase represents an inflection point in Valeant's share price. Between 2011 and the end of 2015, Valeant would spend more than $32 billion on more than 24 acquisitions. Purchases ranged from paying $22 million in 2012 for Eyetech, an ophthalmology biotech, to $14.5 billion in 2015 for gastrointestinal medication maker Salix Pharmaceuticals. Exhibit 3 lists Valeant's major acquisitions.

The majority of deals complemented Valeant's core of dermatology; however, the company diversified into ophthalmology and eye care with its $8.6 billion purchase of contact lens maker Bausch and Lomb, and the global consumer market with cough and cold company Natur Produkt (Russia) and Priobiotica, the Brazilian sports nutrition concern. The common thread that ran through all acquisitions, according to Pearson, was a focus on "mispriced products."[17] Investors loved the Valeant strategy, rocketing Valeant's shares into the stratosphere. The stock went from $18.87 the day after the Biovail merger to a high of $262.52 in August 2015, for total shareholder return of 1,391 percent.

The Big Pharma model grounded long-term company profitability in the creation of new patented drugs, and then pricing those drugs so as to recover the development costs of between $1 and $2.6 billion, generate cash to fuel the next round of innovation, and provide shareholders with a return.[18] Valeant eschewed that model by cutting its own R&D, replacing that driver with debt-fueled acquisitions. To recover the cost of that debt and provide attractive returns to shareholders, Valeant chose to raise prices on key drugs in its expanding portfolio. For some of its purchases—Valeant's drugs had not yet come "off-patent" (subject to competition from generic formulations)—the company used its monopoly position to raise prices between 60 and 2,850 percent (Exhibit 4 provides a list of some of Valeant's price increases.).

A report from Deutsche Bank indicated that the average Valeant price increase was 66 percent, more than five times the rates of competing pharmaceutical companies.[19] An investigation by the United States Government noted that "from 2014 to 2015, Valeant increased the prices of more than 20 additional 'US Prescription Products' by more than 200 percent. Valeant raised the prices of several of these products multiple times from 2014 to 2015, in some cases by as much as 800 percent."[20] CFO Howard Shiller admitted in May of 2015 that about 80 percent of Valeant's revenue growth for the quarter was driven by price increases.[21]

Valeant chose the drugs to add to its portfolio based on the level to which a drug had been "mispriced" in the market, but the company also focused on drugs that were used to treat the chronic nature of dermatological and other conditions. Valeant's price increases would result in long-term substantial increases in cash flow and profitability. The impact on drug consumers would mean a long-term increase in their out-of-pocket drug costs. One consumer saw their cost for Cuprimine, a drug that treats Wilson's disease (an inherited malady that can affect the liver and nervous system), rise from $366 per month to more than $1,800. For retirees and other middle-income patients, Valeant's gain was their loss.[22]

Valeant defended its price increases on three grounds. Internally, the company noted that increases (often major) in price did not affect demand. A consultant's report on heart medication Nitropress noted that, "With roughly one year of data showing essentially

EXHIBIT 2   Valeant Pharmaceuticals, Selected Financial Data

	2015	2014 (restated)	2013	2012	2011	2010	2009	2008
Revenues								
Product sales	$ 10,292.20	$ 8,046.10	$ 5,640.30	$ 3,288.59	$ 2,255.05	$ 1,133.37	$ 789.03	$ 714.55
Other revenues	$ 154.30	$ 159.90	$ 129.30	$ 191.80	$ 208.04	$ 47.87	$ 31.40	$ 42.63
Selected Expenses								
Cost of goods sold	$ 2,531.60	$ 2,177.70	$ 1,846.30	$ 905.10	$ 683.75	$ 395.60	$ 204.31	$ 197.67
Cost of other revenues	$ 53.10	$ 58.40	$ 58.80	$ 64.60	$ 43.08	$ 10.15	$ 13.85	$ 23.03
Selling, general and administrative	$ 2,699.80	$ 2,026.30	$ 1,305.20	$ 756.10	$ 572.47	$ 276.55	$ 167.63	$ 188.92
Research and development	$ 334.40	$ 246.00	$ 156.80	$ 79.10	$ 65.69	$ 68.31	$ 47.58	$ 69.81
Restructuring, integration and other costs	$ 361.90	$ 381.70	$ 462.00	$ 267.10	$ 97.67	$ 140.84	$ 30.03	$ 70.20
Operating income (loss)	$ 1,527.40	$ 2,000.70	($ 409.50)	$ 79.70	($ 110.08)	$ 181.15	$ 181.15	$ 124.11
Interest income	$ 3.30	$ 5.00	$ 8.00	$ 6.00	$ 4.08	$ 1.29	$ 1.12	$ 9.40
Interest expense	($ 1,563.20)	($ 971.00)	($ 844.30)	($ 481.60)	($ 333.04)	($ 84.31)	($ 24.88)	($ 1.02)
Net income (loss) attributable to Valeant	($ 291.70)	$ 880.70	($ 866.10)	($ 116.00)	$ 159.56	($ 208.19)	$ 176.45	$ 199.90
Earnings (loss) per share for Valeant								
Basic	($ 0.85)	$ 2.63	($ 2.70)	($ 0.38)	$ 0.52	($ 1.06)	$ 1.11	$ 1.25
Diluted	($ 0.85)	$ 2.58	($ 2.70)	($ 0.38)	$ 0.49	($ 1.06)	$ 1.11	$ 1.25
Weighted-average common shares (in millions)								
Basic	342.70	335.40	321.00	305.40	304.65	195.81	158.23	159.73
Diluted	342.70	341.50	321.00	305.40	326.12	195.81	158.23	159.73
Selected Assets								
Current assets:								
Cash and cash equivalents	$ 597.30	$ 322.60	$ 600.34	$ 916.09	$ 164.11	$ 394.27	$ 114.46	$ 317.55
Accounts receivable	$ 2,686.90	$ 2,075.80	$ 1,184.76	$ 913.83	$ 569.27	$ 274.82	$ 112.16	$ 90.05
Inventories, net	$ 1,256.60	$ 889.20	$ 882.96	$ 531.25	$ 355.21	$ 229.58	$ 82.77	$ 59.56
Total current assets	$ 5,507.20	$ 4,131.70	$ 3,885.89	$ 2,777.45	$ 1,357.51	$ 1,020.16	$ 342.87	$ 490.36
Goodwill	$ 18,552.80	$ 9,361.40	$ 9,752.10	$ 5,141.36	$ 3,581.51	$ 3,001.38	$ 100.29	$ 100.29
Total assets	$ 48,964.50	$ 26,304.70	$ 27,970.79	$ 17,950.38	$ 13,108.12	$ 10,795.12	$ 2,059.29	$ 1,623.56
Selected Liabilities								
Current liabilities:								
Accounts payable	$ 433.70	$ 398.00	$ 326.97	$ 277.38	$ 157.62	$ 101.32	$ 72.02	$ 41.07
Total current liabilities	$ 5,312.60	$ 2,708.40	$ 2,512.39	$ 1,822.75	$ 924.27	$ 692.46	$ 249.15	$ 267.17
Long-term debt	$ 30,265.40	$ 15,228.00	$ 17,162.95	$ 10,535.44	$ 6,539.76	$ 3,478.37	$ 313.97	$ –
Total liabilities	$ 42,934.70	$ 20,903.00	$ 22,737.47	$ 14,232.98	$ 9,178.29	$ 5,884.02	$ 704.92	$ 421.97
Total equity	$ 5,911.00	$ 5,279.40	$ 5,233.32	$ 3,717.40	$ 3,929.83	$ 4,911.10	$ 1,354.37	$ 1,201.60
Total liabilities and equity	$ 48,964.50	$ 26,304.70	$ 27,970.79	$ 17,950.38	$ 13,108.12	$ 10,795.12	$ 2,059.29	$ 1,623.56

Source: Company 10K filings, various years.

EXHIBIT 3 Valeant Pharmaceuticals, Selected Acquisitions, 2008–2015

Year	Target	Purchase Price (millions)	Key Products
2008	Coria Laboratories	$ 95	Dermatology products
	Derma Tech (Australia)	$ 13	Dermatology products
2009	Dow Pharmaceutical Services	$ 285	Dermatology products
	Tecnofarma (Mexico)	$ 33	Branded/private label generics
	Laboratoire Dr. Renaud	$ 18	Dermatology/aesthetic products
2010	Aton Pharmaceuticals	$ 318	Ophthalmology
	Brazilian Generics Maker	$ 56	Dermatology products
	Biovail	Reverse Merger	Moves to Canada for tax breaks
2011	PharmaSwiss (Switzerland)	$ 481	Generic drug maker with markets in Eastern Europe
	Ortho Dermatologics	$ 345	Dermatology products, Retin-A Micro, Ertaczo, Renova
	AB Sanitas (Lithuania)	$ 500	Generics, plus dermatology and ophthalmology
	Inova (Australia)	$ 698	OTC and prescriptions in Australia, South Pacific, and Africa
	Afexa Life Science	$ 76	Cold and flu remedies
	Dermik	$ 425	Dermatology products, including BenzaClin and Sculptra
2012	Medicis Pharmaceutical	$ 2,600	Dermatology products
	Probiotica (Brazil)	$ 44	Sports nutrition
	Eyetech, Inc	$ 22	Ophthalmology biotech company
	Pedinol	$ 27	Podiatry specialty pharma
	AcneFree	$ 64	Dermatology products
	Orapharma	$ 312	Oral health including Arestin (antibiotic)
	Atlantis Pharma (Mexico)	$ 71	Generics, gastrointestinal, analgesics, and anti inflammatory
2013	Natur Produkt (Russia)	$ 180	Cough and cold medications
	Obagi Medical Products	$ 344	Dermatology products
	Bausch & Lomb	$ 8,600	Contact lenses
2014	Solta Medical	$ 250	Medical aesthetics
	PreCision Dermatology	$ 475	Dermatology products, including acne
2015	Salix Pharmaceuticals	$ 14,500	Gastrointestinal Medications
	Mercury Holdings (Cayman)	$ 800	Holding co for Amoun Pharma (Egypt)
	Sprout Pharmaceuticals	$ 1,000	Women's libido drug Addyi
	Brodalumab (from AstraZeneca)	$ 445	Psoriasis treatment
	Synergetics USA	$ 192.00	Eye surgery products
	Paragon vision services	undisclosed	Gas permeable contact lens products

Source: Casewriter research.

static volume performance after a substantial price increase (350%), [the consulting firm] believes pricing flexibility may still exist for the product up to the perceptual price point of $1,000 per vial. . . . With current WAC [Wholesale Acquisition Cost] pricing at $214 per vial, Nitropress is likely to still have flexibility by multiple orders of magnitude."[23] Nitropress had apparently not reached its economic price ceiling, where demand would begin to decrease.

Externally, Valeant claimed that its price increases were justified by the money saved from drug therapies versus hospitalization or other intensive treatments. Northern California's KQED reported on

EXHIBIT 4   Valeant Pharmaceuticals, Selected Drug Price Increases

Product	Initial Price	New Price	Percentage	Usage
Seconal	$ 1,500	$ 3,000	100%	Assisted suicide pill
Benzaclin	$ 150	$ 500	202%	Acne treatment
Nitropress	$ 258	$ 806	212%	Cardiac drugs from Salix Pharmaceuticals
Wellbutrin	$ 480	$ 1,400	190%	Antidepressant
Oxsoralen-Ultra	$ 1,227	$ 5,204	324%	Psoriasis treatment
DHE 45	$ 3,090	$ 14,000	356%	Migraine treatment
Retin-A micro	$ 175	$ 900	414%	Acne treatment
Isuprel	$ 4,489	$ 36,811	720%	Treats abnormal heart rhythm
Glumetza	$ 1,000	$ 10,000	900%	Diabetes treatment
Syprine	$ 1,395	$ 21,267	1,425%	Wilson's disease
Targetin	$ 1,687	$ 30,320	1,697%	Cutaneous T-cell lymphoma treatment
Carac	$ 159	$ 2,865	1,702%	Treats precancerous skin lesions actinic keratoses
Curprimine	$ 888	$ 26,189	2,849%	Used in treatment of Wilson's disease

Source: Casewriter research, various primary sources.

Valeant's price increase of Seconal, an assisted suicide drug: "'Valeant sets prices for drugs based on a number of factors,' the company said in a statement, including the cost of developing or acquiring the drug, the availability of generics, and the benefits of the drug compared with costly alternative treatments. 'When possible, we offer patient assistance programs to mitigate the effects of price adjustments and keep out-of-pocket costs affordable for patients.'"[24]

Those patient assistance programs represented the third element of Valeant's justification for its strategy. The company argued that few consumers bore the brunt of their price increases—most of the higher bills would be paid by third-party payers, either private health insurers or government agencies such as Medicare or Medicaid. Valeant's anti-depressant Wellbutrin provides an example. Patients who visited the Wellbutrin website learned that, depending on their insurance plan, they may pay between zero and $50 for "unlimited use." Doctors were told that if they prescribed Wellbutrin XL, and specified "no generic substitution" would find "no hassles and no need for call-backs—guaranteed. Your prescription decision is never questioned by the pharmacy."[25] Wellbutrin had been on the market for three decades and was available in generic form for about $30 per month. Valeant had increased the price 11 times to more than $1,400 a month. The drug's 2015 revenue was projected to top $300 million, double its 2013 level.[26]

THE FALLOUT OF VALEANT'S ACQUISITION STRATEGY

Valeant's drug pricing strategy came under criticism as the US presidential election heated up in the fall of 2015. Democratic candidate Bernie Sanders called for an investigation in August 2015, and Hillary Clinton followed in September. Her tweet pledged action around "outrageous price gouging" by pharmaceuticals and put investors in the sell mode. Valeant's shares, trading at more than $250 per share in August, began to fall. On September 28 alone, Valeant's shares dropped 16 percent.[27] Valeant had no response to these attacks. Just over two weeks later, on October 15, Australian hedge fund manager—and short seller of Valeant stock—John Hempton reported a questionable connection between Valeant and Philidor, a specialty pharmacy that distributed a number of Valeant products. Hempton claimed that Philidor was a "captive pharmacy" rather than an independent agent.[28] Information emerged during the next couple of weeks showing the Valeant staff, posing as Philidor employees, fraudulently wrote "dispense as written" on prescriptions to avoid generic substitution. They also deceived insurers by listing the drugs as being filled by smaller pharmacies in order to avoid attracting suspicion of too many high-priced prescriptions filled by Philidor.[29]

Valeant's response showed that the executive team and the board failed to understand the threat. The company initially (and emphatically) denied the charges of any improper affiliation with Philidor; however, the company later disclosed that it was, in fact, quite entwined with Philidor. Valeant blended Philidor's financials with its own, and the company had invested $100 million in the pharmacy. Valeant pledged to cut ties with Philidor and launched an internal investigation. Valeant held a conference call on October 30 to quell investor fears; instead, Valeant's poor handling of the call and the overall situation stoked investor concern. The stock dropped another 16 percent.[30] Problems with Philidor would affect the company's financial results and were responsible for the delay in Valeant releasing its 2015 annual report—a move that threatened to throw the company into default with its creditors. In late December of 2015, Valeant announced that Pearson would take a leave of absence because of a severe case of pneumonia; CFO Howard Shiller would assume Pearson's role and serve as temporary CEO. Robert Ingram would become board chairman and Valeant would finally split the roles of chairman and CEO. Pearson returned to work at the end of February 2016, but Ingram remained board chairman.[31] Throughout the winter of 2016, Valeant continued to exhibit a surprisingly nonchalant public attitude about its drug pricing troubles.

In February 2016, Clinton continued her assault: "[Valeant] is one of these companies that is absolutely gouging American consumers and patients," she said. "I'm going after them. We are going to stop this. This is predatory pricing. It is unjustified, it is wrong, and we're going to make sure it is stopped."[32] Between August 2015 and February 2016, Valeant's shares lost more than 60 percent of their value. As Valeant's troubles became front-page news, the US Congress and the US Department of Justice jumped on the bandwagon, the former calling for hearings and the latter opening an investigation into Valeant's pricing behavior.[33]

Other Valeant problems came to light. Its 2013 acquisition of Bausch & Lomb resulted in a commanding market position in the contact lens market. When Valeant purchased Paragon Vision Services in 2015, the company held an estimated 80 percent market share in orthokeratology "buttons," a key input to gas permeable hard contact lenses. The US Federal Trade Commission opened another investigation, and a contact lens manufacturer filed a class action suit to stop Valeant. Jan Svochak, president of the Contact Lens Manufacturers Association described the threat: "The issue is the orthokeratology market . . . We believe they have a monopoly situation in that market," Svochak said. "They significantly raised prices in the orthokeratology market, and they've also taken control of distribution channels." Valeant used the Paragon acquisition to raise prices for the buttons by more than 100 percent.

In a final blow to the now-beleaguered company, investors began to raise concerns about CEO Michael Pearson's compensation package. In 2014, activist investor William Ackman noted that Pearson held stock options in Valeant worth more than $1.3 billion, on top of $10.275 million in salary and bonus compensation for the year. Ackman noted that the pay plan would richly reward the Valeant team and Pearson for raising share price over the long term. The company's proxy statement included this description of the pay plan: "Our compensation philosophy is to align management's pay with long-term TSR [Total Shareholder Return] . . . We richly reward for outstanding TSR performance, but pay significantly less for below-average TSR performance." Executives would receive their shares only if the stock price hit an annual return of 15 percent; however, if the stock returned 45 percent, shares tripled. They quadrupled if the stock went up 60 percent. Valeant claimed its "executives could be among the best-paid in the industry."

Because of Valeant's collapse, neither Pearson nor other Valeant executives would receive stock compensation for the period of 2013–2016, as their options would not vest until 2017. The late-filed 2015 10K report included the board's investigation of the Philidor scandal. The board admitted "the company has determined that the tone at the top of the organization, with its performance-based environment, in which challenging targets were set and achieving those targets was a key performance expectation, was not effective in supporting the control environment . . . [and] may have been contributing factors resulting in the company's improper revenue recognition." The company also noted the burgeoning number of federal and state investigations underway; the SEC, the United States Senate, and state-level inquiries in Massachusetts, New York, New Jersey, and North Carolina.

Doctors, hospitals, and other activist groups began targeting the company. With its future revenue growth increasingly uncertain, investors jumped off the Valeant bandwagon and continued to sell their shares. With the prospect of increased scrutiny from stakeholders in the public and private sectors, Valeant's ability to find, acquire, and re-price "mispriced" drugs appeared in jeopardy. On March 21, Valeant announced that Pearson would be leaving the company and a search for a new CEO would begin immediately.[34] Valeant's stock finally hit bottom on March 31, tumbling to $26.30, down almost exactly 90 percent from its peak seven months earlier.

CONCLUSION

The shares had come back to Earth, leaving long-term holders of Valeant stock with a company valued at its 2010 price. Consumers who saw their prescription bills skyrocket were clearly worse off. Who were the real winners in Valeant's rise and fall? These and other questions gave Ingram pause as he considered how to work with the new CEO and directors Valeant named to its board. The investing community was waiting to see how new CEO Joe Papa would alter Valeant's strategy and lead the company toward a new future. As the board chairman, Ingram wanted to see Valeant return to profitability, but he also wanted to ensure that Valeant, and the board, proved more responsive to the charged stakeholder environment in the health care industry. Had Valeant simply transferred wealth from consumers to shareholders through its price increases? How should it set prices in the future to reflect the real value of the drugs but avoid excessive, "gouging" price increases? How should the board govern the company in order to avoid further fraud or accounting scandals? Finally, Ingram wondered about how to address Papa's compensation and other board-level policies: How could they incentivize long-term sustainable growth and build an ethical culture?

References

1 Material in this paragraph from "ICN Pharmaceuticals, Inc. History," Funding Universe, http://www.fundinguniverse.com/company-histories/icn-pharmaceuticals-inc-history/, accessed October 28, 2021.

2 Ibid.

3 Ibid.

4 Ibid.

5 "Company News: ICN Pharmaceuticals names chief to replace founder," *New York Times*, 21 June 2002, available at https://www.nytimes.com/2002/06/21/business/company-news-icn-pharmaceuticals-names-chief-to-replace-founder.html, accessed October 28, 2021.

6 M. Sheridan, "ICN Pharmaceuticals changes its name to Valeant Pharmaceuticals," ICIS, 12 November 2003. Available at https://www.icis.com/explore/resources/news/2003/11/12/534218/icn-pharma-changes-name-to-valeant-pharma-international/, accessed October 28, 2021.

7 Financial data for 2003 comes from Valeant's (ICN) 2003 10-K filing, available at www.edgar.sec.gov, search for Valeant Pharmaceuticals International.

8 Data from Merck's 2003 Annual Report, http://www.merck.com/finance/annualreport/ar2003/pdf/merck2003ar.pdf, accessed October 13, 2021.

9 S. Silcoff, "How Valeant Became Canada's Hottest Stock," *The Globe and Mail*, February 21, 2013, http://www.theglobeandmail.com/report-on-business/rob-magazine/how-valeant-became-canadas-hottest-stock/article8889241/?page=all, accessed October 13, 2021.

10 Ibid.

11 Ibid.

12 P. Jorda and E. Dey, "Drugmaker Biovail to Buy Valeant in $3.3 Billion Deal," Reuters, June 21, 2010, http://www.reuters.com/article/us-biovail-valeant-idUSTRE65K1LA20100621, accessed October 28, 2021.

13 Silcoff.

14 "Biovail to Merge with Valeant," *New York Times* (June 21, 2010), http://dealbook.nytimes.com/2010/06/21/biovail-to-merge-with-valeant/?_r=0, accessed October 28, 2021.

15 Jorda and Dey.

16 Ibid.

17 L. Lorenzetti, "Valeant Eases Up on Strategy to Buy Up 'Mispriced Drugs'," *Fortune* (October 19, 2015), http://fortune.com/2015/10/19/valeant-backs-down-drug-prices/, accessed October 13, 2021.

18 A. E. Caroll, "$2.6 Billion to Develop a Drug? New Estimate Makes Questionable Assumptions," *New York Times* (November 18, 2014), http://www.nytimes.com/2014/11/19/upshot/calculating-the-real-costs-of-developing-a-new-drug.html?_r=0, accessed October 13, 2021.

19 Ibid.

20 "Emails Reveal Turing, Valeant (VRX) Price Increases Were Basis for Revenue Growth," Biospace, February 3, 2016, http://www.biospace.com/News/emails-reveal-turing-valeant-price-increases-were/407561, accessed October 13, 2021.

21 S. Armour and J. Rockoff, "Valeant, Turing Boosted Drug Prices to Fuel Preset Profits," *Wall Street Journal* (February 2, 2016), http://www.wsj.com/articles/valeant-turing-boosted-drug-prices-to-fuel-preset-profits-1454445342, accessed October 13, 2021.

22 A. Pollack and S. Tavernise, "Valeant's Drug Price Strategy Enriches It, but Infuriates Patients and Lawmakers," *New York Times* (October 4, 2015), http://www.nytimes.com/2015/10/05/business/valeants-drug-price-strategy-enriches-it-but-infuriates-patients-and-lawmakers.html, accessed October 28, 2021.

23 Ibid.

24 L. Lopez, "Valeant Bought a Drug that Helps Terminally Ill People Die and Doubled the Price," *Business Insider* (March 23, 2016), http://www.businessinsider.com/valeant-seconal-price-increase-2016-3, accessed October 13, 2021.

25 Ibid.

26 N. Weinberg and R. Langreth, "How Valeant Tripled Prices, Doubled Sales of Flatlining Drug," *Bloomberg* (January 8, 2016), http://www.bloomberg.com/news/articles/2016-01-08/how-valeant-tripled-prices-doubled-sales-of-flatlining-old-drug, accessed October 13, 2021.

27 S. Gandel, "What Caused Valeant's Epic 90% Plunge," *Fortune* (March 20, 2016), http://fortune.com/2016/03/20/valeant-timeline-scandal/, accessed April 26, 2016.

28 S. Gandel, "Valeant: A Timeline of the Big Pharma Scandal," *Fortune* (October 31, 2015), http://fortune.com/2015/10/31/valeant-scandal/, accessed April 29, 2016.

29 J. Hempton, "Philidor 2.0: Valeant and Stephen King Play Chess with a Lot of Pharmacies," November 26, 2016, http://brontecapital.blogspot.com/2015/11/philidor-20-valeant-and-stephen-king.html, accessed October 13, 2021.

30 Gandel, "Valeant".

31 A. Pollack, "Valeant Pharmaceuticals Chief Returns from Medical Leave," *New York Times* (February 28, 2016), http://www.nytimes.com/2016/02/29/business/valeant-pharmaceuticals-j-michael-pearson-ceo.html?_r=0, accessed October 13, 2021.

32 D. Crow, "Price of Valeant Drug Singled Out by Clinton Rose 356% in a Year," *Financial Times*, https://www.ft.com/content/fff89b8e-c922-11e5-be0b-b7ece4e953a0, accessed October 28, 2021.

33 A. Pollack, "2 Valeant Dermatology Drugs Lead Steep Price Increases, Study Finds," *New York Times* (November 25, 2015), http://www.nytimes.com/2015/11/26/business/2-valeant-dermatology-drugs-lead-steep-price-increases-study-finds.html?_r=0, accessed October 13, 2021.

34 N. Vardi, "Mike Pearson Is on His Way Out of Valeant, Former CFO Refuses to Leave Board," *Forbes* (March 21, 2016), http://www.forbes.com/sites/nathanvardi/2016/03/21/mike-pearson-is-on-his-way-out-of-valeant-amid-more-drama-former-cfo-refuses-to-leave-board/#2c7f12525c1a, accessed October 13, 2021.

Culture and Ethical Leadership—Mary Barra at General Motors

Mary Barra left her office on the thirty-ninth floor of the Renaissance Center, a seven-building complex on the banks of the Detroit River that served as the headquarters of one of America's industrial titans, General Motors (GM). As she pushed the button to call the elevator, she reflected that it had been over seven years since she assumed the office of chief executive officer (CEO) in January of 2014. She had broken the glass ceiling in the male-dominated auto industry when she took the role. The past seven years had put her leadership style on display for the world. In her first weeks on the job, she faced her first crisis, an ignition switch problem that had cost over 120 lives and several hundred injuries. That event had tested her mettle, but it also allowed her to reorient the behemoth company and its over 200,000 worldwide employees toward an uncertain future.

Just before leaving the office, she had glanced at the annual report from GM's internal diversity, equity, and inclusion team (DE&I). The company had made strides in so many areas, but DE&I would require an ongoing effort. One element of the report stood out to her and was an issue near and dear to her heart: gender diversity. Female employment at GM lagged leaders in the industry, and the industry as a whole lagged the rest of corporate America. There was work to do. As she climbed aboard the elevator and began her descent, she wondered how she could leverage her past successes to help GM continue to become a global leader in ethical, sustainable business practices.

MARY BARRA: A BRIEF HISTORY

Barra was born on Christmas Eve of 1961 and she joined a GM family. Mary's father worked for the Pontiac division for thirty-nine years. Mary followed in his footsteps. She graduated from the General Motors Institute (Kettering University since 1985) with a degree in electrical engineering and went to work at a GM plant. Managers at GM identified her as a potential leader early in her career, and the company sent Mary for an MBA on a GM fellowship. She received her degree in 1990 from Stanford and returned to Michigan. The next twenty-years would see her manage several production operations and GM's human resources department. In 2011, she was appointed the head of GM's product portfolio.[1]

Barra had developed a unique leadership style in her more than three decades at GM. She led meetings that were models of efficiency. She gathered the relevant parties to make a decision, identified the critical issues, and invited a focused discussion to understand the situation and options. Mary had a reputation for making decisions and moving on, but those decisions relied heavily on others. Her attitude about being a manager was "My rules are your rules," and she managed by persuasion rather than fiat (exerting her authority). "The day they say, 'I'm doing it because Mary told me to do it' is the day I lose."[2]

Although she had worked at GM her entire career, she felt no inherent loyalty to the traditional ways of doing things at GM. Neither hierarchy nor precedent mattered to her. For example, as the head of GM's HR function, she cut through the bureaucratic fog to provide simple, actionable results. HR leaders from around the company were working to revise and update GM's ten-page dress code. Barra threw out the handbook and reduced the rules for on-the-job apparel to two words: "Dress appropriately."[3] She brought each of these skills with her when she assumed the role of CEO on January 15, 2014. A little over two weeks later, she would face her first crisis, one that had been brewing for almost fifteen years: a deadly problem with an ignition switch.

THE IGNITION SWITCH CRISIS

In 2001, GM engineers were hard at work designing a new model for the company's Saturn brand, the Ion. The car incorporated a newly designed ignition switch, an important part of powering and controlling many electronic systems in the car. Located in the steering column adjacent to the ignition lock cylinder (where the key is inserted and turned), the switch has several positions that power on or off different systems as the key is turned.[4]

The New GM Ignition Switch

The new GM switch was springier than it should be, which resulted in weaker tension on the ignition keys. If the key was jiggled or moved during travel, the switch moved from "run" to "accessory" mode, meaning that the vehicle's electrical systems, and even the engine, would cease working.[5] Engineers worked on the problem, but could find no easy solution. Exhibit 1 provides a general time line of the problem.

The Ion came on the market in 2003, and GM engineers believed that if the ignition key was changed to reduce the key from moving as much, the problem would be solved. The new switch was a component of the Chevy Bolt, introduced in 2004. Engineers for the Bolt soon discovered the same problem. One suggestion was to redesign the key head so that it would have less opportunity to move. That suggestion was rejected. In March of 2005, product leaders rejected a potential fix because it cost too much and would take too long to redesign. Part of the decision calculus may have been that in the same quarter, GM reported a loss of $1.1 billion.[6]

The ignition switch problem moved from an internal challenge to one with real-world consequences on July 29, 2005. Amber Marie Rose, sixteen and a Maryland resident, died when her Chevy Cobalt crashed into a tree and the airbags failed to deploy. In December of that year, GM notified dealers of the problem and recommended that they advise customers to remove "unessential items from their key chains."[7] Federal officials at the National Highway Transportation and Safety Administration would investigate complaints about the switch after three other people died that year but would find no link between the switch and the accidents.

As the number of crashes and fatalities from the ignition switch piled up, they were overshadowed by the financial problems at GM.

GM Ignition Switch Time Line, 2001–2014

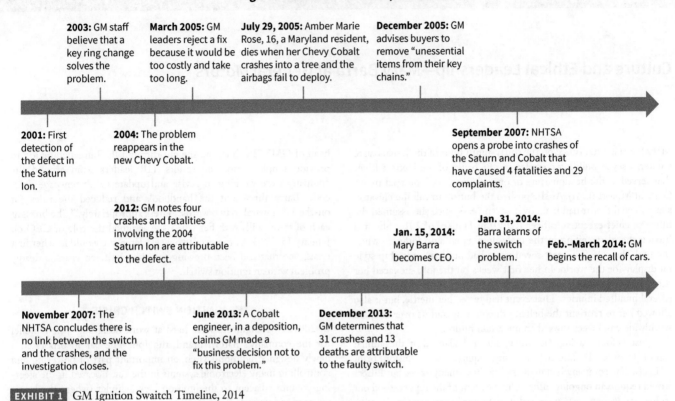

2003: GM staff believe that a key ring change solves the problem.

March 2005: GM leaders reject a fix because it would be too costly and take too long.

July 29, 2005: Amber Marie Rose, 16, a Maryland resident, dies when her Chevy Cobalt crashes into a tree and the airbags fail to deploy.

December 2005: GM advises buyers to remove "unessential items from their key chains."

2001: First detection of the defect in the Saturn Ion.

2004: The problem reappears in the new Chevy Cobalt.

September 2007: NHTSA opens a probe into crashes of the Saturn and Cobalt that have caused 4 fatalities and 29 complaints.

2012: GM notes four crashes and fatalities involving the 2004 Saturn Ion are attributable to the defect.

Jan. 15, 2014: Mary Barra becomes CEO.

Jan. 31, 2014: Barra learns of the switch problem.

Feb.–March 2014: GM begins the recall of cars.

November 2007: The NHTSA concludes there is no link between the switch and the crashes, and the investigation closes.

June 2013: A Cobalt engineer, in a deposition, claims GM made a "business decision not to fix this problem."

December 2013: GM determines that 31 crashes and 13 deaths are attributable to the faulty switch.

EXHIBIT 1 GM Ignition Swaitch Timeline, 2014

GM lost $3.2 billion in the second quarter of 2006 as it absorbed the costs of shrinking its workforce by 30,000 manufacturing employees. When the Great Recession hit in 2007 and 2008, new car sales plummeted. GM would lose $30.9 billion in 2008.[8] Through the close of 2008, company executives lobbied Congress for a financial bailout to save the company. The Bush administration provided $13.4 billion in funding through its Troubled Asset Relief Program (TARP); however, the infusion of cash still left GM in dire straits. On June 1, 2009, GM filed for bankruptcy protection, and the company exited bankruptcy on July 10, 2009, with the U.S. Treasury as its controlling shareholder. The government sold the last of its stake in late 2013.[9]

In June of 2013, a GM engineer for the Cobalt brand claimed in a deposition that GM made a "business decision not to fix this problem," which meant that GM may have decided to launch a vehicle it knew was defective. By December of 2013, the company would attribute the switch to thirty-one crashes and deaths. The failed switches would later be linked to as many as 124 deaths.[10] On the last day of January 2014, Mary Barra, still adjusting to her new role, would learn of the switch problem.

Mary Barra Responds to the Crisis

In a 2018 interview, Barra described the nature of the challenge she faced: "When you are in a crisis, it's not like you have perfect information on day one. In our situation specifically, we learned we had an issue, and we acted. But then there was a lot to unfold."[11]

She immediately pulled together a small team to manage the crisis. The team would meet each day for as few as twenty minutes to over two hours to handle the emerging crisis. Barra employed a tactic she'd seen used in the GM production process: a "read-across."

This protocol provided a structure through which the team looked beyond the source (the Ion) and looked for manifestations of the problem in other areas of the organization. To guide the efforts, Mary and the team relied on the company's core values: As events unfolded, Mary resolved to respond to the crisis "with an action plan based on our values of customer service and transparency."[12] The company would be open with regulators and the public. This represented a dramatic change in GM's typical behavior; indeed, from 2012 through 2014, "GM, through its agents and employees, concealed a potentially deadly safety defect from [the National Highway Safety and Traffic Administration] and the public."[13]

As the crisis unfolded, Mary spent many sleepless nights thinking "this just doesn't feel right" about one path of action or another. Barra recognized that transparency had an important corollary value: accountability for mistakes. To that end, she commissioned former U.S. Attorney Anton Valukas to conduct an independent investigation to get to the bottom of the problem. She recounted, "No, we're going to say we're sorry. . . . We're going to do an independent investigation. . . . We're going to release the independent investigation. . . ." She had been offered advice by "everyone," but in this case she went with her gut.[14]

During February and March of 2014, GM began to recall cars as the "read-across" process identified millions of affected vehicles. Over the next months and year, GM would recall 2.6 million cars with faulty ignition switches. The recall and switch replacement cost GM $2.8 billion.[15] GM would recall an additional 3 million cars for a wiring problem and 2.4 million more vehicles for faulty seatbelts and transmissions.[16] Over the next six years, the ignition switch scandal would cost $900 million in a criminal settlement to the U.S. Department of Justice (DOJ), $300 million to the New York Teachers fund for lost shareholder equity, $626 million for a settlement fund, and unrelated judgments of $275 million in 2015 and $120 million in 2020. Over 400 suits are still outstanding. That's a total of $2.2 billion, on top of the $2.8 billion to perform repairs.[17]

On March 17, 2014, Mary Barra issued a statement that "something went very wrong"[18] at GM and that "terrible things happened."[19] Valukas's investigation would come to the same conclusions and found "a pattern of incompetence and neglect" and "a pattern of management deficiencies and misjudgments"[20] at GM. Following the Valukas report, Barra disciplined five employees and fired fifteen more.[21] In September of 2015, GM agreed to pay $900 million to the DOJ as a part of a "deferred prosecution agreement," where the company avoided criminal prosecution. "We didn't do our jobs. . . . As part of our apology to the victims, we promised to take responsibility for our actions," Barra said, and "so we accept the penalties being announced today because they are part of being held accountable."[22]

MARY BARRA CHANGES GM AND ITS CULTURE

Barra worked hard to make sure GM would recover from the aftereffects of the ignition switch scandal, but her changes did not stop there. She wanted to ensure that the organizational culture and structure that led to the ignition switch crisis would change forever. She also realized that the current organization was losing in the marketplace, and that changing the ethical climate at GM could also change its business climate and culture. Exhibit 2 provides information about GM's business performance.

Remaking GM: Organizational Structure

Setting up an executive team to manage the crisis was an important first step that allowed Barra to work through the turbulent days of 2014. Eight of the fifteen employees Barra fired were company executives, and Barra remade her top leadership team. An outsider, former investment banker Dan Ammann, assumed the role of president, and Barra promoted Chuck Stevens from North American chief financial officer (CFO) to corporate CFO. She retained Mark Reuss as product chief, and the four would work over the next several months and years to transform GM.

Barra created a "speak up for safety" hotline to give employees a chance to speak up without involving management. GM had been a culture of confrontation and division for many years, and the hotline gave employees an anonymous way to report business or ethics concerns around product or workplace safety. She also created a product integrity team in 2014, with a goal to increase product quality and safety while products were still in the design stages, before problems got "baked in" to a new car's complex systems.[23] Barra noted that both of these steps would improve ethical *and* business performance: "The best time to solve a problem is the minute you know about it. Most problems don't get smaller with time."[24]

Barra and her team created a set of cross-functional "co-labs" across the organization. These teams brought people from different business functions (HR, finance, production, supply chain). The goal was to break down the bureaucracy and silos that existed within the company. From an ethics perspective, having a more diverse team in

EXHIBIT 2   General Motors Business Performance, 2015–2020

(All numbers in thousands)	2020	2019	2018	2017	2016	2015
Revenue by segment						
GM North America	$96,733	$106,366	$113,792	$111,345	$119,113	$106,744
GM International	$11,586	$ 1,611	$ 19,148	$ 21,920	$ 20,943	$ 22,970
GM Finance	$13,831	$ 14,554	$ 14,016	$ 12,151	$ 8,983	$ 5,867
EBIT—Adjusted						
GM North America	$ 9,071	$ 8,204	$ 10,769	$ 11,889	$ 12,388	$ 11,354
GM International	$ (528)	$ (202)	$ 423	$ 1,300	$ 767	$ 533
GM Finance	$ 2,702	$ 2,104	$ 1,893	$ 1,196	$ 763	$ 679
Wholesale Vehicles Sold						
GM North America	2,707	3,214	3,555	3,511	3,958	3,558
GM International	663	995	1,152	1,267	1,255	1,372
Market Share (Selected Markets and Vehicles)						
North America	16.5%	15.9%	16.2%	16.6%	16.6%	16.8%
China	11.6%	12.2%	13.7%	14.3%	13.8%	14.9%
Total Worldwide	8.7%	8.5%	8.9%	10.2%	10.8%	11.1%
U.S. Cars	7.1%	8.4%	10.7%	11.5%	12.9%	12.5%
U.S. Trucks	31.0%	29.7%	32.3%	26.4%	27.0%	27.2%

Source: GM 10-K filing, various years.

place would foster questions about safety or other concerns and would push for answers that went beyond an engineering mindset. She encouraged collaboration in the executive suite as well as on the shop floor. Each quarter, Barra hosted an offsite for her top sixteen reports. The topic of discussion was not strategy or product marketing; it was "transformational leadership." If GM produced better executive leaders who could work together, the rest of the organization was more likely to follow. HR chief John Quattrone explained, "Mary believes that if we change the behaviors [of top managers], people who work for us will see that and emulate it. There won't be this dysfunction that we had before."[25]

Mary drew from her experience with the dress code as she worked to push decision making down in the hierarchy and truly empower managers. She recalled that her "dress appropriately" simplification of the dress code has drawn blowback from, ironically, HR managers around the company. "They were concerned that, for example, employees would show up wearing T-shirts with inappropriate slogans or images," she later said. One manager was worried that employees would show up to important meetings wearing jeans; believing "dress appropriately" could be easily misconstrued. Barra called the manager directly and challenged him and his direct reports to formulate their own solution. They devised a simple, yet ingenious way to avoid problems: Employees would keep dress clothes in their lockers at work just in case important officials showed up for a meeting. Barra would later recount this as an "a-ha!" that guided her work to empower GM managers and employees after the crisis. "If they couldn't handle dress codes on their own, then what else couldn't they handle?" she said.[26] Her goal was to empower people to make decisions without a cumbersome set of rules.

Remaking GM: The Culture

At an internal town hall meeting in 2014, Barra told the GM family, "I never want to put this behind us. I want to put this painful experience permanently in our collective memories."[27] A natural human (and GM's historical default) impulse would be to find a quick solution that solved the immediate crisis, and then return to life as normal. Barra realized that the ignition switch problem provided her, and the company, an opportunity to do more than just apply a Band-Aid to the problem; they could truly change the cultural foundations at GM. She wanted to create a culture where ethical behavior would be the new default, a culture that emphasized "always doing the right thing, even when it's the hard thing."[28] The first step was to let people know that she had a clear set of values, the ones the company espoused, and she would work to make them real. She noted, "You get lots of conflicting advice from lots of sources during times like that, but if you have values and your teams aligned with them, that guides you on what to do."[29]

Another core element of the GM culture she worked to change was a mindset of turf battles and the logic that everything at GM was a zero-sum game. She hoped that many of the structural changes she initiated, particularly the co-lab teams and moves to empower decision making, would root out a culture of blame and bureaucracy and provide the fertile soil in which a culture of accountability, speed, and collaboration would grow. Accountability and collaboration would provide an antidote to poisoned ethical reasoning and behavior, and speed would help the company more effectively compete in its markets. "In this area of rapid transformation, you have to have a culture that's agile," she said. She also noted three years into the process that, "We still have a lot of work to do."[30]

A cultural flaw that the crisis exposed was a proclivity to think solely within the walls of the company and fail to account for customer needs and concerns. This had been a problem at GM for decades. A generation ago, GM workers would put coke bottles or screws inside the door panels of cars. The customer would hear the noise but never be able to figure out the source or fix it. The customer got a lousy car, but factory employees, in the culture of conflict at GM, saw this as another victory in its war with management.[31] That culture was slowly dying, and Barra wanted to replace its last vestiges with a future-oriented, nimble, and customer-focused culture. She emphasized the role of customers in ethics and business, "by listening carefully to their hopes, their concerns, and their expectations and then applying the talent and resources that we have, we can develop solutions that demonstrate that customers are truly at the center of everything we do."[32]

Moving GM Beyond the Scandal

Barra knew that creating a new GM was a longer journey than merely resolving the ignition switch crisis. It would be an evolution to "reimagine" GM.[33] She noted in 2016 that people shouldn't "confuse progress with winning, It's not like, 'Check, check, check, done.' It's, 'Okay, the table is barely set. This is a huge opportunity. So, what are we going to do?'" She knew that for GM to be all it could be, the company needed to win, and every GM employee would have to work hard. People's "best efforts" alone would not be enough to cut it. "Are you doing what you can?" she asked. "Or are you doing what it takes to *win*?"[34]

That drive to win led to a series of post-crisis strategic shifts to establish GM as a leader in creating a new, sustainable auto industry. In 2016, Barra announced that GM was moving into ride sharing, autonomous vehicles, and electric vehicles (EVs). In January, GM invested $500 million in ridesharing leader Lyft. GM created its "Express Drive" program that lets Lyft drivers rent GM cars at heavy discounts. Two weeks after announcing its investment in Lyft, Barra announced Maven, a new car-sharing service. GM purchased electric vehicle (EV) maker Cruise in March for $580 million, giving GM a presence in this market.[35] GM felt that it had much to offer these start-up companies. As Mike Ableson, head of GM's strategy group, said, "The Silicon Valley culture of developing fast and iterating fast can be a strength. But if you're going to put this stuff in production, sooner or later you've got to turn it into hardware at high volume. That's the Detroit side of the discussion."[36]

The transformation continued in 2017 with the adoption of a new vision, which was published the next year in the company's sustainability report: "Guided by the vision of a future with zero crashes, zero emissions, and zero congestion, the company is addressing societal and environmental challenges while transforming the future of mobility. By tackling these issues, General Motors has the potential globally each year to help save some of the 1.25 million lives lost in vehicle crashes; help eliminate the more than 2 billion metric tons of carbon dioxide from vehicle emissions; and reduce congestion, giving commuters back time otherwise spent in traffic."[37] In the United States, about 40,000 people die in traffic accidents annually, and 90 percent of those accidents involve human error. GM's investments in autonomous vehicles reflected the hope to dramatically reduce those numbers.

Electric vehicles would become the mechanism that would lead to zero emissions, and zero traffic congestion can be achieved with "a combination of autonomous and different modes of travel, not just the individual driving their vehicle, but ridesharing and car sharing." Designing cities differently may also be necessary. The new vision tied together each of these business moves, and Barra stated that "all of this we look at as General Motors' responsibility."[38]

She continued that theme of responsibility in 2019 as GM became one of 181 corporations to adopt the Business Roundtable's new "Statement on the Purpose of a Corporation" document.[39] On January 28, 2021, Barra announced that by 2035 GM would produce and sell only vehicles with "zero tailpipe emissions." This would make good on the promise of the vision, and it would transform GM and the automobile ecosystem further. Traditional auto jobs such as manufacturing, service, and repair technicians would give way to new jobs in battery manufacturing, mining, charging stations, and software development.[40]

THE NEXT CHALLENGE

As the elevator finished its downward journey and opened into the executive parking garage, Mary Barra felt satisfied with the work she had done; however, she knew that much work remained to be done to create a twenty-first-century automaker, one that was ethical, profitable, and sustainable. She reminded herself of a comment she had made as she approached her first anniversary at GM's helm. "We're improving, but we have a lot of work to go," she had said.[41] The next challenge was a set of reports in her briefcase. Exhibit 3 provides some of this important data. Although GM had made many strides, the company lagged behind both the industry and American industry in gender diversity. Gender diversity was not like the ignition switch scandal: It was not a "bet the company" crisis that allowed her to make sweeping changes at GM. Gender diversity was an ongoing problem. She cared deeply about this issue, and she wanted to create opportunities for every woman at GM to reach her full potential. As she climbed into her car, she sent herself a quick text to think about over the weekend: "How can I use my position as a female CEO to help improve gender diversity at GM and in the auto industry? How can I leverage what I've done so far at GM to improve gender diversity?"

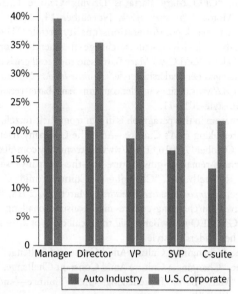

Percentage of U.S. corporate executives who are women vs. percentage of auto industry executives

Source: Data from USA Today article.

EXHIBIT 3 Statistics on Women in the Auto Industry (From *USA Today* article)

References

[1] Alex Taylor, "Mary Barra: GM's next CEO," *Fortune*, December 17, 2012, https://web.archive.org/web/20131214071920/http://management.fortune.cnn.com/2012/12/17/gm-mary-barra/.

[2] Taylor, "Mary Barra: GM's next CEO."

[3] Taylor, "Mary Barra: GM's next CEO."

[4] Your Mechanic, "Symptoms of a bad or failing ignition switch: Here's what you should be looking for," *Autoblog*, January 11, 2016, https://www.autoblog.com/2016/01/11/symptoms-of-a-bad-or-failing-ignition-switch/.

[5] Tanya Basu, "Timeline: A History Of GM's Ignition Switch Defect," NPR, March 31, 2014, https://www.npr.org/2014/03/31/297158876/timeline-a-history-of-gms-ignition-switch-defect.

[6] Basu, "Timeline: A History Of GM's Ignition Switch Defect."

[7] Basu, "Timeline: A History Of GM's Ignition Switch Defect."

[8] Dan Bigman, "How General Motors Was Really Saved: The Untold True Story Of The Most Important Bankruptcy In U.S. History," *Forbes*, November 18, 2013, https://www.forbes.com/sites/danbigman/2013/10/30/how-general-motors-was-really-saved-the-untold-true-story-of-the-most-important-bankruptcy-in-u-s-history/?sh=6d69b627eea2.

[9] Basu, "Timeline: A History Of GM's Ignition Switch Defect."

[10] David Muller, "In ignition switch debacle, GM's Mary Barra tells employees: 'We didn't do our jobs'," Michigan Live, last updated January 20, 2019, https://www.mlive.com/auto/2015/09/in_ignition_switch_debacle_gms.html.

[11] "How GM's Mary Barra Drives Value," Knowledge@Wharton, May 3, 2018, https://knowledge.wharton.upenn.edu/article/how-gms-mary-barra-drives-value/.

[12] "How GM's Mary Barra Drives Value."

[13] Muller, "In ignition switch debacle, GM's Mary Barra tells employees: 'We didn't do our jobs'."

[14] "How GM's Mary Barra Drives Value."

[15] Chris Isidore, "GM's total recall cost: $4.1 billion," CNN Business, February 4, 2015, https://money.cnn.com/2015/02/04/news/companies/gm-earnings-recall-costs/index.html.

[16] "GM: Steps to a recall nightmare," CNN Money, July 2014, https://money.cnn.com/infographic/pf/autos/gm-recall-timeline/index.html.

[17] Clifford Ativeh, "GM, After Six-Year Battle, Settles Another Ignition-Switch Lawsuit for $120 Million," *Car and Driver*, March 28, 2020, https://www.caranddriver.com/news/a31965015/gm-settles-lawsuit-ignition-switch-car-values/.

[18] Basu, "Timeline: A History Of GM's Ignition Switch Defect."

[19] Chris Isidore, "GM's total recall cost: $4.1 billion."

[20] Muller, "In ignition switch debacle, GM's Mary Barra tells employees: 'We didn't do our jobs'."

[21] Chris Isidore, "GM's total recall cost: $4.1 billion."

[22] Both quotes are from Muller, "In ignition switch debacle, GM's Mary Barra tells employees: 'We didn't do our jobs.'"

[23] Jill Jusko, "CEO Mary Barra is Driving Culture Change at General Motors," *Industry Week*, November 14, 2014, https://www.industryweek.com/operations/quality/article/21964120/ceo-mary-barra-is-driving-culture-change-at-general-motors.

[24] Richard Feloni, "GM CEO Mary Barra said the recall crisis of 2014 forever changed her leadership style," *Business Insider*, November 14, 2018, https://www.businessinsider.com/gm-mary-barra-recall-crisis-leadership-style-2018-11.

[25] All information in this paragraph is drawn from Rick Tetzeli, "Mary Barra Is remaking GM's Culture—And The Company Itself," *Fast Company*, October 17, 2016, https://www.fastcompany.com/3064064/mary-barra-is-remaking-gms-culture-and-the-company-itself.

[26] Andrew R. McIlvaine, "Changing a Culture Amid Constant Challenge," *Human Resource Executive*, March 26, 2018, https://hrexecutive.com/changing-culture-amid-constant-challenge/.

[27] Feloni, "GM CEO Mary Barra said the recall crisis of 2014 forever changed her leadership style."

[28] McIlvaine, "Changing a Culture Amid Constant Challenge."

[29] McIlvaine, "Changing a Culture Amid Constant Challenge."

[30] Tetzeli, "Mary Barra Is remaking GM's Culture—And The Company Itself."

[31] Ira Glass (interviewer), NUMMI, (2010), *This American Life*, March 26, 2010, https://www.thisamericanlife.org/403/nummi-2010.

[32] Jusko, "CEO Mary Barra is Driving Culture Change at General Motors."

[33] Tetzeli, "Mary Barra Is remaking GM's Culture—And The Company Itself."

[34] Tetzeli, "Mary Barra Is remaking GM's Culture—And The Company Itself."

[35] Tetzeli, "Mary Barra Is remaking GM's Culture—And The Company Itself."

[36] Tetzeli, "Mary Barra Is remaking GM's Culture—And The Company Itself."

[37] GM's Vision Drives Value for the Company, Communities and Future Mobility, GM Corporate Newsroom, press Release, June 12, 2018, https://media.gm.com/media/us/en/gm/news.detail.html/content/Pages/news/us/en/2018/jun/0612-sustainability.html.

[38] "How GM's Mary Barra Drives Value."

[39] Business Roundtable Redefines the Purpose of a Corporation to Promote 'An Economy That Serves All Americans'," August 19, 2019, https://www.businessroundtable.org/business-roundtable-redefines-the-purpose-of-a-corporation-to-promote-an-economy-that-serves-all-americans.

[40] Neal E. Boudette and Coral Davenport, "G.M. Will Sell Only Zero-Emission Vehicles by 2035," *New York Times*, January 28, 2021, https://www.nytimes.com/2021/01/28/business/gm-zero-emission-vehicles.html.

[41] Jusko, "CEO Mary Barra is Driving Culture Change at General Motors."

Global Ethics—Ethical Challenges for Apple in China

Tim Cook settled into his seat and prepared for the fight from Apple's production facility in Austin, Texas, to company headquarters in Cupertino, California. Cook, Apple's chief executive officer (CEO), had just toured the facility with an eye toward expanding its production capabilities. The past week had been a difficult one for Cook. On May 3, the company's dispute with Epic Games went to trial. Epic was suing Apple over the exorbitant fees it earned from developers on its App Store.[1] Just three days earlier on April 30, the European Union's competition commission charged Apple with antitrust violations based on the same fee structure.[2] All this happened on the heels of the company reporting record revenue for the quarter just ended.[3] The year 2021 was proving to be a wild ride for Mr. Cook and his company.

Cook's trip to Austin was unrelated to these current challenges. The long-planned trip marked the beginning of a longer, more important question for Apple and Cook. He had come to Apple in 1998 to help Steve Jobs build a world-class supply chain, one that matched Apple's world-class product innovations. Apple now assembled essentially 100 percent of its products in China, with the majority of that production being done by its contract partner Foxconn. That supply chain had been built because it made economic sense for Apple. Apple's involvement in China had opened the company to criticism of its ethical practices (critics would say the lack of ethical practices) in the country. Cook, and many others in the Western world, hoped that the economic, political, and social benefits of trade would empower Chinese workers and citizens, encourage the evolution of democratic political institutions, open borders, and reduce barriers to the flow of goods and services across borders. As of 2021, that hoped had dimmed.

Cook pulled out his iPad and jotted down several questions: Over the longer term, should Apple continue its reliance on China for manufacturing? Could the company ever resolve some of its ethical challenges in the country? Should Apple reduce its manufacturing footprint in China? If so, by how much? Where should the company begin to establish a new manufacturing hub? His mind full of difficult questions, Cook set his iPad down and looked out to see the beautiful Texas prairies below him.

Apple Inc.

Steve Jobs and Steve Wozniak formed the partnership that would eventually become Apple on April 1, 1976. The young entrepreneurs hoped to capitalize on their newest product, a personal computer they dubbed the Apple I. The company continued to innovate, and in 1984 it revolutionized personal computing with the introduction of the Macintosh, a ground-breaking machine with a sleek design, the first graphical user interface (GUI), TrueType fonts, and a "closed" architecture that featured only Apple software and hardware. That closed architecture represented a barrier to imitation, and it allowed the company to capture all the value added in its creation. With all of its innovation, the Mac sold at a hefty price premium over the then dominant IBM personal computer (PC).

Jobs had proven himself to be an adept designer and visionary, but he also was difficult to work with. He was forced out of the company in 1985. Over the next twelve years, the company would see John Sculley, Michael Spindler, and Gil Amelio sit in the CEO's chair and preside over the fall of a once innovative giant.[4] The company lost market leadership and become a niche player in education and desktop publishing, and its overall PC market share fell to 4 percent.

Jobs returned to Apple in 1996, when Apple bought his company NeXT. Under his leadership, the company produced a series of ground-breaking, game-changing products: the iMac, a redesigned and improved PC, in 1998, a new retail concept known as the Apple Store in 2000, the iPod in 2001, the iTunes store in 2002, the iPhone in 2007, and the iPad in 2010. Each of these products or services echoed the state-of-the-art Macintosh and each commanded a hefty price premium in the market.

In 1998, Jobs realized that innovative products would only be part of the Apple story; the other part would be exceptional, world-class manufacturing. To design and implement his vision, he hired a thirty-seven-year-old supply chain manager from Compaq named Tim Cook. Cook, an Alabama native with degrees from both Auburn (industrial engineering) and Duke (MBA), became a fixture in Apple's rise, initially by reducing the number of suppliers—from one hundred to twenty-four—and inventory stocks from two months to six days.[5] Early in his tenure, Cook saw the potential of China as a manufacturing and assembly center and set about building a world-class supply chain and manufacturing operation there.

During Jobs's second tenure at Apple, the company's stock moved from a low of $3.56 in 1997 to a high of $51.39 in 2011. The stock experienced two 2-for-1 stock splits in 2001 and 2005. The stock split 7-for-1 in June of 2014 and 4-for-1 in August of 2020.[6] One hundred shares purchased in 1997 for $356 were worth $148,445 in May of 2021, for a compound annual growth rate of 28.58 percent. In May of 2021, Apple had a market capitalization of $92.2 trillion.[7] Apple's brand equity had risen in similar fashion. Exhibit 1 displays Apple's current brand equity versus that of other prominent technology companies. Exhibits 2, 3, and 4 provide selected financial performance data for the company.

Apple's World-Class Supply Chain

Exhibit 5 provides a visual representation of Apple's global supply chain. Design, engineering, sales coordination, and overall administration were managed from the company's California headquarters. Apple sourced raw materials and intermediate components from several countries and regions throughout the world. For example, in a recent trade dispute, Apple had written then U.S. Trade Representative Robert Lighthizer that Apple's supply network in the United States accounted for over two million American jobs, and the company had committed to direct contributions to the U.S. economy of $350 billion between 2018 and 2023. The company spent about $60 billion in support of its U.S. suppliers in 2017.[8] The letter noted Apple was the largest corporate payer of U.S. income

EXHIBIT 1 InterBrand Best Brands 2020 Rankings, technology companies

Global Ranking	Name	Brand Value (millions)	Change from 2019
1	Apple	$322,999	+38%
2	Amazon	$200,687	+60%
3	Microsoft	$166,001	+53%
4	Google	$165,444	–1%
5	Samsung	$ 62,289	+2%
12	Intel	$ 36,971	–8%
13	Facebook	$ 35,178	–12%
14	IBM	$ 34,885	–14%

Source: Interbrand, https://interbrand.com/best-global-brands/?filter-brand-sector=.

taxes and paid billions more in state and local property, sales, and employment taxes.[9]

The company sourced other components from a number of European, Asian, and Chinese companies. Apple differed from a typical electronics company in that it often invested in machinery and other production-related costs to support its high-volume suppliers. It also made firm commitments to its supply partners for future orders, which facilitated dedicated investments by suppliers to meet strict demands for quality. In return, suppliers provided Apple with cost information about their products. Because of its huge volumes, Apple became the dominant customer for many of these suppliers, as shown in the following example:

> Apple struck a deal with GT Advanced Technologies, Inc., a maker of furnace equipment that is used to produce sapphire materials that cover smartphone lenses and home buttons. Apple received an exclusivity agreement from GT Advanced for the furnaces in exchange for making a pre-payment of $578 million. GT Advanced said it would repay Apple back

EXHIBIT 2 Apple, Inc. Selected Financial Data (millions)

	2020	2019	2018	2017	2016
Net sales:					
Products	$220,747	$213,883	$225,847	$196,534	$ 191,291
Services	$ 53,768	$ 46,291	$ 39,748	$ 32,700	$ 24,348
Total net sales	$274,515	$260,174	$265,595	$229,234	$ 215,639
Cost of sales:					
Products	$151,286	$144,996	$148,164	$126,337	
Services	$ 18,273	$ 16,786	$ 15,592	$ 14,711	
Total cost of sales	$169,559	$161,782	$163,756	$141,048	$ 131,376
Net income	$ 57,411	$ 55,256	$ 59,531	$ 48,351	$ 45,687
Earnings per share:					
Basic	$ 3.31	$ 11.97	$ 12.01	$ 9.27	$ 8.35
Diluted	$ 3.28	$ 11.89	$ 11.91	$ 9.21	$ 8.31
Cash dividends declared per share	$ 0.795	$ 3.00	$ 2.72	$ 2.40	$ 2.18
Total cash, cash equivalents and marketable securities	$191,830	$205,898	$237,100	$268,895	$ 237,585
Total assets	$323,888	$338,516	$365,725	$375,319	$ 321,686
Non-current portion of term debt $	$ 98,667	$ 91,807	$ 93,735	$ 97,207	$ 75,427
Other non-current liabilities	$ 54,490	$ 50,503	$ 48,914	$ 44,212	$ 39,986

Source: 2019, 2016 10-K.

EXHIBIT 3   Apple, Inc. Sales by Category (millions)

	2020	2019	2018	2017	2016
Net sales by category:					
iPhone	$ 137,781	$ 142,381	$ 164,888	$ 139,337	$ 136,700
Mac	$ 28,622	$ 25,740	$ 25,198	$ 25,569	$ 22,831
iPad	$ 23,724	$ 21,280	$ 18,380	$ 18,802	$ 20,628
Wearables, Home and Accessories	$ 30,620	$ 24,482	$ 17,381	$ 12,826	$ 11,132
Services	$ 53,768	$ 46,291	$ 39,748	$ 32,700	$ 24,348
Total net sales	$ 274,515	$ 260,174	$ 265,595	$ 229,234	$ 215,639

Source: 2019, 2016 10-K.

EXHIBIT 4   Apple, Inc. Sales by Geography (millions)

	2020	2019	2018	2017	2016
Americas:					
Net sales	$ 124,556	$ 116,914	$ 112,093	$ 96,600	$ 86,613
Operating income	$ 37,722	$ 35,099	$ 34,864	$ 30,684	$ 28,172
Europe:					
Net sales	$ 68,640	$ 60,288	$ 62,420	$ 54,938	$ 49,952
Operating income	$ 22,170	$ 19,195	$ 19,955	$ 16,514	$ 15,348
Greater China:					
Net sales	$ 40,308	$ 43,678	$ 51,942	$ 44,764	$ 48,492
Operating income	$ 15,261	$ 16,232	$ 19,742	$ 17,032	$ 18,835
Japan:					
Net sales	$ 21,418	$ 21,506	$ 21,733	$ 17,733	$ 16,928
Operating income	$ 9,279	$ 9,369	$ 9,500	$ 8,097	$ 7,165
Rest of Asia Pacific:					
Net sales	$ 19,593	$ 17,788	$ 17,407	$ 15,199	$ 13,654
Operating income	$ 8,808	$ 6,055	$ 6,181	$ 5,304	$ 4,781
	2020	**2019**	**2018**	**2017**	**2016**
Segment operating income	$ 91,240	$ 85,950	$ 90,242	$ 77,631	$ 74,301
Research and development expense	$(18,752)	$(16,217)	$(14,236)	$(11,581)	$(10,045)
Other corporate expenses, net	$ (6,200)	$ (5,803)	$ (5,108)	$ (4,706)	$ (4,232)
Total operating income	$ 66,288	$ 63,930	$ 70,898	$ 61,344	$ 60,024
	2020	**2019**	**2018**	**2017**	**2016**
Net sales:					
U.S.	$ 109,197	$ 102,266	$ 98,061	$ 84,339	$ 75,667
China (1)	$ 40,308	$ 43,678	$ 51,942	$ 44,764	$ 46,349
Other countries	$ 125,010	$ 114,230	$ 115,592	$ 100,131	$ 93,623
Total net sales	$ 274,515	$ 260,174	$ 265,595	$ 229,234	$ 215,639

Source: 2019, 2016 10-K.

Supply Chain Map of Apple Inc.

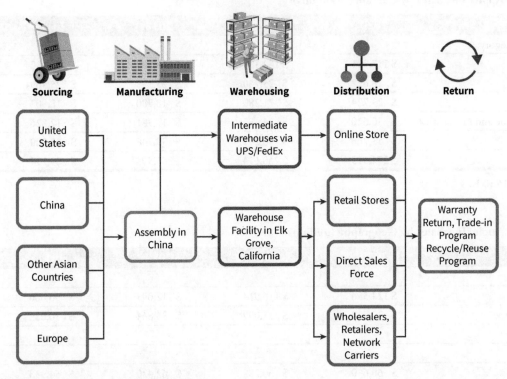

Source: Sourced from supplychain247.com.

EXHIBIT 5 Supply Chain Map of Apple Inc.

over five years, starting in 2015. The deal has "limited our ability to take additional" business, Thomas Gutierrez, GT Advanced's CEO, said in a conference call with analysts.[10]

Raw materials and inputs often "hopscotched" around the globe for processing into subcomponents at several locations, and each of those subcomponents eventually ended up in China at one of two primary final assemblers, Hon Hai Precision Industry Co., Ltd. (also known as Foxconn), and Pegatron, another Taiwan-based manufacturer. Foxconn was by far the largest assembler of iPhones at more than 50 percent; Pegatron produced about 30 percent of iPhones sold.[11] Moving those subcomponents around the world and within China required a complex mix of physical infrastructure (airports, warehouses, roads) and logistics partners, from packers to security teams to truck drivers. Apple's supply chain represented a global ecosystem working in finely tuned harmony to produce and bring to market hundreds of millions of iPhones, iPads, Mac computers, and other accessories.

Foxconn, as the largest producer of Apple products, ran its own ecosystem at its facilities in China, exemplified by its largest facility in Zhengzhou. Dubbed "iPhone City," the sprawling campus of a dozen factories and numerous support buildings was home to 350,000 employees, just over a fourth of the company's 1.3 million workers in China (90% of its worldwide workforce was located in China). The campus extended over two square miles.

Foxconn was China's largest exporter, accounting for 4.2 percent of the country's exports, and authorities received value-added-tax (VAT) payments on Apple products before they moved around the world. Foxconn and other Apple manufacturers were seen as central

to the Chinese government's "Made in China 2025" campaign for economic growth.[12] Both China and Apple benefited from the company's focus on the country.

The Foxconn network provided more than just final assembly of Apple products; the company had its own network of dedicated suppliers that provided critical inputs to the final product. Apple learned this in 2012 when the company wanted to move some Mac production to its Austin, Texas, facility. The company could bring most components to Texas; however, the company had no supplier that could produce customized miniature screws needed for final assembly. Foxconn had a dedicated, high-volume manufacturing partner that could produce tens of thousands of screws in custom sizes on short notice. Apple's Texas supplier could produce at most 1,000 screws per day. In order to produce Macs in Texas, Apple imported screws from China.[13]

The Foxconn and Pegatron networks drew from and included more than just production employees and logistics partners. They included knowledge workers as well. As Tim Cook noted during a conference in China: ". . . the skill here is just incredible. . . . In the United States, you could have a meeting of tooling engineers and I'm not sure we could fill the room," he said. "In China, you could fill multiple football fields."[14]

Foxconn built on huge tracks of land, and their factories and infrastructure underpinned a network of suppliers, developers, and other businesses that supported the core product. For example, their proposed factory in Wisconsin would build 8,000 LCD screens and support a community of glass panel makers, component suppliers, app developers, and traditional logistics companies to move products in, around, and from Racine as well as services such as restaurants, laundromats to support its large workforce.[15] Foxconn's plant in Wisconsin featured an initial $10 billion investment, and that would likely be matched or exceeded by other supply chain partners in and around the new facility.

In addition to building manufacturing facilities, many of Foxconn and Apple's global logistics partners (DHL, FedEx, UPS) built world-class, massive distribution centers in these communities. Analyst Jason Jing noted that, "In September [of 2011], DHL also came in big time to Zhengzhou, announcing the creation of what it claims will be one of its five largest logistics bases in China. UPS, FedEx, and TNT are also present there."[16]

Those logistics bases proved important for two reasons. First, as Exhibit 5 shows, Apple never took physical possession of iPhones and other products ordered over the Web. FedEx, UPS, and other shipping partners hold and deliver that inventory. Second, those companies shipped product to the United States and other destinations on their own aircraft. "FedEx ships Apple handsets to the United States mainly using Boeing 777s. . . . Those planes can make the fifteen-hour flight from China to the main U.S. hub for freight shipments in Memphis, Tennessee, without refueling."[17]

Ethical Problems in China

Apple faced numerous complaints over the years that the company earned profits on the backs of exploited labor and was not concerned about the environmental impacts of its operations. In 2006, the British publication *Mail on Sunday* wrote that Foxconn paid assembly workers at its Longhua plant as little as £27 (about $54) per month. Employees at the facility in Suzhou, Shanghai, earned £54 per month (about $110), and these employees paid about one-half of their salaries for lodging and food in company dormitories.[18] The average wage in China for manufacturing employees working in urban areas for that year was $1.56 an hour.[19] Employees rarely worked a typical eight-hour shift; with overtime, the more typical workday was eleven to thirteen hours, six days a week.[20] In 2010, conditions at Longhua induced fourteen suicides at the huge plant, and officials talked another twenty people down from the tall dormitories.[21]

Foxconn, and by implication Apple, experienced constant criticism over its treatment of workers, including hiring an inordinate number of temporary workers, withholding promised bonuses, and failing to provide adequate safety training.[22] Critics accused Apple of turning a blind eye to many of these violations and profiting from its assembly partners exploiting workers. The violations were abetted by an illiberal political system that neglected worker concerns and provided little avenue for dissent or protest to change conditions. Signs outside the Longhua facility, for example, informed visitors that, "This factory area is legally established with state approval. Unauthorized trespassing is prohibited. Offenders will be sent to police for prosecution!"[23]

The provincial government of Henan province, one of China's historically poorest regions, provided over $600 million in 2010 to get another Foxconn campus up and running. The province continued to support Foxconn with tax incentives and infrastructure development, including the construction of power plants to keep the facility running. Henan also enforced quotas for employees that local villages and cities must make available to Foxconn.[24] Some considered these quotas forced labor requirements, which contributed to the criticism of Apple's operations in a country with little respect for human rights. Said one Chinese activist, "Without China, Apple wouldn't be the company it is today. No other country can provide labor so cheaply and make its products so quickly."[25]

Apple responded to the challenges at Foxconn by creating a supplier code of conduct in 2015. The code states:

Apple is committed to the highest standards of social and environmental responsibility and ethical conduct. Apple's suppliers are required to provide safe working conditions, treat workers with dignity and respect, act fairly and ethically, and use environmentally responsible practices wherever they make products or perform services for Apple. Apple requires its suppliers to operate in accordance with the principles in this Apple Supplier Code of Conduct ("Code") and in full compliance with all applicable laws and regulations. This Code goes beyond mere compliance with the law by drawing upon internationally recognized standards to advance social and environmental responsibility. When differences arise between standards and legal requirements, the stricter standard shall apply, in compliance with applicable law.[26]

While the code created strong incentives for compliance, critics noted that Apple absolved itself of direct responsibility for the ethical violations and pushed the responsibility to their suppliers.[27] Given the scale and scope of Apple's investments in China, how firm could the company afford to be in enforcing its code?

That scale caused problems in China beyond issues with labor; analysts had also tracked increases in air pollution around Zhenghou's "iPhone City" to the release of the iPhone 12 in the fall of 2020. Morgan Stanley tracked the ramp-up in production with increases in atmospheric nitrogen dioxide, a molecule that decreases crop yields and becomes acid rain. Apple's Chinese factories, like most of the country's industrial base, ran on fossil fuels.[28] In 2018, Apple and ten of its largest suppliers agreed to invest $300 million by 2022 to generate one gigawatt of electricity through renewable sources.[29] One gigawatt of electricity would power 300,000 homes. China currently had 2,200 gigawatts of generating capacity, and one gigawatt would represent less than 0.045 percent of China's power.[30] Given that Apple accounted for 4.2 percent of Chinese exports, critics wondered if this investment was more symbolic than substantive.

Given the complexity and sophistication of its operations in China, moving production to other countries would be an endeavor fraught with difficulties. "'It is nearly impossible to replicate the ecosystem we have in China quickly,' says Jean-Frederic Kuentz, a senior partner at McKinsey. 'The first problem is that there is not enough manpower. The second is the network of suppliers—panel makers, molding companies, component makers. It is a big, big headache.'"[31] Analysts predicted it would take Apple at least two to three years, and billions in invested capital, to begin to replicate "iPhone City" somewhere else on the planet.

Cook had spent the better part of twenty years developing, implementing, and perfecting a best-in-class global manufacturing and supply chain. If not for ethical concerns, there would be little economic reason to question the value of his baby and consider moving some of that production out of China.

Cook's Questions

As his plane approached the San Jose airport, Tim Cook reopened his iPad and pondered the questions he'd written earlier. After thinking through the issues, he had basically the same questions as he wrote at the beginning of his flight. He knew that because private activists and government regulators had increased their scrutiny of tech companies, he needed to think seriously about Apple's involvement in China.

Were the codes of conduct and investments in environmental remediation sufficient? If not, how could they be strengthened? Should he begin to dismantle his supply chain baby and seek additional markets for assembly? If so, how much should he move, and where should Apple go? As he was thinking long term, he jotted down one more question:

Over the long term, what, if any, considerations should the company take when doing business in politically illiberal countries, ones without many protections for workers and the environment as well as those that limit many freedoms he took for granted? He made a note to contact several consultants to get a variety of opinions, options, and scenarios.

References

[1] Sarah E. Needleman, "Epic Games CEO Slams Apple's Fees as Unfair on Trial's First Day," *Wall Street Journal*, last updated May 4, 2021, https://www.wsj.com/articles/apple-and-fortnite-maker-epic-games-to-square-off-in-court-11620034202.

[2] Sam Schechner, "EU Charges Apple With App Store Antitrust Violations in Spotify Case," *Wall Street Journal*, last updated April 30, 2021, https://www.wsj.com/articles/apple-faces-eu-antitrust-charges-over-app-store-payments-in-spotify-case-11619777595.

[3] Apple Newsroom, "Apple Reports Second Quarter Results," press release, April 28, 2021, https://www.apple.com/newsroom/2021/04/apple-reports-second-quarter-results/.

[4] Walter Isaacson, 2011, Steve Jobs, New York: Simon and Schuster, 296.

[5] Walter Isaacson, 2011, Steve Jobs, New York: Simon and Schuster, 360–361.

[6] "Investor Relations: FAQ," Apple, accessed September 9, 2021, https://investor.apple.com/faq/default.aspx#:~:text=back%20to%20top-,How%20many%20times%20has%20Apple's%20stock%20split%3F,%2C%20and%20June%2016%2C%201987.

[7] "Y-Charts," Apple Inc., https://ycharts.com/companies/AAPL/market_cap.

[8] Jack Nicas, "A Tiny Screw Shows Why iPhones Won't Be 'Assembled in USA'," *New York Times*, January, 28 2019, https://www.nytimes.com/2019/01/28/technology/iphones-apple-china-made.html.

[9] "Apple's letter to the U.S. Trade Representative," Philip Elmer-DeWitt's Apple 3.0, June 20, 2019, https://www.ped30.com/2019/06/20/apple-letter-robert-lighthizer/.

[10] Adam Satariano, "Apple's $10.5B on Robots to Lasers Shores Up Supply Chain," *Bloomberg*, November 13, 2013, https://www.bloomberg.com/news/articles/2013-11-13/apple-s-10-5b-on-robots-to-lasers-shores-up-supply-chain.

[11] See Edward Humes, "Your iPhone's 500,000-Mile Journey to Your Pocket, *Wired*, April 12, 2016, https://www.wired.com/2016/04/iphones-500000-mile-journey-pocket/; and Sam Costello, "Where Is the iPhone Made?," *Lifewire*, last updated January 27, 2021, https://www.lifewire.com/where-is-the-iphone-made-1999503.

[12] Kathrin Hille, "Foxconn: why the world's tech factory faces its biggest tests," *Financial Times*, June 9, 2019, https://www.ft.com/content/0f57109e-8845-11e9-a028-86cea8523dc2.

[13] Nicas, "A Tiny Screw Shows Why iPhones Won't Be 'Assembled in USA'."

[14] Nicas, "A Tiny Screw Shows Why iPhones Won't Be 'Assembled in USA'."

[15] John Schmidt, "How would Foxconn complex compare to China twin?," *Milwaukee Journal Sentinel*, August 25, 2017, https://www.jsonline.com/story/money/business/2017/08/25/twin-foxconn-factories-one-china-one-wisy-campus-low-cost-china-could-compete-proposed-wisconsin-sit/580671001/.

[16] Jason Jing, "Wiley Foxconn," *Supply Chain Asia*, January/February 2012, http://supplychainasia.org/wp-content/uploads/2016/03/SCA_Jan_Feb_2012.pdf.

[17] Tim Worstall, "It's Cheaper To Send Apple's iPhones By Air Than By Sea," *Forbes*, September 12, 2013, https://www.forbes.com/sites/timworstall/2013/09/12/its-cheaper-to-send-apples-iphones-by-air-than-by-sea/#c80eb2935f7a.

[18] Macworld staff, "Inside Apple's iPod factories," Macworld, June 12, 2006, https://www.macworld.co.uk/news/inside-apples-ipod-factories-14915/.

[19] "International Labor Comparisons 2002 - 2009," U.S. Bureau of Labor Statistics, accessed September 9, 2021, https://www.bls.gov/fls/china.htm, obtained from search string "Chinese average manufacturing wage 2006."

[20] Harrison Jacobs, "Inside 'iPhone City,' the massive Chinese factory town where half of the world's iPhones are produced," *Business Insider*, May 7, 2018, https://www.businessinsider.com/apple-iphone-factory-foxconn-china-photos-tour-2018-5.

[21] Brian Merchant, "Life and death in Apple's forbidden city," *The Guardian*, June 18, 2017, https://www.theguardian.com/technology/2017/jun/18/foxconn-life-death-forbidden-city-longhua-suicide-apple-iphone-brian-merchant-one-device-extract.

[22] Reed Albergotti, "Apple accused of worker violations in Chinese factories," *Washington Post*, Sept 9, 2019, https://www.washingtonpost.com/technology/2019/09/09/apple-accused-worker-violations-chinese-factories-by-labor-rights-group/.

[23] Merchant, "Life and death in Apple's forbidden city."

[24] Jacobs, "Inside 'iPhone City,' the massive Chinese factory town where half of the world's iPhones are produced."

[25] Thomas Clarke and Martijn Boersma, "Apple, the $1 trillion company searching for its soul," *The Observer*, August 5, 2018, https://theconversation.com/apple-the-1-trillion-company-searching-for-its-soul-101030.

[26] "Apple Supplier Code of Conduct," Apple.com, January 1, 2015, https://www.apple.com/anzsea/supplier-responsibility/pdfs/supplier_code_of_conduct.pdf.

[27] Clarke and Boersma, "Apple, the $1 trillion company searching for its soul."

[28] Ben Lovejoy, "Air pollution in China's 'iPhone city' blamed on iPhone 12 production," 9to5Mac, October 29, 2020, https://9to5mac.com/2020/10/29/air-pollution-in-china/.

[29] Apple Newsroom, "Apple-launched China Clean Energy Fund invests in three wind farms," press release, September 24, 2019, https://www.apple.com/newsroom/2019/09/apple-launched-china-clean-energy-fund-invests-in-three-wind-farms/#:~:text=Launched%20in%202018%2C%20the%20China,1%20gigawatt%20of%20renewable%20energy.

[30] "Installed capacity of Electric Power Generation in China between 2010 and 2020," Statista, February 25, 2021, https://www.statista.com/statistics/302269/china-installed-power-generation-capacity/.

[31] Hille, "Foxconn: why the world's tech factory faces its biggest tests."

Power, its Use and Abuse—The Wrong Hallway

I was excited to start my new job at Blaine, Schultz, and Zenger. It was one of Detroit's largest advertising agencies. BSZ, as it was known in the local market, had begun doing print advertising in the early 1920s. The firm had navigated the transition to radio that decade, television in the 1950s, and the Internet in the 1990s and was considered one of the premier digital agencies in the Midwest. To land a job like this had been my dream since I settled on an advertising major at Michigan State University (MSU) four years earlier.

Getting to MSU was not easy for me. Raised by a single mother in Ferndale, one of Detroit's poorest areas, I had come a long way from a childhood surrounded by crime, drug use, and economic despair. Michigan State had provided me with a great education and a new set of friends who taught me about life beyond the hood, and with one of the top-rated advertising programs in the nation, I knew the basics of the ad business. BSZ was a dream job for anyone in the program. During my senior year, I signed on to MSU's entry in the annual BSZ advertising challenge. We took third place, but several BSZ partners told me I had a solid grasp of advertising fundamentals and could really help them understand the emerging digital marketing and social media world. It didn't hurt my chances that by hiring a woman of color BSZ would also meet its minority and diversity goals.

That summer had been a whirlwind of activity with firm onboarding and my first assignment. I got put on a high-profile account. While the products were very traditional consumer packaged goods, our team was going to help our client move into the digital age and reach emerging millennial and Gen Z customers through new social media outlets such as Facebook. Our team leader was Don Johannsen, an MBA graduate from Northwestern in his mid-forties. Don was creative and had really great client-management skills, which made him a valuable and respected partner in the firm. He pretty much walked on water with his ability to bring in new business.

Don was also driven. He expected excellent work from his team, and he worked long hours right alongside all of us. We knew we'd have to bring our A game every day. What a great learning experience! As summer turned to fall, I gained confidence and completed several early tasks well. Don told me I had a future in the business and that I had a sixth sense for what clients needed in what was then the "Wild West" world of social media advertising. No one knew what campaigns would hit a home run, but we had some great early successes with that high-profile account.

One Friday evening in late September, I came out of the digital media workroom and, to save time getting back to my cubicle, I walked down the wood-paneled hallway where the partners, including Don, had their offices. I walked past his office and saw him, as usual, hard at work. He saw me, dropped the paper he was reading, and hustled to meet me in the hallway. I stopped and turned, thinking we'd have a brief conversation before I hit the road.

That's when things got ugly. The next thing I knew, Don had slammed me against the paneled wall, was kissing my neck, and had slipped his hands on my breasts. I was stunned and just reacted.

I put my hands up and pushed his away. I created a couple of inches between us and saw the look in his eye turn even more violent. He told me that I was "totally hot" and that he had wanted me since he first saw me at the BSZ competition. He let me know that he was the reason I had been hired. Yes, I had talent, but if I gave him what he wanted, he could put me on the glide path to success in the firm and industry. He also told me that if I refused him, he could make sure I never advanced beyond my current role.

I pushed him away, turned, and walked down that hall as confidently as I could. I did not look back and left with my head and shoulders high. When I got to my car, I locked the door and cried for several minutes. My body was shaking, and my soul was shaken. I had lived in the ghettos of Detroit and gone to sleep at night to the sounds of gangbangers and gunfire. But I had never, until this very moment, thought I'd be a victim of sexual assault. I had always been tough and wily, and I was as filled with embarrassment at my own weakness as I was terrified by the encounter.

The weekend was awful. I could hardly sleep or eat, and I had to figure out whether or not to return to work on Monday. I didn't want to go back, but I knew that I couldn't just walk away from an agency as prestigious as BSZ after only three months. That would be career suicide, even if I never said a word to anyone. I also had to figure out what to do about Don. There was no way I'd sleep with a guy like that, not for any promotion in the world. I had seen enough at the firm to know that he had real power, and if he wanted to, he could stall my career. Much of what counts as "great work" in an agency is all subjective, and whether or not you are a "team player" is totally up to your boss.

I went to work on Monday morning and acted as if everything was normal, as if the incident in the hallway had been a bad dream. Don said nothing. He soon realized that I had no intention of filing a complaint or making his life miserable, and we worked together just fine. I completed my work on the high-profile account and moved on to work with several other major clients. I put in two years at the firm, gained great experience, and then moved to Los Angeles to get an MBA at USC's Marshall School. I never walked down that wood-paneled hallway again. Ever.

Funny thing, the day I left the firm, Don came to my farewell party and wished me well.

I've looked back on that experience with a mix of shame and revulsion, but also some pride. I wonder how many other women Don had found "totally hot" and how many had suffered what I did, or worse. Did I do the right thing? I'm now a partner at a new firm, Jackson-Lieberman, in Los Angeles and work on great accounts. Don didn't stall my career, and I've done very well. I feel like I let part of myself down—the part my friends at MSU encouraged me to be, the woman who wanted to build a better world. There was another part of me, the girl from the violence of Ferndale who knew how to survive, who thought I was incredibly brave, and had done what I needed to do be done—and maybe even thrive.

Conflicts of Interest—Challenges Within the World of Investing

Example 1   A Questionable Trade

Sarah Johnson earned a degree in finance at the University of Minnesota in 2021 and had graduated cum laude. Many people believed the COVID-19 pandemic was just ending thanks to vaccinations and, while several entry-level positions were available in the financial services sector, she found herself competing against graduates from 2020 as well as her own class. It had taken a few months for her to land a job at Elliott Securities, a Chicago-based brokerage firm. Elliot focused on helping young investors, people like Sarah, who were just starting to build their portfolios and retirement accounts. The company pitched itself as a perfect fit for investors with long-time horizons and a corresponding appetite for risk. Elliot's brokers focused on helping clients create wealth by capitalizing on cyclical and thematic market movements identified in various equity sectors and industries. Elliot specialized in "actively traded portfolios"; traders rotated through companies in a specific industry—or across sectors—based on which stocks were appreciating. Clients would make money based on daily, weekly, or quarterly price volatility, capitalizing on trends with high volume trading. Elliot made its money by charging a small fee on each transaction.

Sarah joined the company's new Minneapolis office. Sarah liked the setup. Elliot had a marketing team that generated qualified leads for Sarah to close. She would be paid a base salary of $90,000 a year, plus 3 percent of trading volume beyond a projected base level. The first year's salary was guaranteed, but after that, her salary would be a draw against commissions paid on her average trading volume from the previous two years. Since this was her first year, she had a year to generate $3 million in trading volume. Sarah felt confident that she would meet those goals. The marketing team provided solid leads, and she would need to close those leads and then use the firm's research, investment tools, and her expertise to help her clients earn great returns.

Things went well for the first three quarters and Sarah began to create a sizable book of assets under management. The major challenge was that, because most of her accounts were small, she had to be very active with these accounts to meet her trading volume goal. She found that, like several of her colleagues, she could execute trades that "made money" for the client on a pre-fee basis. After accounting for fees, however, some clients made nothing, and a few lost money.

Sarah's preferred trading strategy involved rotating between large "blocks" of a given security based on an analyst's reports and potential "momentum" for a given security. She would rotate (trade) in to a stock when she saw upside momentum or rotate out when she saw momentum declining. Timing was essential, and most of her trades had proven successful. Over the course of the year, her clients had learned to trust her judgment.

Sarah, like most brokers at Elliot, did not have limited power of attorney (LPOA) for her client accounts. Technically, she could not trade on a client's behalf without their approval. In practice, as a client and broker became familiar with each other and made money, both the client and the broker became flexible in following this rule. For example, clients often chided Sarah when they missed out on portfolio movements because Sarah could not reach them when an opportunity arose. Many told Sarah to make the trades she felt would increase their portfolio value. Sarah began to use this lack of oversight and "informal" authority to become more active in trading.

As Sarah neared the end of her first year, she found herself in a difficult position. She had generated just shy of $3 million in trading volume, and her manager approached her with some new information. She already knew that her base salary for the next year would reflect her first-year trading volume; she could potentially get a raise or see her salary go down. This would be tough because she had begun to adjust her lifestyle to that of a successful broker: a newly leased BMW, the latest fashions, and lunches and dinners at many of Minneapolis's finest and most popular restaurants. The new information was that if Sarah could beat her $3 million base, she would not only earn more next year, but she also would qualify for a broker-enhanced sales incentive, or "spiff": a week of skiing at Banff resort in the Canadian Rockies.

When her boss left, Sarah began searching for trades that she could execute. She found a couple of large blocks she could rotate to reach her volume goal. For both blocks, there were very early signals that the shares might be losing momentum. A couple of analysts had become negative on these companies, taking a contrarian view. Sarah would not normally move on this type of news, but she could make an argument that this "defensive rotation" would be prudent. These trades would, however, guarantee her income level for the next year and earn the trip to the resort. As she looked through her client portfolios, she realized that a few of her clients would benefit from these trades, many would lose value on the transaction fee, and others would see a clear loss.

Example 2   To Fee or Not to Fee?

Briana Mason had worked at Cook and Company, a national private wealth management boutique, for over three years. The firm, located in Memphis and founded in the early twentieth century, held accounts for many of Tennessee's wealthiest families. The firm had a stellar reputation for client service and investment returns. Housed in the city's historic Brodnax Building, most in the industry considered the firm to be a plumb employment opportunity. After Mason received her MBA from Vanderbilt, she felt honored to join the firm. She became the fourth African American, and first woman of color, among a staff of twenty-five wealth advisors. Advisors ranged in age from twenty-eight to seventy, and most advisors only left the firm when they retired.

A year ago, Mason joined a new group at the firm. Cook managed a lot of "old money," and the firm hoped to shed its solid, and maybe staid, image and target "new money" in the city. New money meant young entrepreneurs and up-and-coming executives in the area. Briana targeted several HENRY (high earning, not rich yet) clients and began to establish relationships and build her book of business among this group. She found many HENRYs to be savvy investors; however, she also found that many had preconceived biases and blind spots that made her job challenging. Like all Cook advisors, her goal was to develop long relationships with her clients while helping them create substantial wealth.

Tom Schmidt was a perfect example of a HENRY with strong opinions of what he wanted out of his investment portfolio, sometimes to his detriment. Briana had been working with Tom for about nine months and met with him earlier in the day. The meeting had not gone well. Schmidt was enamored with a technology-sector mutual fund offered through a national firm. The fund had no up-front fee and an annual management fee of forty-five basis points (bps). Schmidt saw himself as a long-term investor and he was certain that paying the commission on a similar Cook Fund would reduce his long-term returns. The amount was a smaller allocation of his portfolio, but Schmidt seemed committed to the strategy. Mason felt that her differentiating value proposition in her firm's similar portfolio was her advice and the research of her firm. Her competing technology fund had a great long-term performance, and a "buy and hold" in this sector might be best for his portfolio allocation. Cook's similar offering was a fund that did not have a front-end commission structure and carried a slightly higher expense ratio (75 bps). The competing in-house national fund would pay a trailing management fee to Mason.

Mason illustrated that the benefit to her technology fund was that she came with the transaction. Technology is a volatile sector of the S&P 500 and both her expertise and Cook's research would likely be valuable in the future. Two facts about the national fund were unknown to Schmidt: (1) The prospectus of the fund stated a surrender charge of a declining percentage scale of 3%–2%–1%, over three years, and (2) although illustrating a competitive long-term performance, recently the portfolio manager had left the fund to start his own asset-management company.

Schmidt pushed Mason to put his money in her company's fund. Mason knew the Cook fund was more aligned with Schmidt's propensity to be headstrong and independent, causing him to easily lose confidence in the markets and possibly do what was counterintuitive to the savvy, long-term money manager. When Schmidt came on as a client, Mason had plowed through his accounts and tracked his trading history. Schmidt was an impulsive investor with a history of switching between funds and stocks regularly. Mason presented that the higher management fee bought the benefits of Cook's research, Mason's service, and solid long-term performance. When it came to the surrender fee, all the information was clearly printed in the prospectus. Every transaction in a mutual fund requires a prospectus to accompany the purchase.

As Briana sat in her office and pondered the situation, she wondered how to move forward. On the one hand, it was Schmidt's money, and her role as his wealth manager was to manage his money according to his goals and risk tolerance. If she could persuade him to follow her recommendation, she would keep the assets under management. If she put him in his desired fund, she would still make something on Schmidt's portfolio. On the other hand, the Cook culture was to "do right by our clients" and Briana knew the trading history of Schmidt. As she thought more about her options, she wondered how comfortable she could be with a "It's my client's money" justification.

Example 3 Picking an Investment Custodian

Shelia Oaks managed large client portfolios for Nelson and Nelson Capital. The Nelson sisters had founded their capital management fund when they realized that working for the big players did not offer the lifestyle or professional environment they wanted. Charlotte Nelson had worked for Solomon Brothers, and Beth Nelson cut her teeth at Merrill Lynch. After a decade of that grind, the sisters had a life-changing conversation over lunch. They found out that neither of them enjoyed what they were doing. The sixty-hour workweeks had left little time for much else, and even the extravagant vacations they could afford failed to recharge their batteries. Plus, both sisters faced significant pressure to cut ethical corners to make the numbers, whether their own income numbers or to keep costs in their business units under control. With that, they decided to launch their own management firm. The past ten years had been fruitful and fulfilling, and the sisters now managed $6 billion in total assets.

Oaks had been one of their first hires. Shelia had graduated with a finance degree from Arizona State University and had been drawn to the "whole-person" culture that Nelson and Nelson was trying to build. She was very good at what she did, and she had the trust of several of the firm's largest clients. She put the needs of her client first, and that had always paid off for her. Her compensation was more than adequate, and she made more working for this small boutique than many of her friends made in commissions for the larger institutional asset managers.

Shelia had just closed a major new account: Nelson and Nelson would be the managers of the $1.2 billion retirement fund for Stockholm Parks, an Auburn, Alabama, owner and operator of amusement and theme parks in thirty-seven U.S. states. Stockholm Parks was legendary for their commitment to customer service and was considered a premier amusement park operator. As the account manager, Oaks now began to operate in a consultative role for Stockholm's investment committee, the plan sponsor. Oaks would help the sponsor fill out their "investment lineup": the portfolio managers who would manage the various funds. In addition to the portfolio holdings, the plan design and custodian would be reviewed. The custodian would be an outside firm, usually a large brokerage house or bank, and would assume responsibility for plan administration, record keeping, and filing critical IRS and other relevant compliance documents. Nelson worked with a variety of custodians to administer client plans.

The size of the Stockholm deal created a challenge for Shelia. She felt two firms would do a good job for this size and complexity of account: Funds First and Jones-Blackwell. Both firms served as custodians for hundreds of billion dollars of plan assets. Funds First catered to retirement plans the size of Stockholm's. They offered services that would be an excellent fit. Stockholm would have the attention of the top people at Funds First. Jones-Blackwell could handle the work but, frankly, Stockholm would be a small client for Jones-Blackwell and would not have the attention of senior leaders in administering the account.

The Stockholm account would, however, put enough Nelson and Nelson assets under contract with Jones-Blackwell for the firm to qualify as a tier 1 client. That status would entitle Nelson and Nelson to many "soft dollar" benefits from Jones. For example, Nelson and Nelson would have access to Jones-Blackwell's huge, industry-leading research operations and marketing support dollars, and they also would be included in the Jones-Blackwell referral network. In addition, Oaks and other staff members would be invited to Jones-Blackwell conferences. The soft dollar benefits from Jones would deepen Nelson and Nelson's expertise and better position the firm to attract more and larger clients.

As Shelia pondered her decision, she knew that either Funds First or Jones-Blackwell would meet the basic needs of the Stockholm account. Funds First would provide better service for the account; however, if she went with Jones-Blackwell, Nelson and Nelson would grow their retirement plan expertise and qualified plan status and be better off as a firm. Shelia would get credit for moving Nelson and Nelson to tier 1 status and that would only help her reputation.

Example 4   Designing an Ethical Investment Firm

Jackson Blackner was excited as he thought about his new opportunity. He had studied finance at John Carroll College and hoped to land a job with a top money-management firm. After graduating, he went to work for Lehman Brothers as a financial consultant. In every role at Lehman, he had been successful. His status at the firm, and his compensation, reflected that success. He had a growing book of business where his clients were regularly providing referrals, and his work schedule had reached a point where the constant grind had started to subside. His peers in the business felt he was in an enviable place.

Despite his success, his nagging conundrum was his perception of the rampant ethical minefields that were endemic to the industry. Two things had long bothered him about the industry. First, ethical challenges sometimes accompanied the pressure to perform. He had seen investment advisors fail to disclose important information about funds and investment products to their clients. These disclosures often stopped clients from purchasing services, and Jack saw a willingness to omit the disclosure as a conflict of interest that favored the investment advisor. He had also seen several sales presentations where advisors favored in-house products that carried higher commissions and often provided added sales incentives. The complexity of markets, combined with confusing industry jargon, left many investors susceptible to the advisor's knowledge, experience, and counsel. In addition, the appropriate risk tolerance and asset allocation were sometimes discarded if an investment offering with a higher commission could

interest the investor. Sales targets were often a greater focus than the needs of the client. The pressure to succeed invited even the best people to compromise.

Second, Jack had come to see the focus on income, sales targets, sales spiffs, and other perks as responsible for a shallow definition of success among advisors. In pursuit of ever-higher incomes, he had seen many of his colleagues not only trade in their ethics (which was bad enough), but also neglect their families, their friends, and even their health and sanity in the relentless pursuit of more. Jack was committed to pursuing a dream that was focused more on meaning than money. The pressures of performing in alignment with the demands of a Wall Street firm challenged his image of fulfilling his dream. Achieving his dream would require living and operating counter to the wisdom of Wall Street. He knew that his commitment to living a meaningful life congruent with his values would ultimately build and define his character. His favorite definition of character was, "the ability to carry out a worthy decision after the emotion of making the decision has passed."

With his dream firmly in mind, Jack decided to branch out on his own and start a new firm. His goal was to create a fee-based investment versus a transactional environment where investment advisors and clients would operate in a non-conflict-of-interest relationship. The non-conflict-of-interest environment would promote full disclosure, accentuate investment performance, and ultimately create a culture where deep and trusting relationships between investment advisor and client could flourish. He intuitively believed that such a firm would attract the best people who would operate at a high level of integrity and engagement. He wanted employees who not only wanted to come to work, but who also wanted to go home and be with family or friends. He knew that he had workaholic tendencies, and he wanted to create a culture that would encourage people to work for more than just money. Given his experience in the world of investing, he knew that such a firm was not impossible. He needed to attract the right type of people, with the right business model, operating to first meet the needs of the client. The result would be something very rare.

Jack was excited to launch his own firm, but he wondered what concrete steps he should take to create the firm he really wanted.

Goldman Sachs and 1MDB—Rogue Employee or Failed Oversight?

Goldman Sachs Chief Legal Officer (CLO) Kathryn H. Ruemmler retreated to her private office after a meeting of the firm's management committee, the most senior leaders of the firm. It had been six months since Goldman had agreed to pay a $2.9 billion fine to the United States Department of Justice (DOJ), which closed out one chapter of the bank's involvement with the 1Malaysia Development Berhad (1MDB) scandal. The company paid $2.3 billion to the DOJ and disgorged $600 million in "ill-gotten gains."[1] The fine represented the organization-wide penalty for its work involving $6.5 billion in bond raises for the 1MDB, a purported investment fund that ended up enriching the country of Malaysia's ex-prime minister Najib Razak and his coterie of cronies and advisors.[2]

The DOJ sought to recover $2.1 billion in pilfered 1MDB assets from entities around the globe. Goldman was the subject of investigations in fourteen countries. The DOJ alleged that Goldman violated the U.S. Foreign Corrupt Practices Act (FCPA) by bribing foreign officials to garner and/or keep business. Further, the DOJ and Securities and Exchange Commission (SEC) alleged that Goldman misled investors over the 1MDB bond sales. Goldman's Malaysian unit had already pled guilty to FCPA violations.

Goldman Sachs agreed to pay $3.9 billion to the Malaysian government to drop criminal charges related to 1MDB. They had paid the Hong Kong stock market regulatory agency $350 million for "serious lapses and deficiencies in management controls" that led to misappropriation of funds. Goldman's lead banker on the deal, Tim Leissner, pled guilty in 2019 to charges from the DOJ.[3] The 1MDB bond sales had been good business at the time for Goldman; the firm earned almost $600 million in profits for helping the fund place $6.5 billion, no-bid bond placements. To date, the bank had paid just over $6.6 billion in fines and penalties, roughly twelve times the amount it made on the three deals.

Ruemmler realized that the fines and resolutions of criminal charges were only one chapter in the scandal. As the organization's chief compliance officer, she wanted to ensure that the bank did not repeat such a scandal. When the scandal broke, Goldman portrayed it as the work of a single rogue banker, Tim Leissner. That stance had sown doubt among Goldman's senior ranks and even more in the market. Ruemmler realized she had a golden opportunity to change the bank in a fundamental way. As she walked back to her office, she pondered what organizational and cultural levers she could pull to help Goldman change.

THE 1MDB SCANDAL

Then prime minister Najib Razak founded 1MDB in July of 2009. 1MDB stood for 1Malaysia Development Berhad (or limited).[4] The purported goal of the fund was to provide development funds to build and unify the country; thus, 1 Malaysia (Exhibit 1 provides a timeline of key activities of the fund and its managers). 1MDB's original funding came from a Goldman- (and Leissner-) backed $1.4 billion bond offering. The Malaysian state of Terengganu guaranteed the bond

offering with its oil revenues.[5] Razak associate and informal advisor Jho Low had already siphoned funds from the Terengganu fund. Low needed the backing of a sovereign wealth fund to cover his tracks, and he sold Razak on the fund as a way to generate foreign capital that could be diverted into his political accounts and pay off his political supporters and voters.[6]

In September of 2009, Low and Razak had convinced a Saudi business, PetroSaudi, to invest $1 billion into a joint venture with little investigation or due diligence. Low siphoned $700 million of this money into a shell corporation; he relied, as he would throughout the life of the fund, on offshore banks with weak institutional and compliance infrastructure.[7] From those proceeds, Low kicked back $153 million to Tarek Obaid, $33 million to Patrick Mahony, and $77 million to Prince Turki, all members of the PetroSaudi executive team. Low would use some of this money, as well as other funds he purloined through his shell companies, to underwrite Red Granite Pictures and turn the company over to Razak's stepson, Riza Aziz. Ironically, Red Granite would produce *The Wolf of Wall Street* at a cost of $100 million, a film depicting the scandalous dealings of American financier Jordan Belfort (played by Leonardo DiCaprio).[8]

The corruption, graft, and fraud continued, and it continued to involve Goldman's Leissner. In 2012, for example, 1MDB purchased the assets of Tanjong Energy Holdings, owned by Malaysian billionaire Ananda Krishnan. 1MDB offered $2.7 billion for the assets and hired U.S. investment banking firm Lazard to value the properties. Lazard returned a valuation far lower than $2.7 billion: "Lazard believed the whole deal smelled of political corruption. It is common in Malaysia for the government to award sweetheart deals to companies in return for kickbacks and political financing."[9] Krishnan obliged and, after the deal closed, made a "donation" of $170 million to 1MDB's "charity arm." Later that year, 1MDB would write off $400 million of the purchase price to reflect the plants' true value.[10] By the time the fraud came to light in 2015, 1MDB leaders, including Razak, would pilfer more than $4.5 billion from the fund.

The money siphoning became so blatant and so egregious that when the third bond sales were completed, Low transferred $681 million into Razak's personal account. Razak then used the money to help with his reelection campaign. The money was used to pay off local officials to help swing the election in his favor. The Razak campaign also used some of the money to sponsor events that would convince voters to cast their votes for Razak. Razak was reelected in 2013 after a contentious election.[11] The DOJ would later describe 1MDB in these terms: "kleptocracy at its worst."[12]

GOLDMAN SACHS AND THE BOND ISSUES

After the Lazard valuation, Goldman, through Leissner, became the underwriter of a $1.75 billion bond issue to help finance the Tanjong purchase. The bank would assume all the risk and purchase the whole bond offering, and 1MDB would get the cash immediately. For its services, Goldman would earn $190 million in fees. Exhibit 2 presents

1MDB Scandal Timeline

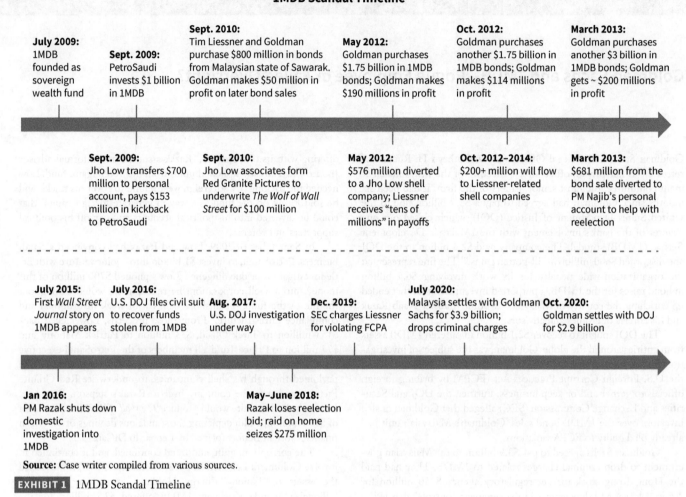

July 2009:
1MDB founded as sovereign wealth fund

Sept. 2009:
PetroSaudi invests $1 billion in 1MDB

Sept. 2010:
Tim Liessner and Goldman purchase $800 million in bonds from Malaysian state of Sawarak. Goldman makes $50 million in profit on later bond sales

May 2012:
Goldman purchases $1.75 billion in 1MDB bonds; Goldman makes $190 millions in profit

Oct. 2012:
Goldman purchases another $1.75 billion in 1MDB bonds; Goldman makes $114 millions in profit

March 2013:
Goldman purchases another $3 billion in 1MDB bonds; Goldman gets ~ $200 millions in profit

Sept. 2009:
Jho Low transfers $700 million to personal account, pays $153 million in kickback to PetroSaudi

Sept. 2010:
Jho Low associates form Red Granite Pictures to underwrite *The Wolf of Wall Street* for $100 million

May 2012:
$576 million diverted to a Jho Low shell company; Liessner receives "tens of millions" in payoffs

Oct. 2012–2014:
$200+ million will flow to Liessner-related shell companies

March 2013:
$681 million from the bond sale diverted to PM Najib's personal account to help with reelection

July 2015:
First *Wall Street Journal* story on 1MDB appears

July 2016:
U.S. DOJ files civil suit to recover funds stolen from 1MDB

Aug. 2017:
U.S. DOJ investigation under way

Dec. 2019:
SEC charges Liessner for violating FCPA

July 2020:
Malaysia settles with Goldman Sachs for $3.9 billion; drops criminal charges

Oct. 2020:
Goldman settles with DOJ for $2.9 billion

Jan 2016:
PM Razak shuts down domestic investigation into 1MDB

May–June 2018:
Razak loses reelection bid; raid on home seizes $275 million

Source: Case writer compiled from various sources.

EXHIBIT 1 1MDB Scandal Timeline

EXHIBIT 2 Goldman Sachs Investment Banking Segment Results, 2012–2020

$ In Millions	2020	2019	2018	2017	2016	2015	2014	2013	2012
Financial Advisory	$3,065	$3,197	$3,444	$3,188	$2,932	$3,470	$2,474	$1,978	$1,975
Equity Underwriting	$3,406	$1,482	$1,628	$1,243	$ 891	$1,546	$1,750	$1,659	$ 987
Debt Underwriting	$2,670	$2,119	$2,358	$2,940	$2,450	$2,011	$2,240	$2,367	$1,964
Total Underwriting	$6,076	$3,601	$3,986	$4,183	$3,341	$3,557	$3,990	$4,026	$2,951
Corporate Lending	$ 282	$ 801	$ 748						
Net Revenues	$9,423	$7,599	$8,178	$7,371	$6,273	$7,027	$6,464	$6,004	$4,926
Operating Expenses	$6,134	$4,685	$4,473	$3,526	$3,437	$3,713	$3,688	$3,479	$3,333
Pre-Tax Earnings	$1,665	$2,581	$3,581	$3,845	$2,836	$3,310	$2,776	$2,525	$1,593

Source: Company 10-K filings.

Goldman's revenues and profits from its investment banking operation, the division of the firm responsible for underwriting debt and equity. The May bond issue would account for 10 percent of Goldman's 2012 revenue for debt underwriting. The revenue reflected a Goldman strategy of "monetizing the state" in Asia by seeking revenues and profits from dealing with government entities and sovereign wealth funds.[13] The bank underwrote three separate bond issues; two for $1.75 billion in 2012 and one for $3.5 billion in 2013. The firm earned $600 million in fees over the three sales.

Tim Leissner

Leissner's Goldman compensation for the year was around $10 million, but over the next two years he would receive payments (through shell companies) of over $200 million from 1MDB. The descent into taking bribes and corruption was not a sudden shift of behavior for Leissner. He had skirted Goldman compliance rules for a number of years. He had worked in Asia for many years and as a part of gaining access to deals, he often paid middlemen a fee for making introductions. While the fees were common in Asia at that time, the practice ran up against the guardrails of the FCPA; it would be difficult to discern legitimate payments from bribes.

Skirting the rules was part of Leissner's modus operandi. In 1993, he received a doctorate degree from England's University of Somerset, which was later shut down as a for-profit degree mill. While advising on an IPO for an Asian company, Leissner began a romantic relationship with the company's chief financial officer, and rival banks complained that Leissner had a sweetheart deal with the company. In the summer 2010, Leissner arranged a summer internship for the daughter of the Malaysian ambassador to the United States. She worked at Goldman's Singapore office and engaged in a sexual relationship with Leissner. Many thought the internship appeared to violate the FCPA if it encouraged 1MDB or other Malaysian government entities to do business with Goldman. A junior banker at Goldman described Leissner: "He never operated within boundaries. He would offer clients [whatever they needed to close the deal] and get permission later. It was tolerated because he brought in deals."[14]

Goldman Sachs

Marcus Goldman, a German immigrant to New York City in 1869, began buying the promissory notes of merchants to help finance their operations during a time of expensive credit. He would then sell this "commercial paper" to New York banks at a profit. In 1885, Marcus, his son Henry, and son-in-law Samuel Sachs formed Goldman Sachs & Co. Over the next century, the firm would become one of the world's leading investment banking firms, helping corporations raise money through equity and debt offerings to public markets. In the 1970s, Goldman began moving into areas other than investment banking, such as investing and lending.[15] By 2012, investment banking would contribute 15 percent of revenues and 14 percent of the firm's profits. In the early twenty-first century, and particularly after the financial crisis of 2008–2009, Goldman looked abroad for revenue and profit-making opportunities.[16]

As a large commercial bank, Goldman was subject to all major banking laws and regulations. The FCPA prohibited the payment of bribes to obtain business from foreign governments. The Bank Secrecy Act of 1970 required banks to establish internal control systems to monitor transactions and prevent money laundering, terrorist funding, and other types of international fraud.[17] As such, Goldman had an extensive global compliance unit to verify conformance to all applicable laws and regulations. The bank also had layers of executive review to ensure compliance. Senior leaders of regions and the bank as a whole were aware of major deals and had obligations to ensure compliance.

The compliance function in any organization faces a challenge: It is seen as an impediment to money making. This is particularly true in non-U.S. environments where customary practices may appear to violate U.S. laws, sometimes do, and sometimes do not. Given this reality, compliance groups are under tremendous pressure to "turn a blind eye" to questionable activities. Many compliance groups were a "weak appendage" in a bank and buried in the legal architecture of the bank.[18] In fact, Goldman's compliance group had raised alarms over Leissner's dealings with Low as early as 2009. As Goldman underwrote the first set of 1MDB bonds in 2012, several executives aware of the deal raised concerns that the excessive profits Goldman stood to make on the deal were a signal of potential fraud. These concerns had no effect on Leissner, and the firm as a whole took no action to stop this, or any other, transaction with 1MDB.

THE AFTERMATH

The scandal came to light in 2015 when Clare Newcastle Brown, a British journalist who ran the blog *Sawarak* (a Malaysian state) *Report*, published an expose on 1MDB under the headline "Heist of the Century." She had been investigating 1MDB since 2010 and finally had the evidence she needed to go public.[19] The *Wall Street Journal* published its own account in July of that year. A year later, in July of 2016, the DOJ and SEC moved to recover $2.1 billion in funds stolen from 1MDB and in 2017 began investigating Goldman, Leissner, and others. The SEC charged Leissner with violating the FCPA in December of 2019 and announced a settlement with Goldman in October of 2020. The complaints noted:

> Specifically, in an attempt to win Goldman bond deals with 1Malaysia Development Berhad ("1MDB"), a Malaysian state-owned investment fund, Leissner engaged Low, whom he knew had connections to Malaysian government officials who could influence the transactions. The officials in turn would use their influence to award Goldman bond deals and other financial deals and Leissner, along with other Goldman management, worked to misappropriate the bond proceeds and divert them as bribes to officials or misappropriate funds for themselves.
>
> The SEC alleged that Leissner was aware of Goldman's refusal to approve any business relationships with Low, as Goldman's compliance and legal groups had concerns about Low after conducting a screen, however Leissner continued to work with Low in securing deals for Goldman Sachs and "actively concealed highly relevant information" [from] Goldman Sach's financial, executive, and legal teams about his work with Low, causing Goldman Sachs to inaccurately and improperly record the payments made with respect to the 1MDB bond deals.[20]

Charles Cain, chief of the SEC's FCPA enforcement group, noted, "Individual conduct lies at the heart of all bribery schemes. Here, Leissner abused his leadership role at Goldman Sachs by engaging in a massive bribery scheme targeting the highest levels of two foreign governments in order to bring in lucrative business to the firm and enrich himself."[21] The SEC alleged that Leissner had engaged Low to bribe officials in the Emirate of Abu Dhabi, and that Leissner had received $43 million in illicit payments. Leissner consented to the SEC's finding of bribery and lack of internal accounting control.

Goldman's defense centered on the "rogue banker" theory. They claimed that Leissner had single-handedly misled the bank and that "he was able to outfox some of the smartest, highest paid bankers in the world, and a bank with a huge audit, compliance, and legal staff."[22] The DOJ did not buy that argument and proceeded to investigate the bank. In terms of Goldman Sachs, DOJ assistant director William F. Sweeney said:

> When government officials and business executives secretly work together behind the scenes for their own illegal benefit, and not that of their citizens and shareholders, their behavior lends credibility to the narrative that businesses don't succeed based on the quality of their products, but rather their willingness to play dirty. Greed eventually exacts an immense cost on society, and unchecked corrupt behavior erodes trust in public institutions and government entities alike. This case represents the largest ever penalty paid to U.S. authorities in an FCPA case.[23]

The total cost to Goldman for its part in the scandal was $6.6 billion, slightly more than the total of its 1MDB bond purchases. Razak was ousted as Prime Minister in 2018 and received a twelve-year prison sentence in 2020.[24] Low continues to live in hiding. The Malaysian people saw no development and now find themselves burdened with the financial and reputational costs of the scandal. It may take several years to work through those issues.

THE RED FLAGS

As outside critics unpacked the bank's involvement, they identified ten issues that raised concerns early in the process:

1. The amount of Goldman profits on the deals. Usually, a bond underwriting fee would be about $1 million. Goldman's tally for the three issues was $600 million, or 200 times the normal fee. One argument was that Goldman took substantial risk in the private placement—Goldman bought the bonds with its own cash—but in reality, it had a large network of buyers ready to purchase the government-backed securities.[25]

2. Goldman enriched itself at the expense of a poor country (in 2019, the Malaysian average gross domestic product based on purchasing power parity [GDPPP] was $11,414 per person,[26] compared with $65,297 for the United States). The bond offerings allowed Razak, a kleptocrat, to remain in power and push Malaysia toward a more authoritarian regime. In July of 2018, police raided the home of the former prime minister and removed $274 million worth of items, including 12,000 pieces of jewelry, 567 expensive handbags, 243 watches, and $28 million in cash.[27]

3. The bank acted contrary to the advice and counsel of its own compliance group. "While there is some dispute about who knew what, when, about Mr. Low's involvement in 1MDB, Goldman's compliance department was adamant that 'the bank should not do business with him' [Jho Low] in 2010 and again later in 2013. That was reportedly because Goldman's compliance group couldn't determine how he obtained his wealth, one of innumerable glaring red flags about him and often a sure sign of criminal activity."[28]

4. A review of 1MDB's financials should have raised questions about the distribution of funds, and about the lack of physical assets (the group owned a couple of oil-drilling ships and a couple of power plants). Both EY and KPMG resigned as auditors.[29]

5. On the power plant sale, Goldman hired Lazard, an investment banking firm that indicated that the pricing for the deal reeked of graft and corruption. State agencies often buy from private investors at inflated prices and then receive kickbacks from the seller.

6. A review of 1MDB's staff and due diligence would reveal an inexperienced group of people running the firm.

7. Goldman's own compliance team had identified Low as a bad risk. "He was rejected as a client of the private bank because the origin of his wealth couldn't be determined (a huge red flag, as stated above) and 'a few years later' was rejected as a direct client on a deal involving the Abu Dhabi state energy investment company IPIC in 2013. Nevertheless, a Goldman executive's email to others at Goldman on March 27, 2012 (just two months before the first 1MDB bond offering in May 2012) 'acknowledged that Low was a "1MDB Operator or intermediary in Malaysia"'."[30]

8. David Ryan, president of Goldman's Asia business, "had visited 1MDB's staff in Malaysia and came away with concerns over its plans to take on so much debt and the inexperience of its management, none of whom seemed to have overseen multi-billion-dollar investments before." He also "voiced concerns"[31] about the unusual and incredibly lucrative no-bid contracts, which "struck" him "and other Goldman executives as possibly too good to be true."[32]

9. Other groups in Goldman refused to get involved: "another red flag was the structure of the very first 1MDB offering. Goldman had suggested that it be guaranteed by the $70 billion Abu Dhabi state energy investment fund, International Petroleum Investment Company (IPIC). "Leissner's colleagues at Goldman's Middle Eastern headquarters in Dubai, who did regular business with IPIC, found the idea preposterous and declined to get involved."[33]

10. The use of BSI, a poorly capitalized and small Swiss bank, as a transaction partner raised concerns. BSI lacked the compliance architecture, which allowed private banker Yeo Jiawei to help Low and 1MDB move large amounts of money to offshore shell companies. There was no effective compliance function at BSI. Yeo would be convicted of money laundering and was sentenced to over six years in prison.[34]

Author Matt Taibbi would write of Goldman that the fabled bank was "a great vampire squid wrapped around the face of humanity, relentlessly jamming its blood funnel into anything that smells like money."[35]

CONCLUSION: RUEMMLER'S NEXT MOVES

As she returned and sat at her desk, Katherine glanced at two open files. The first had a one-page summary of the ten red flags to which external critics had pointed. The second file provided a summary of Leissner's main arguments in defense of his role in the 1MDB fraud. Leissner had blamed the corporate culture at Goldman and had implied to prosecutors that, for leniency, he would help them shine a light on the "aggressive methodology" at the core of Goldman's business philosophy.[36] One reporter noted that "Goldman Sachs's former top banker in Asia says the culture of secrecy at the investment bank led him to conceal wrongdoing from the company's compliance staff. In his guilty plea, which was unsealed in early November, Mr Leissner said others at the bank helped him conceal bribes used to retain business in Malaysia."[37] Leissner's own words directed blame at Goldman: "I conspired with other employees and agents of Goldman Sachs very much in line of its culture of Goldman Sachs to conceal facts from certain compliance and legal employees of Goldman Sachs."[38]

The DOJ investigation noted that Goldman's "system of internal accounting controls could be easily circumvented" and that the "business culture, particularly in southeast Asia, was highly focused on consummating deals, at times prioritized this goal ahead of the proper operation of its compliance functions."[39] Ruemmler wondered how much the 1MDB scandal had influenced the DOJ's new rules on compliance with the FCPA and Bank Secrecy Act. The DOJ was responsible for prosecuting offenses under either act and had established clear guidelines for designing and administrating compliance programs. In June of 2020, the agency issued new guidelines for determining the robustness of a bank's compliance programs. Prosecutors would ask three "fundamental questions" when evaluating compliance: "Is the compliance program well designed? Is it applied earnestly and in good faith? Does it work in practice?"[40]

Ruemmler was smart enough to know that neither Goldman's "rogue banker" theory nor Leissner's "I'm a product of a culture" argument was entirely true, but both likely held nuggets of wisdom as she pondered her next move. If Leissner had been a rogue banker, how could she strengthen the compliance group at the bank to ensure that compliance had a greater voice in decision making around deals, particularly in countries with cultures and political systems that encouraged bribery, corruption, and graft? If Leissner was indeed the product of a culture that valued profit above ethics, how could she work to create change in the storied Goldman culture?

As she pondered these thoughts, she took out a piece of paper. At the top, she wrote "I'm a member of the C-Suite." She then divided the paper into two columns. At the top of the first, she wrote, "What resources do I have at my disposal?" and at the top of the second, "How can I deploy these resources to enact change?"

References

1 Rozanna Latiff, "Understanding Goldman Sachs' role in Malaysia's 1MDB mega scandal," Reuters, October 22, 2020, https://www.reuters.com/article/us-goldman-sachs-1mdb-settlement-explain/understanding-goldman-sachs-role-in-malaysias-1mdb-mega-scandal-idUSKBN2772HC.

2 Tom Wright and Bradley Hope, *Billion Dollar Whale* (New York: Hachette Books, 2019). This chronicles the rise, fall, and fraud that was the 1MDB.

3 Latiff, "Understanding Goldman Sachs' role in Malaysia's 1MDB mega scandal."

4 Hannah Ellis-Petersen, "1MDB scandal explained: a tale of Malaysia's missing billions," *The Guardian*, July 28, 2020, https://www.theguardian.com/world/2018/oct/25/1mdb-scandal-explained-a-tale-of-malaysias-missing-billions.

5 John Burton, "Malaysian state plans bond sale to finance SWF," *Financial Times*, May 18, 2009, https://www.ft.com/content/b5eefe9a-43bc-11de-a9be-00144feabdc0.

6 Wright and Hope, *Billion Dollar Whale*, 63.

7 Wright and Hope, *Billion Dollar Whale*, 167.

8 Wright and Hope, *Billion Dollar Whale*, 77. The Red Granite connection appears throughout the text.

9 Wright and Hope, *Billion Dollar Whale*, 184.

10 Wright and Hope, *Billion Dollar Whale*, 184–186.

11 Wright and Hope, *Billion Dollar Whale*, 216–226.

12 "Timeline: How Malaysia's 1MDB financial scandal unfolded," *Al Jazeera*, July 28, 2020, https://www.aljazeera.com/news/2020/7/28/timeline-how-malaysias-1mdb-financial-scandal-unfolded.

13 Felix Salmon, "How Goldman Sachs facilitated the heist of the century," *Axios*, September 12, 2018, https://www.axios.com/goldman-sachs-billion-dollar-whale-malaysia-9f6c10d1-85a7-4576-9f92-90c4c5498777.html.

14 Wright and Hope, *Billion Dollar Whale*, 57.

15 "A Brief History of Goldman Sachs," https://www.goldmansachs.com/our-firm/history/a-brief-history-of-gs.pdf.

16 Goldman Sachs, 2016 10-K. See Salmon, "How Goldman Sachs facilitated the heist of the century," for information on Goldman's expansion into Asia and other global markets.

17 Reena Shani, Mark Chorazak, and Timothy Byrne, "Banking Regulations, 2021 | USA," Global Legal Insights, 2021, https://www.globallegalinsights.com/practice-areas/banking-and-finance-laws-and-regulations/usa.

18 Wright and Hope, *Billion Dollar Whale*, 160–161.

19 Sarah Hoffman, "Lone brave journalist exposes 1MDB corruption," *Fraud Magazine*, May/June 2018, https://www.fraud-magazine.com/article.aspx?id=4295001869.

20 Shearman and Sterling, "In the Matter of Tim Liessner (2019)," accessed October 29, 2021, https://fcpa.shearman.com/siteFiles/FCPA%20Cases/Leissner%20-%20Case%20Summary.pdf.

21 "SEC Charges Former Goldman Sachs Executive With FCPA Violations," U.S. Securities and Exchange Commission, press release, December 2019, https://www.sec.gov/news/press-release/2019-260.

22 Dennis Kelleher, "Goldman Sachs and the 1MDB Scandal," Harvard Law School Forum on Corporate Governance, May 14, 2019, https://corpgov.law.harvard.edu/2019/05/14/goldman-sachs-and-the-1mdb-scandal/.

23 "Goldman Sachs Charged in Foreign Bribery Case and Agrees to Pay Over $2.9 Billion," United States Department of Justice, press release, October 22, 2020, https://www.justice.gov/opa/pr/goldman-sachs-charged-foreign-bribery-case-and-agrees-pay-over-29-billion.

24 Rebecca Radcliffe, "1MDB scandal: Najib Razak handed 12-year jail sentence," *The Guardian*, July 28, 2020, https://www.theguardian.com/world/2020/jul/28/1mdb-scandal-najib-razak-verdict-malaysia.

25 Wright and Hope, *Billion Dollar Whale*.

26 "GDP per capita (current US$) – Malaysia," The World Bank, accessed November 1, 2020, https://data.worldbank.org/indicator/NY.GDP.PCAP.CD?locations=MY.

27 Wright and Hope, *Billion Dollar Whale*, 378.

28 Kelleher, "Goldman Sachs and the 1MDB Scandal."

29 Wright and Hope, *Billion Dollar Whale*.

30 Kelleher, "Goldman Sachs and the 1MDB Scandal."

31 Emily Flitter, Matthew Goldstein, and Kate Kelly, "Goldman Chairman Met Privately With Fugitive Accused in Malaysian Fraud,"

New York Times, November 22, 2018, https://www.nytimes.com/2018/11/22/business/goldman-blankfein-1mdb-malaysia.html.

[32] Kelleher, "Goldman Sachs and the 1MDB Scandal."

[33] Kelleher, "Goldman Sachs and the 1MDB Scandal."

[34] Fathin Ungku," Singapore sentences ex-BSI banker to more jail time in 1MDB linked case," Reuters, July 12, 2017, https://www.reuters.com/article/us-malaysia-scandal-bsi/singapore-sentences-ex-bsi-banker-to-more-jail-time-in-1mdb-linked-case-idUSKB-N19X0MC. See also Wright and Hope, *Billion Dollar Whale*, for an extensive description of BSI's role in the scandal.

[35] Quoted in Kelleher, "Goldman Sachs and the 1MDB Scandal."

[36] Kelleher, "Goldman Sachs and the 1MDB Scandal."

[37] Andrew Sachs-McLeod, "Goldman Sachs star Tim Leissner ends 2 year 1mdb saga with bank getting $2 billion punch in the face," *Finance Feeds*, October 20, 2020, https://financefeeds.com/goldman-sachs-star-tim-leissner-ends-4-year-1mdb-saga-bank-getting-2-billion-punch-face/.

[38] Sachs-McLeod, "Goldman Sachs star Tim Leissner ends 2 year 1mdb saga with bank getting $2 billion punch in the face."

[39] Kelleher, "Goldman Sachs and the 1MDB Scandal."

[40] Douglas Jensen and Ashley Williams, "Bribery & Corruption Laws and Regulations 2021 | USA," April 12, 2020, https://www.globallegalinsights.com/practice-areas/bribery-and-corruption-laws-and-regulations/usa.

Integrity and Mercy—A Question of Loyalty

I faced an ethical dilemma in the summer of 2019. It was a classic question of whom I should be loyal to, my firm or my friend. I'd taken an ethics class as an undergrad student at the University of Washington (UW), but I thought the cases were so kitschy and unreal. Who knew that within two years of taking the class I'd find myself in the very situation I had laughed over? Life is funny that way, but this was no laughing matter.

After graduating from UW, I moved to the Bay Area in California to work as an analyst for Briggs Venture Funding. Briggs was short for Briggs, Ford, and Evenson. Mr. Briggs had been an early investor in Intel back in the 1960s, and the firm was one of the most prestigious, but never one of the biggest, in Silicon Valley. Our latest fund, the Vision IV Fund, was only worth $3.5 billion, and we were actively seeking new investments in the life sciences. We were putting money into animal health, biotech pharma, and medical device start-ups. Unlike our investments in Silicon Valley and in software—where we invested early and often—our approach in the life sciences was to take bigger stakes later in the life cycle. The payoffs were bigger, but so were the risks.

I owed my job at Briggs to my best friend and roommate Jordan Jensen. Jordan was a year older than I, and I met her on the first day of rush at UW my freshman year. After I joined the Beta Lambda Sigma sorority, she became my big sister and mentor. We were both finance majors and ended up sharing an apartment during her senior year. When she took a job at Providian Equity Partners in San Jose, California, we were both thrilled. The following December, Jordan invited me to come to the Bay Area for the weekend and attend a holiday party for her office. While there, I met Tom Matheson from Briggs. Tom eventually helped me get a job at Briggs, and while we were not on the same project team, we became good friends.

As soon as I started at Briggs, Jordan and I began looking for a place to share. We found one in Sunnyvale on Palo Alto's Sandhill Road, halfway between her job in San Jose and mine. We lived on the second story of a remodeled 1950s apartment complex, complete with swimming pool, multiple hot tubs, and a common area where we could host friends and family. We established a rule very early: Since we were both working in venture-related finance, we'd keep any client-related discussions out of the apartment. We shared many of the travails of working in Silicon Valley, and we often gave each other advice about how to handle work-related situations.

We always used code words if we even mentioned a client project in order to keep confidentiality. As you can imagine, that wasn't always a smooth process. We were both smart, and the Valley turned out to be a very small community, so it was hard not to know what everyone was working on. An example of this was a project Jordan and I referred to as "sunrise," or eValve. Jordan was on the "sunrise" team at Providian, and Tom's team at Briggs was handling our work on the project.

eValve was a medical device company founded on some patents developed at the University of California San Francisco. eValve used some cutting-edge composite materials to create a breakthrough in replacement heart valve efficacy and longevity. Briggs was the lead investor in a Series E round of $700 million. Providian was a major partner in the consortium and would be contributing about $225 million to the round.

As the months went by, I noticed that the work culture of Providian was far different from the one at Briggs. Jordan worked an 8 a.m. to 5 p.m. job, and Providian really emphasized work–life balance. They could do this because their investing strategy was different from ours. While Providian dabbled in pre-IPO companies, the bulk of their business was with larger, well-established companies. Providian had a culture much more like a traditional bank, slow and hierarchical, with a California twist of a laid-back style and real concern for having a personal life.

Briggs, for being one of the older venture capital (VC) firms in the Valley, reflected the culture of Sandhill Road. Venture capital was a fast and heady business, with employees expected to work whenever and wherever. Decision making devolved to each financing team. The name of the game was thorough research and a risk-assessment process that looked heavily at upside potential. The Silicon Valley VC community is pretty cutthroat as well, so speed mattered on getting any deal locked down. Briggs had a reputation as a smart firm; we did our homework and brought together financing consortiums that helped our portfolio companies grow and move toward liquidity events, either IPOs or acquisitions.

I bought into the culture of Briggs and became very loyal to the firm. Given how hard I worked, when I got home, I was ready to unwind and not think about the helter-skelter world of VC. When I arrived home one Friday evening in June, I found Jordan very upset. The tear stains had totally mangled her makeup, and she was obviously agitated. I asked what was up, and Jordan said she couldn't say. I had a hard time with this because we were best friends and shared everything. She told me that she didn't want to put me in an uncomfortable position, but if I promised to keep the information confidential, she would tell me.

I agreed, figuring this was likely something to do with Jayden, her boyfriend of several months. Jordan told me that she received her "walking papers" earlier that afternoon from Providian. She lost her job and would be out of work in a couple of weeks. My first thought, and hers, was concern about how we would pay the rent on our killer apartment. My second thought was about what kind of opportunity she would pursue. She was a smart woman with good experience, and I told her that this would just be a bump in the road for her.

My third thought was about "sunrise." I asked her what the shake-up at Providian meant for the project and she began to cry again. She explained that Max Creer, the managing director of Providian, had decided to completely exit Providian from all things biotech. He felt that the runway for success was too long, and the need for capital was too great to build a sustainable business. Providian would be backing out of the eValve deal.

Max was out of the country until Monday morning, and he wanted to announce Providian's new strategy at a press conference that morning. If Jordan's disclosure to me were revealed, it could jeopardize any severance she received from the firm.

I left Jordan in her room and went to the living room and sat on the couch. I opened my laptop and pulled up the eValve file on our secure server. With this Series E round, Briggs would have put a total of $900 million into the venture. We were by far the leading investor in the company to date and the most vulnerable to the risks of eValve failing. This Series E round would give eValve the capital to move the initial product through the FDA approval process. As a Class III medical device, the FDA had to certify that the product was both safe and efficacious. If eValve crossed this last hurdle, they could begin selling the product. Having the capital in hand would allow eValve's team to be really well prepared for a process scheduled to start in ninety days. Delays of even a couple weeks could jeopardize—or substantially delay—the FDA approval process.

The financing round would also be used to help build out the company's marketing and sales team. To date, eValve was primarily a research company with a strong capability in basic and applied research and testing. Without a strong branding and marketing team, and a robust sales force, eValve would be dead in the water. The thoracic surgery market was very technical, and it took a long time for companies to build the level of trust with surgeons that led to a product being used in an operating theater.

The "sunrise" deal was well advanced and the junior consortium members had already transferred funds into escrow. Briggs would have to cover Providian's stake, at least until another investor could be found. The problem for Briggs was that our scheduled investment took us to the limit of an ownership stake in the Vision IV Fund covenants. The firm would have to come up with the additional $225 million in less than a week. That would require raiding our own investment fund, plus short-term borrowings of about $50 million.

Tying up our own funds would limit our flexibility to invest in other projects, and the interest rates we'd need to pay to come up with $50 million would put a real dent in the profitability of our eValve investment. Bonuses for everyone at Briggs could very well disappear.

I thought about the ramifications for Tom and the firm in general. Like I said, the Valley is a very small world and Tom would look like a fool if he were caught off guard by the Providian announcement. It wouldn't look good that Tom's team was surprised by a slow and methodical private equity (PE) firm. Briggs would take a serious hit to our reputation as well. Briggs could lose out on some upcoming investment deals because no one wants a laggard on their team.

Jordan told me what had happened, so I wondered if someone else on the Providian team had done the same thing. Would the news get leaked to the press? Silicon Valley news feeds were every bit as competitive as the VC firms they covered, and a story like this would be too good not to publish immediately.

After looking through the file, I thought about how valuable a couple days' advance notice would be to Tom and his team. There was no question that they'd work all weekend to lessen the blow of Providian's pullout, and given their track record, sixty hours were an eternity. I thought about my friendship with Tom. He was really one of the good guys at Briggs and had been able to avoid the arrogance that plagues so many VCs. I opened my Gmail account and started to compose a new message.

Then I just stopped. What was I thinking? Was I really ready to violate a promise of confidence I'd made to my best friend in order to be loyal to my work? Did I have a life outside work? I always thought that the only reason I'd break a promise was if someone faced physical harm, but what about economic harm? I loved working at Briggs, and I had a ton of respect for Tom. Jordan, on the other hand, was my best friend.

Corporate Social Responsibility—CSR at Microsoft

Bill Gates and Paul Allen met each other in the 1960s, when both were students at Seattle's Lakeside High School. The two would often meet at the school's lone computer terminal to work and learn.[1] That friendship led the two to eventually drop what they were doing and found Microsoft in 1975. Allen was working as a programmer in Boston for Honeywell, and Gates was a student at Harvard. They relocated to Albuquerque, New Mexico, and began writing software for one of the first microcomputers, the Altair 8800. Four years later, annual revenues exceeded $1 million, and the two moved their company to Bellevue, Washington. At that time, the company had a simple mission statement: "a computer on every desk and in every home."[2]

Microsoft's big break came in 1980 as computing giant IBM found itself caught off guard by the exploding market for small, personal computers. IBM needed to build a computer as fast as possible, and they chose to outsource many of the machine's key systems. IBM chose Microsoft's MS-DOS to provide the operating system for the new IBM PC.[3] Over the next few years, the company would come to dominate the market for PC software, both operating systems and applications. The company went public in 1986, raising $61 million in its initial public offering (IPO).[4]

By 1998, Microsoft had become so powerful that the U.S. Department of Justice filed suit to break the company up. Microsoft dominated the personal computer operating system market with a 95 percent share[5] and the workplace application market with a 93 percent global share for its Office suite of programs.[6] Its status threatened competition in the nascent Internet search market and imperiled then leader Netscape's ability to generate revenue from its browser.[7] In 2000, federal Judge Thomas Penfield Jackson ruled that Microsoft had violated the Sherman Antitrust Act. Microsoft entered into a consent decree and agreed to disclose fundamental code to third-party developers for its application software, and, most important, allow consumers to easily uninstall Internet Explorer as the default Web browser.[8]

Microsoft followed the world and the industry onto the World Wide Web in the late 1990s and into the twenty-first century. The company continued to develop its flagship Windows product throughout that period. The company's Xbox game station holds a 42 percent share of the gaming device market and continues to close the gap with Sony's PlayStation.[9] Microsoft Office has moved to an online subscription model, and when combined with the Microsoft Cloud architecture, the company offers a turnkey solution for home, small business, and large corporate users. During the COVID-19 pandemic, the company's Teams product—a competitor to Zoom—saw it user base grow from 20 million to 95 million during the year 2020.[10]

Corporate Social Responsibility at Microsoft

Microsoft began a corporate giving program in 1983, one of the first in the rapidly growing high-technology sector.[11] Thirty years later, Microsoft and its employees had donated over $6.5 billion in cash, services, and software to nonprofits around the world.[12] In 2020 alone, the company donated $1.9 billion in services or products to global nonprofits.

The company began to document and report on its citizenship activities in 2003. That report has evolved over the years and is now titled the "Corporate Social Responsibility Report." The 2003 report focused on five key stakeholders: communities, customers, employees, partners and developers, and the natural environment. The report also detailed six core values that would drive Microsoft's social commitments in the years ahead:

- Integrity and honesty
- Passion for customers, partners, and technology
- Open and respectful with others, and dedicated to making them better
- A willingness to take on big challenges and see them through
- Self-critical, questioning, and committed to personal excellence and self-improvement
- Accountable for commitments, results, and quality to customers, shareholders, partners, and employees

Then chief executive officer Steve Balmer and board chair Bill Gates wrote that "global citizenship, like the rest of our business, is a work in progress. This overview simply provides a snapshot of where we stand today because every program and activity highlighted here is active and ongoing. We look forward to continuing to make a lasting difference in the lives we touch and the communities where we do business and to empowering more people who—because of age, geography, physical disability, or economic barriers—could not otherwise reap the benefit of technology."[13]

In 2017, CEO Satya Nadella unveiled a new vision statement for the company:

> Microsoft is a technology company whose mission is to empower every person and every organization on the planet to achieve more. We strive to create local opportunity, growth, and impact in every country around the world. Our strategy is to build best-in-class platforms and productivity services for an intelligent cloud and an intelligent edge infused with artificial intelligence ("AI").
>
> The way individuals and organizations use and interact with technology continues to evolve. A person's experience with technology increasingly spans a multitude of devices and becomes more natural and multi-sensory with voice, ink, and gaze interactions. We believe a new technology paradigm is emerging that manifests itself through an intelligent cloud and an intelligent edge where computing is more distributed, AI drives insights and acts on the user's behalf, and user experiences span devices with

a user's available data and information. We continue to transform our business to lead this new era of digital transformation and enable our customers and partners to thrive in this evolving world.[14]

The shift in vision from putting computers in every home to empowering every person and organization to increase their achievements represented a much broader focus. Corporate social responsibility (CSR) at Microsoft had broadened its focus as well. While the 2003 report detailed actions around five stakeholder groups, the 2020 report represented a shift to much broader areas of involvement. The company labels these commitments as:

- Support Inclusive Opportunity
- Protect Fundament Rights
- Commit to a Sustainable Future
- Earn Trust[15]

Several groups have recognized the company's efforts in CSR. In 2019, the company received a 100 percent rating on the Human Rights Campaign Corporate Equality Index. The company was also recognized by Ethisphere as one of the world's most ethical companies, a list on which Microsoft has appeared for nine straight years. The Carbon Disclosure Project put Microsoft on its "Climate A" list for leadership in sustainability. *Corporate Responsibility Magazine* ranked Microsoft as one of its 10 Best Corporate Citizens for 2019. Overall, the company garnered CSR awards from sixteen different organizations.[16]

The Case Assignment

This case takes place in real time. The background materials for this case can be found in current public documents. You should begin by viewing and studying Microsoft's Web page devoted to its CSR activities. You can find this through any search engine. You should then become familiar with Microsoft's detailed CSR report. You should be able to find a link to the latest report through the website, or

by typing "Microsoft Corporate Social Responsibility Report" into any search engine. You'll also need some familiarity with the United Nations Sustainable Development Goals, which you can find online through any search engine.

You will see that Microsoft is involved in several different and discrete areas of CSR. Your instructor may assign you, or your class team, to focus on one or more of these areas. As you prepare for this discussion, you should focus on the following questions:

- What is Microsoft doing well in this area?
- How does their involvement in this area converge with and leverage their core business skills and competences? How does the CSR activity fill their mission?
- How do their activities "map on" and contribute to the United Nations Sustainable Development Goals?
- What gaps do you see in Microsoft's work in this area? What other unsolved problems could Microsoft help solve? Note: This may require that you become familiar with the broader area in which Microsoft works.
- How well does work in your area of focus mesh with the other areas of CSR for Microsoft?
- What challenges do you see ahead for Microsoft in its CSR agenda?
- If you were advising the Microsoft vice president of the Corporate and Technology Responsibility group, what would you recommend that Microsoft stop doing? Start doing? Keep doing?

You or your group should assume that you have fifteen minutes with Microsoft's VP of Corporate and Technology Responsibility. You should prepare a presentation, based on the questions and research above, that evaluates Microsoft's performance in your CSR area of focus and makes recommendations for changes going forward. You should also anticipate that the VP will have questions about your reasoning and recommendations.

References

[1] David Levesley, "Paul Allen and Bill Gates: a brief history of their friendship," *GQ*, October 16, 2018, https://www.gq-magazine.co.uk/article/paul-allen-bill-gates-microsoft.

[2] Mary Jo Foley, "Microsoft's new mission statement: No more computer on every desk," *ZDNet*, October 7, 2013, https://www.zdnet.com/article/microsofts-new-mission-statement-no-more-computer-on-every-desk/.

[3] History.com editors, "1975, April 04, Microsoft founded," History.com, This Day in History, last updated April 1, 2020, https://www.history.com/this-day-in-history/microsoft-founded.

[4] History.com editors, "1975, April 04, Microsoft founded."

[5] "Windows in 95% of PCs by 1999," CNET.com, June 17, 1998, https://www.cnet.com/news/windows-in-95-of-pcs-by-1999/.

[6] Joel Brinkley, "Microsoft Has A Stronghold In Office Suites," *New York Times*, May 27, 1998, https://www.nytimes.com/1998/05/27/business/microsoft-has-a-stronghold-in-office-suites.html.

[7] What was the Microsoft Antitrust Case?," Corporate Finance Institute, https://corporatefinanceinstitute.com/resources/knowledge/strategy/microsoft-antitrust-case/.

[8] Victor Lukerson, "'Crush Them': An Oral History of the Lawsuit That Upended Silicon Valley," *The Ringer*, May 18, 2018, https://www.theringer.com/tech/2018/5/18/17362452/microsoft-antitrust-lawsuit-netscape-internet-explorer-20-years.

[9] "Xbox Closes Gap But Playstation Still More Popular - 57.54% Of Market Share," *Scoop Independent News*, press release, February 24, 2021, https://www.scoop.co.nz/stories/WO2102/S00257/xbox-closes-gap-but-playstation-still-more-popular-5754-of-market-share.htm#:~:text=The%20data%20indicates%20that%20as,42.15%25%20share%20of%20the%20market.

[10] David Curry, "Microsoft Teams Revenue and Usage Statistics (2021)," Business of Apps, last updated July 29, 2021, https://www.businessofapps.com/data/microsoft-teams-statistics/.

[11] *Microsoft Citizenship Report*, 2003.

[12] "Microsoft Employees Raise $1 Billion for Communities Around the World," Microsoft, press release, October 18, 2012, https://news.microsoft.com/2012/10/18/microsoft-employees-raise-1-billion-for-communities-around-the-world/#:~:text=Microsoft%20employees%20have%20donated%20%241,the%20corporate%20match%2C%20since%201983.&text=Since%201983%2C%20Microsoft%20and%20its,sponsored%20giving%20and%20volunteer%20campaigns.

[13] *Microsoft Citizenship Report*, 2003, 1.

[14] Nat Levy, "Microsoft's new corporate vision: artificial intelligence is in and mobile is out," *GeekWire*, August 2, 2017, https://www.geekwire.com/2017/microsofts-new-corporate-vision-artificial-intelligence-mobile/#:~:text=Microsoft%20is%20a%20technology%20company,every%20country%20around%20the%20world.

[15] See Microsoft Corporate Social Responsibility, accessed September 9, 2021, https://www.microsoft.com/en-us/corporate-responsibility.

[16] Microsoft Corporate Social Responsibility, Awards and Recognition, accessed September 9, 2021, https://www.microsoft.com/en-us/corporate-responsibility/recognition#:~:text=Microsoft%20again%20ranked%20within%20the,companies%20across%20the%20United%20States.

Ethics and Technology—Facebook's Oversight Board and its Effect in 2021

> Maybe there are some calls that just aren't good for the company to make by itself.[1]
> — Mark Zuckerberg, Facebook CEO

Jennifer Newstead sighed heavily as she glanced at the headline of her news feed, "Facebook Oversight Board upholds Trump ban but calls indefinite suspension 'not appropriate.'"[2] As vice president and general counsel of the technology giant, she knew that the board's ruling would create work for her and her team. Facebook had issued an indefinite ban of then President Donald Trump from its platform in January of 2021 for posts that the company claimed were disinformation that sparked the violence that led groups to storm the U.S. Capitol on January 6 as Congress met to affirm and count the Electoral College votes. The ban had moved to a review by the company-sponsored but independent oversight board, a kind of "supreme court" body that was designed to review company decisions that dealt with freedom of speech issues.

In announcing its decision, the board said that "At the time of Mr. Trump's posts, there was a clear, immediate risk of harm and his words of support for those involved in the riots legitimized their violent actions.... Given the seriousness of the violations and the ongoing risk of violence, Facebook was justified in suspending Mr. Trump's accounts." The board seemed to play the role of appellate court for Facebook's actions. The statement went on, however, and noted that if Facebook was hoping to "avoid its responsibilities" through "a vague, standardless penalty" of an indefinite suspension, the company would be disappointed. "The Board declines Facebook's request and insists that Facebook apply and justify a defined penalty," the board noted in its decision.[3]

Newstead realized that the board request for a well-defined policy of what types of violations would justify a permanent ban, a temporary ban, or no ban, would fall to her. As a lawyer, she could offer a set of clear, legalistic standards, but she realized that defining the company's free speech policy would need to include lawyers, leaders of Facebook's business units, academics, and ethicists. This was uncharted territory for the company, and the technology industry in general, and Newstead knew that her actions would set an important precedent.

THE RISE OF SOCIAL MEDIA

Facebook competed in and dominated the social media industry, defined as "websites and applications that enable users to create and share content or to participate in social networking."[4] The idea that technology and tools could improve networking, social interaction, and relationships did not begin with the Internet. Each improvement in communications technology, from the advent of postal services through the telegraph and to the telephone, enhanced people's ability to communicate, share news and ideas, and deepen relationships.

The first real digitally based, online, and scalable social media application appeared in 1979 in the form of USENET, a platform that allowed users to communicate via a newsletter, articles, or posts to newsgroups. The year 1997 marked a new era in social media with the advent of SixDegrees.com, a site on the World Wide Web where users could upload pictures and connect with others.[5] LinkedIn and Myspace were both founded in 2003. LinkedIn was, and is, the most popular social media platform for business professionals. Myspace represented the first large-scale site where users could create a unique profile and share information about themselves with others. The fore-runner of Facebook, thefacebook.com, launched to a limited audience of Harvard students in 2004. Twitter followed in 2006, the same year Facebook launched its service under a new name and URL.[6]

The rise of social media, along with the advent of the smart-phone in 2007, changed how Americans interacted with each other, how they shared information, and how they received news of events and happenings in the larger world. See Exhibit 1 for a ranking of the most popular social media sites. As of the end of 2014, Pew Research estimated that two-thirds of the American population used social media, with rates among young users (18–29) approaching 90 percent. During the 2016 election cycle, 62 percent of Americans received their news from social media, with 18 percent reporting that they used social media "often" and another 26 percent using it "sometimes."[7] By 2021, those figures had changed, with over two-thirds of Americans getting their news from news websites or apps, and only 53 percent using social media "often" (23%) or "sometimes (30%).[8]

FACEBOOK

Mark Zuckerberg, a psychology student at Harvard with a penchant for computer programming, created thefacebook.com in 2004. The site represented his third effort; he had developed Coursematch, which allowed users to see who else at Harvard had the same major, and Facemash, a site where users could rate the physical attractiveness of others. The original thefacebook.com site allowed users to create a personal profile and to share with others. Within twenty-four hours of launching thefacebook.com, over 1,200 Harvard students had signed up for the site, which soon spread to the rest of the Ivy League schools. By May of 2007, Facebook was already the sixth most visited website in the United States,[9] and by mid-2008, the site had signed up its first 100 million subscribers. At the close of 2020, Facebook had 2.7 billion monthly users. Exhibit 2 details Facebook's growth. Exhibit 3 provides details of Facebook's financial performance.

Facebook prospered because it had a strong vision: "I'm here to build something for the long term," Zuckerberg said. The core Facebook idea was that by providing an open platform where users could share information, human relationships would improve and the world would become a better place.[10] The company grew because, unlike its original competitor Myspace, Facebook allowed its users—and the market in general—to set its direction and inform how the site would evolve in terms of features and functionality. The company worked to create technology that would enable its users to do what they wanted, from finding new friends on the site to playing games (think *FarmVille*), and to easily upload content.[11] Facebook

Most Popular Social Networks Worldwide as of January 2021, Ranked by Number of Active Users (In Millions)

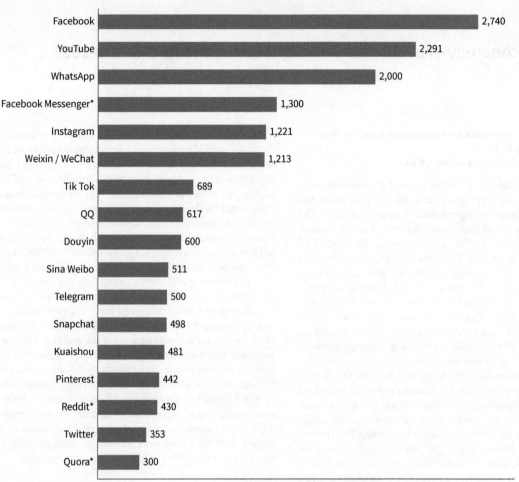

Facebook	2,740
YouTube	2,291
WhatsApp	2,000
Facebook Messenger*	1,300
Instagram	1,221
Weixin / WeChat	1,213
Tik Tok	689
QQ	617
Douyin	600
Sina Weibo	511
Telegram	500
Snapchat	498
Kuaishou	481
Pinterest	442
Reddit*	430
Twitter	353
Quora*	300

Number of active users in millions

Source: We Are Social; Various sources (Company data); Hootsuite; DataReportal © Statista 2021.
*Platforms have not published updated user figures in the past 12 months, figures may be out of date and less reliable.

EXHIBIT 1   Research shows Facebook is the most popular social media platform[13]

Facebook Average Monthly Users

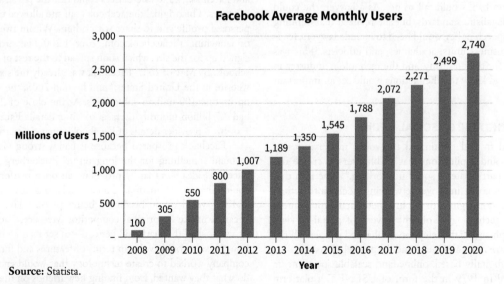

Year	Millions of Users
2008	100
2009	305
2010	550
2011	800
2012	1,007
2013	1,189
2014	1,350
2015	1,545
2016	1,788
2017	2,072
2018	2,271
2019	2,499
2020	2,740

Source: Statista.

EXHIBIT 2   Facebook experienced continuous growth

EXHIBIT 3   Facebook Financial Performance

Consolidated Statements of Income - USD ($)			12 Months Ended			
Shares in Millions, $ in Millions	Dec. 31, 2020	Dec. 31, 2019	Dec. 31, 2018	Dec. 31, 2017	Dec. 31, 2016	Dec. 31,2015
Revenue	**$ 85,965**	**$ 70,697**	**$ 55,838**	**$ 40,653**	**$ 27,638**	**$ 17,928**
Costs and expenses:						
Cost of revenue	$ 16,692	$ 12,770	$ 9,355	$ 5,454	$ 3,789	$ 2,867
Research and development	$ 18,447	$ 13,600	$ 10,273	$ 7,754	$ 5,919	$ 4,816
Marketing and sales	$ 11,591	$ 9,876	$ 7,846	$ 4,725	$ 3,772	$ 2,725
General and administrative	$ 6,564	$ 10,465	$ 3,451	$ 2,517	$ 1,731	$ 1,295
Total costs and expenses	$ 53,294	$ 46,711	$ 30,925	$ 20,450	$ 15,211	$ 11,703
Income from operations	$ 32,671	$ 23,986	$ 24,913	$ 20,203	$ 12,427	$ 6,225
Interest and other income, net	$ 509	$ 826	$ 448	$ 391	$ 91	$ (31)
Income before provision for income taxes	$ 33,180	$ 24,812	$ 25,361	$ 20,594	$ 12,518	$ 6,194
Provision for income taxes	$ 4,034	$ 6,327	$ 3,249	$ 4,660	$ 2,301	$ 2,506
Net income	**$ 29,146**	**$ 18,485**	**$ 22,112**	**$ 15,934**	**$ 10,217**	**$ 3,688**
Less: Net income attributable to participating securities			$ (1)	$ 14	$ 29	$ 19
Net income	**$ 29,146**	**$ 18,485**	**$ 22,111**	**$ 15,920**	**$ 10,188**	**$ 3,669**
Earnings per share						
Basic (in dollars per share)	$ 10.22	$ 6.48	$ 7.65	$ 5.49	$ 3.56	$ 1.31
Diluted (in dollars per share)	$ 10.09	$ 6.43	$ 7.57	$ 5.39	$ 3.49	$ 1.29
Basic (in shares)	2,851	2,854	2,890	2,901	2,863	2,803
Diluted (in shares)	2,888	2,876	2,921	2,956	2,925	2,853

Source: Company 10-K filiings, various years.

encouraged people to use their real names, a practice that soon became commonplace throughout the social media sphere.[12]

No feature set Facebook apart more effectively than its News Feed, added in September of 2006. Before the News Feed came online, Facebook users had to visit the individual profiles of friends to see new posts or information; they had to search the platform to find what they wanted. News Feed now brought the power of the platform to users. It became the new landing page that would constantly update to feature the latest posts and activities of the user's friends as well as provide news content that appealed to particular users. The News Feed made Facebook a dynamic website that offered users a constant set of new ways to interact on the site.[14] The company's post announcing the launch of the News Feed touted this dynamic capability: "[News Feed] updates a personalized list of news stories throughout the day, so you'll know when Mark adds Britney Spears to his Favorites. Now, whenever you log in, you'll get the latest headlines generated by the activity of your friends and social groups."[15]

In 2009, the company allowed users to "like" posts, pictures, or other content. The company added an algorithm to predict the news stories that would be most relevant to users based on their Facebook visit history, calling the concept "your own personal newspaper."[16] Users also gained the ability to self-filter their News Feed to only receive updates from people and groups they selected.[17] In 2011, the News Feed began to display a user's News Feed by interests rather than chronology.[18] These developments on the News Feed mirrored other algorithms at Facebook that allowed the company to micro-target advertising to a user's known—and anticipated—preferences. This micro-targeting capability contributed to strong revenue and profit growth at the company since its initial public offering (IPO) in 2012.

Facebook dealt with the problem of users facing overwhelming information in their feed by narrowing the funnel. Critics noted that the News Feed led to an "echo chamber," or a platform where users only get exposed to content with which they are likely to agree. Academic studies confirmed the existence of this echo chamber;

one study found that "the algorithm suppresses the diversity of the content you see in your feed by occasionally hiding items that you may disagree with and letting through the ones you are likely to agree with. The effect wasn't all or nothing: For self-identified liberals, one in thirteen diverse news stories were removed, for example. Overall, this confirms what many of us had suspected: that the Facebook algorithm is biased towards producing agreement, not dissent."[19]

Facebook's News Feed allowed users "to promote their favorite narratives, form polarized groups, and resist information that doesn't conform to their beliefs."[20] Ironically, the News Feed turned Facebook into a site that, instead of bringing people together, drove them apart. Facebook had developed a set of capabilities that allowed it to effectively filter information that users saw, and to make sure they saw the types of information they wanted to see and were likely to act upon and didn't see things that challenged their opinion or worldview. These capabilities would become central to the 2016 U.S. presidential election, for good or for ill.

THE 2016 U.S. PRESIDENTIAL ELECTION

Facebook's entry into the 2016 election fray came in winter of 2016 with the publication of an awkward post by the news site *Gizmodo* of an internal question for an all-hands meeting: "What responsibility does Facebook have to help prevent President Trump in 2017?" *Gizmodo* would follow that post with a headline in May: "Former Facebook workers: we routinely suppressed conservative news."[21] Facebook was seen by many, on the left and the right, as anything but a neutral platform for the sharing of ideas. Conservatives, liberals, and company executives began to worry that the platform was, or could be, much more than a mere facilitator of information; Facebook, with its dominant position in news dissemination, might be a powerful tool for influencing public opinion and individual electoral attitudes and behaviors. *Gizmodo*'s posts sparked a letter from Senator John Thune (R-SD) asking for answers from Facebook about potential bias. Facebook responded by hosting a day-long event for prominent conservatives at its Menlo Park Headquarters. The company's main message, as recounted by conservative icon Glenn Beck: "I asked [Zuckerberg] if Facebook, now or in the future, would be an open platform for the sharing of ideas or a curator of content. Without hesitation, with clarity and boldness, Mark said there is only one Facebook and one path forward: 'we are an open platform.'"[22]

Late in the election cycle itself, and in the immediate aftermath of Mr. Trump's unexpected victory, allegations surfaced that Russian intelligence agencies, often working through intermediaries, had used these same tools and capabilities to influence the outcome of the election illegally and surreptitiously through the dissemination of false news stories and posts aimed at making political issues more divisive. An army of Russian "trolls," government agents and actors who posed as American citizens and created false profiles on Facebook, disseminated stories, opinion posts, videos, and memes that focused on such divisive issues as gun control, immigration, LGBT rights, and movements such as Black Lives Matter. Posts by Russian trolls were written to amplify and exacerbate divisions and tensions around these issues among readers.[23] Exhibit 4 displays a sample of ads traced to Russian sources.

Trolls initiated posts that were "scathing or defamatory towards Hillary Clinton. Widely circulated fake stories include accounts of Pope Francis endorsing the Republican candidate, Hillary Clinton murdering an FBI agent, and President Obama 'admitting' he was born in Kenya." These hoax stories appeared in the News Feed alongside fact-based posts, and many of these stories were picked up and shared by people sympathetic to the political ideology in the posts.[24]

The Internet Research Agency, posing as an independent organization, but allegedly sponsored by the Russian Government, bought political advertisements on Facebook, an open violation of U.S. election laws. Alex Stamos, Facebook's chief security adviser, reporting on the company's own internal investigation, noted that "In reviewing the ads buys, we have found approximately $100,000 in ad spending from June of 2015 to May of 2017—associated with roughly 3,000 ads—that was connected to about 470 inauthentic accounts and Pages in violation of our policies. Our analysis suggests these accounts and Pages were affiliated with one another and likely operated out of Russia."[25] Estimates of the impact of these ads vary, with estimates ranging from 10–135 Million Americans viewing these false ads.[26,27] Five hundred posts from six known Russian-backed groups had been shared a total of 340 million times between Facebook groups and users.[28]

In an analysis of use of Facebook by Russian entities, researchers concluded:

> **Following the 2016 U.S. presidential election, many have expressed concern about the effects of false stories ("fake news"), circulated largely through social media.... Drawing on web browsing data, archives of fact-checking websites, and results from a new online survey, we find: (i) social media was an important but not dominant source of election news, with 14 percent of Americans calling social media their "most important" source; (ii) of the known false news stories that appeared in the three months before the election, those favoring Trump were shared a total of 30 million times on Facebook, while those favoring Clinton were shared 8 million times; (iii) the average American adult saw on the order of one or perhaps several fake news stories in the months around the election, with just over half of those who recalled seeing them believing them; and (iv) people are much more likely to believe stories that favor their preferred candidate, especially if they have ideologically segregated social media networks.[29]**

The Director of U.S. National Intelligence concluded: "Moscow's influence campaign followed a Russian messaging strategy that blends covert intelligence operations—such as cyber activity—with overt efforts by Russian Government agencies, state-funded media, third-party intermediaries, and paid social media users or "trolls.""[30]

THE AFTERMATH AND FACEBOOK'S RESPONSE

On November 7, 2016, Donald J. Trump won the U.S. presidential election; he earned 306 votes in the Electoral College (270 votes are needed to win), even though he lost the popular vote by just under three million votes. Trump's election took pundits by surprise as most polls showed Secretary Clinton winning the election.[31] Within days, accusations of Russian manipulation of the election emerged as a cause of the unexpected election outcome, and attention soon focused on the role of false news on Facebook.

On November 11, 2016, Mr. Zuckerberg publicly questioned how much influence Facebook might actually have, saying "I think the idea that fake news on Facebook—of which it's a very small amount of the content—influenced the election in any way is a pretty crazy idea.... Part of what I think is going on here is people are trying to understand the results of the election," Zuckerberg said. "I think there is a certain profound lack of empathy in asserting that the only reason why someone could have voted the way they did is because they saw some fake news."[32]

As findings from the investigations came forward, Facebook executives realized that the Russian influence was anything but a "crazy idea." In September of 2017, Facebook officials responded to the

Being Patriotic shared their event.
Sponsored · 🌐

Hillary Clinton is the co-author of Obama's anti-police and anti-Constitutional propaganda

JUL
23
Down With Hillary!
Sat 1 PM EDT · 1 Pierrepont Plz, New York City, ...
180 people interested · 45 people going

★ Interested

763 Reactions 76 Comments

👍 Like   💬 Comment

LGBT United
Sponsored · 🌐

👍 Like Page

You can color your own Bernie Hero!

There is a new coloring book calling "Buff Bernie: A coloring Book for Berniacs" is full of very attractive doodles of Bernie Sanders in muscle poses.

The author of the book said that she wanted people to stop taking this whole thing too serious. The coloring is something that suits for all people. ...
See More

40 Reactions 2 Comments 3 Shares

👍 Like   💬 Comment   ➤ Share

Blacktivist

Black Panthers were dismantled by US government because they were black men and women standing up for justice and equality.

never forget that the Black Panthers, group formed to protect black people from the KKK, was dismantled by us govt but the KKK exists today

😮❤️ 6.2K   205 Comments 29K Shares

BM shared their event.
Sponsored · 🌐

People are genuinely scared for their futures!
Racism won, Ignorance won, Sexual assault won

STOP TRUMP! STOP RACISM! JOIN THE PROTEST at Union Sq.
Saturday 12 PM
Bring signs, snacks, water!

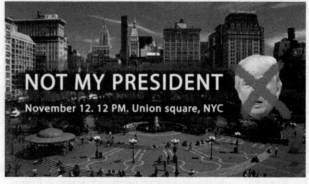

NOT MY PRESIDENT
November 12. 12 PM. Union square, NYC

NOV
12
Trump is NOT my President. March aga...
Sat 12 PM EST · Union Square - 14th & Broadwa...
33,140 people interested · 16,760 people going

★ Interested

👍 Like   💬 Comment

EXHIBIT 4 Russian-backed ads and posts on Facebook

reality of the Russian activity during the 2016 election. The company admitted that its site and systems had been abused but highlighted the difficulties it faced in monitoring and mitigating such abuse. Eliot Schrage, Facebook's vice president of public policy, stated:

Even when we have taken all steps to control abuse, there will be political and social content that will appear on our platform that people will find objectionable, and that we will find objectionable. . . . We permit these messages because we share the values of free speech—that when the right to speech is censored or restricted for any of us, it diminishes the rights to speech for all of us, and that when people have the right and opportunity to engage in free and full political expression, over time, they will move forward, not backwards, in promoting democracy and the rights of all.[33]

Facebook moved away from the "crazy idea" that nation-states might use its platform and embraced the idea that the events surrounding the 2016 election—if replicated—could pose a threat to the integrity of democratic elections around the globe. Facebook began to move away from an open platform and toward being a curator of content, the opposite of what Zuckerberg had told Glenn Beck months earlier. Chief operations officer (COO) Sheryl Sandberg noted that her company owed the American public an apology and described the mood at the company: "It's not just that we apologize. We're angry, we're upset. But what we really owe the American people is determination."[34]

Facebook announced sweeping changes in its News Feed in January of 2018. These changes, according to the company, would provide a further layer of protection against false information and news, making it harder, but not impossible, for malicious content to appear and spread. The driving objective of the News Feed would change from providing "relevant content" that may interest a user and toward content that would encourage "meaningful interaction" among users on the site. For example, users would see fewer posts from third parties, such as news organizations, and more posts from friends and family, the logic being that posts from the latter would be more likely to encourage a meaningful response or even human interaction.[35]

According to Mark Zuckerberg, the changes to the News Feed were designed to encourage users to spend less overall time on Facebook. While this change responded to long-time critiques of the company that saw Facebook as addictive, the threat to revenue could be very real. If users failed to spend enough time on the site, or continue patterns of use and "likes," Facebook's advertising algorithms might not serve up the types of targeted ads that sponsors loved. In spite of the business risks, Zuckerberg saw the changes to the News Feed as a part of an ongoing evolution at Facebook—an iterative and interactive evolution that included the billions of Facebook users: "The world feels anxious and divided and Facebook has a lot of work to do—whether it's protecting our community from abuse and hate, defending against interference by nation states, or making sure that time spent on Facebook is well spent."[36]

That evolution continued. In 2018, Harvard Law School professor Noah Feldman was visiting his old college friend and Facebook COO Sheryl Sandberg. As he thought about the challenge of policing political content on the site, "[I]t suddenly hit me: Facebook needs a Supreme Court." He raced home and wrote up the idea, arguing that social-media companies should create "quasi-legal systems" to weigh difficult questions around freedom of speech." He wrote a memo on the subject, which he gave to Sandberg, who gave it to Zuckerberg. Zuckerberg liked the idea as he found himself spending inordinate amounts of time deciding what high-profile posts to delete. Zuckerberg ordered the company to set up a board. Soon after, Feldman noted, "I was kind of stunned. Like, holy sh*t, this is actually going to happen."[37] Facebook scoured the globe for opinions about the board and held a number of focus groups to see which posts people in different countries and cultures would reject.

It was a long and arduous process, but the company eventually established a board of twenty experts from around the world, including former political leaders, human rights activists, and others. Facebook provided a $130 million endowment to fund the independent board. The board would review and rule on the company's decisions about free speech and would, in theory, act as the final decision maker regarding issues of free speech on the site. Many of the board's initial decisions had ruled against Facebook in favor of free speech rights.[38] Co-chair of the oversight board Michael McConnell noted that in the Trump case, as with any other one, the board's "sole job is to hold this extremely powerful organization, Facebook, accountable."[39]

NEWSTEAD'S CHALLENGE

The oversight board had agreed with the decision to ban Trump from the site; however, the board found that an "indefinite ban" was a vague standard. The board instructed Facebook to determine whether Trump's ban would be time bound or permanent. An "indefinite" suspension created an unacceptable "gray zone" and that further clarity around the ultimate duration of any suspension, and the reasoning behind that duration. Jennifer Newstead knew that Mark Zuckerberg and the rest of the Facebook leadership team would look to her for initial guidance about these standards. She realized that standards would need to be clear and firm enough to withstand legal challenges. She also knew that fairness and a default goal to protect free speech were central to Facebook's business model. She knew that underneath both the legal and business questions were two ethical ones: What ethical principles should she use to create the standards? What would be the ethical impact on free speech and global democratic institutions of the guidelines?

References

[1] Kate Klonick, "Inside the Making of Facebook's Supreme Court," *New Yorker*, February 12, 2021, https://www.newyorker.com/tech/annals-of-technology/inside-the-making-of-facebooks-supreme-court.

[2] Brooke Singman, "Facebook Oversight Board upholds Trump ban but calls indefinite suspension 'not appropriate,'" *FOXBusiness*, last updated May 5, 2021, https://www.foxbusiness.com/politics/facebook-trump-ban-upheld-oversight-board-decision.

[3] Shannon Bond, "Facebook Ban On Donald Trump Will Hold, Social Network's Oversight Board Rules," NPR, last updated May 5, 2021, https://www.npr.org/2021/05/05/987679590/facebook-justified-in-banning-donald-trump-social-medias-oversight-board-rules.

[4] Definition taken from *Oxford English Dictionary*, CF social media, https://en.oxforddictionaries.com/definition/social_media.

[5] Martin Beck, "Pew Survey: Nearly Two-Thirds Of All Americans Use Social Media," MarTech, October 9, 2015, at https://marketingland.com/pew-survey-nearly-two-thirds-of-all-americans-use-social-media-146026; and Christopher McFadden, "A Chronological History of Social Media," Interesting Engineering, July 2, 2020, https://interestingengineering.com/chronological-history-of-social-media. Material also is drawn from Monica Riese, "The definitive history of social media," *The Daily Dot*, last updated May 26, 2021, https://www.dailydot.com/debug/history-of-social-media/.

[6] McFadden, "A Chronological History of Social Media"; and Riese, "The definitive history of social media."

[7] Jeffrey Gottfried and Elisa Shearer, "News Use Across Social Media Platforms 2016," Pew Research Center, Journalism and Media report, May 26, 2016, http://www.journalism.org/2016/05/26/news-use-across-social-media-platforms-2016/.

[8] Elisa Shearer, "More than eight-in-ten Americans get news from digital devices," Pew Research Center, January 12, 2021, https://www.pewresearch.org/fact-tank/2021/01/12/more-than-eight-in-ten-americans-get-news-from-digital-devices/.

[9] Ellen McGirt, "Facebook's Mark Zuckerberg: Hacker. Dropout. CEO.," *Fast Company*, May 1, 2007, https://www.fastcompany.com/59441/facebooks-mark-zuckerberg-hacker-dropout-ceo.

[10] McGirt, "Facebook's Mark Zuckerberg: Hacker. Dropout. CEO."

[11] Adam Hartung, "How Facebook beat MySpace," *Forbes*, January 14, 2011, https://www.forbes.com/sites/adamhartung/2011/01/14/why-facebook-beat-myspace/#2399b722147e.

[12] Marc Schenker, "Former MySpace CEO explains why MySpace lost out to Facebook so badly," Digital Trends, May 12, 2015, https://www.digitaltrends.com/social-media/former-myspace-ceo-reveals-what-facebook-did-right-to-dominate-social-media/.

[13] "Most popular social networks worldwide as of July 2021, ranked by number of active users (in millions)," statista, https://www.statista.com/statistics/272014/global-social-networks-ranked-by-number-of-users/.

[14] Samantha Murphy, "The Evolution of Facebook News Feed," Mashable, March 12, 2013, http://mashable.com/2013/03/12/facebook-news-feed-evolution/#Q3pKQwZUQPqj.

[15] Murphy, "The Evolution of Facebook News Feed."

[16] Murphy, "The Evolution of Facebook News Feed."

[17] Murphy, "The Evolution of Facebook News Feed."

[18] News Feed, Wikipedia, accessed January 18, 2018, https://en.wikipedia.org/wiki/News_Feed.

[19] Zeynep Tufekci, "Facebook Said Its Algorithms Do Help Form Echo Chambers. And the Tech Press Missed It.," *Huffington Post*, last undated May 11, 2016, https://www.huffingtonpost.com/zeynep-tufekci/facebook-algorithm-echo-chambers_b_7259916.html.

[20] Christine Emba, "Confirmed: Echo chambers exist on social media. So what do we do about them?," *Washington Post*, July 14, 2016, https://www.washingtonpost.com/news/in-theory/wp/2016/07/14/confirmed-echo-chambers-exist-on-social-media-but-what-can-we-do-about-them/?utm_term=.b32eee072391.

[21] Thompson and Vogelstein.

[22] Thompson, N. and Vogelstein, F. Inside the Two Years that Shook Facebook—and the world. Wired, 12 February, 2018. Available at https://www.wired.com/story/inside-facebook-mark-zuckerberg-2-years-of-hell/.

[23] Carol D. Leonnig, Tom Hamburger, and Rosaline S. Helderman, "Russian firm tied to pro-Kremlin propaganda advertised on Facebook during election," *Washington Post*, September 6, 2017, https://www.washingtonpost.com/politics/facebook-says-it-sold-political-ads-to-russian-company-during-2016-election/2017/09/06/32f01fd2-931e-11e7-89fa-bb822a46da5b_story.html?utm_term=.72c155c33d88.

[24] "US Election 2016: Trump's 'hidden' Facebook army," BBC Trending, November 15, 2016, http://www.bbc.com/news/blogs-trending-37945486.

[25] Alana Abramson, "Facebook Says Russian Accounts Bought $100,000 in Ads During the 2016 Election," *Time*, September 6, 2017, http://time.com/4930532/facebook-russian-accounts-2016-election/.

[26] Tony Romm, "10 million people saw Russian ads on Facebook around the 2016 presidential election," Recode, October 2, 2017, https://www.recode.net/2017/10/2/16405900/russian-advertisements-facebook-2016-us-presidential-election-trump-clinton.

[27] Bruce Thornton, "Social Media, Fake News, and Free Speech," *Frontpage Magazine*, December 4, 2017, https://www.frontpagemag.com/fpm/268572/social-media-fake-news-and-free-speech-bruce-thornton.

[28] Thompson and Vogelstein.

[29] Hunt Allcott and Matthew Gentzkow, "Social Media and Fake News in the 2016 Election," NBER Working Paper #23089, last updated June 2017, https://www.nber.org/papers/w23089.

[30] "Intelligence community assessment: Assessing Russian Activities and Intentions in Recent US Elections," Office of the Director of National Intelligence, January 6, 2017, https://www.dni.gov/files/documents/ICA_2017_01.pdf.

[31] For example, Nate Silver of the website 538 had the odds of a Clinton victory at 71 percent based on a number of polls. See Nate Silver, "Final Election Update: There's A Wide Range Of Outcomes, And Most Of Them Come Up Clinton," 538.com, November 8, 2016, http://fivethirtyeight.com/features/final-election-update-theres-a-wide-range-of-outcomes-and-most-of-them-come-up-clinton/.

[32] Kia Kokalitcheva, "Mark Zuckerberg Says Fake News on Facebook Affecting the Election Is a 'Crazy Idea'," *Fortune*, November 11, 2016, http://fortune.com/2016/11/11/facebook-election-fake-news-mark-zuckerberg/.

[33] Tony Romm, "10 million people saw Russian ads on Facebook around the 2016 presidential election."

[34] *Guardian* staff, "Sheryl Sandberg: Facebook owes US an apology over Russian meddling," *The Guardian*, October 12, 2017, https://www.theguardian.com/technology/2017/oct/12/sheryl-sandberg-facebook-owes-us-an-apology-over-russian-meddling.

[35] Sapna Maheshwari and Sydney Ember, "The End of the Social News Era? Journalists Brace for Facebook's Big Change," *New York Times*, January 13, 2018, https://www.nytimes.com/2018/01/11/business/media/facebook-news-feed-media.html.

[36] Maheshwari and Ember, "The End of the Social News Era?"

[37] Klonick, "Inside the Making of Facebook's Supreme Court."

[38] Cecilia Kang, "What Is the Facebook Oversight Board?," *New York Times*, May 5, 2021, https://www.nytimes.com/2021/05/05/technology/What-Is-the-Facebook-Oversight-Board.html.

[39] Mike Isaac, "Facebook Oversight Board Upholds Social Network's Ban of Trump," *New York Times*, May 5, 2021, https://www.nytimes.com/2021/05/05/technology/facebook-trump-ban-upheld.html.

Ethics and Capitalism—The Other Side Academy

As Joseph Grenny, chairman of the board, and executive director Dave Durocher walked from the Quorum Room toward the main entrance of The Other Side Academy, they spoke softly about how much progress the Academy had made in fewer than five years of operations in Salt Lake City, Utah. The Other Side Academy (TOSA) is a therapeutic community (TC), a long-term, peer-run, residential treatment facility with the goal of rehabilitating people with problems of addiction and/or criminal behavior.[1] TCs came of age in the middle of the twentieth century as an outgrowth of the self-help recovery movement. TOSA serves people with a wide variety of substance abuse problems and criminal histories; the average participant in the TOSA community (referred to as students) has been arrested twenty-five times before being accepted into the program. Most have exhausted all their relationships with family and friends and are totally alone when they take a seat on "the bench" at TOSA and wait for an intake interview.

Grenny, Durocher, and their team had guided TOSA to remarkable success. The State of Utah's recidivism rate, the likelihood than an offender will reoffend, stood at about 70 percent in 2018.[2] For a TOSA student who completes the two-year program, that rate will be 15 percent. TOSA measures success by a different criterion, DCE, which means drug free, crime free, and employed. For those who complete the two-year program, that number has been 70 percent. Those who remained in the program for an additional year average a DCE rate of 89 percent. TOSA was so successful in such a short time that the organization opened a second facility in Denver, Colorado, in 2019.

Grenny, Durocher, and chief executive officer (CEO) Tim Stay had spent the last couple of hours reviewing the success of the operation to date. Their meeting ended with a challenging question to which none of them had a great answer: What would be the next set of challenges facing TOSA, its business model, and its challenge to help those who desired to abandon lives of addiction and crime?

FOUNDING

Joseph Grenny has gray hair, is slight of build, founded two very successful companies, and coauthored several best-selling business books. In 2005, Grenny and his business partners began research for the book that would later become *Influencer: The New Science of Leading Change*, a best-seller business book designed to help people create meaningful change in their lives and organizations. Grenny interviewed Stanford psychology guru Albert Bandura about organizations that could serve as models of behavioral change. Grenny recalled, "We'd been to Africa and Asia and South America, lots of interesting kinds of projects, but I was also really interested in criminal recidivism. I wanted to find anybody that was doing well-researched work in that regard. Bandura said, 'Well, that one's easy. You don't have to get on a plane; you can just drive up the peninsula here to Delancey Street.'"[3] Grenny took Bandura's advice and met with Mimi Silbert, who had founded the Delancey Street Foundation in 1971.

Mimi Silbert partnered with ex-convict John Maher to design and deploy a new model for helping people trapped in poverty, substance abuse, or criminal behavior. Their model would look like an extended family. Rather than relying on therapists and traditional interventions, the new organization would "empower people with the problems to become the solution."[4] Those who could work worked, and their salaries helped pay the costs of housing and feeding others. Those who could not work maintained the facility, cooked, and cleaned. Within two years, the group had purchased the former Russian Embassy in one of San Francisco's poshest neighborhoods. The organization supported itself through some donations but mostly by operating businesses such as a moving company, restaurants, and construction operations. Delancey Street grew from its initial four residents to own and operate facilities in San Francisco, Los Angeles, New Mexico, New York, and North Carolina.

Grenny had an incredible experience at Delancey Street's San Francisco location. He had certainly found a research site for the book, but over the next decade, he found himself unable to forget the amazing community he had seen and the work that community did to change the lives of some of America's most broken people. A deeply religious member of the Church of Jesus Christ of Latter-day Saints (LDS), Grenny saw the Delancey Street model as an example of Christ's teachings about love, human development, and community. He felt a deep spiritual calling to become involved in the work. He knew he didn't need to reinvent the wheel; he just needed to begin with the Delancey Street model. To get started, he reached out to Charlotte Harper, a thirty-eight-year Delancey Street leader who was the de facto chief operations officer (COO) of the organization, for help, advice, and leadership. Grenny described the meeting with Harper:

> We flew her out [to Salt Lake City] and we had this marathon group of meetings, and she asked us all the hard questions about whether we were really naïve and whether we were serious about this, or this was just sort of a dream that would go away in a week or two. She said, 'All right, I'm going to admit something to you. Yesterday, before I boarded the plane, I got a call from a guy named Dave Durocher.' She continued, 'Dave said that he's been out of Delancey Street for a few years, but he really wants to get back into saving lives.' She [told Dave], 'You know what, I'm going to meet with these folks in Provo, Utah, tomorrow. If they're not insane, I'll let you know.'

Dave Durocher is the polar opposite of Joseph Grenny. Durocher has no hair and a muscular, stocky build that makes him look like the person you'd least want to meet in a dark alley. Durocher was born in Anaheim, California, and spent his childhood in Cerritos and Huntington Beach. At age thirteen, he was arrested for the first time, and over the next quarter century he would serve four consecutive prison terms. To learn more about his story, visit the following website: https://www.youtube.com/watch?v=8vsuW9rZWHg. Durocher traded a twenty-nine-year prison sentence for a chance to change his life at Delancey Street. He finished the two-year program and stayed another six as a staff member. He moved on to work in North Dakota's oil boom:

I was making completely stupid money," Durocher said. "Here's a guy that had been out of the workforce since the '80s, making anywhere between $10,000 and $15,000 a month. So. I'm literally having an affair with my checkbook, but I'm putting money in the bank. I'm watching my bank account grow. But I had a hole in my heart. I missed the people part. It wasn't long after I had graduated Delancey Street when I quickly realized that making money was fun, but saving lives was rewarding. So, I came back from North Dakota. I went back to Southern California and I went back to work for Brkich Construction.

Durocher met Grenny and Stay for dinner in Los Angeles. He described the encounter:

We met at a restaurant called Fleming's. We probably had a two-and-a-half-, three-hour meeting over dinner. And before they said anything, when Joseph and Tim sat down, I said, 'Don't you say a word. Don't ask me any questions. Who in the hell are you? What is the genesis of thought behind this? What makes you think you can do this? Why would you want to? Make me understand who you do-gooders are.' And it didn't take long before both of them told me their stories and who they were, and I realized I was in the presence of some great men. And that was the only interview we ever did. They asked me if I'd be willing to come to Utah to help get it started. I said, 'I'm willing to go to the moon if you don't quit in six months when it gets hard.'

Here's a couple of just devout LDS guys who want to make a difference in the world. They want to help people, but never been drug addicts themselves. You only know what you think you know, and sometimes that makes people dangerous. But they were the right guys obviously.

GETTING STARTED

Durocher completed one critical piece of the TOSA puzzle: leadership. Over the next several months, Durocher, Grenny, and Stay combed the Salt Lake Valley for a location. They kept coming back to one of the first sites they visited, the old Francis Armstrong house just east of the downtown area. Grenny and his business partners raised money to buy the nineteenth-century property that had fallen into disrepair. Grenny explained: "While self-reliance is a critical piece of what we do here, I didn't want it to be saddled with so much debt that we would sit in this room and say 'We have to rush more students in here because we got to get revenues up, because we got to. . . .' I wanted to make sure this was a sacred space where the only criterion for admitting somebody was, we can help them, and it was good for them to be here." Location was puzzle piece number two.

The third piece of the puzzle was students. That meant building support among local politicians and community leaders. Grenny realized that the Delancey Street model had converted him, and it would likely convert skeptical politicians, law enforcement, and businesspeople:

I know that direct experience is the ultimate influence strategy, that if people have been immersed in something and seen it and touched it and experienced it, that they're going to be far more emotionally committed to it. So, I took a group of thirty people, a combination of government leaders, criminal justice system leaders, business leaders, out to San Francisco to have the same experience I did. I took them to dinner after that. After two days at Delancey Street, we went to the Delancey Street restaurant

and we sat in the room and I said, 'Do you want this in Utah? Is this something that would be important enough that you'd be willing to sacrifice to make it happen?'

We had the head of adult probation and parole, which was critical. We had Jeff Buhman, the county prosecutor for Utah Valley, a number of people that were important positions for what we were going to do. Every one of them said 'Absolutely.' They'd seen the revolving door; they'd seen how many lives are being destroyed by our criminal justice system. People make bad choices, but then we put them in a system that ensures they'll continue to make bad choices in the future. We had that buy-in.

Getting buy-in at a conceptual level did not equal students. That took more work, as Dave Durocher explained:

We had to convince the courts, prosecutors, and sheriffs to let us go in the jails and do interviews. We had to convince the judges to send their inmates to us. I'll never forget in one of our meetings the judge said, 'Mr. Durocher, let me see if I've got this straight. What you're telling me is right now you don't have an address and you don't have a phone number. So this is just a pipe dream. But I'm supposed to send you my inmates, some of whom have sworn to kill each other in jail and in prison. And they're going to go live under your roof peacefully?'

I said, 'Absolutely, your honor.' He says, 'You mind telling me how you're going to keep them from killing each other?'

I said, 'Sure. We're going to ask them not to.' And he looked at me kind of dumbfounded. 'Your honor,' I said. 'I spent my life in and out of prison. When was the last time this population was asked not to do that? And besides none of them really want to. If they want to continue with that behavior, they wouldn't be writing us and asking for help. What do you have to lose?

'They've been arrested twenty-five times already. You've sent them to jail or sent them to prison multiple times. They keep coming back. What you're doing isn't working. What do you have to lose? It worked for me. I had done four prison terms and then the judge finally gave me the shot to go to Delancey Street. I stayed eight and a half years and completely turned my life around. So you can continue to incarcerate them or send them to the thirty-, sixty-, ninety-day [treatment and rehabilitation] models over and over and over and over again to no avail.

'These short-term programs don't work. But at least they're expensive. Or you can send them to us and allow them to stay with us for a few years for free and completely recalibrate their moral compass and give us a shot at changing them.' And lo and behold, as the months wore on, they started to send people to us. And the rest is history.

TOSA admitted its first student in September 2015, fewer than six months after Durocher, Grenny, and Stay had broken bread in Los Angeles.

THE OPERATING MODEL

TOSA's work builds on three basic principles:[5]

1. **Peer run.** TOSA does not rely on a model of professional therapy; the model employs peer accountability and a highly structured, family-like environment. Both students and staff come from the same background. Everyone is not only responsible for their own behavior, but also for the success of the entire enterprise. Students describe the model as *each one teach one*.

2. **Self-funded.** TOSA runs a number of social enterprises that generate the revenue that covers all operational expenses. These businesses represent a therapeutic context for healing through

work and accountability. Character weaknesses are exposed and addressed in the process of doing real work and living a real life. The problem becomes the solution. Vocational training also helps students enter the economy after graduation.

3. **Behaviors not drugs.** TOSA does not focus on addiction or criminal behaviors in and of themselves. In fact, students are prohibited from talking about their past with others. TOSA uses an evidenced-based approach of dealing with the underlying behaviors and a view of self that, for many, originally led to their addiction and criminality. For example, addicts are often liars, manipulators, and thieves. Take away the addiction, and those underlying behaviors remain. TOSA's model helps students become honest, open, and respectful members of a community.

Selection

TOSA accepts men and women from ages eighteen to sixty-four. Because the days are long and the work is hard, applicants must be relatively healthy, aside from addictions. Because the model does not use therapists or other clinicians, TOSA will not accept individuals with mental health issues requiring medication. They also will not accept sex offenders, arsonists, those with murder charges, or those who have assaulted law enforcement personnel. TOSA works with the criminal justice system, homeless agencies, and mental health providers to receive or make referrals.

Many candidates write to TOSA from jail or short-term treatment facilities. Those candidates will be interviewed while in the facility. Other candidates just walk in the door and take a seat on the bench. (Exhibit 1 is a picture of the bench.)

Shiloh, a student now in his third year at TOSA, explained the intake process:

I'll tell you about the bench. That was the first place I came to when I got here. That is just exactly what it sounds like, a big wooden bench that you're told to sit on. 'Sit there and we'll be with you.' It's not, 'we'll be with you shortly.' There's really nothing nice about it. It's just sit there, and we'll be with you when we get to you.

I sat on a bench for eight hours. Eight hours. You're confronted with so many things in that period of time. I mean, you're reflecting on who you are, where you've been, and the situation that you're in. You're placed right in the center of the house. You see people walking past, you see these values posted

EXHIBIT 1 The Bench

EXHIBIT 2 The 12 beliefs of TOSA

1. You alone can do it, but you can't do it alone.
2. Make and keep promises.
3. Self-reliance. There is no free lunch.
4. Impeccable honesty.
5. Act as if.
6. Embrace humility.
7. Each one teach one.
8. 200% accountability.
9. Forgiveness.
10. Boundaries.
11. We are faith friendly.
12. Pride in work.

Source: TOSA Internal Documents.

up right in front of you like, 200 percent accountability, integrity, honesty, pride in work. (Exhibit 2 displays TOSA's twelve beliefs.) You're reflecting on those and 'Who am I?' You have all this just swirling through your brain and knowing the fact that this is a two-year commitment and the hole you're in and how you're going to fill that.

You see people walking past with this sense of purpose and smiles and laughs, and for me, I just wanted that. I just wanted what they had. I didn't know if these were students. I could assume they were students. I didn't know if they were staff members. I didn't know if they were visitors. I just saw that they were extremely happy and were walking with a purpose. I just knew that I wanted that, I had to have that, and I think that's what gave me the strength to sit there for eight hours. I said I'm going to sit here till they tell me I've got to go, or 'We'll give you a shot.' That's kind of what it was like for me on the bench.

During the initial interview,

The primary element that the interviewer is looking for is for the applicant to show a willingness to change their life and if they are willing to make the sacrifice it will require to change their behaviors. The interviewer is also going to test whether or not the applicant can take an emotional punch, because they are going to get a lot of them as hear about themselves and receive feedback about their behaviors. If they believe that and if they meet the acceptance criteria, then the applicant will be accepted as a student.[6]

Progression

Once admitted, students realize how different TOSA is from anything they've experienced. Dave Durocher explained in a nutshell how TOSA's guiding philosophy shapes every aspect of life at the facility:

The minute you get here, you're part of the solution rather than part of the problem. We don't take any money from the city, the county, the state, federal government, rich mommy and daddy, Medicaid, insurance, nothing. [Students] go to work in one of the social enterprises; all the money that we generate comes back into the facility so we can continue to support ourselves, continue to grow, continue to take more students. Then [they're] paying it forward, just like those who came in before that generated the revenue that allowed [them] to be there. Now [they're] doing the same for somebody else. I'll be damned. That's the balm for our wounds: service, helping others.

Students move through four distinct phases during their two years.

- **Orientation.** For the first two weeks, a student gets to observe life at TOSA. They participate much as freshmen do, but they don't take part in Games and don't face the same level of consequences. Students get to see the program in action and decide if they want to stay. About a third walk out at that point.
- **Freshman.** A student is a freshman for two to four months. Freshmen learn some basic life skills, and work entails cleaning and maintaining the house, other buildings, or the surrounding grounds. They do not leave the facility at any time. Freshmen take part in Games and other team-building activities. They are members of a "tribe"—a small group of students who act as family to each other. Freshmen earn no money, but they incur no expenses.
- **Sophomore and Junior.** These phases make up the bulk of a student's time at TOSA, until about month eighteen. Students work in one of the social enterprises to learn job skills, but also to help support the operation. As they learn life skills and become productive members of the community, they are given more responsibilities and more privileges.
- **Senior.** At about eighteen months, students become seniors. They begin to receive an allowance of $25 each month. This small amount of money helps them learn another crucial skill—money management. They begin to actively plan for life after TOSA and reentry into the larger community. Later in the senior phase, students will begin working in regular jobs while still living at TOSA. This allows them to adjust to having a stable income and becoming self-supporting.

Some students apply to stay at TOSA for another year or more. They may become a "master" student and continue to work in their current role at TOSA. Some become "scholars in residence" and work toward a community college, technical school, or university degree. Others may apply for a "staff-in-training" position, which puts them in a paid position of greater responsibility at TOSA.

Games

The house is run by a number of strict rules; obedience to those rules helps students gain a sense of stability and structure they never had in a life of crime or substance abuse. The only rule many knew was "Do whatever it takes to survive or stay high." This included lying, manipulating, stealing, and a host of other negative behaviors. Life at TOSA is very different. Students receive no mail for the first thirty days, and those with spouses/partners or children may have no contact with them for fifteen months. Contact between men and women is strictly forbidden—even talking to a member of the opposite gender violates the rules.

The rules exist to enable peer accountability, the basis of the TOSA family and individual progress. Violations of the smallest rules may be brought up immediately, or they may be reserved for "The Game," a group feedback session held every Tuesday and Friday night. It's called The Game, students say, because it teaches you how to play the game of life in an honest, open, and loving way. Students will write the names of those they want to "play" with on a slip of paper. Groups of twenty are formed, including those who want to play The Game or for whom others have Games. The group confronts the individual with the evidence of their poor behavioral choices and rule violations. Games often include loud and profane language. Shiloh explained the importance of The Game:

The Game here is 80 percent of what we came to get. It is the majority of why we're here. So I just kind of look at it as the game of life in this community.

I remember getting The Game for speaking to a woman. I was a freshman and you cannot engage with the women for the first year you're here, unless it's strictly work related; even then, probably just stay away from it. So there was a woman by the name of Sierra here, and she was talking with one of her women peers. They were asking something about who invented the light bulb. I chime in as the guy with all the answers and she quickly said, 'You can't say that.' So I kind of was dumbfounded. Anyway, I get a haircut [TOSA's term for a reprimand] later from one of the other staff members: 'Why are you talking to the women? What do you do? Who do you think you are?' To me, it just wasn't a big deal. I was just trying to be the guy with all the answers, trying to be helpful, but now I see how it was a big deal. Then I remember getting The Game.

This was my first Game, and you're in a room with twenty to thirty of your peers. Sierra gives me The Game and I'm thinking, 'Okay, I got it. We're done.' But then I'm getting the perspective of twenty other people. I thought it was just unnecessary. But it was their opinion and it was the way they saw me, and that's what I'm here to change, the perception of me. That's what I'm doing. Because I was completely unaware of it. I was unaware that I couldn't follow rules. I just felt ganged up on is what it was. That was my feeling at first.

Then the more I got into it, the more I played, I saw the purpose of it. I then I fixed that behavior. The longer I was here, I began to see the purpose. Then you start to gain the skills of The Game. Who am I working with? What are their core behaviors? I have to build a relationship with this person so that they're going to want to take this feedback. Because if I'm somebody that they despise, I can't give them any feedback. It's not going to do any good. So I've got to build this relationship with people so when I'm in a Game setting, they want to hear my feedback.

The Game isn't just an opportunity to vent frustrations or unload on people you don't like. Kjerstie, another student, explained:

It's really important that your motives are in the right place. If you're truly trying to help [someone] out and help them fix behaviors that aren't healthy for them, that they're just portraying, that are bringing them down, and you're attacking that behavior, that's good. But if you're going in a Game because you're wanting to hurt them or hurt their feelings, or make them feel bad about themselves, that's the wrong way to go about it.

Work

The typical day starts at 6 a.m. with a shower, morning meeting, and breakfast. Students then work until lunch and participate in a daily seminar and then go back to work until 5 p.m. The evenings are filled with classes, seminars, and The Game. Students have about an hour of free time, and the lights go out at 11 p.m. They work Saturdays, and there is a social function in the evening. Sundays are a day off. Most students rest and get ready for the next week.

Students have the opportunity to work and gain job skills in either an internal (non-revenue-generating) function or an external business unit. The internal functions are the following:[7]

- **Bookkeeping and Accounting**—Bookkeeping, invoicing, accounts receivable, accounts payable, and banking services for the organization and for the other departments.

- **Food Services**—Menu planning, nutritional planning, purchasing, warehousing, food safety oversight and training, culinary instruction, and food production for all meals for the campus population.
- **Construction and Maintenance**—Basic repair, construction, and maintenance for all campus facilities; includes plumbing, framing, basic electrical, finishing, tile work, stonework, concrete work, and general construction and maintenance skills.
- **Legal and Intake**—Work with various governmental agencies, including district courts, district attorneys, adult probation and parole, jail staff, and other judicial or correctional officers.
- **Corporate Development**—Work to obtain donations (cash or in kind) from businesses and community organizations. Students master basic computer skills, including Word, email, and Excel.
- **Cleaning**—Provide quality professional cleaning, including proper use of cleaning chemicals, proper techniques, and safety issues related to cleaning services.

TOSA runs three businesses that generate the revenue to sustain operations. While TOSA's goal is to help people change their lives, they also have to make a profit and sustain operations. CEO Tim Stay believed that running a successful business was essential to the social mission. Stay and Grenny had been involved in social enterprises before, and they had learned valuable lessons that helped TOSA succeed. Stay summarized these lessons:

- We have to have business competency within the organization. We have seen plenty of social enterprises where they are really good at providing services to their clients but are really bad at running a business. You have to be able to master the block and tackle of the basics of business, and that requires people on the team with business competency.
- We have to have a competitive product or service that the market wants to buy at a price they are willing to pay. Any social mission aspect to the product is secondary and may help build goodwill and loyalty, but the product or service has to be competitive. Many nonprofits that are trying to sell something to generate revenue miss this point. They think that if people know they are providing some social good, that this is enough to attract customers. It isn't.
- We learned that it is healthy to have a natural tension between the mission and the business in a double-bottom-lined business. You need to have people on the team who are pushing what is best for the business and people on the team pushing what is best for the mission. Of course, when it has to be one or the other, the mission always wins. But the beauty of The Other Side Academy is that so often both business and mission are so well aligned.
- As a nonprofit, there are many, many benefits to being self-sufficient where we can cover all our operational costs with the revenues that we generate. One benefit is not having to build a large fundraising team where a significant amount of the daily attention by top leadership is spent trying to raise money. Another benefit is we can do what is best for the students rather than be constrained by requirements placed upon us by outside funders such as the government or insurance agencies. Another benefit is that we get to model self-sufficiency to our students as an organization as we work to help them reach that same point in their lives.[8]

TOSA operates three main businesses:

- **The Other Side Movers.** The top-rated moving company in the Salt Lake Valley. Students learn to estimate, schedule, and manage the logistics of efficient allocation of labor and vehicles. They drive commercial vehicles and safely lift and carefully move items as well as deal with billing, sales transactions, customer feedback, and insurance claims.

CEO Tim Stay explained the challenges behind convincing people to let a bunch of ex-cons have access to all their valuables, neatly packaged and easy to move:

We determined we could gain market share with superior customer service. In our market research, we saw that most competitors had poor ratings, were unreliable, weren't trustworthy, and had lousy attitudes. Superior customer service for us included the hard work and hustle of our students, their charm and politeness, meeting all of our commitments (such as showing up early) and never exceeding an estimate, and a fierce determination to do whatever it takes to make the customer satisfied, such as owning up to mistakes and taking care of them.

- **The Other Side Thrift Boutique.** A retail store where students sort, catalog, store, and price incoming inventory. They learn warehousing skills and management, including organization, forklift operations, and inventory management. Students learn how to display merchandise and how to market and advertise using print, online, social media, and billboard advertising. Students master principles of retail management, cash management, and customer service.

Competing in the thrift store business also had strategic challenges, as Tim Stay noted.

Most people have an image of a dreary, poorly lighted, smelly thrift store with piles of junk and lousy customer service. We felt we could compete by establishing the following attributes:

- Superior customer service with sales associates who were friendly, attentive, and charming and not pushy.
- A clean, welcoming, attractive sales floor. We set up the store with good space, lighting, and flow so you don't feel claustrophobic or that something might fall on you. The fixtures, shelving, and environment are more like a Gap than a Goodwill.
- Quality items at great value. Our students sort through all the clothes that are donated and only select the very best to put out on the floor. We easily put only 10 percent of clothing we receive through donations on the floor. The clothes we do not select are sold in bulk to another nonprofit.
- Lower customer hassle. Other thrift stores rely on you to bring your donated item to their store for drop-off. They also do not deliver items when you purchase them. We saw a great gap in the market [we could fill] if we provided donation pick-up services and delivery services for large, purchased items. This has ensured that we continue to get high-quality furniture donated to us. Many people have large furniture or appliances that they want to donate to a good cause, but they don't know how to get the item out of their house. Since we will pick up donations, it becomes a simple task to pick up the phone or send an email.

- **The Other Side Construction.** A TOSA graduate was able to obtain a general contractor's license. The construction team of students bids on remodels, demolitions, and other construction projects.

Stay described the value of the construction business: Many who have had no construction experience learn highly marketable skills. The work ethic, pride in work, punctuality, and impeccable integrity that are the core of TOSA differentiate TOSA grads from other competitors in this industry.

TOSA opens its books to all students and stakeholders. On a quarterly basis, CEO Tim Stay will present the financial status, good and bad, of the last quarter to the students and explain where the money generated is being used, which helps teach basic understanding of the financial statements. Students are allowed to ask detailed questions about any of the finances. Because the students earn no wages, and because most of them come from highly manipulative environments where someone is always scamming others, they often wonder where the money goes. Grenny, for example, drives a Tesla. While he receives no compensation from TOSA, his affluence can raise suspicion. It's important for students to understand that they are not being exploited—most of them have been exploited a number of times in their life. Grenny noted that students gain a greater sense of appreciation for TOSA, and their own work, when they understand where the money comes from and goes to. (Exhibit 3 shows the 2018 financial report for TOSA.)

Impact on Students

Joseph Grenny started TOSA because he hoped to change lives for the better. Dave Durocher quit a high-paying job because making money wasn't fulfilling. He wanted to change lives in the same way his own life had changed.

Students learn how to have authentic relationships with others. One of the harshest rules at TOSA is that students can't see their children for the first fifteen months of their stay. Grenny explained how this challenged him and what he had learned:

That's a debate that I have had to be persuaded on slowly, because my thought is that if these are your children, for example, you have a moral duty to be involved in their life, so we ought to be getting them back there, taking that responsibility as soon as we can. You ought to learn how to reconnect with them as soon as possible.

What I've come to learn over time is that number one, they were never parents, so the fact that you've fathered or mothered a child doesn't make you a parent. If you've been arrested twenty-five times and spent six out of the last ten years incarcerated, you've been nothing but a negative influence in that child's life. And I mean negative influence. Basically, what happens is I go to jail, and that's the first time I'm paying attention to them because I want jail visits. And I don't want a jail visit because I want to be a positive influence in my child's life, I want jail visits because the girlfriend is going to bring them and that's going to give me a chance to make sure she's not sleeping with other people and ask her to put money on my books.

It's that kind of self-serving, narcissistic motivation that is at least a significant piece of that. [Students] need to push away the entire [relationship] until [they] can learn to have that connection only for the purpose of loving that child.

Kjerstie, who experienced this harsh reality when she couldn't see her son, explained what she has learned about relationships:

You're doing it for the right reasons, because you genuinely care about that person, not because you like them, or because you want something from them. It's because you built this relationship that's built on trust and honesty, and you can depend on them.

TOSA provides students with a future and confidence that they can succeed. Shiloh explained the decisions he's facing, and his excitement to make them:

That's where I'm at right now. I can't stop thinking about the future. I can't stop, . . . but it's in a healthy way. I used to be so crippled by mistakes and obstacles. Now, I just, I can't wait for them. I can't wait to figure out how to build credit. I can't wait to figure out what a mortgage looks like. I can't wait to figure out what a vehicle looks like. What's a sensible vehicle? What makes sense?

Then holding off on a relationship, having the ability to delay gratification for what's overall best, not being able . . . I can see past just a few inches in front of me. I can see the future and . . . I'm excited. Education, career, I've got a multitude of different paths that I know that I can take, and I've just got to figure out. . . . Right now, I'm trying to stay in the moment I'm in, because I've committed to a third year and I need to stay here in the house. But I do give myself some time to think about the future. Financially, what is that going to look like? Do I need an education? Family-wise, I mean, I can't wait to be the person in my family, my immediate family that shows up with the steaks and the barbecue to actually barbecue for them. You know what I mean? To invite them to the lake and put on a party for them. That's . . . I just can't wait.

Taylor, who runs The Other Side Movers, described what the future looks like for him:

I'm excited. I just committed to a third year, so I still got quite a bit of time left. It doesn't make it easy because it's a big commitment. But understanding the principle of being able to sacrifice what you want right now, because what I want right now is to

EXHIBIT 3　TOSA Financial Report

Item	2017	2018
Contributions and Grants	$ 1,876,709	$ 8,523,983
Program Service Revenue	$ 1,376,231	$ 1,974,087
Investment Income		$ 59
Other Revenue	$ 212,777	$ 862,309
Total Revenue	**$ 3,465,717**	**$ 11,360,438**
Salaries Paid	$ 690,053	$ 1,128,408
Professional Fundraising Fees		$ 42,500
Oher Expenses	$ 2,111,960	$ 3,670,823
Total Expenses	**$ 2,802,013**	**$ 4,841,731**
Revenue Less Expenses	$ 663,704	$ 6,518,707
Total Assets	$ 3,409,259	$13,839,833
Total Liabilities	$ 341,315	$ 4,253,182
Net Assets of Fund Balances	$ 3,067,944	$ 9,586,651

Source: IRS Form 990, available at https://www.theothersideacademy.com/assets/docs/TOSA%202018%20Form%20990.pdf.

get my life together and rush back out there and fix everything, but to sacrifice what I want right now for what I want most. And what I want most is just to have a consistent, and not even a crazy life, just like a normal life with a job and a family and just having a good life.

Being here as long as I have now, for the first time I actually have confidence because I have consistency. All I need to do out there is what I've been doing. Get up every single day with a purpose, get up early, go to work, work hard. Just be a good man, have integrity, be honest. If something's not okay, say something about it.

Kjerstie saw both what's ahead and the role that TOSA had played, and would continue to play, in her life:

I'm really close to starting my workout [preparing to reenter society], and what that looks like is going and getting a job out in the community and transitioning back out there. I'm not in any hurry, but I'm ready for that next chapter. I know The Other Side Academy supports me a hundred percent. I've had multiple conversations with Dave about the career path I want to go, and what I want to get my feet into. Never in my life have I ever had as much confidence in myself that I could do anything I want to do. I just have to actually put forth the work and the effort to get there. That's kind of where I'm at.

There's multiple things that I want to try and if I don't like it, okay, I'll move onto the next thing, but there's a few things that I'm excited for. I might go dabble in the medical field.

I really want to also dabble in maybe becoming a personal trainer and doing all these things. But I know in my heart that whatever path I choose, I'm going to stay close to The Other Side Academy because this is the family that I've learned to love and gained by choosing to do something different. So I'm really grateful for that.

I never can forget where I've come from though because that's important. But I also know that having the support system here and having my family who I'm excited to start building relationships that I've broken and that's a slow process. When that happens, it will happen. I'm ready to start fixing my credit, doing all that stuff that is going to help me be a productive member of society, and I'm really excited for it.

CONCLUSION

As Grenny and Durocher reached the main entrance and looked at the bench that had offered a new life to over 400 people in the last four years, they took in the moment with joy. Like Shiloh, Taylor, and Kjerstie, they were excited about the future. The future brought its own set of challenges, however. How would the economic shock of the COVID-19 virus affect their operation, model, and revenues? What challenges would the new Denver facility create? What opportunities? Could, or should, they grow the model and work to transform more lives? What kinds of changes might help them do so? As they parted, each man knew that, while they had done much, there was more to do.

References

[1] "What Are Therapeutic Communities?," National Institute on Drug Abuse, last modified July 2015, https://www.drugabuse.gov/sites/default/files/therapueticcomm_rrs_0723.pdf.

[2] Brian Wood, "Behind Bars: Give Utah's inmates an opportunity to reform and they'll succeed," *Standard-Examiner*, May 1, 2017, https://www.standard.net/opinion/beyond-bars/2017/may/01/behind-bars-give-utahs-inmates-an-opportunity-to-reform-and-theyll-succeed/.

[3] Case writer interview with Joseph Grenny, July 3, 2020. All quotations from Mr. Grenny in this case are from this interview.

[4] "Our Story," Delancey Street Foundation, About Us, delanceystreet-foundation.org, accessed July 11, 2020, http://www.delanceystreetfoundation.org/ourstory.php.

[5] TOSA internal documents.

[6] TOSA internal documents.

[7] The following text is adapted slightly from TOSA internal policy documents.

[8] Case writer communications with Tim Stay, July 17, 2020.

Name Index

Company Index

Subject Index